SIXTH
EDITION

Perspectives on Personality

Charles S. Carver
University of Miami

Michael F. Scheier
Carnegie Mellon University

PEARSON
A B
and

Boston • New York • San Francisco
Mexico City • Montreal • Toronto • London • Madrid • Munich • Paris
Hong Kong • Singapore • Tokyo • Cape Town • Sydney

Sponsoring Editor: Michelle Limoges
Production Supervisor: Karen Mason
Marketing Manager: Karen Natale
Editorial-Production Service: Omegatype Typography, Inc.
Manufacturing Buyer: JoAnne Sweeney
Cover Administrator: Linda Knowles
Text Designer: Joyce Weston
Electronic Composition: Omegatype Typography, Inc.

For related titles and support materials, visit our online catalog at www.ablongman.com.

Between the time website information is gathered and published, some sites may have closed. Also, the transcription of URLs can result in typographical errors. The publisher would appreciate notification of any problem with URLs so that they may be corrected in subsequent editions.

Library of Congress Cataloging-in-Publication Data

Carver, Charles S.
    Perspectives on personality / Charles S. Carver, Michael F. Scheier. — 6th ed.
        p. cm.
    Includes bibliographical references and indexes.
    ISBN-13: 978-0-205-52262-0 (hardcover)
    ISBN-10: 0-205-52262-9 (hardcover)
  1. Personality—Textbook.   I. Scheier, Michael. II. Title.
  BF698.C22 2008
  155.2—dc22

                                        2007008463

Printed in the United States of America

10 9 8 7 6 5 4 3   11 10 09

Photo credits are on page 539, which constitutes a continuation of the copyright page.

To Linda Cahan
For her boundless enthusiasm,
energy, devotion, and courage
CSC

To Karen Matthews
For her wisdom, support, and love
through the good times, and
also the hard times
MFS

Contents

Preface

PERSPECTIVES ON PERSONALITY, Sixth Edition, examines one of the most engaging and mysterious topics in all of life: human personality. As the book's title implies, there are many perspectives on personality, many ways to think about human nature. This book describes a range of viewpoints that are held by personality psychologists today.

WHAT'S THE SAME IN THIS EDITION?

As in the five earlier editions, the book's content reflects two of our strongly held beliefs. The first is that *ideas* are the most important part of a first course on personality. For this reason, we stress concepts throughout the book. Our first priority has been to present as clearly as we can the ideas that form each theoretical viewpoint.

The second belief is that *research* is important in personality psychology. Ideas and intuitions are valuable, but an idea shouldn't lie around too long before someone checks to see whether it actually works. For this reason, along with each theory, we discuss research that bears on the theory. This emphasis on the role of research stresses the fact that personality psychology is a living, dynamic process of ongoing scientific exploration.

As in previous editions, we present the theories in groups, which we've labeled *perspectives*. Each group of theories depends on a particular sort of orienting viewpoint, an angle from which the theorists proceeded. Within a given perspective, there often are several theories that differ from one another. In each case, however, the theories of a given perspective share fundamental assumptions about human nature.

Each perspective on personality is presented in a pair of chapters that are introduced by a prologue. The prologue provides an overview of that perspective's orienting assumptions and core themes. By starting with these orienting assumptions, you'll be placed right inside the thought processes of the theorists as you go on to read the chapters themselves. Each chapter concludes with a discussion of current problems within that theoretical viewpoint and our own best guess about its future prospects.

The perspectives are presented in an order that makes sense to us, but they can easily be read in other orders. Each theoretical section of the book is intended to stand on its own, with no assumptions about previous exposure to other parts of the book. Thus, instructors can move through the perspectives in whatever order they prefer.

As in the previous editions, the final chapter takes up the question of how the different viewpoints relate to each other. The main goal of this chapter is to tie together ideas from theories discussed separately in earlier chapters. A second goal is to consider the usefulness of blending theoretical viewpoints, treating theories as complementary to each other, rather than competing.

This edition also continues our use of the boxed feature "The Theorist and the Theory." These boxes focus on how the personal experiences of some of the theorists have influenced the forms their theories took. In several cases, theorists almost literally took events from their own lives as models of human events more generally and went on to derive entire theories from those personal experiences. Not all cases are quite this striking, but personal experiences do appear to have played a role in the development of several views of personality.

In this revision, we've continued to try very hard to make the content accessible. We use an informal, conversational style throughout to try to draw you into the ideas. We've also included examples of how the ideas can apply to your own life. We hope these qualities make the book engaging and enjoyable, as well as informative.

What's Different about This Edition?

This edition retains the prior structure (the same chapters, in the same perspectives). However, the content of this edition differs in several ways from that of the fifth edition. These changes reflect four years of rapid change in the continually evolving research literature of personality psychology. Updates have been made to every substantive chapter. In fact, we used information from over 300 new sources. Although updates have been made everywhere, several areas of change are major enough that we should note them explicitly.

First, work has continued at a rapid rate on the trait structure of personality and the implications of that structure for behavior. Most of this work is taking place within the framework of the five-factor model. This has resulted in considerable change in Chapter 4 (Types, Traits, and Interactionism). It has also resulted in the inclusion of additional material bearing on the five-factor model in several other chapters.

Second, *incredibly* rapid advances continue to be made in work concerning behavioral genetics, molecular genetics, temperament, neurotransmitters, and other biological processes and how they relate to aspects of personality. Theorists have approached these processes and their relations to personality from several directions. As a result, Chapters 6 and 7 have both undergone major updates, and Chapter 7 has been reorganized.

Another area of rapid expansion is work on adult attachment patterns and their implications for personality and social behavior. This explosion of work has resulted in major changes in the chapter dealing with psychosocial theories in the neoanalytic perspective (Chapter 11).

Rapid expansion has also taken place in work on self-actualization and related models. Research deriving from self-determination theory, terror management theory, and related theories has continued to be very active. The information produced by this work has re-invigorated interest in this view of personality, resulting in changes to Chapter 14.

Finally, we've included a good deal of new material in the chapters of the cognitive self-regulation perspective. This new material includes a discussion of connectionist models of cognitive processes and the related idea that cognition takes two somewhat distinct forms. We've also expanded information on contextual models of behavior and the process by which intentions are implemented.

Despite adding a great deal of new information, we've also been able again to shorten several of the book's longer chapters. We did this by simplifying and tightening the writing. We hope the result is more readable but with no loss of clarity.

For more information on *Perspectives on Personality,* Sixth Edition, consult its webpage at www.mypsychkit.com.

Acknowledgments

WE HAVE SEVERAL DIFFERENT KINDS of acknowledgments to make, in recognition of people who have been helpful and important in one way or another. First, we would like to express our thanks to some of those who played roles in the continuing evolution of the book. In particular, we are grateful to Mia Weinberger Biran, Miami University; Amy Corbett, Siena College; M. Brent Donnellan, Michigan State University; and Brian H. Stagner, Texas A&M University, who reviewed the previous edition and offered comments and suggestions.

A second set of acknowledgments is more diffuse in focus. These acknowledgments are not about this book, but rather about how we grew to be academic psychologists who were able to write a book at all. These acknowledgments pertain to the mentors and educators who inspired us, taught us, and opened doors of opportunity to us. These people include (alphabetically) Mark Bickhard, Arnie Buss, Kenneth Craik, David Glass, Lew Goldberg, Al Riley, and Bob Wicklund. We owe them a great debt of gratitude. Without their influence, this book (and, for that matter, our careers in psychology) would have been much less likely.

Each of us also has some individual acknowledgments:

• From Coral Gables, my thanks to those who've been part of my life during the past four years, particularly Linda Cahan, Sheri Johnson, Youngmee Kim, André Perwin, Rod Gillis, Mike Antoni, Jean-Philippe Laurenceau, and Rod Wellens. A special bow to Linda Cahan, whose Herculean efforts are presently being applied to getting well. Major thanks to Danny Garzon, who entered all 300 of the new references in this edition. I am unceasingly grateful to my family: Jeff, Allysen, Alexandra, and Julia; Carol; Nancy Lorey; all the Sherricks; and Mike, Karen, Meredith, and Jeremy. Finally, a very special thank you to my shag terrier, Calvin (www.psy.miami.edu/faculty/ccarver/CCdog.html), who continues to amaze me with his deep insights about life and his ability to sleep upside down.

• From Pittsburgh, thanks go first to my partner in life, Karen Matthews, and to our two children, Jeremy and Meredith. Thanks also to the following group of friends and colleagues: Chuck Carver, Sheldon Cohen, Ed Gerrard, Vicki Helgeson, David Klahr, Ken Kotovsky, Rich Schulz, and Jim Staszewski. I'd also like to express my gratitude to Ginger Placone, my administrative assistant, for her help in keeping my professional life somewhat organized and under control. Finally, I'd like to thank my project director, Suzanne Colvin. Her dedication and effort have made it possible to keep my research program moving forward in the face of many conflicting demands.

About the Authors

Charles S. Carver and **Michael F. Scheier** met in graduate school at the University of Texas at Austin, where they both earned Ph.D. degrees in personality psychology. After graduation, they took jobs at the University of Miami and Carnegie Mellon University, respectively, where they have remained throughout their careers. They've collaborated for over three decades in work that spans personality, social, motivational, clinical, and health psychology. In 1998, they received awards for Outstanding Scientific Contribution (Senior Level) from the Division of Health Psychology of the American Psychological Association. Mike was the 2003–2004 president of the Division of Health Psychology of the American Psychological Association and currently serves as department head at CMU. Chuck is currently editor of the *Journal of Personality and Social Psychology*'s section on *Personality Processes and Individual Differences.* Along with six editions of *Perspectives on Personality,* the authors have published two books on self-regulation (the more recent titled *On the Self-Regulation of Behavior,* in 1998) and over 260 articles and chapters. Mike is an avid outdoorsman, hunter, and fisherman. Chuck keeps intending to take up painting but gets distracted by things that need fixing.

www.psy.miami.edu/faculty/ccarver
www.psy.cmu.edu/faculty/scheier/index.html

An Introduction

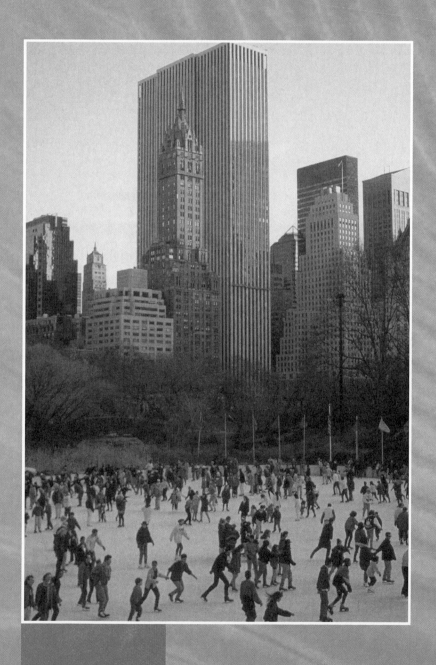

What Is Personality Psychology?

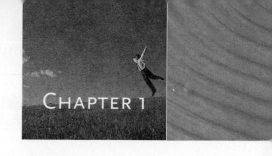
Sue met Rick in a philosophy class when both were sophomores. They started to date casually, and their relationship gradually deepened. Now, two years later, they're talking seriously of marriage. Sue describes Rick this way: "He's attractive to me in so many ways. He's good looking, and athletic, and smart, and he likes the same music I like. He knows how to do lots of things you don't expect a guy to know, like cooking. But the best part I don't even know how to describe, except to say he has a really wonderful personality."

EVERY NOW and then, someone surveys the qualities people value in a potential husband or wife. Most people want their mate to have a sense of humor, good looks, and a streak of romance. Almost always, though, a high priority is placed on the person's personality. Most people want someone who has a "good personality."

A good personality. What does that mean? If you were to describe a friend of yours who *does* have a good personality, what would you say? "Rick has a really wonderful personality. . . ." But then what?

Describing someone's personality means trying to portray the essence of who the person is. It means crystallizing something from the things you know about the person. It means taking a large pile of information and reducing it to a smaller set of qualities. Personality is reflected partly in what people do and say. Partly, though, it's a matter of *how* they do what they do—the style that puts a unique stamp on their actions.

Defining Personality

Trying to describe someone's personality is an exercise in being a psychologist. Each of us is a psychologist part of the time, because we all spend part of our lives trying to understand what other people are like. When you think about how to describe someone and what reveals those qualities to you, you're doing informally what personality psychologists do more formally.

There's a little difference in focus between what you do in daily life and what personality psychologists do. Use of the word *personality* in everyday speech tends to focus on the *specific* personalities of specific persons (Rick, for instance). Psychologists are more likely to focus on personality as an abstraction. When psychologists use the word *personality,* they usually are referring to a conception of what everyone's personality is like.

What *is* personality, viewed that way? Psychologists have argued for a long time about exactly how to define personality. Many definitions have been offered, but none is universally accepted. Personality is, in fact, something of an elusive concept.

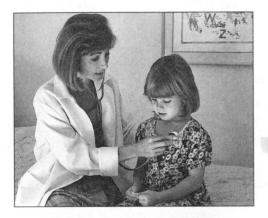

WHY USE PERSONALITY AS A CONCEPT?

In trying to define personality as a concept, a good way to start is to think about why the word is used. Understanding why it's used should help us decide what it means. When *you* use the word *personality,* why do you use it? What makes you use that word instead of another one?

One reason people use the word *personality* appears to be the desire to convey a sense of *consistency* or *continuity* about a person. There are several kinds of consistency. All of them evoke the concept of personality. You may see consistency in a person across time (Sue talked a lot when you first met her, and years later she still dominates conversations). You may see consistency across similar situations (André is very polite to waiters in restaurants and has been that way every time you've had dinner with him). You sometimes even see consistency across situations that are quite different from each other (Virginia tends to order people around—in stores, at work, even at *parties*). In each of these, there's the sense that it's undeniably the same person from one instance to another, because the person acts (or talks, or thinks, or feels) in consistent ways from time to time and from setting to setting. One reason for using the word *personality,* then, is to imply this consistency or continuity within the person.

A second reason people use the word *personality* is to convey the sense that whatever the person is doing (or thinking or feeling) *originates from within.* The idea that behavior comes from inside the person may seem so obvious that it hardly deserves mention, but not everyone sees it that way. Nonetheless, using the term *personality* conveys the sense of a causal force *within* the person, influencing how the person acts. There is, in fact, very good reason to assert that personality has very important behavioral consequences (Ozer & Benet-Martínez, 2006).

These two reasons for using the term *personality* come together when you try to predict and understand people's behavior (even your own). It can be important to predict behavior. When you choose a roommate for next year, you're predicting you'll get along well. When you tell a chronically late friend that the movie starts at 8:00 when it really starts at 8:30, you're predicting that this will get her to arrive more or less on time. An important contributor to these predictions is your view of the other person's personality.

Personality produces consistencies in behavior across different contexts. Although this woman finds herself in different situations, her warm and caring nature comes through in all of them.

The term *personality* is also used for another reason. It often conveys the sense that a few qualities can summarize what a person is like because they're so prominent in that person's behavior. Saying that Karen has a sociable personality implies that sociability stands out in her actions. Saying that Tanya has a hostile personality implies that hostility is a key quality in her. Taking note of the most prominent characteristics of a person brings to mind the concept of personality, because those characteristics seem to capture the person's personality.

This patchwork of reasons for using the term *personality* moves us closer to having a definition for it. That is, the word *personality* conveys a sense of consistency, internal causality, and distinctiveness. As it happens, these elements are in almost all definitions of personality.

A WORKING DEFINITION

Here's one definition. We're not saying it's the "right" one, but we think it comes close. We've adapted it slightly from one written decades ago by Gordon Allport (1961): *Personality is a dynamic organization, inside the person, of psychophysical systems that create the person's characteristic patterns of behavior, thoughts, and feelings.*

Individual differences in behavior and reactions are an important part of personality.

This definition makes several points:

- Personality isn't just an accumulation of bits and pieces; it has organization.
- Personality doesn't just lie there; it has *processes* of some sort.
- Personality is a *psychological* concept, but it's inextricably tied to the *physical* body.
- Personality is a *causal force* that helps determine how the person relates to the world.
- Personality shows up in individualized *patterns*—recurrences and consistencies.
- Personality is displayed not just in one way but in *many ways*—in behaviors, thoughts, and feelings.

This definition covers a lot. It points to several elements that should be part of any conceptualization of personality. As good as it is, though, it isn't perfect. Even this careful definition seems to let something about the concept slip through your fingers. This elusiveness is something that personality psychologists have struggled with for many years.

TWO FUNDAMENTAL THEMES IN PERSONALITY PSYCHOLOGY

From what we've said so far, two core themes stand out in thinking about personality. One of them is the existence of **individual differences.** Each person who ever lived is different from everyone else. No two personalities are quite alike—not even those of identical twins. Some people are happy, some are sad. Some people are sociable, some are shy and reclusive. As we said earlier, one reason to use the word *personality* in the first place is to capture central features of a person. This couldn't happen if the features didn't differ from one person to another. Thus, the notion of individual differences is key to everyday use of the term *personality*.

Individual differences are also important to the theorist who tries to understand personality. To be useful, any approach to personality has to have something to say about these differences. A really complete account of personality should consider where the differences come from. A complete account should also consider the questions of why the differences matter.

The other theme concerns what we'll call **intrapersonal functioning.** By this phrase, we mean the processes within the person that Allport (1961) referred to as a "dynamic organization" of systems. The idea here is that personality isn't like a rubber stamp that you pound onto each situation you enter. Instead, there are processes that go on inside you, leading you to act the way you do. Such processes create a sense of continuity within the person, even if the person acts differently in different circumstances. That is, the same processes are engaged, even if the results differ in different situations.

Here's an example. Some theorists believe that behavior is a product of motives. Motivational tendencies rise and fall as time passes and situations change. Which motive is strongest at any given time determines what the person does at that time. A person may work in isolation for four hours, then spend a couple of hours socializing, then go eat dinner, followed by some reading. The behaviors differ, but they all stem from motives within the person that vary in strength over the course of the day. This view of personality treats the motives as key variables. The processes by which motives vary in strength are some of the processes of intrapersonal functioning.

This is just one example of an intrapersonal process. It's not the only kind of process that has been argued for. Regardless of what processes are assumed, though, the idea of *process* is important. A complete account of personality should say what kinds of processes underlie personality and how and why they work.

Various approaches to personality place differing emphases on these two themes. Some approaches emphasize process and consist largely of a view of intrapersonal functioning, with little attention to differences among people. Other approaches treat individual uniqueness as the most important aspect of personality and are more vague about the processes underlying the uniqueness. These differing emphases contribute to the diversity among personality theories.

Why have we spent so much effort here describing what personality psychology is about? We've placed you in the role of a theorist in this discussion. Theorists have to keep in mind what aspects of human experience they want to understand. To understand the theories, you'll have to do that too.

Theory in Personality Psychology

Much of this book is a series of statements of theoretical principles. Because theories are so important, let's spend a little time on what they are, what they do, and how to evaluate them.

WHAT DO THEORIES DO?

What *is* a theory? A **theory** is a summary statement, a general principle or set of principles about a class of events. More informally, a theory is a set of ideas about how to think about that class of events. A theory can apply to a very specific class of events, or it can be broader. Some theories in psychology are about processes in a single nerve cell. Others concern complex behaviors, such as maintaining close relationships, playing chess, and living all of life.

Theories are used for two purposes (no matter what the theory is about). The first purpose is to *explain* the phenomena it addresses. A theory always provides a way to explain some things that are known to be true. For example, some biological personality theories hold that heredity influences personality. This idea provides a way to explain why children act like their parents in certain ways (things we know to be true).

Every theory about personality provides an account of at least some phenomena. This first purpose of the theory—explanation—is fundamental. Without giving an explanation for at least some of what's already known, a theory would be useless.

Theories also have a second purpose, though. A theory should suggest possibilities you don't yet know for sure are true. To put it differently, a theory should allow you to *predict new information*. A theory of personality should let you predict things you haven't thought to look for yet—maybe things *nobody* has thought to look for yet. For the psychologist, this is where much of the excitement lies.

Psychologists generally want to make predictions about large numbers of people, but the same principle holds when you make predictions in your own life. It's exciting to take an idea about personality and use it to predict how your roommate will react to a situation you haven't seen her in before. It's particularly exciting when your prediction turns out to be right!

The predictive aspect of theories is more subtle and more difficult than the explanatory aspect. The difficulty lies partly in the fact that most theories have a little ambiguity. This often makes it unclear exactly what the prediction should be. In fact, the broader the theory (the more things it has to account for), the more likely it is to be ambiguous. As you've seen, personality is a very broad concept. This forces theories of personality to be broad and complex. As a result, it's sometimes hard to use them to make predictions.

EVALUATING THEORIES: THE ROLE OF RESEARCH

How do psychologists decide whether a theory is any good? In describing the predictive function of theories, we've revealed a bias held by many personality psychologists: Theories should be *testable,* and they should be *tested*. It's important to find out whether a theory makes predictions that receive support.

We want to be quite clear about what we're saying here. Personality is so important in life that lots of people besides psychologists think about it. Theologians, philosophers, artists, poets, novelists, and songwriters have all written about personality, and many of them have had good insights about it. We don't mean to diminish the value of these insights. But are they enough?

People have different opinions on this question. Some believe that insight stands on its own and requires nothing more. Even some personality theorists have believed this. Sigmund Freud, who's often viewed as the father of personality psychology, wasn't much interested in whether his ideas were supported in research by others. He saw the insights as sufficient in themselves.

The view that dominates today's psychology, however, is that ideas—even brilliant ideas—have to be tested before they can be trusted. Too often, things that *seem* true turn out not to be true after all. Unfortunately, until you test them, you never know which ideas are brilliant and right and which are brilliant but wrong. Because of this, today's personality psychology is a scientific field, in which research counts for a lot. Studies of personality provide information about how accurate or useful a theory is. The studies either confirm or disconfirm predictions and thereby support or undermine the theory.

When theories are used to generate predictions for research, a continuous interplay arises (see Figure 1.1). If a theory makes predictions, the result is research—scientific studies—to test the predictions. Results often support the predictions. Sometimes, however, the result either fails to support the theory or supports it only partly. The outcome may suggest a limit on the theory—perhaps it

FIGURE 1.1

In a scientific approach to personality psychology, there is a continuous cycling between theory and research. Theory suggests predictions to be tested, and the results of studies suggest the need for new or modified theory.

predicts accurately under some conditions but not others. Such a finding leads to revision of the theory.

Once it's been revised, the theory must be tested again, because it's no longer quite the same theory as before. Its new elements must be examined for other predictions they might make. The cycle of prediction, testing, revision or refinement, and additional prediction and testing can be virtually never ending.

WHAT ELSE MAKES A THEORY GOOD?

An important basis for deciding whether a theory is good is whether it does what a theory's supposed to do: explain and predict. But that's not the only way people evaluate theories. There are several more criteria for why one theory may be preferable to another (Maddi, 1980).

One criterion is the breadth of the information behind the theory. Some theories are criticized because they're based heavily on the theorists' experiences conducting therapy. Other theories are criticized because they're based on studies of laboratory animals in highly artificial situations. Others are criticized because they rest largely on information from long sets of rating scales. None of these sources of information is bad in itself. But to base a theory on just one source of information weakens the theory.

A theory should also have the quality of **parsimony**. That is, it should include as few assumptions (or concepts) as possible. To put it differently, it should be as simple as possible. This criterion is important, but there's a danger in applying it too rigidly to personality theories. Knowledge about personality is far from complete. A theory that looks parsimonious today may not be able to account for something that will be discovered tomorrow. A theory that looks too complex today may be the *only* one that can handle tomorrow's discovery. Nevertheless, excess theoretical "baggage" is a cause for concern.

Another basis for evaluating theories is highly subjective. To put it bluntly, some theories "feel" better than others. Some theories you'll read about will fit your personal worldview better than others. You're not the only one who reacts this way. So do psychologists. There's even evidence that behavioral scientists prefer theories that fit their images of *themselves* (J. A. Johnson, Germer, Efran, & Overton, 1988). William James, an important figure in the early years of psychology, said people will prefer theories that "are most interesting, . . . appeal most urgently to our aesthetic, emotional, and active needs" (James, 1890, p. 312). Which theories feel best to you, then, depends partly on how you see the world. This shouldn't be the only criterion you use, but it can be an important one.

A theory should also be *stimulating* (Maddi, 1980). Being stimulating may mean provoking enthusiasm, interest, or excitement, but a theory can also be stimulating by provoking outrage and efforts to show how wrong it is. Provoking either kind of reaction is good, because it leads to efforts to test the theory. Theories so dull that they provoke no reaction at all are less useful, because no one bothers to study their implications.

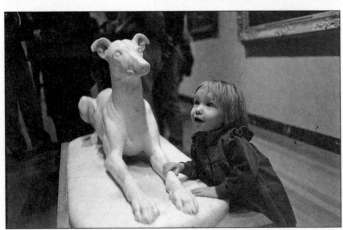

Like a good work of art, a good theory should evoke some sort of reaction, either positive or negative, but not indifferent.

Perspectives on Personality

Next let's preview the theories about personality you will be reading about in this book. The theories range considerably in their starting points, which can make matters a little confusing. The starting point, in some sense, is always a vague conception of human nature. How often have you heard someone say "It's just human nature"? That phrase implies a view of what people are like. But what *is* human nature? *In what terms* should we think about people? Different theorists have had very different answers to these questions.

GROUPINGS AMONG THEORIES

Theories bearing on personality tend to form groups. Each group is characterized by a broad viewpoint on human nature. Each group's view of human nature differs (sometimes slightly, sometimes radically) from those of the other groups. Throughout the book we refer to each of these views as a *perspective* on personality.

Another term that means much the same as this is **metatheory.** A metatheory is a set of orienting assumptions *within which* theories are devised. These orienting assumptions are more general than are the assumptions of a particular theory. Metatheories are guides to what kinds of concepts are appropriate to use in theories. For example, the view that life involves competition among energy systems is a metatheory. There are lots of ways to think about energy systems, which could lead to many theories. But all of them would be grounded in the idea that life is about energy systems. Each perspective, or metatheory, thus provides a core metaphor for human nature. The metaphor becomes a guide for developing specific theories.

In this book we discuss seven perspectives on personality, each in a separate part. The perspectives are termed *dispositional, biological, psychoanalytic, neoanalytic, learning, phenomenological, and cognitive self-regulation*. Most of them include several theories. The theories of a given perspective sometimes differ substantially from one another, but they seem to share a set of orienting assumptions.

For each perspective, we start with a brief prologue that describes the basic themes and core assumptions of that section's metatheory. This is the metaphor of human nature that serves as a foundation for that view on personality. This prologue is followed by two content chapters, each covering a theoretical view of personality within that perspective. Each of these chapters ends with a statement on problems that type of theory faces, and our guesses about its prospects for future development. Here are brief overviews of the perspectives you'll be reading about.

The *dispositional perspective* (Part Two) is based on the idea that people have fairly stable qualities (dispositions) that are displayed across diverse settings but are deeply embedded in the person. Theorists of this perspective vary in how they view dispositions. Some emphasize that various dispositions exist, and don't say much about how they go about influencing behavior. Others focus on the idea that dispositions pertain to motive forces, which influence behavior. These two sets of ideas are described in separate chapters in the dispositional section.

Another way of thinking about human nature, the *biological perspective* (Part Three), emphasizes the fact that humans are biological creatures. One biological view resembles dispositional theories, but with a different emphasis. This approach says personality is genetically based: Dispositions are inherited. Indeed, some theorists take this idea a step further to suggest that many qualities of human behavior exist precisely because long ago they had evolutionary benefits. Another part of the biological perspective stems from the idea that personality reflects the workings of the body we inhabit. This kind of biological theory focuses on how the nervous system and hormones influence the kind of person you are.

The *psychoanalytic perspective* (Part Four) is a very different view of the world. It's based on the idea that personality is a set of internal forces that compete and conflict with one another. The focus of this perspective is on the dynamics of these forces (and the way they influence behavior). Human nature, from this viewpoint, involves a set of pressures inside the person that sometimes work with each other and sometimes are at war with each other. This perspective is the most tightly focused of all, in the sense that one theory dominates it—the theory of Sigmund Freud.

We've termed the next perspective *neoanalytic* (Part Five). In a sense, neoanalytic theories aren't really a distinct perspective: they all derive in one way or another from psychoanalytic theory (thus the name *neoanalytic*). One might argue that this makes them all variations on the psychoanalytic perspective. (Indeed, that's what we said in the first edition of this book.) On the other hand, the theories evolved in ways that make them very different from Freud's theory. For this reason, we believe they no longer share the worldview assumed in Freud's theory. The ideas that form the core of the neoanalytic perspective concern the development of the ego (the person's executive functions), and the importance of social relationships in personality.

The next perspective, the *learning perspective* (Part Six) begins with a view of human nature in which *change,* rather than constancy, is paramount. That is, the key quality of human nature, from this perspective, is that behavior changes systematically as a result of experience. Because there are several views of how learning takes place, several theories link learning to personality. Though they differ, they share a single metatheory, holding that a person's personality is the integrated sum of what the person has learned up till now.

Next comes the *phenomenological perspective* (Part Seven). The roots of this perspective trace to two ideas. The first is that everyone's subjective experience is important, valuable, meaningful—and unique. The second is that people tend naturally toward self-perfection and that all people can move themselves in that direction by exercising their free will to do so. The sense of self-determination is central to this view of human nature. A person's personality, in this view, is partly a matter of the uniqueness hidden within, and partly a matter of what the person chooses to make of that uniqueness.

We've labeled the final perspective *cognitive self-regulation* (Part Eight). This view holds that cognitive processes underlie personality. The nervous system is a huge matrix of neurons, sending messages to one another. Somehow the nervous system yields systematic sets of decisions. It uses information in organized, coherent, patterned ways, rather than randomly. In this view, these patterns give rise to personality. Another aspect of this perspective is that people are self-regulating systems, setting goals and progressing toward those goals. Again, there is an assumption of organization, coherence, patterning.

How Distinct Are the Perspectives?

The brief description we just gave makes it clear that different perspectives on personality start with different views of human nature. There are also links among the perspectives, however. For example, phenomenological theories emphasize the concept of *self* and the need for the self to grow and develop naturally. The concept of self isn't too different from the concept of *ego,* which is a focus of neoanalytic theories. Thus, there's a conceptual link between neoanalytic and phenomenological theories. As another example, George Kelly, a phenomenological theorist, developed ideas that were reflected in later cognitive theories. This creates a link between the phenomenological and cognitive self-regulation views.

Is our linking of each theory to particular perspectives arbitrary, then? No, but it's imperfect. Here's an analogy. Think of theories as hot-air balloons (certainly a dangerous metaphor). All are attached by mooring ropes to posts in the ground. Each post represents a metatheory. Each balloon is tied quite firmly to one post, with a boarding ramp for passengers. However, most also have second ropes (and sometimes third and fourth ones) tied to other posts. Some posts have lots of balloons tied to them, others have only one or two. Some of the mooring ropes are strong and heavy, some are lighter. In an analogous way, each theory in this book is placed according to the metatheory it's tied to most firmly, but theories often have secondary ties to other metatheories.

ANOTHER KIND OF PERSPECTIVE

One more thing about our use of the term *perspective*. There was a time when personality psychologists created grand theories aimed at explaining the total complexity of personality. Freud's theory is the clearest example (and some would say the only good example). However, this has become less common. More common today are theories that deal with some *aspect* of personality. Most of these theories weren't really intended to be full models of personality, and it's a little misleading to present them (and judge them) as though they were.

The fact that a theory isn't a grand-scale theory doesn't mean it has nothing important to say about personality. It does mean, though, that such a theory won't say *everything* about personality. It gives us a particular viewing angle on the subject (a more literal meaning of the word *perspective*). This viewing angle may be special and may yield insights you can't find from other angles. But it yields only part of the picture. This limitation is important to keep in mind as you think about the various theories and what each has to say.

The fact that specific theories today tend to focus on smaller pieces of the puzzle also has another implication. Many people who have contributed to today's understanding of personality have made contributions to *several* points of view. Don't be surprised when you see the same name show up in two or three different places. In today's personality psychology, people whose work informs us about psychoanalytic concepts may also have had useful things to say about principles of self-regulation. People who helped us to understand learning may also have contributed to trait psychology.

This is one reason why, in general, we haven't focused the chapters in this book on particular individuals. Rather, in each chapter, we've emphasized *concepts* emphasized by a given theoretical viewpoint.

Organization within Chapters

Each chapter in a given perspective addresses a specific type of theory. Most of the content of each chapter is a description of the basic elements and processes of personality, as viewed from that theoretical view. Each chapter thus tells you something about individual differences and intrapersonal functioning, as seen by that theory.

Each chapter also addresses two more subjects. One is the process of measuring personality, called *assessment*. The other is the potential for problems to arise in human experience, and the processes by which behavior is changed for the better through therapy. Here's a brief preview of what these sections will be like.

Personality does not always function smoothly. Each perspective on personality has its own view about why problems occur.

ASSESSMENT

Personality psychologists give considerable attention to the process of measuring personality, for at least three reasons. First, psychologists want to be able to portray the personalities of specific individuals, in much the same way as you characterize the personalities of people you know. To be confident these pictures are accurate, psychologists need good ways to measure personality.

A second reason for assessing personality concerns the effort to study personality. To study qualities of personality, psychologists have to measure those qualities. Without good ways to assess individual differences or intrapersonal functioning, it's impossible to study them. Good assessment, then, lies at the heart of personality research.

A third reason to measure personality strays a bit from the main focus of this book. Specifically, assessing people's personality is an important part of applied psychology. For example, organizational psychologists use personality to help make hiring decisions (e.g., you might want to be sure you're hiring someone with a desired pattern of motives). Clinical psychologists also use personality assessment to help diagnose problems.

Assessment is a goal that's important throughout personality psychology. Some issues in assessment are the same for all viewpoints. (These are addressed in Chapter 3.) In other ways, assessment is viewed somewhat differently from different perspectives. As a result, theoretical views often differ in the assessment techniques they emphasize. In discussing assessment in each later chapter, we focus on how assessment from that viewpoint has its own special character.

PROBLEMS IN BEHAVIOR, AND BEHAVIOR CHANGE

The other topic included in each theory chapter concerns the fact that people's lives don't always go smoothly. Each view of normal personality also suggests a way to think about the nature of problems (more formally, *psychopathology*). Indeed, it can be argued that a theory of personality gains in credibility from saying useful things about problems. To clarify how each approach to personality views problems, we briefly take up this issue in each chapter from that chapter's viewpoint. As with assessment, our emphasis is on the special contribution made by that theoretical orientation to thinking about problems.

Finally, we describe how the theoretical orientation under discussion contributes to understanding the therapeutic management of problems. If each view has a way of thinking about normal processes and about how things can go wrong, each view also has a way to think about how to try to deal with the problems. Each suggests ways to turn problematic functioning back into effective and satisfying functioning.

· SUMMARY ·

Personality is a hard concept to define. Thinking about how people use the concept, however, suggests three reasons for its use. People use it to convey a sense of consistency or continuity within a person, to convey the sense that the person is the origin of behavior, and to convey the sense that the essence of a person can be summarized or captured in a few salient qualities.

The field of personality addresses two fundamental themes. One is the existence of differences among people. The other is how best to conceptualize intrapersonal functioning—the processes that take place within all persons, giving form and continuity to behavior.

Much of this book deals with theories. *Theories* are summary statements, sets of principles that pertain to certain classes of events. Theories have two purposes: to explain things that are known and to predict possibilities that haven't yet been examined. One way to evaluate the worth of a theory is to ask whether research supports its predictions. Scientific psychology has a continuing cycle between theory and research, as theories are tested, modified on the basis of results, and tested again.

Theories can be evaluated on several grounds other than research. For example, a theory shouldn't be based on a single kind of information. Theories benefit from being *parsimonious*—from having relatively few assumptions (or concepts). Theories also are judged as better when they fit well with one's intuitions and when they stimulate interest (and thus efforts to test them).

The theories described in this book derive from seven different perspectives, or viewpoints, on human nature. They are identified with the terms *dispositional, biological, psychoanalytic, neoanalytic, learning, phenomenological,* and *cognitive self-regulation.* Each theory chapter focuses on assumptions about the nature of personality within a particular theoretical framework. Also included are a discussion of assessment from the viewpoint of the theory under discussion, and a discussion of problems in behavior and how they can be remedied.

· GLOSSARY ·

Individual differences   Differences in personality from one person to another.

Intrapersonal functioning   Psychological processes that take place within the person.

Metatheory   A set of orienting assumptions about reality that provides guidelines for what kinds of ideas to use to create theories.

Parsimony   The quality of requiring few assumptions; simplicity.

Personality   A dynamic organization, inside the person, of psychophysical systems that create the person's characteristic patterns of behavior, thoughts, and feelings.

Theory   A summary statement, a principle or set of principles about a class of events.

Methods in the Study of Personality

Sam and Dave are at the lounge taking a break from studying. Sam says, "My roommate got a letter yesterday from his girlfriend at home—breaking up with him. People around here better watch out 'cause he's gonna be looking for some serious partying to help forget her."

"What makes you think so?"

"What kind of question is that? It's obvious. That's what *I'd* do."

"Huh. I know several guys whose hometown girls dumped them, and *none* of them did that. It was exactly the opposite. They lay around for a few weeks moping. I think you're wrong about how people react to this kind of thing."

W HEN PEOPLE try to understand personality, where do they start? When people create theories, where do the theories come from? How are theories tested? How do personality psychologists decide what to believe? These are all questions about the methods of science. They can be asked in all areas of scientific study, from astronomy to zoology. They are particularly challenging, though, when applied to personality.

Gathering Information

SOURCES: OBSERVE YOURSELF AND OBSERVE OTHERS

A simple way to gather information about personality is to look inward to your own experience (a process called *introspection*). This technique (used by Sam in the opening example) is open to everyone. Try it. You have a personality. If you want to understand personality in general, perhaps you should take a look at yours as an example. Sit back and think about recent events in your life. Think about what you did and how you felt, and pull from those recollections a thread of continuity. From this might come the start of a theory—a set of principles to explain your thoughts, feelings, and actions.

Examining your own experience is an easy beginning, and it can be a useful one, but it has a drawback. Specifically, your own consciousness has a special relationship to your memories (and to your present behavior) because they're your own. It's hard to be sure that this special relationship doesn't distort what you're seeing. For instance, you can misrecall something you experienced yet feel sure your memory is correct.

This problem lessens when you look at someone else instead of yourself (as Dave did in the opening example). That's the second method of gathering information: observe someone else. This method also has a problem, though—the opposite of introspection's problem. Specifically, it's impossible to be "inside another person's head," to really know what that person is thinking and feeling. This difference in perspective can create vast differences in understanding (cf. Jones & Nisbett, 1971). It can lead to misinterpretation.

Which starting point is better? Most psychologists would say that each has a place in the search for truth, though each also has problems. Each can lead to theories and research.

SEEKING DEPTH: CASE STUDIES

Some psychologists interested in personality seek explicitly to understand the entire person at once, rather than just part of the person. Henry Murray (1938), who emphasized the need to study persons as coherent entities, coined the term **personology** to refer to this effort. Many other early personality theorists took a similar view.

This view leads to the use of a technique called the **case study.** A case study involves in-depth examination of one person. It usually entails a long period of observation and typically includes unstructured interviews. Sometimes it involves spending a day or two interacting with the person or just being around the person to see how he or she interacts with others. The repeated observations let the observer confirm initial impressions or correct impressions that were wrong. Confirming or disconfirming an impression is hard to do if you make only one observation. The depth of probing that's possible in a case study can reveal detail about the person that otherwise wouldn't be apparent. This, in turn, can yield important insights.

Case studies are rich in detail and can create vivid descriptions of the person under study. Particularly compelling incidents or examples can be seen as illustrating broader themes in the person's life. There are other advantages to case studies, as well. Because they examine the person in his or her life situation, instead of settings created by the researcher, the information pertains directly to normal life. Because they're open ended, the observer can follow whatever leads seem interesting, rather than asking only questions chosen ahead of time.

Many case studies (though not all) are also *clinical studies*. That is, people who do case studies often focus on persons who have some kind of problem. Typically, these are therapists studying people they're treating. Clinical case studies give information about ways personality goes awry, as well as information about the normal workings of the person. Indeed, several theories of personality arose largely from case study observations in the context of therapy.

As an illustration of how a case study might be used to generate broader ideas about personality, consider this excerpt from the brief case study of a college student who's having personal difficulties: John is 19 years old, slender, and of medium height. His typical manner of dress conveys no particular style other than "average college student." The middle of three sons, he grew up in a small city in the Midwest. His father is a factory worker, and his mother works as an aide in a nursing home. Their combined income provides a modest living and lets the sons attend the state university, but does not permit many luxuries. John's older brother (by four years) had been a star athlete in high school, but his college career ended with an injury, and he now works in the same factory as his father. John's younger brother (by three years) shows a talent for math and science, and his father refers to him as "the engineer," clearly reflecting his hope for the boy's future.

Asked to talk about his high school years, John said he thought they had been mostly good, but maybe not as good for him as for others. Asked to clarify this, he related several minor disappointments in high school, none of which seemed to carry much weight by itself. Then he described an incident in which he had done poorly on a test for which he'd felt fully prepared. He shrugged, as if to suggest that the event wasn't important, but he seemed more tense than at other times during the conversation (or in other interviews).

John has had consistent academic difficulties at the university, despite having higher than average SAT scores. Academic Services referred him to the university's counseling center in the hope of resolving the difficulties. At first, John was all bravado with his counselor, but he didn't maintain that stance for long. In their second meeting, John said to his counselor that he didn't want to disappoint his parents, but he had doubts about whether he belonged in college. Other people in his dorm never seemed to question their abilities, but John felt a constant nagging sense that he wasn't up to the challenge.

After just a few discussions, it became apparent to John's counselor that he was lacking in self-esteem. As the counselor updated her notes on the case, she thought again about an idea that had crossed her mind more than once before: Students low in self-esteem don't seem to perform up to their potential in college. This idea has many implications, and the counselor made some more notes on it.

Thus, a series of observations—even brief observations—made in the course of examining one person's life situation can lead an observer to conclusions about how personality is involved in important categories of events.

SEEKING GENERALITY: STUDIES OF MANY PEOPLE

Case studies can provide insights into the human experience. They provide useful information for researchers and often serve as an important source of ideas. But currently they aren't the main source of information about personality. In large part, this is because a case study, no matter how complete, is lacking in an important respect: It deals with just one person. When you're forming theories or drawing conclusions from observations, you want them to apply to many people—if possible, to *all* people.

The generality of a conclusion can be established only by studying a mix of people from different backgrounds.

The breadth of applicability of a conclusion is called its **generality** or its **generalizability.** For a conclusion to be generalizable, it must be based on many people, not just one or two. The more people you look at, the more convinced you can be that what you see is true of people in general, instead of only a few people. In most research on personality done today, researchers look at tens—even hundreds—of people to increase the generality of their conclusions.

To truly ensure generality, researchers should study people of many ages and from all walks of life—indeed, from all cultures. For various reasons, this isn't always done, though it is becoming more common. As a matter of convenience, a lot of research on personality has examined only college students.

Do college students provide a reasonably good cross-section of the processes that are important in personality? Maybe yes, maybe no. College students differ from older adults in several ways; for one, they have a less fully formulated sense of self. This may make a difference in the research findings. How big a difference is a matter of conjecture. It does seem clear, though, that we should be cautious in assuming that conclusions drawn from research on college students always apply to "people in general."

Similarly, most observations on personality come from research done in the United States and western Europe. Most of the research has been done with middle- to upper-middle-class people. Some of it has used only men or only women. One must be cautious in assuming that the conclusions of a study apply to people from other cultures, other socioeconomic groups, and (sometimes) both genders.

Generalizability, then, is a kind of continuum. Rarely does any study range broadly enough to ensure total generalizability. Some are better than others. How broadly a conclusion can be generalized is an issue that must always be kept in mind in evaluating results of studies.

The desire for generality and the desire for in-depth understanding of a person represent competing pressures for observers of personality. They force a trade-off. That is, given the same investment of time and energy, you can know a great deal about the life of one person (or a very few people), or you can know a little bit about the lives of a much larger number of people. It's nearly impossible to do both at once. As a result, researchers tend to choose one path or the other, according to which pressure they find more important.

Establishing Relationships among Variables

Insights from introspection, observation, or systematic examination of a person by a case study can suggest relationships between variables. A **variable** is a dimension along which variations exist. There must be at least two values or levels on that dimension, though some variables have an infinite number of values. For example, *sex* is a variable with values of *male* and *female*.
Self-esteem is a variable that has a virtually limit-less number of values (from *very low* to *very high*) as you make finer discriminations among people.

It's important to distinguish between a variable and its values, because conclusions about relationships involve the whole dimension, not just one end of it. Thus, researchers always study at least two levels of the variable they're interested in. For example, you can't see effects of low self-esteem by looking only at people low in self-esteem. If there's a relationship between self-esteem and academic performance, the only way to find out is to look at people with *different levels* of self-esteem (see Figure 2.1). If the relationship does exist, people with very low self-esteem should have poor grades and people with higher self-esteem should have better grades.

The last part of that statement is every bit as important as the first part. Knowing that people

FIGURE 2.1

Whether a relationship exists between variables can be determined only by looking at more than one value on each variable. For instance, knowing that people low in self-esteem have poor academic performances leaves open the question of whether everyone else's performances are just as poor. This question is critically important in establishing a relationship between the two variables.

A correlation between two variables means they covary in some systematic way. Here there is a correlation between height and place in line.

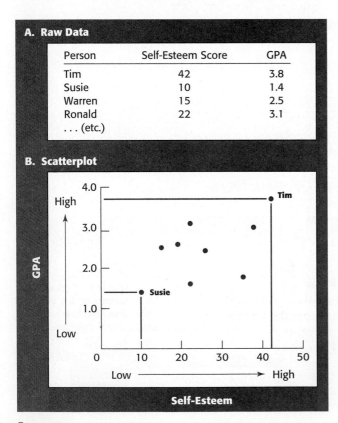

A. Raw Data

Person	Self-Esteem Score	GPA
Tim	42	3.8
Susie	10	1.4
Warren	15	2.5
Ronald	22	3.1
. . . (etc.)		

B. Scatterplot

FIGURE 2.2

Thinking about the meaning of correlation (with hypothetical data): (A) For each person, there are two pieces of information, a self-esteem score and a grade-point average (GPA). (B) The data can be arranged to form a scatterplot by plotting each person's self-esteem score along the horizontal dimension and GPA along the vertical dimension, thereby locating the combination in a two-dimensional space.

low in self-esteem have poor grades isn't informative if people high in self-esteem also have poor grades. It can be hard to keep this in mind. In fact, people often fail to realize how important this issue is. If you don't keep it in mind, though, you can make serious errors in the conclusions you reach (for illustrations, see Chapman, 1967; Crocker, 1981).

The need to examine people across a range of variability is a second reason why it's important to go beyond case studies. (The issue of generality was the first reason.) Indeed, the importance of examining a range of variability is what leads to the methods on which we focus for the rest of this chapter.

CORRELATION BETWEEN VARIABLES

There are two kinds of relationship that can be found between variables. The first is called **correlation.** A correlation between two dimensions means that as you examine them across many examples or instances, the values tend to go together in a systematic way. There are two aspects of this relationship, which are separate from each other: the *direction* of the correlation and the *strength* of the correlation. To clarify what these terms mean, let's return to the example of self-esteem and academic performance.

Suppose you've decided to investigate whether these two variables go together. You've gone out and found 40 students to study. They've completed a measure of self-esteem and given you their current grade-point average (GPA). You now have two pieces of information for each person (Figure 2.2, A). One way to organize this information is to create a scatterplot, (Figure 2.2, B). In a scatterplot, the two variables are represented by lines at right angles (the axes of the graph). The point where the lines meet is zero for both variables. Being farther away from zero on each line means having a higher value on that variable. Because the lines are at right angles, the combination of any score on one variable and any score on the other variable can be portrayed as a point in a two-dimensional space. For example, in Figure 2.2, Tim has a self-esteem score of 42 (thus being to the right side on the horizontal line) and a GPA of 3.8 (thus being toward the top on the vertical line). The scatterplot for your study would be the points that represent the combinations of self-esteem scores and GPA for each person in the study.

To ask whether the two variables are correlated means (essentially) asking the following question about the scatterplot: When you look at points that represent low versus high values on the *horizontal* dimension, do they differ in how they line up regarding the *vertical* dimension? If low values tend to go with low values and high values tend to go with high values (as in Figure 2.3, A), the two variables are said to be *positively* correlated. If people low in self-esteem tend to have low GPAs and people high in self-esteem tend to have high GPAs, you would say that self-esteem correlates positively with GPA. This finding has, in fact, emerged from actual studies of these variables (Scheirer & Kraut, 1979; Wylie, 1979).

Sometimes, however, a different kind of correlation occurs. Sometimes high values on one dimension tend to go along with low values on the other dimension (and vice versa). When this happens (Figure 2.3, B), the correlation between the variables is termed *inverse,* or *negative.* This kind of correlation might have emerged if you had studied the relation between GPA and the frequency of going to parties. That is, you might have found that students who party the most tend to have lower GPAs, whereas those who party the least tend to have higher GPAs.

The *direction* of the association between variables (positive versus negative) is one aspect of correlation. The second aspect—entirely separate from the first—is the *strength* of the correlation. Think of strength as the "sloppiness" of the association between the variables. More formally, it refers to the degree of accuracy with which you can predict values on one dimension from values on the other dimension. For example, assume a positive correlation between self-esteem and GPA. Suppose that you knew that Victoria had the second-highest score on self-esteem in your study. How accurate a guess could you make about Victoria's GPA?

The answer to this question is determined by how strong the correlation is. Because the correlation is positive, knowing that Victoria is on the high end of the self-esteem dimension would lead you to predict a high GPA. If the correlation is also *strong,* you're very likely to be right. If the correlation is weaker, you're less likely to be right. A perfect positive correlation—the strongest possible—means that the person who has the very highest value on one variable also has the very highest value on the other, the person next highest on one is also next highest on the other, and so on, throughout the list (Figure 2.4, A).

The strength of a correlation is expressed by a number called a **correlation coefficient** (often labeled with a lowercase *r*). An absolutely perfect positive correlation (as in Figure 2.4, A) is expressed by the number 1.0. This is the largest numerical value a correlation can take. It indicates a totally accurate prediction from one dimension to the other. If you know where the person is on one variable, you can tell with complete confidence where he or she is on the other.

The scatterplot of a somewhat weaker correlation is shown in Figure 2.4, B. As you can see, there's more "scatter" among the points than in the first case. There's still a noticeable tendency for higher values on one dimension to match up with higher ones on the other and for lows to match up with lows, but the tendency is less exact.

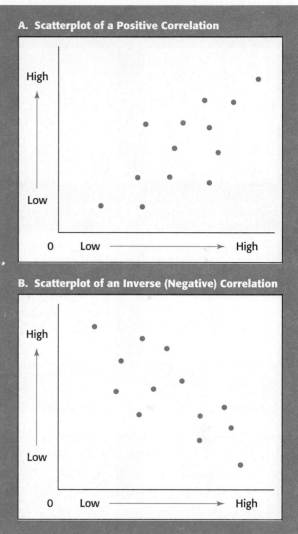

A. **Scatterplot of a Positive Correlation**

High

Low

0   Low ⟶ High

B. **Scatterplot of an Inverse (Negative) Correlation**

High

Low

0   Low ⟶ High

FIGURE 2.3
(A) If high numbers on one dimension tend to go with high numbers on the other dimension (and low with low), there is a positive correlation. (B) If high numbers on one dimension tend to go with low numbers on the other dimension, there is an inverse, or negative, correlation.

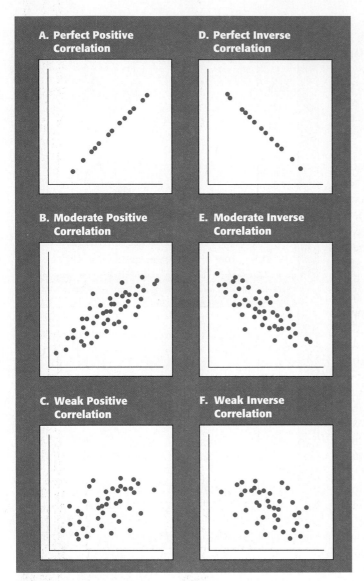

FIGURE 2.4

Six correlations: (A) Perfect positive correlation, (B) Moderate positive correlation, (C) Weak positive correlation, (D) Perfect inverse correlation, (E) Moderate inverse correlation, and (F) Weak inverse correlation. The weaker the correlation, the more "scatter" in the scatterplot.

As the correlation becomes weaker, the number representing it becomes smaller (thus, virtually all correlations are decimal values). Correlations of 0.6 to 0.8 are strong. Correlations of 0.3 to 0.5 are moderately strong. Below 0.3 or 0.2, the prediction from one variable to the other is getting poorer. As you can see in Figure 2.4, C, weak correlations have even more scatter. The tendency toward a positive relation is there, but it definitely isn't strong. A correlation of 0.0 means the two variables aren't related to each other at all. A scatterplot of a zero correlation is random dots.

As we said before, a correlation's strength is entirely separate from its direction. *Strength* refers only to degree of accuracy in prediction. Thus, it is eminently sensible to talk about a perfect inverse (negative) correlation as well as a perfect positive correlation. A perfect inverse correlation (Figure 2.4, D) means that the person who had the highest value on one variable also had the very lowest value on the other variable, the person with the next-highest value on one had the next-to-lowest value on the other, and so on.

Negative correlations are expressed in numbers, just as are positive correlations. But to show that the relationship is an inverse one, a minus sign is placed in front. Thus an r value of -0.75 is precisely as strong as an r value of 0.75. The first represents an inverse correlation, though, whereas the second represents a positive correlation.

TWO KINDS OF SIGNIFICANCE

We've been describing the strength of correlations in terms of the size of the numbers that represent them. Although the size of the number gives information about its strength, the size of the number by itself doesn't tell you whether the correlation is believable or real. Maybe it's a fluke. This is a problem, in fact, for all kinds of statistics. You can't tell just by looking at the number or looking at a graph whether the result is real. You need to know whether the result is **statistically significant.**

Significant in this context has a very specific meaning: It means that the correlation would have been that large or larger only rarely if no true relation exists. When the probability is small enough (just under 5%), the correlation (or whatever statistic it is) is said to be statistically significant (see also Box 2.1). At that point, the researcher concludes that the relationship is a real one rather than a random occurrence.

A second use of the word *significant* has also become common in psychology. This use more closely resembles the use of the word in day-to-day language. An association is said to be **clinically significant,** or **practically significant,** if the effect is both statistically significant (so it's believable) and large enough to have some practical importance. How large it has to be varies from case to case. It's possible, though, for an

BOX 2.1 STATISTICS AND STATISTICS

Description versus Inference

When people think of *statistics,* they often think of the statistics that portray a set of events—for example, "The average American earns $37,000 a year," or "She averaged 21.6 points per game." These are called **descriptive statistics** because their purpose is to give a description.

Psychologists also use statistics in a different way, discussed in the body of the chapter. These statistics are called **inferential statistics** because they let the researcher make inferences. The information they provide guides the scientist in deciding whether to believe something is true. Interestingly enough, it isn't possible to *prove* something is true. What statistics do is show how probable the finding was, provided that there was no true relation. If it can be shown that the effect was very *unlikely*

to have occurred, the researcher infers that it's real.

An example of the ability of inferential statistics to reveal patterns, and the limitations on what they can say, took place after the 2000 presidential election in the United States. Voters in Palm Beach County, Florida, had encountered an unfamiliar and confusing ballot format on election day. Many later reported accidentally voting for one candidate (Pat Buchanan) while trying to vote for another one (Al Gore). The election, won by George W. Bush, was extremely close. Its outcome might have turned on such errors. Were these people just complaining because their candidate lost? Or was there really a problem with the ballot?

Social scientists Greg Adams and Chris Fastnow (2000) used inferential statistics to test whether the pattern of votes in Palm Beach County differed from patterns in other Florida coun-

ties. In every county but Palm Beach, the more votes cast for Bush, the more votes also cast for Buchanan. If Palm Beach had been like every other county in Florida, Buchanan would have gotten around 600 votes instead of 3,407. The inference was clear: The chances were extremely small that this difference in pattern would have occurred if there were no true relation. Something apparently was throwing off the voting pattern in Palm Beach.

We say "apparently" to emphasize something about the nature of inferential statistics. Whenever you use them to make a judgment, the conclusion is always probabilistic. The odds that the inference was wrong in this case are *extremely* small. But the possibility does exist. Inferential statistics thus are best viewed as procedures that allow us to attach "confidence units" to our judgments, rather than procedures that lead infallibly to correct choices.

---

association to be statistically significant but to account for only a tiny part of the behavior. The practical significance of such an association usually isn't very great.

CAUSALITY AND A LIMITATION ON INFERENCE

Correlations tell us whether two variables go together (and in what direction and how strongly). But they don't tell us *why* the variables go together. The *why* question takes us beyond the realm of correlation into a second kind of relationship. This relationship is called **causality**—the relationship between a cause and its effect. Correlational research isn't able to provide evidence on this second kind of relationship. A correlational study often gives people strong *intuitions* about causality, but no more.

Why? The answer is illustrated in Figure 2.5. Each arrow there represents a possible path of causality. What this figure shows is that there are always three ways to account for the results of a correlation. Consider the correlation between self-esteem and academic performance. What causes that association? Your intuition may say the best explanation is that having bad academic outcomes causes people to have lower self-esteem, whereas having good outcomes causes people to feel good about themselves (arrow 1 in Figure 2.5). Or maybe you think the best explanation is that having low self-esteem causes people not to try as hard in their courses, thus resulting in poorer performances (arrow

Random assignment is an important hallmark of the experimental method. The experimenter randomly assigns participants to a condition, much as a roulette wheel randomly catches the ball in a black or red slot.

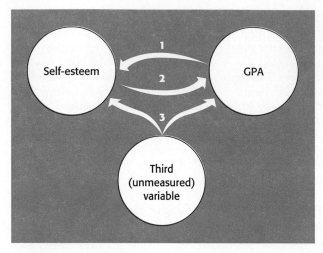

FIGURE 2.5
Correlation does not imply cause and effect, because there are always three possibilities: (1) variations in one variable (academic performance) may be causing variations in the second (self-esteem); (2) variations in the second may be causing variations in the first; or (3) a third variable may actually be causing both observed effects. Knowing only the single correlation between self-esteem and GPA doesn't allow you to distinguish among these possibilities.

2). Both of these explanations are plausible, though they represent opposite cause–effect relationships.

It could also be, however, that a third variable—not measured, perhaps not even thought of—actually exerts a causal influence over both variables that were measured (the pair of arrows labeled 3). Perhaps having a high level of intelligence causes a positive sense of self-esteem and also causes better academic performance. In this scenario, both self-esteem and academic performance are effects, and something else is the cause.

The possible involvement of another variable behind a correlation is sometimes called the **third-variable problem.** It's a problem that can't be handled by correlational research. That method cannot tell which of the three possibilities shown in Figure 2.5 is actually correct.

SEARCH FOR CAUSALITY: EXPERIMENTAL RESEARCH

There *is* a method that allows one to demonstrate cause and effect, however. It's called the **experimental method.** Think of it as having two defining characteristics. First, in an experiment, the researcher "manipulates" one variable—creates the existence of at least two levels of it. The one the researcher is manipulating is called the **independent variable.** It's the one the researcher is testing as the possible *cause* in a cause–effect relationship. When we say the researcher is "creating" two (or more) levels of this variable, we mean exactly that. There's some kind of event that *actively creates* a difference between the experience of some people and the experience of other people.

Sometimes researchers do experiments in order to better understand what they've seen in correlational studies. Let's illustrate the experimental method by doing just that. Let's pursue further the example we just discussed. Suppose you have a hunch that variations in academic performance have a causal effect on self-esteem. (Unlike John's counselor, you think poor performances make people get down on themselves and good performances make them happy with themselves.) To study this possibility, you conduct an experiment in which you hypothesize (predict) that academic outcomes affect self-esteem.

You can't really manipulate GPA in this experiment, but it's fairly easy to manipulate other things with overtones of academic performance. For instance, you could arrange to have some people experience a success and others a failure (using a task rigged to be easy or impossible). By arranging this, you would *create* the difference between success and failure. You'd manipulate it—not measure it. You're sure that a difference now exists between the two sets of people in your experiment, because you *made* it exist.

As in all research, you'd do your best to treat every participant in your experiment exactly the same in all ways other than that one. Treating everyone the same—in fact, making everything be exactly the same except for what you manipulate—is called **experimental control.** Exerting a high degree of experimental control is important to the logic of the experimental method, as you'll see momentarily.

Control is important, but you can't control everything. It's rarely possible to have every person be in the research at the same time of day or the same day of the week. More obviously, perhaps, it's impossible to be sure the people in the experiment are exactly alike. One of the main themes of this book, after all, is that people differ. Some people in the experiment are just naturally going to have higher self-esteem when they walk in the door than are others. How can these differences be handled?

This question brings us to the second defining characteristic of the experimental method: Any variable that can't be controlled—such as individual differences—is treated by **random assignment.** In your experiment, you would randomly assign each participant to either the success experience or the failure experience. Random assignment is often done by such means as tossing a coin or using a list of random numbers.

The use of random assignment rests on a specific assumption: that if you study enough people in the experiment, any important differences between people (and from other sources as well) will balance out between the groups. Each group is likely to have as many tall people, fat people, depressed people, and confident people as the other group—*if* you have a fairly large number of participants and use random assignment. Anything that matters should balance out.

So you've brought people to your research laboratory one at a time, randomly assigned them to the two conditions, manipulated the independent variable, and exerted experimental control over everything else. At some point, you would then measure the variable you think is the effect in the cause-and-effect relationship. This one is termed the **dependent variable.**

In this experiment, your hypothesis was that differences in success and failure cause people to differ in their self-esteem. Thus, the dependent measure would be a measure of self-esteem (for example, self-report items asking people how they feel about themselves). After getting this measure for each person in the experiment, you would compare the groups to each other (by statistical procedures that need not concern us here). If the difference between groups was statistically significant, you could conclude that the experience of success and failure *causes* people to differ in self-esteem.

What would make you so confident in that cause-and-effect conclusion? The answer, despite all the details we've gone through, is really quite simple. The logic is displayed graphically in Figure 2.6. At the beginning of the experiment, you separated people into two groups. (By the way, the reasoning applies even if the independent variable has more than two levels.) If the assumption about the effect of random assignment is correct, the two groups don't differ from each other at this point. Because you exercise experimental control throughout your procedures, the groups still don't differ as the experiment unfolds.

At one point, however, a difference between groups is introduced—when you manipulate the independent variable. As we said before, you know there's a difference now, and you know *what* the difference is, because you created it yourself. For this reason, if you find the groups differ from each other on the dependent measure at the end, you know there's only one thing that could have caused the difference (Figure 2.6). It *had* to come from the manipulation of the independent variable. That was the only place where a difference between groups was created. It was the only thing that could have been responsible for causing the effect.

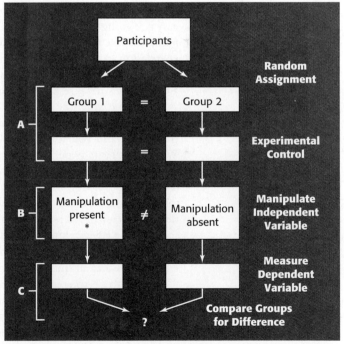

FIGURE 2.6
The logic of the experimental method: (A) Because of random assignment and experimental control, there is no systematic difference between groups at first. (B) The experimental manipulation creates—for the first time—a specific difference. (C) If the groups then are found to differ in another fashion, the manipulation must have caused this difference.

This reasoning is straightforward. We should note, however, that this method isn't entirely perfect. Its problem is this: When you do an experiment, you show that the *manipulation* causes the difference on the dependent measure—but you can't always be completely sure *what it was* about the manipulation that did the causing. Maybe it was the aspect of the manipulation that you were focused on, but maybe it was something else.

For example, in the experiment we've been considering, low self-esteem may have been caused by the failure and the self-doubt to which it led. But it *might* have been caused by other things about the manipulation. Maybe the people were worried that they had spoiled the results of your experiment by not solving the problems. They didn't feel a sense of *failure* but were angry with themselves for creating a problem for you. This interpretation of the result wouldn't mean quite the same thing as your first interpretation of it. This issue requires us always to be a bit cautious in how we view results, even from experiments.

RECOGNIZING TYPES OF STUDY

When you read about correlational studies and experiments later in this book, how easy is it going to be for you to tell them apart? At first glance, it seems simple. An *experiment* makes a comparison between groups, and a *correlational study* gives you a correlation, right? Well, no. Results of correlational studies aren't always reported as correlations. Sometimes the study compares two (or more) groups with each other on a dependent measure, and the word *correlation* is never even mentioned.

Suppose you studied some people who were 40% overweight and some who were 40% underweight. You interviewed them individually and judged how sociable they were, and you found that heavy people were more sociable than thin people. Would this be an experiment or a correlational study? Recall the two defining characteristics of the experiment: manipulation of the independent variable and random assignment of people to groups. You didn't randomly assign people to be heavy or thin (and didn't *create* these differences). Therefore, this is a correlational study. The limitation on correlational research (the inability to conclude cause and effect) applies to it.

A good rule of thumb is that any time groupings reflect *naturally occurring differences* or are formed on the basis of a *characteristic that you measure,* the study is correlational. This means that all studies of personality differences are, by definition, correlational.

Why do personality researchers make their correlational studies look like experiments? Sometimes it's because they select participants from the extreme ends of some personality variable—people who are very low and very high, respectively, on some dimension of personality. This strategy maximizes the chances of finding differences. That is, removing the people who are average on that dimension helps to remove clutter and make the picture clearer. It has the side effect, however, of making it hard to express the finding as a correlation. The result is correlational studies that look at first glance like experiments.

WHAT KIND OF RESEARCH IS BEST?

Another question that's often asked is, Which kind of research is better, experiments or correlational studies? The answer is that both have advantages, and the advantage of each is the disadvantage of the other. The advantage of the experimental method, of course, is its ability to show cause and effect, which the correlational method cannot do.

But experiments also have drawbacks. For one (as noted), there's sometimes uncertainty about which aspect of the manipulation was important. For another, experiments on people usually involve events of relatively short duration in carefully controlled conditions. The correlational method, in contrast, lets you examine events that take place over long periods (even decades) and events that are much more elaborate. Correlational studies also let us get information about events in which experimental manipulation would be unethical—for example, the effects of being raised by a divorced parent or the effects of cigarette smoking.

Personality psychologists sometimes also criticize experiments on the grounds that the kinds of relationships they reveal often have little to do with the central issues of personality. Even experiments that seem to bear on important issues in personality may tell less than they seem to. Consider the hypothetical experiment described earlier, in which you manipulated academic success and failure and measured self-esteem. Assume for the moment that participants given a failure had lower self-esteem afterward than participants given a success. You might be tempted to infer from this experiment that having poor academic outcomes over the course of one's life causes people to develop low self-esteem.

This conclusion, however, may not be justified. The experiment dealt with a brief task outcome, manipulated in a particular way. The broader conclusion you're tempted to reach deals with a basic quality of personality. This latter quality may differ in many ways from the momentary state you manipulated. The "reasoning by analogy" you're tempted to engage in is dangerous, and it can be misleading.

To many personality psychologists, the only way to really understand personality is to look at naturally occurring differences between people (Underwood, 1975). These psychologists are willing to accept the limitation on causal inference that's inherent in correlations; they regard it as an acceptable price to pay. On the other hand, many of these psychologists are comfortable *combining* the correlational strategy with experimental techniques, as described next.

MULTIFACTOR STUDIES

We've been talking about studies as though they always involved predicting a dependent variable from a single predictor variable (either an experimental manipulation or an individual difference). In reality, however, studies often look at the effects of several predictors at once by using multifactor designs. In a **multifactor study,** two (or more) variables are varied *separately,* which means creating all combinations of the various levels of the predictor variables. The study shown in Figure 2.7 has two factors, but more than two can be used. The more factors in a study, of course, the larger is the resulting array of combinations, and the trickier it is to keep track of things.

Sometimes the factors are all experimental manipulations. Sometimes they're all personality variables. Often, though, experimental manipulations are crossed by individual-difference variables. The example shown in Figure 2.7 is such a design. The self-esteem factor is the level of self-esteem the people had when they came to the study. This is a personality dimension (thus correlational). The success–failure factor is an experimental manipulation, which takes place during the session. In this particular experiment, the dependent measure is performance on a second task, which the participants attempt after the experimental manipulation.

FIGURE 2.7
Diagram of a hypothetical two-factor study. Each square represents the combination of the value listed above it and the value listed to the left. In multifactor studies, all combinations of values of the predictor variables are created in this fashion.

These designs allow researchers to examine how different types of people respond to variations in situations. They thus offer a glimpse into the underlying dynamics of the individual-difference variable. Because this type of study combines experimental procedures and individual differences, it is often referred to as **experimental personality research.**

FIGURE 2.8
Two hypothetical outcomes of a two-factor study looking at self-esteem and an initial success-versus-failure experience as predictors of performance on a second task. (A) This graph indicates that experiencing a failure causes people low in self-esteem to perform worse later on than if they had experienced a success, but that experiencing a failure does not have any effect on people high in self-esteem. (B) This graph indicates that experiencing a failure causes people low in self-esteem to perform worse later on, but that experiencing a failure causes people high in self-esteem to perform *better* later on. Thus, the failure influences both kinds of people but does so in opposite ways.

READING FIGURES FROM MULTIFACTOR RESEARCH

Because multifactor designs are more complex than single-factor studies, what they can tell you is also potentially more complex. Indeed, people who do experimental personality research use these designs precisely for this reason.

You don't *always* get a complex result from a multifactor study. Sometimes you find only the same outcomes you would have found if you had studied each predictor variable separately. When you find that a predictor variable is linked to the outcome variable in a systematic way, completely separate from the other predictor, the finding is referred to as a **main effect.** For example, the study outlined in Figure 2.7 might find only that people of both self-esteem levels perform worse after a failure than after a success.

The complexity occurs when a study finds what's termed an **interaction.** Figure 2.8 portrays two interactions, each a possible outcome of the hypothetical study of Figure 2.7. In each case, the vertical dimension portrays the dependent measure: performance on the second task. The two marks on the horizontal line represent the two values of the manipulated variable: initial success versus failure. The color of the line depicts the other predictor variable: the color line is participants high in self-esteem, and the black line is those low in self-esteem.

We emphasize that these graphs show *hypothetical* outcomes. They are intended only to give you a clearer understanding of what interactions are about. Figure 2.8, A, portrays a finding that people who are low in self-esteem perform worse after an initial failure than after a success. Among people high in self-esteem, however, this doesn't occur. Failure apparently has no effect on them. Thus, the effect of one variable (success versus failure) differs across the two levels of the other variable (degree of self-esteem). That is the meaning of the term *interaction.* In the case in Figure 2.8, A, a failure has an effect at one level of the second variable (in the low self-esteem group) but has no effect at the other level of the second variable (the high self-esteem group).

Two more points about interactions: First, to find an interaction, it's *absolutely necessary* to study more than one factor at a time. It's impossible to find an interaction unless both variables involved in it are studied at once. This is one reason researchers often use complex designs: They allow the possibility for interactions to emerge.

The second point is revealed by comparing Figure 2.8, A, with Figure 2.8, B. This point is that interactions can take many forms. In contrast to the interaction we just described, the graph in panel B says that failure has effects on both kinds of people, but opposite effects. People low in self-esteem perform worse after failure (as in the first graph), but people high in self-esteem actually perform better after a failure, perhaps because the failure motivates them to try harder.

These two graphs aren't the only forms of interactions. Exactly what an *interaction* means always depends on the form it takes. Thus, exploring interactions always requires checking to see in what way each group was influenced by the other variable under study.

· SUMMARY ·

Research in personality relies on observations of both the self and others. The desire to understand a person as an integrated whole led to *case studies,* in-depth examinations of specific persons. The desire for *generalizability*—conclusions that would apply to many rather than to a few people—led to studies involving systematic examination of many people.

Gathering information is only the first step toward examining relationships between and among variables. Relationships among variables are examined in two ways, corresponding to two kinds of relationships. *Correlational research* determines the degree to which two variables tend to go together in a predictable way when measured at different levels along the dimensions. This technique determines two aspects of the relationship: its direction and its strength. The special relationship of cause and effect cannot be determined by this kind of study, however.

A second technique, called the *experimental method,* allows testing for cause and effect. In an experiment, an independent variable is manipulated, other variables are controlled (made constant), and anything that cannot be controlled is treated by random assignment. An effect caused by the manipulation is measured in the dependent variable. Experimental and correlational techniques are often combined in multifactor studies. This is termed *experimental personality research.* Multifactor studies permit the emergence of interactions.

· GLOSSARY ·

Case study   An in-depth study of one individual.

Causality   A relationship such that variation in one dimension produces variation in another.

Clinically significant   An association large enough to have some practical importance.

Correlation   A relationship in which two variables or dimensions covary when measured repeatedly.

Correlation coefficient   A numeric index of the degree of correlation between two variables.

Dependent variable   The variable measured as the outcome of an experiment; the effect in a cause–effect relation.

Descriptive statistics   Statistics used to describe or characterize some group.

Experimental control   The holding constant of variables that are not being manipulated.

Experimental method   The method in which one variable is manipulated to test for causal influence on another variable.

Experimental personality research   A study involving a personality factor and an experimental factor.

Generality (generalizability)   The degree to which a conclusion applies to many people.

Independent variable   The variable manipulated in an experiment, tested as the cause in a cause–effect relation.

Inferential statistics   Statistics used to judge whether a relationship exists between variables.

Interaction   A finding in which the effect of one predictor variable differs depending on the level of another predictor variable.

Main effect   A finding in which the effect of one predictor variable is independent of other variables.

Multifactor study   A study with two (or more) predictor variables.

Personology   The study of the whole person, as opposed to studying only one aspect of the person.

Practical significance   An association large enough to have practical importance.

Random assignment   The process of putting people randomly into groups of an experiment so their characteristics balance out across groups.

Statistical significance   The likelihood of an obtained effect occurring when there is no true effect.

Third-variable problem   The possibility that an unmeasured variable caused variations in both of two correlated variables.

Variable   A dimension along which two or more variations exist.

Issues in Personality Assessment

On the first day of class, Jeff saw a woman he didn't know, and he's been trying ever since to get an idea of what she's like. He watches how she acts and dresses, listens to what she says to people. He asks friends if they know anything about her. After a while he starts to wonder how "good" the information he's gathering is. Pat always sees things in a slanted way, so whatever she says has to be taken with a grain of salt. Jennifer hardly notices things that are right in front of her, so who knows what to make of what she says? When the stranger raises her hand and gives opinions in class, do they represent who she really is, or is she trying to convince the teacher she's an intellectual? When she turned down a date with Chris after class the other day, was that a trace of scorn in her voice? Or was she just flustered?

THE MEASURING of personality is called **assessment.** It's something we all do informally, all the time. We want to have an idea of the personalities of the people we interact with so we know what to expect of them. For this reason, we develop ways of gauging people, judging what they're like. You probably don't think of this as *assessment,* but what you're doing informally is much the same—in principle—as what psychologists do more formally.

Forming impressions of what other people are like can be hard. It's easy to get misleading impressions. Personality assessment is also hard for psychologists. All the problems you have, they have too. But personality psychologists work hard to deal with those problems.

Sources of Information

Informal assessment draws information from many sources, and so does formal assessment. In fact, as you'll see, each way of getting information that was mentioned in the opening example has a counterpart in a formal assessment technique.

Many measures of personality come from someone other than the person being assessed (Funder, 1991; Paunonen, 1989). The broad name for this technique is **observer ratings.** There are many kinds of observer ratings. Sometimes observers make judgments about the person being assessed without interacting directly with the person. The judgments may be based on watching the person's actions. The judgments may be opinions, ratings made by people who know the person well enough to say what he or she is like.

Other observer assessments involve interviews. People being assessed may talk in their own words about themselves, and the interviewer draws conclusions from what's said and how it's said. Sometimes the people being interviewed talk about something *other than* themselves. In so doing, they reveal something indirectly to the interviewer about what they're like.

Though many techniques of assessment rely on the impressions of outside observers, not all do. A great many measures of personality—indeed, the vast majority—are **self-reports.** In self-reports, people themselves indicate what they think they're like or how they feel or act. Self-reports thus resemble the process of introspection described in the last chapter. Although self-reporting can be done in an unstructured descriptive way, usually it's not. Most self-reports ask people to respond to a specific set of items.

There are many different types of observer ratings. Here an observer is directly rating a research participant's overt behavior.

Self-report scales can be created in many formats. An example is the true–false format, where you read statements and decide whether each one is true or false for you. Another common format is a multipoint rating scale. Here a wider range of response options are available—ranging, for example, from "strongly agree" to "strongly disagree."

Some self-reports focus on a single quality of personality. Often, though, people who develop tests want to assess *several* aspects of personality in the same test (as separate scales). A measure that assesses several dimensions of personality is called an **inventory.** The process of developing an inventory is no different from the process of developing a single scale. The only difference is that in this case, you must go through each step of development for *each scale of the inventory,* rather than just one.

As you can see, the arsenal of possible assessment techniques is large. All require two processes, though. First, in each case the person who's being assessed produces a sample of "behavior." This may literally be an action that someone else observes, it may be internal behavior such as a change in heartrate, or it may be the behavior of answering self-report items. Second, someone then uses the behavior sample as a guide to some aspect of the person's personality.

Some measures are termed **subjective,** whereas others are termed **objective.** In subjective measures, an interpretation is part of the measure. An example is an observer's judgment that a person he or she is watching looks nervous. The judgment renders the measure subjective, because it's an *interpretation* of the behavior. If the measure focuses on a concrete physical reality that requires no interpretation, it's said to be objective. For example, you could count the number of times a person stammers while talking. This would involve no interpretation yet. Although this count might later be used to infer nervousness (an interpretation), the measure itself is objective.

To some extent, this issue cuts across the distinction between observer ratings and self-reports. An observer can make objective counts of acts, or can develop a subjective impression of the person. In the same way, a person making a self-report can report counts of specific events, or can give a subjective impression of what he or she is like. It should be apparent, though, that self-reports are particularly vulnerable to incorporating subjectivity. Even reports of specific events, if they're retrospective, permit unintentional interpretations to creep in.

Reliability of Measurement

All techniques of assessment confront several kinds of problems, or issues. One issue is termed **reliability** of measurement. The nature of this issue can be conveyed by putting it as a question: Once you've made an observation about someone, how confident can you be that if you looked again a second or third time, you'd see about the same thing? When an observation is reliable, it has a high degree of *consistency,* or *repeatability.* Low reliability means that what is measured is less consistent. The measure isn't just reflecting the person being measured. It's also including a lot of randomness, termed **error.**

All measurement procedures have sources of error. (Error can be reduced but not eliminated.) When you use a telescope to look at the moon, a little dust on the lens, minor imperfections in the glass, flickering lights nearby, and swirling air currents can all contribute error to what you see. When you use a rating scale to measure how independent people think they are, the way you phrase the item can be a source of error because it can lead to different interpretations. When you have an observer watching a child's behavior, the observer is a source of error because of variations in how closely he's paying attention, thinking about what he's seeing, or being influenced by a thousand other things.

How do you deal with the issue of reliability in measurement? The general answer is to repeat the measurement, make the observation more than once. Usually this means measuring the same quality from a slightly different angle or using a slightly different measuring device. This lets the diverse sources of error in the different devices cancel each other out.

Reliability actually is a family of problems, not just a single problem, because it crops up in several different contexts. Each version of the problem has a separate name, and the tactic used to treat each version differs slightly from the tactics used on the others.

INTERNAL CONSISTENCY

The simplest act of assessment is the single observation or measurement. How can you be sure it doesn't include too much error? Let's take an illustration from ability assessment. Think about what you'd do if you wanted to know how good someone was at a particular type of problem—math problems or word puzzles. You wouldn't give the person just a *single* problem to solve, because whether he or she solved it easily might depend too much on some quirk of that particular problem. If you want to know (reliably) how well the person solves that kind of problem, you'd give him or her *several* problems.

The same strategy applies to personality assessment. If you were using a self-report to ask people how independent they think they are, you wouldn't ask just once. You'd ask several times, using different items that all reflect independence, but in different words. In this example, *each item* is a measuring device. When you go to a new item, you're shifting to a different measuring device, trying to measure the same quality in the same person. In effect, you're putting down one telescope and picking up another.

Human judges are not infallible. They sometimes perceive things inaccurately.

The reliability question is whether you see about the same thing through the different telescopes.

This kind of reliability is termed **internal reliability** or **internal consistency.** This is reliability within a set of observations of a single aspect of personality. Because different items have different sources of random error, using many items should tend to balance out the error. The more observations, the more likely it is that the random error will cancel out. Because people using self-report scales want good reliability, most scales contain many items. If the items are reliable enough, they're then used together as a single index of the personality quality.

How do you find out whether the items you're using have good internal reliability? Just having a lot of items doesn't guarantee it. Reliability is a question about the correlations among people's responses to the items. Saying that the items are highly reliable means that people's responses to the items are highly intercorrelated.

As a practical matter, there are several ways to investigate internal consistency. All of them examine correlations among people's responses across items. Perhaps the best way (although it's cumbersome) is to look at the average correlation between each pair of items taken separately. A simpler way is to separate the items into two subsets (often odd- versus even-numbered items), add up people's scores for each subset, and correlate the two subtotals with each other. This provides an index called **split-half reliability.** If the two halves of the item set measure the same quality of personality, people who score high on one half should also score high on the other half, and people who score low on one half should also score low on the other half. Thus, a strong positive correlation between halves is evidence of internal consistency.

INTER-RATER RELIABILITY

As noted, personality isn't always measured by self-reports. Some observations are *literally* observations, made by one person watching and assessing someone else. Use of observer ratings creates a slightly different reliability problem. In an observer rating, the *person making the observation* is a measuring device. There are sources of error in this device, just as in other devices. How can you judge reliability in this case?

Conceptually, the answer is the same as it was in the other case. You need to put down one telescope and pick up another. In the case of observer ratings, you need to check this observer against another observer. To the extent that both see about the same thing when they look at the same event, reliability is high. This dual observation is logically the same as using two items on a questionnaire. Raters whose judgments correlate highly with each other across many ratings are said to have high **inter-rater reliability.**

In many cases, having high inter-rater reliability requires the judges to be thoroughly trained in how to observe what they're observing. Judges of Olympic diving, for example, have witnessed many thousands of dives and know precisely what

If all judges are seeing the same things when they rate an event, then inter-rater reliability will be high.

to look for. As a result, their inter-rater reliability is high. Similarly, when observers assess personality, they often receive considerable instruction and practice before turning to the "real thing," so their reliability will be high.

Table 3.1 Three Kinds of Reliability. Each assesses the consistency or repeatability of an observation by looking a second time, either with the same measuring device or with a slightly different one.

Type of Reliability	Measuring Device	Type of Consistency
Internal reliability	Test item	Consistency within the test
Inter-rater reliability	Rater	Agreement between raters
Test–retest reliability	Entire test	Consistency across time

STABILITY ACROSS TIME

There's one more kind of reliability that's important in the measurement of personality. This type of reliability concerns repeatability across time. That is, assessment at one time should agree fairly well with assessment done at a different time.

Why is this important? Remember, personality is supposed to be stable. That's one reason people use the word—to convey a sense of stability. If personality is really *stable*—doesn't fluctuate from minute to minute or from day to day—then *measures* of personality should be reliable across time. People's scores should stay roughly the same when measured a week later, a month later, or four years later.

This kind of reliability is termed **test–retest reliability.** It's determined by giving the test to the same people at two different times. A scale with high test–retest reliability will yield scores the second time (the retest) that are fairly similar to those from the first time. People with high scores the first time will have high scores the second time; those with lower scores at first will have lower scores later on. (For a summary of these three types of reliability, see Table 3.1.)

Validity of Measurement

Reliability is a starting point in measurement, but it's not the only issue that matters. It's possible for measures to be highly reliable but completely meaningless. Thus, another important issue is what's called **validity.** This issue concerns whether what you're measuring is what you *think* you're measuring (or what you're *trying* to measure). Earlier we illustrated the concept of reliability in terms of random influences on the image in a telescope as you look through it at the moon. To extend the same analogy, the validity issue is whether the image you're seeing is really the moon, or just a street light (see also Figure 3.1).

How do you decide whether you're measuring what you want to measure? There are two ways to answer this question. One is an "in-principle" answer, the other is a set of tactics. The in-principle answer is that people decide by comparing two kinds of definitions with each other. When you see the word *definition,* what probably comes to mind is a conceptual, or dictionary, definition, which spells out the word's meaning in terms of conceptual qualities or attributes. It tells us what information the users of a language have agreed the word conveys. Psychologists also talk about another kind of definition, however, called an **operational definition.** This is a description of some kind of physical event.

The difference between the two kinds of definition is easy to illustrate. Consider the concept of *love.* Its conceptual (dictionary) definition might be something like "a strong affection for another person." There are many ways, however, to define *love* operationally. For example, you might ask the person you're assessing to indicate on a rating scale how much she loves someone. You might measure how often she looks into that person's eyes when interacting with him. You might measure how willing she is to give up events she enjoys in order to be with him. These three measures differ considerably from one another. Yet each might be taken as an operational definition (or operationalization) of *love*.

The essence of the validity issue in measurement can be summarized in this question: How well does the *operational* definition (the event) match the *conceptual* definition (the abstract quality that you have in mind to measure)? If the two are close, the measure has high validity. If they aren't close, validity is low.

How do you decide whether the two are close? Usually, psychologists poke at the conceptual definition until they're sure what the critical elements are and then look to see whether the same elements are in the operationalization. If they aren't (at least by strong implication), the validity of the operationalization is questionable.

The validity issue is important. It's also tricky. It's the subject of continual debate in psychology, as researchers try to think of better and better ways to look at human behavior (Borsboom, Mellenbergh, & van Heerden, 2004). The reason the issue is important is that researchers and assessors form conclusions about personality in terms of what they *think* they're measuring. If what they're really measuring isn't what they think they're measuring, they will draw false conclusions. Likewise, a clinician may draw the wrong conclusion about a person if the measure doesn't measure what the clinician thinks it measures.

Validity is important whenever anything is being observed. In personality assessment, the validity question has been examined closely for a long time. In trying to be sure that personality tests are valid, theorists have come to distinguish several aspects of validity from one another. These distinctions have also influenced the practical process of establishing validity.

FIGURE 3.1
A simple way to think about the difference between reliability and validity, using the metaphor of target shooting. (A) Sometimes when people shoot at a target, their shots go all over. This result corresponds to measurement that's neither reliable nor valid. (B) Reliability is higher when the shots are closer together. Shots that miss the mark, however, are not valid. (C) Good measurement means that the shots are close together (reliable) *and* near the bull's-eye (valid).

CONSTRUCT VALIDITY

The idea of validity you have in mind at this point is technically called **construct validity** (Campbell, 1960; Cronbach & Meehl, 1955). Construct validity is an all-encompassing validity, and is therefore the most important kind (cf. Hogan & Nicholson, 1988; Landy, 1986). Construct validity means that the measure (the assessment device) reflects the construct (the conceptual quality) that the psychologist has in mind. Although the word *construct* sounds abstract, a construct is just a concept. Any trait quality, for example, is a construct.

Establishing construct validity for a measure is a complex process. It uses several kinds of information, each treated as a separate aspect of the validation process. For this reason, the various qualities that provide support for construct validity have names of their own. Several are described in the following paragraphs.

CRITERION VALIDITY

One important part of showing that an assessment device has construct validity is showing that it relates to other manifestations of whatever quality it's supposed to measure (Campbell, 1960). The other manifestation usually is a behavioral index, or the judgment of a trained observer, as an external *criterion* (a standard of comparison). The researcher collects this information and sees how well the assessment device correlates with it. This aspect of validity is sometimes referred to as **criterion validity** (because it uses an external criterion) or **predictive validity** (because it tests how well the measure predicts something else it's supposed to predict).

As an example, suppose you were interested in criterion validity for a measure of dominance you were developing. One way to approach this problem would be to select people who score high and low on your measure and bring them to a laboratory one at a time to work on a task with two other people. You could tape each group's discussion and score the tape for the number of times each person made suggestions, gave instructions, took charge of the situation, and so on. These behaviors would be viewed as criteria of dominance. If people who scored high on your measure did these things more than people who scored low, it would indicate a kind of criterion validity.

Another way to approach the problem would be to have a trained interviewer spend 20 minutes with each of the people who completed your scale and rate each person's dominance after the interview. The interviewer's ratings would be a different kind of criterion for dominance. If the ratings related to scores on your measure, it would indicate a different kind of criterion validity for the measure.

Criterion validity is usually regarded as the most important way to support construct validity. In recent years, though, a controversy has arisen over the process of establishing it. Howard (1990; Howard, Maxwell, Weiner, Boynton, & Rooney, 1980) has pointed out that people often assume the criterion that's chosen is a perfect reflection of the construct. In reality, though, this is almost never true. In fact, far too often, researchers choose criterion measures that are *poor* reflections of the construct. We raise this point to emphasize how critical it is to be careful in deciding what criterion to use. Unless the criterion is a good one, associations with it are meaningless. Despite this issue, however, criterion validity remains the keystone of construct validation.

CONVERGENT VALIDITY

Another aspect of support for construct validity involves showing that the measure relates to characteristics that are similar to, but not the same as, what it's supposed to measure. How is this different from criterion validity? It's just a very small step away from it. In this case, though, you know the second measure aims to assess something a little different from what your measure assesses. Because this sort of information gathering often proceeds from several angles, it's often termed **convergent validation** (Campbell & Fiske, 1959). That is the findings converge on the construct you're interested in, even though any single finding by itself won't clearly reflect the construct.

For example, a scale intended to measure dominance should relate at least a little to measures of qualities such as leadership (positively) or shyness (inversely). The correlations shouldn't be perfect because those aren't quite the same constructs, but they shouldn't be zero either. If you developed a measure to assess dominance and it didn't correlate at all with measures of leadership and shyness, you'd have to start wondering whether your measure really assesses dominance.

DISCRIMINANT VALIDITY

It's important to show that an assessment device measures what it's intended to measure. But it's also important to show that it does *not* measure qualities it's *not* intended to measure—especially qualities that don't fit with what you have in mind as a construct (Campbell, 1960). This aspect of the construct validation process is termed establishing **discriminant validity** (Campbell & Fiske, 1959).

The importance of discriminant validity can be easy to overlook. However, discriminant validation is a major line of defense against the third-variable problem in correlational research, discussed in Chapter 2. That is, you can't be sure why two correlated variables correlate. It may be that one influences the other. But it may be that a third variable, correlated with the two you've studied, is really responsible for their correlation. In principle, it's always possible to attribute the effect of a personality dimension on behavior to some other personality dimension. In practice, however, this can be made much harder by evidence of discriminant validity. That is, if research shows that the dimension you're interested in is unrelated to another variable, then that variable can't be invoked as an alternative explanation for the effect of the first.

To illustrate this, let's return to an example used in discussing the third-variable problem in Chapter 2: a correlation between self-esteem and academic performance. This association *might* reflect the effect of an unmeasured variable, for instance, IQ. Suppose, though, that we know this measure of self-esteem is unrelated to IQ, because someone checked that possibility during the process of its validation. This would make it difficult to claim that IQ is what really underlies the correlation between self-esteem and academic performance.

The process of discriminant validation is never ending because new possibilities for third variables always suggest themselves. Ruling out alternative explanations thus is a challenging task, but it's also a necessary one.

FACE VALIDITY

There's one more kind of validity that should be mentioned. It's much simpler, a little more intuitive, and most people think it's less important. It's called **face validity.** Face validity means that the assessment device appears, on its face, to be measuring the construct it was intended to measure. It *looks* right. A test of sociability made up of items such as "I prefer to spend time with friends rather than alone" and "I would rather socialize than read books" would have high face validity. A test of sociability made up of items such as "Green is my favorite color" and "I prefer imported cars" would have low face validity.

Many researchers regard face validity as a convenience, for two reasons. First, some believe that face-valid measures are easier to respond to than measures with less face validity. Second, researchers sometimes focus on distinctions between qualities of personality that differ in subtle ways. It often seems impossible to separate these qualities from each other except by using measures that are high in face validity.

On the other hand, face validity can occasionally be a detriment. This is true when the assessment device is intended to measure something that the person being assessed would find threatening or undesirable to admit. In such cases, the test developer usually tries to obscure the purpose of the test by reducing its face validity.

Whether face validity is good, bad, or neither, it should be clear that it does not substitute for other aspects of validity. If an assessment device is to be useful in the long run, it must undergo the laborious process of construct validation. The "bottom line" is always construct validity.

CULTURE AND VALIDITY

Another important issue in assessment concerns cultural differences. In a sense, this is a validity issue; in a sense, it's an issue of generalizability. Let's frame the issue as a question: Do the scores on a personality test have the same meaning for a person from an Asian culture or a Latino culture or an African American culture as they do for a middle–American European culture?

There are at least two aspects to this question. The first is whether the psychological construct *itself* has the same meaning from one culture to another. This is a fundamental question about the nature of personality. Are the elements of personality the same from one human group to another? Many people assume the basic elements of personality are universal. That may, in fact, be a dangerous assumption.

The second aspect of the question concerns how the items of the measure are interpreted by people from different cultures. If an item has one meaning for middle-class Americans but a different meaning for people in some other culture, responses to the item will also have different meanings in the different cultures. A similar issue arises when a measure is translated into a different language. This usually involves translating into the new language and then translation back into the original language by someone who's never seen the original items. This process sometimes reveals that items contain idiomatic or metaphorical meanings that are hard to translate. Adapting a measure from one culture for use in another culture is a complex process (Butcher, 1996). It must be done very carefully, if the measure is to be valid in the new culture.

RESPONSE SETS AND LOSS OF VALIDITY

Any discussion of validity must also note that there are problems in self-reporting that can interfere with the validity of the information collected. We've already mentioned that biases in recall can distort the picture and render the information invalid. In the same way, people's motivational tendencies can also get in the way of accurate reporting.

There are at least two biases in the way people respond in assessment. These biases are called **response sets.** A response set is a psychological orientation, a readiness to answer in a particular way (Berg, 1967; Jackson & Messick, 1967; Rorer, 1965). Response sets create distortions in the information assessed. Personality psychologists want their assessments to provide information that's free from contamination. Thus, response sets are problems.

Two response sets are particularly important in personality assessment. One of them emerges most clearly when the assessment device is a self-report instrument that, in one fashion or another, asks the person questions that require a yes-or-no response (or a response on a rating scale with *agree* and *disagree* as the opposite ends of the scale). This response set, called **acquiescence,** is the tendency to say yes (Couch & Keniston, 1960).

Everyone presumably has a bit of this tendency, but people vary greatly on it. That's what causes the problem. If the set isn't counteracted somehow, the scores of people who are highly acquiescent become inflated. Their high scores reflect the response set instead of their personality. People who have extreme personalities but not much acquiescence will also have high scores. But you won't know whose high scores are from personality and whose are from acquiescence.

Many view acquiescence as an easy problem to combat. The way it's handled for self-reports is this: Write half the items so that *yes* indicates being at one end of the personality dimension. Write the other half of the items so that a *no* response means being at that end of the personality dimension. In the process of scoring the test, then, any bias that comes from the simple tendency to say yes is canceled out.

This procedure takes care of the problem of overagreement, but not everyone is convinced it's a good idea. Negatively worded items often are harder to understand or more complicated to answer than positively worded items. The result can be responses that are less accurate (Converse & Presser, 1986; Schriesheim & Hill, 1981). For this reason, some people feel it's better to live with the acquiescence problem than to introduce a different kind of error by using complex wording.

The tendency to provide socially desirable responses can sometimes mask a person's true characteristics or feelings.

A second response set is perhaps more important than acquiescence and also more troublesome. It's called **social desirability,** reflecting the fact that people tend to portray themselves in a good light (in socially desirable ways) whenever possible. Once again, this tendency is stronger among some people than others (see Crowne & Marlowe, 1964; Edwards, 1957). As with acquiescence, if it isn't counteracted, people with strong concerns about social desirability will produce scores that reflect the response set, rather than their personalities.

For some personality dimensions, this isn't much of a problem. This is because there's really no social approval or disapproval at either end of the dimension. In other cases, though, there's a consensus that it's better to be one way (for example, honest or likable) than the other (dishonest or unlikable). In these cases, assessment becomes tricky.

In general, psychologists deal with this problem by trying to phrase items so that the issue of social desirability isn't salient. As much as anything else, this is a process of trying to avoid even bringing up the idea that one kind of person is approved of more than the other. Sometimes this means phrasing undesirable responses in ways that make them more acceptable. Sometimes it means looking for ways to let people admit the undesirable quality indirectly. A different way to deal with the problem is to include items that assess the person's degree of concern about social desirability and use this information as a correction factor in evaluating the person's responses to other items. In any event, this is a problem that personality psychologists must constantly be aware of and constantly guarding against in trying to measure what people are like.

Two Rationales behind the Development of Assessment Devices

Thus far, this chapter has considered issues that arise in trying to measure any quality of personality. What it hasn't taken up yet is how people decide what qualities to measure in the first place. This question won't be answered completely here, because the answer depends partly on the theoretical perspective underlying the assessment. There is, however, a general issue to address. In particular, development of personality measures usually follows one of two paths, each of which has its own kind of logic.

RATIONAL, OR THEORETICAL, APPROACH

One strategy is termed a **rational, or theoretical, approach** to assessment. This strategy is based on theoretical considerations from the very start. The psychologist first develops a rational basis for believing that a particular dimension of personality is important. The next task is to create a test in which this dimension is reflected validly and reliably in people's answers. This approach to test development often leads to assessment devices that have a high degree of face validity.

It's important to realize that the work doesn't stop once a set of items has been developed. Instruments developed from this starting point must be shown to be reliable, to predict behavioral criteria, and to have good construct validity. Until these steps are taken, the scale shouldn't be considered a useful measure of anything.

It's probably safe to say that the majority of personality measurement devices that now exist were developed using this path. Some of these measures are single scales; others are inventories. Most of the measures that are discussed in later chapters were created by first deciding *what* to measure and then figuring out *how* to measure it.

EMPIRICAL APPROACHES

The theoretical approach isn't the only way to start in scale development, though. A second strategy is usually characterized as an **empirical, or data-based, approach.** The basic characteristic of this approach is that it relies on data, rather than on theory, to decide what items go into the assessment device.

There are two important variations on this theme. One of them is an inductive approach in which the person developing the measure uses the data to decide what qualities of personality even exist (Cattell, 1947, 1965, 1979). Because this line of thought is an important contributor to trait psychology, we're going to wait to discuss it until the chapter on trait psychology. We'll focus here on another empirical approach. This one reflects a very pragmatic orientation to the process of assessment. It's guided less by a desire to understand personality than by a practical aim of sorting people into categories. If a quick or inexpensive technique can be found to do this, the technique provides an important benefit.

Instead of developing the test first and then validating it against a criterion, this approach works in the opposite direction. The groups into which people are to be sorted represent the criteria for the test. Developing the test is a matter of starting out with a very large number of possible items and finding out which items are answered differently by members of one criterion group than by other people. This is termed the **criterion keying** approach to test development. This label reflects the fact that the items retained are those that empirically distinguish between the *criterion* group and other people. If such an item set can be found for each criterion group involved, then the entire test (all the item sets together) can be used to tell who belongs to which group.

In the point of view reflected in this approach, it doesn't matter at all what the items of the assessment device look like. It only matters that they distinguish people who fit a criterion from those who don't. Items in a scale based on this approach are chosen because members of a specific group (defined on some other basis) tend to answer them differently than other people.

The best illustration of the use of this method is the Minnesota Multiphasic Personality Inventory, better known as the MMPI (Hathaway & McKinley, 1943), revised in 1989 as the MMPI-2 (Butcher, Dahlstrom, Graham, Tellegen, & Kaemmer, 1989). The MMPI was a very long true–false inventory developed as a measure of abnormality. The first step in its development was to collect a large number of self-

Table 3.2 Content Scales of the MMPI-2 and Interpretation of Each Scale's Meaning.
Source: MMPI-2TM (Minnesota Multiphasic Personality Inventory-2) TM Manual for Administration, Scoring, and Interpretation, Revised Edition. Copyright © 2001 by the Regents of the University of Minnesota. Used by permission of the University of Minnesota Press. All rights reserved. "MMPI-2" and "Minnesota Multiphasic Personality-2" are trademarks owned by the Regents of the University of Minnesota.

Clinical Scales	Interpretation
Hypochondriasis	High scorers are cynical, defeatist, over-concerned with physical health
Depression	High scorers are despondent, distressed, depressed
Hysteria	High scorers report frequent symptoms with no apparent organic cause
Psychopathic deviate	High scorers are adventurous, have disregard for social or moral standards
Masculinity/femininity	Scores provide indication of level of "traditional" male/female interests
Paranoia	High scorers are guarded and suspicious, feel persecuted
Psychasthenia	High scorers are anxious, rigid, tense, and worrying
Schizophrenia	High scorers exhibit social alienation, bizarreness in thinking
Hypomania	High scorers are emotionally excitable, impulsive, hyperactive
Social introversion	High scorers are shy, withdrawn, uninvolved in social relationships

descriptive statements. The statements then were given to a group of normal persons and to groups of psychiatric patients—people already judged by a clinician to have a specific disorder. Thus, the criterion already existed. The next step was to test the items. Do people with one psychiatric diagnosis either agree or disagree with the item more often than normal people and people with different diagnoses? If so, that item was included in the scale for that psychiatric diagnosis.

The original MMPI was developed long ago using a sample that had a narrow age range and was restricted ethnically and geographically (largely from Minnesota). Concern arose that scores from other populations might not be interpreted properly. In addition, some of the items were hard to understand. The people developing the MMPI-2 reworded about 20% of the original items for clarity, wrote 154 new ones, and distilled the total to 567. They collected data from people who varied more widely in ethnicity, age, and gender. Thus, interpretation of responses is now more consistent with the contemporary U.S. populace.

As was true of the original, the MMPI-2 has ten basic content scales (see Table 3.2). It also has six validity scales. The content scales indicate similarity of a person's responses to those of patients with a particular diagnosis. The validity scales provide an estimate of how meaningful the person's response profile is. For example, the Lie scale measures people's tendencies to present themselves too favorably to be true. As another example, frequent "cannot say" responses—an inability to choose the true or false option—may mean that the person is being evasive. If too many of these responses are made, the meaning of the other responses is called into question.

Better Assessment: A Never-Ending Search

As was just described, even one of the most widely used tests in the world wasn't considered "finished" just because it was widely used. It was subjected to further refinement, additional data gathering, and a continuing examination of how people respond to its items. The result was an improvement in what the test can tell the psychologists who use it.

The MMPI isn't the only measure to be re-examined and revised in this way. Most personality scales in widespread use have been revised once or more and restandardized periodically. The process of establishing construct validity requires not just a single study but many. It thus takes time. The process of establishing discriminant validity is virtually never ending. Tremendous effort is invested in creating and improving tests of personality. This investment of effort is necessary if people are to feel confident of knowing what the tests measure. Having that confidence is an important part of the assessment of personality.

The characteristics of personality tests discussed in this chapter distinguish these tests from those you see from time to time in newspapers, magazines, on TV, and so forth. In some cases, the items in a magazine article were written specifically for that article. It's unlikely that anyone checked on their reliability. It's even less likely that anyone checked on their validity. Even if the items were taken from a carefully developed instrument, the entire set of items usually isn't used; it can be hard to be sure how well the ones that were chosen reflect the entire scale. Unless the right steps have been taken to create an instrument, you should be careful about putting your faith in the results that come from it.

· SUMMARY ·

Assessment (measurement of personality) is something that people constantly do informally. Psychologists formalize this process into several distinct techniques. Observer ratings are made about people by someone else—an interviewer, someone who watches, or someone who knows the people well enough to make ratings of what they are like. Observer ratings often are somewhat subjective, involving interpretations of the person's behavior. Self-reports are made by the people being assessed, about themselves. Self-reports can be single scales or multiscale inventories. Assessment devices can be subjective or objective. Objective techniques require no interpretation as the assessment is made. Subjective techniques involve some sort of interpretation as an intrinsic part of the measure.

One issue for all assessment is *reliability* (the reproducibility of the measurement). Reliability is determined by checking one measurement against another (or several others). Self-report scales usually have many items (each a measurement), leading to indices of internal reliability, or internal consistency. Observer judgments are checked by inter-rater reliability. Test–retest reliability assesses the reproducibility of the measure over time. In all cases, high correlation among measures means good reliability.

Another important issue is *validity* (whether what you're measuring is what you want to measure). The attempt to determine whether the operational definition (the assessment device) matches the concept you set out to measure is called *construct validation*. Contributors to construct validity are evidence of criterion, convergent, and discriminant validity. Face validity is not usually taken as an important element of construct validity. Validity is threatened by the fact that people have response sets (acquiescence and social desirability) that bias their responses.

Development of assessment devices proceeds along one of two paths. The rational path uses a theory to decide what should be measured and then figures out the best way to measure it. Most assessment devices developed this way. The empirical path involves using data to determine what items should be in a scale. The MMPI was developed this way, using a technique called *criterion keying,* in which the test developers let people's responses tell them which items to use. Test items that members of a diagnostic category answered differently from other people were retained.

· GLOSSARY ·

Acquiescence   The response set of tending to say yes (agree) in response to any question.

Assessment   The measuring of personality.

Construct validity   The accuracy with which a measure reflects the underlying concept.

Convergent validity   The degree to which a measure relates to other characteristics that are conceptually similar to what it's supposed to assess.

Criterion keying   The developing of a test by seeing which items distinguish between groups.

Criterion validity   The degree to which the measure correlates with a separate criterion reflecting the same concept.

Discriminant validity   The degree to which a scale does *not* measure unintended qualities.

Empirical approach (to scale development)   The use of data instead of theory to decide what should go into the measure.

Error   Random influences that are incorporated in measurements.

Face validity   The scale seeming on its face to measure what it's supposed to measure.

Internal reliability (internal consistency)   Agreement among responses made to the items of a measure.

Inter-rater reliability   The degree of agreement between observers of the same events.

Inventory   A personality test measuring several aspects of personality on distinct subscales.

Objective measure   A measure that incorporates no interpretation.

Observer ratings   An assessment in which someone else produces information about the person being assessed.

Operational definition   The defining of a concept by the concrete events through which it is measured (or manipulated).

Predictive validity   The degree to which the measure predicts other variables it should predict.

Rational approach (to scale development)   The use of a theory to decide what you want to measure and then deciding how to measure it.

Reliability   Consistency across repeated measurements.

Response set   A biased orientation to answering.

Self-report   An assessment in which people make ratings pertaining to themselves.

Social desirability   The response set of tending to portray oneself favorably.

Split-half reliability   Assessing internal consistency among responses to items of a measure by splitting the items into halves and then correlating them.

Subjective measure   A measure incorporating personal interpretation.

Test–retest reliability   The stability of measurements across time.

Theoretical approach   See **Rational approach.**

Validity   A measure's "truthfulness," or the degree to which it actually measures what it is intended to measure.

The Dispositional Perspective

r

The Dispositional Perspective: Major Themes and Underlying Assumptions

A key theme of the *dispositional perspective* on personality is the idea that people display consistency in their actions, thoughts, and feelings. A human being's dispositional nature doesn't shift aimlessly from moment to moment—it endures across changes in time and place. Indeed, the very concept of *disposition* is a way of representing the fact that people remain the same people, even as time passes and as they move from one situation to another. Dispositions are qualities that people carry around with them, that belong to them, that are part of them.

Certainly, we all experience periods in which we're unpredictable, in which we may feel buffeted by the psychological winds around us. But for most people that experience is the exception rather than the rule. It certainly isn't the essence of personality. Rather, personality implies stability, constancy, something that doesn't vary too much from one time to another. You—like most people—undoubtedly feel within yourself a sense of coherence, a kind of permanence across time, events, and experiences. You're the person you are, and you'll still be that person tomorrow, and next week, and next year. This is the core meaning of disposition.

A second theme of the dispositional perspective derives from the fact that people differ from each other in many ways. As indicated in Chapter 1, the entire field of personality psychology is guided in part by an emphasis on differences among people. This emphasis is particularly central to the dispositional perspective. From this perspective, each person's personality consists of a pattern of dispositional qualities. The composition of the pattern differs from one person to another. The intersection among these dispositions in any given person constitutes the defining nature of that person's personality.

These assumptions are important throughout the dispositional perspective. They're dealt with differently, however, by different kinds of theorists. One approach emphasizes the mere existence of dispositions. It focuses primarily on trying to measure and catalog them in better ways, to reach a clearer understanding of what the dimensions are that are most important in personality and to find better ways to place people on those dimensions. This trait-and-type approach is discussed in Chapter 4. This trait approach most clearly exemplifies the dispositional perspective.

This isn't the only way to approach the concept of disposition, though. A second way is to think of dispositions as enduring motivational characteristics that vary in strength from person to person. These differences in the motive tendencies that underlie people's actions are reflected in differences in the qualities that the people display in their behavior. This needs-and-motives approach to dispositions is examined in Chapter 5.

Types, Traits, and Interactionism

"I want you to meet a friend of mine from high school. He's really outgoing. He's friendly, but he doesn't go along with the crowd all the time. You might say he's sociable, but he's also independent."

"My psychology professor is *so* predictable. He's smart, but he's such a geek. He must spend all his time in his office. I can't imagine him doing anything interesting or fun. He can't help it, I guess. It's just his personality."

I**T'S COMMON** to assume that each person has a set of dispositions that are fairly easy to observe. When you find out what people are like, you know what to expect of them in the future. This idea applies to all of personality psychology, of course. But it's particularly prominent in the trait-and-type view of personality. The words *trait* and *type* convey slightly different meanings. They converge, though, on the idea that people have stable characteristics that they display across different circumstances and across time.

Types and Traits

The idea that people could be divided into different types, or categories, goes back at least to Hippocrates (about 400 B.C.), whose ideas were later embellished by Galen (about A.D. 150). People were thought to form four groups: *choleric* (irritable), *melancholic* (depressed), *sanguine* (optimistic), and *phlegmatic* (calm). Each personality type was thought to reflect an excess of one of four basic bodily fluids.

More recently, Carl Jung (1933) argued that people are either introverts or extraverts. An **introvert** tends to be alone a lot and prefers solitary activities. When facing stress, introverts tend to withdraw into themselves. An **extravert** prefers to spend time with others rather than be alone. When facing stress, extraverts tend to seek out other people.

In true typologies, the **types** are regarded as distinct and discontinuous categories. An example of a discontinuous category is *gender:* People are either male or female. Jung often portrayed the categories of introvert and extravert as discontinuous in the same way (see Figure 4.1). Type theories have generally faded from personality psychology. (For dissenting views, see Gangestad & Snyder, 1985; Meehl, 1992; Robins, John,

45

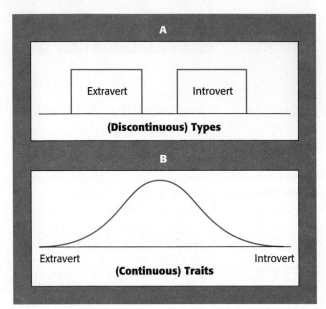

FIGURE 4.1
(A) Early type theories assumed a discontinuity between or among categories of people. (B) Trait theories assume that traits are continuous dimensions of variability on some characteristic and that the degree of presence versus absence of the characteristic is distributed across a population.

Caspi, Moffitt, & Stouthamer-Loeber, 1996; Strube, 1989; York & John, 1992.)

In contrast to categorical typologies, **trait** theories assume that people occupy different points on continuously varying dimensions (Figure 4.1). For that reason, this is sometimes called a *dimensional* approach. In trait theories, differences among people are seen as *quantitative* rather than qualitative. People are seen as differing in *how much* of various characteristics they incorporate in their personalities.

This difference in terminology has been maintained by most theorists, but not all. Hans Eysenck (1967, 1970, 1975) muddied the water a little, using the word *type* not to indicate discontinuity, but to imply a *supertrait*—a trait that's very broad and important.

NOMOTHETIC AND IDIOGRAPHIC VIEWS OF TRAITS

Thus far, we've implied that traits pertain to every person and that people just vary in how much of each quality they have. The belief that traits exist in the same way in every person is called a **nomothetic** view of personality (Allport, 1961). The term *nomothetic* derives from the Greek word meaning *law*. This view holds that everyone stands somewhere on each trait that exists. This allows comparisons among people. (You can't compare people unless the trait is the same for everyone.) The nomothetic view has dominated trait psychology for at least 50 years.

In contrast is the **idiographic** view (Allport, 1961), which emphasizes each person's uniqueness (see also Lamiell, 1981). The term *idiographic* has the same source as *idiosyncratic*. This view holds that traits are individualized. A given trait may be possessed by only one person in the world. This view suggests that people often can't be compared, because everyone is on a different scale. Even if the same term applies to two people, its connotations will differ between people (Dunning & McElwee, 1995). Even if the connotations are the same, the trait may differ in importance, so the people can't be compared meaningfully (Britt & Shepperd, 1999).

Does the nomothetic view deny uniqueness? No, not really. Those who favor the nomothetic view think instead that uniqueness means unique *combinations* of levels on many trait dimensions, though the dimensions themselves are the same for everyone. As Eysenck put it, "the unique individual is simply the point of intersection of a number of quantitative variables" (1952, p. 18).

Psychologists who emphasize the idiographic view believe that nomothetic views always are oversimplifications (even though they sometimes use them). To Allport, we should never lose sight of that fact: Even traits that people share always have a special flavor (maybe from differences in how the trait is expressed) that varies from person to person.

Most trait psychologists do keep this point in the back of their minds. But most tend to disregard the strongest version of the idiographic approach: the idea that traits themselves differ from person to person.

What Traits Matter?

Thinking of personality in terms of traits quickly leads to this question: *What are the traits that make up personality?*

This is a hard question to answer with complete certainty. In fact, there have been serious disagreements about where to *start* in answering it. Before we describe this disagreement, let's back up and consider a problem that all trait theorists share, and a tool that helps deal with it.

A Key Tool: Factor Analysis

Personality is reflected in many ways—for example, in descriptive words. If each word describing personality meant a different trait, a psychologist would go crazy trying to organize things. That, in a nutshell, is a problem every trait psychologist faces: bringing order to such diversity. Perhaps, however, the many words may reflect a small number of underlying trait dimensions. If so, how do you figure out what the dimensions are?

A tool that's often used for this is a statistical technique called **factor analysis.** The basic idea is simple: If two qualities correlate when assessed across many people, they may reflect a trait that contributes to both of them. *Patterns* of correlation, then, may reveal trait dimensions that lie beneath the measured qualities. Factor analysis is essentially a more complex version of correlation. Instead of looking at one correlation between *two* variables, a factor analysis looks at correlations among *many* variables. Because the process is very complex, it was not widely used until the computer age. The huge rise in computing power over the years has led to far greater sophistication in these procedures (Bentler, 1990; Jöreskog & Sörbom, 1979).

The process starts by collecting measurements on many variables from large numbers of people. The measures can take any form, but typically they are self-reports or observer ratings. Once the data are collected, correlations are computed between every pair of variables (see Box 4.1). The set of correlations is then put through a procedure called *factor extraction*. This distills the correlations to a smaller set of **factors.** Each factor represents shared variations (underlying commonalities) among several of the measures (rather than two at a time).

Once the factors are extracted, each can be described by a set of **factor loadings.** Think of these as correlations between the factor and each item (rating) that contributes to its existence. Items that correlate strongly with the factor (usually higher than 0.30 or so) are said to "load on" that factor. Items that don't correlate strongly with the factor are said not to load on it. The items that load on the factor tell you what the factor is about.

The final step in the analysis is labeling the factors. Remember that a factor is defined by which items load on it. Thus, you choose a label to denote as closely as possible the essence of those items, particularly those with the highest loadings. In analyses on personality, the factor is viewed as the statistical reflection of a trait. When you name the factor, you are naming the trait.

Factor naming is very subjective. Several names might seem equally good. Which name is chosen, however, can have important consequences. People often forget that the label is an inference from the pattern of correlations. They rely on the label to tell them what the trait is. If the label you choose is misleading, it can create problems of interpretation later.

Factor analysis as a tool in trait psychology does three things. First, it reduces the multiple reflections of personality to a smaller set of traits (tells you what traits underlie the reflections). Second, it provides a basis for arguing that some traits matter more than others. That is, if a factor accounts for a lot of variability in the ratings, it reflects an important trait; if it accounts for less, it's less important. Third, factor analysis helps in developing assessment devices. You keep items (or ratings) that load strongly (greatly reflect the trait) and discard items that don't. Through repeated item creation and analysis, items that don't do a good job of measuring a particular trait are replaced by better ones.

Box 4.1 A Closer Look at Factor Analysis

The process of factor analysis is complex, but its logic is fairly simple. It's an attempt to find patterns of association in a set of variables.

The first step is collecting data. This is more complicated than it might seem. First you have to decide what aspects of behavior you want to measure. Do you want self-reports? Observer ratings? As you can see, the first step—collecting data—entails many decisions.

Let's use an example. Imagine you're interested in how people cope with stress (Lazarus & Folkman, 1984). You've decided to use self-reports: people's ratings of how much they did certain things during their most stressful event of the past year. To "collect data," get 300 or so of your friends to recall a stressful event and respond to each of 28 items (listing things people sometimes do under stress). Among the items are these:

1. Took action quickly, before things could get out of hand
2. Refused to believe that it was real
3. Did something concrete to make the situation better
4. Tried to convince myself that it wasn't happening
5. Went on thinking things were just like they were
6. Changed or grew as a person in a new way
7. Tried to look on the bright side of things

The second step is to compute the correlation of every item with every other item (panel A, right). Each correlation reflects the degree to which the 300 people tended to answer one item the same as the other item. There are strong correlations between items 1 and 3; between 6 and 7; and between 2 and both 4 and 5 (which also strongly relate to each other). The others are quite weak.

Because you had people rate 28 items (instead of just these seven), your correlation matrix is huge (each item with each other item). Interpreting the pattern of correlations would be a real chore. The chore is lessened by the third step, called *factor extraction*. It reduces your matrix to a smaller number of underlying dimensions (for example, the links among items 2, 4, and 5 would contribute to one dimension). These dimensions of underlying commonality are called *factors*. Factors are hazy entities you can imagine but can't see.

The next step is to compute the *factor loadings* of each item on each factor. Loadings tell you the relations between the items and the factors (panel B, right). Each loading indicates how much the item reflects the underlying dimension. A large number (a high loading) means the item is closely linked to that dimension, a small number means it's not. As shown, items 1 and 3 load on factor A (but no other factor), items 6 and 7 load on factor B (but no other factor), and items 2, 4, and 5 load on factor C (but no other factor). Similar loadings emerge for all your 28 items, letting you know which items go together.

Once it's clear which items form which factors, you're at the final step: naming the factors. You want to convey the essence of the underlying quality, but your only guide is which items load on it. Often the items are ambiguous or have several elements, clouding the picture. In our example, a

A. Hypothetical Correlation Matrix

Item	1	2	3	4	5	6	7
1	*	0.10	0.75	−0.05	0.03	0.12	0.00
2		*	−0.02	0.52	0.61	−.007	−0.08
3			*	0.17	0.00	0.09	0.15
4				*	0.71	0.11	0.08
5					*	0.06	−0.04
6						*	0.59
7							*

B. Hypothetical Factor Loadings

Factor	A	B	C
Item 1	0.62	0.15	0.01
Item 2	0.03	−0.08	0.49
Item 3	0.54	0.04	−0.20
Item 4	0.10	0.11	0.56
Item 5	0.07	0.08	0.50
Item 6	−0.02	0.72	0.12
Item 7	0.08	0.48	0.08

couple of factors are easy. The items on factor A show a tendency to try to solve the problem. This might be called *problem-focused coping.* Given the content of items 2, 4, and 5, factor C might be *denial.* Factor B seems to be *positive reinterpretation* or *posttraumatic growth* or *looking on the bright side,* but it's hard to be sure which is best. It's important to be careful, though, because the name you use will guide your future thinking.

Factor analysis is a very useful tool. It's only a tool, though. What we've told you has a big hole in it. We haven't said anything about *what measures to collect in the first place*. A factor analysis can tell you only about what you put into it. Thus, the decision about what to measure has a huge impact on what emerges as traits.

How do you decide what measures to collect? As noted earlier, different people have started off differently. Let's now return to that question.

LET REALITY REVEAL ITSELF: CATTELL'S APPROACH

The answer some give is that researchers should determine *empirically* what traits make up personality, not impose preconceptions. If you start with preconceptions, you'll lead yourself astray. This was the argument of Raymond Cattell, an early contributor to trait psychology and one of the first users of factor analysis (Cattell, 1947, 1965, 1978; Cattell & Kline, 1977). This reasoning had a strong influence on many other trait researchers (Goldberg, 1993b).

Whereas extraverts prefer exciting activities involving other people, introverts like to be alone.

One empirical approach focused on language as a source of information (see Goldberg, 1982). A language that's evolved over thousands of years has words to describe many human qualities. Presumably, any trait that matters has words that describe it. In fact, the more words for a quality of personality, the more it probably matters. This is called the **lexical criterion** of importance. Following this idea, Cattell (1947, 1965) took a set of trait terms, removed obvious synonyms, collected ratings on the terms, and factor analyzed the ratings. The resulting factors were the traits he believed are important.

Cattell came to believe that personality is captured in a set of 16 dimensions (see Table 4.1). The dimensions re-emerged in analyses across various types of data, and he saw them as the primary traits in personality. These 16 primary factors provided a name for the resulting inventory: the 16 Personality Factor inventory, or 16PF (Cattell, Eber, & Tatsuoka, 1977).

Table 4.1 The 16 Factors in Cattell's View of Personality (as defined by the characteristics of high and low scorers on each trait dimension). The factors are listed in order of variance accounted for by each factor. The labels listed are the currently used verbal approximations for the content of each factor. *Source:* Copyright © 1993 by the Institute for Personality and Ability Testing, Inc., Champaign, IL 61824-1188. Reproduced by permission.

Reserved	Warm	Trusting	Vigilant
Concrete-reasoning	Abstract-reasoning	Practical	Imaginative
Reactive	Emotionally stable	Forthright	Private
Deferential	Dominant	Self-assured	Apprehensive
Serious	Lively	Traditional	Open to change
Expedient	Rule-conscientious	Group-oriented	Self-reliant
Shy	Socially-bold	Tolerates disorder	Perfectionist
Utilitarian	Sensitive	Relaxed	Tense

START FROM A THEORY: EYSENCK'S APPROACH

Not all agreed that an empirical starting point is best. Another major contributor to trait psychology, Hans Eysenck (e.g., 1967, 1970, 1975, 1986; Eysenck & Eysenck, 1985) argued that we should begin instead with well-developed ideas about what we want to measure. Then we should set about measuring those qualities well.

In framing his theory, he began with the typology of Hippocrates and Galen and related observations made by Jung and Wundt (Eysenck, 1967). He set out to investigate whether the four types identified by Hippocrates and Galen (and re-identified by others) could be created by combining high and low levels of two supertraits.

The two supertraits Eysenck posed as the key dimensions of personality are introversion–extraversion and emotionality–stability (or neuroticism). The extraversion dimension concerns tendencies toward sociability, liveliness, activeness, and dominance (all of which characterize extraverts). The neuroticism dimension concerns the ease and frequency with which the person becomes upset and distressed. Moodiness, anxiety, and depression reflect greater neuroticism.

These dimensions can create more diversity than you might guess. Table 4.2 portrays four sets of people, with combinations of highs and lows on these dimensions. The ancient type label for each group is printed in color. In considering these people, keep two things in mind: First, although the form of Table 4.2 suggests discontinuity, both dimensions are continuous. Second, the descriptions apply to fairly extreme and clear-cut cases. Most people are closer to the middle on both dimensions and thus have less-extreme characteristics.

As Table 4.2 indicates, people who are introverted and also emotionally stable tend to be careful, controlled, calm, and thoughtful in their actions. The combination of introversion and emotional *instability,* on the other hand, creates a more moody sense of unsociable reserve, a pessimistic and anxious quality. Thus, introverts can differ substantially, depending on their levels of emotional stability or instability.

Table 4.2 Traits Common among Four Categories of People Deriving from the Two Major Personality Dimensions Proposed by Eysenck. Each category results from combining introversion or extraversion with either a high or a low level of emotional stability. *Source:* Adapted from Eysenck, 1975.

	Emotionally Stable		Emotionally Unstable	
Introvert	Passive Careful Thoughtful Peaceful Controlled Reliable Even tempered Calm	Phlegmatic	Quiet Pessimistic Unsociable Sober Rigid Moody Anxious Reserved	Melancholic
Extravert	Sociable Outgoing Talkative Responsive Easygoing Lively Carefree Leaderly	Sanguine	Active Optimistic Impulsive Changeable Excitable Aggressive Restless Touchy	Choleric

So can extraverts. When extraversion combines with emotional stability, the result is an easygoing, carefree sociability. Emotional *instability* in an extravert introduces an excitable aggressive quality. Thus, the impact of one dimension differs as a function of the person's location on the other trait dimension. In the terms used in Chapter 2, the traits *interact*.

Eysenck assessed these dimensions by a self-report measure called the Eysenck Personality Questionnaire, or EPQ (Eysenck & Eysenck, 1975). He used factor analysis to help create it, but he did so with a different goal in mind than Cattell had. Cattell used factor analysis to find out what dimensions *exist*. Eysenck used factor analysis to refine his scales by selecting items that loaded well and to confirm that the scales measure two factors, as he intended.

Although Eysenck and Cattell started out very differently, they produced trait structures with distinct similarities. The two dimensions Eysenck saw as supertraits resemble two of the first three factors of Cattell's 16PF (Table 4.1). The similarities are even stronger in **second-order factors** from the 16PF. A second-order analysis tells whether the factors *themselves* form factors (correlate in clusters). One second-order factor from the 16PF is virtually identical to extraversion (Cattell & Kline, 1977); another is similar to neuroticism.

Another reflection of the convergence can be seen in Eysenck's argument that extraversion and neuroticism are at the top of an unfolding hierarchy of qualities (see Figure 4.2). Each supertrait is made of component traits (which resemble Cattell's primary traits). Component traits contribute to the supertrait. Component traits, in turn, reflect habits, which derive from specific responses. Eysenck believed all levels are involved in behavior, but he saw supertraits (which he called *types*) as the most important.

Two more points about Eysenck's view: First, he believed that extraversion and neuroticism link to aspects of nervous system functioning. That aspect of his theory comes up in Chapter 7. Second, there's a third dimension in Eysenck's view, which has had less attention than the others, called *psychoticism* (Eysenck & Eysenck, 1976). It involves, in part, a tendency toward psychological detachment from, and lack of concern with, other people. People high in this trait tend to be hostile, manipulative, and impulsive (Eysenck, 1992).

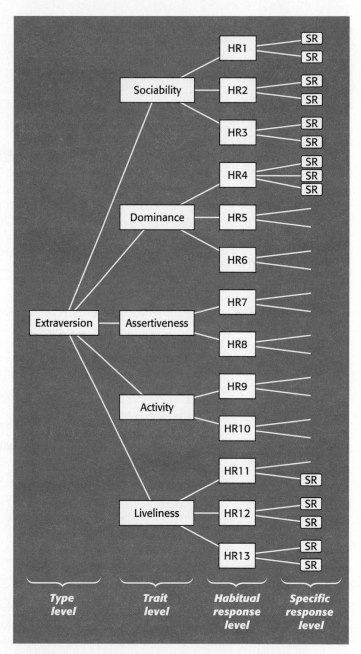

FIGURE 4.2

Eysenck's hierarchical view of personality as applied to extraversion. The top level of the model (types) subsumes the elements represented at the next-lower level (traits). These elements, in turn, are made up of yet lower-order qualities (habits), which are made up of associations between stimulus and response. *Source: Adapted from* The Biological Basis of Personality *(1967, p. 36), by H. J. Eysenck. Reprinted courtesy of Charles C Thomas, Publisher, Springfield, IL.*

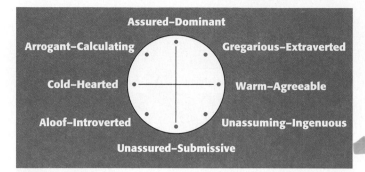

FIGURE 4.3

The *interpersonal circle,* a set of personality patterns portrayed in terms of their relative prevalence of two traits: love (the horizontal dimension) and dominance (the vertical dimension). The midpoint of each trait is the point where the lines cross.

Source: Adapted from Wiggins, Phillips, & Trapnell, 1989.

ANOTHER THEORETICAL STARTING POINT: THE INTERPERSONAL CIRCLE

Another theoretical starting point emphasized interpersonal aspects of personality. Jerry Wiggins and his colleagues (Wiggins, 1979; Wiggins, Phillips, & Trapnell, 1989) argued that the core human traits influence interpersonal life. Wiggins proposed a set of eight patterns, which he calls the interpersonal circle, arrayed around two dimensions that underlie human relations (see Figure 4.3). The core dimensions are dominance (or status) and love.

Wiggins argued (as did Eysenck) that diverse personalities arise from combinations of values on the two core dimensions. A person who's high in dominance and toward the cold-hearted end of love will seem arrogant and calculating. Put the same degree of dominance with warmth on the love dimension, though, and you get a person who's gregarious and extraverted.

Introversion and extraversion appear on this interpersonal circle (in lower-left and upper-right corners), but here they aren't a fundamental dimension. Instead, they are seen as resulting from the intersection of two other qualities.

The Five-Factor Model: The Basic Dimensions of Personality?

Despite the different starting points taken by various people, a substantial consensus has begun to emerge about what traits are basic. The emerging consensus has overtones of several ideas we've already presented, but it extends beyond them. The emerging consensus is that the basic structure of personality may incorporate five superordinate factors. These are often referred to as the *five-factor model,* or the *"big five"* (Goldberg, 1981; McCrae & Costa, 2003; Wiggins, 1996).

Evidence in support of a five-factor view of personality structure accumulated slowly for a long time (Digman, 1990). In 1949, Fiske couldn't reproduce Cattell's sixteen factors but instead found five. That finding sat in obscurity until the early 1960s, when Norman (1963), Borgatta (1964), and Smith (1967) all addressed the same general issue with different measures. Each reached the same conclusion: Five factors provided the best account of the data.

During the 1980s and 1990s, there was an explosion of work on this topic, which has continued to the present. Diverse samples have been collected, including teachers' ratings of children (Digman & Inouye, 1986) and peer ratings (McCrae & Costa, 1987). Some studies used a kind of self-rating called a *Q-sort* (Lanning, 1994; McCrae, Costa, & Busch, 1986); others assessed frequencies with which people engage in particular kinds of actions (Botwin & Buss, 1989); others used nonverbal assessments (Paunonen, Jackson, Trzebinski, & Forsterling, 1992). The model was also tested against measures developed from entirely different lines of thought (Costa & McCrae, 1988a; McCrae & Costa, 1989a). Peabody and Goldberg (1989; Peabody, 1984) used scales that were chosen to be sure there were enough *common* trait words instead of words that mean more to psychologists than to other people. Haas (2002) even explored the idea that proverbs capture the five factors.

Data have now been collected from many cultures and languages. The findings as a group suggest that the five factors may transcend many boundaries of language and culture (e.g., Benet-Martínez & John, 1998; Church, 2001; Katigbak, Church,

Guanzon-Lapeña, Carlota, & del Pilar, 2002; McCrae & Costa, 1997; McCrae, Zonderman, Costa, Bond, & Paunonen, 1996; Paunonen et al., 1992; Saucier & Ostendorf, 1999; Somer & Goldberg, 1999; Stumpf, 1993). The cultures examined in this work are as diverse as those of Turkey (Somer & Goldberg, 1999) and the Philippines (Katigbak et al., 2002). One study of observer ratings collected data in 50 cultures (McCrae, Terracino, et al., 2005). It has even been argued (Gosling, 2001) that the factors (or at least some of them) apply to lower animals!

There have been some failures to find the pattern and some imperfections in the findings (e.g., Benet & Waller, 1995; Church & Burke, 1994; Di Blas & Forzi, 1991; Lanning, 1994). And Saucier and Simonds (2006) caution that the pattern is clearest in Western languages and not at all easy to find in some other languages. Yet the body of work as a whole is impressive in the fit to the five-factor model (Digman, 1990; John, 1990; McCrae & Costa, 1997, 2003; McCrae & John, 1992; Ozer & Reise, 1994).

WHAT ARE THE FIVE FACTORS?

Given what we've said so far, what comes next may surprise you. There's still a fair amount of disagreement as to exactly what the five dimensions *are* (Briggs, 1989; John, 1990; Johnson & Ostendorf, 1993; Pytlik Zillig, Hemenover, & Dienstbier, 2002; Saucier, 1992).

The disagreement has at least two sources. First, recall that naming factors can be hard. You do it by looking at the items that load on the factor and trying to extract the underlying thread that connects them. But most words have several connotations, and trait terms often represent blends of factors rather than one factor per word (Hofstee, de Raad, & Goldberg, 1992). Naturally, then, there are disagreements in interpretation.

Second, exactly what a factor looks like depends on what items are in the study. If a particular quality is left out or is not well represented in the items, its importance to a trait will be missed (Peabody & Goldberg, 1989). Thus, studies with slightly different measures can lead to different conclusions about the meaning of the factors, even when there's agreement that more or less the same factors have emerged.

Table 4.3 displays the five traits, using a variety of names for each. Peabody and Goldberg (1989) suggested that the five factors are the metaphorical equivalent of a piece of music, in which there's a theme and a series of variations on it. That's pretty much what you see in Table 4.3. The labels listed under each factor all share a theme, but there are also variations. Some of the basis for the variation is displayed in Table 4.4, which lists examples of the descriptive terms that loaded on the five factors in one study or another.

Table 4.3 Labels Used by Various Authors to Refer to the "Big Five" Factors in Personality. Labels in the rows are from (in order) Fiske (1949), Norman (1963), Borgatta (1964), Digman (1990), and Costa and McCrae (1985). The final row provides a characterization by Peabody and Goldberg (1989) of the life domain to which the trait pertains.

1	2	3	4	5
Social adaptability	Emotional control	Conformity	Will to achieve	Inquiring intellect
Surgency	Emotionality	Agreeableness	Conscientiousness	Culture
Assertiveness	Emotionality	Likeability	Responsibility	Intelligence
Extraversion	Neuroticism	Friendly compliance	Will to achieve	Intellect
Extraversion	Neuroticism	Agreeableness	Conscientiousness	Openness to experience
Power	Affect	Love	Work	Intellect

Table 4.4 Bipolar and Unipolar Adjective Scales Reflective of the Five Major Personality Factors. *Source:* Based on Digman & Inouye, 1986; McCrae & Costa, 1987; Norman, 1963; Peabody & Goldberg, 1989.

Factor	Item	
Extraversion	Bold–timid	Gregarious
	Forceful–submissive	Outspoken
	Self-confident–unassured	Energetic
	Talkative–silent	Happy
	Spontaneous–inhibited	Seclusive (inverse)
Neuroticism	Nervous–poised	Concerned
	Anxious–calm	Nervous
	Excitable–composed	Fearful
	Relaxed–high strung	Tense
Agreeableness	Friendly–unfriendly	Jealous (inverse)
	Warm–cold	Considerate
	Kind–unkind	Spiteful (inverse)
	Polite–rude	Touchy (inverse)
	Good natured–irritable	Complaining (inverse)
Conscientiousness	Cautious–rash	Neat
	Serious–frivolous	Persevering
	Responsible–irresponsible	Planful
	Thorough–careless	Careful
	Hardworking–lazy	Eccentric (inverse)
Intellect	Imaginative–simple	Knowledgeable
	Intellectual–unreflective	Perceptive
	Polished–crude	Imaginative
	Uncurious–curious	Verbal
	Uncreative–creative	Original

The first factor is usually called *extraversion,* but there's a good deal of variation in what it includes. This helps account for the different labels. Sometimes it seems based in assertiveness, sometimes in spontaneity and energy. Sometimes it's based in dominance and confidence, sometimes in a tendency toward happiness. Extraversion is often thought of as implying a sense of sociability (Watson, Clark, McIntyre, & Hamaker, 1992), but some argue that that's actually a by-product of other features of extraversion (Lucas, Diener, Grob, Suh, & Shao, 2000).

There's more agreement (though still not unanimity) about the meaning of the next factor. *Neuroticism,* or *emotional stability,* is regarded by most people as being what Eysenck referred to with those labels. Digman and Takemoto-Chock (1981) called it *emotional disorganization,* because items loading on it convey more than mere presence of emotion. What's at the heart of this factor, though, seems to be the subjective experience of anxiety and general distress.

The next factor in Table 4.4 is most commonly called *agreeableness.* This trait is often characterized as being concerned with the maintaining of relationships. Digman and his colleagues (Digman, 1990; Digman & Inouye, 1986; Digman & Takemoto-Chock, 1981) held that it's not just a quality of being warm and likeable versus being cold; it may extend to a kind of docile compliance. It can also imply nurturance and emotional supportiveness, which requires inhibition of negative affect (Graziano &

Eisenberg, 1999). The opposite pole of this dimension has an oppositional or antagonistic quality verging toward hostility (Digman, 1990). Fitting this, people low in agreeableness choose displays of power as a way of resolving social conflict more than people higher in agreeableness (Graziano, Jensen-Campbell, & Hair, 1996). There's also evidence that they actually *experience* more conflicts (Asendorpf & Wilpers, 1998).

The essence of the next factor is also a little hard to capture. The most commonly used label is *conscientiousness*. However, this label doesn't fully reflect its qualities of planning, persistence, and purposeful striving toward goals (Digman & Inouye, 1986). Indeed, because the word *conscientious* itself has two shades of meaning, it loads both on this factor and on agreeableness, which hints that conscientiousness may not be the perfect name for this factor. Noting that this quality relates to educational achievement, Digman (1990) suggested that it be thought of as will to achieve, or simply *will*. Other suggested names include *constraint* and *responsibility*. Roberts, Walton, and Bogg (2005) recently examined the qualities various theorists consider part of conscientiousness and concluded that no measure includes all of them.

The largest disagreement may concern the next factor. The disagreement stems at least partly from differences in measures. Early on, Cattell measured qualities of *intelligence*. Then he stopped doing so and started using the term *culture* to refer to the qualities that remained. The label stuck. Peabody and Goldberg (1989) pointed out, though, that when intelligence-related measures are reintroduced, they join with culture. These authors suggested the factor should more properly be labeled *intellect*. Costa and McCrae (1985) favor yet another label: *openness* to experience.

Peabody and Goldberg (1989) argued that Costa and McCrae's measure of this factor taps one aspect of intellect (the imaginative side) but misses the other side (the logical side). They said that when both sides are measured, they merge (implying that this factor is really intellect). McCrae and Costa (1987) disagreed. They argued that intelligence just provides a basis for the broader sense of openness. The concept of openness to experience is newer to psychology than is intelligence. However, McCrae (1996) has reviewed a wide range of ways in which openness relates to social experience and shown that it may be far more important than people realize.

REFLECTIONS OF THE FIVE FACTORS IN BEHAVIOR

Until fairly recently, most work on the five-factor model was aimed at the factors themselves: showing that they exist in diverse cultures and emerge from many ways of assessment. More recently, however, researchers have turned more to looking at how these five traits are reflected, or expressed, on the broader canvas of people's lives.

Let's start with the traits that are most social in nature: extraversion and agreeableness. Several projects have focused on the idea that extraversion and agreeableness are both tied to social situations, but in different ways. Extraversion seems to relate to *having social impact;* agreeableness seems to relate to *maintaining positive relations with others* (Jensen-Campbell & Graziano, 2001). Fitting this, extraversion predicts being prominent in fraternities and sororities (Anderson, John, Keltner, & Kring, 2001), but agreeableness does not. In a study of adolescents (Jensen-Campbell, Adams, Perry, Workman, Furdella, & Egan, 2002), extraversion and agreeableness both related to peer acceptance, but agreeableness also protected against being victimized by peers. Adults high in agreeableness also feel they have greater social support from family members (Branje, van Lieshout, & van Aken, 2004). All of this makes sense, if agreeableness is largely about maintaining good relations.

A variety of other findings fit that idea, as well. Agreeableness predicts endorsement of conflict resolution tactics among children (Jensen-Campbell, Gleason, Adams,

People high in agreeableness care about maintaining positive relations with others.

& Malcolm, 2003). Agreeable adults get less angry over bad outcomes caused by other people than do less agreeable adults (Meier & Robinson, 2004). In fact, agreeableness seems to short circuit aggressive responses (Meier, Robinson, & Wilkowski, 2006).

Agreeableness has been found to predict more empathy and responsiveness in parenting (Clark, Kochanka, & Ready, 2000), less negativity in marital interactions (Donnellan, Conger, & Bryant, 2004), less seeking of revenge after being harmed (McCullough & Hoyt, 2002), and greater attempts to control negative emotions (Tobin, Graziano, Vanman, & Tassinary, 2000). Agreeableness also predicts less poaching of romantic partners and less responsiveness to poaching attempts by others (Schmitt & Buss, 2001). Agreeableness has also been linked to less substance abuse (Chassin, Flora, & King, 2004; Lynam, Leukefeld, & Clayton, 2003; Walton & Roberts, 2004) and less antisocial behavior (J. D. Miller, Lynam, & Leukefeld, 2003).

Extraversion is helpful socially. Extraverted men interact better with women they don't know than introverts do (Berry & Miller, 2001), and extraverts have the firm handshake that conveys confidence (Chaplin, Phillips, Brown, Clanton, & Stein, 2000). But there can be a dark side to the desire for social impact. There's evidence that extraverts are less cooperative than introverts when facing a social dilemma over resources, whereas agreeableness relates to being more cooperative (Koole, Jager, van den Berg, Vlek, & Hofstee, 2001).

Studies have also found that these two traits relate in consistent ways to personal values and life goals. Extraversion relates to valuing achievement and stimulation; agreeableness relates to valuing benevolence and tradition (Roccas, Sagiv, Schwartz, & Knafo, 2002). Extraversion relates to the desires for a high-status career, political influence, an exciting lifestyle, and children; agreeableness relates to desires for goals of group welfare and harmonious family relations and actually relates inversely to desires for wealth, political influence, and an exciting lifestyle (Roberts & Robins, 2000).

Conscientiousness has also received a good deal of attention in recent years. Greater conscientiousness predicts avoidance of unsafe sex (Trobst, Herbst, Masters, & Costa, 2002) and other risky behaviors (Markey, Markey, & Tinsley, 2003). Conscientious people are less likely to try to steal someone else's romantic partner, and are less responsive to being lured away (Schmitt & Buss, 2001). Conscientiousness has been linked to more responsive parenting of young children (Clark et al., 2000) and to use of negotiation as a conflict-resolution strategy (Jensen-Campbell & Graziano, 2001). Conscientiousness has been related to a desire for a career, but not necessarily a high standard of living (Roberts & Robins, 2000). Conscientiousness in adolescence predicts higher religiousness in adulthood (McCullough, Tsang, & Brion, 2003) and higher academic achievement (Chamorro-Premuzic & Furnham, 2003).

Conscientiousness also seems to have health implications. In a study of cancer risk, conscientiousness led to more restrictive household bans on smoking (Hampson, Andrews, Barckley, Lichtenstein, & Lee, 2000). People who are high in conscientiousness even seem to live longer, presumably because they take better care of themselves (Christensen et al., 2002; Friedman et al., 1995). Consistent with this, conscientiousness relates to various kinds of health-linked behaviors (Bogg & Roberts, 2004; Roberts et al., 2005). In fact, conscientiousness in childhood has been related to health behaviors 40 years later (Hampson, Goldberg, Vogt, & Dubanoski, 2006). Conscientiousness has also been related to lower levels of substance abuse (Chassin et al., 2004; Lynam et al., 2003; Roberts & Bogg, 2004; Walton & Roberts, 2004) and to less antisocial behavior more generally (J. D. Miller et al., 2003).

Openness to experience has been found to predict greater engagement with the existential challenges of life (Keyes, Shmotkin, & Ryff, 2002). Openness relates to more favorable inter-racial attitudes (Flynn, 2005). Openness relates to greater sexual satisfaction in marriage (Donnellan et al., 2004). People high in openness say they desire artistic expression, and they devalue traditional marriage and the possibility of an easy, lazy life (Roberts & Robins, 2000). On the other hand, openness has also been found to predict more prior arrests among prisoners (Clower & Bothwell, 2001).

Neuroticism has been studied for decades. High levels of neuroticism relate to distress in a wide variety of difficult circumstances. For example, it relates to more difficult interactions among married partners (Donellan et al., 2004) and less satisfaction in marriages. People who are highly neurotic are also more likely to distance themselves from their partners after a negative event (Bolger & Zuckerman, 1995). Neuroticism impairs academic performance (Chamorro-Premuzic & Furnham, 2003), and it even predicts a negative emotional tone when writing stories about oneself (McAdams et al., 2004).

THE FIVE-FACTOR MODEL IN RELATION TO EARLIER MODELS

Today, when people think of trait psychology, they tend to think first of the five-factor model. However, recall from earlier in the chapter that several other trait models preceded this one. Let's consider how the five-factor model relates to them.

The easiest comparison is to Eysenck's theory. It's obvious from Table 4.3 that two of the "big five" are virtually the same as Eysenck's supertraits: extraversion and emotional stability. It's been suggested that Eysenck's third dimension, psychoticism, is a blend of agreeableness and conscientiousness (Goldberg, 1993b; Zuckerman, Kuhlman, Joireman, Teta, & Kraft, 1993).

A second similarity to Eysenck is that the five factors are superordinate traits, incorporating narrower traits. For example, Paul Costa and Robert McCrae (1985, 1992) developed a measure called the NEO Personality Inventory (NEO-PI-R; NEO stands for *neuroticism, extraversion,* and *openness;* agreeableness and conscientiousness were added after the name was coined; the R stands for *revised*). The NEO-PI-R includes measures of six narrow traits for each domain of the five-factor model. The six narrow traits combine into a score for that supertrait. Thus, many people who use the five-factor model share with Eysenck the idea that the core traits are supertraits, which in turn are composed of more specific facet traits.

Another useful comparison is with the interpersonal circle of Wiggins and his colleagues. The basic dimensions there are *dominance* and *love*. Love may be equivalent to agreeableness. If dominance were seen as roughly equivalent to extraversion, the interpersonal circle would comprise two factors of the five-factor model (McCrae & Costa, 1989b; Peabody & Goldberg, 1989). Trapnell and Wiggins (1990) expanded a measure of the interpersonal circle to have additional scales and an even better fit to the five-factor model (see also Saucier, 1992).

This comparison with the interpersonal circle also raises an issue, however. As noted earlier (Figure 4.3), Wiggins saw extraversion as a combination of two qualities in the circle, not as a basic dimension. Doesn't that conflict with the five-factor model? It depends on how you define *extraversion*. Remember, there are diverse opinions on how to view that factor. If it's really about dominance and assertiveness, it would fit with the interpersonal circle.

To summarize some of the points made in this part of the chapter, the five-factor model of personality structure has emerged as a candidate to integrate a variety of earlier models. The data make this set of broad traits look very much as though they represent universal aspects of personality (McCrae & Costa, 1997). Remember, though, that what comes out of a factor analysis depends on what goes into it. It can be dangerous to draw solid conclusions too quickly. Nonetheless, at present the five-factor model seems to offer the best promise of a consensus about the dimensions of personality that trait psychology has ever seen.

SOME ADDITIONAL VARIATIONS AND SOME CAUTIONS

Consensus is not the same as *unanimity,* however. People have disagreed with this view for a variety of reasons (e.g., Block, 1995, 2001; Eysenck, 1992, 1993; Zuckerman, 1992). One line of dissent claims that work from the lexical approach omitted a set of words that shouldn't have been left out—words that are purely evaluative (e.g., *excellent, evil*). When these words are included, two more factors emerge: *positive valence* and *negative valence* (Almagor, Tellegen, & Waller, 1995; Benet & Waller, 1995).

We should also note that there are other influential trait models that differ from the five-factor model in various ways. One of them is Tellegen's (1985) model. It greatly resembles that of Eysenck (1975, 1986) in having three supertraits, though with somewhat different origins and different overtones. Tellegen (1985) recast *neuroticism* as a tendency to experience negative emotions, and he recast *extraversion* as a tendency to experience positive emotions. Positive emotionality (like extraversion) has been tied to social success and negative emotionality (like neuroticism) to various indices of poor adjustment (Shiner, Masten, & Tellegen, 2002). Tellegen's third factor, called *constraint,* resembles psychoticism in Eysenck's model, but viewed from the opposite direction. It predicts the same kinds of outcomes, too. Low constraint has been linked to criminal and antisocial behavior (Krueger, 2002; Shiner et al., 2002) and (in interaction with high negative affectivity) to drug use (Shoal & Giancola, 2003).

The idea of five factors was carried in another direction by Zuckerman and his colleagues (1993), who proposed an "alternative five." Remember that what comes out of the factor analysis depends partly on what goes into it. Zuckerman et al. (1993) put slightly different things in. The sociability factor in this model resembles extraversion (if you view extraversion as mostly social). Neuroticism–anxiety is most of neuroticism but without the hostility that others include there. That hostility is incorporated in aggression–hostility, which otherwise looks like agreeableness (reversed). Impulsive sensation seeking looks like conscientiousness (reversed). The last factor in this model is *activity.* What may be the most important difference between this and the other five-factor model is that Zuckerman et al., located hostility outside neuroticism. There are reasons to believe that's a better location for it (Carver, 2004; Jang, Livesly, Angleitner, Riemann, & Vernon, 2002; Peabody & DeRaad, 2002; Saucier & Goldberg, 2001).

The idea that what comes out depends on what goes in is reflected in several other findings. Saucier and Goldberg (1998) found evidence of several dimensions beyond the five factors but concluded that they lie outside personality (for example, religiousness and attractiveness). Paunonen and Jackson (2000) looked at the same evidence and saw nine or ten dimensions that they thought should be viewed as traits, albeit narrow ones (religiousness, dishonesty, seductiveness, humorousness, and conventionality). They argued that some of these narrow traits might even coalesce to form *honesty,* which might be a sixth supertrait (see also Ashton, Lee, & Son, 2000).

Ashton and his colleagues have carried this argument even further. They found a sixth supertrait in multiple studies involving seven languages (Ashton et al., 2004). They refer to it as *honesty/humility.* Subsequent work established that that factor can also be found in analyses of English words (Ashton, Lee, & Goldberg, 2004).

Ashton and his colleagues argue that this trait is a distinct quality that tends to be absorbed into agreeableness but stands out on its own, if allowed to do so.

Although some researchers have argued for more factors, others have argued that the five-factor model can be distilled into two dimensions (Digman, 1997). That is, putting the five traits into a higher-order analysis yields two factors. The first is defined by agreeableness, conscientiousness, and (low) neuroticism. Digman characterized it as reflecting *socialization,* because these qualities all influence whether people get along in social units. The second is defined by extraversion and openness. Digman characterized it as reflecting *personal growth,* because these two qualities influence whether people expose themselves to new things, thereby fostering growth.

These various lines of work all represent qualifications on the idea that the "big five" are the basic dimensions of personality. It should be clear that a number of issues still must be resolved. In sum, the consensus on the five-factor model is substantial, but not complete.

ARE SUPERORDINATE TRAITS THE BEST LEVEL TO USE?

At least one more question needs to be raised, even if you accept the five-factor model. As we said, this is a model of supertraits. Supertraits have facets. As noted earlier, Costa and McCrae's NEO-PI-R measures six facets of each factor. Those who use the five-factor model sometimes point to the utility of examining patterns of traits within each factor (Costa & McCrae, 1995; Goldberg, 1993a), but this strategy is not used very often.

Is anything lost when lower-level traits are combined to form the supertraits? This is essentially what Cattell and Eysenck argued about when they disagreed about the meaning of second-order factors (see also Briggs, 1989; H. E. P. Cattell, 1993; Funder, 1991; John, 1990). The evidence now suggests that something is indeed lost when facet traits are merged.

Paunonen and Ashton (2001a) compared the "big five" factors to specific facet scales as predictors of 40 behaviors, which were measured by self-reports and peer ratings. The behaviors were chosen because they had some social importance (altruistic behavior, smoking, alcohol consumption, religiosity, and so on). For a substantial number of these behaviors, facet scales added significantly to prediction after the five factors had been entered as predictors. Thus, something was lost if only the "big five" were used. Conceptually similar findings have come from a number of other studies (Mershon & Gorsuch, 1988; Paunonen, 1998; Paunonen & Ashton, 2001b; Schimmack, Oishi, Furr, & Funder, 2004; Wolfe & Kasmer, 1988).

Better prediction from specific narrow traits comes at a cost, though. The cost is that to understand the findings, you have to hold a larger number of traits in mind at once. In general terms, that's the trade-off: Using supertraits creates a picture that's more intuitive and easier to hold in mind. Using the narrower traits may often give greater accuracy.

Traits, Situations, and Interactionism

We turn now to a very different part of the trait approach. Trait psychology experienced an important controversy from about 1970 to about 1990. How researchers reacted to this controversy had a big impact on today's views of traits, although this impact is separate from anything we've discussed so far.

IS BEHAVIOR ACTUALLY TRAITLIKE?

The question that shook the foundations of trait psychology in the early 1970s is whether behavior actually shows traitlike consistency. Traits are assumed to be *stable* aspects of personality that influence behavior in a *wide range of settings*. The reason for assuming traits in the first place was to account for consistency in people's thoughts and actions across time and circumstances. Differences on a trait should predict differences in trait-related behaviors.

It was somewhat surprising, then, that trait measures and behavior often didn't correlate well (Mischel, 1968; P. E. Vernon, 1964). Walter Mischel (1968) coined the phrase **personality coefficient** to characterize the modest correlations between trait self-reports and actual behavior, which often were around 0.30. This correlation means that the trait accounts for less than 10% of the variation in the behavior, with the remaining 90% unaccounted for. Later estimates ranged a little higher (around 0.40). Even so, the proportion of variance accounted for didn't seem high.

What, then, are we to think about traits? If traits don't predict people's actions, then why should the trait concept be considered useful? (Indeed, some people went so far as to ask why the concept of *personality* should be considered useful.)

SITUATIONISM

An extreme form of the attack on traits was called **situationism.** This is the idea that situational forces determine behavior, not personality. This view was held by some social psychologists, who traditionally emphasize the role of the social environment, rather than personality, as a cause of actions. This view argued that correlations between traits and behavior were low because situational variables overwhelmed the effect of personality. This turned out to be quite wrong.

Funder and Ozer (1983) pointed out that effects of situations and effects of traits usually are reported with different statistics. This makes it hard to compare them. Funder and Ozer returned to several famous studies of the impact of situations on behavior and converted the original statistics to correlations. To the astonishment of many, these correlations were *about the same size* as the personality coefficients that had been criticized so sharply.

INTERACTIONISM

Another approach to understanding inconsistency between traits and actions is called **interactionism** (e.g., Ekehammer, 1974; Endler & Magnusson, 1976; Magnusson & Endler, 1977; Ozer, 1986; Pervin, 1985). Interactionism is the idea that traits and situations interact to influence behavior. Neither the setting alone nor the person alone provides a complete account.

FIGURE 4.4

Sometimes there is an interaction between a situation and a trait variable, such that variations in the situation affect some people but not others. This particular interaction is one that has, in fact, been hypothesized by Abramson, Seligman, and Teasdale (1978). The type of interaction displayed here is only one type of potential interaction between people and situations (see text).

The term *interactionism* is tied in part to an "analysis-of-variance" understanding of how two variables (or in this case, two classes of variables) influence an outcome. To explain this, we return to an idea from Chapter 2. We described there how experimental personality research often combines two variables as factors in a single study. We now state that point again in terms of persons and situations.

When a situation and a trait are examined in the same study, there are three systematic sources of influence on behavior. Sometimes variations in the *situation* have an effect on all persons—for example, stressful situations may induce depression. Sometimes variations on a *trait* have an effect in all situations—for example, people who are susceptible to depression may be more depressed across situations than people who are less susceptible.

It's also possible, however, for the situation and trait to *interact* (see Figure 4.4). An interaction here means that variations in situation affect some people in one way and others in a different way. For example, stress may cause an increase in depression among people who are prone to depression but not among others. This interaction may occur in addition to one or both of the overall effects, or it may occur *instead of them*. In the latter case, it would create a picture of weak effects for both the trait and the situation.

In this analysis-of-variance view, situations and dispositions can interact in several ways to determine behavior. Perhaps most obvious (the case shown in Figure 4.4) is that a situation may influence one kind of person but not others. Sometimes a situational variable causes one behavior in one person and a *different* behavior in another person. For example, a stressful situation may cause extraverts to seek out others and introverts to withdraw from others.

Here's another way to describe such interactions: Some situations permit easy expression of personality. Other situations force behavior into channels, thus preventing expression of personality (Monson, Hesley, & Chernick, 1982; Schutte, Kenrick, & Sadalla, 1985). The first set is called *weak* situations; the second set is called *strong* situations (Mischel, 1977). As an example, the lawn of a college campus on a Sunday afternoon is a weak situation. Individual differences can be expressed easily; in fact, the situation seems to invite it. An army boot camp is a strong situation. It dampens any expression of individual differences.

INDIVIDUAL DIFFERENCES IN CONSISTENCY

Apparently, dispositions can also be strong and weak in the same sense. That is, some people are so consistent that they overwhelm the situations they're in. Other people are more willing to let situational influences guide them and thus are less consistent.

This depiction fits a trait called *self-monitoring* (M. Snyder, 1974, 1987). People high in self-monitoring like to fit smoothly into situations they encounter. They look to others for cues about what actions are appropriate, and they bend to the needs of the situation. People low in self-monitoring behave the way they think they *are,* no matter the situation. It follows that high self-monitors should be less consistent from one situation to another than low self-monitors. This turns out to be true (see M. Snyder, 1987).

There is also evidence that people vary in consistency on *specific* traits. People who saw themselves as being inconsistent on a trait acted in ways that didn't relate well to their trait self-reports (Bem & Allen, 1974). Among those who reported being consistent, however, the trait reports predicted their actions quite well. Others have found much the same things (Kenrick & Stringfield, 1980; Woodruffe, 1985; Zuckerman, Bernieri, Koestner, & Rosenthal, 1989; Zuckerman, Koestner, DeBoy, Garcia, Maresca, & Sartoris, 1988).

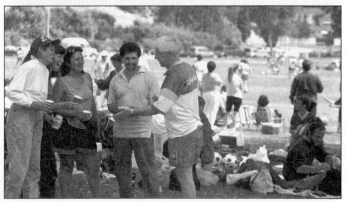

Some situations act to constrain behavior and hide individual differences. Other situations allow personality free expression.

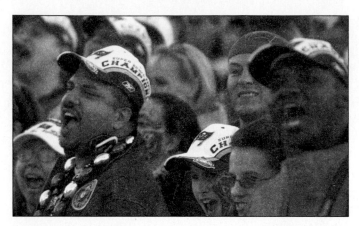

People exercise choice over the settings they enter, which influences the behaviors they engage in. Some people choose to go to football games, other people do not.

OTHER ASPECTS OF INTERACTIONISM

The analysis-of-variance model derives from lab research, a context in which researchers put people into identical situations. It tends to imply that people outside the lab also enter identical situations. This, of course, is wrong—a point made by a number of authors (D. M. Buss, 1984; Emmons & Diener, 1986; Emmons, Diener, & Larsen, 1986; Magnus, Diener, Fujita, & Pavot, 1993; Plomin, DeFries, & Loehlin, 1977; Scarr & McCartney, 1983; M. Snyder & Gangestad, 1982). In life outside the lab (and rarely, but occasionally, even in the lab), people exercise considerable choice over which environments they enter.

Some people choose to go to church, others choose not to. Some people choose to go to basketball games, some to rock concerts, some to country meadows. By exercising choice over the settings they enter, people thereby influence the behaviors they engage in. Indeed, there's evidence that people choose their *marriage partners* partly by whether the partner lets them be who they are (Caspi & Herbener, 1990). The choices that people make about what situations to enter depend partly on their personalities (Brandstätter, 1983; Emmons & Diener, 1986; Emmons et al., 1986).

Another way persons and situations interact is that people differ in the kinds of responses they elicit from others (Scarr & McCartney, 1983). Some people naturally bring a smile to your face, others can make you frown just by entering the room. Introverts tend to steer conversations in one direction, extraverts in another (Thorne, 1987). Indeed, people actively manipulate each other using such tactics as charm, coercion, and silence (Buss, Gomes, Higgins, & Lauterbach, 1987). All these effects change the situation, so *the situation is actually different for one person than it is for another*. This reciprocal influence is another way persons and situations interact.

WAS THE PROBLEM EVER REALLY AS BAD AS IT SEEMED?

Trying to understand weak links from trait to behavior has led to a great deal of information about how they relate. We should note, however, that doubt has arisen about whether the problem ever was actually as bad as it seemed to be.

After Mischel (1968) said that personality correlated with behavior around 0.30, others pointed out that the studies leading to that conclusion weren't the best of studies (Block, 1977; Hogan, DeSoto, & Solano, 1977). There seems to have been some truth to that. More recent studies, which were more carefully designed (e.g., Conley, 1985; Deluty, 1985; Funder & Block, 1989; Funder & Colvin, 1991; Moskowitz, 1994; Woodruffe, 1985), have found much stronger relationships than those Mischel had summarized.

There also turn out to be statistical reasons why a correlation of 0.30 isn't so bad! Many actions are influenced by more than one trait. For example, when you get to a party where you don't know anyone, what you'll do next will depend on how extraverted you are, but it will also depend on how anxiety prone you are. As it happens, whenever a behavior is influenced by several traits at once, the *mere fact of multiple influence* puts limits on how strong a correlation can be for any single trait (Ahadi & Diener, 1989). This limit looks, in fact, very nearly the same as the much maligned personality coefficient.

Maybe the core problem really wasn't ever as bad as it seemed in 1968. But the work addressing the problem has told us a lot about how behavior emerges. Indeed, this work has led many people to hold a more elaborate view of the trait construct than they might otherwise hold. We consider this view next.

Interactionism Becomes a New View of Traits: Context-Dependent Expression of Personality

Psychologists put a lot of effort into developing the ideas known collectively as *interactionism*. Nonpsychologists, however, seem to approach traits naturally with what seems an interactionist mentality. That is, people seem to recognize intuitively that whether a trait influences behavior varies from setting to setting. You shouldn't expect a given trait to operate all the time—only in situations to which it's relevant.

This is reflected in the fact that people often use verbal hedges in discussing personality (Wright & Mischel, 1988). A *hedge* (in this context) means a word or phrase that limits a trait's applicability. As examples, you might describe someone as "shy *with strangers*" or "aggressive *when teased*." The ultimate hedge is *sometimes*. Using a hedge implies you think the trait-based behavior occurs only in certain kinds of situations (see also Shoda, Mischel, & Wright, 1989).

Such evidence, along with the insights of interactionism more generally, led Mischel and Shoda (1995) to a more elaborated analysis of how traits influence behavior (see also Cervone, 1997, 2004; Mischel, Shoda, & Mendoza-Denton, 2002). In this view, traits are not freestanding tendencies to act, but patterns of linkages between situation and action. Given situation *x,* action *y* is likely. A key point of this idea is that a given action shouldn't be expected to occur all the time, because the situation that brings it out isn't always present. Thus, a person's behavior may appear inconsistent across situations, especially situations that differ a lot. But in situations that seem similar to the person, the behavior is consistent (Furr & Funder, 2004). Thus, there's a lot of consistency, despite the variability (see also Box 4.2).

Another key point in this theory is that the pattern of linkage between situation and behavior differs from one person to another. This is a source of individuality, uniqueness: the pattern of situation–behavior links the person has established over time and experience. Even if two people tend toward the same kind of behavior, the situations that elicit that behavior may differ from one person to the other. If so, these two people will act differently from each other in many situations, even though they have the same trait. This, in fact, may be a way in which idiographic traits can exist. Each person's unique pattern of links from situation to action creates a trait that is just a little different from that of any other person.

The idea that traits represent patterns of situation–action links opens other possibilities as well. For example, imagine a person who is mostly an introvert but occasionally acts like an extravert—for example, by becoming talkative. From the perspective of the linkage model, this would mean that there are classes of situations (perhaps infrequent in their occurrence) that link to those actions for this person. From this way of thinking, there would be no contradiction in the idea that a person can display qualities from one end of a trait dimension in one situation and qualities from the opposite end of the dimension in another.

Considerable support for this argument has been reported by Fleeson (2001). For example, he found that most people do things that reflect the entire range of a trait

Box 4.2 How Consistent Is Personality over *Long* Periods?

When we talk about consistency and stability in personality, we often focus on fairly short time periods. However, the trait concept implies stability over much longer periods. We should also ask about whether people's personalities stay the same even years later.

Several projects have contributed information on this issue (for more, see Caspi, Roberts, & Shiner, 2005). Helson and Moane (1987) described women who were studied as college seniors, then at age 27, and again at age 43. Across each span, traits had high test–retest correlations. On the other hand, the women also changed as a group, becoming more dominant and independent from age 27 to 43. How can that be? The answer is that there was a lot of rank-order stability in the group over time. Even as the women became more independent as they all grew older, the ones who were most independent at 22 were still the most independent at 27 and at 43.

Wink and Helson (1993) found that the change toward more competence and self-confidence continued to age 52. There was also evidence that women who changed the most were those who had begun families or had career development during this period—activities that changed role demands, which changed how the women saw themselves. Analyses of even later assessments showed that dominance and independence had peaked in middle age but that various kinds of change continued into old age (Helson, Jones, & Kwan, 2002).

Several studies have looked at the transition from adolescence to young adulthood. Robins, Fraley, Roberts, and Trzesniewski (2001) looked at personality reports across the college years and found some change in mean levels, but large correlations over time. Roberts, Caspi, and Moffitt (2001) found changes from ages 18 to 26 that were consistent with a group shift toward greater maturity. For the most part, though, correlations of traits across time were quite strong. Yet people appear to think their personality has changed more over this period than it really has (Robins, Noftle, Trzesniewski, & Roberts, 2005).

One interesting project focused on two specific qualities of childhood personality—shyness and temper—and how they predict adult behavior (Caspi, Elder, & Bem, 1987, 1988). This study started with mothers of 8- to 10-year-old children describing what the children were like. The children themselves were interviewed when they were 30 and 40, along with their spouses and their own children. Boys with frequent temper tantrums in childhood grew up to be ill-tempered men. Girls with frequent tantrums in childhood were seen by their *families* as ill-tempered mothers, but this didn't come across in interviews with the researchers. Childhood shyness also reverberated later on. Shy boys married late and were slow to establish stable careers. Shy girls weren't slower to marry but were more likely to follow a conventional pattern of family and homemaking than were less-shy girls.

On the whole, research seems to confirm two ideas. They may seem at first glance to be contradictory, but they really aren't. First, people change as they age. They become more conscientious and more agreeable (Helson, Kwan, John, & Jones, 2002; Roberts et al., 2005)—more "mature" (Caspi et al., 2005). Second, there is a lot of rank-order stability within any given group over long periods of time. Indeed, a review of the evidence from 152 longitudinal studies found that correlations of personality grow increasingly strong from college, through midadulthood, to later adulthood (Roberts & Del Vecchio, 2000; see also Costa & McCrae, 1988b, 1989; McCrae, 1993). This kind of consistency is one more reason to believe that traits are real.

---

dimension. It's just that the things they do most often reflect a narrower portion of that dimension (see Figure 4.5). In the same way, more recent research (Fleeson, Malanos, & Achille, 2002) shows that the positive emotions that are tied to extraversion vary from hour to hour, right along with the degree of extraverted behavior the person is engaging in.

The linkage viewpoint seems to deal well with some problems people have had in thinking about traits. It doesn't distort the trait concept, but it clearly adds something to the concept, as it was discussed in the first part of this chapter. This theory has other elements that are considered in Chapter 16. For now, the point is that the impact of traits seems to be context dependent (see also Fleeson & Leicht, 2006). This conclusion is very consistent with an interactionist view of personality.

Fitting the Pieces Together: Views of Traits and Behavior

Let's pull these ideas together with what came earlier. If you had read only the first half of this chapter, you might have been tempted to assume that most trait theorists hold the view in Figure 4.6, panel A or B, in which traits have a *constant* influence on behavior. People who discuss the five-factor model tend not to talk much about how traits and situations interact. It can be easy to infer from their statements that that's what they assume.

But traits don't work that way. Research described in the previous sections makes that clear. Traits sometimes influence behavior a lot, and sometimes not at all. Whether the trait matters depends on the situation (Figure 4.6, C). This dynamic approach to the role of traits in the constantly varying social environment recognizes complexities in the creation of behavior.

This picture is certainly more compelling than the simple ones. Interestingly enough, though, the core idea isn't all that new. Some trait theorists of earlier years said much the same thing. They didn't say it in as much detail as it's being said today, however. As early as 1937, Gordon Allport wrote that "traits are often aroused in one situation and not in another" (p. 331). His conception of a trait explicitly included the assumption that the trait doesn't influence all behaviors and that it may not influence a given category of behavior at all times (Zuroff, 1986). Rather, the effect of the trait depends on whether it's evoked in that situation. Allport even believed that people have *contradictory* traits. The fact that the different traits are aroused by different situations keeps this from being a problem (Fleeson, 2001, 2004).

Allport also anticipated another contemporary theme when he noted that people choose the situations they enter and actively change the situations they're in (Zuroff, 1986). Thus, the ideas that would become known as *interactionism* have roots that go back a long way.

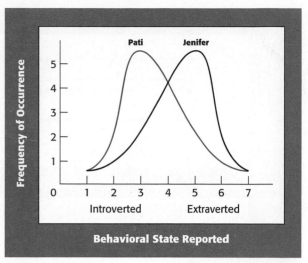

FIGURE 4.5

Traits as situation-linked frequency distributions of states. People occasionally act extraverted, even if they are essentially introverts (such as Pati); people occasionally act introverted, even if they are essentially extraverts (such as Jenifer). The person's generalized trait is reflected in the fact that particular sorts of behavioral states are most frequent. *Source: Based on Fleeson, 2001.*

Assessment

More than is true of most viewpoints on personality, the trait approach focuses a great deal on the process of assessment. Indeed, the first part of this chapter discussed how various theorists developed measures. In this section, we consider briefly how the measures are used.

COMPARING INDIVIDUALS: PERSONALITY PROFILES

The trait approach makes extensive use of self-report inventories. Those self-reports ask people to describe their view of themselves by making ratings of one kind or another. The most common ratings involve indicating whether a descriptive adjective applies to you or not, or where on a dimension (anchored by opposing adjectives) you'd fall, or whether you agree or disagree with a statement. The ratings may be made as yes–no or agree–disagree decisions, or they may be made on multipoint scales.

Recall that traits are seen as fundamental qualities of personality, reflected in diverse behaviors. For this reason, self-reports of traits usually include ratings for several reflections of each trait being measured. A scale using adjectives would have several adjectives for each trait; a scale made up of statements would include statements implying diverse ways the trait might be expressed.

Regardless of the exact form of the inventory, the nomothetic version of trait psychology assumes that anyone can be placed somewhere along each trait dimension

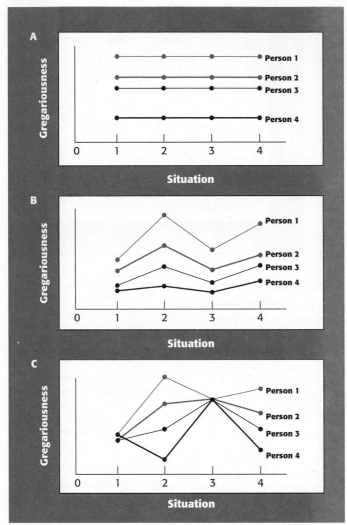

FIGURE 4.6
Three models of the effects of traits on behavior (portrayed for the trait of gregariousness). (A) A naive model, in which people are assumed to display their traits at a relatively constant level, no matter what situation they're in (what Magnusson & Endler, 1977, called *absolute consistency*). (B) A model in which situations influence the *overall* levels at which the trait is displayed, but people retain the same ordering (*relative consistency*). (C) An *interactionist model,* in which some situations (2 and 4) permit or even elicit individual differences, whereas others (1 and 3) don't do so.

assessed. Inventories measuring these traits are used to create *profiles.* A personality profile describes a person's place on each trait dimension the inventory measures (see Figure 4.7). Knowing the dimensions and the person's place on each can create a sense of what the person is like and how the person will behave in a variety of situations.

The profile in Figure 4.7 illustrates the kind of information a personality inventory gives. At first glance, a profile can seem like nothing more than a string of beads. (Allport [1961] said that's exactly what they are.) Perhaps a better metaphor is the bar code used by supermarkets to identify products. Nomothetic theorists believe that the profile is where uniqueness lies. You can see from Figure 4.7 that a shift on a single trait changes the balance of a person's qualities. It can thereby change how the person will act in various settings and how the person will seem to someone else. Since everyone has a unique combination of trait levels, everyone is different from everyone else.

Further, trait theorists believe traits can *interact* with one another. To put it differently, how a given level of one trait influences behavior may differ from person to person, as a function of where the people are on other traits. For example, two adventuresome people may display their boldness differently as a function of how sociable they are. The highly sociable one may engage in risky interpersonal exchanges, the less sociable one may climb mountains. Thus, a given trait can be reflected in unique ways for each person because of the modifying effect of differences on *other* traits (recall the earlier discussion of extraversion and emotionality and Table 4.2). This is true even though any particular trait dimension is the same from one person to another.

Problems in Behavior, and Behavior Change

The trait approach was the starting point for some of the earliest efforts to assess disorder. Those efforts were based on the idea that problems directly reflect people's traits. Differences among categories of problems occur because each trait (or group of traits) relates to a different kind of problem.

The attempt to understand psychopathology from this trait-based viewpoint was largely an attempt to categorize it. Categorizing was a matter of determining the trait indicators in people's behavior that relate to a given class of problem. This process led to a taxonomy for identifying and labeling problems (Wiggins, 1973), which has been revised several times.

Some traits relate to problems because the trait itself *is* problematic. As noted earlier, Eysenck's model has a dimension termed *psychoticism*. Psychoticism is a tendency toward certain kinds of problem behaviors, such as antisocial actions and alcohol and drug abuse (Sher, Bartholow, & Wood, 2000). Because people vary in psychoticism, they will vary in the degree to which they can be expected to display those problems. *Neuroticism* is a tendency toward experiencing emotional distress. Many psychopathologies are characterized by high levels of distress. Thus, people who are high in neuroticism are more likely to display those problems than people lower in neuroticism.

THE FIVE-FACTOR MODEL AND PERSONALITY DISORDERS

The emerging influence of the five-factor model of personality has led especially to renewed interest in the traits related to personality disorders (see Costa & Widiger, 2002; Watson & Clark, 1994). A *personality disorder* is a stable, enduring pattern of behavior that deviates from normal cultural expectations and interferes with a person's life or the lives of others. Many theorists are interested in whether personality disorders are essentially extreme manifestations of several of the "big five" traits (Larstone, Jang, Livesley, Vernon, & Wolf, 2002; Markon, Krueger, & Watson, 2005; Widiger, Trull, Clarkin, Sanderson, & Costa, 2002).

Recent research indicates this might be the case. For example, O'Connor and Dyce (2001) found that all personality disorders are represented within the five-factor model. Reynolds and Clark (2001) also found that the "big five" did a good job of representing personality disorder and that the facet scales (the narrow scales within the five domains) did even better. An edited volume containing diverse reviews of relevant evidence, and theoretical statements on the relation between the "big five" and the personality disorders is now in its second edition (Costa & Widiger, 2002). One recent study has even found that clinicians find the "big five" more useful clinically than the categories of the diagnostic system (Samuel & Widiger, 2006).

This exploration of the five factors and disorder is not limited to personality disorder. The question is being raised more generally about abnormalities of all types (Krueger, Watson, & Barlow, 2005; Nigg et al., 2002; O'Connor, 2002). Might they turn out to reflect extremes of specific traits? This area of work is likely to continue to be an important focus for more exploration in future years.

FIGURE 4.7

An illustration of a personality profile, adapted from the NEO-PI-R. The NEO-PI-R provides both an overall profile of the five major factors (top portion) and a profile of the facets within each of the "big five" (lower portion). The top profile provides a quick and simple summary for the person's personality; the other provides a more detailed picture.

Source: Reproduced by special permission of the Publisher, Psychological Assessment Resources, Inc, 16204 North Florida Avenue, Lutz, Florida 33549, from the NEO Personality Inventory Revised, by P. T. Costa, Jr., and R. R. McCrae, PhD, copyright 1978, 1985, 1989, 1992 by Psychological Assessment Resources, Inc. (PAR). Further reproduction is prohibited without permission of PAR.

Even a person prone to experiencing fear will not experience fear unless a fear-producing situation is encountered.

INTERACTIONISM IN BEHAVIOR PROBLEMS

As described earlier in the chapter, evidence suggesting a poor relationship between traits and actions led to development of *interactionism*. The logic of interactionism is useful not just for understanding normal behavior, but also for understanding problems.

One basic idea of interactionism is that individual differences matter in some situations but not others. As applied to problems, the idea takes on slightly different connotations. They are easiest to understand if you think of a trait as a *vulnerability* or *susceptibility* to a problem. Saying a person is susceptible to a problem doesn't mean that the person *has* the problem. It means the problem will emerge more easily for this person than for someone else. To put it in terms of interactionism, there are situations in which the susceptibility matters and others in which it doesn't (recall Figure 4.4).

The susceptibility usually matters in situations involving a lot of stress. Therefore, this approach to problems is called a **diathesis-stress model.** (*Diathesis* means susceptibility.) In this model, an interaction is required between the diathesis and a stress before the problem will develop (Meehl, 1962). Diathesis-stress models have been quite common in thinking about psychological problems.

BEHAVIOR CHANGE

What of the process of therapeutic behavior change? The trait approach is inherently a little pessimistic about change. If traits define a person's personality, how much can problems be resolved without changing the person's personality? Traits are stable. Any change that therapy produces is likely to be in how traits are displayed, rather than in the traits themselves.

On the other hand, the interactionist approach also has an implication here. If problems arise through an interaction between susceptibilities and difficult situations, then it should be helpful for the susceptible person to avoid entering situations in which the relevant stresses are likely to occur. Avoiding such situations should prevent the problems from arising.

This, of course, is something that people often do on their own. As we said earlier in the chapter, people exercise some control over what situations they choose to enter. Just as some people choose to go to church and some do not, some people choose to avoid situations in which their vulnerabilities place them at risk. Shy people may avoid singles bars. People with short tempers may try to avoid arguments. People who routinely overspend their credit cards may cancel the cards and switch to using only cash. Avoidance isn't always possible. Yet if people learn which stressors they can and cannot handle, this knowledge should make them more effective in managing their lives.

Trait Psychology: Problems and Prospects

The trait view is in many respects the most basic approach to personality of all. The very concepts of type and trait arose literally thousands of years ago, to account for consistency in behavior across time and circumstances. The concepts have been elaborated and embellished over the years, but in some ways their core remains the same.

Although the trait view on personality is the most basic, some people find it unsatisfying. It's been criticized on several grounds in recent years. (For opinions on both sides, see Pervin, 1994, and commentaries that follow it.) One problem is that trait theories have had little to say about how personality works (Block, 1995) or how the person gets from trait to action (Pervin, 1994). A clear exception to this characterization is the more recent work of Mischel and Shoda (1995), their colleagues, and others pursuing their ideas. This work is not at all typical of the trait approach of years past, but it may represent the trait approach of the future.

To put it differently, until the recent past, the trait approach has had little to say about intrapersonal functioning. This has resulted in a picture of personality that feels static and empty. McAdams (1992) called *trait psychology* the "psychology of the stranger," because it provides information that would be important if you knew nothing about a person, but it doesn't portray the dynamic aspects of personality. Labeling a person as *friendly,* or *sociable,* or *dominant* gives a name to what you see. But it doesn't tell you much about how or why the person acts that way. This is a major criticism of the trait concept.

The idea that the trait viewpoint has had little to say about the process side of personality is often made jointly with a second, related criticism. This second criticism is that trait theories sometimes resort to circular explanation in trying to deal with causality. As an example, imagine a woman who acts in a dominant manner— not just occasionally but often; not just in one situation or with one set of people, but in many situations, with whoever else is around. You might conclude from this that she has a high level of the trait of dominance.

But that can be a hollow conclusion. Ask yourself two questions and think about your natural responses. Question: Why does she behave that way? (Answer: Because she's dominant.) Question: How do you know she's dominant? (Answer: Because she behaves that way.) The problem is that the information about behavior is being used to infer the existence of a trait, which is being used in turn to explain the behavior. This is called *circular reasoning,* because it can go around and around in an endless circle. There's no point here at which the presumed trait is used to predict anything but the evidence that was used to presume it initially. The circularity can be broken if the trait is used to predict something new, and sometimes trait theorists do that. However, this view on personality is more vulnerable than most to the criticism of circularity.

A final problem that was raised in years past concerns the issue of consistency. As noted earlier, the concepts of trait psychology were developed to account for consistency in behavior across time and situations. The discovery that people's behavior sometimes fails to display this consistency created a crisis. There have been many creative and thoughtful responses to this discovery. Thus, this problem has served to promote evolution in this viewpoint. There has been a growing awareness among trait theorists that to view traits as having a constant impact on behavior is too simple. This view is being replaced by approaches in which situational forces and the interaction between situations and dispositions are taken into account. These insights hold further promise for the possibility of linking the trait approach to other views that have a more prominent place for process.

A final point favoring the future of the trait approach is this: No matter how hard various people have tried to dispense with the use of traits as explanatory mechanisms, the trait concept has retained an active place in the working vocabulary of the personality psychologist. The long history of these concepts attests to their hardiness. Somehow it appears as though the personality psychologist needs them. The fact that they've endured the test of time seems to imply a fundamental correctness that is hard to deny.

· SUMMARY ·

The trait-and-type approach begins with the assumption that personality consists of stable inner qualities, which are reflected in behavior. *Types* are discontinuous categories of personalities, with each person falling into one category or another. This concept has largely disappeared from use in personality psychology. *Traits* are continuous dimensions of variability, along which any person can be placed. Most trait approaches are nomothetic, emphasizing how people differ but assuming that the trait dimensions are the same for everyone. The idiographic approach emphasizes persons' uniqueness and treats some dimensions as unique to specific persons.

Factor analysis is a tool used by many trait psychologists. Factor analysis tells what items (or ratings, etc.) go together. Further, the more variability in ratings a factor accounts for, the more important the factor. Factor analysis also lets you tell which observations do and don't reflect a factor well, thus helping refine scales.

An important question in trait psychology is what traits are basic and important. Some theorists believe we must let reality tell us the structure of personality. Others believe we must start with a theory. Several theoretical views have been developed, including one that emphasizes traits that have a long history in ideas about personality (extraversion and neuroticism) and one that emphasizes traits that are relevant to social interaction (the interpersonal circle).

Many now favor the idea that there are five major factors in personality. Evidence to that effect is strong, and a relatively successful attempt has also been made to fit these five factors to the models of personality structure already mentioned. There is disagreement about the precise nature of the five factors, but commonly used labels for them are *extraversion, agreeableness, conscientiousness, emotionality,* and *openness.* Recent research has examined how these traits relate to behaviors and experiences in people's lives.

A question about the usefulness of the trait concept was raised by the finding that people's behavior often wasn't well predicted from trait self-reports. This led some to question whether traits actually influence behavior. *Situationism,* the idea that behavior is controlled primarily by situational influences, was a poor alternative. *Interactionism* holds that personality and situations interact in several ways to determine behavior. For example, some situations permit or even elicit individual differences, whereas other situations don't. People also choose which situations to enter, and then they influence the nature of situations by their own actions. Indeed, people also vary in how consistent they are, and they often know whether they're consistent or not.

The idea that the influence of traits on behavior is dependent on situations has expanded into a broader view of personality structure, in which traits are individualized linkages between situations and actions. This view accounts for stability over time within the person as well as for variability across situations. This view of the nature of traits provides a sense of process for trait models.

Personality assessment from the viewpoint of trait psychology is a matter of developing a personality *profile* of the person being assessed—a description of where the person falls on all the dimensions being measured by the inventory. To these psychologists, the profile holds the key to understanding the person's uniqueness.

Regarding problems in behavior, trait theorists say that some problems result from having a trait that is intrinsically problematic, such as psychoticism or neuroticism. Other kinds of problems stem from having an extreme position on some trait dimension. Interest in the relation between personality disorder and the five-factor model is growing. The interactionist position suggests the following possibility (termed a *diathesis-stress model*): Certain dispositions may create a susceptibility to some kind of problem, but the problem occurs only under certain conditions, usually involving stress. Therapeutic behavior change, from the trait perspective, may mean changing how a trait is reflected in behavior, because a person's traits are not easily altered. Alternatively, it may mean avoiding situations in which the problem behavior arises.

· GLOSSARY ·

Diathesis-stress model   A theory holding that a vulnerability plus stress creates problems in behavior.

Extravert   A person who is outgoing and prefers social and exciting activities.

Factor   A dimension that underlies a set of interrelated measures, such as items on a self-report inventory.

Factor analysis   A statistical procedure used to find basic dimensions underlying a set of measures.

Factor loading   A correlation between a single measure and the factor to which it is being related.

Idiographic   Pertaining to an approach that focuses on an individual person's uniqueness.

Interactionism   The idea that situations and personality interact to determine behavior.

Interpersonal circle   Personality patterns deriving from varying levels of dominance and love.

Introvert   A person who prefers solitary activities.

Lexical criterion   An index of the importance of a trait from the number of words that refers to it.

Nomothetic   Pertaining to an approach that focuses on norms and on variations among persons.

Personality coefficient   A stereotypic correlation between personality and behavior of about 0.30.

Second-order factor   A factor that emerges from a factor analysis performed on a set of previously found factors.

Situationism   The idea that situations are the primary determinants of behavior.

Traits   Dimensions of personality on which people vary.

Types   Distinct and discontinuous categories of persons.

Needs and Motives

"I'm in the pre-med program here, and I really want to get into a good medical school. The courses aren't that easy for me, so I have to study more than some people. I can't even take time off on weekends because I'm taking an extra heavy load. I don't mind, though, because I'm really motivated to go to med school, and that makes it worth the effort."

"I've been going with my boyfriend for over two years now. I care for him a lot. But lately I've been wondering if this is really the right relationship for me. It's hard to describe it. It's not anything about *him*, exactly, but it's like the relationship isn't meeting my needs. I don't know how else to put it."

THINK ABOUT the concerns that occupy your daily thoughts. Many college students are concerned about what they will do after college. Some have ambitions they're already pursuing full speed (for example, the pre-med student quoted above). Others aren't sure what they want to do, and worry about it. Yet others don't think it's a big deal one way or another.

Many college students are concerned about close relationships. Some envision being married in the years to come and wonder whether the person they're with is the right one. Some don't have this kind of relationship but wish they did. For some people, this is the most serious issue in their lives. For others, it's not a big deal.

These two concerns are probably familiar to you. Work and love are issues in everyone's life. They aren't everything, of course. Most of us have other things on our minds a lot of the time. Some people are trying to find order and meaning in life's experiences. Some seek truth, some seek beauty. For others, what really matters isn't truth *or* beauty but having the laundry done, the kitchen clean, or new high-performance tires on their SUV.

There's a lot of diversity in the concerns we've touched on here. Despite the diversity, they have something in common. They imply the existence of needs and motives behind people's thoughts and actions. How do people describe their preoccupations? I *need* to find a lover. I *need* to have a direction for my future. I *want* to do well in school. I *need* to find a sense of purpose in life. I *have* to get caught up on my chores. I *need* to get an A on this test. There are also individual differences here. For any aspect of life you might imagine, some people feel a deep need within it, others don't.

If needs and motives influence people's thoughts and actions this way, they're surely important. It can even be argued that they define who a person is. This idea forms the basis for the viewpoint on personality that's examined in this chapter.

Basic Theoretical Elements

Needs

The fundamental principle of this approach is that human behavior is best understood as a reflection of needs. A **need** is an internal state that's less than satisfactory, a lack of something that's necessary for well-being. Henry Murray (1938), who began this approach to personality (see Box 5.1), defined a need as an internal directional force that determines how people seek out or respond to objects or situations in the environment.

Some needs are based in our biological nature (needs for food, water, air, sex, and pain avoidance). Murray called these **primary needs.** Others, such as the need for power and the need for achievement, either *derive* from biological needs or are inherent in our *psychological* makeup. Murray called these **secondary needs.**

When you take up need theories, it's easiest to start with biological needs, because biology is a good model for how needs work. Biological needs must be satisfied

Box 5.1 The Theorist and the Theory:

Henry Murray and Human Motives

The history of Henry Murray, the father of the motive view of personality, contains tantalizing suggestions about how his theory drew on his life's experiences. Murray was born to a wealthy family in New York in 1893. He got on well with his father but had a poor relationship with his mother, feeling that she gave him less attention than his sister and brother. The emotional separation created a deep-seated need to stand on his own, which was central to his personality. It's tempting to speculate that this experience led Murray to be especially aware of social needs, and may have led him toward the idea that such needs are the determinants of personality.

Murray's education was varied, but none of it was in psychology (he disliked his only psychology course). He majored in history, completed medical school, got a master's degree in

biology, did an internship in surgery, and then earned a Ph.D. in biochemistry. His focus after college was on the biology of human functioning. This biological emphasis is also apparent in Murray's thinking about personality. As noted, the ideas behind his theory are most easily illustrated by biological motives. Indeed, he believed that even psychological motives have biological roots.

Murray's medical background also influenced his approach to research. The program he led at the Harvard Psychological Clinic was very much a team approach. This seems to reflect the view that personality is best assessed by a team of specialists working together, much as a team of physicians collaborates on diagnosing patients.

A turning point in Murray's life occurred seven years into his marriage, when he fell in love with Christiana Morgan. This was a turning point in at least two ways. First, Murray was faced with a serious conflict. He didn't want

to leave his wife, but neither did he want to give up his lover. Wanting both women in his life surely made Murray acutely aware of the conflicting pressures that differing motives exert on a person.

The experience was a turning point in a second way, as well. Morgan had been fascinated by the psychology of Carl Jung. At her urging, Murray visited Jung in Switzerland. Jung, it turned out, was living in much the same situation as Murray but without discomfort. Jung's advice was to continue with both relationships, which Murray proceeded to do for 40 years (see Douglas, 1993; Robinson, 1992). The experience of bringing a problem to a psychologist and receiving an answer that seemed to work had a great impact on Murray, leading him to seriously consider psychology as a career (J. W. Anderson, 1988). When given the opportunity to assist in founding the Harvard Psychological Clinic, which was being set up to study personality, he jumped at the chance.

Every need has associated with it some category of "goal objects." When thirsty, you need water, not food.

repeatedly over time. As time passes, the needs gradually become more intense, and the person acts in ways that cause the need to be satisfied. For example, over time your body starts to need food. When the need gets strong enough, you'll do something to get some food. That reduces the need.

The strength of a need influences the intensity of the related behavior. The stronger the need, the more intense the action. Intensity can be reflected in several ways: vigor, enthusiasm, and thoroughness. But intensity can also be expressed in less obvious ways. For example, need strength can help set priorities—which action you do first versus put off until later. The stronger the need, the sooner it's reflected in action. Figure 5.1 shows how this prioritizing can create a continually changing stream of actions, as need strengths build and subside. The need that's greatest at any given point is the one that shows up in behavior.

Needs are directive: They help determine which of many possible actions occurs at a given time. They are directive in two senses. First, when you have a need, it's a need for something in particular. When you need water, you don't just *need;* you need *water.* Needs thus pertain to classes of goal objects or events. Needs are also directive in that they create movement either *toward* the object or *away* from it. A need is either to get something or to avoid something. Thirst reflects a water-related need, but it's more than just water *related.* After all, fear of going swimming also reflects a water-related need. Thirst reflects a need to *get* water. Moving toward versus moving away is part of the directionality of all needs.

MOTIVES

Theorists assume that needs work through **motives.** Motives take the underlying need and move it a step closer to behavior. David McClelland (1984), an important contributor to this view of personality, said motives are clusters of *cognitions with affective overtones, organized around preferred experiences and goals.* Motives appear in your thoughts and preoccupations. The thoughts pertain to goals that are either desired or undesired. Thus they are affectively toned. Motives eventually produce actions.

To illustrate, the need for food occurs in the tissues of the body, but it gives rise to a motive state called *hunger.* Unlike the need for food, hunger is experienced directly. It creates mental preoccupation and leads to behavior that will reduce the hunger (and the need for food). Thus, people who distinguish needs from motives do so partly by whether there is a subjective experience. The need is a physical condition you don't sense directly. It creates a motivational state that you *do* experience subjectively.

PRESS

Motives are influenced by internal needs, but they're also influenced by external events. Murray (1938) used the term **press** to refer to such external influences. A press

FIGURE 5.1
A graphic display of how changes in behavior over time can be explained by variations in the relative strengths of several motives over the same time. The letters at the top of the diagram indicate which of three activities the person is engaged in at any given time (shifting from one to the other). The three lines indicate the levels of the three motives related to these three activities. As one motive rises above the other two, the behavior changes. *Source: Adapted from Seltzer, 1973.*

(plural is also *press*) is an external condition that creates a desire to obtain (or avoid) something. It thus has a motivational influence, just as does an internal need (see Figure 5.2).

It's probably easiest to get a feel for the effects of need and press with a biological motive. Imagine your need for food creates a hunger motive. You respond by eating lunch. Your peanut butter sandwich, though dry and crumbly, satisfies the need for food. But just as you finish, someone walks in with an extra-large pizza (or whatever you find irresistible). Suddenly you don't seem as satisfied as you did a moment before. The motive to eat has been rekindled—not by a need but by a press.

The concept of press also applies to motives from secondary needs. Seeing someone else receive an honor can increase your motive for recognition. Being around someone who's in a close relationship may increase your motive to be with someone. Being around a new mother brings out caretaking motives in some people, making them wish they had a baby to care for. These are all examples of motive states induced by environmental press.

Although needs and motives clearly *can* be distinguished from each other, people don't always do so. One reason is that it's harder to keep the concepts distinct for psychological needs than biological needs. A need for achievement involves no deficit in the body. It's hard to say how the need to achieve differs from the motive to achieve. For this reason, it's common for people writing about needs and motives in personality to use the two terms interchangeably.

FIGURE 5.2
Internal need states and external press can both influence motives to engage in particular kinds of action, which in turn become realized in overt behavior.

Needs, Motives, and Personality

When motives are strong, they influence behavior. Motive strength has two aspects, however. There are temporary variations in needs across time and situations. But people also vary in *dispositional* needs. That is, some people naturally have more of a given need much of the time than other people do. Such dispositions begin to form a picture of the person's personality.

MOTIVE STATES AND MOTIVE DISPOSITIONS

We've already shown how to think about temporary fluctuations of needs (Figure 5.1, earlier). People shift from doing one thing to doing something else, as one need is satisfied and others build up. Ongoing behavior reflects whichever need is now greatest. That model provides a sense of how people shift from one action to another over time.

Now let's add the idea that people vary in their dispositional levels of needs. This can be portrayed as differences in the overall heights of the lines. Such differences can have large effects on moment-to-moment behavior. For example, John has a high dispositional need for achievement, whereas George's dispositional need for achievement is lower. Assume that the achievement motive goes up and down in the same pattern for both across time. Assume also that they have identical patterns in all their other needs.

As Figure 5.3 shows, John and George would display quite different patterns of behavior over time. Why? Because *even when John's other needs are also up, his need for achievement is so high it tends to remain above the others.* As a result, he tends to do achievement-related things a lot of the time. For George, the achievement motive rarely gets

FIGURE 5.3
John has a high dispositional need for achievement; George's is lower. Assume this need fluctuates for both of them in the same pattern across time. John's and George's levels of two other needs are identical (and also fluctuate). The difference in the dispositional need for achievement creates a great difference in the overt actions John and George display (the bars above the lines).

high enough to be the strongest motive. Thus, George doesn't engage in achievement-related behavior very often.

MURRAY'S SYSTEM OF NEEDS

Murray (1938) developed a view of personality organized in terms of needs, press, and motives. He and his colleagues made a list of needs, emphasizing the secondary ones. Some of them are listed in Table 5.1. These, to Murray, are the motives that underlie important human behavior, the needs that form personality. Murray believed that everyone has all these needs but that everyone has a dispositional tendency toward *some particular level* of each need.

Each need stands on its own, but Murray argued that needs can also interrelate in several ways. Needs sometimes *fuse* and are expressed in the same act. For example, Sarah's mother has a high need to dominate and a high need to nurture. She often acts toward Sarah in a caring way (nurturing) but at the same time disregards Sarah's wishes and preferences (dominating). A single action thus satisfies two needs for her at the same time.

Needs can also act *in the service of* one another. For instance, a person may have a need for order, which works to the benefit of a more general need for achievement. As another example, sexual activity, which is motivating in its own right, can serve and support a variety of other motives (Cooper, Shapiro, & Powers, 1998). Needs can also *conflict* with one another. For instance, the need for independence can conflict with the need for intimacy. Someone with a strong need to be independent and also a strong need to share experiences with someone else may feel conflicted in social relations.

Just as needs can interrelate in complex ways, so can needs and press. As one need can work in the service of another, a press can work in the service of a need. For example, Jane, who has a high need for achievement, works at an advertising firm. Her office surrounds her with challenging tasks; each of them is a press for achievement. Having this constant press at work facilitates and supplements her already high motive to achieve.

MEASURING MOTIVES: THE THEMATIC APPERCEPTION TEST

To study the motive approach to personality, researchers had to measure motives. For several reasons, they began not by just asking people about their motives but with another strategy. This turns out to have been a very fortuitous decision. *Why* gets us ahead of our story, however.

What was this alternative strategy? Morgan and Murray (1935) suggested that needs are *projected* into a person's fantasy, just as a movie is projected onto a screen. (This idea derives from psychoanalytic theory; we'll say more about it in Chapter 9.) Murray termed the process of projecting imagery **apperception.** The idea that people

Table 5.1 Partial List of Psychological Needs. *Source:* Adapted from Murray, 1938.

Domain	Need for . . .	Representative Behavior
Pertaining to Ambition		
	Achievement*	Overcoming obstacles
	Recognition	Describing accomplishments
	Exhibition	Attempting to shock or thrill others
Pertaining to Inanimate Objects		
	Acquisition	Obtaining things
	Order	Making things neat and orderly
	Retention	Hoarding things
	Construction	Building things
Pertaining to Defense of Status		
	Inavoidance	Concealing a handicap or a failing
	Defendance	Giving an explanation or excuse
	Counteraction	Retaliating for something
Pertaining to Human Power		
	Dominance*	Directing others' behavior
	Deference	Cooperating with or obeying someone
	Autonomy	Standing up to authority
	Contrariance	Being oppositional
	Aggression	Attacking or belittling others
	Abasement	Apologizing or confessing
	Blame avoidance	Stifling blameworthy impulses
Pertaining to Affection between People		
	Affiliation*	Spending time with others
	Rejection	Snubbing others
	Nurturance*	Taking care others
	Succorance	Being helped by others
	Play	Seeking diversion through others
Pertaining to Exchange of Information		
	Cognizance	Asking questions of others
	Exposition	Delivering information to others

* Needs that have received the most research attention.

normally do this led to the **Thematic Apperception Test,** or **TAT** (Morgan & Murray, 1935; Murray, 1938; C. P. Smith, 1992).

When your motives are being assessed by TAT, you view a set of pictures in which it isn't clear what's going on. You're asked to create a story about each one. Your story should describe what's happening, the characters' thoughts and feelings, the relationship among characters (if there's more than one), and the outcome of the situation. Through apperception, the themes in your stories should reflect your implicit motives.

Do fantasy stories really reflect people's needs? Yes. Several early validation studies were done. One of them looked at a biological need, the need for food. Participants were deprived of food for varying lengths of time, so they'd have different needs for food. They turned out to differ in their food-related TAT imagery (Atkinson & McClelland, 1948).

Other research manipulated people's achievement motive, by giving some a success and others a failure. A failure should temporarily increase the achievement need, because it creates an achievement deficit (just as passing time creates a food deficit). A success should reduce the achievement motive because it satisfies the need. As predicted, success and failure led to differences in TAT achievement imagery (McClelland, Atkinson, Clark, & Lowell, 1953). In another study, people who were led to be concerned about their social acceptability displayed more affiliation imagery (Atkinson, Heyns, & Veroff, 1954).

Studies of Specific Dispositional Needs

Once it had been validated by such studies, the TAT was used extensively to measure individual differences in *dispositional* needs. Researchers studied several dispositional needs in detail.

NEED FOR ACHIEVEMENT

Of the various needs identified by Murray, the first to receive research attention was the **need for achievement.** This motive has been studied for decades by David McClelland, John Atkinson, and many other people (e.g., Atkinson & Birch, 1970; Atkinson & Raynor, 1974; Heckhausen, 1967; Heckhausen, Schmalt, & Schneider, 1985; McClelland et al., 1953).

Achievement motivation is *the desire to do things well, to feel pleasure in overcoming obstacles.* The need for achievement is reflected in TAT responses that mention performing well at something, reaching goals or overcoming obstacles to goal attainment, having positive feelings about success, or negative feelings about failure.

People who differ in achievement motivation differ in several ways in achievement-related situations. Consider, for instance, the very act of choosing a task. Tasks (or problems within a task) can be easy, hard, or somewhere in between. Given a choice, which would you prefer? (When you plan your course schedule for next semester, do you choose easy courses and professors, hard ones, or ones in between?)

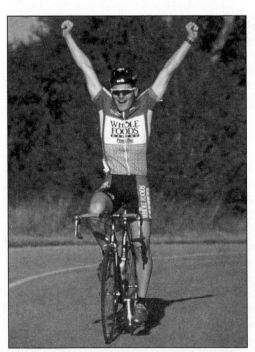

Persons high in achievement motivation have a strong need to succeed.

People with low need for achievement prefer tasks that are either very easy or very hard (Atkinson, 1957). It's easy to understand the easy ones. There isn't much achievement pressure in an easy task, and it's nice to get something right, even if everyone else gets it right too. Why, though, would people with low achievement needs choose a hard task? Apparently it's not for the challenge. It seems to be more that doing poorly on a hard problem doesn't reflect badly on you. And there's always the possibility (however remote) that you'll get lucky and succeed. People high in the need for achievement, in contrast, tend to prefer tasks of moderate difficulty. They also work harder on moderately difficult tasks than on very hard or very easy ones (Clark & McClelland, 1956; French, 1955).

Why do those high in achievement motivation prefer tasks of middle difficulty? Maybe because these tasks give the most information about ability (Trope, 1975, 1979). If you *do well* at an *easy* task, you don't learn much about your ability, because *everyone* does well. If you *fail* at a *hard* task, you don't learn much about your ability, because almost *no one* does well. In the middle, though, you can find out a lot. Perhaps people high in achievement motivation want to find out about their abilities. Trope (1975, 1980) tested this by having people choose test items. He figured out a way to manipulate (separately) the items' difficulty and their **diagnosticity** (how much they tell about ability). People with high achievement needs had a strong preference for diagnostic items (see Figure 5.4), whereas difficulty in itself turned out not to be important.

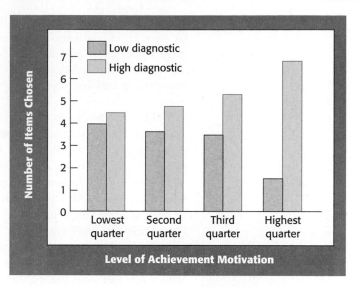

Effects of achievement motivation have been studied in a variety of domains. The need for achievement relates to persistence in the face of failure (e.g., Feather, 1961). It relates to task performances (e.g., Lowell, 1952) and to grades in school (Schultz & Pomerantz, 1976). This need thus plays an important role in a variety of achievement-related behaviors. Indeed, it's even been suggested that the need for achievement may play a role in the economic rise and decline of entire cultures. This idea led to studies of literature from several civilizations, at several distinct points in their history. The literature is interpreted for its themes, in much the same way as TAT responses are interpreted. The economic growth and decline of that civilization are then plotted over the same period.

One impressive study of this sort was done by Bradburn and Berlew (1961), who examined the literature and economic history of England from 1500 to just after 1800. They divided this period into 50-year segments and coded achievement imagery and economic development in each. Achievement imagery was stable for 100 years, fell off, then rose sharply. The index of economic development followed a nearly identical pattern of falling then rising—but 50 years later. This suggests that shifts in achievement motives had economic consequences.

Another, even more complex study of this sort was done by D. C. McClelland (1961). This study focused on a much more narrow period (1925 to 1950) but looked at 23 cultures across the world. McClelland coded achievement imagery from children's schoolbooks at both points in history. He developed two measures of economic growth over the intervening period and compared the achievement imagery to economic growth. A moderately strong association emerged between achievement imagery in 1925 and economic growth from 1925 to 1950. As in the Bradburn and Berlew study, there was virtually no relation between economic growth and later achievement imagery. This pattern suggests that motivation (reflected in the imagery) produced the economic achievement, not vice versa.

Achievement motivation predicted economic success in these studies, but in some situations a need for achievement can be a problem. For example, people who serve in high-level managerial or political positions don't have opportunities for personal achievement. Their task is to mobilize others (which draws on a different need). If people in this situation try to do too much themselves, it can backfire, producing worse outcomes. Consistent with this idea, Spangler and House (1991) found that the need for achievement related inversely to the effectiveness of U.S. presidents.

FIGURE 5.4
Participants in this study chose items to work on that they expected to be either highly diagnostic of their abilities or not diagnostic. This figure divides participants into four levels of achievement motive, ranging from very low to very high. There is an increasingly strong preference for highly diagnostic items among those with higher levels of achievement motivation. *Source: Adapted from Trope, 1975.*

An interesting aspect of the literature on the achievement motive is that at first, far more was known about its effects among men than among women, because most early studies included only males. Eventually, however, researchers looked at achievement needs among women. Some of this work suggests that achievement needs are expressed in varying ways among women, depending on the direction taken by their lives.

Elder and MacInnis (1983) recruited two sets of 17- to 18-year-old girls. One group was family oriented, the other group had a mix of family and career interests. Achievement motives, assessed at the same time, predicted different outcomes in the two groups as they moved into adulthood. Among family-oriented women, those with high achievement needs invested energy in activities leading to marriage and family. In effect, they expressed achievement by creating and sustaining a family. Among career-minded women, high achievement needs led to putting off marriage and family. Presumably this was because they were focusing on their careers. Thus, what women value as a goal determines what behaviors follow from achievement needs.

Another way of putting this is to say that women with achievement needs pursue achievement in ways that fit their views of themselves and the world they live in. It seems reasonable that this principle should also influence what careers women consider. Jenkins (1987) looked at career choices made by women who were college seniors in 1967. Those high in the need for achievement were likely to become teachers but not to go into business. Why? Teaching gave them an outlet for their achievement needs but didn't conflict with traditional women's roles. Business careers didn't fit those roles as well. Thus, the achievement needs of these women were channeled by other aspects of their social environments.

NEED FOR POWER

Another motive that's been studied extensively by David Winter (1973) and others is the **need for power.** The need for power is *the motive to have impact on others, to have prestige, to feel strong* compared to others. TAT responses that reflect the need for power have images of forceful, vigorous action—especially action that evokes strong emotional responses in others. Responses showing concern about status or position also reflect need for power.

What kinds of behavior reflect the power motive? Not surprisingly, people high in the need for power seek out positions of authority and influence and surround themselves with symbols of power (Winter, 1972, 1973). For example, students high in the power motive are likely to be office holders in student organizations (Greene & Winter, 1971). People high in this motive also are more sexually active than persons lower in this motive (Schultheiss, Dargel, & Rohde, 2003). People high in the need for power are concerned about controlling the images they present to others (McAdams, 1984). They want to enhance their reputations. They want others to view them as authoritative and influential. Not surprisingly, they tend to be somewhat narcissistic, absorbed in their importance (Carroll, 1987).

This quality can work for you or against you. People high in the power motive are less likely to make concessions in diplomatic negotiations than those lower in this motive (Langner & Winter, 2001), which can lead to better outcomes in the negotiations. Power-motivated people learn more from victories than do other people (Schultheiss, Wirth, Torges, Pang, Villacorta, & Welsh, 2005). On the other hand, they learn less from failures than other people.

There's evidence that the power motive can enhance effectiveness in managing others. For example, among U.S. presidents, those high in the power motive were more effective than those lower (Spangler & House, 1991). One way in which this motive may enhance effectiveness is by fostering a more active response to problems. For example, people high in the need for power respond to inefficiency in work groups by becoming more aroused or activated (Fodor, 1984).

Who do power-motivated persons relate to in their personal lives? Men with high power needs are more likely than those with lower power needs to say that the ideal wife is a woman who's dependent (Winter, 1973). An independent woman is a potential threat. A dependent woman allows the man to feel superior. A later study found that the wives of men high in the need for power were indeed less likely to have careers of their own than other wives (Winter, Stewart, & McClelland, 1977).

The need for power is often expressed in the tendency to acquire high-status possessions and to surround oneself with symbols of power.

This isn't to say that the need for power is something that matters only among men. Women vary in this need as well, and it has proved to predict important outcomes among women. One study (Jenkins, 1994) found that women high in the need for power had more power-related job satisfactions than women lower in this need but also more *dis*satisfactions. These women also made greater strides in career development over a 14-year period—but only if they were in power-relevant jobs.

The level of a person's need for power can also influence the manner in which the person relates to others. The need for power relates to taking an active, assertive, controlling orientation in peer interactions (McAdams, Healy, & Krause, 1984). Power-motivated students are also more argumentative in class and eager to convince others of their point of view (Veroff, 1957). The desire for dominance is reflected in the social signals that are rewarding to them. That is, people high in the need for power are rewarded by low-dominance expressions from others and they're disrupted by high-dominance expressions (Schultheiss, Pang, Torges, Wirth, & Traynor, 2005). Not surprisingly, they are also more attentive to low-dominance expressions (Schultheiss & Hale, in press). The dominating style of interacting that characterizes the need for power can also have more ominous overtones: Men high in power needs are more likely than men with lower power needs to physically abuse their female partners during arguments (Mason & Blankenship, 1987).

The desire for dominance sometimes leads to success but sometimes is frustrated by failure. Both of these experiences can be stressful but for different people (see Figure 5.5). Those with a high need for power have an increase in the stress hormone cortisol after a failure (Wirth, Welsh, & Schultheiss, 2006). But people with low power needs have an increase in cortisol after a success! Apparently, what constitutes a stressor differs between these two sorts of people. Stress seems to be the occurrence of an outcome other than the one you are motivated for or accustomed to.

.   Oliver Schultheiss and his colleagues have found that the need for power also relates to the sex hormone testosterone. (We say more about this hormone and its

FIGURE 5.5
Increase in the stress hormone cortisol after a failure was greater among persons *higher* in the need for power; increase in cortisol after a success was greater among persons *lower* in the need for power. Source: Adapted from Wirth et al., 2006.

influence on personality in Chapter 7.) There is a slight link between power needs and baseline testosterone (Schultheiss et al., 2005). More interesting, however, is what happens to testosterone after success and failure. Among men, higher need for power related to a larger increase in testosterone after a success and also to a greater reduction in testosterone after a failure. Among women, however, the associations were much more complex.

Winter has suggested that the power motive is manifested in two paths, depending on whether the person has acquired a sense of responsibility during socialization (Winter, 1988; Winter & Barenbaum, 1985). For those high in the sense of responsibility, the power motive yields "conscientious" pursuit of prestige, where power is expressed in socially accepted ways. For those lower in responsibility, though, the need for power can lead to more problematic ways of influencing others—what Winter calls "profligate, impulsive" power. This includes aggressiveness, sexual exploitation, and alcohol and drug use.

Winter and Barenbaum (1985) found considerable support for this argument. In one sample of low-responsible men, the need for power related to drinking, fighting, and sexual possessiveness. Among high-responsible men, the need for power related inversely to all these tendencies. Similar findings have emerged from other samples. It has since been found that men with high need for power without the sense of responsibility also have a rise in testosterone when imagining and experiencing a power-related success (Schultheiss, Campbell, & McClelland, 1999; Schultheiss & Rohde, 2002).

NEED FOR AFFILIATION

Another motive that received a good deal of early attention in motive research is the motive to affiliate. The **need for affiliation** is *the motive to spend time with others and form friendly social ties.* This isn't a need to dominate others but to be in social relationships, to interact with others. Social interactions here aren't a means to an end; they're a goal in their own right. In TAT responses, the need for affiliation is reflected in concern over acceptance by others and by active attempts to establish or maintain positive relations with others.

Studies have uncovered several reflections of this motive. For example, people who want to affiliate want to be seen as agreeable. If a group exerts pressure on them, they will more likely go along than will people with lower affiliation needs (Hardy, 1957). People with a high affiliation need get nervous if they think others are judging their interpersonal skills (Byrne, McDonald, & Mikawa, 1963). They show a strong preference for interaction partners who are warm compared to those who are reserved (Hill, 1991). They're more likely to make concessions in negotiations (Langner & Winter, 2001) and more likely to initiate contacts and try to establish friendships (Crouse & Mehrabian, 1977). They are especially sensitive to angry expressions from others (Schultheiss et al., 2005).

The active initiation of social contact suggests that affiliative needs go beyond worry about acceptance from others. These needs can also lead to active participation in social events. For example, Sorrentino and Field (1986) studied the emergence of leadership in discussion groups, which met in five weekly sessions. At the end, group members were asked to indicate whom they viewed as group leaders. People high in the need for affiliation were nominated more often than people lower in the need for affiliation.

As suggested by the Sorrentino and Field research, people with a strong affiliation motive spend more time engaged in social activities than people lower in this motive. They make more phone calls (Lansing & Heyns, 1959), and when paged, they're more likely to be engaged in social activities—conversing or letter writing (Constantian, 1981; McAdams & Constantian, 1983). When they're alone, they're more likely to express a wish to be interacting with others (McAdams & Constantian, 1983; Wong & Csikszentmihalyi, 1991).

The affiliation motive influences satisfaction in relationships (Meyer & Pepper, 1977) in a complex way. Happiness depends partly on the balance of affiliation needs between partners. That is, well-adjusted husbands and wives had affiliation needs that *correlated* with each other. To put it concretely, if you have a low affiliation need, you're best off with someone else with a low affiliation need. If your affiliation need is high, you're best off with someone whose affiliation need is also high.

We noted in Chapter 4 a difference of opinion about whether traits should be measured as broad supertraits or as more narrow traits. A similar question has been raised about affiliation motivation, and by implication about the entire motive approach to personality. Hill (1987) pointed out that affiliation can occur for several reasons. Perhaps the different reasons for affiliation should be considered as separate motives.

To do this, Hill developed self-report scales for four affiliation needs: social comparison, emotional support, positive stimulation, and attention from others. He then created hypothetical situations, each of which related to a particular type of affiliation need. For example, one of them described a job interview that was confusing and ambiguous; this should relate to a need for social comparison (but not to other affiliation motives). As expected, the social comparison scale predicted responses to this situation better than any other scale. The same pattern held for each situation: In each case, the theoretically relevant scale was the best predictor of responses.

These findings have a more general implication. They suggest that there is merit in focusing on specific, rather than global, needs. As with traits, the question seems to be whether the better prediction is worth the trade-off of having to hold more variables in mind.

NEED FOR INTIMACY

Another motive that has emerged as a research focus is the **need for intimacy.** It's been studied intensively by Dan McAdams (1982, 1985, 1989) and his collaborators. Intimacy motivation is *the desire to experience warm, close, and communicative exchanges with another person, to feel close to another person.* Carried to an extreme, it's the desire to merge with another person. Intimacy motivation shares with affiliation motivation a wish to be with others as an end, rather than as a means. It goes beyond the need for affiliation, though, in its emphasis on closeness and open sharing with another person.

Interestingly, intimacy motivation wasn't on Murray's list. McAdams proposed it partly because he felt the need for affiliation didn't focus enough on the positive, affirmative aspects of relationships. Additionally, the need for affiliation is an active, striving, "doing" orientation, whereas the need for intimacy as McAdams views it is a more passive "being" orientation (McAdams & Powers, 1981). The two aren't entirely distinct, of course. McAdams and Constantian (1983) reported a correlation of 0.58 between them.

What kinds of behaviors reflect the intimacy motive? In one study, people higher in the need for intimacy reported having more one-to-one exchanges with other people, though not more large-group interaction (McAdams et al., 1984). The interactions reported by intimacy-motivated people involved more self-disclosure, as well. To put it differently, people with a high intimacy need are more likely to share with friends their hopes, fears, and fantasies. The sharing goes both ways: People with a

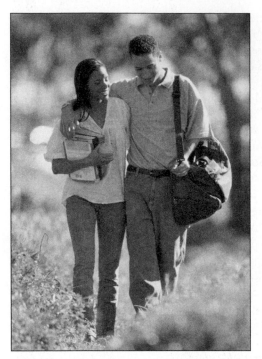

Need for intimacy is the desire to experience warm, close, and meaningful relationships with others.

high intimacy need report doing more *listening* than people with a low intimacy need, perhaps because they are more concerned about their friends' well-being. Indeed, intimacy seems to entail both self-disclosure and partner disclosure (Laurenceau, Feldman Barrett, & Pietromonaco, 1998).

Because close interactions are important to people with high intimacy needs, it should be no surprise that these people define their lives partly in terms of such interactions. McAdams (1982) collected autobiographical recollections among students high and low in intimacy needs. They were asked to report a particularly joyful or transcendent experience from their past and then an important learning experience. The content of each was coded several ways. For instance, some events involved considerable psychological or physical intimacy with another person; others did not. Analysis revealed that intimacy motivation was strongly correlated with memory content that also implied intimacy.

How do people high in the intimacy motive act when they're with others? They laugh, smile, and make more eye contact when conversing than people with lower intimacy needs (McAdams, Jackson, & Kirshnit, 1984). They don't try to dominate the social scene. (People with the need for power do that.) Instead, they seem to view group activities as chances for group members to be involved in a communal way (McAdams & Powers, 1981).

There's evidence that the desire for intimacy may be good for people. Men in this study (McAdams & Vaillant, 1982) wrote narrative fantasies at age 30 and were assessed 17 years later. Men with higher intimacy motivation at 30 had greater marital and job satisfaction at 47 than did those with less intimacy motivation. Another study found that women high in the intimacy motive reported more happiness and gratification in their lives than those low in the intimacy motive—unless they were living alone (McAdams & Bryant, 1987). On the other hand, intimacy needs (needing to be close) don't coexist well with power needs (needing to influence or dominate others). Persons who are high in both needs are often poorly adjusted (Zeldow, Daugherty, & McAdams, 1988).

PATTERNED NEEDS: INHIBITED POWER MOTIVE

Thus far, we've mostly discussed needs individually. Indeed, for many years that's how they were examined—one at a time. However, some have examined patterns involving several needs at once, sometimes in combination with other characteristics. One well-known pattern combines a low need for affiliation with a high need for power, in conjunction with the tendency to inhibit the expression of the latter. This pattern is called **inhibited power motivation** (McClelland, 1979). The reason for interest in this pattern depends on the context in which it's examined.

One context is *leadership*. The line of reasoning goes as follows: A person high in the need for power wants to influence people. Being low in the need for affiliation lets the person make tough decisions with no worry about being disliked. Being high in self-control (inhibiting the use of power) means the person will want to follow orderly procedures and stay within the framework of the organization. Such a person should do very well in the structure of a business.

This pattern does seem to relate to managerial success (McClelland & Boyatzis, 1982). Those with the inhibited power pattern moved to higher levels of management in a 16-year period than others, but only those who were nontechnical managers. Among managers whose jobs rested on engineering skills, personality didn't matter. This is understandable, because the managerial value of those people depends heavily on their particular skills.

There is also evidence that people with this pattern are especially effective at persuasion (Schultheiss & Brunstein, 2002). Their persuasiveness stems both from greater verbal fluency and from an effective use of nonverbal cues such as gesturing. Presumably being more persuasive helps these people be effective in mobilizing others.

The pattern of high power motivation and low affiliation motivation may be good for getting others mobilized, but even this may be a mixed blessing. Winter (1993) has argued that this pattern is actually conducive to starting wars! Historical data show that high levels of power imagery and low levels of affiliation imagery in the statements of politicians predicted going to war. For example, speeches by the rulers of Great Britain contained more power imagery than affiliation imagery in the year before Britain entered a war, whereas the reverse was true during years before a no-war year (see Figure 5.6). In another case (the Cuban Missile Crisis of 1962), greater affiliation than power imagery occurred before the successful avoiding of a war.

FIGURE 5.6
Balance of power motive imagery versus affiliation motive imagery in sovereign's speeches during the year before Great Britain entered a war (18 cases) compared to the year before Britain did *not* enter a war (36 cases). *Source: Adapted from Winter, 1993, Table 3.*

Implicit and Self-Attributed Motives

As we noted earlier in the chapter, the motivational view is that personality is a system of multiple needs. Every motive exists in every person. Behavior at any given time depends partly on how intense various motives are.

INCENTIVE VALUE

This analysis sounds reasonable, but it's missing something. It predicts that if your need for affiliation is more intense than your other needs, you'll engage in an affiliative act. But what act? Additional concepts are needed to address that question (McClelland, 1985).

One such concept is **incentive,** the degree to which a given action can satisfy a need for you. It's sort of a personalized weighting of how relevant an act is to the need. Incentive values determine how a motive is expressed behaviorally. For example, a person with a high need for affiliation who values long conversations with special friends but not impersonal crowds will avoid parties. Avoiding parties might seem strange for a person with a high need for affiliation. But people don't engage in all conceivable need-related behaviors. They choose ways to satisfy their needs, based on the incentive values that various activities have for them.

We didn't introduce the concept of *incentives* earlier in the chapter. It should be clear, however, that something like it is needed to account for behavior's diversity. People vary in the activities they engage in, even when satisfying the same need. As noted earlier, some women satisfy the need for achievement through careers, others by achieving strong family lives. These activities differ greatly, yet each can satisfy the need to achieve.

This principle relates to a point made in Chapter 4 regarding interactionism: We said there that people choose for themselves which situations to enter and which to avoid, thus creating an interaction between person and situation. We didn't say *why* different people choose different situations. One answer is that various situations have different *incentive* values to different people, even if the situations fulfill the same need.

Needs and incentives both influence behavior but in different ways. McClelland (1985) said that need strength relates to long-term *frequencies of need-relevant actions of any type*. Incentive values, on the other hand, should relate to *choices within a domain of action*. In this view, needs influence behavior primarily at a nonconscious level, whereas values influence the more conscious process of choice.

IMPLICIT MOTIVES ARE DIFFERENT FROM SELF-ATTRIBUTED MOTIVES

The last paragraph was deceptively simple, but it has a great many implications. Earlier in the chapter, we described development of the TAT to assess needs. We said there that the decision to use that strategy instead of asking people about their needs was fortuitous. Why? Because it allowed the discovery of something that today seems very important.

The TAT was used in the vast majority of the work described thus far. We feel relatively confident from the wide range of findings that it does assess people's motives. Given the large effort required to score the TAT, however, other researchers created self-report scales to assess motives. They intended those self-reports to measure the same motives as the TAT. But the self-reports turn out to correlate poorly with TAT assessment (McClelland, Koestner, & Weinberger, 1989; Pang & Schultheiss, 2005; Schultheiss & Brunstein, 2001). Why? What's going on?

McClelland and his colleagues argued that the two kinds of assessments are, in fact, measuring different things (McClelland et al., 1989). They used the term **implicit motive** to refer to what the TAT measures. They called the motives *implicit* because the person may or may not be aware of them. They used the term **self-attributed motive** to refer to what's measured by self-reports. An increasing body of evidence indicates that implicit motives and self-attributed motives are different from each other. Implicit motives seem to be what we have been calling *motives*. Self-attributed motives are closer to what was described in the preceding section as *incentives*.

McClelland et al. (1989) held that implicit motives are the more basic. They are the recurrent preferences for classes of affective experiences that McClelland believed lie at the heart of motives (the feeling of "doing better" for the achievement motive, the feeling of "being strong" for the power motive, the feeling of "being close" for the intimacy motive). Implicit motives are thought to be primitive and automatic (Schultheiss, 2002). Because they are basic, they are good predictors of broad behavioral tendencies over time. In contrast, self-attributed motives relate to specific action goals. They tell how a person will act in a particular situation. For this reason, they're better at predicting responses in structured settings.

This distinction has been pursued further in several projects. Brunstein and Maier (2005) expanded on the idea that both implicit and self-attributed achievement motives play important, but distinct, roles in achievement behavior. They found evidence that the implicit achievement motive acts primarily as an energizer, boosting effort when the person falls behind. The self-attributed achievement motive, in contrast, acts primarily as an influence on decision making, influencing how people seek information about their skills compared to other people (for example, by choosing whether to continue a task or not).

Evidence that these qualities are distinct also comes from research in which people first completed TAT and self-report measures and then kept records of memorable experiences over 60 days (Woike, 1995). The records were coded for motive relevance and for feelings. Strength of implicit motives (TAT) related to the frequency of reporting feelings that relate to that motive, but strength of self-attributed motives did not. Self-attributed motives related to the frequency of reporting motive-related events with no feelings (but TAT scores did not). It seems, then, that the two aspects of motivation link to different aspects of memory. Further evidence that they link to different aspects of memory comes from studies showing that self-attributed motives predict recall of general memories related to the self-concept, whereas implicit motives predict recall of specific events (Woike, Mcleod, & Goggin, 2003).

As a final example of the value of distinguishing between implicit and self-attributed motives, consider a set of studies by Baumann, Kaschel, and Kuhl (2005). They argued that people sometimes form motive-related intentions (conscious) that fit poorly with their implicit motive dispositions (thus making it clear the two are different). When this happens, the person is stressed, which has adverse effects on well-being. Finally, they argued that this tendency is particularly pronounced among persons who are poor at regulating negative emotions. Evidence from three studies fits that picture.

McClelland believed that both the implicit motive and the self-attributed motive are important, but that they should be viewed separately. The evidence appears to support that belief. Sometimes it makes sense to expect an implicit motive to predict an outcome but not a self-attributed motive. Sometimes the opposite is true. For this reason, it's important to be sure which one you want to measure and to measure it correctly (McClelland, 1989). The distinction between implicit and self-attributed motives is one aspect of the motive view on personality that is receiving increasingly close attention.

Approach and Avoidance Motives

Another distinction that is also becoming increasingly important is between *approach* and *avoidance*. As noted early in the chapter, a motive is either a readiness to approach something or a readiness to avoid something. Thus far, we've written only about approach: for example, people who want to achieve try to approach success. But whenever there's an achievement task, the possibility of failure is also present. It seems likely that the desire to avoid failure also plays a motivational role here. Just as Atkinson (1957) tied the need for achievement to the capacity to feel pride in success, the motive to avoid failure relates to a tendency to feel shame after failure (McGregor & Elliot, 2005).

A simple way to avoid failure is to avoid achievement situations altogether. Never trying keeps you from failing. Another way to avoid failing is *by the very act of succeeding*. It may be that some people who struggle to achieve don't care so much about gaining success as they care about the fact that gaining success lets them avoid failure.

Much early research on achievement actually measured both of these motives. A lot of it derived from Atkinson's (1957) theory of achievement behavior. That theory makes its clearest predictions for people whose only motivation is to approach success and people whose only motivation is to avoid failure. Predictions are less clear for people high in both motives and people low in both motives. For that reason, studies often included only the two groups who were high in one motive and low in the other.

That strategy was guided by theory, but it has a bad side effect: It completely confounds the two motives. This causes ambiguity in interpretation (Chapter 2). If the groups act differently, is it because of the difference in the motive to approach success, or because of the difference in the motive to avoid failure? There is no way to know, though interpretations tend to focus on the motive to approach success.

In recent years, the distinction between approach and avoidance motivation has re-emerged as a focus for research on achievement, much of it by Andrew Elliot and his colleagues (e.g., Elliot, 2005; Elliot & Harackiewicz, 1996; Elliot & McGregor, 2001). Part of their theory is that achievement can reflect either of these motives. Which motive is central, however, will influence many aspects of the person's experience.

Elliot and McGregor (2001) found that the motive to succeed in mastering course material (approach) related to study strategies that involved thoughtfully elaborating on the material. The avoidance motive related to memorization. Avoidance motivation also related to having difficulty organizing study time effectively. Elliot and Sheldon (1997) found that the two motive tendencies also had different effects on subjective experiences. People who spent their effort trying to avoid failure reported less emotional well-being and less satisfaction with their performances than did people who were trying to approach success.

Though it might generally be better to approach than to avoid, there is also evidence that people do better when they're doing what's familiar to them. Specifically, people with high fear of failure are made uneasy and upset by imagining success (Langens & Schmalt, 2002). As suggested in the context of the power motive, it may be that what is stressful to you is what you're unfamiliar with.

APPROACH AND AVOIDANCE IN OTHER MOTIVES

Once you grasp the idea of separate approach and avoidance motives, you realize that the idea has implications for *every* motive you can think of (see also Carver, Lawrence, & Scheier, 1999; Higgins, 1997; Ogilvie, 1987). Try it out. Pick a motive from Table 5.1 (or think of one that's not there). Identify a behavior that reflects that motive. Then see if you can spot the opposing motive that might create the same behavior. For example, acts of affiliation can come from the desire to *be with others* (need for affiliation), but they can also come from a desire to *avoid being alone* (Boyatzis, 1973; Pollak & Gilligan, 1982). These aren't the same. One is a motive to approach; the other is a motive to avoid. The same issue can be raised for any need you can think of.

Just as with achievement behavior, evidence is beginning to accumulate that approach and avoidance motives have different consequences in other domains. A powerful example is a study of commitment among romantic partners. Frank and Brandstätter (2002) found that commitment based in approach predicted more relationship satisfaction six and thirteen months later. However, commitment based in avoidance (i.e., avoiding the process of breaking up) predicted lower relationship satisfaction at the follow-ups.

The idea that a given behavior can be based on either an approach motive or an avoidance motive (or some combination of the two) raises very broad questions about why people do the things they do. Are people generally moving toward goals, or are they trying to avoid or escape from things? Do actions differ, depending on which motive is more prominent? Do the feelings that go with the actions differ? The general idea that any approach motive has a corresponding avoidance motive has very broad implications. It complicates the picture of human behavior enormously. We will put this idea aside for the rest of this chapter, but you should keep in mind that it's always in the background.

The Methods of Personology

Research examining the effects of motive patterns tends to take one of two forms. Some studies examine how people respond to particular events, in the laboratory or in the field. Other studies collect evidence of a dispositional motive (or set of motives) at one time and relate the motive to some outcome that occurs considerably later.

These two ways of studying motives both differ greatly from the approach favored by Henry Murray, the father of this viewpoint. Murray believed the way to understand personality is to study the *whole person* and to do so over an extended period. The work on which he based his theory was an intensive study of 51 college men (Murray, 1938). Each was tested in many ways and also interviewed by a staff of professionals. These people then presented their impressions to what Murray called the Diagnostic Council, the most experienced members of the team. This group came to know each participant's personality quite thoroughly.

This approach was idiographic. It focused on the pattern of qualities that made each person unique. Murray disliked nomothetic methods. He thought their focus on comparison prevented them from probing deeply into a person's life. To Murray, the nomothetic approach yielded only a superficial understanding.

In fact, Murray's concern about the inadequacies of nomothetic approaches led him to coin the term **personology** to refer to the approach he preferred. He defined *personology* as the study of individual lives and the factors that influence their course. He believed that personology was more meaningful than other approaches because of its emphasis on the person's life history. According to Murray (1938, p. 604), "The history of a personality *is* the personality."

Recent years have seen a resurgence of interest in this way of thinking about personality. For example, Dan McAdams, whose work on intimacy motivation was described earlier, has written extensively on the idea that identity takes the form of an extended narrative—a life story that each of us writes and lives out over time (McAdams, 1985; McAdams & Pals, 2006). This narrative has chapters, heroes, and thematic threads that recur and permeate the story line (see also Rabin, Zucker, Emmons, & Frank, 1990).

As an example of how individual narratives can differ from person to person, the themes they express sometimes emphasize growth ("I found out how to make our relationship better") and sometimes safety ("I hope that never happens again"; Bauer, McAdams, & Sakaeda, 2005). As another example of a narrative focus, McAdams (2006) has identified a constellation of themes focused on personal redemption—a transition from a state of suffering to a better psychological state—which characterizes the lives of some middle-aged Americans.

From this point of view, the person's identity lies in keeping a coherent narrative going across time (McAdams & Pals, 2006; Singer, 2004). This way of thinking speaks directly to the uniqueness of each person, because every life story is unique (Singer, 2005). Whether this approach will become more prominent in personality psychology in the future remains to be seen, but it surely is a development that Murray would have applauded.

Assessment

Assessment of personality from the motive viewpoint is a matter of determining the dispositional levels of a person's needs. As noted earlier, there are several ways to assess this information. The assessment technique most distinctly associated with assessment of needs, however, is the TAT (C. P. Smith, 1992; Winter, 1996).

Box 5.2 The Process Behind the TAT

Take a good look at the picture on the right. Something's happening in the minds of these people, but what? Decide for yourself. Make up a story that fits the picture. Include the following information (and whatever else you want to include): *What's just happened to these people? What's the relationship between them? What are their present thoughts and feelings? What will be the outcome of the situation?* Take your time, and make your story as long and detailed as you wish.

What you've just done is similar to what people do when completing the Thematic Apperception Test, or TAT (Morgan & Murray, 1935). The idea is that people's needs will show up in the

thoughts they generate from their imaginations when they try to make sense out of ambiguous pictures. The ambiguity of the picture makes it less likely that environmental press will dictate your story's content and more likely that your needs will influence what you write. When people complete the TAT, they write stories for several pictures. One of them is completely blank, the ultimate in ambiguity!

Different pictures tend to elicit stories with different themes. Some pictures naturally elicit achievement-related stories; others are more amenable to stories with affiliation themes. Over the course of several pictures, however, dispositional tendencies emerge in the narratives

that people compose. Presumably these storytelling tendencies reflect the motives that characterize the person's personality. If you're interested in the motives that dominate your own personality, look at the story you wrote to see if there's evidence of the motives listed back in Table 5.1.

Illustration by Stephen P. Scheier. Reproduced by permission.

Earlier in the chapter, we described the essence of the procedure by which the TAT is administered (see also Box 5.2). People who are completing the TAT view a set of ambiguous pictures, in which it isn't clear what's happening. They're asked to create a story about each picture. The story should describe what's happening, the characters' thoughts and feelings, their relationship to each other (if there's more than one character), and the outcome of the situation. Through apperception, the themes that are manifested in the stories reflect implicit motives.

Scoring people's responses can be complex (Winter, 1994), but here's a simple version. Look to see what kinds of events take place in the story and what themes and images are in it. Events that involve overcoming obstacles, attaining goals, and having positive feelings about those activities reflect the achievement motive. Events in which people choose to be with other people and stories that emphasize relationships among people reflect the affiliation motive. Stories with images of one person controlling another reflect the power motive. More than one theme can occur in a given story. These can be scored separately, so the story can be used to assess several different motives at the same time.

The use of stories written in response to ambiguous pictures is the core method for assessing motives in research deriving from this theoretical viewpoint. It's not just stories that can be scored for motive imagery, of course. Anything that is written can potentially be scored in the same way (Winter, 1994). However, variations on the TAT remain the most popular method of assessing implicit motives.

The TAT is widely used to measure motives, but it has had its share of criticism. Questions have been raised about its relatively low internal consistency and test–retest reliability (Entwisle, 1972; Lilienfeld, Wood, & Garb, 2000). Defenders of the technique reply that there are good reasons for both of these to be low. The pictures in the TAT vary considerably in content. It's not surprising that they bring out different kinds of stories. This reduces internal consistency. It is also arguable that being instructed to tell several stories creates some implicit pressure to avoid repetition. This can reduce both internal consistency and test–retest reliability (e.g., Atkinson & Raynor, 1974). There's evidence, though, that the reliability of the TAT need not be as low as was once believed (Lundy, 1985; Schultheiss & Pang, in press).

Another criticism of the TAT is far more pragmatic. It takes a lot of time and effort to give and score it. This is a key reason people wanted to develop self-report measures of motives. Several attempts were made to create self-reports of the needs Murray saw as basic. An early effort was the Edwards Personal Preference Schedule (Edwards, 1959). A more recent one was the Personality Research Form, or PRF (Jackson, 1984). As with any inventory, these can be used to create personality profiles. In this case, however, the traits measured are self-attributed motivational traits.

As was noted earlier in the chapter, there is now substantial evidence that self-attributed motives (assessed by self-report scales) and implicit motives assessed (by story imagery) are not the same. Each captures something different about human motivational experience.

MOTIVES AND THE FIVE-FACTOR TRAIT MODEL

Do the qualities measured by inventories of motives resemble those that are measured by scales with different starting points? Chapter 4 described the idea that the basic traits of personality fall largely within five supertraits. Does the five-factor model absorb the qualities that Murray saw as important?

Several researchers have addressed this question. As a starting point, several analyses of the PRF yielded five factors. Stumpf (1993) concluded that all of the "big five" except neuroticism were captured in the PRF. Costa and McCrae (1988a) looked at associations of PRF scales with the NEO-PI-R, a "big five" measure. Their findings also suggested that many PRF scales reflect underlying qualities of the five-factor model. On the other hand, several PRF scales loaded on two or more of the five factors, rather than one. This appears to indicate that those motives relate to several traits. For example, the need for dominance related to openness, extraversion, and (inversely) agreeableness. It seems, then, that the five-factor model doesn't perfectly absorb the needs reflected in the PRF.

This general pattern of loadings has been replicated by Paunonen et al. (1992). In contrast, somewhat better support for a fit to the five-factor model has been found using the Edwards measure of needs (Piedmont, McCrae, & Costa, 1992).

TRAITS AND MOTIVES AS DISTINCT AND COMPLEMENTARY

Although the attempt to fit these motives to the five-factor model can be seen as an effort to integrate across theoretical boundaries, some believe that the effort is misguided and that traits and motives are fundamentally different from each other (Winter, John, Stewart, Klohnen, & Duncan, 1998). In taking this position, Winter et al. noted that all the evidence reviewed in the previous section involved self-attributed motives, not implicit motives. The fact that self-attributed and implicit motives are not strongly related is reason enough to be cautious about concluding that traits and motives are the same. In fact, there is separate evidence that implicit motives relate poorly to the five-factor model (Schultheiss & Brunstein, 2001).

Winter et al. (1998) proposed an integration, but of a different sort: They proposed that motives are fundamental desires and that traits channel how those desires are expressed. Thus, they argued, motives and traits interact to produce behavior. In some respects, this resembles the argument described earlier in the chapter about

Table 5.2 Sample Hypothesis about the Interaction between the Affiliation–Intimacy Motive and the Trait of Introversion–Extraversion. *Source:* Adapted from Winter et al., 1998.

	Affiliation–Intimacy Motive	
	Low	High
Extravert	Intimate relationship not salient as a desire	Desire for intimate relationship leads to single stable relationship
Introvert	Intimate relationship not salient as a desire	Desire for intimate relationships but difficulty maintaining them, because high focus on inner world is disruptive of a connection to the other person

implicit motives and incentive values. In the view taken by Winter et al., traits may represent patterns of incentive preferences.

In support of their argument, Winter et al. (1998) presented two studies of the trait of extraversion and (TAT-derived) needs. The studies examined women's lives across many decades. Winter et al. (1998) predicted that intimacy needs would have different effects among introverts and extraverts (see Table 5.2). For women with a low intimacy need, it shouldn't matter much whether they are introverts or extraverts. Intimacy isn't a big need for them. The complicated situation occurs among those with high intimacy needs.

An extravert with a high intimacy need should do fine in relationships, because extraverts are comfortable with and good at various kinds of social interaction. In contrast, introverts with high intimacy needs should have more problems. Their highly inner-directed orientation should interfere with relationships. Their partners may see them as remote or withholding. The result should be more likelihood of marital problems. This is exactly what Winter et al. (1998) found.

Problems in Behavior, and Behavior Change

People working within the motive approach to personality have been interested in specific domains of human activity (e.g., achievement, affiliation, power, intimacy) and in the more general idea of motivation as a concept. They haven't addressed the question of problems in behavior in great detail, nor have they suggested a particular approach to therapy. Nevertheless, the literature in this area has at least tentative links to some problems in behavior and to the processes of behavior change.

NEED FOR POWER AND ALCOHOL ABUSE

It's been suggested that the need for power can play a role in developing a drinking problem (McClelland, Davis, Kalin, & Wanner, 1972). This idea stems partly from the finding that drinking alcohol leads to feelings of power. Thus, a person with a need for power can satisfy that need, at least somewhat, by drinking. This doesn't satisfy the need for long, of course, because the feeling of power is illusory. It goes away when the person sobers up.

The idea that alcohol abuse may reflect a need for power leads to some recommendations for treatment. In particular, it suggests that people who are using alcohol this way aren't aware of doing so. They'd probably benefit from realizing what they're doing. By encouraging other ways to satisfy the power motive, a therapist can treat the issue productively, rather than simply treating a symptom. Evidence from one study (Cutter, Boyatzis, & Clancy, 1977) indicates that this approach can be more effective than traditional therapies, yielding nearly twice the rate of rehabilitation at one-year follow-up.

Focusing On and Changing Motivation

Those contributing to the motive approach to personality have also had relatively little to say about therapeutic behavior change. Murray, the father of this approach, was a therapist, but he didn't develop new therapy techniques. In general, he tended to apply the currently existing psychodynamic techniques to people's problems.

Motivation seminars are often used to enhance achievement motivation among people in business.

It would seem, however, that one of the studies just discussed makes some suggestions about behavior change. As indicated, some people appear to use alcohol as a way of temporarily satisfying a desire for power. A treatment program developed for these people had two focuses. It made them more aware that this motive was behind their drinking. It also helped them to find other ways to satisfy the need for power, thus making drinking unnecessary.

A broader implication of this discussion is that people may *often* be unaware of the motives behind problem behaviors. Many problem behaviors may reflect needs that are being poorly channeled. If so, taking a close look at the person's motive tendencies might tell something about the source of the problem. Knowing the source may make it easier to make changes.

Another program of work with indirect implications for therapy was conducted by McClelland and his colleagues (McClelland, 1965; McClelland & Winter, 1969). This training program was developed to raise achievement motivation among businesspeople (see also Lemann, 1994). It was rooted in the idea that thinking a lot about achievement-related ideas increases your motive to achieve.

The program began by describing the nature of the achievement motive and instructing people on how to score TAT protocols for achievement imagery. People then were taught to use achievement imagery in their thoughts as much as possible. By teaching themselves to think in terms of achievement, they increased the likelihood of using an achieving orientation in whatever activity they undertook.

Achievement-related thinking is important. By itself, however, it isn't enough. A second purpose of the training was to link these thoughts to specific concrete action patterns. It's also important to be sure the patterns work outside the training program. Participants were encouraged to think in achievement terms everywhere—not just in training sessions—and to put the action patterns into motion. People who completed the course wrote down their plans for the next two years. They were encouraged to plan realistically and to set goals that were challenging but not out of reach. Creating this plan was a way of turning the achievement orientation they had learned into a self-prescription for a course of activity. This prescription then could be used in guiding actual achievement later on.

Was the course effective? The answer seems to be yes. In a two-year follow-up, participants had greater business achievement, were more likely to have started new business ventures, and were more likely to be employing more people than previously compared to control participants (McClelland & Winter, 1969).

The outcomes of this program show it's possible to change people's achievement-related behavior, but a question remains about whether their underlying needs are

BOX 5.3 THEORETICAL CONTROVERSY:

Are Motives Biologically Based or Rooted in Cognition?

As we've noted, McClelland and his colleagues developed a training program to increase achievement motive. This program seemed to produce the desired results, but its success raises questions about the nature of the achievement motive—indeed, about all psychological motives.

Early motive theorists such as Murray assumed that even psychological and social needs derive from biological processes. Biology is used here more as a metaphor than an explanatory device. Still, it's generally assumed that individual differences in need profiles are stable, determined by the person's basic nature.

McClelland (1965), on the other hand, came to believe that psychological motives are learned and thus can be altered. The success of his program

stands as a testament to this idea. The program is very simple. Participants get a clear understanding of what the motive is and how it shows up in thought and action. They're then taught to think and act that way. Because McClelland knew a lot about how need for achievement is manifested, it was easy for him to tell people what to do.

These procedures produced the intended changes, but they raise questions. If motives are so easily altered—if motives are learned—why have the concept of motive at all? There are, after all, some psychologists who see the concept of motive as useless and even misleading (Chapters 12 and 13). Isn't this a case in which a motivational theorist is turning around and embracing a competing approach?

Another question is raised by the training program's emphasis on cognitive processes. The program entails elaborately coding in memory the nature of the motive the people are

trying to acquire. It also includes drawing explicit mental associations between that motive and concrete actions and emphasizing the monitoring of outcomes. These processes look suspiciously like the things that would be emphasized by people who take a cognitive or self-regulation approach to personality (Chapters 16 and 17). Are the effects of the program, then, really motivational?

One possible response to these questions is that the program developed by McClelland may change people's motives but not their needs. Recall that theorists sometimes distinguish needs from motives and that motives are influenced by both needs and press. It's possible to think of McClelland's training program as teaching people how to surround themselves with press to evoke the achievement motive. This way of thinking would account for the fact that the motive changes but still allow the assumption that needs are enduring dispositions.

---

changed, as well (see Box 5.3). It also remains uncertain how much these effects can be generalized to the domain of therapy. Nonetheless, the studies do seem to provide intriguing suggestions about behavior change.

Need and Motive Theories: Problems and Prospects

The chapter before this one dealt with trait theorists. As a group, those theorists are more concerned about describing the structure of personality than in describing the mechanics by which traits are expressed. Theorists of *this* chapter, in contrast, look to motivational processes and the pressures they place on people as a way to specify how dispositions influence actions. By providing a way to think about how dispositions create behavior—by specifying a type of intrapersonal functioning—this approach to dispositions evades one of the criticisms of trait theories.

A criticism that's harder to evade is that decisions about what qualities to study have been arbitrary. Murray developed his list of needs from his own intuition (and other people's lists). Others working in this tradition have tended to go along uncritically. Yet McAdams noted one omission from that list—the need for intimacy—that is strikingly obvious as a human motive. This suggests that Murray's intuitive list was incomplete. A response to this criticism is that the motives that have been examined most closely in research are those that fit with ideas also appearing elsewhere in psychology, including trait psychology. This convergence across views suggests that the needs in question really are fundamental.

Another criticism bears less on the theory than on its implementation. Murray was explicit in saying that the dynamics of personality can be understood only by considering multiple needs at once. However, research from the motive approach to personality has rarely done that. More often, people have studied one motive at a time to examine its dynamics. Occasionally, researchers have stretched to the point of looking at particular clusters of two or three needs, but this has been rare. On the other hand, it's important to keep in mind that, despite Murray's wishes, the motive view of dispositions is not the same as the practice of personology. It's certainly possible to investigate the former without adopting the latter.

Despite these limitations, work on personality from the viewpoint of motive dispositions has continued into the present. Indeed, such work has enjoyed a resurgence in the past decade or so. The idea that people vary in what motivates them has a good deal of intuitive appeal. Further appeal derives from the idea that motive states wax and wane across time and circumstances. This builds in a way to incorporate both situational influences and dispositional influences in an integrated way. Given these pluses, and a growing interest in understanding how implicit motives and self-attributed motives work together, the future of this approach seems strong.

· SUMMARY ·

The motive approach to personality assumes that behavior reflects a set of underlying needs. As a need becomes more intense, it is more likely to influence what behavior occurs. Behavior is also influenced by press: external stimuli that elicit motivational tendencies. Needs (and press) vary in strength from moment to moment, but people also differ from each other in patterns of chronic need strength. According to this viewpoint, this difference is the source of individual differences in personality.

Murray cataloged human needs, listing both biological (primary) and psychological (secondary) needs. Several of the psychological motives later received systematic study by others. One (studied by McClelland, Atkinson, and others) was the need for achievement: the motive to overcome obstacles and to attain goals. People with high levels of the achievement motive behave differently from those with lower levels in several ways: the kinds of tasks they prefer, the level of task difficulty they prefer, their persistence, and their performance levels. Early research on achievement tended to disregard how approach and avoidance motives might separately influence behavior. More recent work has begun to examine those distinct influences.

The need for power—the motive to be strong compared to other people—has also been studied extensively. People who score high in this need tend to seek out positions of influence, to surround themselves with the trappings of power, and to become energized when the groups they are guiding have difficulties. People with a high level of the power motive tend to choose as friends people who aren't influential or popular, thereby protecting themselves from undesired competition. Power-motivated men prefer wives who are dependent, and these wives tend not to have their own careers. The power motive can lead to unpleasant forms of social influence unless it's tempered by a sense of responsibility.

The need for affiliation is the desire to spend time with other people, to develop and maintain relationships. People who score high in this need are responsive to social influence, spend a relatively large proportion of their time communicating with other people, and when alone often think about being with others. A related motive that isn't represented in Murray's list but has received research attention in recent years is the need for intimacy. People high in this need want warm, close, and communicative relationships with other persons. People with a strong intimacy need tend to spend more time in one-to-one interaction and less in groups. They tend to engage in interactions that involve lots of self-disclosure and are especially concerned about their friends' well-being.

Recent research has also begun to investigate patterns of motives, such as inhibited power motive. This pattern is defined by having more of a need for power than a need for affiliation and by restraining the power need. People with this pattern do well in managerial careers, but the pattern has also been linked to political orientations preceding wars.

Theorists of this view also use other concepts in talking about behavior. Incentive value—the extent to which a given action will satisfy a given need for a person—helps to explain why people with the same need express the need in different ways. Indeed, the concept of incentive provides an opening into a broader issue. Specifically, assessment of needs by the Thematic Apperception Test (TAT) does not relate well to assessment by self-report. The former have come to be called *implicit motives* and the latter, *self-attributed motives.* The former are thought to function mostly nonconsciously and the latter consciously. One active area of interest is how these two aspects of motives function.

Murray emphasized the study of individual lives in depth over extended periods of time. He coined the term *personology* to refer to the study of the whole person, and he saw personology as his goal. This emphasis has not been strong in the work of most others, but it has re-emerged more recently in the work of McAdams and his colleagues.

The contribution to assessment that is most identified with the motive approach is the TAT. It is based on the idea that people's motives are reflected in the imagery they *apperceive,* that is, read into ambiguous stimuli—a set of pictures depicting people in ambiguous situations. There are also self-report measures of needs, which appear to measure something different from what the TAT measures.

The motivational approach to personality has largely ignored the issue of analyzing problems in behavior, although at least some evidence links the need for power to the misuse of alcohol. It's possible to infer from this evidence, however, that many problems in behavior may stem from inappropriate channeling of motives. It's also reasonable that people can be helped by increasing their awareness of the motive that underlies the problem, so the motive can be channeled in alternative ways. Research on increasing the need for achievement suggests that it may be possible to alter people's dispositional levels of the motives that make up personality.

· GLOSSARY ·

Apperception The projecting of a motive onto an ambiguous external stimulus via imagery.

Diagnosticity The extent to which a task provides information about something.

Implicit motive A motive assessed indirectly by fantasy or other narrative.

Incentive The degree to which an action can satisfy a particular need for a person.

Inhibited power motivation The condition of having more need for power than for affiliation but restraining its use.

Motive Cognitive–affective clusters organized around readiness for a particular kind of experience.

Need An unsatisfactory internal condition that motivates behavior.

Need for achievement   The need to overcome obstacles and attain goals.

Need for affiliation   The need to form and maintain relationships and to be with people.

Need for intimacy   The need for close communication with someone else.

Need for power   The need to have influence over other people.

Personology   The study of the entire person.

Press   An external stimulus that increases the level of a motive.

Primary need   A biological need, such as the need for food.

Secondary need   A psychological or social need.

Self-attributed motive   A motive that is consciously reported.

Thematic Apperception Test (TAT)   A method of assessing the strength of a motive through narrative fantasy.

The Biological Perspective

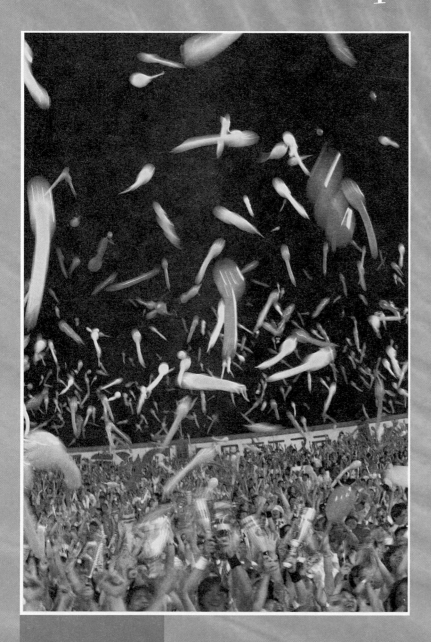

The Biological Perspective: Major Themes and Underlying Assumptions

We human beings are biological creatures, members of the animal kingdom. We carry around all of the characteristics implied by citizenship in that kingdom. We eat, drink, breathe, void wastes, and engage in sexual activities that ensure the continuation of our species. We're also influenced by a number of more subtle forces that reflect our animal nature.

How deeply rooted are these biological pressures? How pervasive is their influence? Are the qualities of personality determined by genes? Is the existence of personality itself a product of evolution? How much of an influence do biological processes have on personality? What adaptive functions do these influences serve? These are some of the questions that underlie the biological perspective on personality.

Biological approaches to personality have varied widely in focus over the years. Some theories of this group are only vaguely biological. Others are tied to specific biological processes and structures. The nature of the research also varies widely, from studies of inheritance to studies examining the nature of biological functions. In some ways, the biological perspective is still a scattered approach to personality. There are, however, threads of thought running below the fragmented surface, linking many of the pieces together.

The biological orientation to personality has two main thrusts. Theorists of the first group focus on the idea that personality characteristics are genetically determined. The biological mechanisms by which inherited differences influence behavior aren't well understood yet, and until recently, they were rarely explored. That is changing quickly, however. The interest of this group lies largely in knowing what characteristics of personality and social behavior are influenced by heredity. The view of these theorists is something of a cross between the biological perspective and the dispositional perspective.

Many of these same people are also interested in the broader idea that the qualities of personality resulted from the evolutionary pressures that produced the human species. This view has grown rapidly in recent years. It's now suggested that far more of human social behavior is a product of our evolutionary heritage than anyone would have guessed two decades ago. These two ideas—that many personality characteristics are genetically determined and that human behavioral tendencies derive from our evolutionary history—form the basis of Chapter 6.

The second focus of the biological perspective is the idea that human behavior is produced by a complex biological system. The processes that make up this system reflect the way we're organized as living creatures. In this view, many ongoing biological processes have systematic influences on people's behavior and experience. To understand these influences, theorists first try to follow the biological systems that exist, to see exactly what they're about and how they work. They then think about how the workings of these systems might influence the kinds of phenomena that are identified with personality.

This idea has its roots in antiquity, but it's been revolutionized by methodological advances of the recent past. The component processes and functions of the nervous system are becoming better understood. We're also coming to understand how hormones affect behavior. The viewpoint represented in this work is a process approach to personality, looking at how biological functions influence human action. As you'll see, however, this focus on process doesn't mean ignoring individual differences. That is, the processes often operate to different degrees in different people, thereby creating the patterns of uniqueness we know as personality. This type of biological approach to personality is considered in Chapter 7.

CHAPTER 6

Inheritance, Evolution, and Personality

Two 3-day-old babies are lying in cradles behind the glass window. One of them lies peacefully for hours at a time, rarely crying and moving only a little. The other thrashes his arms and legs, screws up his face, and rends the air with piercing yowls. What could possibly have made these two children so thoroughly different from each other so soon in life?

A group of young men, 16 to 18 years old, have been hanging around the pool hall all afternoon, acting cool, eyeing women who pass by, and trying to outdo one another with inventive insults. Occasionally tempers flare, the lines of faces harden, and there's pushing and taunting. This time, though, the one doing the taunting went too far. There's a glint of dark steel, and the hot air is shattered by gunshots. Later, the dead one's grieving mother cries out, "Why do men do these things?"

PART OF who you are is the body you walk around in. Some people have big bodies, some have small ones. Some bodies are strong, some are frail. Some bodies are coordinated, some are klutzy. Some bodies turn toward dolls at a certain stage of life, others turn to Legos.

Your body is not your personality. But does it influence the personality you have? The idea that our bodies determine our personalities goes back at least to Hippocrates and Galen. As was said in Chapter 4, Hippocrates proposed four personality types; Galen added the idea that each type reflects an excess of some bodily fluid. The idea that people's physical makeup determines their personalities has re-emerged repeatedly ever since.

The term *physical makeup* has meant different things to theorists at different times, however. In the early and mid-twentieth century, it meant physique, or body build (see Box 6.1). Today, physical makeup means genes. Many people now believe most qualities of personality are partly—maybe even largely—genetically determined.

Box 6.1 EARLY BIOLOGICAL VIEWS

Physique and Personality

The idea that people's bodies relate to their personalities is reflected in popular stereotypes: the jolly fat man, the strong adventurous hero, the frail intellectual. Is there any truth to it?

Several theorists have thought so over the years. Kretschmer (1925) classified people as *thin, muscular,* or *obese,* and found that each group was prone to a different set of disorders. William Sheldon (1942) expanded the idea from categories to dimensions and looked at normal personality. What he called a **somatotype** is defined by placing a person on three dimensions corresponding to Kretschmer's categories. It's designated by three numbers (from 1 to 7), indicating the degree to which the person has that quality. Sheldon believed each quality reflects an emphasis on one of three layers of the embryo. For that reason, he named them after the layers.

Endomorphy is the tendency toward plumpness (reflecting an emphasis on digestion). Endomorphs are soft and round. **Mesomorphy** is the tendency toward muscularity (reflecting a predominance of bone, muscle, and connective tissue). Mesomorphs are rectangular, hard, and strong. **Ectomorphy** is the tendency toward thinness (reflecting predominance of skin and nervous system). Ectomorphs are delicate and frail, easily overwhelmed by stimulation.

Most people have a little of each quality. Someone who's generally muscular but a little pudgy might be a 4-6-2 (endo-meso-ecto). A person who's frail but has a potbelly might be a 6-1-7. A person who's absolutely average would be a 4-4-4.

In parallel with the physical dimensions, Sheldon proposed three aspects of *temperament.* **Viscerotonia** is qualities such as relaxation, tolerance, sociability, love of comfort, goodwill, and easygoingness. **Somatotonia** is qualities such as boldness, assertiveness, and a desire for adventure and activity. **Cerebrotonia** includes avoidance of social interaction, restraint, high pain sensitivity, and a mental intensity approaching apprehensiveness. As with somatotypes, most people have some of each of these three temperaments.

As he'd predicted, Sheldon found that temperaments and somatotypes go together. Mesomorphy related to somatotonia, endomorphy to viscerotonia, and ectomorphy to cerebrotonia. Later studies also supported this view in ratings of children (Walker, 1962), in self-reports (e.g., Cortes & Gatti, 1965; Yates & Taylor, 1978), and in other ways (M. A. Davidson, McInnes, & Parnell, 1957; Glueck & Glueck, 1956; Parnell, 1957).

These studies all say that body types relate to personality. But why? Does physique cause personality? Is the link more roundabout? The body types reflect well-known stereotypes, which include expectations about how people act. If we have such expectations, we may induce people to act as expected (Gacsaly & Borges, 1979). This can produce an association between physique and behavior. It would stem from social pressure, though, not body type per se.

It's hard to know why associations exist between body type and personality. Partly for this reason, many people were skeptical and interest waned. Sheldon's ideas as such are no longer influential, but he stressed a theme that re-emerged only a couple of decades later. He believed that personality, along with body type, was inherited. He didn't test this belief. Indeed, in his time, it wasn't widely understood *how* to test it. Others found ways to do so, however, leading to the findings presented in the first half of this chapter.

Determining the Role of Inheritance in Personality

How do researchers decide whether a given quality is inherited? Family resemblance is a starting point, but it has a serious problem. Family members could be similar for two reasons: They may be similar because of inheritance. Or they may be similar because they're around each other a lot and have learned to act like each other (see Chapter 13).

To get a clearer picture requires better methods. Psychologists turned to the discipline of genetics for ideas. The result was a mix of psychology and genetics called **behavioral genetics.** This is the study of genetic influences on behavioral qualities, including personality qualities, abnormalities, and even cognitive and emotional processes (Plomin, 1997; Plomin, DeFries, & McClearn, 1990; Plomin & Rende, 1991).

TWIN STUDY METHOD

A method that's widely used in behavioral genetics is the **twin study.** It takes advantage of two unusual events in reproduction, which produce two types of twins. One kind of event occurs shortly after conception. A fertilized egg normally divides into two cells, then four, then eight, eventually forming a person. Sometimes, though, the first two cells become separated, and each grows *separately* into a person. These persons are identical twins, or **monozygotic (MZ) twins.** Because they came from what was a single cell, they are 100% alike genetically.

Comparisons between identical and fraternal twins can provide information about the heritability of characteristics.

The second kind of event occurs in conception itself. Usually, only one egg is released from the mother's ovary, but occasionally, two are. If both happen to be fertilized and begin to develop simultaneously, the result is fraternal twins, or **dizygotic (DZ) twins.** Genetically, DZ twins are like any pair of brothers, pair of sisters, or brother and sister. They just happen to be born at the same time rather than separately. As with any pair of **siblings** (brothers or sisters), they are, on the average, 50% alike genetically (though the overlap of specific pairs ranges from 0% to 100%). Interestingly enough, many twins are wrong about which kind they are, and errors are just as common for MZ as DZ twins. One study found that in about 30% of pairs, one twin was wrong; in about 12% of pairs, both twins were wrong (Scarr & Carter-Saltzman, 1979).

In a twin study (see Figure 6.1), pairs of identical twins are related to each other on the characteristic of interest by a correlation; the same is done with pairs of same-sex fraternal twins. The two *correlations* are then compared. If identical twins are more similar to each other than fraternal twins, presumably it's because of the difference in degree of genetic similarity.

The index of genetic influence on personality is termed a **heritability** estimate. This index represents the amount of interpersonal variability in the trait under study that's accounted for by inheritance. The higher the heritability, the stronger the evidence that genes matter in some way. It's important to be careful here, because people sometimes read too much into this term. It does *not* represent the probability that a behavioral characteristic is inherited, *nor* does it mean we know *why* genes matter, only that they seem to matter.

The twin study method is based on the assumption that co-twins who are raised together are exposed to much the same life experiences as each other, *whether they are identical or fraternal twins.* This

FIGURE 6.1

A basic twin study method examines pairs of identical and same-sex fraternal twins raised together. Members of each twin pair are assessed on the variable of interest, and a separate correlation is computed for each type of twin. The correlation for fraternal (DZ) twins is subtracted from the correlation for identical (MZ) twins. Multiplying this difference by 2 gives an index of the heritability of the characteristic—an estimate of the proportion of variance in that characteristic that is accounted for by inheritance.

is critically important. You couldn't conclude that a difference between correlations comes from heredity if parents treated DZ twins differently from MZ twins. The difference in genetic overlap would be confounded with the difference in treatment.

Are the two kinds of twin pairs treated more or less the same? The answer seems to be a very cautious yes. MZ twins are more likely than DZ twins to be dressed alike, but the differences are slight (Plomin et al., 1990). MZ twins also don't seem to resemble each other more in personality if they were treated alike than if they were not (Loehlin & Nichols, 1976). On the other hand, one study found that DZ twins who thought they were MZ twins were more alike than other DZ twins (Scarr & Carter-Saltzman, 1979). A more recent study found that MZ pairs recalled somewhat more similar experiences than DZ twin pairs, but these similarities did not relate to personality similarity (Borkenau, Riemann, Angleitner, & Spinath, 2002).

ADOPTION RESEARCH

Another way to study inheritance is termed the **adoption study.** An adoption study looks at how the adopted child resembles the biological parents and the adoptive parents. Resemblance to biological parents is viewed as genetically based, whereas resemblance to the adoptive parents is environmentally based.

Another method combines features of the twin study with features of the adoption study. It's sometimes possible to study MZ twins who were adopted and raised separately (see Box 6.2). Because they grew up in different homes, environmental impacts should cause *differences*, rather than similarities. Similarity between these

---

BOX 6.2 TWINS SEPARATED AT BIRTH, REUNITED AS ADULTS

Some Startling Similarities

Our emphasis here is on systematic studies of genetics and personality. However, some of the most striking indications that personality qualities can be inherited are more anecdotal. The information comes from identical twins who were separated early in life, raised in different homes, and then reunited later on (Segal, 1999).

This combination of circumstances occurs when identical twins are put up for adoption separately as newborns, a practice that once was fairly common but no longer is. In many cases, the infants grew into adults who had no idea they were twins. In some cases, though, they were reunited as adults. Imagine the surprise of discovering someone else who looks just like you!

What's it like to discover your identical twin after you're both grown?

Reunited twins sometimes discover astonishing similarities (Rosen, 1987; Segal, 1999). Fascinating stories have emerged from projects studying twins raised apart, such as the Minnesota Center for Twin and Adoption Research. Two of their participants, brothers from New Jersey, didn't meet—didn't even know the other existed—until they were adults. At that time, both were volunteer firefighters, both held their beer bottles in the same unusual way, both drank the same brand, and both tended to make the same remarks and gestures when joking, which both did frequently. Another pair of twins discovered that they both smoked the same brand of cigarettes, drove the same kind of car, and did woodworking as a hobby.

A pair of women from Finland provide another amazing example. They were raised in economic circumstances that were very different from each

other, but both grew up to be penny pinchers. Each had a fear of heights, each had had a miscarriage, then three healthy children. Not long after they first met, they were so in tune with each other that they began finishing each other's sentences—all this despite being raised totally separated from each other.

Examples such as these are striking, but it's hard to say how much they capitalize on chance. That is, although reunited twins do tend to be similar in many ways, not every pair of twins displays such dramatic patterns of unlikely similarities. Nonetheless, dramatic examples such as these do tend to stick in people's minds and influence their thinking about the nature of personality. Such illustrations convey the impression that inheritance not only influences broad qualities such as activity level and emotionality but also affects personality in more subtle ways.

pairs can be contrasted with MZ twins raised together and DZ twins raised together. If heredity is important to the trait under study, then MZ twins—even if they were raised apart—should be more similar than DZ twins. If heredity is *really* important, then MZ twins raised apart should be nearly as similar as MZ twins raised together.

What Personality Qualities Are Inherited?

Twin and adoption study methods have been used for over three decades to study genetic influences on personality. An early body of work focused on **temperaments.** This term has been used in several ways. Some people have used *temperament* (singular) to refer to a person's overall "emotional nature" (Allport, 1961; Gallagher, 1994; Kagan, 1994). Arnold Buss and Robert Plomin (1984) used the plural *temperaments* to refer to "inherited personality traits present in early childhood."

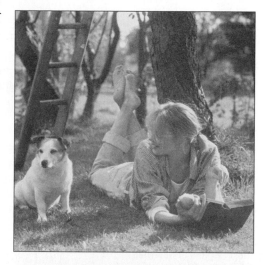

TEMPERAMENTS: ACTIVITY, SOCIABILITY, AND EMOTIONALITY

Buss and Plomin (1984) argued that three normal personality qualities deserve to be called temperaments: *activity level, sociability,* and *emotionality*. Each of these is a dimension of individual differences.

Activity level is the person's overall output of energy or behavior. This temperament has two aspects that differ conceptually but are highly correlated: *vigor* (the intensity of behavior) and *tempo* (speed). People high in vigor prefer high-intensity action. People whose tempo is high prefer fast-paced activities. Those whose vigor and tempo are lower take a more leisurely approach to things.

Sociability is the tendency to prefer being with other people, rather than alone. Sociability is a desire for other people's attention, sharing activities, and the responsiveness and stimulation that are part of interaction. Sociability is *not* a matter of desiring social rewards such as praise or respect. Rather, to be sociable is to value intrinsically the process of interacting with others.

Emotionality is the tendency to become physiologically aroused—easily and intensely—in upsetting situations. This temperament was conceptualized as pertaining to distress, anger, and fear, and the measure of temperaments for adults has three subscales, measuring proneness to these three emotions. It's of interest that anger proneness isn't highly correlated with the others (Buss & Plomin, 1984). Perhaps this temperament of emotionality is actually two distinct traits.

Temperaments influence many kinds of behavior; for example, activity level expresses itself through the kinds of leisure activities people choose to engage in. Some activities are more laid back, others are more fast paced and require lots of energy.

The temperaments proposed by Buss and Plomin resemble those proposed earlier by Sheldon more than is usually recognized (see Box 6.1). The resemblances are quite intriguing. Activity level—and the impact on the world this concept implies—resembles somatotonia. Sociability was part of viscerotonia. Emotionality (apprehensiveness) was part of cerebrotonia.

What's the evidence that these temperaments are inherited? In several twin studies, parents rated their children on these qualities (Buss & Plomin, 1975; Plomin, 1974;

FIGURE 6.2
Average correlations for parental ratings of identical and fraternal twins on temperaments of emotionality, activity level, and sociability. (Correlations are averaged across four samples, totaling 228 pairs of identical twins and 172 pairs of fraternal twins, with an average age of 5 years, 1 month. *Source: Adapted from Buss & Plomin, 1984.*

Plomin & Rowe, 1977). Correlations between parent ratings of activity, emotionality, and sociability were strong for MZ twins; they were next to nonexistent for DZ twins (see Figure 6.2).

Concerns have been raised, though, about rater bias when parents rate their children (Neale & Stevenson, 1989; Saudino, McGuire, Reiss, Hetherington, & Plomin, 1995). If DZ twins fail to much resemble each other, parents tend to contrast the two, which would amplify differences. Parents of MZ twins, seeing more similarity, wouldn't do this. There's also evidence that mothers of young children aren't very good reporters of their children's behavior (Seifer, Sameroff, Barrett, & Krafchuk, 1994).

It's important, then, that other sources of evidence exist. Adoption research (Loehlin, Willerman, & Horn, 1985) also supports a genetic influence for activity level and sociability. This study compared adopted children with their biological parents and their adoptive parents. Measures were self-reports, with several scales that reflect sociability and activity level. Table 6.1 shows some of the correlations from this study. Although the children had spent their lives with their adoptive parents (from a few days after birth), there was remarkably little resemblance between them (column A). On the other hand, despite the separation from their biological parents, there was a pattern of moderate correlations between them (column B).

The data also allowed comparisons between the adopted children and both biological and adoptive siblings (columns C and D). The pattern is less consistent than for parents, but the same general picture emerges: Adopted children are more like their biological brothers and sisters than their adoptive brothers and sisters.

OTHER VIEWS OF TEMPERAMENTS

Developmental researchers have become increasingly interested in temperaments in the past two decades. Mary Rothbart and her colleagues have argued for the existence

Table 6.1 Correlations between Adopted Children and (A) Their Adoptive Parents, (B) Their Biological Parents, (C) Their Adoptive Siblings, and (D) Their Biological Siblings, on Three Measures of Sociability and Two Measures of Activity. *Source:* Data adapted from Loehlin, Willerman, & Horn, 1985. Parent correlations are averages of child–father and child–mother correlations; sibling correlations are also averaged.

Measure	(A) Adoptive Parent	(B) Biological Parent	(C) Adoptive Siblings	(D) Biological Siblings
Sociability (CPI)*	0.04	0.17	0.04	0.22
Social presence (CPI)	0.12	0.34	−0.08	0.70
Sociable (TTS)**	0.02	0.18	−0.13	0.38
Active (TTS)	0.02	0.16	−0.12	0.06
Vigorous (TTS)	0.06	0.33	0.18	0.42

* CPI is the California Psychological Inventory.
** TTS is the Thurstone Temperament Schedule.

of basic temperaments for approach and avoidance (e.g., Derryberry & Rothbart, 1997; Rothbart, Ahadi, & Evans, 2000; Rothbart, Ahadi, Hershey, & Fisher, 2001; Rothbart & Bates, 1998; Rothbart, Ellis, Rueda, & Posner, 2003; Rothbart & Posner, 1985; see also Eisenberg, 2002; Eisenberg et al., 2004; Kochanska & Knaack, 2003; Nigg, 2000). To some extent, the avoidance temperament resembles Buss and Plomin's (1984) view of emotionality. There also seems to be some resemblance between the approach temperament and sociability, though that resemblance is a little less clear.

Rothbart also proposes a third temperament termed **effortful control**. This temperament is about being focused and restrained. In part, it reflects attentional management (e.g., persistence of attention during long-lasting tasks). It also reflects the ability to suppress an approach behavior when doing so is situationally appropriate. This temperament seems to imply a kind of planfulness versus impulsiveness. High levels of this temperament early in life relate to fewer problems with antisocial behavior later in life (Kochanska & Knaack, 2003).

In thinking about this temperament, it is very interesting that Buss and Plomin (1975) originally saw impulsivity as a possible temperament. They dropped it, because evidence of heritability had not been strong. Later on, a new study found a genetic effect on impulsiveness (Pedersen, Plomin, McLearn, & Friberg, 1988). This later study was unusual in that it examined older adults (average age 58), whereas Buss and Plomin had relied mostly on parent ratings of children.

Another possible candidate to be a temperament is intelligence. Intelligence is not usually regarded as a *personality* trait (for a dissenting opinion see Eysenck & Eysenck, 1985), but it has the characteristics Buss and Plomin used to define temperaments. It's genetically influenced (Bouchard, Lykken, McGue, Segal, & Tellegen, 1990; Loehlin, Willerman, & Horn, 1988; Plomin, 1989), and its effects on behavior are broad, manifest early in life, and continue throughout the life span. Perhaps intelligence should also be seen as a temperament.

INHERITANCE OF TRAITS

We began this discussion with temperaments. Are other traits genetically influenced? Yes. An early twin study (Loehlin & Nichols, 1976) found correlations among MZ twins were higher than among DZ twins on a wide range of characteristics (an average of about 0.50 versus an average of about 0.30). Other early studies (reviewed by Carey, Goldsmith, Tellegen, & Gottesman, 1978) found similar results.

Early twin studies were done before trait theorists had begun to converge on the idea that personality is described by five basic factors. With the emergence of the five-factor model, however, work has increasingly focused on whether those dimensions are genetically influenced (Bergeman et al., 1993; Heath, Neale, Kessler, Eaves, & Kendler, 1992; Jang, Livesley, & Vernon, 1996; Jang, McCrae, Angleitner, Riemann, & Livesley, 1998; Loehlin, 1992; Tellegen et al., 1988; Viken, Rose, Kaprio, & Koskenvuo, 1994). The answer again is yes. Indeed, the effects are substantial and remarkably consistent across factors (Bouchard, 2004).

Most twin studies of adult personality use self-reports or reports of people close to the twins. This suggests the same criticism as was made when mothers rated their infants. That is, the potential exists for contrast effects that exaggerate differences between twins that are only slightly dissimilar. To deal with this possibility, Borkenau, Riemann, Angleitner, and Spinath (2001) did a twin study in which participants were videotaped and then rated by people who didn't know them. They also found evidence of genetic contribution to all five factors.

TEMPERAMENTS AND THE FIVE-FACTOR MODEL

The supertraits that make up the five-factor model are broad and pervasive in influence. In that respect, they're a lot like temperaments. In fact, the five factors have considerable conceptual similarity to qualities that others call temperaments (Digman & Shmelyov, 1996; Halverson, Kohnstamm, & Martin, 1994; Loehlin, 1992). One obvious similarity is that the temperament Buss and Plomin (1984) called *emotionality* and Rothbart and Posner (1985) called an *avoidance* temperament closely resembles neuroticism.

Extraversion from the "big five" has overtones of not one but two temperaments (plus some other qualities). Extraversion suggests a preference for being with others, implying a possible link to sociability (Depue & Morrone-Strupinsky, 2005). Eysenck (1986) also included activity in his view of extraversion. This suggests extraversion may blend sociability with activity level. On the other hand, extraversion has come to be viewed partly in terms of social dominance or agency (Depue & Collins, 1999), which isn't directly implied either by sociability or by activity.

Another of the five factors—agreeableness—also has overtones of sociability, although again not being identical to it. Agreeableness suggests liking to be with people. It goes beyond that, however, in having connotations of being easy to get along with. Whether agreeableness derives from a temperament of sociability is something of an open question.

Examination of conscientiousness suggests that it's defined partly by the absence of impulsiveness. That is, conscientiousness is a planful, persistent, focused orientation toward life's activities. The possibility that impulsivity, or effortful control, is a temperament (Pedersen, Plomin, McClearn, & Friberg, 1988; Rothbart et al., 2003) suggests another link between temperaments and the five-factor model.

The last of the "big five" is openness to experience, or intellect, culture, or intelligence. Given the diverse labels for this factor, it's unsure whether this is the same as intelligence, mentioned earlier as a potential temperament. (Indeed, it's not entirely clear exactly what intelligence is, cf. Sternberg, 1982.) But if this part of the five-factor model did reflect what intelligence tests measure, there would be yet another link between temperament and trait models.

In sum, although the fit is not perfect, the set of qualities proposed as biologically based temperaments bears a great deal of resemblance to qualities in the five-factor model. The places where the resemblance is less clear serve partly to raise interesting questions. For example, why should activity and sociability be considered fundamental, rather than extraversion? Is extraversion really one trait, or two? As we said in Chapter 4, there are many ways to divide up the qualities of behavior, and it's hard to know which is best.

It's likely that these questions will continue to be of interest. More specifically, it seems likely that the five-factor model will continue to have an increasing influence on how behavioral genetics researchers decide which qualities of personality to study in their research.

GENETICS OF OTHER QUALITIES: HOW DISTINCT ARE THEY?

The evidence that inheritance influences personality goes beyond studies of traditional traits. A number of other effects have emerged, some of which relate fairly readily to personality. For example, there's a genetic effect on risk of divorce (McGue & Lykken, 1992), which operates through personality (Jockin, McGue, & Lykken, 1996). There's a genetic effect on having impactful life events, which again appears to operate via personality (Saudino, Pedersen, Lichtenstein, McClearn, & Plomin, 1997). Heredity influences how much social support people have (Kessler, Kendler, Heath, Neale, & Eaves, 1992), which probably reflects personality (Brissette, Scheier, &

Carver, 2002; Kendler, 1997). There's also a genetic contribution to people's attitudes on various topics (Eaves, Eysenck, & Martin, 1989; Olson, Vernon, Harris, & Jang, 2001; Tesser, 1993), which again seems likely to reflect personality.

Findings such as these raise a question: To what extent are the various effects distinct and separate? The temperaments and supertraits discussed earlier are very broad. When evidence is found that a quality is genetically influenced, it raises a question. Is this a *separate* effect? Or is the effect there because the quality under study relates to a temperament or supertrait?

The question of how many distinct qualities are *separately* influenced by inheritance is one that hasn't been explored much. However, it's an important question in understanding how inheritance affects personality. One recent study began to explore it, within the framework of the five-factor model (Jang et al., 1998). This study found that not only were the five supertraits heritable, but so were most of the facet traits. Indeed, the genetic influences on facets were separate from the genetic influences on the overall traits. This suggests that *many* distinct qualities may be genetically influenced, not just a few broad ones.

INHERITANCE AND SEXUAL ORIENTATION

A topic about which there's been much discussion in recent years is the possible role of genetics in determining a person's sexual orientation. Some people would regard this topic as outside the realm of personality, but others would say it's very much a part of personality.

Evidence of a possible genetic role in sexual orientation goes back over 40 years, with the report of a higher incidence of homosexuality among men whose MZ twin was gay than men whose DZ twin was gay (Eysenck, 1964a). Later on, twin studies were done with homosexual men (Bailey & Pillard, 1991) and homosexual women (Bailey, Pillard, Neale, & Agyei, 1993). In both cases, a co-twin was more than twice as likely to be homosexual if the twins were MZ than if they were DZ. (Similar findings were also reported by Whitam, Diamond, and Martin [1993].) A later twin study of men found much weaker effects (Bailey, Dunne, & Martin, 2000), but it did find evidence of genetic influence on childhood gender nonconformity (low feelings of male gender identity and participation in gender-typed activities).

Other research has found evidence of a genetic basis for male homosexuality using an entirely different approach. A study of families of gay men found there were more gay male relatives on the mother's side (maternal uncles and sons of maternal aunts) than on the father's side. This suggests that a gene related to homosexuality might be on the X chromosome (because a son always receives it from his mother). Examination of genetic material revealed a region of the X chromosome that was similar among most of the gay participants. This suggests a genetic basis for at least some instances of homosexuality. Genetics cannot explain all of the instances, though, because this region was *not* similar for all gay men (see also Pool, 1993). A later study found further (and more complicated) evidence of the involvement of the X chromosome in men's sexual orientation (Bocklandt, Horvath, Vilain, & Hamer, 2006).

It's long been wondered why homosexuality hasn't died out over generations, because gay men don't reproduce at the same rate as other men. If the gene is on the X chromosome, that would account for it. That is, the X chromosome is carried by women as well as men. The gene can be passed on without being reflected in behavior.

The biological basis for homosexuality almost certainly involves several paths, rather than one. The findings just reviewed focus on a particular chromosome. However, there is other evidence that multiple gene locations are involved (Mustanski, Dupree, Nievergelt, Bocklandt, Schork, & Hamer, 2005).

Indeed, other possibilities are biological without being genetic. For example, the probability of a man's being homosexual increases with the number of older brothers he has but not with the number of older sisters (Blanchard, 2004; Blanchard, Cantor, Bogaert, Breedlove, & Ellis, 2006). This led to the idea that mothers develop antibodies to male qualities when pregnant with boys. Repeated occurrence (having more sons) causes the antibody response to strengthen to the point that it prevents full masculinization of the fetal brain.

MOLECULAR GENETICS AND NEW SOURCES OF EVIDENCE

In the preceding discussion, a new issue crept in. Specifically, there now are ways to study genetic influences that weren't available even a short time ago. The effort to map the human **genome**—the genetic blueprint of the body—was wildly successful. A first draft was completed in 2000, years ahead of schedule. It's increasingly possible to identify specific genes that cause differences among people. Differences range from vulnerability to physical and psychological disorders to normal personality qualities. Many believe the ability to identify genes linked to such differences will revolutionize medicine, psychiatry, and psychology (Plomin, 1995; Plomin & Crabbe, 2000; Plomin, DeFries, Craig, & McGuffin, 2003).

A huge proportion of the human genome is identical for everyone. Interest focuses on the parts that vary. When different forms or patterns of DNA (genetic material) occur at a particular location, they are called **alleles.** The existence of the differences is called a **polymorphism.** A **genotype** difference between persons means the persons have different alleles at some particular location. Whereas twin research is referred to as quantitative behavioral genetics, the attempt to relate differences in particular gene locations to other measurable differences among persons is often called **molecular genetics** (Carey, 2003).

The question for personality, then, is which locations influence a given personality quality. The answer to this is not likely to be at all simple. It is very likely that many genes relate to a given personality quality (Plomin & Crabbe, 2000). Indeed, different genes may connect to different aspects of behavior that all relate to the same trait.

The first discoveries in this area were mostly single genes relating to broad outcomes, such as disorders (which we return to later on). A few genes have also been identified that have clear relevance to normal personality. For example, a gene has been identified that relates to the use of dopamine in the brain. This gene has several alleles, one of which is longer than the others. Two research teams (Benjamin, Li, Patterson, Greenberg, Murphy, & Hamer, 1996; Ebstein et al., 1996) found almost simultaneously that people with the long allele have high scores on personality scales that relate to novelty seeking. A different candidate gene for dopamine function has also been linked to a different measure of fun seeking (Reuter, Schmitz, Corr, & Hennig, 2006). Some have been able replicate such associations, but a good many others have not. Ebstein (2006) recently reviewed a series of meta-analyses (involving many specific studies) and concluded that the support is not very strong after all.

Another gene has been identified that appears to relate to use of serotonin in the brain. Several groups have found a link of the short allele of that gene to high scores on neuroticism and low scores on agreeableness (e.g., Greenberg et al., 2000; Lesch et al., 1996; Sen et al., 2004). There is even some suggestion that this gene is partly responsible for the moderately high inverse correlation between neuroticism and agreeableness (Jang et al., 2001). Again, the association has been difficult to replicate. Several meta-analyses have also been done on studies of this polymorphism, and support for a relation to neuroticism is not strong overall (Ebstein, 2006). It is important to note, however, that these meta-analyses have all failed to look at the association with agreeableness. There is reason to believe that that one may be the more important of the two (Carver & Miller, 2006).

Single-gene discoveries such as these have received huge publicity when first announced. We repeat, though, that it's very likely that most genetic influences on behavior will involve small contributions from many genes (Plomin & Crabbe, 2000). Indeed, that may be one reason why the discoveries have been hard to replicate. News programs and magazines will probably continue to trumpet every new discovery as *the* gene for something, but that's misleading (Kendler, 2005). Despite this caution, it's clear that the tools of molecular genetics have greatly changed the way in which researchers pursue the genetic contributions to many aspects of the human experience, including personality.

Environmental Effects

There are two more issues to raise in this part of the chapter. They concern the other effects in twin and adoption studies—the part we haven't emphasized. Specifically, studies always find that nonhereditary factors contribute to personality. The issues are how great a contribution they make and what kind of contribution they make.

THE SIZE OF ENVIRONMENTAL INFLUENCES

A topic that's been debated as long as twin and adoption studies have been done is the size of genetic versus environmental influence. The argument seems easy enough to resolve. Don't the statistics of the study tell you? Unfortunately, it's not that simple. There are reasons why the statistics may have built-in biases. The arguments are subtle and complex. Here are two of them.

Dickens and Flynn (2001) said that there often are unrecognized correlations between genetic influences and environmental influences on the same outcome. The example they used is intelligence. People with high intelligence gravitate to environments that foster learning more than do people with less intelligence. In those environments, they learn more. Their IQs go up. The *environment* had an effect on their IQ. But the possibility for that to happen stemmed indirectly from their genetic makeup. Thus, the two influences are correlated.

Why does this matter? The size of an environmental effect on an outcome is judged by how much variability is not explained by the genetic effect. If an environmental effect is mistaken to be a genetic effect (because they're correlated), the genetic effect gets the credit for what the environment is doing. The genetic statistical effect from the study is larger than it should be, and the environmental statistical effect is smaller than it should be.

Dickens and Flynn (2001) made this argument in the context of IQ, but it also can be applied to personality. As was said in Chapter 4, people gravitate to environments that suit their interests, that let them be who they are. Maybe those environments even induce people to have more of the quality that first led them there. Someone who's slightly introverted and who starts reading more or keeping a diary may discover the joys of solitary pursuits and become even more introverted. Someone who's slightly extraverted and who gets involved in group activities may discover he or she likes being in charge of groups and develop greater extraversion.

Another argument begins with the fact that influences on societies as a whole change over extended periods of time. These broad influences may have an impact on personality. There is evidence, for example, that people of a given age in the United States were more anxious in 1993 than in 1952 (Twenge, 2000). Indeed, in that study, the average child in the 1980s reported more anxiety than did children who were psychiatric patients in the 1950s! Age-cohort effects have also been found for extraversion (Twenge, 2001) and self-esteem (Twenge & Campbell, 2001).

Why does this matter? It matters because these seem to be environmental influences on personality (perhaps across the entire population). But this very broad environmental influence is never included in the computations of genetic and environmental effects in twin studies. It's controlled out of the entire analysis (Twenge, 2002). Again, this would mean that the genetic effects seem larger in the studies than they really are.

THE NATURE OF ENVIRONMENTAL INFLUENCES

The studies that establish a powerful role for inheritance in personality also show an important role for nonhereditary factors. Surprisingly, however, the evidence on the whole suggests that families don't make children alike, as you might assume. The environment has an impact on personality but primarily at an *individual* level (Plomin & Daniels, 1987).

What might be the sources of nonshared environmental influence? There isn't a lot of information on this. Several guesses sound reasonable, though (Dunn & Plomin, 1990; Rowe, 1994). For example, siblings often have different sets of friends, sometimes totally different. Peers have a big influence on growing children—some think even stronger than the influence of parents (Harris, 1995). Differences in peer groups may cause children's personalities to become different. If that happens, it's an environmental influence, but it's not shared by the siblings.

Another point is that siblings in families don't exist side by side. In their interactions, they develop roles that play off each other (e.g., Daniels, 1986; Hoffman, 1991). For example, if one child often helps another child with schoolwork, the two are developing styles of interacting that diverge. As another example, parents sometimes favor one child over another. This can affect the children's relationship, perhaps inducing differences between them. Again, the effects would be environmental, but they would differ from one child to the other.

The exact manner in which the environment influences personality remains to be clarified. Questions also remain about the impact of the shared versus the unshared environment. When behavior measures are used instead of rating scales, the shared environment seems to matter more (Turkheimer, 1998). For example, in the study described earlier, in which videotaped behavior was rated by strangers, Borkenau et al. (2001) found a much larger effect for shared environment than is typically found. Thus, variations in research methods may influence what conclusion emerges.

Evolution and Human Behavior

We now change directions somewhat. Evidence that inheritance plays a role in personality is one contributor to the emergence of a broader current of thought. The broader current is the idea that evolutionary processes have a major influence on present-day human behavior. This line of thought is tied to several labels, including behavioral ecology, sociobiology, and evolutionary psychology (Barkow, Cosmides, & Tooby, 1992; Bjorklund & Pellegrini, 2002; D. M. Buss, 1991, 1995; Caporael, 2001; Heschl, 2002; Segal, 1993; Tooby & Cosmides, 1989, 1990). Work deriving from this group of ideas has grown explosively in recent years.

SOCIOBIOLOGY AND EVOLUTIONARY PSYCHOLOGY

Sociobiology (Alexander, 1979; Barash, 1977, 1986, 2001; Crawford, 1989; Crawford, Smith, & Krebs, 1987; Dawkins, 1976; Lumsden & Wilson, 1981; Wilson, 1975) is the study of the biological basis of social behavior. The core assumption is that many—perhaps all—of the core elements of social interaction in humans are products of evolution. That is, the patterns were retained genetically because at some point in prehistory they conferred an adaptive advantage.

In some respects this view resembles one presented earlier by people working in **ethology,** the study of animals' behavior in their natural environment. Two ideas from ethology are often mentioned in psychology. One is *imprinting,* in which the young of many species attach to their mothers (Hess, 1973). Another is the idea that animals mark and defend territories (cf. Ardrey, 1966). Ethologists suggested that humans have similar patterns.

Ethologists addressed human behavior mostly by making analogies. Sociobiologists, in contrast, focused on evolutionary genetics and the question of how behavior patterns might get built in (see also Box 6.3). This view is more radical. To a sociobiologist,

---

BOX 6.3   THEORETICAL ISSUE

Specieswide Adaptations and the Existence of Individual Differences

The basic concepts of natural selection and population genetics are simple. If a characteristic differs from person to person, it means each gene behind that characteristic has several potential forms, or alleles. Some people have one allele, some have another one. (Actually, it's even more complicated, because everyone has two of each chromosome, so you can also have mixed alleles even if there are only two versions available.)

Selection means one form of the gene is more likely to show up in the next generation because it's been helpful in survival or reproduction, or is less likely to show up because it's *interfered* with survival or reproduction. This is **directional selection.** It means a shift toward a greater proportion of the adaptive allele in the population's next generation. If it goes on long enough, directional selection reduces or even eliminates individual differences. Over many generations, those without the

adaptive allele fail to reproduce, and a larger proportion of the next generation have the adaptive one. In principle, this is how a characteristic can become universal in the population.

Many characteristics might influence survival. For example, in a world where strength matters (which probably was true during human evolution), strength makes you more likely to survive long enough to reproduce. That sends genes for strength into the next generation. As long as these genes are well represented in the population, the population will tend to survive and create yet another generation.

But wait. If some characteristics are more adaptive than others, why are there individual differences at all? Why aren't we all large and strong and smart and stealthy and whatever else is a good thing to be? A tricky thing about selection is that whether a particular value is adaptive depends on the context. Sometimes a value that's useful in one environment is not just useless—but fatal—in another. In the long run, genetic variability in the population is necessary for it to survive in a world that changes over time. Thus, the importance of another kind of selec-

tion, termed **stabilizing selection,** which maintains genetic variability (Plomin, 1981). Stabilizing selection occurs when an intermediate value of some characteristic is more adaptive than the value at either extreme. Presumably, intermediate values reflect combinations of alleles, rather than a specific allele, and probably involves multiple genes. Predominance of intermediate values thus implies genetic variability.

How can an intermediate value of a characteristic be more adaptive than an extreme value? Consider this example. It's important for people to have some sociability because we are such a social species. Having too little sociability isn't adaptive. But neither is it adaptive to have too *much* sociability. A person with extremely high sociability can hardly bear to be alone, and life sometimes requires people to be alone.

Intermediate values are especially adaptive in many of the domains that are relevant to personality. That's why personality traits vary from person to person: There's genetic diversity on those traits. Otherwise, there'd be only a single personality, which everyone would have.

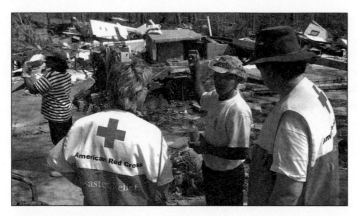

Evolutionary psychologists believe that even acts of altruism, such as doing disaster relief work for the Red Cross, may have a genetic basis.

a behavior pattern might exist in humans *but in no other species* because of a unique adaptation among humans.

This reasoning led in some surprising directions. For example, it led to a way to account for altruism, a tendency that seems very hard to explain in evolutionary terms. *Altruism* is acting for the welfare of others, to the point of sacrificing one's own well-being (potentially one's life) for someone else. Altruism would seem to confer a biological *dis*advantage. That is, being altruistic may help someone, but it also might get you killed. This would prevent your genes from being passed on to the next generation. If the genes aren't passed on, a genetically based tendency toward altruism should disappear very quickly.

Sociobiologists point out, however, that the process of evolution isn't really a matter of individual survival. What matters is a *gene pool,* distributed across a population. If one *group* in a population survives, prospers, and reproduces at a high rate, its genes move onward into subsequent generations more than other groups' genes.

This means there are ways to get your genes carried forward besides reproducing on your own. Your genes are helped into the next generation by anything that helps *your part of the gene pool* reproduce, an idea called **inclusive fitness** (Hamilton, 1964). If you act altruistically for a relative, it helps the relative survive. If an extremely altruistic act (in which you die) saves a great many of your relatives, it helps aspects of your genetic makeup be passed on because your relatives resemble you genetically. This process is sometimes called *kin selection.*

Thus, it's argued, the tendency to be altruistic may be genetically based. This argument implies that people will be more altruistic toward those in their kinship group than strangers (especially competitors). This seems to be true (Burnstein, Crandall, & Kitayama, 1994). Also fitting this view, there seems to be a genetic contribution to empathic concern for others, which may underlie altruism (Burnstein et al., 1994; Matthews, Batson, Horn, & Rosenman, 1981; Rushton, Fulker, Neale, Nias, & Eysenck, 1986). Indeed, there's evidence that emotional closeness, which increases with genetic relatedness, underlies the effect of relatedness on altruism (Korchmaros & Kenny, 2001).

The idea that altruistic tendencies are part of human nature has been extended to suggest an evolutionary basis for cooperation even among nonrelatives. The idea is essentially that our far ancestors survived better by cooperating than by being individualists. Thus, they acquired a tendency toward being helpful more generally. One person helps the other in the expectation that the help will be returned, an idea termed **reciprocal altruism** (Trivers, 1971).

Can this possibly have happened? Wouldn't people cheat, and take without giving? Sometimes. But those who do get punished (Fehr & Gächter, 2002). From an evolutionary view, the issue is whether cooperation leads to better outcomes for the group. There's evidence that it does, at least in the cooperative situations studied by psychologists (Axelrod & Hamilton, 1981). This has led some to conclude that a tendency to cooperate is part of human nature (Guisinger & Blatt, 1994; Kriegman & Knight, 1988). There's also evidence that punishing those who don't cooperate leads to better group outcomes (Fehr & Gächter, 2002). Maybe punishing those who don't go along with the group is also genetically built into human nature.

GENETIC SIMILARITY AND ATTRACTION

The idea that people act altruistically toward relatives has been extended by Philippe Rushton and his colleagues (Rushton, 1989a; Rushton, Russell, & Wells, 1984) to what he calls **genetic similarity theory.** The basic idea is what we've said before: A gene "survives" (is represented in the next generation) by any action that brings about reproduction of any organism in which copies of itself exist. That may mean being altruistic to your kinship group, but Rushton says it means other things as well.

Rushton and his colleagues (1984) argued that genetic similarity has an influence on who attracts you. Specifically, you're more attracted to strangers who resemble you genetically than to those who don't. How does this help the survival of the gene? If you're attracted to someone, you may become sexually involved, which may result in offspring. Offspring have genes from both parents. By making you attracted to someone with genes like yours, your genes increase the odds that genes like themselves will be copied (from one parent or the other or both) into a new person, surviving into the next generation.

Are people attracted to others whose genes resemble their own? Maybe so. Rushton (1988) had couples take blood tests that give a rough index of genetic similarity. He found that sexually involved couples had in common 50% of the genetic markers. When he took the data and paired people randomly, the pairs shared only 43% of the markers, significantly less. Rushton went on to compare couples who'd had children with those who hadn't. Those with a child shared 52% of the genetic markers; those with no child shared only 44%. Thus, among sexually active couples, those most similar were also most likely to have reproduced.

This attraction effect isn't limited to the opposite sex. People also tend to form friendships with others who are genetically similar to them. Rushton (1989b) repeated his study with pairs of men who were close friends (all heterosexual). The pairs of friends shared 54% of the genetic markers, the random pairs shared only 48%. Again, genetic similarity related to attraction.

How would friendships with genetically similar people of the same sex be adaptive? The point is to get the genes into offspring. Having same-sex friends won't do that directly. There are two ways it can help, though. The first is similar to the idea discussed earlier about altruism and kin selection. You're more likely to be altruistic for a close friend than a stranger, making the friend more likely to live to reproduce. The second possibility is that you may meet the same-sex friend's opposite-sex sibling. If the sibling is also genetically similar to you, an attraction may develop, with potential sexual activity, resulting in offspring.

How do people detect genetic similarity in others? It's hard to say. One possibility is that we are drawn to others who share our facial and body features. People who look like you seem like family and therefore attract you. Another possibility is that genetic similarity is conveyed by smell. Consistent with this, there is evidence that women prefer the odor of men who are genetically similar to their fathers (Jacob, McClintock, Zelano, & Ober, 2002). Outside your awareness, you may recognize those who are like you by subtle physical cues.

It's also likely that culture plays a role here. If you are descended from eastern Europeans, you may feel more comfortable around people who share your (eastern European) traditions. It might be the familiar traditions that bring you close, but the result is that you are drawn to people who come from your part of the gene pool.

The general idea that people choose mates on the basis of particular characteristics is called **assortative mating** (Thiessen & Gregg, 1980). Mating definitely isn't

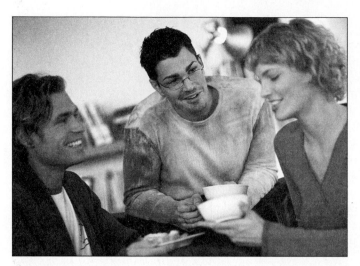

Both men and women are in competitions for desirable mates.

random. People select their mates on the basis of a variety of characteristics, though there are limitations on how fine grained this selection is (Lykken & Tellegen, 1993). Often the features that influence mate selection are similarities to the self (Buss, 1985; Rushton & Bons, 2005).

MATE SELECTION AND COMPETITION FOR MATES

We've talked at some length about the importance of getting genes to the next generation. (From this viewpoint, it's sometimes said that a person is a gene's way of creating another gene [Barash, 2001].) Obviously, then, the evolutionary view on personality focuses closely on mating (Gangestad & Simpson, 2000). Indeed, from this view, mating is what life's all about (although other issues do arise when you think about the complexities of mating). Just as certain qualities confer survival advantage, certain qualities also confer reproductive advantage.

Mating involves competition. Males compete with one another; females compete with one another. But what's being competed for differs between the sexes. Trivers (1972) argued that males and females evolved different strategies, based on their roles in reproduction. Female humans have greater investment in offspring than males: They carry them for nine months, and they're more tied to caring for them after birth. The general rule across species is that the sex with the greater investment can generate fewer offspring over the life span, because of the commitment of time and energy to each. It thus is choosier about a mate (though not everyone agrees on this; see Small, 1993). The sex with less investment can generate more offspring and thus is less discriminating.

Given the difference in biological investment, the strategy of women is to tend to hold back from mating until they identify the best available male. "Best" here is defined as quality of genetic contribution, parental care, or material support for the mate and offspring. In contrast, the strategy of males is to maximize sexual opportunities, copulating as often as possible. This means seeking partners who are available and fertile (Buss, 1994a, 1994b). In this view, men tend to view women as *sex objects,* whereas women tend to view men as *success objects.*

These differences in orientation should produce different strategies for trying to get the opportunity to mate (which both males and females want). David Buss and David Schmitt (1993) examined differences in how men and women compete for and select mates and how the strategies differ from short term to long term (see also Buss, 1994a, 1994b; Feingold, 1992; Schmitt & Buss, 1996). If men are interested in finding fertile partners, women should compete by emphasizing their attributes that relate to fertility—youth and beauty. If women want to find partners that will provide for them and their babies, men should compete by emphasizing their status, personal dominance and ambition, and wealth or potential for wealth (Sidanius, Pratto, & Bobo, 1994; Sprecher, Sullivan, & Hatfield, 1994).

What do men and women actually *do* to compete for mates? College students report doing pretty much what we just described (Buss, 1988). Women enhance their beauty with makeup, jewelry, clothing, and hairstyles. Women also play hard to get, to incite widespread interest among many males. This permits the women to be choosy once candidates have been identified (see also Kenrick, Sadalla, Groth, & Trost, 1990). Men brag about their accomplishments and earning potential, display expensive possessions, and flex their muscles. In fact, just seeing women around makes men display these qualities even more (Roney, 2003).

Buss (1989) examined mate preferences in 37 different cultures around the world. Cultural differences were relatively rare. The preferences of U.S. college students didn't differ much from those of people elsewhere. Males (more than females) were drawn to cues of reproductive capacity. Females (more than males) were drawn to cues indicating resources (see also Singh, 1995). The resource issue may not be a case of "more is better." It may just be that men who aren't at an acceptable level are out of the running (Kenrick, Sundie, Nicastle, & Stone, 2001). Females are also drawn to cues of dominance and high status (Cunningham, Barbee, & Pike, 1990; Feingold, 1992; Kenrick et al., 1990; Sadalla, Kenrick, & Vershure, 1987), especially dominance expressed in socially positive ways (Jensen-Campbell, Graziano, & West, 1995).

Despite these gender differences, the qualities just listed don't always rank high in people's lists of desired characteristics. This leads some to be skeptical of their importance. But rankings can also be deceiving. Other research gave people tight "budgets" for getting what they want in a partner (Li, Bailey, Kenrick, & Linsenmeier, 2002). In this situation, men treated physical attractiveness as a necessity rather than an option, women treated status and resources as necessities, and both treated kindness and intelligence as necessities. That is, given that they couldn't be choosy about everything, they went for these qualities first.

People have investigated implications of the evolutionary model in several ways. For example, research shows that men prefer younger women, especially as they themselves grow older, consistent with the seeking of reproductive capacity. This comes from a study of the age ranges specified in singles' ads (Kenrick & Keefe, 1992). As can be seen in Figure 6.3, men past age 25 specified a range that extended increasingly below their own age. Women, in contrast, tended to express a preference for men slightly older than themselves.

Also consistent with predictions from the evolutionary model are results from several other studies of gender differences (see also Table 6.2). Men are more interested in casual sex than are women (Bailey, Gaulin, Agyei, & Gladue, 1994; Buss & Schmitt, 1993; R. D. Clark & Hatfield, 1989; Oliver & Hyde, 1993), want more sexual variety (Schmitt, 2003), and are less selective in their criteria for one-night stands (Kenrick, Groth, Trost, & Sadalla, 1993). Men are more easily turned on by visual erotica than are women (Bailey et al., 1994). Men's commitment to their relationship is shaken by exposure to a very attractive woman, whereas women's commitment is shaken by exposure to a very dominant man (Kenrick, Neuberg, Zierk, & Krones, 1994). Men's confidence in their own value as a mate is shaken by exposure to a very dominant man (but not an attractive one), and women's confidence in their value as a mate is shaken by exposure to a very attractive woman (but not a dominant one; Gutierres, Kenrick, & Partch, 1999). Men overinterpret women's smiles and touches as implying sexual interest, and women are overly conservative in judging men's commitment in relationships that are forming (Buss, 2001).

Both men and women experience jealousy, but it has been suggested that there's a difference in what creates this emotion. In theory, it's evolutionarily important for men

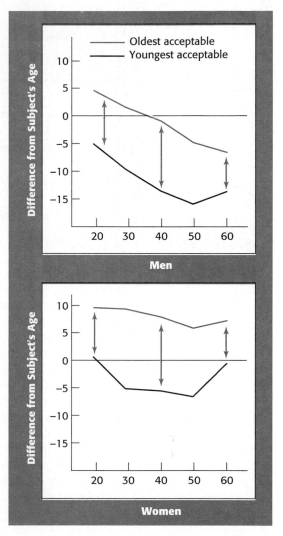

FIGURE 6.3
Singles' ads placed by men and women often specify the age range of persons of the opposite sex whom the placer of the ad would like to meet. In this sample of ads, as men aged, they expressed an increasing preference for younger women. Women tended to prefer men slightly older than they were, and the extent of that preference didn't change over time.
Source: Adapted from Kenrick & Keefe, 1992.

Table 6.2 Summary of Predictions from Evolutionary Psychology for Sex Differences in Mating Tendencies.

Issue	Females	Males
Reproductive constraints	Can produce only a limited number of children over life	Can reproduce without limit through life
Optimal reproductive strategy	Locate and hold onto best-quality mate	Mate as widely and often as possible
Desired quality in potential mate	Resources to protect and support them and offspring	Childbearing capability
Basis for evaluating mate potential	Earning capacity, status, possessions, generosity	Physical attractiveness, health, youth
Prime basis for jealousy	Partner's emotional attachment to another	Partner's sexual infidelity

to be concerned about paternity. (They want to support their *own* children, not someone else's.) Thus, men should be especially jealous about sexual infidelity. In theory, women are most concerned about whether the man will continue to support her and her children. Thus, women should be jealous about a man's having emotional bonds with another woman, rather than sex per se.

Data from several studies fit this view: Men were more disturbed by thoughts of sexual infidelity, and women were more disturbed by thoughts of emotional infidelity, (Buss, Larsen, Westen, & Semmelroth, 1992; see also Bailey et al., 1994). This particular finding has been challenged, however, partly because asking the question differently erases the gender difference (DeSteno, Bartlett, Braverman, & Salovey, 2002; Harris, 2002, 2003) and partly because it's been hard to obtain the effect in nonstudent samples (Sabini & Green, 2004).

Jealousy is partly about what your partner may have done, but it's partly about the presence of rivals. Again, there is evidence of a gender difference in what qualities matter. Men are more jealous when the potential rival is dominant than when he is physically attractive; women are more jealous when the potential rival is physically attractive (Dijkstra & Buunk, 1998).

MATE RETENTION AND OTHER ISSUES

The first challenge in mating is getting a mate. The next challenge is *keeping* the mate. Men and women both have the potential to stray, and other people sometimes try to make that happen (Schmitt, 2004; Schmitt & Buss, 2001). People use various tactics to prevent this (Buss & Shackelford, 1997). Some are used by men and women alike, but others differ by gender. For example, men report spending a lot of money and giving in to their mates' wishes. Women try to make themselves look extra attractive and let others know their mate is already taken.

Use of retention tactics also relates predictably to other factors in the relationship but differently for men and women. Men use their tactics more if they think their wife is physically attractive. Men also work harder at keeping a wife who is young, independent of the man's age and the length of the relationship. In contrast, women work harder at keeping husbands with higher incomes. They also make more efforts if their husbands are striving for high status (independent of current income).

Although mating strategies are the starting point for much of this research on gender differences, others have applied the theme more broadly. (As noted earlier, issues involved in mating lead to several other complexities in life.) Several have suggested that evolutionary differences cause men and women to have very different styles—indeed different *needs*—in communication (e.g., J. Gray, 1992; Tannen, 1990). Men are seen as having an individualistic, dominance-oriented, problem-solving approach. Women are seen as having an inclusive, sharing, communal approach. The argument is also made that these differences in goals and patterns of communication lead to a good deal of misunderstanding between men and women.

We should note that our discussion has emphasized gender differences, not similarities. There are, of course, many similarities. Both genders are looking for partners who have a good sense of humor and a pleasing personality (Feingold, 1992), who are agreeable and emotionally stable (Kenrick et al., 1993), intelligent (Li et al., 2002), and kind and loving (Buss, 1994b). Both also seem to prefer partners whose faces are symmetrical (Grammer & Thornhill, 1994). The way men and women look at each other goes far beyond seeing each other as sex objects and success objects (Buss, 1994b). Nevertheless, gender differences also seem important.

AGGRESSION AND THE YOUNG MALE SYNDROME

Competition for mating opportunities leads to a lot of male posturing. It has also been blamed for many problem aspects of young men's behavior, including their risky driving (Nell, 2002). But it can also lead to more. When males face hard competition for scarce resources (females), the result sometimes is confrontation and potentially serious violence of several sorts (Hilton, Harris, & Rice, 2000).

This pattern has been referred to as the *young male syndrome* (Wilson & Daly, 1985). It's viewed as partly an effect of evolutionary pressures from long ago and partly a response to situations that elicit the pattern. That is, although the pattern of behavior may be coded in every man's genes, it's most likely to emerge when current situations predict reproductive failure. The worst case would be a single man who is unemployed and thus a poor candidate as a mate.

In line with this analysis, there's clear evidence that homicide between competitors is primarily a male affair (Daly & Wilson, 1990). Figure 6.4 displays the homicide rates in Chicago during a 16-year period, omitting cases in which the person killed was a relative. Males are far more likely to kill one another than are females. It's also obvious that the prime ages for killing are the prime ages for mating. According to Daly and Wilson, these killings come largely from conflicts over "face" and status (see also Wilson & Daly, 1996). Trivial events escalate into violence, and someone is killed.

Why killing instead of ritualized displays of aggressiveness? No one knows for sure. It is certain that easy access to guns in the United States plays a role. When weapons aren't there, the same pressures are more likely to result in punching and shouting. Deadly violence certainly is possible without weapons, but weapons make it far more likely.

We should point out explicitly that the theory underlying this area of study is very different from ideas about aggression and human nature of only a few years ago. This view isn't that aggression is part of human nature, expressed indiscriminately. Rather,

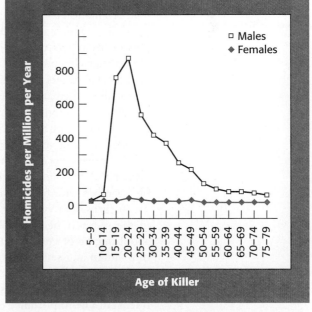

FIGURE 6.4
Homicide rates for males and females killing nonrelatives of the same sex in Chicago during the period 1965–1981.
Source: Adapted from Daly & Wilson, 1990.

physical aggression is seen as largely a male phenomenon, which occurs specifically as a result of sexual selection pressures in the competition for mates (Buss, 2005b).

Our focus here is on violence by young men toward their genetic competitors. It's worth noting that genetic competition also may play a role in violence within family units. In particular, children—especially very young children—are far more likely to be killed by stepparents than by genetic parents (Daly & Wilson, 1988, 1996). The overall frequency of this event is low; most parents don't kill children. Yet if it happens, a stepparent is far more likely to be the perpetrator than a biological parent. As is true of the young male syndrome, this finding may reflect a deep-rooted desire to help one's own genes into the next generation instead of a competitor's genes.

We noted earlier that part of mating is retaining one's mate. People have a variety of tactics for doing this. Most of them are quite benign. Some can even be viewed as efforts at solidifying the relationship to make it resistant to temptation. However, some tactics of mate retention are coercive. Some men are so concerned about losing their mates—or unknowingly supporting a rival's child—that they become quite controlling. Tactics to control the woman sometimes escalate to violence against her (Hilton et al., 2000; Wilson & Daly, 1996). Sometimes that violence is a warning: Don't stray. Sometimes the violence is murder, ending all possibility of straying (Buss, 2005b). When killings occur *within* families, most victims are wives.

Although male violence against women is cause for great concern, we should also be clear that it is not just men who do this. Aggression against partners also occurs among women (Hilton et al., 2000).

Assessment

The orientation to personality that was discussed in the first part of this chapter developed as a branch of the dispositional perspective. In general, its ways of assessing personality reflect the dispositional view. What it offers primarily is content—some ideas about which traits to assess. As we said earlier, those who take the genetic view on personality feel that certain dispositions are inherited as biological substrates of personality. These, then, are the qualities to assess.

A second point made by this approach to personality concerns a more general issue regarding assessment in research. The issue is what kind of data to collect to measure the trait you want to study (an issue also discussed in Chapter 3). For example, in some twin studies, the data were self-report scales. In other studies, children were rated by their parents or by teachers. Occasionally, but not often, behavioral observations have been made of children at play.

It turns out that it may matter considerably which of these sources of data is used in the research, because different types of data don't always give the same answers about degree of genetic influence (Plomin & Foch, 1980). In general, parent ratings of children and self-ratings indicate genetic influence more reliably than do behavioral observations. (In fact, they may well overestimate the size of genetic effects [Saudino et al., 1995].) This raises questions about which kind of data to be most confident in. The importance of deciding which kind of measure to use is not unique to the biological approach. But it may be particularly important here because of the fact that twin studies are difficult and expensive.

Given the rise in influence of molecular genetics, some have raised the possibility that gene assessment will eventually be done as a better way of determining personality. Although it is too soon to be sure, many people prominent in this area see this as unlikely (e.g., Plomin & Crabbe, 2000). The reason is the belief that personality traits are influenced by many, many genes, each exerting a small effect. It will be hard enough to identify those genes, never mind use them as convenient personality tests.

Problems in Behavior, and Behavior Change

Let's turn now to problems in behavior. The genetic approach has made a major contribution here. Behavior geneticists have examined the possibility that several kinds of vulnerabilities to problems may be influenced by inheritance (see also Box 6.4). Molecular genetics is also starting to weigh in, but with the same problem as it has with respect to normal personality: that many genes are likely to be involved in any given problem rather than one or two.

SCHIZOPHRENIA AND BIPOLAR DISORDER

For many years, research on the behavior genetics of problems focused mainly on schizophrenia and bipolar disorder. Most of the research has been on schizophrenia, which is characterized by disorientation, confusion, cognitive disturbances, and a separation from reality.

Box 6.4 LIVING IN A POSTGENOMIC WORLD

The human genome is mapped. Researchers today know more than ever about the makeup of the human body and the functions of some of our genes (Plomin et al., 2003). The technology behind these advances is continuing its rapid development, with no signs of slowing down.

Mapping the human genome will surely yield benefits. Some disorders are caused by single genes. Knowing the map makes it easier to locate the genes. (For example, the gene for cystic fibrosis is in the middle of chromosome 7.) This information can be used in genetic counseling. People can be warned if they carry a gene for a disorder they may pass on to a child. Another benefit is genetic therapies, which now exist for some disorders— for example, to correct defects in producing blood cells. Some say the map of the genome, by allowing identification of genetic weaknesses, will usher in a new era of preventive medi-

cine, dramatically changing the way we deal with disease (Lewin, 1990).

The mapping of the genome excites imaginations, but it also raises concerns (Buchanan, Brock, Daniels, & Wikler, 2000; Fukuyama, 2002; Lynn, 2001; Stock, 2002). Knowing what genes control body and behavior raises serious ethical issues. For example, a great deal of pressure will doubtlessly arise to modify genes to create specific characteristics in new children, creating so-called designer babies (Plomin & Crabbe, 2000; Stock, 2002). Should this happen? Who is to decide what characteristics should be created? What happens to people whose genetic characteristics are viewed by society as inferior?

Knowledge about disorders also raises ethical issues. Will there be discrimination against people with particular genetic profiles? What happens to the cost of medical insurance when it's possible to know who is susceptible to what diseases? Will insurance even be *available* to people with susceptibilities? This isn't an idle

question. Already, insurance policies have been cancelled for entire families because of genetic problems in specific family members (Stolberg, 1994).

The same issue arises with respect to psychological disorders. If it's known that your genes predispose you to mania or depression, will you be able to get a job? Will you be able to have insurance against the possibility of needing treatment? The other side of this issue, however, is that it is likely that many patterns now seen as disorders are simply extremes of personality (Plomin & Crabbe, 2000). Clarity on this issue would follow from knowing what genes are involved in both the problem patterns and normal patterns. Such a realization might go a long way toward removing stigma from disorders.

In short, the project to map the genome holds out much promise, but it also raises very difficult issues that will have to be addressed. You may want to start thinking about them, because they're issues that are in your future—and the future of your children.

A well-known early study of genetic influence on schizophrenia by Gottesman and Shields (1972) began by recruiting twins admitted to a hospital with a diagnosis of schizophrenia. They sought out each one's co-twin and evaluated the co-twin's status. The term **concordance** is used to describe similarity of diagnosis. A pair of twins were concordant if they were both diagnosed as schizophrenic. This study found concordance rates of 50% among identical twins and 9% among fraternal twins. It thus appears that inheritance plays a role in schizophrenia. Indeed, this conclusion follows from over a dozen studies similar to this one.

It should be noted that the twin study data also indicate that life circumstances play a role in determining who shows schizophrenic symptoms openly (Plomin & Rende, 1991). Some people have the genetic susceptibility but don't develop the disorder. This interaction between a susceptibility and a suitable context to touch it off reflects a diathesis-stress view of disorder (discussed in Chapter 4). This is a theme that recurs in studying genetics and disorder.

Molecular genetic studies have also been done to try to isolate gene locations that relate to schizophrenia. Several locations have been suggested (Faraone, Taylor, & Tsuang, 2002; Owen, Williams, & O'Donovan, 2004; Straub et al., 2002). However, findings from studies such as these are often very difficult to repeat (DeLisi et al., 2002). Thus, there remains great uncertainty about what genes may be involved in schizophrenia.

A second disorder that appears to be affected by heredity is bipolar (manic–depressive) disorder. *Mania* is characterized by episodes of frenetic, hyperactive, grandiose, and talkative behavior, accompanied by a rush of ideas. Often the manic pattern is accompanied by positive emotion, but anger is also common. The onset of this disorder is usually sudden. As with schizophrenia, twin studies reveal very strong evidence of genetic contribution (McGuffin, Rijsdijk, Andrew, Sham, Katz, & Cardno, 2003).

There has also been molecular genetics research on this problem. One study linked bipolar disorder to a specific dominant gene on chromosome 11 in a group of Amish families (Egeland, Gerhard, Pauls, Sussex, & Kidd, 1987). Two other studies, however, found no link from the disorder to that chromosome, so this gene can't be the only one responsible for the disorder (Detera-Wadleigh, Berrettini, Goldin, Boorman, Anderson, & Gershon, 1987; Hodgkinson, Sherrington, Gurling, Marchbanks, & Reeders, 1987). Scientists continue to look for genetic markers of bipolar disorder, using the techniques of molecular genetics (Badner & Gershon, 2002).

It is clear that biology plays a major role in bipolar disorder. However, it is also clear that events in the environment are important to how the disorder is expressed. In this case, at least a little is known about what environmental influences matter. For example, lack of sleep makes people with the disorder especially vulnerable to manic episodes; so does experiencing success in attaining goals (S. L. Johnson, 2005; S. L. Johnson et al., 2000). Once again, at least in the short term, there is an interaction between genetic and environmental influences.

SUBSTANCE USE AND ANTISOCIAL BEHAVIOR

Another focus of research on the genetics of problems is substance abuse. Quite some time ago, Eysenck (1964b) found that MZ twins were more likely to share tendencies toward alcoholism than DZ twins. Similar findings, with information about the metabolic processes that underlie the difference, were reported by Schuckit and Rayses (1979). Another finding provides an interesting reflection of the interweaving of genetic and environmental influences (Dick & Rose, 2002). Genetic contributions to drinking in this study increased from about a third of the variance at age 16 to half the variance—in the same sample—at age 18.

Recent research has also implicated a specific gene in the craving for alcohol that some people experience after having a little (Hutchison, McGeary, Smolen, Bryan, & Swift, 2002). The gene turns out to be the long allele of the dopamine-related gene described earlier in the chapter. That was the gene that related to measures of reward seeking. That allele has also been linked to heroin addiction (Kotler et al., 1997; Li et al., 1997; Shao et al., 2006).

Another fast-growing area of research concerns genetics and antisocial behavior. Long ago, Eysenck (1964a) reported higher concordance rates among MZ than DZ twins on childhood behavior problems and adult crime. Further research on adult criminality tends to fit the picture of a genetic influence (DiLalla & Gottesman, 1991; Wilson & Herrnstein, 1985). Other research suggests that antisocial personality disorder is genetically influenced (Rowe, 1994; Vandenberg, Singer, & Pauls, 1986; Willerman, Loehlin, & Horn, 1992), and most observers now believe there are clear genetic influences on antisocial behavior (Moffitt, 2005b; Rhee & Waldman, 2002).

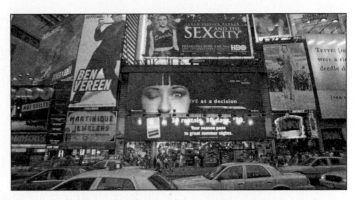

Some people believe that our cultural evolution has outstripped the ability of our biological evolution to keep up.

Once again, however, there appears to be evidence of an interaction between predisposition and environment. Moffitt (2005) reviewed research on antisocial behavior, looking specifically for interactions between genetics and environment and finding them. One of her conclusions was that we should not be framing questions in terms of whether genes influence this disorder but rather who is at greatest risk when placed in circumstances that pull for problem behavior. The search for interactions between genes and environment is likely to remain an important focus for studies of diverse problems, including this one (Moffitt, Caspi, & Rutter, 2006).

EVOLUTION AND PROBLEMS IN BEHAVIOR

A somewhat different view of certain behavior problems is suggested by sociobiology. Barash (1986) argued that many difficulties in human life stem from the fact that two kinds of evolution influence people. There is biological evolution, a very slow process that occurs over millennia. There is also cultural evolution, which is much faster. Your experiences of life stem partly from what biological evolution shaped humans to be during prehistory and partly from the cultural circumstances in which you live.

Barash pointed out that biological evolution prepared us for life in a world very different from the one we live in now. Cultural evolution has raced far ahead, and biological evolution can't keep up. Being in a world to which we don't quite belong, we are conflicted and alienated. Barash's point is a general one, not specific to a particular disorder, but it's an interesting one: That is, problems emerge when behavioral tendencies that have been built in as part of human nature conflict with pressures that are built into contemporary culture.

BEHAVIOR CHANGE: HOW MUCH IS POSSIBLE?

A major question about therapeutic behavior change is raised by the view under discussion in this chapter. Biologically based personality qualities—whether temperaments or not—are by definition firmly anchored in the person's constitutional functioning. How easy can it be to alter these aspects of personality in any major way, through *whatever* therapeutic processes are used? Psychotherapy may change the person to some extent. But how far against their biological nature can people be expected to bend?

This is an interesting issue, about which little is known. It's been suggested that even true temperaments can be modified, within limits (Buss & Plomin, 1984). But what are the limits? It seems likely that some kinds of therapeutic change are more difficult to create and sustain for some people than for others. For example, it will be harder for a therapy aimed at reducing emotional reactions to be effective for someone with high emotionality than for someone lower in that temperament. In fact, there may be some people whose constitutions make certain kinds of therapy so difficult as to be impractical.

Nonetheless, it should also be recognized that the heritability of personality, though strong, is not complete. There's a good deal of influence from experiences. Thus, the data that establish a genetic influence on personality also show that genetic determination is not total. The extent to which genetically coded tendencies limit behavior change is an important issue. The answer is not at all clear. It is clear, however, that psychological processes do matter, even for disorders that are strongly influenced by inheritance, such as bipolar disorder. Although medication is very important in the management of this disorder (see Chapter 7), psychological treatments of various kinds have also proven beneficial (Johnson & Leahy, 2003).

Inheritance and Evolution: Problems and Prospects

The biological perspective on personality has roots that go far back in the history of ideas. Yet today's views are in many ways quite new. Research on heritability of personality is still fairly recent in origin. Application of the ideas of evolutionary psychology is even more recent. With the advent of advances in molecular genetics, people are now trying to link particular genes with qualities of personality, an approach that's newer still.

In considering the usefulness of these biological ideas in thinking about personality, several issues arise. For example, temperaments are broad tendencies reflected in fundamental aspects of behavior. The fact that temperaments are so basic, however, raises a question about how to view their role in personality. Does it make more sense to think of temperaments as all of personality, as part of personality, or as the bedrock on which personality is constructed? Since many personality traits seem heritable and many of the traits relate conceptually to temperaments, perhaps we should view temperaments as the starting point from which the conceptually related traits emerge.

Another question is, How many traits are genetically influenced, and how many *look* heritable because they derive from the first group? Recent evidence suggests that facets of the five supertraits are separately heritable. This puts a different twist on the question. Maybe we should be asking whether the temperaments are really unitary, broad qualities that are just displayed in diverse ways or whether they are convenient aggregates of what are really separate traits.

A final question concerns the methods of behavioral genetics as a discipline. Although we didn't address this point in discussing the research, some have questioned whether the methods in this research really tell investigators what they believe they are being told (e.g., Haviland, McGuire, & Rothbaum, 1983; Wahlsten, 1990). Questions have also been raised about what kind of bridge can be built between quantitative *behavioral genetics*—which is about identifying sources of variability in data—and *molecular genetics*—which is about particular gene locations and what they do. These are extremely different phenomena (Greenberg, 2005; Partridge, 2005), yet we are treating them as though they were closely related. The issues here are very technical, and it's difficult to know how they will be resolved. But until they *are* resolved, there will remain at least a small cloud on the horizon of the genetic approach to personality.

Another aspect of the viewpoint discussed in this chapter is sociobiology and evolutionary psychology. This view on personality has been controversial during its relatively brief existence and has been criticized on several grounds (e.g., L. C. Miller, Putcha-Bhagavatula, & Pedersen, 2002). The early arguments of sociobiology were very theoretical, with little supporting evidence. Sociobiology was seen by some as a game of speculation, rather than a serious science. More than a few people scorned the ideas under discussion as unfalsifiable and indeed untestable.

In the past decade and a half, however, this situation changed dramatically. As more precise ideas were developed about the implications of evolutionary theory, this way of thinking led to a surge of studies. Evolutionary psychology is now an area of vigorous research activity. It seems clear that evolutionary thinking provides a wealth of hypotheses for researchers. Moreover, the hypotheses are becoming more and more sophisticated.

Nevertheless, there remains concern about whether the hypotheses being studied by these researchers really *depend on* evolutionary theory, as opposed to merely *being consistent* with it. Indeed, one recent critic has argued that support for many key evolutionary hypotheses is highly ambiguous and does not support the conclusions drawn (Buller, 2005a, 2005b). One challenge evolutionary psychology faces today is that of making clear predictions that resist alternative interpretations. This issue, of course, is faced by all views on personality, not just the evolutionary one. The issue, however, seems likely to remain an especially important one for this approach for some time.

Sociobiology and evolutionary psychology have also been criticized because their statements have disturbing political and social overtones. Some regard arguments about how human nature evolved as thinly veiled justifications for unfair social conditions in today's world (Kitcher, 1987, and the succeeding commentaries; see also Lewontin, Rose, & Kamin, 1984). That is, these ideas explain why men are bullies, why there's a double standard of sexual behavior for men and women, and why race and class differences exist. These explanations provide a basis for considering such conditions to be natural. This is only a small step from saying they should continue to exist (see Pratto & Hegarty, 2000). These overtones of evolutionary thinking are seen by some as racist and sexist and have prompted considerable hostility toward the theories among some people.

One response to this sort of criticism is to point out that evolution is a natural force that works dispassionately, based on the principles of reproduction and survival. In the arena of evolution, issues of equal rights and equal opportunities have no meaning. It may well be that in today's world, some of the results of evolution work against some people because evolution prepared us to fit not this world but the world of prehistory. If people are disadvantaged by the consequences of evolution, though, it's something that must be dealt with by the cultures that people have built. The fact that the theory explains why inequity exists can't be used as an argument that the theory is wrong. As you might expect, this response is not entirely satisfying to critics.

Despite controversies such as these, there remains a huge interest in evolutionary ideas in today's personality psychology. These ideas will not go away any time soon.

· SUMMARY ·

The approach to personality rooted in inheritance and evolution has two facets. One emphasizes that your personality is tied to the biological body you inherit. This idea goes far back in history, but today's version of the idea is quite different, emphasizing the role of genes.

Behavior genetics provides ways to find out whether personality differences are inherited. In twin studies, correlations among identical twins are compared with correlations among fraternal twins; in adoption studies, children are compared with their biological and adoptive families. Studies of identical twins raised apart provide yet a different look at the effects of inheritance and environment.

Twin research has been used to look at genetic contributions to a variety of dispositions, starting with temperaments: broad inherited traits that appear early in life. Evidence supports genetic influences on activity level, emotionality, and sociability. Other temperaments have been suggested, including temperaments for approach, avoidance, and effortful control. There also is evidence of genetic influence in the "big five" supertraits and other variables. It's unclear whether the "big five" derive from (or duplicate) the temperaments studied under other names. It is also unclear whether hereditary influences on other variables depend on associations between the other variable and a temperament. Recent developments in molecular genetics provide a new tool in the search for genetic influences on personality. Now there is evidence of specific genes playing roles in traits, including novelty seeking and neuroticism.

The idea that dispositions are genetically influenced can be extended a step further, to the suggestion that many aspects of human social behavior are products of evolution. This idea is behind an area of work termed *sociobiology* or *evolutionary psychology*. Sociobiologists propose ways to account for various aspects of human behavior, even behavior that on the face of it seems not to provide an evolutionary advantage. Altruism, for example, is understood as people acting for the benefit of their family groups, so that the family's genes are more likely to be continued (kin selection). This idea has been extended to the notion that people are attracted to other people who share their genetic makeup.

The evolutionary view also has implications concerning mate selection, including the idea that males and females use different strategies. The male strategy is to mate whenever possible, and males are drawn to signs of reproductive capability. The female strategy is to seek the best male available, and females are drawn to signs of resources. People use the relevant strategies and act in ways that make them seem better candidates as mates. Mating pressures also may lead to aggression among young men. Theory suggests that violence is most likely among men of reproductive age who are in poor reproductive circumstances. Evidence seems to bear this out, along with the idea that much violence concerns conflicts over status.

The genetic approach to personality says little about assessment except to suggest what dispositions are particularly important to assess—those that have biological links. Assessment directly from genes seems unlikely soon, due to the probable involvement of many genes in any given trait. With regard to problems in behavior, there is substantial evidence that schizophrenia and manic–depressive disorder are affected by heredity, as are substance abuse tendencies and antisocial tendencies. As elsewhere, this area is beginning to use the tools of molecular biology to search for genetic influences.

With regard to therapeutic behavior change, this approach raises a question on the basis of studies of temperament: How much can people be expected to change, even with therapy, in directions that deviate from their biological makeup?

· GLOSSARY ·

Activity level   The overall output of a person's energy or behavior.

Adoption study   A study of resemblances between children and their adoptive and biological parents.

Allele   Some version of a particular gene.

Assortative mating   Mating based on choice of specific characteristics rather than random.

Behavioral genetics   The study of inheritance of behavioral qualities.

Cerebrotonia   A mental overintensity that promotes apprehensiveness and social inhibition.

Concordance   Agreement on some characteristic between a twin and a co-twin.

Directional selection   Evolution in which one extreme of a dimension is more adaptive than the other.

Dizygotic (DZ) twins   Fraternal twins (overlapping genetically 50%, on average).

Ectomorphy   A tendency toward frail thinness.

Effortful control   A tendency to be focused, restrained, and planful.

Emotionality   The tendency to become emotionally aroused easily.

Endomorphy   A tendency toward obesity.

Ethology   The study of animals in their natural environment.

Genetic similarity theory   The idea that people work toward reproducing genes similar to their own.

Genome   The sequence of the genes contained in the full complement of chromosomes.

Genotype   The particular version of a gene that a given person or group has.

Heritability   An estimate of how much variance of some characteristic is accounted for by inheritance.

Inclusive fitness   The passing on of genes through the survival of relatives.

Mesomorphy   A tendency toward muscularity.

Molecular genetics   The study of how alleles of specific genes relate to other observed differences.

Monozygotic (MZ) twins   Identical twins (overlapping genetically 100%).

Polymorphism   The characteristic of having more than one allele for a given gene.

Reciprocal altruism   Helping others with the expectation the help will be returned.

Siblings   Brothers and sisters.

Sociability   The tendency to prefer being with people over being alone.

Sociobiology   The study of the evolutionary basis for social behavior.

Somatotonia   Energetic desire for adventure and physical activity.

Somatotype   The description of a person's body configuration along three dimensions.

Stabilizing selection   Evolution in which intermediate values of a dimension are most adaptive.

Temperaments   Inherited traits that appear early in life.

Twin study   A study comparing similarity between MZ twins against similarity between DZ twins.

Viscerotonia   A relaxed sociability and love of comfort.

CHAPTER 7

Biological Processes and Personality

Gina craves adventure. She always seems to be widening her circle of friends and activities. It's as though she needs the stimulation to keep her alive and happy. Her boyfriend, Leo, shies away from it. All the noise and action seem too much for him. He's more comfortable when things are less intense and he can plan his activities. Oddly enough, both of them feel their bodies are telling them what's best for them, even though what's "best" is so different from the one to the other.

THE IDEA that people's personalities are somehow embedded in the makeup of their bodies was the starting point for Chapter 6. There we focused on the idea that genetics play a big role in what people are like. That idea accounts for why people are different from one another (they inherit different traits). It also accounts for why people are the same (evolution shaped certain tendencies into the human species as a whole).

The ideas in Chapter 6 are definitely biological. If something is genetically caused, the influence has to occur through a biological process. But the ideas in Chapter 6 say little about how the effects are *exerted*. That is, knowing that traits are inherited says nothing about the process by which genes influence the behaviors that eventually emerge.

In this chapter, we take the same starting point: the idea that personality is embedded in people's bodies. This time, though, we focus on the idea that personality is influenced by the *workings* of the body. Now we consider some questions about what the body is organized to do. The view taken now is that personality reflects the operation of these processes of the body.

As in the last chapter, there's room for similarities among people and also differences. The similarities reflect the fact that everyone has a nervous system and an endocrine system. The systems have the same basic structure and functions from one person to another. The differences reflect the fact that parts of the nervous system and endocrine system are more active or more responsive in some people than in others.

Eysenck: Extraversion, Neuroticism, and Brain Functions

One of the first modern attempts to link personality to biological functions was that of Hans Eysenck (see Box 7.1). Recall from Chapter 4 that Eysenck saw personality as composed largely of two supertraits: neuroticism and extraversion. He saw both of these as rooted in the body.

EXTRAVERSION AND CORTICAL AROUSAL

Introverts are quiet, introspective, and disinterested in social activity; extraverts are outgoing, uninhibited, and immersed in social activity. Eysenck (1967, 1981) argued that this difference derives from the degree to which the cerebral cortex is activated. When the context is highly activated, the person is alert. When it's not, the person is sluggish and drowsy. Eysenck proposed that introverts normally have higher cortical arousal than extraverts. Because they have higher base levels, it's easy for them to get overaroused. They may refrain from social interaction because it gets them overstimulated. Extraverts, with lower baseline levels, seek stimulation to bring their arousal up.

BOX 7.1 THE THEORIST AND THE THEORY

The Many-Faceted Contributions of Hans Eysenck

Hans Eysenck was one of the most eclectic theorists in psychology. As described in Chapter 4, he played a major role in the dispositional view of personality. He also studied inheritance and tried to understand how the nervous system relates to personality. His interests didn't stop there, however. Eysenck wrote about topics as diverse as intelligence, politics, the links between personality and health, parapsychology, and astrology. He published more than 50 books and hundreds of articles and was often embroiled in controversy (which he appeared to relish).

Eysenck's parents were actors in Germany, where he was born in 1916. His parents divorced when he was two, and he lived with his grandmother for years afterward. Eysenck grew quickly into a self-confident and strong-willed young man. Two anecdotes illustrate his tenacity (Gibson, 1981). When he was about 8, he was called on during singing class to perform a solo passage. He declined on the grounds that his voice wasn't any good, but the teacher insisted. He finally went ahead but sang so poorly the teacher thought he was mocking the lesson. The teacher was about to punish him, but Eysenck struck first: He took the teacher's thumb in his teeth and held on like a bulldog, not letting go until the headmaster intervened.

The second incident occurred when Eysenck was in high school, during the period when the Nazis were seizing power. His teacher said that Jews were known to be lacking in military valor. Eysenck set off to explore this issue and returned with the fact that Jewish soldiers had earned an extra-high rate of military honors during World War I. This incident illustrates his tendency to take on controversy willingly and also his dedication to scientific evidence.

Eysenck later went to England for university studies. He had decided to study physics and astronomy, but he made an error that changed the path of his life—and that of psychology. Prospective students had to take a set of exams in the areas of their intended study. Eysenck inadvertently took the wrong exams, making him eligible to major only in subjects other than his chosen ones. Because psychology was the most scientific of the majors available at that point, he decided to study psychology.

In short, the qualities that mark Eysenck's contributions to personality psychology can be seen in his own life, including an extremely diverse range of interests, a tenacity about sticking with what he believed, and an enjoyment of controversy and being the center of attention. All those qualities were apparent early in his life. The same qualities also play a role in a central construct of his theory: extraversion.

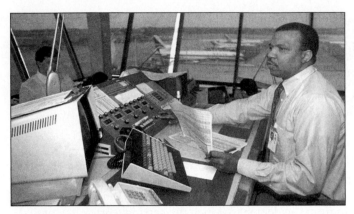

Laboratory studies suggest that introverts may do better than extraverts at tasks that require the monitoring of slowly changing visual displays, as is required in the work of air traffic controllers.

This influences the kinds of situations introverts and extraverts prefer. Introverts should prefer lower levels of stimulation—but not *too* low, or it will get boring even to them. Extraverts should prefer higher levels—but not *too* high, or it will get overwhelming even to them. Research has shown not only that the two groups prefer different levels of stimulation but that they also function better with different levels of stimulation (Geen, 1984).

Other evidence also fits the idea that introverts and extraverts differ in alertness. Consider *vigilance tasks,* which require you to be alert for specific stimuli. For example, you might have to listen to a long series of numbers and press a button whenever you hear three odd ones in a row. If your mind wanders, you will miss some of what you're listening for. Introverts miss less than extraverts (Claridge, 1967). Another source of evidence is drug effects. If introverts are already alert, they shouldn't need as much of a stimulant to reach a given level of arousal. On the other hand, introverts should need *more* of a depressant drug to reach a given level of unalertness. This seems to be the case (Claridge, 1967; Eysenck, 1983).

NEUROTICISM AND EMOTIONAL AROUSAL

Eysenck also proposed a neural basis for neuroticism (emotionality). He said that people who are higher on this trait are more easily aroused in the brain's emotion centers. Eysenck thought this had two implications. First, emotional arousal causes behavioral reflections of both extraverts and introverts to emerge more fully. It makes both of them become "more of what they are."

Second, emotional arousal can set the stage for conditioning, because emotional reactions sometimes result in conditioning (see Chapter 12). Eysenck said that introverts condition easily, because they're high in cortical arousal. If they also happen to be highly emotional, they'll have emotions in many settings and thus many opportunities for conditioning. Because much of the conditioning during childhood arises from punishment, the emotions that get conditioned are mostly negative. As a result, Eysenck argued, neurotic introverts should be vulnerable to anxiety and depression.

When neuroticism combines with extraversion, the effects are different. Extraverts don't condition well, because they're less aroused cortically. Thus, they don't learn from punishment. Extraverts who happen also to be highly emotional therefore respond to the emotions especially impulsively. They display a lack of socialization.

Eysenck's effort to link personality to aspects of brain function was a path-breaking one. However, brain functioning was not as well understood when he wrote as it is now. Changes in knowledge have greatly changed people's views of how brain functions and personality relate.

Incentive Approach System

Within the past 20 years or so, a number of theorists have proposed ideas about how the nervous system relates to personality. The ideas vary in focus. Some concern what parts of the brain are involved in certain kinds of actions. Some concern what brain chemicals are involved in certain kinds of actions. As did Eysenck, all of them take what might be called a *functional approach*. That is, they ask, what *functions* do particular kinds of behavior serve? The various types of behavior then are linked to ideas about brain processes, and both are also linked to personality.

Many people are working hard on this topic, and the literature is growing explosively. There are broad areas of agreement, but there are also disagreements. There's a lot of consensus about major themes, but there are also lots of ways to slice the pie. People differ in where they draw the lines for slicing.

BEHAVIORAL APPROACH, ACTIVATION, ENGAGEMENT, OR FACILITATION

Most theorists of this group believe there's a set of brain structures that cause animals to approach **incentives**: things they desire. Several theorists have made assertions about parts of the brain involved in this system, though they're not in full agreement (Cloninger, 1988; Davidson, 1992, 1995; Davidson, Jackson, & Kalin, 2000; Depue & Collins, 1999; Depue & Iacono, 1989; J. A. Gray, 1982, 1991). Although there is a great deal of ongoing effort to figure out what parts of the brain are involved, we will say only a little about that here. We will focus instead on the functional properties of the brain systems—how they are believed to be reflected in behavior and experience.

The structures involved in approach have been given several names: the *activation system* (Cloninger, 1987; Fowles, 1980), *behavioral engagement system* (Depue, Krauss, & Spoont, 1987), *behavioral facilitation system* (Depue & Iacono, 1989), and **behavioral approach system** (J. A. Gray, 1987, 1990, 1994a, 1994b), often abbreviated as **BAS.** You might think of this system as regulating the psychic gas pedal, moving you toward what you want. It's a "go" system, a reward-seeking system (Fowles, 1980).

This set of brain structures is presumed to be involved whenever a person is pursuing an incentive. It is likely that certain parts of the brain are involved in the pursuit of food, others in the pursuit of sex, and others in the pursuit of shade on a hot summer day. But it is thought that the separate parts also link up to an overall BAS. Thus, the BAS is seen as a general mechanism to go after things you want. BAS doesn't rev you up "in neutral," though, with no incentive in mind (Depue & Collins, 1999). It's engaged only in the active pursuit of incentives.

The BAS is also held to be responsible for many kinds of positive emotions (e.g., hope, eagerness, and excitement). These emotions can be viewed as reflecting the anticipation of getting incentives. Researchers have pursued this idea in studies of brain activity. Richard Davidson and his colleagues (and others) have studied what brain areas are active by recording electrical activity (Davidson, 1988, 1992, 1995; Davidson & Sutton, 1995) or by using imaging techniques that capture activity in other ways. While that's happening, the people are exposed to stimuli such as video clips or still images that were chosen to create specific kinds of emotional reactions. The question is which parts of the brain become more active in various situations.

A variety of evidence indicate that incentives (and thus positive feelings) activate the left prefrontal cortex. More left prefrontal activity has been found in adults presented with incentives (Sobotka, Davidson, & Senulis, 1992) or positive emotional adjectives (Cacioppo & Petty, 1980), and in 10-month-olds viewing their mothers approaching (Fox & Davidson, 1988). Higher *resting* levels in that area predict positive responses to happy films (Wheeler, Davidson, & Tomarken, 1993). Self-reported BAS sensitivity also relates to higher resting levels in that area (Harmon-Jones & Allen,

1997; Sutton & Davidson, 1997). Findings such as these led Davidson and his colleagues to two conclusions: First, the tendency to experience many positive emotions relates to an approach system. Second, that system is based partly in the left prefrontal cortex.

More Issues in Approach

Recent evidence suggests that what underlies left-prefrontal activation is not positive feelings but something else about the approach motivational process (Harmon-Jones, Lueck, Fearn, & Harmon-Jones, 2006). Sometimes a desire to approach is thwarted. Sometimes a desire to approach is specifically a desire to inflict pain on someone. In both cases, the approach system is engaged, but the emotions—frustration and anger—have a negative valence rather than a positive one. Several studies have linked such emotional experiences to left-prefrontal activation and BAS sensitivity (Carver, 2004; Fox & Davidson, 1988; Harmon-Jones & Allen, 1997; Harmon-Jones & Sigelman, 2001; Harmon-Jones, Vaughn-Scott, Mohr, Sigelman, & Harmon-Jones, 2004).

Another project has linked BAS sensitivity to conditioning. Because the BAS responds selectively to incentives, BAS sensitivity should relate to conditioning involving *positive* outcomes, but not to conditioning involving *negative* outcomes. Research by Zinbarg and Mohlman (1998) supports this idea. A self-report measure of BAS sensitivity predicted speed at learning cues of reward in a conditioning task. This scale did not relate to speed at learning cues of punishment.

One more thing about the approach function: Some neurobiological evidence suggests that there may be social incentive and social threat systems, which overlap partially but not entirely with the more general approach and avoidance systems (Depue & Morrone-Strupinksy, 2005; Panksepp, 1998). Thus, there may be specialized sensitivities to incentives and threats *within relationships*. In support of this idea, Gable (2006) found that hope for affiliation predicted social approach goals and fear of rejection predicted social avoidance goals. Elliot, Gable, and Mapes (2006) have developed a measure to assess social approach and avoidance goals to investigate this idea further.

To sum up, people with reactive approach systems are highly sensitive to incentives, or to cues of good things about to happen. Those whose approach systems are less reactive don't respond as much (either behaviorally or emotionally) to such cues. For example, consider two people with tickets to an upcoming concert by a band they like. Melanie gets excited whenever she thinks about the concert (although it isn't until next week). Every time she thinks about it, she's ready to jump in the car. Melanie is very high in incentive reactivity, or BAS sensitivity. Barbara, on the other hand, is more calm about it. She knows she'll enjoy the concert, but she's not so responsive to thoughts of potential reward. Barbara has less incentive reactivity.

Neurotransmitters and the Approach System

Operation of the approach system has been tentatively linked to a specific **neurotransmitter** in the brain. A *neurotransmitter* is a chemical involved in sending messages along nerve pathways. There are many of them, and they seem to have somewhat different roles. Several theorists have argued that a neurotransmitter called **dopamine** is involved in the approach system (Cloninger, 1988; Depue & Collins, 1999; Zuckerman, 1994).

As we noted in Chapter 6, two research teams (Benjamin et al., 1996; Ebstein et al., 1996) linked dopamine to a specific gene, though subsequent research found the link wasn't as reliable as it seemed at first (Ebstein, 2006). The finding was that people with one version of that gene scored higher on personality scales related to approach (novelty seeking). That finding linked *genetics* (variation in a particular gene) to a biological *process* variable (dopamine function) to an aspect of *behavior* (approach of incentives).

Others have used very different methods to study dopamine function. One technique is to assess individual differences in dopamine reactivity using biomedical indicators of response to drug challenges. In several studies, higher dopamine reactivity related to higher trait levels of positive emotionality (Depue, 1995; Depue, Luciana, Arbisi, Collins, & Leon, 1994). Others have used similar procedures to relate dopamine to novelty seeking (Hansenne et al., 2002). Depue and Collins (1999) linked dopamine to aspects of extraversion, including social dominance, enthusiasm, assertiveness, and energy. Research using monkeys also linked dopamine function to greater social dominance (Kaplan, Manuck, Fontenot, & Mann, 2002).

Dopamine function has also been related to performance on particular kinds of tasks (Wacker, Chavanon, & Stemmler, 2006). Higher levels of dopamine relate to being able to hold larger amounts of information in working memory (Barch, 2004; Seamans & Yang, 2004). A link from dopamine to approach is suggested by the fact that people who report high BAS sensitivity also can hold more information in working memory (J. R. Gray & Braver, 2002).

It's also been suggested that low dopamine levels tend to keep people focused on one goal, whereas higher levels produce a flexible shifting among goals (Dreisbach & Goschke, 2004). Of course, shifting of goals can also be seen as distractibility. Consistent with this is evidence that links high levels of dopamine explicitly to distractibility (Frank & O'Reilly, 2006).

It has long been believed that dopamine is involved in reward-based learning (Frank & Claus, 2006; Holroyd & Coles, 2002). For example, a substance that disrupts dopamine function impairs instrumental learning and performance (Andrzejewski, Spencer, & Kelley, 2006). The idea that dopamine is involved in reward-based learning has evolved over the years. One current view is that bursts of dopamine in response to reward increase the learning (and the execution) of approach behavior and that dips in dopamine after nonreward increase the learning (and the execution) of avoidance responses (Frank, Seeberger, & O'Reilly, 2004).

It may be, however, that the effect of dopamine is more on the performance than on actual learning. Studies of mice seem to show that the mice don't need dopamine to learn from reward and that dopamine doesn't increase the value of the reward. However, dopamine is necessary for the mice to *want* the reward and *seek* it in goal-directed action (Peciña, Cagniard, Berridge, Aldridge, & Zhuang, 2003; Robinson, Sandstrom, Denenberg, & Palmiter, 2005). Some have concluded that dopamine is mainly about motivation rather than learning—more specifically, that dopamine is involved in attaching motivational importance to stimuli (Wise, 2004).

Others have looked at these effects from a different angle. Dopaminergic neurons respond intensely when a reward occurs unpredictably, but respond less to rewards that are expected, and diminish responses when an expected reward fails to occur (Schultz, 2000, 2006). This pattern has been seen as indicating that dopamine neurons are involved in detecting unexpected events of two kinds—better and worse than expected. That is, there's an increase in activation when a desirable event is better than expected, no change in activity when an event occurs as expected, and a decrease in activity when an event is worse than expected (Schultz, 2006).

Although discussion of dopamine usually focuses on the context of approach, there is also some evidence of its involvement in stressful situations. There have been a number of reports of dopamine release in animals in response to stress (see Pruessner, Champagne, Meaney, & Dagher, 2004). People undergoing a stressful, anxiety-inducing task have also been shown to experience dopamine elevation (Pruessner et al., 2004). It seems certain that dopamine has multiple functions, rather than one (Seamans & Yang, 2004). Though some of these functions relate to the management of approach, it may not be that all do.

Behavioral Avoidance, or Withdrawal, System

The prior section described an approach system. Many theorists also assume a somewhat distinct system that reacts to punishers and threats, rather than incentives. Gray (1987, 1990, 1994a, 1994b) called it the **behavioral inhibition system (BIS).** Others have labeled a threat-responsive system as an *avoidance system* (Cloninger, 1987) or *withdrawal system* (Davidson, 1988, 1992, 1995). Activity in this system may cause people to *inhibit* movement (especially if they are currently approaching an incentive) or pull back from what they just encountered. You might think of this system as a psychic brake pedal, a "stop" system. You might think of it instead as a "throw-it-into-reverse" system.

The avoidance system is responsive to cues of punishment or danger. When this system is engaged, the person may stop and scan for further cues about the threat, or the person may pull back. Since this is the system that responds to threat, danger, or other to-be-avoided stimuli, this system is also thought to be responsible for feelings such as anxiety, guilt, and revulsion.

Once again, research on cortical activity is consistent with this general view. We said earlier that left-prefrontal areas are more active when people are happy. Right-prefrontal areas are more active when people are feeling anxiety or aversion: for example, when viewing film clips that induce fear and disgust (Davidson, Ekman, Saron, Senulis, & Friesen, 1990). Higher resting levels in that area predict more negative feelings when seeing such films, and they also relate to self-reports of BIS sensitivity (Harmon-Jones & Allen, 1997; Sutton & Davidson, 1997). Findings such as these led Davidson and his colleagues to argue that anxiety relates to a behavioral withdrawal system, which involves the right-prefrontal cortex.

Research on conditioning has also examined the sensitivity of this system. The BIS was theorized to be reactive to punishments, not incentives. Thus, BIS sensitivity should relate to conditioning for *negative* outcomes, not positive ones. This was found by Zinbarg and Mohlman (1998). A self-report measure of BIS sensitivity predicted speed at learning cues of punishment (but not cues of reward). Similar results were reported by Corr, Pickering, and Gray (1997).

To sum up this section, people with reactive avoidance systems are sensitive to threat. This dimension reflects a trait of anxiety proneness. As an example of how it influences experiences, think of two people who just took a psychology test and suspect they did badly. Anxiety-prone Randy is almost in a panic about it. Jessica, who is less anxiety prone, is bothered hardly at all. One of them is reacting emotionally to the sense of threat; the other isn't.

Threat sensitivity and incentive sensitivity are thought to be relatively separate. People presumably differ from each other on both. As a result, all combinations of high and low BAS and BIS sensitivity probably exist. As an example, it might be intuitive to think of sociability as being the opposite of shyness, but that's too simple (Schmidt, 1999). It's possible to be both very sociable (drawn to social incentives) and very shy (fearful of social interaction and avoiding it).

A REVISED VIEW OF BIS FUNCTION

Thus far, we've treated the label *BIS* as equivalent to the label *withdrawal system*. However, differences of opinion have arisen about what to call what. In 2000, Gray and McNaughton revised Gray's (1987, 1990) theory. In the revision, inhibition, instead of threat sensitivity, is the core feature of the BIS (fitting its label: behavioral inhibition system). In the new view, the BIS responds to conflict—of any kind—by inhibiting action and searching for more information. In the new view, a different system altogether is sensitive to threat. Thus, use of the term BIS from the newer Gray and McNaughton (2000) point of view differs from previous use.

This change obviously creates potential for confusion. To minimize confusion, in the rest of the chapter, we do not refer to *BIS* at all. We continue to refer to a threat sensitivity system as managing avoidance. Later on in the chapter, we take up the inhibition of action, because that is a very important function. When we do so, however, we use new terms altogether.

NEUROTRANSMITTERS AND THE AVOIDANCE SYSTEM

As with incentive sensitivity, there have also been efforts to link threat sensitivity to a particular neurotransmitter, but with less consensus. **Serotonin** has long been believed by some people to be involved in threat sensitivity or anxiety (Cloninger, 1987; Handley, 1995; Lesch & Mössner, 1998). However, that view has been strongly challenged (Depue, 1995; Depue & Spoont, 1986; Panksepp & Cox, 1986; Soubrié, 1986; Zuckerman, 2005). The dispute isn't over, and the evidence is complex. Our interpretation of it, however, suggests that serotonin's main influence lies elsewhere (Carver & Miller, 2006). We return to this issue later on.

Another candidate for involvement in anxiety is *gamma-aminobutyric acid,* more commonly known as *GABA* (Roy-Byrne, 2005). There is some research linking sensitivity of GABA receptors to neuroticism (Glue, Wilson, Coupland, Ball, & Nutt, 1995). However, most of what is known about GABA and anxiety comes from studies of anxiety disorders. In fact, most of the studies focus specifically on panic disorder (Zwanzger & Rupprecht, 2005). People with panic disorder have relatively low levels of GABA (Goddard et al., 2001). Treatments that increase GABA reduce anxiety in panic patients (Zwanzger & Rupprecht, 2005).

Yet another likely contributor to the biology of threat is *norepinephrine*. Norepinephrine is produced in response to stress (Morilak et al., 2005), and there is evidence linking it to panic reactions (Bailey, Argyropoulis, Lightman, & Nutt, 2003). Recent research has also shown that problems in regulation of norepinephrine relate selectively to anxiety disorders (Cameron, Abelson, & Young, 2004). This seems to link this chemical specifically to threat sensitivity.

Although there are several candidates for involvement in the brain systems that manage anxiety and avoidance, it may be wise to resist jumping to conclusions. This is an active area of research, and it seems likely that the eventual answer will involve some complexity.

Relating Approach and Avoidance Systems to Traits or Temperaments

Let's stop and look at what we've said thus far in the chapter. Many theorists converge on the idea that one brain system manages approach of incentives and another manages withdrawal from threats (Cacioppo, Gardner, & Berntson, 1999; Watson, Wiese, Vaidya, & Tellegen, 1999). The one that manages approach also creates excitement and other positive feelings. The one that manages withdrawal creates anxiety. How do these ideas fit with ideas from previous chapters?

It's possible to draw some very strong connections. The avoidance system links easily to the trait of neuroticism. As noted in Chapter 6, although some labels for that trait are neutral, anxiety is always at its core. Thus, Larsen and Ketelaar (1991) found that neuroticism predicts susceptibility to a manipulation of anxiety; Carver and White (1994) found the same effect for a measure of threat sensitivity. In sum, neuroticism and anxiety proneness have a great deal in common. (Elliot and Thrash [2002] also provide support for this idea.) In fact, there's little doubt that the brain system we've been describing regarding avoidance is critical to neuroticism.

As also noted in Chapter 4, Tellegen (1985) postulated a temperament termed **negative emotionality.** The idea is that some people are built to have negative emotions frequently and others less frequently (see also Watson & Clark, 1984; Watson & Tellegen, 1985; Watson et al., 1999). This concept resembles both neuroticism and threat sensitivity. As noted in Chapter 6, developmental theorists have also posited an avoidance temperament (e.g., Derryberry & Rothbart, 1997; Eisenberg, 2002; Eisenberg et al., 2004; Kochanska & Knaack, 2003; Rothbart, Ahadi, & Evans, 2000; Rothbart, Ahadi, Hershey, & Fisher, 2001; Rothbart & Bates, 1998; Rothbart & Posner, 1985). Again, there is a good fit.

With respect to approach, there appears to be a link between the BAS and extraversion. Fitting these two together is a little trickier than matching neuroticism and avoidance, partly because theorists differ about what defines *extraversion.* Definitions usually include a sense of activity and agency (Morrone, Depue, Scherer, & White, 2000). Extraversion also suggests a preference for being with others, or sociability (Depue & Morrone-Strupinsky, 2005). Sometimes there's a quality of social dominance or potency (Depue & Collins, 1999). All definitions seem to include a tendency to experience positive emotions.

These various extraversion packages resemble BAS function fairly well. Extraverts are responsive to positive mood manipulations (Larsen & Ketelaar, 1991); those high in BAS sensitivity similarly have more positive feelings to impending reward (Carver & White, 1994). Measures of extraversion correlate with measures of BAS sensitivity (Carver & White, 1994). As noted in Chapter 4, Tellegen (1985) postulated a temperament termed **positive emotionality,** which relates closely to extraversion, and developmental theorists also assume an approach temperament. Zelenski and Larsen (1999) found that measures of extraversion and several BAS constructs all were interrelated, and as a set, they predicted positive feelings. Thus, there is a good deal of consistency.

THE ROLE OF SOCIABILITY

Still, when fitting extraversion to approach sensitivity, there are a couple of areas of uncertainty. Table 7.1 lists several theorists who have written about extraversion and similar traits. The table also lists some qualities the theorists see as belonging to these

Table 7.1 Several Theorists and Qualities They Believe Belong to Extraversion (and alternative traits closely related to extraversion). All incorporate pursuit of incentives and a tendency to experience positive emotions. Many, though not all, include a quality of sociability. A few also include impulsiveness.

Theorist	Preferred Term	Term Incorporates:			
		Pursuit of Incentives	Sociability	Impulsivity	Positive Emotions
Eysenck	Extraversion	x	x		x
Costa & McCrae	Extraversion	x	x		x
Depue	Extraversion	x	x	x	x
Zuckerman	Sociability	x	x		x
Tellegen	Positive emotionality	x	x		x
Cloninger	Novelty seeking	x		x	x
Gray	BAS–Impulsivity	x		x	x

traits. As you can see, there are two qualities for which some difference of opinion arises.

One issue concerns the social quality that's usually considered part of extraversion. That quality is missing from Gray's view of the BAS. That may be simply because Gray ignored sociability altogether. One way to resolve things would be to view BAS sensitivity as sensitivity to *social* incentives. Given that humans are a very social species, it might make sense to think of human approach primarily in terms of approaching social interaction. As noted earlier in the chapter, however, some postulate a separate approach subsystem that's specialized to regulate social approach. Perhaps extraversion actually is a blend of overall BAS sensitivity and social-specific BAS sensitivity.

On the other hand, several recent studies seem to suggest that sociality per se is not the core quality of extraversion. One of these projects, mentioned in Chapter 4, was by Lucas, Diener, Grob, Suh, and Shao (2000). Their studies led them to conclude that the core of extraversion is *reward sensitivity* and the tendency to experience *positive affect*. They inferred that extraverts' social tendencies stem from the fact that social interaction is one source of positive experiences. Indeed, Lucas and Diener (2001) found extraverts were drawn to situations that offered opportunities for pleasant experiences, whether social or nonsocial.

THE ROLE OF IMPULSIVITY

The second issue on which conceptualizations of extraversion differ concerns impulsivity. In this case, however, fewer people currently argue that it should be part of extraversion. Gray used the word *impulsivity* for incentive sensitivity, but it was an unfortunate choice, as he didn't seem to have issues of impulse control in mind. Cloninger includes a kind of impulsiveness in his construct of novelty seeking, but impulsiveness is also involved in his threat sensitivity construct (see Carver & Miller, 2006). Eysenck included impulsiveness in extraversion for years, but he moved it to psychoticism because it consistently related better to psychoticism than to extraversion. Depue and Collins (1999) said that impulsivity with positive affect (the key to extraversion) belongs in extraversion but impulsivity without it doesn't.

Relevant to this issue is a study by Zelenski and Larsen (1999) mentioned earlier. They factor analyzed several personality measures, including measures of impulsivity and threat and incentive sensitivity. They found that measures of impulsivity loaded on a different factor than did extraversion (which loaded on the BAS factor). Also relevant to this issue is evidence from monkey research. One study (Fairbanks, 2001) found that social dominance, which many see as part of extraversion, relates to moderate impulsivity—not high or low.

On the whole, the evidence suggests that impulsivity does not belong in extraversion. Where, then, does it belong?

Impulse, Constraint, Sensation Seeking, and Effortful Control

Many people believe that there's at least one more biologically based dimension of personality. It has had several labels. In each case, the construct incorporates a quality of planfulness versus impulsivity. One label for this dimension is **sensation seeking.** Marvin Zuckerman (e.g., 1971, 1985, 1991, 1992, 1993, 1994, 2005) and his colleagues have studied this variable extensively.

People high in sensation seeking are in search of new, varied, and exciting experiences. Compared to people lower on this trait, they're faster drivers (Zuckerman & Neeb, 1980). They are also more likely to use drugs (Zuckerman, 1979), to increase alcohol use over time (Newcomb & McGee, 1991), to do high-risk sports such as skydiving (Hymbaugh & Garrett, 1974), and to engage in risky antisocial behaviors (Horvath & Zuckerman, 1993). They are more sexually experienced and sexually responsive (Fisher, 1973), and when in relationships, they're more dissatisfied (Thronquist, Zuckerman, & Exline, 1991). In the army, they're more likely to volunteer for combat units (Hobfoll, Rom, & Segal, 1989).

FUNCTIONS OF THE SENSATION-SEEKING DIMENSION

We said earlier that theorists of this group tend to use a functional approach—that is, look for the purpose that a given system might serve. What might be the function of a dimension of sensation seeking? At least two possibilities have been suggested. An early view was that it regulates exposure to stimulus intensity (Zuckerman, 1979, 1991, 1994). High sensation seekers open themselves to stimulation; low sensation seekers protect themselves from it.

Both of these tendencies would have advantages and disadvantages. People high in sensation seeking should function well in overstimulating conditions such as combat, but they may display antisocial and even manic qualities when the situation is less demanding. People lower in sensation seeking are better adapted to most circumstances of life, but they may "shut down" psychologically when things get too intense.

Another broader view of this trait's function relates it to the demands of social living. Zuckerman (1991, 1993) found a higher-order factor he calls **impulsive unsocialized sensation seeking (IUSS).** He thinks IUSS concerns a capacity to inhibit behavior in service of social adaptation. People high on IUSS don't do this very well. IUSS relates

Sensation seekers like to seek out new, varied, and exciting experiences.

inversely to sociability and positively to trait aggressiveness (Zuckerman, 1996; Zuckerman, Kuhlman, Joireman, Teta, & Kraft, 1993). It has been implicated in antisocial personality disorder (Krueger et al., 1994; Rowe, 2001; Zuckerman, 1994). There is also evidence that IUSS involves a focus on the immediate consequences of behavior, rather than longer-term consequences (Joireman, Anderson, & Strathman, 2003). All of these qualities seem to reflect (in part) qualities of impulse versus restraint.

RELATING IUSS TO TRAITS OR TEMPERAMENTS

As with the approach system and the avoidance system, it's useful to stand back and ask how these ideas fit with ideas from previous chapters. There are strong links to several trait models, discussed in Chapter 4 (for more detail see Carver, 2005).

With regard to the five-factor model, IUSS relates inversely to both conscientiousness and agreeableness (Zuckerman, 1996). Recall that low levels of these traits relate to a variety of problems in getting along in life. IUSS also relates positively to psychoticism in Eysenck's model, which concerns disregard of social restraint in pursuit of intense sensations. Similarly, it relates inversely to constraint from Tellegen's (1985) model, which is virtually the opposite of IUSS. Constraint is the holding back of impulses. A description of constraint sounds like a reverse description of the sensation-seeking dimension.

In discussing temperaments in Chapter 6, we noted that impulsivity has been discussed as a temperament. The most elaborate view of that possibility was developed by Rothbart and her colleagues (e.g., Rothbart et al., 2000; Rothbart et al., 2001; Rothbart, Ellis, Rueda, & Posner, 2003; see also Eisenberg, 2002; Eisenberg et al., 2004; Kochanska & Knaack, 2003). The temperament that she called *effortful control* bears a good deal of resemblance to IUSS. It's about being focused and restrained, and it implies a kind of planfulness and an awareness of others' needs. High levels of this temperament early in life relate to fewer problems with antisocial behavior later on (Kochanska & Knaack, 2003).

TWO SOURCES OF IMPULSE AND RESTRAINT

In making comparisons to these trait-and-temperament models, one more thing is worth noting explicitly. In each case, whatever trait IUSS relates to is distinct and separate from the traits relating to extraversion and neuroticism (or to approach and avoidance sensitivities). Clark and Watson (1999) reviewed considerable evidence and concluded that constraint is consistently separate from extraversion (or positive affectivity) and neuroticism (or negative affectivity). Similarly, Depue and Collins (1999) reviewed 11 studies in which two or more personality inventories were jointly factor analyzed. All identified a distinct higher-order trait reflecting impulse versus constraint.

FIGURE 7.1

Impulse can arise from high subcortical incentive sensitivity compared to threat sensitivity; restraint can arise from high threat sensitivity compared to incentive sensitivity. Addition of a system of effortful control can override either of these: impulse *or* constraint.

Why, then, did early views of extraversion—and some current views—incorporate impulsivity? One reason seems to be that there are two ways for the separation of impulse and restraint to occur (Carver, 2005). One possibility derives entirely from the balance between incentive sensitivity and threat sensitivity (see the bottom of Figure 7.1). A person with strong appetites and little anxiety will approach impulsively (Arnett, Smith, & Newman, 1997; Avila, 2001); a person with weak appetites and strong anxiety won't behave impulsively (and would certainly not seek out unusual sensations). But with the addition of a system that exerts effortful control (top of Figure 7.1), restraint can have a different source (as can action). People can restrain themselves in order to get along better with other people, or in order to get better outcomes over the long term (Carver, 2005). They can also make themselves do things they don't want to do, such as look happy when they get a gift they don't really like (Kieras, Tobin, Graziano, & Rothbart, 2005). These influences on behavior need not involve anxiety at all.

The planfulness of this system of effortful control is quite different in character from responses involving "grabbing" or "freezing" (or "fleeing"). The latter are more basic, more reactive. Theory relates reactive control to subcortical brain areas (Eisenberg, 2002; Rothbart & Bates, 1998). Effortful control is believed to relate to the part of the brain that manages executive functioning: the prefrontal cortex.

NEUROTRANSMITTERS AND IMPULSE VERSUS CONSTRAINT

Is there a particular brain chemical tied to sensation seeking or constraint? Zuckerman (1994, 1995) suggested a role for an enzyme called *monoamine oxidase (MAO)*. MAO helps regulate several neurotransmitters. MAO levels relate to personality traits such as sensation seeking and novelty seeking (Ruchkin, Koposov, af Klinteberg, Oreland, & Grigorenko, 2005; Zuckerman, 1994). MAO also relates to dominance, aggression (Rowe, 2001; Zuckerman, 1995), and drunk driving (Paaver, Eensoo, Pulver, & Harro, 2006). A gene related to MAO levels has been linked to aggression and impulsivity (Manuck, Flory, Ferrell, Mann, & Muldoon, 2000). Maybe MAO is one key, then, to this system.

On the other hand, some consider MAO level to be mostly an indicator of the activity of serotonergic neurons (Oreland, 2004). Perhaps the key actually lies in serotonin function. There is, in fact, quite a good deal of evidence linking low serotonin function to impulsivity (reviewed by Carver & Miller, 2006). Much of the research assesses serotonin function by responses to drug challenges of various sorts (see Box 7.2).

Sometimes serotonin function is even manipulated. In one such study, experimentally lowering serotonin led to greater hostility and aggressiveness among persons who were already high in aggressive tendencies, but it didn't do anything among persons lower in aggressiveness (Cleare & Bond, 1995). In a later study (Bjork, Dougherty, Moeller, & Swann, 2000), lowering serotonin created higher aggressiveness among highly aggressive men but had the opposite effect among those low in aggressiveness. These findings suggest that low serotonin function made people act more the way they tend to be anyway. That would fit with the idea that low serotonin function means loosening restraint of one's basic tendencies.

Another source of information is cross-sectional studies linking qualities of personality to serotonin function. Many of these studies focus on patient samples, typically comparing patients to controls. A popular group for this kind of study is people displaying impulsive aggression. A good number of studies have related lower serotonin function to a history of fighting and assault (Coccaro, Kavoussi, Cooper, & Hauger, 1997), domestic violence (George et al., 2001), and impulsive aggression more generally (Cleare & Bond, 1997). Although there is a lot of evidence linking low serotonin function to aggressiveness, most of the researchers appear to believe that the link is more directly to impulsiveness or volatility than to hostility per se.

Studies have also examined personality qualities and serotonin function among nonclinical samples. Several early studies (Cleare & Bond, 1997; Depue, 1995; Netter, Hennig, & Rohrmann, 1999) found relations between low serotonin function and elevated aggression–hostility traits, similar to the findings just described. Depue (1995) also found links from low serotonin function to the impulsivity facet of Tellegen's

BOX 7.2 RESEARCH QUESTION:

How Do You Assess Neurotransmitter Function?

Researchers are now examining the role of neurotransmitters in a wide range of behavior. Many of the techniques for studying this require a way to assess neurotransmitter functions in research participants. How is this done? It's more complicated than assessing how much of that particular neurotransmitter is lying around in the person's brain. What's actually at issue is how the neurotransmitter is being *used*.

Serotonin is a particularly interesting case. Serotonin receptors can vary in sensitivity (as can all receptors for neurotransmitters). If someone has a chronically low serotonin level (call him Eddie), the receptors adjust to become more sensitive. If someone has a

chronically high serotonin level (call him Phil), the receptors adjust to become less sensitive. Because Eddie's receptors are now very sensitive, they can do their work with relatively little serotonin. Because Phil's receptors are now relatively insensitive, they respond less to the same amount of serotonin. Phil needs more serotonin to have the same "processing" effect. Eddie has very responsive serotonin functioning, whereas Phil's is less responsive.

The responsiveness of a neurotransmitter system in humans is often assessed by a biochemical challenge. This means challenging the system's ability to regulate itself by administering an agent that perturbs or disrupts its stable state. The drug that's administered stimulates the system to see how big a response occurs.

For example, a drug called *fenfluramine* causes the release of

serotonin from presynaptic storage areas and also inhibits its reuptake. Thus, it causes an increase (that lasts several hours) in the levels of serotonin available for use in serotonergic neural transmission. Receptors in the hypothalamus sense this increase in serotonin and cause the pituitary gland to release prolactin into circulation. This eventually helps bring the serotonin level back down, but it takes a while. Prolactin concentrations are easy to assess. Researchers track the prolactin level and determine its peak increase over a period of three to five hours after the fenfluramine is taken. That peak prolactin response (the increase over baseline) is an index of how responsive the serotonin system is (e.g., Manuck et al., 2000). A large rise in prolactin means a sensitive or responsive serotonin system.

---

constraint scale, the aggression facet of Tellegen's negative emotionality scale, to two sensation-seeking subscales, and to several indices of impulsiveness. Depue also looked more closely at hostility and found the strongest relations of low serotonin function to subscales for impulsive, action-oriented aggression, rather than more passive, cognitive forms. A more recent study (Hennig, Reuter, Netter, Burk, & Landt, 2005) produced similar results.

Other research has had a broader focus. Several studies have been done using personality inventories, sometimes along with other measures. One of them (Manuck et al., 1998) used the NEO-PI-R plus additional measures in a community sample. All effects that emerged did so only among men. Low serotonin function related to greater life history of aggression and impulsiveness, consistent with previous results. Low serotonin function also related to higher neuroticism (from the NEO-PI-R) and the neuroticism facet angry hostility. (Other facets were not tested.) High serotonin function related to higher conscientiousness (from the NEO-PI-R).

There's also one more interesting twist to the evidence. Zald and Depue (2001) argued that serotonin should inhibit positive reactions as well as negative. To test this, they had men track their emotions for two weeks. They computed averages separately for positive and negative feelings and then related them to the men's levels of serotonin function. Higher serotonin function related to less negative affect, consistent with findings just reviewed. However, higher serotonin function also related to lower levels of *positive* feelings (interested, active, attentive, and enthusiastic). Thus, serotonin may provide a constraining influence over the biological systems that manage affects of both sorts.

The pattern from this research as a whole seems consistent with the view that serotonergic pathways are involved in impulse control (Depue, 1995; Depue & Collins, 1999; Depue & Spoont, 1986; Manuck, Flory, Muldoon, & Ferrell, 2003; Soubrié, 1986; Zuckerman, 2005). Further, it appears to be consistent with a view in which the resulting restraint (when it does occur) is effortful, rather than an involuntary reaction to anxiety.

Why, then, has the idea that serotonin relates to anxiety held on for so long? There probably are several reasons. As noted earlier, one of them is the common assumption that anxiety is the prime reason for restraint. Another concerns the personality measures used in the research. Some measures are better than others at keeping various qualities separate. Those used in some of the early research on this topic tend to blur threat sensitivity with impulsiveness. Indeed, even the better measures do not really sort the pieces out fully unless facets are examined (Carver & Miller, 2006).

Hormones and Personality

We turn now to a different aspect of biology and personality: *hormones.* An important group is sex hormones. They determine a developing embryo's physical sexual characteristics. They also influence physical characteristics at other stages of development. We won't explore all the ways sex hormones influence behavior (see, e.g., Le Vay, 1993; Rubin, Reinisch, & Haskett, 1981; Tavris & Wade, 1984), but we'll examine a few of them, focusing on testosterone.

HORMONES, THE BODY, AND THE BRAIN

Sex hormones are important in a variety of ways from very early in life. Normal males have higher testosterone than normal females from week 8 to week 24 of gestation, from about the first through the fifth month after birth, and again after puberty (Le Vay, 1993). Testosterone differences in gestation appear essential to changes in the nervous system that create normal male and female physical development. Many believe the hormones also change the brain in ways that result in behavioral differences (Breedlove, 1994; Le Vay, 1993).

The basic template for a human body is female. Only if hormones cause specific changes to occur does a body emerge that looks male. If a genetic male isn't exposed to androgen ("male-making") hormones at critical points in development, the result is an exterior that looks female. If a genetic female is exposed to testosterone at the same points, the result is an exterior that looks male (Breedlove, 1994). During typical fetal development, of course, only males are exposed to enough androgen to be masculinized.

The hormones that guide the body in its sexual development also affect nerve cells (Breedlove, 1992; Le Vay, 1993). They organize the developing brains of males and females differently, in subtle ways (Cohen-Bendahan, van de Beek, & Berenbaum, 2005). Animal research suggests there aren't just two patterns but a broad range of variation, with male and female patterns as the extremes (Panksepp, 1998). The genders tend to differ in linkages among synapses and in the size of some brain structures. For example, the two sides of the cortex are more fully interconnected in women than men (Le Vay, 1993). Men are more visually dominated than women (Panksepp, 1998). Interestingly, there's evidence that the brains of gay men structurally resemble those of women more than those of heterosexual men (Allen & Gorski, 1992; Le Vay, 1991).

How might these differences in the nervous system relate to personality? We said earlier that exposure to androgens may "masculinize" the nervous system. Several things may follow from this.

Early Hormonal Exposure and Behavior

Early exposure to hormones, even prenatal exposure, can influence later behavior. One study (Reinisch, 1981) looked at children whose mothers had received synthetic hormones that act like testosterone while being treated for complications in their pregnancies. Each child thus was exposed to the hormones prenatally (an average of 11 years earlier) during a critical phase of development. The other group was their same-sex siblings (to match as closely as possible on genetic and environmental variables).

Each child completed a self-report measure in which six situations were described, each involving interpersonal conflict. The children made decisions about what they would do in each situation. The measure was the likelihood of responding with physical aggression, verbal aggression, withdrawal, and nonaggressive coping.

The study yielded two separate effects, both bearing on the choice of physical aggression as a response to conflict (see Figure 7.2). The first was a sex difference: Boys chose this response more than girls did. There was also an effect of prenatal exposure to the hormone. Children who'd been exposed chose physical aggression more than did those who hadn't been exposed. This was true both for boys and for girls.

This study is intriguing for a couple of reasons. It's clear that a biological variable—the hormone—influenced the behavior. It's less clear *how* it did so. Animal research indicates that exposure to male hormones during early development increases aggressive displays (Reinisch, 1981). But that wasn't the behavior measured here. This study measured no aggressive acts, just self-reports indicating the choice of aggressive acts. Thus, any masculinizing influence on the nervous system had to filter through a lot of cognition to be displayed.

In another project, Berenbaum and Hines (1992) studied children with a genetic disorder that causes high levels of androgens (masculinizing hormones) prenatally and soon after birth. Years later (ages 3 to 8), these children (and unaffected same-sex relatives) were observed as they played individually. Available were toys that had been determined to be generally preferred by boys and by girls. The question was who would play with which toys.

The androgen-exposed girls spent more time with the boys' toys and less time with the girls' toys than did unexposed girls (see Figure 7.3). In fact, they displayed a preference pattern like that of boys. Preferences among the boys were unaffected by exposure. These findings suggest that a masculinizing hormone can influence the activities children engage in much later in life.

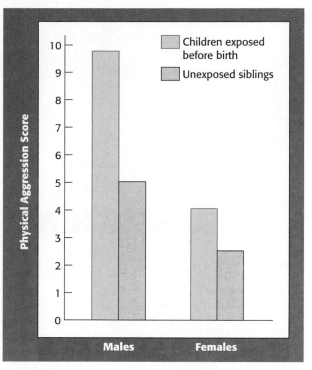

FIGURE 7.2
Average (self-report) physical aggression scores during childhood for boys and girls who had been exposed to synthetic hormones before birth and for their sex-matched siblings who had not been exposed. Exposure to the hormone produced elevated aggression scores for both boys and girls.
Source: Adapted from Reinisch, 1981.

FIGURE 7.3
Amount of time two groups of girls played in a free-play setting with toys generally preferred by boys and toys generally preferred by girls. Some of the girls had been exposed to masculinizing hormones before birth and shortly afterward; the others had not been exposed. *Source: Adapted from Berenbaum & Hines, 1992.*

Androgens come from several sources. Exposure through a mother's medical treatment during pregnancy is one. Another is the adrenal glands, which secrete androgen normally. High levels of natural androgen in girls have been related to greater involvement in sports that involve rough body contact (Kimura, 1999), activities that are more typical of boys. Another study found that higher levels of naturally occurring fetal testostrone predicted lower levels of empathy at age 4 (Knickmeyer, Baron-Cohen, Raggatt, Taylor, & Hackett, 2006).

Other research suggests that hormones also influence play styles. Jacklin, Maccoby, and Doering (1983) found that testosterone levels at birth were related to boldness versus timidity in infant boys over the next 18 months. Boldness was assessed by exposing children to novel (and thus somewhat scary) toys. Higher estradiol (an estrogen) related to more timidity among the boys. No association with a hormone was significant among the girls in the study.

The findings thus are somewhat mixed, but they appear generally consistent with the idea that early exposure to masculinizing hormones can influence behavior. It can increase the potential for aggression, lead to preference for masculine toys, and enhance boldness.

TESTOSTERONE AND ADULT PERSONALITY

A good deal of research on sex hormones and personality examines how current levels of testosterone relate to behavior. That research is several steps away from examining the idea that testosterone masculinizes the nervous system. Yet it shares with it the theme that testosterone is involved in regulating important qualities of behavior. Much of the pioneering research in this area was conducted by James Dabbs and his colleagues (see Dabbs & Dabbs, 2000).

Testosterone is a sex hormone, but research focuses more often on dominance and antisocial behavior than sexual behavior. One study of men in prison (Dabbs, Frady, Carr, & Besch, 1987) found inmates high in testosterone had violated prison rules more often and were more dominant than those lower in testosterone. They were also more likely to have committed violent crimes. Similar results have come from female inmates (Dabbs, Ruback, Frady, Hopper, & Sgoutas, 1988). In a sample of men who had committed murder, those high in testosterone were more likely to have planned the act ahead of time and to have killed people they knew (Dabbs, Riad, & Chance, 2001).

Another study examined testosterone and antisocial behaviors in a noncriminal population: military veterans (Dabbs & Morris, 1990). Men higher in testosterone had larger numbers of sex partners and were more likely to abuse alcohol and other drugs. They were more likely to have gone absent without leave in the military and to have assaulted others. They were also more likely to have had trouble with parents, teachers, and classmates while growing up (see also Box 7.3). These effects were strongest by far among men of low-socioeconomic status (SES).

Being low SES can increase the ill effects of high testosterone, and research also suggests that high testosterone tends to lead men *into* lower-SES occupations (Dabbs, 1992a). This seems to be because high testosterone promotes antisocial behavior and

Box 7.3 Steroids

An Unintended Path to Aggression

Discussing the effects of testosterone on behavior brings up a related topic: bodybuilding and its excesses. The appeal of bodybuilding comes partly from the result: a body that looks as though it's chiseled from rock. Cultural expectations of men's bodies (as reflected in *Playgirl* photos) have shifted over the decades, becoming increasingly dense and muscular (Leit, Pope, & Gray, 2001). These expectations create pressure on men to look that way.

The desire for a well-formed body has led many people into the use of **anabolic steroids.** The word *anabolic* means "building up." Anabolic steroids are chemicals that mimic the body's tendency to rebuild muscle tissues that have been stressed or exercised. Your body gives you small doses of such chemicals, producing growth in muscle size. Using steroids gives you a much bigger dose. Steroids thus let you speed up and exaggerate the building of muscles in ways that exercise alone can't do. That's why people use them.

Indeed, some people are using steroids and steroidlike substances without fully realizing it. So-called dietary supplements, which many use, are often potent drugs. One survey of gym users found that 18% of men said they used adrenal hormones, 25% used ephedrine, and another 5% used anabolic steroids (Kanayama, Gruber, Pope, Borowiecki, & Hudson, 2001). A survey by the National Institute on Drug Abuse found that steroid use more than doubled among high school sophomores from 1992 to 2000.

Many users don't realize that steroids are synthetic hormones. Steroids are related to testosterone (that's why men's muscles tend to be larger than women's). Testosterone is involved in many things, not just building muscle tissue. Consequently, people who use steroids for larger muscles are in for a surprise: There can be unintended and unpleasant side effects.

Some of these effects are physical. If you're a man, part of your body sees the steroids as testosterone. It reacts to what looks like too much testosterone by shutting down production of more. The results are a lowered sperm count and a decreased sex drive. (The steroids don't act like testosterone in those respects.) If you're a woman, steroids cause masculinizing effects: shrinking breasts, a deepening voice, and a growth in facial and body hair (Gruber & Pope, 2000).

Steroids also have behavioral effects, which are of particular interest here. As you've read in the main text, studies link testosterone to dominance and aggressiveness. Steroids produce much the same effects (even among hamsters; Grimes, Ricci, & Melloni, 2006). Because the doses tend to be large, so are the effects. Heavy steroid use can yield irrational bursts of anger that are popularly referred to as "roid rages." Adverse behavioral and psychological responses aren't limited to men, either. In a sample of women users, 56% reported hypomanic symptoms during steroid use, and 40% reported depressive symptoms during steroid withdrawal (Gruber & Pope, 2000). Ominously, evidence from animal research suggests that steroid use during adolescence can create aggressive tendencies that remain after the steroid is withdrawn (Harrison, Connor, Nowak, Nash, & Melloni, 2000).

These effects are bad enough in the average person. But bodybuilding and steroid use aren't limited to the average person. Bodybuilding has considerable appeal for people who already have a strong streak of dominance and aggressiveness. Add steroids to an already aggressive personality, and the result is a potential for serious violence.

---

disruption of education. Both of these factors then lead people away from white-collar occupations.

Differences in testosterone relate to occupations in other ways, as well, fitting a link between testosterone and social dominance (Mazur & Booth, 1998). For example, trial lawyers (of both genders) are higher in testosterone than nontrial lawyers (Dabbs, Alford, & Fielden, 1998). Actors and professional football players have high levels of testosterone (Dabbs, de La Rue, & Williams, 1990), and ministers have low levels. (College professors, if you must know, are in the middle.)

Why are actors so different from ministers? After all, they're both on stage. Dabbs et al. (1990) suggested that actors must be dominant constantly, because their reputation is only as good as their last show. Ministers are in a framework that tolerates more variability. Further, the actor's role is to seek and hold onto glory, whereas a minister's role is to be self-effacing.

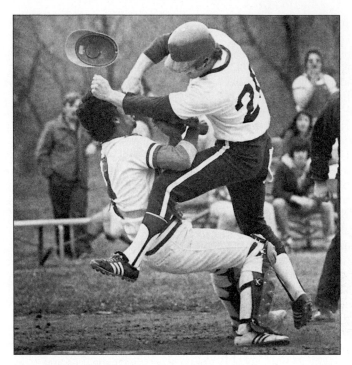

Research suggests a link between testosterone level and aggression.

Effects of testosterone occur in many small ways that are related to social potency and dominance. In one study, testosterone related to deeper voices among men (Dabbs & Mallinger, 1999). In studies of brief interactions with strangers, participants higher in testosterone entered more quickly, focused more directly on the other person, and displayed more independence and confidence than those with less testosterone (Dabbs, Bernieri, Strong, Campo, & Milun, 2001). Even young children high in testosterone are more independent on the playground than those with lower testosterone (Strong & Dabbs, 2000).

The role of testosterone in dominance is displayed in other ways as well. What happens if people low in testosterone are put into positions of high status? What happens if people high in testosterone are put into positions of low status? In both cases, the people become upset and perform poorly (Josephs, Sellers, Newman, & Mehta, 2006). When the situations are reversed, however, everyone feels better and performs better.

The dominance that's linked to high testosterone is useful in many contexts, but it can interfere with relationships. Booth and Dabbs (1993) found that men with higher testosterone were less likely to have married. If they did marry, they were more likely to divorce. They were also more likely to have had extramarital sex and to commit domestic abuse. Men high in testosterone have smiles that are less friendly than men lower in testosterone, and they express more dominance in their gaze when in conversation (Dabbs, 1992b, 1997). Members of low-testosterone fraternities are friendly and smile a lot, whereas members of high-testosterone fraternities are wilder and more unruly (Dabbs, Hargrove, & Heusel, 1996).

Several studies have related testosterone to personality measures. In two studies, personality data and testosterone data were factor analyzed (Daitzman & Zuckerman, 1980; Udry & Talbert, 1988). In both cases, a factor formed around testosterone, with overtones of impulsiveness, sensation seeking, and dominance. Udry and Talbert's (1988) factor included these self-ratings: cynical, dominant, sarcastic, spontaneous, persistent, and uninhibited. Such findings may relate back to work on brain functions and impulsivity, discussed earlier in the chapter.

CYCLE OF TESTOSTERONE AND ACTION

It may be most obvious to think about testosterone in terms of stable individual differences. However, testosterone is also part of a dynamic system that changes over time and events (Dabbs, 1992b). Levels of testosterone shift in response to social situations of several types. These shifts may, in turn, go on to influence the person's later behavior.

Testosterone levels rise after certain kinds of positive experience. As shown in Figure 7.4, testosterone rises after success at a competitive event (Mazur, Booth, & Dabbs, 1992) and falls after a failure or humiliation. It rises when your team wins and falls when your team loses (Bernhardt, Dabbs, Fielden, & Lutter, 1998). It rises when you are confronted with the challenge of an insult (Nisbett & Cohen, 1996). It rises (for both men and women) after sexual intercourse (Dabbs & Mohammed, 1992). Even fooling around with a gun for a few minutes can make testosterone increase (Klinesmith, Kasser, & McAndrew, 2006).

Such changes in testosterone also have implications for subsequent behavior. Increases in testosterone make people more sexually active (Dabbs, 1992b). An increase in testosterone can also make a person more assertive and may lead him to seek out new competition and chances to be dominant (Mazur, 1985; Mazur et al., 1992). It makes people more responsive to possible reward and less responsive to possible losses (van Honk, Schutter, Hermans, Putman, Tuiten, & Koppeschaar, 2004). Decreases in testosterone after a failure may cause a person to be less assertive and avoid new competition. Thus, in either case (success or failure), there's a tendency toward a spiraling effect: A given outcome tends to promote more of the same outcome.

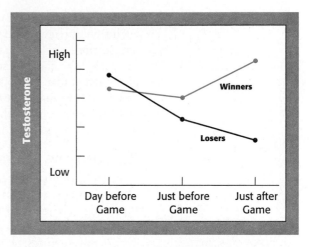

FIGURE 7.4
Testosterone levels among chess players who won or lost close matches in a citywide tournament. *Source: Adapted from Mazur et al., 1992.*

TESTOSTERONE, DOMINANCE, AND EVOLUTIONARY PSYCHOLOGY

Let's step back from these studies to consider a broader implication. The findings as a group seem to fit with one of the themes of evolutionary psychology, discussed in Chapter 6.

Recall that evolutionary thinking includes the idea that selection pressures led to certain gender differences. These differences stem from the fact that human females have greater investment than males in offspring (through the long period of pregnancy and mothering). Females are believed to be choosy about mates for this reason, trying to find one who will provide resources for their children. A gender difference in dominance and aggression is also believed to follow from the differing selection pressures.

In this view, aggression can increase males' opportunities to mate. Aggressiveness helps males establish dominance and status. Evidence for this idea comes from both monkeys and humans. One study found that when male monkeys in a troupe were threatened by an outside rival, their testosterone went up, presumably to facilitate aggression and dominance displays (Cristóbal-Azkarate, Chavira, Boeck, Rodríguez-Luna, & Veà, 2006). An extensive review of relevant literature in humans supports that conclusion and others as well (Archer, 2006). For example, when men are required to care for offspring, testosterone decreases.

There are also interesting individual differences in testosterone effects. For example, after being insulted, testosterone rises more among men from the American South than men from the North (Cohen, Nisbett, Bowdle, & Schwarz, 1996). This has been interpreted as indicating that there is a stronger culture of honor in the South, which increases the impact of insults.

Overt aggressiveness in females doesn't confer the same advantage as it does to men and may even be a disadvantage. It can create the potential for damage to an unborn or young child. It also interferes with their more important activities (bearing and raising children). Nonetheless, testosterone does relate to aggression among women as well as men (Archer, 2006). That this can be a problem for women is suggested by findings that this assertive style interferes with forming alliances in female groups (Archer & Coyne, 2005).

Dabbs (1992b, 1998) notes an interesting irony about testosterone effects. In the evolutionary view, males are high in testosterone and dominance, because physical domination over other males brought access to mates. In recent millennia, however, the rules have changed somewhat. Success is now defined partly in socioeconomic terms, rather than by physical dominance. A man who's too preoccupied with displays and posturing may have trouble gaining the skills needed for economic and social power. Thus, a quality that was important in prehistory may actually interfere with success in today's world.

RESPONDING TO STRESS: MEN, WOMEN, AND OXYTOCIN

Another hormonal influence has drawn considerable attention in recent years. It concerns responses to stress, but extends far beyond. A phrase that's well known in psychology, coined long ago by Cannon (1932) is the *fight-or-flight response*. It refers to the fact that when an animal confronts a predator or competitor, it has two obvious adaptive choices: to attack (hoping to overcome the other) or to flee (hoping to escape). Presumably, the flight response connects in some way to the avoidance that was discussed earlier in the chapter. Apparently, there's a link between the fight response and the system of impulsivity, also discussed earlier in the chapter.

It's often been assumed that these are the only important responses to threat. Shelley Taylor (2002) and her colleagues (Taylor, Klein, Lewis, Gruenewald, Gurung, & Updegraff, 2000) have argued that this assumption is wrong. As they point out, most of the evidence for that view comes from studies of males (and mostly male rats, at that). Females have been studied in a few stressful contexts, but the behavior examined in those studies hasn't been about fight or flight. Rather, the behavior has concerned affiliation, particularly affiliation with other women.

Taylor et al. (2000) argued that focusing on male behavior caused an important set of responses to stress to be widely ignored. They refer to these responses, which are stronger in females than in males, with the phrase *tend-and-befriend*. Taylor et al. think the existence of these responses reflects a difference in evolutionary pressures on males and females, due to differing investment in offspring. That is, as noted just earlier, fighting and fleeing may make good sense for males, who aren't carrying offspring (or pregnant). It makes less sense for females. Females thus may have evolved strategies that benefit both themselves and their offspring.

Tending refers to calming offspring. This protects them from harm. That is, if they don't cry, they (and you) fade into the background, where the threat is less. By extension, you do the same for adults you're close to who are stressed. By soothing them, you put them into a situation of less threat. *Befriending* means affiliating and bonding with others. This reduces certain kinds of risk (there's greater safety in numbers) and increases the chances of receiving tending from each other when needed (Taylor, 2002).

This pattern of response is believed to derive from the system that produces attachment between infant and caregiver. Attachment is often discussed from the perspective of the infant's bond to a caregiver (Chapter 11). It's less often discussed the other way around. Yet there's a good deal of research on this topic (mostly with lower animals), and aspects of the biological mechanism that creates it have been identified (Panksepp, 1998).

This system involves a hormone called *oxytocin*. It acts to relax and sedate (e.g., Light, Smith, Johns, Brownley, Hofheimer, & Amico, 2000), and it reduces fear. Both males and females have this hormone, but females seem to have more of it. Further, androgens inhibit its release under stress, and estrogen increases its effects (see Taylor et al., 2000). Thus, men and women react somewhat differently to stress. Men tend to remove themselves from social interaction; women immerse themselves in nurturing those around them (Repetti, 1989).

The idea that oxytocin is involved (along with endogenous opioids) in mother–infant bonding is a starting point. But it's also argued that oxytocin is involved in social bonding more generally (Carter, 1998; Panksepp, 1998; Taylor et al., 2000; Turner, Altemus, Enos, Cooper, & McGuinness, 1999). Animal research shows oxytocin plays a key role in adult pair bonding in some species. It is released during orgasm, childbirth, massage, and breastfeeding (Matthiesen et al., 2001; Turner et al., 1999). It has been found that greater partner support relates to higher oxytocin (Grewen, Girdler, Amico, & Light, 2005). There is also evidence that receiving a jolt of oxytocin causes people to experience an increase in trust, a willingness to take on risks in the context of a social bond with a stranger (Kosfeld, Heinrichs, Zak, Fischbacher, & Fehr, 2005).

And what of personality? There definitely are individual differences in oxytocin release to particular stimuli. But thus far there's no clear link between these differences and personality traits. This reflects the fact that human research on oxytocin is just getting momentum, in part because it's harder to study than some other hormones. If oxytocin is important in the formation of social bonds, though, it's a key biological influence on human experience. Undoubtedly, its influence on personality will be the subject of work in years to come.

Assessment

The biological view on personality discussed in this chapter assumes that personality derives from events in the nervous system and hormonal system. If personality is biological, then why not just assess the biological characteristics?

There are a couple of problems with this. In many cases, no one's quite sure what the biological mechanism is, so it's hard to know what to measure. It's also hard to assess biological functions in a way that doesn't require a sensor in the body or the drawing of blood. Nonetheless, some biological methods of assessment are now in use.

ELECTROENCEPHALOGRAMS

An indirect indication of what's going on in the brain can be obtained by recording electrical activity from the skin over the skull. The record is called an **electroencephalogram, or EEG.** The reasoning behind it is that neurons throughout the brain fire at various intervals, creating continuous fluctuations in voltage. Electrodes on the scalp sense these changes. This gives a view of aspects of the activity in the cerebral cortex. Cortical activity is very complex, but it forms patterns that relate to different subjective states.

EEGs have been used for some time as a way of investigating normal personality. In fact, some of the work discussed earlier in the chapter used EEGs. Various regions of the cortex are active to different degrees when people are in various psychological states. Mapping EEG activities in different locations shows what areas of the brain are involved in what kinds of mental activity. For example, it's possible to identify a person who's dominated by incentive motivation or by avoidance motivation by looking at left versus right frontal activation levels at rest (Harmon-Jones & Allen, 1997; Sutton & Davidson, 1997).

NEUROIMAGING

Mapping of brain activities has also moved further inside the brain. One technique is called **positron emission tomography (PET).** PET derives a picture of brain functioning from metabolic activity. The person receives a radioactive form of glucose (the brain's energy source). Later, radioactivity in different brain areas is recorded. Presumably, more active areas use more glucose, resulting in higher radioactivity there. A computer color codes the intensities, producing a brain map in which colors represent levels of brain activity.

One application of the PET procedure is measuring neurotransmitter function. To do this, the person receives a radioactively labeled drug with known effects. The person's brain activity is then compared to its activity when in a nondrugged condition. Differences between the PET scans provide information about the receptor systems involved in the drug's effects.

Another technique, called **magnetic resonance imaging (MRI),** relies on a very subtle property of nerve activity. Functioning nerve cells create magnetic fields. With a good deal of computer assistance, the magnetic resonances of a person's brain can be translated into a visual image. Typically, the image is of slices across the brain, as seen from above. Different slices give different information, because they show different parts of the brain.

At first, MRI images were used primarily to look for structural problems in the brain. For example, if you were having blackouts after an auto accident, you might be asked to undergo an MRI to look for possible damage. MRIs are also now being used in a different way. People are being studied to assess levels of activation in various brain structures, both at rest and in other mental states. The picture from this sort of study, called **functional MRI (fMRI),** is much more detailed than what comes from EEG recordings. Of particular importance is that it lets the brain be viewed in slices at different levels. The result is a very detailed three-dimensional picture about what brain centers are active during the scan. As with PET scans, the images are usually created in multiple colors, with each color representing a different level of activity.

Use of fMRI as a tool to understand how the brain works has increased at an incredible rate over the past decade. It's very expensive (it requires a giant, powerful magnet, plus a lot of skilled technical support). But the fact that it can provide a three-dimensional picture means it can show very precise locations of increases and decreases in neural activity as a function of what the person is doing. People can be placed in different motivational and emotional states while in the device and can engage in diverse tasks. This lets researchers determine which parts of the brain are involved in those various experiences. More and more researchers are thinking of possible uses for this tool. This is a research area that unquestionably will continue to grow enormously in the years to come.

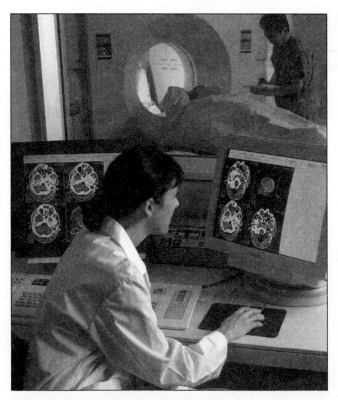

MRIs create an image of the inside of the brain.

Problems in Behavior, and Behavior Change

Let's now turn to problems in behavior. The biological process approach has made large contributions to the understanding of disorders. A full treatment is well beyond the scope of this chapter. We focus here on contributions that relate to the ideas discussed earlier in the chapter.

BIOLOGICAL BASES OF ANXIETY, DEPRESSION, AND ANTISOCIAL PERSONALITY

Recall that a basic assumption of these models is that two motivational systems in the brain manage the approach of incentives and avoidance of threats, respectively. People presumably vary in the strength or sensitivity of these systems. Being too extreme on one or the other system may set a person up for problems.

Perhaps the easiest problem to link to this view is anxiety disorders. The avoidance system creates anxiety in the presence of cues of impending punishment. A person with a very sensitive threat system will experience anxiety easily and frequently. This creates fertile ground for an anxiety disorder to develop. If these people are exposed to frequent punishment during childhood, they learn anxiety responses to many stimuli. The result may be the development of such clinical symptoms as phobias, panic attacks, and obsessive–compulsive disorders.

A related problem is depression. There's less consensus on the biological roots of depression than on those of anxiety (Davidson, Pizzagalli, Nitschke, & Putnam, 2002). Some see depression as a variant of anxiety, reflecting an oversensitive avoidance system. Others tie depression to a weak BAS (e.g., Allen, Iacono, Depue, & Arbisi, 1993; Henriques & Davidson, 1990, 1991). In this view, a person with weak BAS activation has little motivation to approach incentives. The result is the leaden behavioral qualities that typify depression.

Another problem that's often discussed in terms of biological systems is **antisocial personality.** As noted earlier, it involves impulsivity and an inability to restrain antisocial urges. It's sometimes argued that these people have an overactive BAS (Arnett et al., 1997). Thus, they pursue whatever incentive comes to mind. It's sometimes argued that they have deficits in the threat system (Fowles, 1980). Thus, they fail to learn from punishment or aren't motivated to avoid it.

Some think the failure to learn from punishment stems not from a deficient avoidance system but from a failure to stop and think before plowing ahead in pursuit of an incentive (Bernstein, Newman, Wallace, & Luh, 2000; Patterson & Newman, 1993; Schmitt, Brinkley, & Newman, 1999). This would tend to link the antisocial personality to the system that underlies impulsiveness and sensation seeking (Krueger et al., 1994; Rowe, 2001; Zuckerman, 1994). Insufficient MAO (associated with this system) may be a vulnerability, interacting with the environment. In one study (Caspi et al., 2002), boys with genes causing low MAO engaged in more antisocial behavior—but only if they also received maltreatment while growing up (see Figure 7.5). Although men with the combination of low MAO gene and severe maltreatment were only 12% of the male birth cohort, they accounted for 44% of the cohort's

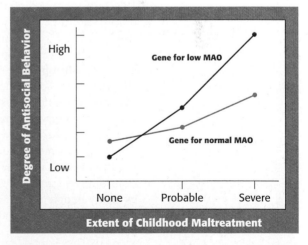

FIGURE 7.5
Scores on an index of antisocial behavior among men with a gene causing low MAO and men with a gene for normal MAO who had experienced either no maltreatment (abuse) during childhood, probably some maltreatment, or severe maltreatment.
Source: Adapted from Caspi et al., 2002.

violent convictions. Indeed, a full 85% of this group developed some sort of antisocial behavior.

Some discussions of antisocial behavior involve other biological systems. Recall that high levels of testosterone relate to various kinds of violent and antisocial behavior (Dabbs & Dabbs, 2000; Dabbs et al., 2001). There's even evidence that high testosterone relates to disruptive behavior in boys as young as 5 to 11 years of age (Chance, Brown, Dabbs, & Casey, 2000). Thus, this set of problems seems to relate to both hormonal and neural processes.

MEDICATION IN THERAPY

The biological process approach to personality also has a relatively straightforward implication for therapy. Many manifestations of problems reflect biological functions. It follows that changing the action of these biological functions should change the manifestation of the disorder. There are several disorders for which this approach seems effective. Because the treatments typically involve administering drugs, they are often called **pharmacotherapy.**

It has long been known that manic–depressive, or bipolar, disorder can be relieved by lithium. About 80% of people with bipolar disorder respond to lithium (Depue, 1979). Besides treating existing symptoms, repeated doses can ward off new symptoms. Unfortunately, lithium has serious unpleasant side effects. Nevertheless, its effectiveness supports two ideas: that the disorder is biological and that its treatment should be (at least in part) biologically based.

A similar case has also been made for treatment of schizophrenia. Research on the biological basis of schizophrenia has looked for ways to treat its symptoms. One hypothesis is that the symptoms reflect too much dopamine (see Walker & Diforio, 1997). As we said earlier, dopamine is a neurotransmitter. With too much dopamine, transmission in certain parts of the nervous system is too easy. With too many messages being sent, communication is disrupted.

This hypothesis is speculative, but it is supported by studies of biochemical treatments for schizophrenic symptoms. Drugs that remove the symptoms of schizophrenia also turn out to lower the levels of usable dopamine in the brain. Apparently the effectiveness of these drugs is related to their ability to block dopamine use. Once again, this finding suggests that the disorder is biological and that treatment should also be biologically based (at least in part).

Drug treatments are also used for disorders that are far less extreme than the two just discussed. Antianxiety drugs are among the most often prescribed of all medications. Current antidepressants—*selective serotonin reuptake inhibitors (SSRIs)*—are used by many people with moderate to mild depression. Indeed, development of this set of antidepressants has led to a far wider use of mood-altering medication than ever before.

The widespread use of these drugs raises a number of questions and issues (Kramer, 1993). One issue concerns the fact that responses to these medications often are much broader than the mere lifting of a depressed mood. People's personalities undergo changes that are subtle but profound and pervasive. People become more confident, more resilient, more decisive—almost more dominant— than they were before. In a sense, they aren't quite the same people as they were before taking the medication. Their very personalities have changed.

Seeing these changes in personality as a function of a slight alteration in brain chemistry raises questions about where personality resides. Personality may consist of the person's biological functioning and the experiences to which it gives rise. Personality may not be a stable entity that stands apart from the symptoms that bring people for therapy. Personality, in the form of the person's biological systems, may be the *source* of the symptoms.

Researchers have gone on to ask whether SSRIs affect people who don't have a disorder. One study (Knutson et al., 1998) gave people either an SSRI or a placebo for four weeks and assessed them before and after. Those given the medication later reported less hostility and negativity (but not greater positive feelings). They also displayed more positive social behavior while working on a cooperative task. Another study (Tse & Bond, 2001) found an increase on a measure of self-direction, which assesses such qualities as purposefulness and resourcefulness.

The availability of drugs with these broad effects on personality raises more questions. How widely should they be prescribed? Should people whose problems aren't severe be given medication if it will make their lives more enjoyable? Should all people have the option of changing their personalities by taking pills? These questions are a long way from being answered.

Biological Processes and Personality: Problems and Prospects

This chapter has discussed the idea that patterns of biological processes have important things to tell us about personality. We wouldn't blame you if you came away feeling that the presentation was a little fragmented. In truth, the ideas themselves are somewhat fragmented. The pieces are coming together, but they're not there yet. As a result, this way of thinking about personality has something of a disjointed feel.

One reason for this is that theories about how the nervous system and hormones influence behavior rely in part on knowledge from other sciences. Ideas in those sciences are continually evolving, causing changes in these ideas about personality. Further, work on these topics is as new as the methodological advances that permit closer looks at how the biological systems function. These methodological advances continue to march forward (Davidson et al., 2000; Lane & Nadel, 2000; Posner & DiGirolamo, 2000). The result is a kaleidoscope of new looks at biological functioning that sometimes have unexpected implications for personality.

For example, many psychologists now have access to PET scans and fMRIs, which illuminate brain functioning in ways only dreamed of a few years ago. The findings generated from these techniques have raised as many new questions as have been answered. Sorting out the picture that such methods reveal will likely be a complex process.

It's clear that there's been progress in these areas of research and thought. To a large extent, theorists agree about what they're trying to account for. There's a general consensus that approach and avoidance (and positive and negative feelings) are important focal points for biological theory building. Almost everyone seems to feel the need to include something more than that, but there's been less consensus about what else to include. Partly for this reason, this way of thinking doesn't yet stand as a fully developed personality theory. It's more of a vantage point, a place from which to look at and consider the nature of personality.

Lest you be tempted to conclude from the disagreements that these theorists aren't doing their homework carefully enough, let us point out that it's not easy to tell what's going on in the nervous system. To really know what connects to what in the brain means tracing neural pathways, which can't be done in human subjects. When animal research is done, the animals can't report directly on the psychological effects of what the researcher is doing. Thus, information often is indirect, and progress can be slow. The functions of the nervous system are being sorted out by research of several types, but there's a long way to go. Until the nature of the organization of the nervous system becomes clearer, personality psychologists of this orientation won't have definitive models.

Although criticisms can be made of various aspects of this way of thinking about personality, this line of work is one of the most active areas of personality psychology today. Many people believe that the mysteries of the mind will be revealed by a better understanding of the brain. They are committed to unraveling those mysteries and their implications for personality. At present, the prospects of this viewpoint seem quite bright indeed.

· SUMMARY ·

The idea that personality is tied to the biological functions of the body leads to a variety of possibilities involving the functions of the nervous system and the endocrine (hormone) system. An initial approach of this sort was Eysenck's theory that brain processes underlie extraversion. He argued that introverts are more cortically aroused than extraverts. Thus, introverts avoid overstimulation, whereas extraverts seek out stimulation.

Others have taken a different path, relying on newer knowledge. It is now often argued that personality rests on an approach system (BAS) that responds to incentives and an avoidance system that responds to threats. Work on emotions suggests that the approach system, which produces positive feelings, involves (in part) the left prefrontal cortex, and that the withdrawal system, which produces feelings such as fear, involves (in part) the right prefrontal cortex. The threat system seems to represent the biological basis for the trait of neuroticism. Some suggest that the BAS represents the biological basis for extraversion.

Many people now believe it is useful to assume another biological variable that is responsible for variations between impulsiveness and sensation seeking (the tendency to seek out novel, complex, and exciting stimuli) and restraint. Sensation seeking relates to Eysenck's dimension of psychoticism and Tellegen's dimension of constraint. Variation in these qualities may concern regulation of exposure to stimulation (as a protective process), and it may concern taking into account other people and long-term goals.

Another aspect of the biological view on personality focuses on the role in behavior played by hormones. Exposure to male hormones before birth can cause people years later to choose more aggressive responses to conflict; it can also increase girls' preference for boys' toys. Testosterone in adults relates to dominance behavior, sometimes expressed in antisocial ways. Testosterone also fluctuates, increasing with challenges and victories and decreasing with failures.

An emerging area of work examines the possibility that another hormone, called *oxytocin,* is important in human social behavior. Oxytocin appears to relate to female responses to stress, termed a tend-and-befriend response. The roots of this response may be in the attachment system, and it may relate to social bonding more generally.

This approach to personality suggests it may be possible to assess personality through biological functions. Although the attempt to do this is in its infancy, some believe recordings of brain activity—particularly fMRIs—hold great promise for the future.

With regard to problems in behavior, high levels of threat sensitivity activity promote disorders involving anxiety. Either a high threat response or a low approach response may contribute to depression. High approach–low avoidance can yield symptoms of antisocial personality, which also relates to impulsive sensation seeking and testosterone. This orientation to personality suggests that therapy based on medication is a means to bring about behavioral change. The idea is that medication can influence the underlying biological system, thereby altering the person's behavior and subjective experience.

· GLOSSARY ·

Anabolic steroids   Chemicals that mimic the body's tendency to rebuild muscle tissues.

Antisocial personality   A person who displays impulsive action with little thought to consequences.

Behavioral approach system (BAS)   The part of the brain that regulates pursuit of incentives.

Behavioral inhibition system (BIS)   The part of the brain that regulates anticipation of punishment.

Dopamine   A neurotransmitter believed to be especially important to approach regulation.

Electroencephalogram (EEG)   A record of overall electrical activity in higher regions of the brain.

Functional MRI (fMRI)   Use of MRI to create a picture of activity inside the brain in different mental states.

Impulsive unsocialized sensation seeking (IUSS)   Trait involving the capacity to inhibit behavior in the service of social adaptation.

Incentives   Things that people desire.

Magnetic resonance imaging (MRI)   A picture of activity inside the brain based on the brain's electromagnetic energy.

Negative emotionality   The predisposition to experience negative feelings frequently.

Neurotransmitter   A chemical involved in sending messages along nerve pathways.

Orienting response   The shift of attention to a stimulus that suddenly appears.

Pharmacotherapy   A therapy based on use of medication.

Positive emotionality   The predisposition to experience positive feelings frequently.

Positron emission tomography (PET)   A picture of activity in the brain based on the brain's metabolism.

Sensation seeking   The tendency to seek out varied, unusual, and exciting stimuli.

Serotonin   A neurotransmitter that some believe is involved in behavioral inhibition.

The Psychoanalytic Perspective

The Psychoanalytic Perspective: Major Themes and Underlying Assumptions

The *psychoanalytic perspective* originated in the writings of Sigmund Freud. His impact on personality psychology was so strong that his ideas form the essence of a distinct perspective on personality (although others have contributed to it besides him). The psychoanalytic view on personality is the subject of Chapters 8 and 9.

One theme of this perspective, which gave rise to the term *psychodynamic,* is the idea that personality is a dynamic set of processes, always in motion. They sometimes work in harmony with one another and sometimes against one another, but they are never still. Personality is a dynamo—or a bubbling spring—from which emerge forces that can be set free, channeled, modified, or transformed. As long as you're alive, these forces never come to rest.

An important implication of this dynamic quality in personality is that the forces sometimes work against each other. The processes of personality sometimes compete or wrestle for control over the person's behavior. The assumption that pressures within the personality can *conflict* with each other is another theme that's very prominent in the psychoanalytic perspective.

An additional assumption goes hand in hand with this one: Specifically, psychoanalytic thinking emphasizes the role of the unconscious in determining behavior. The conflicts that take place among the elements of personality often occur outside awareness. Many of the motives that people have are also unconscious. The emphasis on unconscious influence is a theme that permeates this perspective on personality.

Another theme in the psychoanalytic perspective is the idea that human experience is suffused with qualities of lust and aggression, sexuality and death. These assumptions tie psychoanalytic thinking to Darwin's theory of evolution (see Ritvo, 1990). They serve as a reminder that humans are—first of all—animals whose purpose in life is reproduction. Although this idea doesn't seem so odd today, the extent to which Freud emphasized the role of sexuality in human life was very unusual at the time.

Indeed, Freud's emphasis on sexuality even extended to his ideas about the development of personality. A fifth theme of the psychoanalytic perspective is that personality is strongly affected by early experiences. More specifically, Freud argued that sexuality is involved at all stages of development, even infancy. Many people found the idea of infantile sexuality either absurd or shocking. Nevertheless, the idea that the fundamentals of personality emerge from the crucible of early experience is deeply embedded in psychoanalytic thought.

Another theme that characterizes psychoanalysis is the idea that defense is an important aspect of human functioning. This idea rests on the assumption that there are things about every person that are threatening to him or her. Maybe you have what you regard as shameful desires; maybe you secretly feel you're unworthy as a human being; or maybe you're afraid the social world will reject you. Whatever it is that most threatens you, psychological processes operate to keep these desires or elements of self-knowledge from overpowering you. The notion of defense is an important aspect of psychoanalytic thought.

The psychoanalytic perspective on personality is extremely metaphorical in nature, but it's hard to point to a single metaphor for human nature that dominates this perspective. Rather, it uses multiple metaphors. Freud was a physician, and the idea of biological processes underlying mental processes often appeared in his writing. Similarly, his concepts of life instincts and death instincts resemble the dual processes of metabolic functioning, continually tearing down and building up. Freud used many other metaphors, as well. Sometimes he likened the psyche to a sociopolitical system making reference to censors, economics, compromises, and repression. Sometimes his analogies were from physics, with personality treated as an energy system and the competition among forces compared to hydraulic systems in which energy focused at one point had an inevitable consequence at another point. At other times, he treated psychological phenomena almost as though they were the products of artistic or literary efforts.

Despite the lack of a single orienting point, or perhaps because of it, the psychoanalytic viewpoint on personality may be characterized fairly as one in which the *quality* of analogy or metaphor figures prominently. Human behavior is to be understood not as the product of any one process but as a reflection of multiple processes whose functioning can be captured only imperfectly by any one metaphor.

A final theme of the psychoanalytic perspective is the idea that mental health depends on a balance of forces in one's life. It's good to express your deep desires, but it's not good to let them control your life. It's good to act morally, but a constant effort to be perfect cripples your personality. It's good to have self-control but not to be overcontrolled. Moderation and balance among these forces provide the healthiest experience of life.

CHAPTER 8

Psychoanalytic Structure and Process

John and his girlfriend, Ann, go to different colleges, a thousand miles apart. It's been hard for them to be separated for long periods of time, and John has finally decided he can't go on this way. He's decided to call Ann and break up. He picks up the phone, dials a number, and hears a voice on the other end of the line say "Hello"—at the dorm where Ann lived last year, before she moved off campus. "Now why'd I dial *that* number?" John wonders to himself.

WHY DID I do that? Most people, most of the time, find it easy to answer this question with no doubt that their answer is correct. Most of us assume a direct link between our intentions and actions. Accidents may interfere with those intentions, but accidents are random.

There's a viewpoint on the nature of personality that sharply challenges these assumptions. It sees behavior as determined partly by inner forces that lie outside your awareness and control. Accidents? This view says they rarely happen. What seems accidental, you've usually done on purpose. You just aren't *aware* of the purpose.

The approach to personality that takes this view is called *psychoanalysis.* Psychoanalytic theory is closely identified with a single theorist, an Austrian physician named Sigmund Freud (although it rests more on historical ideas than is widely realized; Ellenberger, 1970; Erdelyi, 1985). The theory, which evolved over the period from 1895 to 1940, stunned the scientific world when it was proposed (see Box 8.1). It's been one of the most influential views ever developed. Its effects have been felt not just in psychology but in anthropology, political science, sociology, and art and literature. It's hard to think of a single aspect of thought in Western civilization that hasn't been touched in some way by psychoanalytic ideas.

One sign of the impact of psychoanalytic ideas is the extent to which they've crept into everyday language. For example, people often use the term *Freudian slip* to refer to an error in speech that seems to suggest an unconscious feeling or desire. Such slips imply that behavior is caused by forces outside our awareness, an idea from psychoanalysis.

Before getting to the theory, we note two features that make it different from any other in personality psychology. First, Freud was fascinated by symbols, metaphors, and analogies. This fascination is reflected

BOX 8.1 PSYCHOANALYSIS IN HISTORICAL CONTEXT

The concepts of psychoanalytic theory were formed earlier than any other theory in this book (starting before the turn of the twentieth century). The cultural and scientific context in which the theory arose differed greatly from that of today, and the context strongly influenced the theory's form. To better understand why Freud's ideas took the form they did and why they had the impact they had, consider the world in which he lived.

Freud did his early writing during the latter part of the Victorian era (late 1800s), a time in which middle- and upper-class society had come to view humans as having reached a lofty state of rational self-control, civilization, and near perfection. It was a smug and self-satisfied society. By today's standards, it would be seen as stuffy and hypocritical. For example, sexuality was rarely even acknowledged publicly, never mind openly discussed.

Into this calm society, Freud dropped a cultural bomb. Instead of rational, he said we are driven by forces from the unconscious. Instead of godlike, we are primitive animals. Instead of intellectual beings, we are driven by sexual and destructive urges, even in infancy.

Freud noted that humanity's admiration of itself had suffered three traumatic shocks: The first was the discovery by Copernicus that the earth is not the center of the universe. The second was the assertion by Charles Darwin that humans evolved as animals. The third was Freud's claim that people are at the mercy of forces that are unconscious and uncontrollable. Soon the horror of World War I showed clearly that the veneer of civilization was far thinner than most assumed.

Freud's ideas jolted the scientific world when they were proposed, partly because they conflicted so sharply with widely held assumptions. Another reason was Freud's emphasis on sexuality, particularly infantile sexuality. This caused many to view him as a pervert, obscene and wicked. The fact that he was a Jew in an anti-Semitic society raised additional suspicion. Further, he presented his theories without much evidence, which didn't sit well in the scientific community. All these factors raised controversy. Ironically, the controversy only brought his ideas more attention.

Although Freud's ideas contradicted the assumptions of Victorian society, they didn't arise in an intellectual vacuum. Darwin's earlier assertion that humans were just one sort of animal carried several other assumptions. For instance, Darwin saw all

creatures as driven by instincts to survive and reproduce. Freud's sexual and life instincts resemble these. Although society at large viewed humanity as rational, philosophers such as Schopenhauer and Nietzsche argued that human behavior is often caused by unconscious irrational forces. This idea is echoed in Freud's work.

Freud was also influenced by the ideas of scientists in other fields (Ellenberger, 1970). For example, Freud's view of the human being as an energy system drew directly from then-current ideas in physics and chemistry. Nineteenth-century physicists had also developed the principle of *conservation,* the idea that matter and energy can be transformed but not destroyed. This conservation principle is reflected in Freud's belief that impulses must eventually be expressed, in one form or another.

If Freud had lived in a different time, his metaphors may well have been different. But psychoanalysis lives on in the terms Freud used. As you read this chapter, keep in mind the cultural and scientific context in which the theory was constructed. We've tried to present the theory as it applies to you, in today's world. If aspects of the concepts seem out of date metaphorically, try to keep in mind the world in which they were conceived.

---

both in the theory's form and in its content. The form of the theory uses many analogies. Freud constantly sought new metaphors. He used different ones at different times, and the metaphor used often had an impact on the theory's form. As a result, it can be hard to be sure which ideas are basic and which are metaphors (Erdelyi, 1985).

Freud's fascination with symbol and metaphor is also reflected in the theory's content. Specifically, Freud came to believe that human behavior itself is highly symbolic. People's acts are rarely quite what they seem to be. Instead, those acts symbolize other, more hidden qualities. This is an idea that permeates psychoanalytic theory.

A second feature is that it's hard to separate Freud's theory from the therapy procedures on which he based it or from the assessment that occurs continually within that therapy. Indeed, the very word *psychoanalysis* is applied to an approach to therapy, Freud's method of research, and his theory of personality. The entanglement of theory with therapy is far greater here than in any other approach to personality, and this tends to color all aspects of the theory.

When viewed in its entirety, psychoanalytic theory is very complex. Underlying this complexity, however, is a fairly small number of principles (Kahn, 2002). The theory can be confusing, because its concepts are deeply interwoven. It's hard to talk about any aspect of the theory separate from other aspects. Perhaps the best place to start, though, is Freud's view of how the mind is organized. This is often termed Freud's **topographical model** of mind.

The Topographical Model of Mind

Many people would say the mind has two regions. One region holds *conscious experience:* the thoughts, feelings, and behaviors you're aware of right now. The other contains *memories,* now outside awareness but able to come to awareness easily. Drawing on ideas of other theorists of his time (Ellenberger, 1970), Freud added a third region to this list. Taken together, the three form what Freud thought of as the mind's *topography,* or its surface configuration.

Freud used the term **conscious** much as we use it today, to mean the part of the mind that holds what you're now aware of. People can verbalize conscious experience and think about it in a logical way. The part of the mind that represents ordinary memory is termed **preconscious.** Things in the preconscious, although now not in awareness, can be brought into awareness easily. For example, if you think of your phone number or the name of the last movie you saw, you're bringing that information from the preconscious to consciousness.

Freud used the term **unconscious** in a way that's considerably different from the way it's used in everyday language. He reserved it to stand for a portion of the mind that's not directly accessible to awareness (see also Box 8.2). Freud viewed the unconscious as being (in part) a repository for urges, feelings, and ideas that are tied to anxiety, conflict, and pain (e.g., Rhawn, 1980). Being unconscious doesn't mean they're gone, though. *They exert a continuing influence* on later actions and conscious experience.

In this view, the mind is like an iceberg. The tip of the iceberg is consciousness. The much larger part—the part below water—is outside awareness. Some of it—the part you can see through the water—is the preconscious. The vast majority of it, however—the part you can't see—is the unconscious. Although the conscious and preconscious influence behavior, Freud saw them as less important than the unconscious. The unconscious is where Freud thought the core operations of personality take place.

The three levels of consciousness form the topographical model of the mind (see Figure 8.1 on page 164). Material passes easily from conscious to preconscious and back again. Material from both of these can slip into the unconscious. Truly unconscious material, however, can't be brought voluntarily to awareness because of psychological forces that keep it hidden. These regions of the mind constitute the theater in which the dynamics of personality are played out.

Box 8.2 Today's Views on the Unconscious

As long as psychology has existed, it has been apparent that events outside awareness influence what happens in awareness. Hardly anyone has assumed an unconscious as contentious and conflicted as Freud did. But many have found it necessary to make assumptions about what's going on in the unconscious.

In recent years, interest in how the mind works has grown dramatically, along with the field of *cognitive psychology* (more about cognitive processes comes up in Chapter 16). Theorists now view the unconscious with a vastly different lens than Freud did (Bargh, 1997; Epstein, 1994). The unconscious is still seen as part of the mind to which we don't have ready access, but for different reasons. Today's theorists sometimes talk of the *cognitive unconscious,* as opposed to the *psychodynamic unconscious* (for a thorough review see Hassin, Uleman, & Bargh, 2005).

From today's point of view, *consciousness* is a sort of workspace where you consider information and make judgments, come to decisions, and form intentions. If these processes become sufficiently routine, they begin to occur automatically, outside awareness. What makes things routine? Some processes are innately routine. You don't have to think about making your digestive juices flow or having your heart beat, and you'd have trouble bringing into consciousness the processes by which those events take place.

Other processes become routine from practice. As you practice anything (a tennis stroke, a new recipe, typing), what happens changes over repetitions. The first few times, you devote lots of attention to it. As you do it over and over, it starts to feel more fluid and go more smoothly. The more you practice, the less attention it needs. When you've done it enough, you disregard it almost totally. When an activity is *very* automatic, the processes have become unconscious. You no longer have access to them as you did when you were just starting out. One well-known study, for example, found that people couldn't accurately report the basis of a decision they'd just made; instead they fell back on stereotypes (Nisbett & Wilson, 1977). Automation seems to occur even for higher mental processes (Bargh & Ferguson, 2000). Even goals can become activated and pursued without the person being aware of it (Bargh, Gollwitzer, Lee-Chai, Barndollar, & Trötschel, 2001).

Seymour Epstein (1994) argues that all these phenomena and more reflect what he calls an *experiential* mode of processing. This mode of processing occurs in parallel to, but distinct from, rational processing. The experiential system is emotional and nonverbal, rather than deliberative and verbal. Its functioning is fast and largely out of awareness. Epstein argues that an unconscious as chaotic as the one Freud assumed is very unlikely. Being so poorly fit to reality, it couldn't possibly have survived. On the other hand, an unconscious such as Epstein argues for has much more adaptive value.

In sum, many aspects of people's experience are influenced by processes that occur outside awareness. Such influences occur when you form perceptions and impressions of other people and when you make judgments about how likely something is to happen. Such influences can also affect your mood states and your actions. Whether you agree with Freud about what defines the *content* of the unconscious, it's clear that he was right about its existence.

Aspects of Personality: The Structural Model

Freud (1962/1923) also developed a **structural model** of personality, which complements the topographical model. He saw personality as having three aspects, which work with each other to create the complexity of human behavior. They aren't physical entities but rather labels for three aspects of functioning. They are known as *id, ego,* and *superego.*

Id

The **id** is the original component of personality, the only one present at birth. *Id* (the Latin word meaning "it") is all the inherited, instinctive, primitive aspects of personality. The id functions entirely in the unconscious. It's closely tied to basic biological

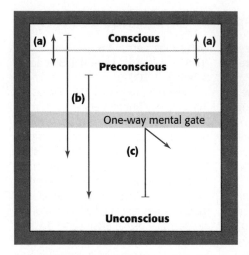

FIGURE 8.1

Graphic representation of Freud's topographical model of the mind. (A) Material can pass easily back and forth between the conscious and preconscious portions of the mind. (B) Material can also move from the conscious and preconscious into the unconscious. But once material is in the unconscious, the person is prevented from having conscious access to it because (C) a mental gate prevents retrieval.

processes, from which it draws energy. Indeed, Freud believed that *all* psychic energy comes through the id. Thus, the id is the "engine" of personality.

The id follows what's called the **pleasure principle:** that needs should be satisfied immediately (Freud, 1949/1940). Unsatisfied needs are aversive tension states. They should be gratified whenever they arise to prevent the tension. Under the pleasure principle, any increase in hunger should cause an attempt to eat. Any twinge of sexual desire should cause an attempt to get sexual gratification.

At first glance, this looks great. Who wants to walk around with inner tensions? There's a problem, though. The pleasure principle doesn't concern *how* needs are to be met. It doesn't say that needs should be met in a way that takes into account risks or problems. It just says that needs are to be met at once.

Acting totally by the pleasure principle would soon get you into a lot of trouble. There's a complex and threatening world out there. A hungry person can't just rush across a street filled with zooming cars to get to food. Social reality also presents problems. For example, if you grab your roommate's pizza before he can get to it (or if you get too friendly with his girlfriend), you may find yourself with an angry roommate on your hands.

Nonetheless, the pleasure principle means that when any tension arises, the id tries to discharge it. The id's mechanism for doing that is called the **primary process.** This entails forming a mental image (fantasy, dream, or hallucination) of an object or event that would satisfy the need and becoming involved with that image. In the case of a hungry infant, the primary process might produce an image of a mother's breast or a bottle. When you're separated from someone you love, the primary process produces images of that person. The experience of having such an image is called **wish fulfillment.**

Tension reduction by primary process has a drawback, however. The primary process can't distinguish between image and reality. Primary process thought may reduce tension briefly, but it can't do so by itself in the long run. The hungry infant that imagines sucking at a nipple won't be satisfied for long. The person who misses a loved one won't be content with fantasies, no matter how vivid. This illustrates again how the id doesn't take reality into account. It's in a world of its own wishes.

Ego

Because the id and its primary process can't deal well with reality, a second set of functions develops, termed **ego** (the Latin word for "I"). The ego evolves from the id and harnesses part of the id's energy for its own use. Ego focuses on making sure id impulses are expressed *effectively,* by taking into account the external world. Because of this concern with the outside world, most ego functioning is in the conscious and preconscious. Given the ego's ties to the id, however, it also functions in the unconscious.

The ego is said to follow the **reality principle:** the taking into account of external reality along with internal needs and urges. The reality principle brings a sense of rationality to behavior. Because it orients you toward the world, it leads you to weigh the risks linked to an action before acting. If the risks seem too high, you'll think of another way to meet the need. If there's no safe way to do so immediately, you'll delay it to a later, safer, or more sensible time.

Box 8.3 Ego Control and Delay of Gratification

A major function of the ego is to delay gratification of impulses and urges until a later time.

Delay of gratification is a mark of a mature personality; it's a major goal of socialization. Children must learn to wait for rewards (e.g., work now but be paid later), if they're to become full members of society. The *inability* to delay gratification predicts use of cigarettes, alcohol, and marijuana among high school students (Wulfert, Block, Santa Ana, Rodriguez, & Colsman, 2002) and may play a role in development of criminal behavior.

Delay of gratification has been studied from a variety of angles. (In fact, it comes up several more times in this book.) Most of the research was prompted by ideas other than psychoanalytic theory, but the findings are relevant to psychodynamic processes.

In most laboratory studies of this phenomenon, children are given the following choice: They can have a smaller, less desired reward now, or they can wait for a while and then get a larger, more desired reward. One focus of this research is on the determinants of delay (for reviews, see Mischel, 1966, 1974). It's harder for children to delay when the desired object is right in front of them (Mischel & Ebbesen, 1970). Delay is easier if the children can mentally transform the situation to make it seem as if the objects aren't really there—for example, to imagine the objects are only "color pictures in their heads" (Mischel & Baker, 1975; Moore, Mischel, & Zeiss, 1976). More generally, delay of gratification seems easiest when children distract themselves, shifting attention away from the desired rewards (Mischel, Ebbesen, & Zeiss, 1973). In effect, the ego tricks the id by getting it involved in something else.

A second line of research on delay of gratification concerns personality correlates of the ability to delay. Ability to delay relates to certain aspects of intelligence (Mischel & Metzner, 1962). Maybe this is because brighter children can more easily transform the situation mentally. Children who are better able to delay also seem more concerned with achievement and social responsibility (Mischel, 1961), fitting the idea that they have well-defined egos.

Longitudinal research by Funder, Block, and Block (1983) suggests that the basis for delay differs slightly from boys to girls. Among boys, delay seems to be closely related to the ability to control emotional and motivational impulses, to concentrate deeply, and to be deliberate in action. This fits the idea that delay of gratification is an ego function, aimed at control over the id's impulse expression. Delay among girls, in contrast, seems most strongly related to intelligence, resourcefulness, and competence. According to Funder et al. (1983), these gender differences stem from differences in the manner in which boys and girls are socialized (see also J. Block, von der Lippe, & Block, 1973; J. H. Block, 1973, 1979).

Thus, a goal of the ego is to *delay the discharge* of the id's tension until an appropriate object or activity is found (see Box 8.3). The ego uses what's called the **secondary process** to match the image of a tension-reducing object to a real object. Until such an object can be found, the ego keeps the tension in check. Ego's goal is *not* to block the id's desires permanently. The ego wants the id's urges to be satisfied. But it wants them satisfied at a time and in a way that's safe—that won't cause trouble because of some danger in the world (Bergmann, 1980).

The ego, using the reality principle and secondary process thought, is the source of intellectual processes and problem solving. The capacity for realistic thought allows the ego to form plans of action to satisfy needs and test them mentally to see whether they'll work. This is called **reality testing.** The ego is often described as having an "executive" role in personality, mediating between the desires of the id and the constraints of the external world.

It's easy to see how the id and ego can conflict. The pleasure principle says needs should be met *now;* the reality principle says *delay.* The pleasure principle orients to internal tensions; the reality principle orients to external constraints. The ego's function, in the short run, is to prevent the id from acting—to hold it up, so its needs can be met in a realistic way. Given all this, there is a vast potential for conflict within the personality.

Freud (1933) used the metaphor of a horse and rider to refer to this pulling of forces within personality. The id is the horse, providing power for movement. The ego is the rider, trying to direct the movement. Often the rider can direct the horse. Sometimes, though, the rider can only guide the horse in small ways, as the horse goes in the direction it wants to go.

The ego can appear to be a positive force, because it exercises restraint over the id. That can be misleading, however, because the ego has no moral sense. It's entirely pragmatic, concerned with getting by. The ego wouldn't be bothered by cheating or stealing or giving free rein to the pleasure principle, as long as there's no danger involved. The moral sense resides in the third part of personality.

SUPEREGO

The final aspect of personality—the last to develop—is the **superego** (a joining of two Latin words meaning "over I"). Freud held that the superego develops while the person resolves a particular conflict during development (discussed later in the chapter).

The superego is the embodiment of parental and societal values. It holds an image of what's right and wrong, and it strives for perfection rather than pleasure. The values in your superego stem from the values of your parents. To obtain the parents' love, the child comes to do what the parents think is right. To avoid pain, punishment, and rejection, the child avoids what the parents think is wrong. The process of "taking in," or incorporating, the values of parents (and wider society) is called **introjection.** Although other authority figures can influence the superego, Freud thought it derived largely from parents.

The superego is further divided into two subsystems. The **ego ideal** is rules for good behavior, or standards of excellence for the person. What the parents approve of, or value, is in the ego ideal. Conforming to those values makes you feel proud. The **conscience** is rules about what behaviors are bad. Prohibitions against things parents disapprove of and punish are in the conscience (Sederer & Seidenberg, 1976). Doing those things causes the conscience to punish you with guilt feelings.

The superego has three interrelated goals. First, it tries to prevent (not just postpone) any id impulse that would be frowned on by your parents. Second, it tries to force the ego to act morally, rather than rationally. Third, it tries to guide the person toward perfection in thought, word, and deed. The superego exerts a civilizing influence on the person, but its perfectionism is quite removed from reality.

Like the ego, the superego operates at all three levels of consciousness. This has important implications for how you experience its effects. When superego processes are conscious, you're aware of your feelings and where they're coming from. If you know you just insulted someone, despite your belief that insulting people is bad, the source of your guilt will be obvious. However, when the superego operates unconsciously to punish an urge of the id (also unconscious), you feel guilty but don't know why. Because guilt can be set off by primary process

DENNIS THE MENACE

"MOM TELLS ME THE STUFF I SHOULDN'T DO AND MY DAD TELLS ME THE STUFF I *SHOULD* DO!"

The superego has two parts. The conscience holds an image of undesirable behavior, and the ego-ideal holds an image of desirable behavior. *DENNIS THE MENACE® used by permission of Hank Ketcham and © by North America Syndicate.*

thought (unconscious id fantasies that don't really occur), the guilt itself may even be irrational.

BALANCING THE FORCES

Once the superego develops, the ego has a hard road. It must deal simultaneously with the desires of the id, the moral dictates of the superego, and the constraints of reality (see Figure 8.2). To satisfy all the demands, the ego would have to release all tension immediately in a way that's both socially acceptable and realistic. This, of course, is highly unlikely. It's much more likely that these forces will conflict. In the psychoanalytic view, such conflicts are part of life.

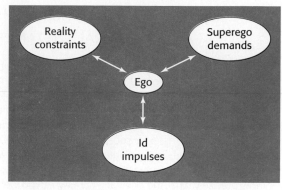

FIGURE 8.2
Graphic representation of how the ego must mediate among the often conflicting demands of the id, the superego, and the constraints of outside reality.

The term **ego strength** refers to the ego's ability to be effective despite these conflicting forces (Barron, 1953). With little ego strength, the person is torn among competing pressures. With more ego strength, the person can manage the pressures. It's possible, however, for the ego to be too strong. Someone whose ego is too strong is very rational and efficient but may also be very boring or cold and distant.

In fact, Freud didn't hold that any aspect of personality is better than the others. Rather, he suggested there should be a balance among them. A person whose superego is too strong may feel guilty all the time or may act in an insufferably saintly way. A person whose id is too strong may be obsessed with self-gratification and completely uninterested in other people. The healthiest personality is one in which the influences of the three aspects are well balanced.

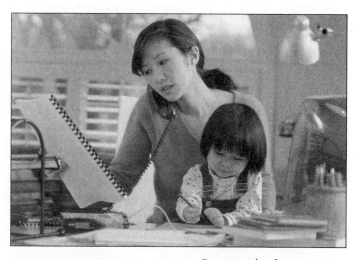

Motivation: The Drives of Personality

At several points we've talked in general terms about energy, impulses, tension states, drives, and urges. Let's now consider these forces more explicitly.

Ego strength refers to a person's ability to deal effectively with competing demands and taxing situations.

In thinking about motivation, Freud borrowed heavily from prevailing views in the biological and physical sciences. He saw people as complex energy systems, in which the energy used in psychological work (thinking, perceiving, remembering, planning, dreaming) is generated and released through biological processes. These biological processes, which operate through the id, have been called *instinct* and *drive*. These two terms differ from each other in other contexts (see Box 8.4), but they are used interchangeably here.

A drive has two related elements: a biological need state and its psychological representation. For example, the need state underlying thirst is a lack of sufficient water in the body's cells. This creates the psychological state of thirst, the desire for water. These elements combine to form a drive to drink water. (This portrayal isn't much different from the picture of motives presented in Chapter 5.)

BOX 8.4 HAVE FREUD'S IDEAS BEEN DISTORTED BY TRANSLATION AND CULTURAL DISTANCE?

Freud wrote in German and lived in a culture very different from ours. His ideas were later translated into English. Translation of any complex or subtle idea is hard, and there is great potential for error. It's hard for any translator to know precisely what the original writer intended to convey, and it's likely that no translation is entirely faithful to the original. Less-than-perfect word choices can greatly distort meaning, however.

How faithful are the translations of Freud's writings? Not very, according to Bruno Bettelheim (1982), an important analyst in his own right. Bettelheim had the background to judge. He came from a Jewish family of Vienna, spoke German from childhood, and lived in the same cultural context as Freud. He was distressed by many aspects of the English translations of Freud. Here are some examples.

Whenever possible, Freud tried to communicate his ideas in words that his readers had used since childhood, adding new insights to those common words. Two names he chose for aspects of personality are among the first words learned by every German-speaking child. In German, the words are personal pronouns. In the pronoun *I (Ich)*, Freud chose a word that virtually forces you to think of yourself, adding the emotional qualities related to your assertive affirmation of your own existence. The translated *ego*, in contrast, is lifeless and sterile.

In the pronoun *it (Es)*, Freud made an allusion that's completely lost to people who speak only English. In German, the word meaning "child" is neuter. For this reason, in early childhood, each German child is referred to as an *it*. This word, as applied to yourself, has clear emotional overtones: It's what you were called when you were so young that you hadn't learned to stifle your impulses or to feel guilty about them. A sense of personalized infancy is conveyed in the original, whereas the translated *id* has no intrinsic associations at all.

Another common word used by Freud was *Trieb,* which is commonly translated as *instinct.* Bettelheim says *drive* is better, because Freud used a different word when he wanted to refer to instincts of animals. By *Trieb,* he meant to convey an inner propulsion, a basic urge, an impulse, but not the sense that the drive was the same as an animal instinct, inborn and unalterable.

Among the few non-German terms Freud used in his theory are *Eros* and *Psyche,* which are the names of characters in a Greek myth. They were characters Freud knew intimately, as did most people to whom he was writing. (Educated people at that time read the classics.) When Freud wrote of *erotic* qualities, he meant to evoke these characters and their qualities: Eros's charm and cunning and the deep love he had for Psyche. Psyche had at first been tricked into believing that Eros was disgusting, and the message of the myth is that this was an

error. For sexual love to be true erotic pleasure, it must be filled with beauty (symbolized by Eros himself) and express the longings of the soul (symbolized by Psyche). These are connotations Freud wanted to convey with the word *erotic.* When they are stripped away (because readers don't know the myth), the word not only loses its true meaning but even takes on connotations opposite to Freud's intention.

Indeed, Bettelheim argued that the word *psyche* itself has also been misrepresented. We're used to thinking of the psyche as the mind, because that's how it's been translated. The German word for *psyche,* however, is *Seele,* which means "soul." Thus, said Bettelheim, Freud's focus was on the metaphysical, but this has been misread as a focus on the mental.

In sum, Bettelheim argued that much of the sense of Freud's ideas has been missed. Freud chose his language to evoke responses not just at an intellectual level but at an emotional level. The latter is lost in translation. Because we don't live in the cultural context in which Freud wrote, we also miss many of his nods to ideas that were common at the time.

Bettelheim also argued that Freud was aware of the distortions and chose to let them go. Why? Freud was annoyed at the U.S. medical establishment, which seemed intent on making psychoanalysis part of medicine, which Freud opposed. Apparently, he simply didn't care enough to correct them.

These processes are continuous. Drive states build up until an action causes their tension to be released. If a drive isn't expressed, its pressure continues to build. This view of motives is called a *hydraulic* model. In this view, trying to prevent a drive from being expressed only creates more pressure toward its expression.

CATHEXES AND THE USE OF ENERGY

Freud believed that psychic energy is generated continuously but gradually. Only so much is available at any given time. The idea that there's only a limited amount available within a given time span has been supported in a good deal of recent research (Baumeister, 2002; Baumeister, Bratslavsky, Muraven, & Tice, 1998; Muraven & Baumeister, 2000; Muraven, Tice, & Baumeister, 1998; Vohs, Baumeister, & Ciarocco, 2005). If you make an effort to control one thing, then there's not as much left to control something else.

Given a limited energy supply at any given time, how energy is distributed becomes an important issue. The three aspects of personality—id, ego, and superego—compete for it. Each gains power only at the expense of the other two.

Early in life, of course, the id has all the energy. The energy is used to satisfy the id's needs and to operate the primary process. Investing energy in an activity or image is called forming a **cathexis.** The more important an object or activity, the more energy invested (cathected) in it. As we said earlier, the id doesn't distinguish reality from unreality. As far as the id is concerned, cathecting an image is as good as cathecting the object. This limitation lets the ego capture part of the id's energy for its own use.

The ego uses secondary process thought to find objects in the world that match the id's images. Because real objects satisfy needs better than images do, the ego gradually comes to control more and more of the id's energy. Over time and experience, the ego controls enough energy that a surplus is available for uses beyond gratifying the id's urges. The ego uses this surplus to bring intellectual functioning to a higher level and to form cathexes of its own. These **ego cathexes** form with objects and activities *associated with* satisfying needs. Regarding hunger, for example, ego might form cathexes with reading restaurant reviews, shopping for food, or watching cooking shows on TV.

The ego also has to use energy to restrain the id from acting irrationally or immorally. The restraining forces are called **anticathexes,** because they prevent cathexes from being expressed. The clearest illustration of an anticathexis is **repression.** Repression is investing energy to keep an upsetting idea or impulse in the unconscious. This keeps the cathexis from being expressed. The harder it pushes to emerge, the more energy must be used to keep it hidden.

In the short run, anticathexes are useful because they keep troubling urges from being expressed. They create problems in the long run, though, because they drain energy from the ego that could be used in other ways. Remember, there's only so much energy to go around at any given time (Baumeister, 2002; Muraven & Baumeister, 2000). If too much of it is tied up in anticathexes, the ego has little left for anything else. When resources are lacking, behavior becomes less flexible and accommodating (Finkel & Campbell, 2001).

The superego also gathers energy from the id, through a process of *identification.* It goes like this: Young children depend on parents for need satisfaction. This leads the child into id-based cathexes toward the parents. As parents impose rules—punishing bad behavior and rewarding good behavior—the child determines which behaviors maximize need satisfaction. The child's affection for the parents (its cathexis to them) leads the child to act in ways the parents value and to *hold* those values. Cathected parental ideals thereby become part of the ego ideal, and cathected prohibitions become part of the conscience.

The competition for energy among the three aspects of personality is never ending. It's yet one more way the aspects conflict with one another. Energy, after all, is the power to control. As one aspect of personality gains control, the influence of the others diminishes.

Two Classes of Drives: Life and Death Instincts

As with many aspects of Freud's work, his ideas about drives changed over time. Ultimately, he contended that all the basic instincts form two classes (Freud, 1933). The first class is termed **life** or **sexual instincts** (collectively called **Eros**). Eros is a set of drives that deal with survival, reproduction, and pleasure. Despite the label *Eros,* not all life instincts deal with erotic urges per se. Hunger and pain avoidance, as well as sex, are life instincts. Collectively, the energy of the life instincts is known as **libido.**

Although not all life instincts are explicitly sexual, sexuality plays an important role in psychoanalytic theory (Freud, 1953a/1905). According to Freud, there's not one sex drive but many. Each is associated with a different area of the body called an **erogenous zone**. The erogenous zones are the mouth, anus, and genitals. Erogenous zones are sources of tension. Manipulating them relieves tension and produces pleasure. Thus, sucking or smoking produces oral pleasure, emptying the bowels produces anal pleasure, and rubbing the vagina or penis produces genital pleasure.

A second set of drives is **death instincts** (also termed **Thanatos**). Freud's view of them is reflected in his statement that "the goal of all life is death" (Freud, 1955/1920). He believed that life leads naturally to death and that people desire (unconsciously) to return to nothingness. The expression of death instincts is usually held back by the life instincts, however. Thus, the effects of the death instincts aren't always visible.

Freud never coined a term for the energy of death instincts, and Thanatos has received less attention than Eros. Today's biology, however, holds that a death instinct does exist in human physiology. That is, there is an active gene-directed suicide process that occurs in human cells in certain circumstances. This process, termed **apoptosis,** is a critical element in development (e.g., W. R. Clark, 1996). It also seems to be involved in the body's defense against cancer (Tyner et al., 2002). The cell death machinery is coded in your cells (Hopkin, 1995). This fact suggests that death is an ultimate goal for parts of the body. Perhaps the principle also extends more broadly into the personality.

An aspect of the death instinct that *has* received attention from psychologists concerns aggression. In Freud's view, aggression isn't a basic drive but stems from the thwarting of the death drive. That is, if Eros blocks expression of the death drive, tension remains. Energy is unspent. It can be used in aggressive or destructive actions against others. In this view, acts of aggression express *self*-destructive urges but turned outward onto others.

Coming Together of Libidinal and Aggressive Energies

Usually sexual and aggressive energies are released in separate activities. Sometimes, however, they exist side by side, with one expressed and then the other. This pattern is termed *ambivalence*. Sometimes the two even fuse and jointly energize a single activity (Freud, 1933). This merging of sex and aggression is termed *sadism*.

Several research areas bear on the interplay between sexual and aggressive energies. One of the more interesting ones sought to examine effects of pornography on aggression, rather than test psychoanalytic theory per se (for reviews, see Donnerstein, 1983, or Malamuth & Donnerstein, 1984). Nevertheless, some of the findings are instructive regarding the competition between these energies and their possible blending.

The major point in this literature is that sexual arousal can facilitate or inhibit aggression, depending on other factors. When a person is angry, exposure to *mild* sexual stimuli typically reduces aggression (e.g., Baron, 1974a, 1974b, 1979; Baron & Bell, 1977; Donnerstein, Donnerstein, & Evans, 1975; Frodi, 1977). In one study (Baron, 1974a), men were angered (or not) and later retaliated. Before retaliation, half viewed pictures of nude women, and the rest saw pictures of scenery, furniture, and abstract art. Exposure to erotica significantly reduced aggression among the angry subjects.

In contrast to this, creation of *intense* sexual arousal *increases* aggression among angry persons. In one study (Zillmann, 1971), male subjects were angered (or not) and later retaliated. Just beforehand, they viewed either a neutral film or a highly erotic, explicitly sexual film. The highly erotic film increased the aggression of angry subjects to a level even higher than was created by watching a violent fight film. Others have found that highly erotic material increases aggression toward women (Donnerstein & Hallam, 1978), especially when the erotic stimuli are themselves aggressive (Donnerstein, 1980). In sum, the evidence suggests that sexual and aggressive urges are sometimes antagonistic to each other but sometimes combine with each other (for broader discussion, see Zillmann, 1998).

CATHARSIS

We said earlier that if a drive's tension isn't released, the pressure remains and even grows. At some point, the buildup of energy may be so great that it can't be restrained any longer. At this point, the impulse is unleashed. The term **catharsis** is used to refer to the release of emotional tension in such an experience. (The term also has a second use that's discussed in Chapter 9.)

This view of catharsis has been studied mostly with respect to aggression. The principle of catharsis leads to two predictions. First, engaging in aggression should reduce tension, because the aggressive drive is no longer being stifled. Second, because this act dissipates the drive's energy, the person should be less likely to be aggressive again in the near future.

This view of aggressive energy and its release is echoed in the ideas of other theorists. Megargee (1966, 1971; Megargee, Cook, & Mendelsohn, 1967) argued that people with strong inhibitions against aggression rarely blow off steam, even when provoked. Over time, though, their feelings build until their restraints can no longer hold. Because so much energy has built up, the aggression released may be quite brutal. Ironically, the final provocation is often trivial (see also N. Miller, Pederson, Earleywine, & Pollock, 2003). Once the episode is over, these people (whom Megargee terms *overcontrolled aggressors*) revert to their overcontrolled, passive ways.

This portrayal is consistent with the psychoanalytic view of aggression, if one assumes the id impulses of these people are overcontrolled by ego and superego processes. The dynamics of overcontrolled aggression have also received a fair amount of verification (see, e.g., Blackburn, 1968a, 1968b; Megargee, 1966). Note, though, that overcontrolled aggressors are a rather select group of people.

How accurate is the catharsis hypothesis for aggression in *most* people? People seem to *think* aggression will make them feel better (Bushman, Baumeister, & Phillips, 2001), but the evidence is mixed (Baron & Richardson, 1994). Aggression can help dissipate arousal (Geen, Stonner, & Shope, 1975; Hokanson & Burgess, 1962a, 1962b; Hokanson, Burgess, & Cohen, 1963), but it's less clear why. For example, in one

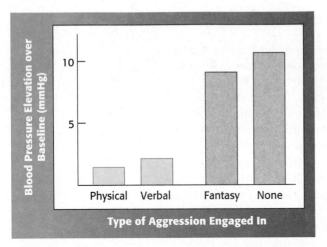

FIGURE 8.3
Tension-reducing effects of aggressive acts. This figure portrays elevations in systolic blood pressure after being provoked and then engaging in various kinds of aggression, in comparison with levels before provocation. Both physical and verbal aggression were relatively effective in returning participants to their initial levels, whereas fantasy aggression was not.

Source: Adapted from Hokanson & Burgess, 1962b.

study (Hokanson & Burgess, 1962b), subjects working on a task were harassed by the experimenter, which raised their blood pressure. Later, some could retaliate physically, others verbally, others in fantasy (writing an aggressive story in response to a TAT picture), and some not at all. As shown in Figure 8.3, the results supported the idea that true retaliation produces emotional catharsis. Subjects who retaliated physically or verbally showed decreases in blood pressure. In contrast, fantasy aggression had little effect.

Although this general pattern of effects has been obtained many times, there are important limiting conditions. The target of the aggression can't be high in status (Hokanson & Shetler, 1961) and must either be the instigator or linked to the instigator (Hokanson et al., 1963). Moreover, tension reduction doesn't require aggression per se. Virtually *any* response that stops a provocation can reduce arousal (e.g., Hokanson & Edelman, 1966; Hokanson, Willers, & Koropsak, 1968; Stone & Hokanson, 1969). There's even evidence that responding to provocation in a friendly fashion reduces arousal among women more than does responding aggressively (Hokanson & Edelman, 1966). This doesn't fit the catharsis hypothesis very well.

What about the other reflection of catharsis? Does aggression make the person less aggressive in the near future? The findings here are even more mixed. Baron and Richardson (1994) concluded that this happens only under very specific conditions. Aggression reduces later aggression only if it's a response to an instigation (e.g., Bramel, Taub, & Blum, 1968; Doob, 1970; Konecni, 1975) and the retaliation is toward the instigator and about equivalent to the instigation (e.g., Berkowitz & Alioto, 1973; Ebbesen, Duncan, & Konecni, 1975; Goldstein & Arms, 1971; Goranson, 1970; Mallick & McCandless, 1966). Interestingly enough, the retaliation may be done by someone else and still reduce aggression (E. J. Murray, 1985). On the other hand, sometimes engaging in aggression actually *increases* later aggression (Geen et al., 1975), contradicting the catharsis hypothesis. Fantasy aggression can also increase later aggression (Bartholow & Anderson, 2001; Bushman, 2002).

In sum, although some evidence suggests catharsis effects, the effects occur only under very specific circumstances. Moreover, other evidence seems to contradict catharsis. Taken together, the evidence doesn't support this aspect of psychoanalytic theory very well.

DISPLACEMENT AND SUBLIMATION OF MOTIVE FORCES

The life and death instincts provide for a wide range of behavior. Behavior is rendered even more diverse by two processes that influence how these drives are expressed. **Displacement** is a change in how energy is used or the object toward which it's used. Displacement lets blocked energy be released in another way or toward another object. For example, a hostile impulse toward your boss might be displaced and vented toward your apartment mate.

Strictly speaking, the word *displacement* applies to any shift in object choice. There's a special kind of displacement, however, that's important enough that it has a special name: **sublimation.** In sublimation, a shift occurs from a socially unacceptable form of action to an acceptable or even praiseworthy form of action.

Consider two students who are angry over criticisms a professor wrote on their term papers. Both want to hit the professor with a baseball bat. Neither does, though. One goes home, kicks his dog, and yells at his roommates. The other writes a letter to the school newspaper, criticizing a policy of the university. In both cases, aggressive energy is released in actions that substitute for the desired act (hitting the professor). Writing the letter, however, is more acceptable than taking out anger on the dog and roommates. The one who kicked the dog was displacing. The one who wrote the letter was both displacing and sublimating.

As another example, consider two women who are experiencing sexual urges toward their best friend's boyfriend. One of them displaces this impulse by acting out the sexual impulses toward the person she happens to be dating. The other one sublimates the sexual energy by composing a poem.

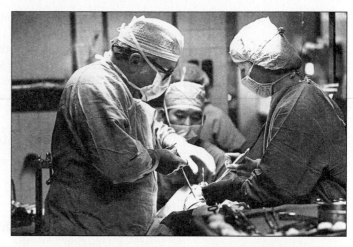

One view of surgery is that it allows unacceptable aggressive energy to be sublimated and released through a more socially acceptable form of activity.

Although displacement presumably occurs for both sexual and aggressive energy, most research on displacement looks at aggression. It's absolutely clear that displacement happens (e.g., Holmes, 1972; Marcus-Newhall, Pedersen, Carlson, & Miller, 2000; N. Miller et al., 2003; Twenge, Baumeister, Tice, & Stucke, 2001). As an example, Fenigstein and Buss (1974) found that people who'd been provoked were more aggressive in the context of a task even when the person on the receiving end was just an innocent bystander.

The concepts of displacement and sublimation are very important in psychoanalytic theory. They give it flexibility to account for the diversity of human behavior. From the psychoanalytic view, such wide-ranging phenomena as works of art and music, altruism, creativity, critical thinking, and excellence in sports can all be attributed to patterns of displaced and sublimated sexual and aggressive energy.

Indeed, the concept of sublimation is even more important than that. Sublimation permits humans to be civilized. Freud believed that without sublimation, people would act wholly from greed and their own desires. Thanks to sublimation, people are capable of acts of altruism and cooperation. Sublimation, then, is the path by which humans can transcend their animal nature and form societies.

Psychosexual Development

Freud derived his ideas primarily from a few case histories of adults in therapy. Despite this, he wrote a lot about how personality develops during childhood. He believed that early experiences are critical in determining a person's adult personality. Indeed, Freud thought that personality is largely determined by age 5. During later life, the expression of personality becomes more symbolic and less literal.

Freud viewed personality development as movement through a series of stages. Each stage reflects a body zone through which sexual energy is discharged in that period. For this reason, they're called *psychosexual stages.* In Freud's view, the child has conflicts at three stages. If the conflict isn't well resolved, too much energy gets permanently invested in that stage, a process called **fixation.** This means less energy is available to handle conflicts in later stages. As a result, it's harder to resolve later conflicts. In this sense, each stage builds on previous ones.

Fixation can occur for two reasons. A person who is overindulged in a stage may be reluctant to leave it and move on. One whose needs are deeply frustrated *can't* move on until the needs are met. In either case, personality gets partly stuck at this stage, as a portion of the libido becomes invested in the concerns of that stage. The stronger the fixation, the more the libido is invested in it. In a very strong fixation, the person is so preoccupied—unconsciously—that there is little energy left for anything else.

THE ORAL STAGE

The **oral stage** extends from birth to roughly 18 months. During this time, much of the infant's interaction with the world occurs through the mouth and lips, and gratification focuses in that area. The mouth is the source of tension reduction (eating) and pleasurable sensations (tasting, licking, and sucking). At the same time, infants are completely dependent on others for their survival. The conflict of this stage concerns the ending of this arrangement: the process of weaning—literal and figurative. That is, toward the end of this stage, children are under increasing pressure to let go of their mother and become less reliant on her.

This stage has two substages. During the first (lasting roughly 6 months), the baby is helpless and dependent. Because the baby is more or less limited to taking things in (food and other experiences), the first part of the oral stage is called the *oral incorporative phase.* Freud thought that several traits develop here, including a general sense of optimism versus pessimism, trust versus mistrust, and dependency on others. Recall Freud's fascination with symbolism and the transformation of the literal into the symbolic. This fascination extended to his ideas about traits. He believed that the trait of gullibility—the tendency to "swallow" everything you're told—arises from events during the oral incorporative phase.

The second part of the oral stage starts with teething. It's called the *oral sadistic phase.* Sexual pleasure now comes from biting and chewing (and even inflicting pain—thus sadistic). During this time, the infant is weaned from the bottle or breast and begins to bite and chew food. Traits arising during this phase trace to this newly acquired ability. This phase is thought to determine who is verbally aggressive later on and who uses "biting" sarcasm.

In general terms, oral characters should relate to the world orally. They should be more preoccupied than others with food and drink. When stressed, they should be more likely than others to engage in activities involving the mouth, such as smoking, drinking, and nailbiting. When angry, they should be verbally aggressive. Oral characters should be concerned with getting support from others, and should do things to ease interactions with people.

Although oral gratification may be most important during infancy, the pleasure of oral stimulation continues throughout life.

Is this characterization accurate? Perhaps. Joseph Masling and his colleagues found that tests of oral imagery relate to both obesity (Masling, Rabie, & Blondheim, 1967; Weiss & Masling, 1970) and alcoholism (Bertrand & Masling, 1969). Orality has also been related to measures of interpersonal interest and social skills. For example, oral imagery has been related to the need to nurture others (Holt, 1966) and to interpersonal effectiveness (Masling, Johnson, & Saturansky, 1974). Persons high in oral imagery also volunteer readily for interpersonal tasks (Bornstein & Masling, 1985; Masling, O'Neill, & Jayne, 1981) and rely on other people's judgments during ambiguous tasks (Masling, Weiss, & Rothschild, 1968).

More generally, people who display oral imagery seem to be highly motivated to gain closeness and support from others and are sensitive to how others react to them. They have greater physiological reactivity to social isolation (Masling, Price, Goldband, & Katkin, 1981) and to subtle cues of rejection (Masling, O'Neill, & Katkin, 1982) than people who display less oral imagery. They also use more physical contact during social interaction (Juni, Masling, & Brannon, 1979) and are more self-disclosing (Juni, 1981) than less oral people.

We should point out that you don't have to be extremely oral to seek oral gratification. Lots of people chew gum. Nor is the expression of sexual energy through oral contact limited to early childhood. Indeed, there's evidence all around you that seeking of oral pleasure continues into adulthood. After all, what is serious kissing but an oral expression of sexuality? Nor is that the only way sexuality is expressed orally among adults. In sum, the mouth seems to be an important part of the body through which the human's sexual nature is expressed.

THE ANAL STAGE

The **anal stage** of development begins at about 18 months and continues into the third year. During this period, the anus is the key erogenous zone, and pleasure comes from stimulation that occurs in defecation. The big event of this period is toilet training. For many children, toilet training is the first time that external constraints are systematically imposed on satisfaction of internal urges. When toilet training starts, children can't relieve themselves whenever and wherever they want. They must learn that there's an appropriate time and place for everything.

The personality characteristics said to arise from fixations during this period depend on how toilet training is approached by parents and caretakers. Two orientations are typical. One involves urging the child to eliminate at a desired time and place and praising the child lavishly for success. This places a lot of attention on the elimination process and reward for the child. This convinces the child of the value of producing things (in this case urine and feces) at the "right" time and place, by whatever means possible. To Freud, this provides a basis for adult productivity and creativity.

The second approach to toilet training is harsher. Rather than praise for a job well done, the emphasis is on punishment, ridicule, and shame for failures. This practice yields two patterns, depending on how the child reacts. If the child adopts an active pattern of rebellion, eliminating forcefully when the parents

An anal retentive personality might be displayed in an excessively neat and tidy workplace.

least want it, a set of *anal expulsive traits* develop. These are tendencies to be messy, cruel, destructive, and overtly hostile.

If the child tries to get even by withholding feces and urine, a set of *anal retentive traits* develops. The anal retentive personality is a rigid, obsessive style. The characteristics that form this pattern are sometimes called the *anal triad:* stinginess, obstinacy, and orderliness. *Stinginess* stems from the desire to retain feces. *Obstinacy* reflects the struggle of wills over toilet training. *Orderliness* is a reaction against the messiness of defecating. This pattern does seem to exist. In one study (Rosenwald, 1972), male students assessed as having the most anal anxiety were also the most compulsively neat (see also Juni & Fischer, 1985; Juni & Lo Cascio, 1985).

THE PHALLIC STAGE

The **phallic stage** begins during the third year and continues through the fifth year. During this period, the focus shifts to the genital organs. This is also the period when most children begin to masturbate, as they become aware of the pleasure that arises from genital manipulation.

At first, the awakening sexual desires are completely *autoerotic* in nature. That is, sexual pleasure is totally derived from self-stimulation. Gradually, however, libido shifts toward the opposite-sex parent, as boys develop an interest in their mothers and girls develop an interest in their fathers. At the same time, the child becomes hostile toward the same-sex parent, due to the perception of competition between them over the affection of the other parent.

Boys' desire to possess their mothers and replace their fathers is termed the **Oedipus complex** (after the character in the play *Oedipus Rex,* who unwittingly marries his mother after killing his father). Comparable feelings in girls are sometimes called an *Oedipus complex* and sometimes an *Electra complex* (after the Greek character Electra, who persuades her brother to kill both their mother and their mother's lover in revenge for the death of their father). These patterns reflect forces that are similar in many ways, but the forces are displayed differently for boys and girls. At this point, the developmental patterns for boys and girls diverge.

Let's consider first what happens to boys. Two changes take place: His love for his mother transforms into sexual desire, and his feelings for his father shift toward hostility and hatred, because his father is a rival for his mother's affection. Over time, the boy's jealousy and competitiveness toward his father may become extreme. Such thoughts may induce feelings of guilt. At the same time, the boy fears that his father will retaliate against him for his desire toward his mother. In traditional psychoanalytic theory, the boy's fear is quite specific: He fears that his father will castrate him to eliminate the source of his lust. Freud termed this **castration anxiety.**

Ultimately, castration anxiety causes the boy to push his desire for his mother into the unconscious. Castration anxiety also causes the boy to **identify** with his father, a term that has a somewhat different meaning here than earlier in the chapter. Here *identification* means to develop feelings of similarity to and connectedness with someone else. This does several things. First, it gives the boy a kind of "camouflage." Being like his father makes it seem less likely that his father will harm him. Second, by identifying with desirable aspects of the father, the boy reduces his ambivalence toward him. Identification thus paves the way for development of the superego, as the boy introjects his father's values.

Finally, by identifying with the father, the boy gains vicarious expression of his sexual urges toward his mother. That is, he gains symbolic access to his mother *through*

BOX 8.5 PENIS ENVY OR VAGINA ENVY?

As discussed elsewhere in the chapter, Freud assumed that developing girls eventually confront the fact that they don't have a penis. He believed this discovery has shattering impact. Girls feel castrated—betrayed—and they blame their mothers for it. This feeling of incompleteness and castration haunts them for the rest of their lives. In his view, the envy women develop for men—penis envy—motivates much of their later behavior, both directly and symbolically.

There are many examples. Women try to recover their lost penises symbolically by incorporating one into their bodies through sex and by giving birth to male children. In today's society, they also seek to obtain the power the penis confers by entering business, law, and other power-related pursuits. Penis envy can also be expressed by desiring others to share the same fate. Thus, some women try to reduce men to the same pitiful state, castrating men symbolically by being "sharp" and "cutting" in social interactions.

This description is entirely compatible with psychoanalytic thought. A case can be made that at least some girls experience a sense that they're missing something boys have, something that may be important. But the idea that penis envy is a prime source of women's motivation is not exactly calculated to win friends among women. Many see this position as condescending and demeaning toward women and a gross distortion (Horney, 1939, 1967).

To point out the arbitrariness of Freud's assumptions, Peterson (1980) proposed a different hypothesis. According to her, Freud got things backward (perhaps because the truth was too threatening to him). It's not women who are envious of men; it's men who are envious of women. Young boys, growing up, sooner or later confront the fact that they have no vagina. This shattering discovery leads to an envy from which they never recover. The resentment that stems from this envy influences all male behavior.

As did Freud, Peterson assumed that the manifestations of this envy are primarily symbolic. This, suggested Peterson, is why men insist on having pockets in their pants. Lots of pockets. Indeed, the three-piece suit (worn by businessmen and others making vain, pathetic attempts to convey an image of power) is a virtual orgy of symbolic wish fulfillment. It has pants pockets, vest pockets, jacket pockets, even an *internal* jacket pocket—symbolism on top of symbolism!

It should be obvious that Peterson's argument was made tongue in cheek. However, she also was making a more serious point about psychoanalytic theory and about theory more generally. There are places in psychoanalytic theory (as in any theory) where assumptions are made that are arbitrary, seemingly based on societal preconceptions rather than theoretical necessity. It's always important to think about the basis for assumptions in order to decide for yourself whether they're sensible.

---

his father. The more the boy resembles the father, the more easily he can fantasize himself in his father's place.

For girls, the conflict of the phallic stage is more complicated. As we said earlier, girls abandon their love relationship with their mother for a new one with their father. This shift occurs when the girl realizes she has no penis. She withdraws love from her mother because she blames her mother for her castrated condition (after discovering that her mother has no penis either). At the same time, the girl's affection is drawn to her father, who does have a penis. Ultimately, the girl comes to wish that her father would share his penis with her through sex or that he would provide her with the symbolic equivalent of a penis—a baby.

Freud referred to these feelings as **penis envy** (though see Box 8.5). Penis envy is the female counterpart of castration anxiety in boys. As do boys, girls resolve the conflict through identification. By becoming more like her mother, the girl gains vicarious access to her father. She also increases the chances that she'll marry someone just like him.

Fixations that develop during the phallic stage result in personalities that, in effect, continue to wrestle with Oedipal conflicts. Men may go to great lengths to demonstrate that they haven't been castrated. The way to do that is to seduce as many

Box 8.6   THE THEORIST AND THE THEORY

Freud's Own Oedipal Crisis

The idea that personal experiences of personality theorists influenced the very form taken by their theories is vividly illustrated by the life of Sigmund Freud. In fact, it's widely believed that several aspects of Freud's life had a direct impact on his theories.

Freud's father, Jakob, a merchant, was 40 years old at the time of Sigmund's birth (1856). By all accounts, he was a strict and authoritarian father. Given this, it would be no surprise that Freud's feelings about his father were ambivalent. Freud's memories were, in fact, of hating his father as well as loving him. A hint of scandal concerning Sigmund's birth may also have had a bearing on his relationship with his father. Two different dates are indicated in various places as his birthdate. This may have been a clerical error. Some believe, however, that the later date was

an effort to disguise the fact that Freud's mother was pregnant when she and his father married (Balmary, 1979).

Jakob Freud had had two sons in a prior marriage and was himself a grandfather when Sigmund was born. His wife, Amalie, on the other hand, was only 20. Sigmund was her first child and her favorite. Sigmund responded by developing a highly idealized image of his mother and a strong affection for her. By all accounts, they had a very close relationship.

In short, the relationships of Freud's childhood had all the elements of what he would later call the *Oedipal conflict.* There was a deep attachment to his mother, which some have said had sexual overtones. There was also a strong ambivalence toward his father. (Freud was even late for his father's funeral, an act he later saw as having been unconsciously motivated.) It seems hard to ignore the possibility that Freud used his own

experiences as a model for what he came to argue were universal aspects of development.

Nor was the Oedipal crisis the only aspect of Freud's thinking to be influenced by events in his own life. World War I, in which 10 million people died, deeply disillusioned Freud, along with many other Europeans. Newspapers were filled with accounts of the slaughter, which seemed truly purposeless. Two of Freud's sons fought in the war, and his fears for their safety must have been a great strain on him. Shortly after the end of the war, Freud wrote his view of the death instinct: that people have an unconscious wish to die, which they turn outward toward others in murderous actions such as war. It seems likely that this view was partly Freud's attempt to understand how the atrocities of that war could have come to happen. Thus, once again, the elements of the theory seem formed by the experiences of the theorist.

---

women as they can or father many children. The attempt to assert their masculinity may also be expressed symbolically by attaining great success in their career. Alternatively, they may fail sexually and professionally (purposely, but unconsciously) because of the guilt they feel over competing with their father for their mother's love.

Among women, the continuation of the Oedipal conflict is displayed by relating to men in a way that is excessively seductive and flirtatious, but with a denial of the sexuality. This style of relating first develops toward the father. She was attracted to him first, but by now has repressed the sexual desire that first drew her. The pattern then applies to her later social interactions. This is a woman who excites men with her seductive behavior and then is surprised when the men want sex with her.

Freud felt that identifying the Oedipus complex was one of his key theoretical contributions. This brief span involves considerable turmoil filled with love, hate, guilt, jealousy, and fear. He believed that how children negotiate the conflicts and difficulties of the phallic stage determines their attitudes toward sexuality, interpersonal competitiveness, and personal adequacy (see also Box 8.6).

Fixations that develop during these first three stages of development presumably form much of the basis of adult personality. Some of the traits said to derive from fixations during these stages are summarized in Table 8.1.

Table 8.1 Personality Qualities Believed to Follow from Fixations in the First Three Stages of Psychosexual Development.

Stage of Fixation	Personality Qualities
Oral	Incorporative: Dependent, gullible, jealous Sadistic: Sarcastic and verbally aggressive
Anal	Expulsive: messy, cruel, destructive Retentive: obstinate, neat and orderly, stingy
Phallic	Among males: macho aggressive sexuality, excessive striving for career power; alternatively, sexual and occupational impotence Among females: flirtatious, seductive behavior that doesn't lead to sexual interaction

THE LATENCY PERIOD

At the close of the phallic stage, the child enters a period of relative calm, termed the **latency period.** This period, from about age 6 to the early teens, is a time when sexual and aggressive drives are less active. The lessening of these urges results partly from the emergence of the ego and superego. During this period, children turn their attention to other pursuits, often intellectual or social in nature. Thus, the latency period is a time when the child's experiences broaden, rather than a time when new conflicts are confronted. As an example, parental identifications during the phallic stage may be supplemented in the latency period by identifications with other figures of authority, perhaps religious figures or teachers.

With the onset of puberty (toward the end of this period), sexual and aggressive urges again intensify. In addition, conflicts of previous periods may be re-encountered. This is a time when the coping skills of the ego are severely taxed. Although adolescents have adult sexual desires, the release of sexual energy through intercourse isn't socially sanctioned. As a result, sexual gratification is sought in other ways.

THE GENITAL STAGE

In later adolescence and adulthood, the person moves into the final stage of psychosexual development, the **genital stage.** If earlier psychosexual stages have been negotiated well, the person enters this stage with libido still organized around the genitals, and it remains focused there throughout life. The sexual gratification during this stage differs, however, from that of earlier stages. Earlier attachments were narcissistic. The child cared only about his or her own sexual pleasure. Others mattered only insofar as they furthered the child's own pleasure. In the genital stage, a desire develops to share mutual sexual gratification with someone. Thus, the person becomes capable of loving others not just for selfish reasons but also for altruistic ones.

Ideally, the person is able to achieve full and free orgasm on an equal basis. This ability to share with others in a warm and caring way and to be concerned with their welfare is the hallmark of the genital stage. Persons in this stage also have more control over impulses, both sexual and aggressive, and are able to release them in smaller amounts (but more frequently) in sublimated, socially acceptable ways. In this manner, the person becomes transformed from a self-centered, pleasure-seeking infant into a well-socialized, caring adult.

Freud believed that people don't enter the genital stage automatically and that this transition is rarely achieved in its entirety (see Fenichel, 1945). Most people have less control over their impulses than they should, and most have difficulty gratifying sexual desires in completely satisfying and acceptable ways. In this sense, the genital personality is an ideal to strive for, rather than an end point to be taken for granted. It is the perfect culmination of psychosexual development from the analytic point of view.

Psychoanalytic Structure and Process: Problems and Prospects

The psychoanalytic view on how personality is organized and functions has been influential since its development. It has also been controversial. From the start, people were reluctant to accept aspects of the theory. Many were incensed by the prominence of sexual themes. They were shocked that anyone would suggest that the behavior of young children is sexually motivated. It also was difficult for many to believe that behavior is determined largely by forces outside awareness.

The scientific community faulted psychodynamic theory on other grounds. The primary problem from a scientific standpoint is that the theory is very hard to test. One reason is that many psychoanalytic concepts are defined ambiguously. An example of this is provided by the term *libido*. Freud used this term to refer to sexual energy, a psychological quality that arises from physiological processes. We know little else about it. Where does it come from? What makes it sexual in nature? How do you measure it? Without some way to measure it, you can't study it. By implication, other ideas to which libido is linked (e.g., psychosexual development, fixation) are also hard to study. Indeed, many psychoanalytic concepts—cathexis, the death wish, id, ego—are also problematic from a research point of view. When a theory's concepts can't be pinned down, the theory can't be tested.

Part of the ambiguity of psychoanalytic concepts comes from Freud's tendency to describe concepts differently from one time to another. Even more ambiguity comes from the fact that Freud thought about personality in such a metaphorical way. This metaphorical approach is deeply embedded in descriptions of the theory. As a result, it's difficult to know when Freud should be read literally and when he should be read metaphorically.

Consider, for example, the Oedipal complex. Should we believe Freud meant literally that every boy comes to desire his mother sexually at around age 4? Or should we assume he was using the Oedipal theme as a metaphor to describe the conflict between young children and their parents? Freud wrote at one point that many of the specific explanatory devices he used could be replaced or discarded without damaging the theory (Silverman, 1976). Clearly, then, parts of what he wrote shouldn't be taken literally. Unfortunately, we don't know which parts.

As a metaphorical statement, the Oedipal theme makes a good deal of sense. As a literal statement, it doesn't hold up as well. As Sears (1943, p. 136) wrote, "Freud's notion of the universal Oedipus complex stands as a sharply etched grotesquerie against his otherwise informative description of sexual development."

Scientific psychologists also criticize the evidence on which psychoanalytic theory rests. One focus of this criticism is Freud's heavy reliance on case studies in developing his ideas, particularly ideas involving infantile sexuality. The case study has several problems. It's very subjective, influenced as much by what the researcher brings to the situation as by what the object of study brings. It's hard to be sure whether the insights gained by one observer would be gained by another, even looking at the same case.

The problem of reliability is even further compounded in this instance. Freud acted both as theorist–researcher and as therapist. Thus, he took an active role in the development of the case history, becoming involved in the interpretation of what was said and done. Freud's actions as a participant–observer may have biased the kinds of things his patients said even more than usual (Powell & Boer, 1994). For example, more sexually toned material emerged as therapy proceeded. Was this because repression was weakening or because patients learned over time that this was what Freud was interested in? Indeed, there is evidence that Freud was sometimes highly directive with patients (Esterton, 1998).

Freud allowed himself to be biased in another way, as well, by relying so much on patients. He carefully screened potential patients and allowed into therapy only those he thought were very good candidates. Thus, he developed his ideas from observations of a biased set of cases. We can't be sure how much or in what ways these people differed from the overall population, but they certainly weren't chosen randomly.

Moreover, the number of cases Freud relied on for a database was distressingly small. In fact, in all his writings and works, Freud described case histories of only a dozen or so people. Yet from this very narrow database—a dozen or so people, all of whom he had carefully chosen and all of whom were in therapy—he went on to formulate what he regarded as universal rules about personality functioning in general. Many researchers find this problematic.

Another criticism of psychoanalytic ideas is the tendency to confuse *facts* with *inferences*. For example, certain observations led Freud to infer the existence (and universality) of an Oedipal complex. He then went on to discuss the Oedipal complex as though its existence were a fact. A general tendency to mix fact with inference has contributed to an intellectual climate in psychoanalytic circles in which basic concepts have gone untested—because it apparently was thought they didn't *need* to be tested (Crews, 1996; Esterson, 1993).

Despite these problems, there's been a resurgence of interest in the ideas that make up both the topographic model of mind and the structural model of personality (Bargh, 1997). With respect to the topography of the mind, many people who start from different perspectives now argue that important aspects of memory cannot be brought to consciousness voluntarily. In some cases, this is because the elements are too small or too hard to locate. Sometimes it apparently is because the thing we're looking for (by its very nature) can be *used* but not *viewed*. Sometimes it's because the thing we might be looking for has become so automatic that, in effect, it's fallen out of our mental "address book" and become lost. Although these aren't quite the same as the unconscious phenomena Freud emphasized, they represent new interest in the idea that the mind has more than two regions.

With respect to the structural model, it is being re-emphasized that we shouldn't get distracted by the idea that the mind has three components. Think of them instead as three modes of functioning (Grigsby & Stevens, 2000). Take the descriptions less literally. The id is simply the psychological nature of the infant. Infantile qualities are overlaid in all of us by effects of socialization, but those infantile qualities remain in some sense the basic structure from which we grew. The id is the part that *wants*—wants as the 1-year-old wants, without regard to dangers or disapprovals. We all still have that part, and it still makes its presence known. The ego is the set of restraints we learn, restraints that diminish the pain we experience from grabbing too fast for what we want without looking for danger. The superego is the abstract rules we learn, to become part of a society in which we can't always have our way, even if we wait patiently.

The idea that humans begin life grabbing for what they want when they first want it, and only gradually learn to restrain themselves, makes a lot of sense. The idea that people later learn abstractions concerning morality also makes sense. So does the idea that the moral abstractions can conflict with the wants. In sum, the structural model expresses a fair amount of truth about the human experience.

What is the future of these ideas? Some see them as being of historical interest only. Others see them as valuable. They remain an important part of the course you're taking. We suspect they'll remain there for a long time.

· SUMMARY ·

Freud's topographical model assumes three regions of mind: the conscious, the pre-conscious (ordinary memory), and the unconscious (a part of mind that isn't accessible to consciousness). The unconscious holds threatening or unacceptable ideas and urges.

Freud's structural model assumes three facets of personality. The id (the original part) is the source of all energy. It follows the pleasure principle (that all needs should be immediately gratified), exists only in the unconscious, and uses primary process thinking (primitive and separate from reality). The ego eventually develops because the id ignores the demands of the external world, and they cannot be ignored. Ego follows the reality principle (that behavior must take into account external reality), operates in all three regions of the mind, and tries to see that the id's impulses are grat-ified in a realistic way. The ego uses secondary process (reality-based) thought. The third facet, superego, is a representation of rules by which parents reward and punish the child. It has two parts: Ego ideal is standards of moral perfection. Conscience is a representation of behaviors that are considered bad. Both function in all three regions of the mind. Once the superego develops, the ego must mediate among id, superego, and reality.

Investing energy in a need is called a *cathexis*. Restraining forces (from the ego) are called *anticathexes*. Id impulses form two categories: Life instincts aim for self-preservation and sexual pleasure. Death instincts are self-destructive and may turn outward as aggression. Catharsis in aggression is releasing an aggressive urge, which is thought to reduce tension and decrease the need to aggress. Displacement releases the impulse onto a different target from that initially intended. Impulses can also be sub-limated, or transformed into socially acceptable acts.

Freud argued that child development proceeds through psychosexual stages and that adult personality is influenced by how crises are resolved at each stage. In the oral stage, sexuality centers on the mouth, and the crisis involves being weaned. In the anal stage, sexuality centers on the anus, and the crisis involves toilet training. In the phal-lic stage, sexuality centers on the genitals, and the crisis (creating Oedipal and Electra complexes) involves lust for the opposite-sex parent and fear of and rivalry with the same-sex parent. The latency period is a calm interval with no serious conflict. The genital period is maturity, in which genital sexuality shifts from selfish narcissism to mutual sharing.

· GLOSSARY ·

Anal stage   The second stage of development, centered around issues in toilet training.

Anticathexis   The investment of energy in suppressing an impulse or image.

Apoptosis   Biologically programmed cell death.

Castration anxiety   A boy's fear (from the phallic stage) that his father will perceive him as a rival and castrate him.

Catharsis   The release of emotional tension.

Cathexis   The investment of psychic energy in a desired activity or image.

Conscience   The part of the superego that punishes violations of moral standards.

Conscious   The part of the mind that holds what one is currently aware of.

Death instincts (Thanatos)   Self-destructive instincts, often turned outward as aggression.

Displacement   The shifting of an impulse from its original target to a different target.

Ego   The rational part of the personality that deals pragmatically with reality.

Ego cathexis   Binding psychic energy in an ego-guided activity.

Ego ideal   The part of the superego that represents perfection and rewards for good behavior.

Ego strength   The ability of the ego to function despite the competing demands of the id, superego, and reality.

Erogenous zone   A sexually responsive area of the body.

Fixation   The condition of being partly stuck in a stage of psychosexual development.

Genital stage   The final stage of development, characterized by mature and mutual sexual involvement with another.

Id   The original, primitive component of personality; the source of all energy.

Identify   To develop feelings of similarity to and connectedness with another person.

Introjection   Absorbing the values of one's parents into one's superego.

Latency period   The period in which the crises of the phallic stage give way to a temporary calm.

Libido   The collective energy of the life instincts.

Life instincts or **sexual instincts (Eros)** Survival and sexual instincts.

Oedipus complex   The mix of desire for the opposite-sex parent and fear of or hatred for the same-sex parent.

Oral stage   The first stage of psychosexual development, in which oral needs create a crisis over weaning.

Penis envy   A girl's envy of males, from feelings of having been castrated.

Phallic stage   The third stage of development, in which a crisis occurs over sexual desire for the opposite-sex parent.

Pleasure principle   The idea that impulses should be gratified immediately.

Preconscious   The region of the mind that corresponds to ordinary memory.

Primary process   The id process that creates an unconscious image of a desired object.

Reality principle   The idea that actions must take into account the constraints of external reality.

Reality testing   The ego's checking to see whether plans will work before they are put into action.

Repression   Preventing an idea or impulse from becoming conscious.

Secondary process   The ego process of rationally seeking an object to satisfy a desire.

Structural model   Freud's model of three components of personality.

Sublimation   Altering an unacceptable id impulse to an activity that's more socially acceptable.

Superego   The component of personality that seeks moral perfection.

Topographical model   Freud's model of three regions, or areas, of the mind.

Unconscious   The region of the mind that's not accessible to consciousness.

Wish fulfillment   The creation of an unconscious image of a desired object.

CHAPTER 9

Anxiety, Defense, and Self-Protection

Dan and Jamie are talking about a club they went to last weekend, at which one of their friends got flagrantly, ostentatiously drunk—something she's done weekly for the past year.

"Man, I can't believe how much Robin *drinks*," says Jamie. "She soaks it up like a sponge."

At this moment, Robin rounds the corner, practically running into them.

"Hey Robin, are you still high from last weekend?" Jamie asks.

"What are you talking about?" replies Robin. "I didn't drink *that* much."

"Seriously, Robin," Dan throws in, "aren't you concerned about how much you've been drinking?"

Robin's face takes on an offended look. "Look, guys, I don't have a problem, so just stay off my back," she says, as she turns and walks away.

Dan and Jamie look at each other and shrug.

Roselyn and Roy, who have been dating for several months, are at a party. Also there is Tim, a very attractive guy they both know. At the end of the evening, after Tim and his date have left, Roselyn is talking with Roy and some friends. She says, "Didn't you see the way Tim was coming on to me? I wish he wouldn't do it, but he does it all the time."

Later, on the way home, Roy says to her, "Roselyn, you just made a fool of yourself—and me—in front of all those people. Tim didn't come on to you at all. I can't imagine where you got such an idea."

CHAPTER 8 described the psychoanalytic view of human nature. In this chapter, we consider more deeply some ways in which human nature is reflected in behavior, according to that view. In many respects, the points made here are extensions of the logic of Sigmund Freud's theory. Some of the ideas, however, came from other people. Most prominent among them was his daughter, Anna Freud (1966).

Anxiety

Much of the activity of personality—in people who are perfectly normal, as well as people with problems—concerns **anxiety.** Freud (1936/1926) saw anxiety as a warning signal to the ego that something bad is about to happen. Naturally, people seek to avoid or escape anxiety.

Freud (1959/1926) distinguished among three types of anxiety, which reflect three kinds of bad things. The simplest is **reality anxiety,** which arises from a threat or danger in the world. It's what you experience when you realize you're about to be bit by a dog, crash your car, be yelled at for a mistake at work, or fail an exam. As its name implies, reality anxiety is rooted in reality. We deal with it by fixing, avoiding, or escaping from the situation producing the feeling.

The second type is **neurotic anxiety.** This is unconscious fear that your id impulses will get out of control and have you do something that will get you punished. People with a lot of neurotic anxiety are constantly worried about the id's escaping from the ego's control (though the worry is unconscious). This isn't a fear of expressing id impulses per se. It's a fear of the punishment that will result from expressing them.

Because people are often punished for impulsive behavior, particularly if it's behavior that society disapproves of, this type of anxiety has a kind of basis in reality. In this case, however, the danger arises from within the person, from the urges of the id. For this reason, neurotic anxiety is harder to deal with than reality anxiety. You can drive carefully, prepare for exams, and avoid dangerous dogs, but you can't escape from your id. It always has the potential to get out of control.

The third type, called **moral anxiety,** is the fear people have when they've violated (or are about to violate) their moral codes. If your moral sense forbids cheating and you're tempted to cheat, you will feel moral anxiety. If your moral sense forbids sex before marriage and you're just about to have sex with someone, you will experience moral anxiety. Moral anxiety is felt as guilt or shame.

Moral anxiety arises from the conscience that's part of your superego. The stronger your superego, the more likely you'll have moral anxiety. Again, it's important to be clear about the difference between this and reality anxiety. People may be punished by society for moral lapses, but the threat of punishment from society isn't the basis of moral anxiety. Its source is internal, in your conscience. As with neurotic anxiety, it's hard to deal with. Just as you can't escape your id, you can't run away from your conscience.

Mechanisms of Defense

If your ego did its job perfectly, you'd never feel anxiety. External dangers would be avoided or dealt with, preventing reality anxiety. Id impulses would be released in degrees at appropriate times, preventing neurotic anxiety. And you'd never let yourself do anything (or even *want* to do anything) that your superego prohibits, preventing moral anxiety. No one's ego works this well, however. As a result, most people experience some anxiety, and many people experience a lot. This is part of normal life.

When anxiety arises, the ego responds in two ways. First, it increases rational problem-oriented coping efforts. It tries to deal (consciously) with the source of the threat. This works pretty well for reality anxiety. Second, it engages **defense mechanisms,** tactics the ego develops to help it avoid the other kinds of anxiety. When defenses work well, they keep anxiety away altogether. Defense mechanisms share two characteristics: First, they all can operate unconsciously. Second, they all distort or transform reality in one way or another.

Varying defense mechanisms have been proposed (A. Freud, 1966). The next sections outline several of them.

REPRESSION

The central mechanism of defense is called **repression.** Indeed, Sigmund Freud often used the terms *defense* and *repression* interchangeably. Repression can be done consciously (which Anna Freud called *suppression*), as the person tries to force something out of awareness (see also Box 9.1). Most discussions of repression, however, focus on it as an unconscious process.

BOX 9.1   UNINTENDED EFFECTS OF THOUGHT SUPPRESSION

People sometimes consciously try to keep particular thoughts out of their minds. If you're trying to quit smoking, you want to avoid thinking about cigarettes. If you're trying to lose weight, you want not to think of food. If you've just broken up with someone, you don't want to think about the things you used to do together. In each case, you try to keep these ideas out of your consciousness.

Sometimes thought suppression works, but trying not to think of something can have unintended side effects. Dan Wegner and his colleagues conducted a program of studies on thought suppression (Wegner, 1989, 1994; Wenzlaff & Wegner, 2000), and their conclusions may surprise you. Trying not to think about something can actually make that thought become *more* likely later on, especially if the thought's an emotionally arousing one (Wegner, Shortt, Blake, & Page, 1990).

The idea of conscious thought suppression contains a paradox. Thought suppression involves two steps: deciding to suppress the thought and then getting rid of all evidence of the thought, including the plan to suppress it. This seems to require you to be

conscious of your intent and not conscious of it, all at once. (If repression occurs unconsciously, of course, this problem is avoided, because the plan to get rid of the thought is unconscious.)

So what happens when people try to suppress a thought? Initial research taught people a think-aloud technique in which they reported all thoughts that came to mind. They then did this for periods of five minutes under two different conditions. In one condition, they were to try not to think of a white bear. Every time a white bear came to mind, they were to ring a bell in front of them. In the other condition, they were to *think* of a white bear and to ring the bell when they did. For some, the suppression came first, then the thinking. For others, the order was reversed.

Two findings emerged. First, it was hard to avoid thinking of a white bear. (The most effective strategy was focusing on something else.) Interestingly, most intrusions of the unwanted thought occurred when the person had just finished another thought and was silent. It was as though the thought could be kept out as long as the mental machinery was fully occupied, but when an opening came up, the thought leaped in. Suppression is hard unless you have a distractor to think of

instead. To put this idea in psychoanalytic terms, it's apparently easier to form an alternative cathexis than to form an anticathexis.

The second finding was that people who suppressed showed a rebound effect. That is, when they were later asked to think of the bear, they did so more frequently and consistently than did the other people. Their reports of the white bear were stable over the five-minute period. In contrast, those who'd started by thinking of the bear wore out fairly quickly, and their reports fell off over the five-minute period. Rebound effects have been found repeatedly, even in dreams! (Wegner, Wenzlaff, & Kozak, 2004).

In practical terms, what are the implications of findings such as these? What should you do if you want *not* to think about something? Wegner (1989) argues that, as odd as it may sound, the best medicine is to let the thoughts in. Experience the feelings associated with the intrusion, and let the experience run its course. Only by relaxing mental control, he says, can we regain it. By lowering your defenses, you eventually reduce the pressure of the unwanted thought, and it will go away on its own (perhaps through the mechanisms of the unconscious).

We said in Chapter 8 that repression can mean forming an anticathexis with an id impulse. This restrains it from being expressed. If you have the impulse to fondle the person next to you in class, your ego (presumably) takes action to keep the impulse out of your awareness. But the idea also applies to information that's painful or upsetting. Sometimes such information is the memory of impulses you already expressed. If you did something last week you're ashamed of, you try not to think about it and eventually may be unable to recall doing it.

Painful and threatening thoughts have many sources, not all of them id impulses. Threat can come from personal lapses—for example, forgetting to lock your apartment, thus letting someone steal your TV. It can come from things about yourself that you see as failings—for example, the fact that you're unpopular or the fact you can't dance. It can come from being part of a group that others put down (Steele, 1997) or from the realization you will eventually die (Pyszczynski, Greenberg, & Solomon, 2000). Threat can come from situations that conflict with your superego's standards—for example, the fact that you're not doing anything about people in the world who are starving or the thought that your parents have an active sex life with certain preferred positions for intercourse.

It's important to realize that repression need not be total. It's easiest to talk about defenses in all-or-nothing terms, but this can be misleading. You can partly hide a moderately distressing memory, so you don't think about it often. In essence, you simply avoid retrieving it (Shane & Peterson, 2004). You haven't forgotten it. If reminded of it, you're still aware it's there. But you'd just as soon not be reminded of it. This would be a partial repression. (For more on repression see Box 9.2.)

DENIAL

Another simple defense occurs when people are overwhelmed by a threatening reality. This defense is **denial:** the refusal to believe an event took place or a condition exists. An example is the mother who refuses to believe the message that her son has been killed in combat. Another is a child abused by a parent who goes on as if nothing were wrong (Freyd, 1996). A less extreme case is a college student who refuses to believe the grade by her name and assumes there's been some sort of mistake. It may also be denial when a young boy plays a superhero, thereby hiding the reality of his weakness.

As people mature and the ego gets better at assessing reality, denial becomes harder. That is, the more you know, the more clearly reality stares you in the face. Denial remains possible at any age, though. It's common for people who have serious problems with alcohol or drugs to deny the problem (as in the opening of the chapter). It's common for someone whose lover is straying to deny it. Many victims of Nazi persecution failed to flee while there was still time, apparently because of denial. Indeed, it's been argued that self-report measures of well-being can be untrustworthy because some people deny to themselves the distress that they're experiencing (Shedler, Mayman, & Manis, 1993).

Denial resembles repression in many ways. Both keep from awareness what the person feels unable to cope with. They differ in the source of the threat. Repression deals with threats that originate within the dynamics of the mind. Denial deals with threats with other sources.

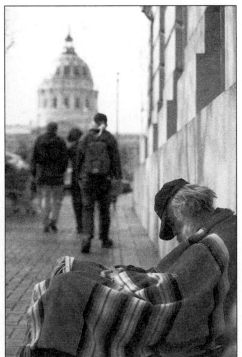

Denial prevents us from becoming aware of unpleasant things in our lives.

Box 9.2 Recall of Traumatic Childhood Memories

Breakdown of Repression, or Events That Never Happened?

Repression can keep memories of past trauma from reaching awareness. If the events can't be recalled, the person is spared any anxiety, anguish, or guilt associated with the experience. It's possible, however, for repression to break down. If that happens, people will recall episodes from their lives they might prefer not to recall. Sometimes, however, the memories that are "recalled" aren't real. This has created a huge controversy.

Consider, for example, a case reported by Elizabeth Loftus (1997). Nadean Cool sought psychiatric help to deal with her reactions to a trauma experienced by her daughter. Through hypnosis and other techniques, she recalled repressed memories of abuse she herself had endured. She became convinced she had repressed memories of having been in a satanic cult, eating babies, being raped, having sex with animals, and being forced to watch the murder of her 8-year-old

friend. In reality, none of these events had ever happened. The therapist's procedures induced her to think they had. When she realized this, she sued the psychiatrist for malpractice and eventually won a $2.4 million settlement. (See Loftus [1997] for other examples of memories being inadvertently planted by therapists.)

Indeed, false memories are surprisingly easy to induce. For instance, researchers had people recall childhood events that relatives recalled (e.g., Loftus, Coan, & Pickrell, 1996; Loftus & Pickrell, 1995). A few events that the relatives didn't mention (because they never happened) were embedded among the real ones. Not surprisingly, most people (80% or so) recalled something about the real events. More surprising was the percentage who reported memories about the events that never happened. Twenty to 30% of people typically report memories of nonexistent events, and the rate sometimes exceeds 60%!

False memories seem to depend partly on the event's being plausible. However, even events that are unusual or highly unlikely can produce false recall (Hyman, Husband, & Billings, 1995; Spanos, 1996). Another

important variable seems to be the extent to which the events are verifiable. False memories are more likely for events that can't be easily verified (Lynn, Myers, & Malinoski, 1997).

Interest in so-called recovered memories runs high today, partly because the memories often lead to accusations of terrible acts that had been repressed. Many persons have been accused of acts of physical and sexual abuse on the basis of such newly recovered memories. Some of them have been shown to be innocent. Yet they've undergone public humiliation in ways that permanently changed their lives.

It's very important to bear in mind that the occurrence of false memories doesn't mean that the spontaneous recall of traumatic events is never true. Children are sometimes the victims of sexual, physical, and emotional abuse. Sometimes those events are repressed to avoid distress. However, it does seem clear that not all cases of recalled trauma are real. Sometimes people are misled into remembering things that never happened. It can be very hard to tell whether a vivid memory is true or false. But a great deal can depend on deciding which it is.

Everyone uses repression and denial because they work (Erdelyi, in press). They save you from pain or anxiety. But too much repression or denial has a cost. These defenses take energy. Energy tied up this way can't be used for other things. If an act of repression continues, the energy is more or less permanently tied up. Thus, despite the fact that repression and denial are sometimes needed, they can eventually work against you.

Perhaps for that reason, other defenses also develop. These other mechanisms operate in combination with repression (and one another). They free some of the energy, while still keeping unacceptable impulses, thoughts, or feelings from registering on consciousness.

PROJECTION

In **projection,** anxiety is reduced by ascribing your own unacceptable qualities to someone else. You project traits, impulses, desires, or even goals (Kawada, Oettingen,

Gollwitzer, & Bargh, 2004). Projection provides a way to hide your knowledge of a disliked aspect of yourself while still expressing that quality, though in a highly distorted form (Mikulincer & Horesh, 1999).

For example, if you feel hostility toward others, you remove the feelings from awareness through repression. The feelings are still there, however. By projecting, you develop the perception that others hate you or are out to get you. In this way, your hostile impulse is expressed, but in a way that's not threatening to you (Schimel, Greenberg, & Martens, 2003). Another example is a woman who has sexual urges toward someone she shouldn't have and accuses him of being seductive toward her (the second example opening the chapter). The impulse gets out in a distorted form, while the woman remains unaware of her own desires.

Thus, projection serves two purposes. It helps to get the id's desires into the open in one form or other, releasing some of the energy required to repress them (Schimel et al., 2003). When you project, you're recognizing that the threatening quality *exists,* because you're seeing it. Just as important, though, the desire emerges in such a way that the ego and superego don't recognize it as belonging to you. Thus, the threat is sidestepped (see Figure 9.1).

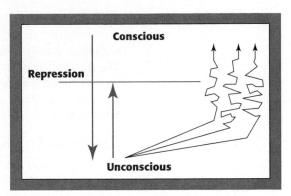

FIGURE 9.1
Defenses begin with repression, removing threatening material from the conscious region of the mind to the unconscious. What has been repressed cannot be brought out directly because it's too anxiety provoking. Repressed material can sneak around the barrier, however, by being transformed so as to make it less recognizable. Though these distortions permit the repressed urges to gain expression, the expression is weaker and less effective than the initial urge. Thus, pressure to express the urge remains.

RATIONALIZATION

Another important defense mechanism is **rationalization.** In rationalization, the person reduces anxiety by finding a rational explanation (or excuse) for a behavior that really was done for unacceptable reasons. For example, the man who cheats on his income tax may rationalize his behavior as reducing the amount of money spent on weapons in the world.

Rationalization also protects against other kinds of threats. For example, after a failure, rationalization maintains self-esteem. If you don't get into medical school, you may convince yourself that you really didn't want to be a doctor anyway. A man who's turned down for a date may convince himself that the woman really wasn't so great after all. Rationalization is very common in people's responses to success and failure. It's been shown repeatedly that people tend to take credit for good performances and blame bad performances on forces outside their control (e.g., Ross & Fletcher, 1985).

INTELLECTUALIZATION

Another defense is the tendency to think about threats in cold, analytical, and emotionally detached terms, which is called **intellectualization.** Thinking about events in a clinical fashion allows people to dissociate their thoughts from their feelings. This process separates and isolates the threatening event from the feeling that normally would accompany it—thus, no anxiety (Feldman, Barrett, Williams, & Fong, 2002).

For example, the woman who finds out her husband is dying of cancer may try to learn as much about cancer and its treatment as she can. By focusing on the disease intellectually and compartmentalizing that information, she shields herself from distress. A man who is sexually aroused by a co-worker may analyze in detail the qualities that make her attractive, considering her from the point of view of an uninvolved connoisseur of beauty. Doing this lets him distance himself from his desires.

Freud (1961/1915) made a more general point about this aspect of defense when discussing the separation of the unconscious from the conscious part of the mind. He suggested that an idea can exist in both parts of the mind at once, in different forms. The intellectual aspect of the idea can be in consciousness, even if it's a threatening idea, such as hating your father. This can be managed if the emotional quality attached to the idea—the deeply personal part that makes the idea psychologically meaningful— remains repressed. This sounds like a perfect description of intellectualization.

REACTION FORMATION

One way to guard against the release of an unacceptable impulse is to make a point of stressing its *opposite*. Doing this is called **reaction formation.** For example, a child may deal with hostile feelings toward a new baby in the family by repressing her hostile feelings and replacing them with effusive positive displays. Adults may react to uncertainty about some aspect of the self by asserting greater confidence in another aspect (McGregor & Marigold, 2003).

Freud believed that it's hard to tell whether an act stems from its apparent motivation or from the opposite impulse. Reaction formation is often inferred from the size of the response. If the person seems to "go overboard" or the response seems out of proportion to the context, you may be seeing reaction formation. Another clue is that the act may incorporate tinges of the impulse being defended against. For example, the child just described may try to "love her new brother to death" by hugging him so hard he begins to hurt. Another example of this is so-called friendly advice that is subtly disparaging.

Further examples are easy to suggest. A man who acts as a superstud, sleeping with one woman after another, may be trying to hide from himself fears about his sexual adequacy. Cases have been reported in which legislators who tried to pass laws against homosexual rights were rumored to be homosexual themselves. They may have been trying to prevent themselves from facing their true nature by behaving in a way that was its opposite.

You can also display reaction formation in interpreting the behaviors of people close to you. For example, people confronting evidence that their romantic partners have important faults may distort their perceptions of the evidence. The result is to turn the faults into virtues (Murray & Holmes, 1993).

REGRESSION

In Chapter 8, we described stages of psychosexual development and how people can become fixated in them. *Fixation* means that energy remains tied up in the cathexes of that stage. Anna Freud (1966) believed that stress causes people to abandon mature coping strategies and use patterns of the stages in which they are fixated. She called this **regression,** because it means giving up a more advanced form of coping in favor of one that's more primitive and infantile.

For example, an adult who's fixated at the oral stage might smoke more or eat or drink more when stressed at work. Someone with an anal fixation may respond to stress by becoming even more obstinate and compulsive than usual. The stronger the fixation, the more likely the person will regress under stress to that mode of functioning. Recall that fixations can arise when needs were well gratified in an early stage of development. Thus, regression often is a return to a way of relating to the world that used to be very effective (A. Freud, 1966).

Regression can occur at any point in development. An older child can regress to patterns of earlier childhood. Adults can also regress. In adult regression, people don't always act literally as they did during the earlier stage (although they may). Rather, the person's thoughts and actions become permeated with the concerns of the earlier stage. The manifestation of these concerns is often symbolic, rather than literal.

IDENTIFICATION

In Chapter 8, we also described how a person who lacks power (or some other desired quality) can acquire it symbolically through **identification.** Identification is linking oneself symbolically with some other person who has the missing quality. Thus, boys in the Oedipal crisis acquire strength and power symbolically through identification with their fathers. This identification also gives them symbolic possession of their mothers. There's evidence that this defense predicts better psychological well-being later on (Cramer & Tracy, 2005).

DISPLACEMENT AND SUBLIMATION

Two final defense mechanisms were introduced in Chapter 8: displacement and sublimation. These are generally considered less neurotic than the others we've described and more adaptive. **Displacement** is shifting an impulse from one target to another. This often happens when the intended target is threatening. Displacement is a defense in such cases because substituting a less threatening target for the original one reduces anxiety.

For example, the student who's angry with her professor and takes out her hostility on her very understanding boyfriend avoids the anxiety that would arise from attacking her professor. The person with an inappropriate lust who displaces that urge onto a permissible target avoids the anxiety that would arise from expressing the desires toward the true target.

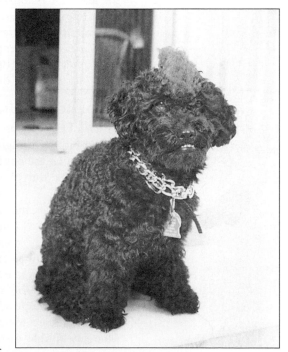

People often express impulses in symbolic form. Sometimes people live out their impulses through their children—or even their pets!

Sublimation also lets impulses be expressed by transforming them to a more acceptable form. In this case, it's not something about the target that creates the threat, but something about the impulse. Sublimation is a defense because anxiety goes down when a transformed impulse is expressed instead of the initial one. Freud felt that sublimation, more than any other mechanism, reflects maturity. Sublimation is a process that keeps problems from occurring, rather than a tactic that people turn to after anxiety is aroused.

RESEARCH ON DEFENSES

What's the scientific status of defense mechanisms? A fair amount of research has been done on this topic; after a quiet period, interest is growing again (Cramer, 2000). Consider a study of projection by Halpern (1977). People who did or did not seem sexually defensive (by a self-report scale) either were or were not exposed to erotic photos before making ratings of someone else. Sexually defensive people rated the other person as more "lustful" if they'd seen erotic photos than if they hadn't. Those who weren't defensive about sexual issues didn't display this projection. This pattern makes sense from a psychodynamic perspective. You project only about things that threaten you.

Research has also tested the idea that projection occurs when people actively try to suppress thoughts about something they don't like about themselves (Newman, Duff, & Baumeister, 1997). This active effort to suppress seems to cause thoughts about the unwanted trait to push back and become even more accessible (recall Box 9.1). This in turn causes the thoughts to be ready to use when someone else's behavior even remotely fits the trait. On the other side, there's also evidence that when a stereotype involving that trait applies to someone else, it makes projection more likely (Govorum, Fuegen, & Payne, 2006).

These studies seem to support the idea of defense. But the literature as a whole is ambiguous, and it's often easy to find alternative interpretations. As a result, different readers draw different conclusions. To Sherwood (1981) there was substantial evidence of projection, whereas to Holmes (1981) there wasn't. Many people are convinced that repression occurs in the short term (e.g., Erdelyi, 1985, in press; Paulhus & Suedfeld, 1988), although in the longer term, there are more questions.

Recent research has begun to take a different angle on the study of repression. This work looks at individual differences in the tendency to repress and asks whether repressors differ in important ways from people who repress less. In one study, participants did a task that required them to make associations to phrases with sexual and aggressive content (Weinberger, Schwartz, & Davidson, 1979). Repressors reported the least distress during this task, but they also showed the most physical arousal. In other research, repressors were less able to recall emotional memories from childhood and from their day-to-day experiences than were other people (Davis, 1987; Davis & Schwartz, 1987). Repressors are also better at suppressing memories of embarrassment than other people (Barnier, Levin, & Maher, 2004). These findings suggest that the search for evidence of repression may be coming closer to fruition.

EVIDENCE OF UNCONSCIOUS CONFLICT

Much of this discussion of ego defenses assumes that conflicts are buried in the unconscious through repression to avoid neurotic or moral anxiety. Although unconscious, the conflicts presumably continue to affect behavior. That is, repressed desires leak out through such processes as projection, reaction formation, and sublimation.

Sometimes, though, the conflicts emerge through symptoms, such as depression. The idea that unconscious conflicts cause symptoms has been studied by Lloyd Silverman and his colleagues (Silverman, 1976, 1983; Weinberger & Silverman, 1987). This idea is hard to test, because it requires arousing the conflict in the unconscious but not letting it reach awareness. The solution was to present material subliminally, at exposures so brief people couldn't tell what they were seeing.

Subliminal stimuli apparently do register. When susceptible people were shown things designed to stir up their unconscious conflicts, their symptoms increased. One susceptible group is depression-prone people. In the psychoanalytic view, depression reflects unconscious death wishes. Such wishes can be stirred up by words (e.g., *cannibal eats person*) or pictures (e.g., one person stabbing another). In several studies, showing such material subliminally to people prone to depression caused them to have deeper feelings of depression (Silverman, 1976). This did *not* happen if the stimuli were allowed to enter consciousness by using longer exposures. This supports the idea that it's the unconscious producing the symptoms.

Other research in this series involved arousing or diminishing Oedipal feelings in men (Silverman, Ross, Adler, & Lustig, 1978). Participants first did a competitive dart-throwing task and then viewed subliminal stimuli. In one condition it said, "Beating Dad is wrong"; in another condition it said, "Beating Dad is OK"; in a third condition the stimuli weren't related to Oedipal issues. Then the men repeated the dart-throwing task. Stirring up Oedipal feelings ("Beating Dad is OK") led to better scores (see Figure 9.2). Presumably, Oedipal feelings translated into stronger competition. Pushing Oedipal desires down ("Beating Dad is wrong") led to worse scores.

In sum, there's evidence that behavior can be influenced by arousing a conflict at an unconscious level. There are limitations. Some effects occur reliably only among people in whom the conflict is already well established. In the last study described, in contrast, the effect was more general, presumably because *all men* have experienced the Oedipal conflict.

We should also note that Silverman's research has been controversial, partly because others have found it hard to obtain the same effects (e.g., Heilbrun, 1980). Another problem is a lack of evidence of processes assumed to underlie the effects (Weinberger & Hardaway, 1990). Despite the controversy—or perhaps even because of it—it seems likely that this technique will continue to be explored as a way to study unconscious conflict.

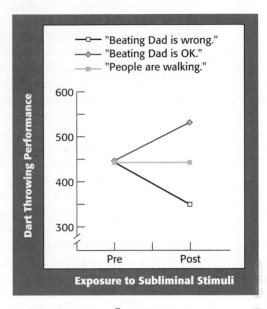

FIGURE 9.2
Effects of subliminal activation (or deactivation) of Oedipal feelings on competitive dart throwing. Participants threw darts for one score before exposure to the subliminal stimuli (pre) and threw again afterward (post). Subjects exposed to "Beating Dad is wrong" got lower scores the second time. Those exposed to "Beating Dad is OK" got higher scores the second time. Those exposed to "People are walking" were not affected. *Source: Adapted from Silverman et al., 1978.*

Exposing the Unconscious

We've been focusing on how the ego handles conflicts. To guard against neurotic and moral anxiety, the ego represses threatening desires. The desires, now unconscious, continue to influence behavior through further ego defenses.

Freud believed that the unconscious is where the vital forces of human life are at work, influencing people in complex ways. There is where the true motives lie. Gaining access to the conflicts and desires of the unconscious seems very hard. Freud believed, though, that it's not as hard as it seems. He thought unconscious impulses are revealed constantly in everyday events. You just have to look for them.

THE PSYCHOPATHOLOGY OF EVERYDAY LIFE

One way such motives are revealed is in people's mistakes. We all make mistakes from time to time. We forget things, get our words jumbled, and have accidents. Freud (1960b/1901) referred to such events as the *psychopathology of everyday life* (a phrase that also conveys his belief that all normal life contains a little of the abnormal). He believed such events, far from being random, stem from urges in the unconscious. The urges emerge in a distorted form, as mistakes. Thus, memory lapses, slips of speech, and accidents provide indirect insights into a person's true desires. (For a contrasting opinion, however, see Reason and Mycielska, [1982].)

Collectively, these events are termed **parapraxes**. (A literal translation from the German term is "faulty achievement" [Bettelheim, 1982].) Perhaps the simplest parapraxis is forgetting. From a psychoanalytic perspective, forgetting reflects repression, an attempt to keep something from consciousness. Sometimes it's easy to see why forgetting occurs (e.g., the student who forgets to return an important book to someone he doesn't like). At other times, it's harder to see the motive. Yet a motive can often be found, if enough is known about the situation.

A simple example comes from a psychology professor we know. He was heading off to a small conference of eminent psychologists, including some he had professional disagreements with. He arrived at the airport only to discover he'd left his wallet at home. As a result, he was unable to board the plane (and would have been unable to pick up his rental car at his destination). The delay caused him to miss the first half-day of the conference.

If forgetting is a successful act of repression, slips of the tongue are partially *un*successful acts of repression. That is, the person expresses all or part of the unconscious thought or wish, despite the effort to keep it hidden. As with forgetting, the hidden meaning may be obvious to observers. Consider the woman who reveals her ambivalent feelings toward her lover by telling him he's exactly the kind of person she'd like to *bury* (instead of *marry*).

There's evidence that these verbal slips are related to anxiety, although the evidence falls short of indicating that the anxiety is unconscious. Motley (1985) and his colleagues induced people to make a certain kind of slip. In this slip, a pair of words is read as a different word pair (for example, saying *flute fry* instead of *fruit fly*). The research requires creating specific pairs that are easy to misread into slips with particular overtones. The research involved creating specific anxieties and seeing whether those anxieties increase relevant slips.

For example, in one case, men were made to feel anxious about receiving electric shocks. In another, the session was run by a provocatively dressed woman to arouse anxiety over sexual issues. Both conditions included word pairs that could be misread as shock related (e.g., *damn shock* instead of *sham dock*) and pairs that could be misread as sex related (e.g., *happy sex* instead of *sappy hex*). As can be seen in Figure 9.3, men led to be nervous about shocks made more shock-related slips than anyone else; men led to think about sex made more slips with sexual connotations than anyone else. Sexual slips were also most frequent among men high on a measure of sex guilt (Motley, 1985).

When accused of making a slip, most people blame fatigue, distraction, or being in a hurry. Freud held that such factors help but don't cause slips. The real cause always comes from the unconscious. A person is more likely to make a slip when tired or inattentive, but the form of the slip depends on unconscious forces.

Accidents, on the other hand, are more complicated. Accidents that are most interesting from a psychoanalytic point of view are those that stem from carelessness. To decide whether something is an accident, you must look at the circumstances. If you learn a man was struck by a motorboat while scuba diving, you might think it was an accident. But if you learn that the man, an experienced diver, failed to put out a diving marker and didn't pause to listen for motors before surfacing, you might be

FIGURE 9.3
Freudian slips induced in the laboratory. When participants expected to receive electric shocks, they made more shock-related slips (left side). When participants had been exposed to a provocatively dressed experimenter, they made more sex-related slips (right side). *Source: Adapted from Motley, 1985.*

more inclined to conclude that (for whatever reason) he had an unconscious desire to do himself harm.

Accidents are complicated for another reason as well. Because they can involve injury, accidents can serve several functions at once. In harming yourself, you can also harm someone else—someone who cares for you. In this sense, an accident can serve both as crime (causing someone else to feel bad) and as punishment (causing you to suffer an injury).

DREAMS

Freud (1953b/1900) believed the unconscious also reveals itself through dreams, which he referred to as "the royal road to the unconscious." Freud began by distinguishing two kinds of dream content. **Manifest content** is the sensory images of the dreamer—what most of us think of as the

Freud believed that accidents often result from an unconscious desire to cause harm.

dream. More interesting, to Freud, was the **latent content**—the unconscious thoughts, feelings, and wishes behind the manifest content. Latent content tells why a dream takes the form it takes (see Box 9.3 for another view).

Freud believed that latent content derives from three sources. The first is the *sensory stimulation* that bombards us as we sleep: a thunderstorm, a passing siren, the barking of a dog. These sounds can prompt dreams and be absorbed into them. When this happens, the stimuli are part of the dream's latent content. Dreams are said to be "guardians of sleep," because absorbing an outside stimulus into a dream prevents it from awakening the sleeper.

The second source of latent dream content is thoughts, ideas, and feelings connected to the sleeper's waking life—**current concerns**—which remain active in the unconscious while you sleep. For example, during the day, you may have been thinking about an upcoming exam, an interesting person you'd just met, or a financial problem you have. Incorporating thoughts about that topic into dreams prevents them from waking you, just as with sensory stimuli.

The third source of latent dream content is unconscious *id impulses* that the ego has blocked from expression while you're awake. Often these impulses relate to childhood conflicts. For this reason, the impulse is often infantile in form and primitive in content. Freud believed that every dream incorporates some unconscious impulse or urge.

Manifest content consists of conscious sensory impressions (usually visual). Manifest content is a fantasy in which the latent wish or impulse is expressed. To use a term from Chapter 8, the dream is *wish fulfillment* on the part of the id.

During early childhood, the tie between latent and manifest content is quite transparent. Consider the dream of a 2-year-old boy a few days after his mother brought home a new baby (Brenner, 1957). The boy reported as manifest content "See baby go away." It takes little imagination to infer the latent content especially because the mother felt the boy had resented the new baby from the moment he learned it was coming. In this case, then, the manifest content was a direct translation of the latent content—the boy's wish to have the new baby no longer a part of his life. The manifest content simply fulfilled this wish in the form of visual images.

Box 9.3 Functions of Sleep and Dreams

Sleep has long been a source of wonder and mystery. Each of us spends a substantial part of each day in a state somewhere between life and death. And what are dreams? Fragmented recollections of journeys to other dimensions? Bits of truth whispered by gods (on the condition we not remember them for long)? Are dreams reflections of the primary process, visual echoes of the snarling and lurid passions of the id? Or are they just a jumble of nonsense, mutterings of a brain left to idle like a car at a red light?

In Freud's time, little was known about sleep and dreams. It seemed natural to him to think of dreams as the pathway to the unconscious, given their surreal and symbolic qualities. In later years, though, scientists have studied sleep and dreaming, and a little more is now known about them (e.g., Domhoff, 2003; Hobson, 1988; Walker, 2005; Winson, 1985, 1990).

For starters, everybody dreams, although many people don't remember the dreams. A sleep state was discovered decades ago, in which people's eyes move rapidly, breathing is irregular, heartrate increases, and movement is suppressed (Aserinsky & Kleitman, 1953). Because rapid eye

movement (REM) is a key feature, it's known as *REM sleep*. Whatever's going on in that state apparently is necessary. When people are kept out of REM (by being awakened whenever it starts), they show an increased tendency to enter it. REM sleep occurs four or five times a night for adults; infants spend nearly eight hours a day in REM sleep.

People awakened from REM sleep almost always report they were dreaming. People awakened from non-REM sleep don't say that as often. It used to be thought that REM is synonymous with dreaming. It's now clear, though, that that's wrong (Nielsen, 2000; Solms, 2000). Nonetheless, because dreaming is more common in REM, most examinations of dreams focus on REM.

Why is REM sleep necessary? What's going on there? Winson (1985) argued that new experiences are integrated with old ones during REM sleep. If this were so, a single set of brain structures could guide action when you're awake and consolidate when you're asleep. This would let us get the most out of our nervous system, because it's being used around the clock, rather than just when we're awake. Others have also suggested that REM sleep is involved in memory consolidation, based on different evidence (Walker, 2005).

Others disagree with that idea (Vertes, 2004). One reason is that antidepressant medications greatly reduce REM sleep but don't negatively affect memory. Vertes (2004) says that REM sleep is the nervous system's way of throwing a little stimulation at the sleeping brain, to keep it from stopping altogether and to prepare it for eventual awakening. He thinks the content of the stimulation is random and the dreaming is without meaning.

Yet another view, with fascinating implications, is that dreaming is an "off-line" model of the world, in which the sleeping brain runs simulations (Revonsuo, 2000). More specifically, this idea is that dreaming is a mechanism for simulating and rehearsing threat perception and threat avoidance. This would account for why dreams are generally somewhat organized and why misfortunes and aggressive interactions are so common in dreams (McNamara, McLaren, Smith, Brown, & Stickgold, 2005). Revonsuo (2000) believes that your nightmares are working for your well-being, preparing you for hazards you may face in your waking life.

These views are extremely different from one another. Although we know more about sleep and dreams than was true in Freud's time, we obviously need to learn much more before we can say we really understand them.

During later childhood and adulthood, the relationship between latent and manifest content becomes less obvious. Indeed, dreams sometimes seem complete gibberish. How can such dreams relate to wish fulfillment? The answer is that, with age, it becomes more important to distort or disguise the dream's latent content. The ego and the superego must remain unaware that an unacceptable impulse is being expressed. Keeping them unaware gets harder as people grow. Thus, even in dreams, the defense mechanisms remain at work.

Two processes allow forbidden impulses to be represented in the manifest content of dreams. In **symbolization,** unacceptable latent content is expressed in manifest content directly but symbolically. The symbol is a form that's less recognizable to the ego and the superego and is thereby less threatening. Symbolization might be considered the dreaming equivalent of sublimation. In **dream work,** latent content is disguised ways other than symbols to make it more acceptable to the ego and the superego. This can be done by jumbling separate thoughts into a single thought. (When they're jumbled, it's harder to tell what's what, and the threat is reduced.) It can be done by the **mechanism of opposites,** in which an unacceptable element of latent content is expressed manifestly as its opposite (much like reaction formation, when awake).

Interpretation of dreams involves examining manifest content, seeking its unconscious meaning. Freud believed many symbols that appear in dreams are unique to the dreamer. He also believed, however, that there are certain categories of shared symbols that have shared meanings. The universality of some symbols makes dream analysis easier.

HUMOR

The unconscious also reveals itself through humor (Freud, 1960a/1905). Humor often rests on threatening desires that are transformed in amusing ways. Much humor reflects hostility, which is blunted by distorting it into something ludicrous. Many jokes depend on there being an underlying inhibited thought. The joke telling slips around the inhibition, diverts attention, and lets the internal censor of the ego relax. When the punchline comes, the forbidden thought is abruptly expressed, too fast for the censor to recover. The energy devoted to restraining the forbidden thought is released in laughter.

Humor is similar to dreams in some respects, but there are also differences. Dreams let the unconscious urges emerge only in a symbolic and unrecognizable form. Humor, in contrast, is communicated from one person to another. Whereas dreams conceal their latent content, humor exposes the underlying content more completely (Oring, 1984). The symbolism and the laughter protect us from the threat, but the latent content is far closer to the surface than in dreams.

Projective Techniques of Assessment

The preceding sections focused on ways in which the unconscious reveals itself in everyday life. We now turn to ways in which the unconscious reveals itself in formal assessment, as practiced from the psychoanalytic perspective.

Formal methods of assessing unconscious processes are called **projective techniques** (Frank, 1939). These tests confront people with ambiguous stimuli. Because there's no obvious response, people's responses are determined primarily by their own feelings, attitudes, desires, and needs. (Recall our discussion of the TAT as a projective technique in Chapter 5.) These tests let people apply the defense of projection to their hidden feelings and put the feelings into their interpretations of what they see. What's projected presumably is beyond the person's conscious control and thus reflects the unconscious.

Several projective techniques exist. In *associative techniques,* people respond to a stimulus with the first word or thought that comes to mind. In *constructive techniques,* they create stories. *Completion techniques* involve completing a thought begun in an incomplete stimulus, such as a sentence that begins, "I wish. . . ." Although the techniques differ in format, they share several features. They all use ambiguous stimuli. The test taker is never told the purpose of the test. Instructions stress that there are no right or wrong answers and that the test takers can respond in whatever way they

FIGURE 9.4
Example of inkblot similar to those used in the Rorschach test. *Source: Courtesy of Jeremy Matthews Scheier and Meredith Matthews Scheier.*

wish. Finally, because of the open-ended and ambiguous nature of the technique, scoring relies heavily on subjective clinical judgments.

We focus for the rest of this section on one device that's often used to assess unconscious processes: the **Rorschach inkblot test.**

RORSCHACH INKBLOT TEST

Swiss psychiatrist Hermann Rorschach is usually credited with formalizing the use of inkblots for assessment (Rorschach, 1942). He finally arrived at a set of ten blots, chosen for their ability to evoke different responses from different groups of psychiatric patients. (His strategy thus made use of the criterion-keying approach to test development, described in Chapter 3.)

The ten inkblots in the Rorschach set are all bilaterally symmetrical, meaning that they are approximately the same on both sides of an imaginary center line (see Figure 9.4). The ink on five of them is all black, but the intensity is uneven, ranging from solid black to light gray. Two have both black and red ink. Three have pastel colors, including blue, green, yellow, and orange.

The Rorschach usually is administered to one person at a time in a two-stage procedure. First the person views the inkblots in a predetermined order and indicates what he or she sees in them, or what the inkblot resembles or suggests, while the examiner records what's being said. Then the person views all 10 cards again. The examiner provides reminders of what was said earlier about the card and asks what it was about the card that made the person say that.

Several systems have been devised for scoring the Rorschach. The most popular is that of John Exner (1974, 1993). In Exner's system, the responses are first compared against those of people with known personality qualities. Then the responses are examined as a progression from one card to the next. Finally, content is analyzed in terms of location, determinants, and content. *Location* is where in the blot the response focuses (the whole blot, a commonly noted detail, an unusual detail, the space surrounding the blot). *Determinants* include form, color, shading, or perceived movement in the location that prompted the response. The *content* of the response is its subject. Table 9.1 has examples of common interpretations of specific responses. Be aware, however, that a given response is interpreted only in the context of the entire test profile.

Although it's interesting as a technique, the Rorschach has serious psychometric problems. Its internal consistency is low, its test–retest reliability and inter-rater reliability are low, and its validity has been hard to establish (Anastasi, 1988; Lilienfeld, Wood, & Garb, 2000). Exner and his collaborators have tried to improve these qualities, but their efforts have not been entirely well received. Wood, Nezworski, and Stejskal (1996a, 1996b) criticized Exner's work on methodological grounds, bearing on issues of reliability and validity (see also Lilienfeld et al., 2000). On the other side, Ganellen (1996a, 1996b) has reported that the Rorschach does better at identifying depressed and psychotic persons than does the MMPI-2. Some of the issues raised in

Table 9.1 Rorschach Inkblot Responses. Here are three categories in which responses to the Rorschach are placed. In the left column is the category name, followed by its definition in the second column. The third column gives examples of responses that would be placed into each category. The far-right (fourth) column gives an interpretation for each example and an indication of why this interpretation is made.

Name of Category	Nature of Category	Example Response	Possible Interpretation (with critical feature identified)
Location	Place on blot from which response arose	"Overall, it reminds me of a cornstalk."	Suggests ability to think conceptually (response is based on whole blot)
		"That thing there looks like a hammer."	Suggests need to be exact and precise (response is based on a commonly noted detail)
Determinant	Quality of blot that led to response	"It's a whale, that's bleeding."	Suggests high degree of emotionality (response is based on color)
		"It's a bat flying."	Suggests high degree of imagination (response is based on perceived movement)
Content	Subject matter of response	"It's a man about to be beaten up by other people."	Suggests anxiety over hostile feelings (response involves aggression)
		"It's a person diving into the ocean waves."	Suggests strong fantasy life (response involves *human* movement)

the critiques of Exner's scoring system are technical; some are not (for example, much of the relevant evidence is unpublished). Not surprisingly, Wood et al.'s conclusions have been disputed by Exner (1996).

Many who favor projective tests respond to criticisms by saying that psychometric criteria are irrelevant to the Rorschach's usefulness. In their view, its value is in the insights it gives the examiner. Perhaps psychologists should stop treating it as a *test* and think of it instead as a *tool*. From this perspective the Rorschach is a supplementary interview aid in the hands of a trained clinician, giving clues and suggesting hypotheses worth further investigation.

It's too early to say how the Rorschach (and instruments like it) will come to be viewed. Continued efforts to standardize scoring procedures may yield better psychometric properties. Even if the Rorschach is viewed only as a clinical aid, though, it is not likely to be discarded soon as part of the psychoanalytic assessment battery.

Problems in Behavior, and Behavior Change

This chapter has emphasized two ideas: First, people use ego defenses to protect themselves from anxiety. Second, repressed urges and memories continue to influence behavior via the defenses. Psychoanalytic theorists believe that everyone uses defense mechanisms. Merely using defense mechanisms is not a sign that the person has a problem.

On the other hand, this is a viewpoint on personality in which normalcy shades easily into abnormality, with no clear boundary. Psychoanalytic theorists tend to distinguish normal from abnormal functioning by how much defenses dominate the person's life. Too much use of defense mechanisms is a sign of problems. Heavy use of defenses can save the person from dealing with conflicts, but it ties up too much energy in anticathexes. This leaves little energy for the person to use in dealing with new challenges. As the person's level of functioning begins to deteriorate, it becomes clearer that he or she has a problem.

Our discussion of problems and how they can be dealt with emphasizes the themes stressed all along. Freud believed the unconscious holds the secrets of people's difficulties in life. Only by delving into the unconscious can those difficulties be identified and resolved. This section begins by considering the psychoanalytic perspective on ways in which problems arise.

ORIGINS OF PROBLEMS

Problems have several possible origins. One origin is childhood experiences. As stated in Chapter 8, Freud believed adult personality is determined by early psychosexual development. If the person handles early stages well, little residue is carried into adulthood. However, it's rare for a person to enter the later stages of development unmarked. Most persons are partly fixated at earlier stages. If fixations are strong, a lot of energy is invested in them. In a very strong fixation, the preoccupation—albeit unconscious—leaves the person with little energy for anything else. This is one source of problems: overinvestment of energy in a fixation. This prevents flexible adult functioning by depleting energy the ego requires (Baumeister, 2002).

Another source of problems is a broad repression of basic needs and urges. If an overly punitive superego or a harsh environment causes too many urges to be buried, the person's basic nature is distorted and denied. The person is cramped and can't function in the way he or she is supposed to function. The repressed needs can squeeze their way past the repression only in twisted forms. This isn't really effective in meeting the needs. Again, the repression required to keep the needs hidden is a constant drain on energy available to the ego.

A third source of problems is buried trauma. Although traumatic incidents can occur at any point in life, most discussion of trauma focuses on early childhood. Indeed, at one point early in the evolution of his thinking, Freud believed most of his patients had suffered childhood sexual abuse. The "seduction theory," as it came to be known, was later abandoned when Freud decided the seductions hadn't actually taken place.

It was this change in his thinking that led to Freud's theory of the Oedipal conflict (Chapter 8), in which children deal with a sexual attraction to their opposite-sex parent. The Oedipal theory accounted for sexual imagery among patients, and it did so in a way that didn't require Freud to believe that large numbers of parents had seduced their children (though see Box 9.4).

BOX 9.4 SEDUCTION FANTASIES, CHILD MOLESTATION, OR NEITHER?

A controversy arose in the 1980s about Freud's abandonment of his seduction theory of the origin of psychological disorder. As indicated in the main text, Freud eventually realized that the accounts he heard from patients weren't true. The women hadn't been seduced as children. Rather, they had unconsciously distorted their own sexual desires for their parents into a symbolic form and projected it outward.

That's the way Freud put it: He'd realized the truth. In 1984, however, Jeffrey Masson challenged that statement. Drawing from previously unpublished letters, he said the seductions were in fact real, that Freud knew it, and that he'd chosen to back away from the reality. Masson said Freud lacked the courage to admit the truth: that child sexual abuse was widespread.

Why would Freud lack the courage to stand up for what he believed? Masson said Freud was concerned for his professional reputation. His first

presentation of the seduction theory, in a speech to a professional society, was met with utter silence. Masson said Freud was later urged not to publish it (though others contradict this assertion; Ellenberger, 1970; Esterson, 2002; McCullough, 2001). Perhaps Freud needed a way out to salvage his career prospects.

Masson also argued that *seduction* is an extremely unfortunate label. He said the word is not at all typical of Freud's first statement of the theory, in which he also used the terms *rape, abuse, attack, assault, aggression,* and *trauma*. Even as the theory was being set aside, Masson held, using the term *seduction* made the theory's implications seem more benign. Perhaps the terminology was one last defense against the truth.

Not everyone found Masson's account convincing. Some criticisms of his view are even less flattering to Freud than Masson's own view. Esterson (1993, 2001) said the seduction theory was a sham from the start—that the alleged evidence of

molestation in patient accounts simply did not exist. Esterson argued that Freud projected his own preconceived ideas onto what patients said. Freud himself even wrote that patients assured him they did not believe their memories were of sexual contact (Esterson, 2001). Thus, to Esterson, the issue is not whether patient reports were recollection or fantasy. The issue is that it wasn't the patients who generated the recollections but Freud himself (see also Schimek, 1987).

What really *is* the truth? We will probably never know. We can't return to Freud's era to study the rate of child abuse. If Freud was aware of frequent abuse, he might have interpreted any hint of sexual contact—even a symbolic hint—in such terms. But perhaps even more worrisome is the assertion that he let himself be guided by his preconceptions, letting them stand in place of patient reports, as Esterson argues. If so, there would be little reason to believe either the seduction theory *or* its successor.

Despite this change, Freud's theory clearly holds a place for traumas such as sexual and physical abuse. His altered view simply reflects his conclusion that abuse isn't common. Still, a child who experiences physical abuse, especially repeated abuse, has a deeply unpleasant part of reality to deal with. The same is true of a child who is sexually abused. Indeed, many events that objectively are far less traumatic can loom large in the experience of a child: rejection by a parent, death of a person (or a pet) close to the child, exposure to fighting parents. Children who experience traumas such as these have large threats to deal with. They're dealt with first and foremost by repression—always the first response to overwhelming anxiety. Once again, the energy invested in forgetting is a constant drain on resources.

These three points of origin for problems differ, and the problems that result may also differ. All three paths, however, share one mechanism: In each case, the original fixation, urge, or trauma is repressed. This repression may protect the person, but it does so at a cost.

BEHAVIOR CHANGE

What can be done about this situation? The therapeutic methods of psychoanalysis developed by trial and error in Freud's practice. His understanding of how to deal with problems evolved along with his views on the *reasons* for the problems. Early on, he found that symptoms could be reduced by hypnotically inducing the person to relive highly emotional (and thus repressed) events—relive them fully and emotionally. The release of energy seemed to free the person from the problem, by diminishing the energy investment in the repressed event. This experience is often referred to as a *catharsis* because of the release of emotional energy.

Two discoveries radically changed Freud's approach. First, he found it wasn't necessary to hypnotize people. If the person just said aloud whatever came to mind—a procedure called **free association**—what was hidden in the unconscious would gradually emerge. In free association, the person is not to censor any thoughts but to say immediately whatever thoughts arise, even if they seem trivial, illogical, or embarrassing. The therapist stays out of view to minimize the person's inhibitions against speaking.

Freud's second discovery was that what emerged often wasn't literally true. As noted earlier, he had initially believed patients had experienced childhood seductions. Eventually he decided those encounters had not taken place. This led to a reorganization in how Freud viewed both the content of free association and also childhood sexuality. Free association was producing something important, but it wasn't quite what it had seemed to be.

In Freud's newer view, unconscious material emerges through free association in *symbolic* form. The symbolism makes it less threatening to the person, thus letting it emerge. Images of seduction are less threatening than images of one's own carnal desires. Free association often creates a jumble of symbols that make no sense on the surface. Yet, as in a crossword puzzle, they provide a partial context from which missing elements may be inferred (Erdelyi, 1985).

As noted earlier, many problems serious enough to produce behavioral problems are thought to stem from repressed conflicts and urges and from suppressed libidinal energy. The goal of therapy is to uncover the conflicts and loose the restrained energy (see also Box 9.5). Free association is a first step, because it allows symbolic access to the problem. It rarely gets to the heart of the problem, though, because of the threat in the repressed material.

Indeed, people in therapy sometimes actively fight against becoming aware of repressed conflicts and impulses. This struggle is called **resistance**. Resistance may be conscious—for instance, when a person has an association that arouses anxiety but doesn't report it. Resistance also may be unconscious, an automatic use of ego defenses against the possibility of anxiety. Its occurrence is usually a sign that something important is nearby, that the person is close to revealing something sensitive.

Whether conscious or unconscious, resistance provides an illustration of how emotionally wrenching psychoanalytic therapy can be. The person in therapy is trying to uncover distressing truths—truths that have been buried in the unconscious precisely *because* they're too painful to admit. It's no wonder that the process of uncovering them is hard.

An important element in psychoanalytic therapy is **transference**. Transference is a set of *displacements*. Feelings toward other people in the patient's life are displaced (transferred) onto the therapist. The feelings can be love or hatred. Transference serves as another defense, in that the therapist provokes less anxiety than does the original object of the feelings.

Transference can interfere with therapy because the patient may become caught up in his or her feelings toward the therapist. These feelings don't reveal the real

Box 9.5 Repression, Disclosure, and Physical Health

Our main discussion focuses on the idea that repression has a psychological cost. Evidence is accumulating, however, that holding back thoughts and feelings can also have a *physical* cost. An example is a study of women undergoing breast biopsies (Greer & Morris, 1975). Women who reported suppressing their emotions (most notably anger) were more likely to have cancer than those who didn't (see also Jensen, 1987). Another study looked at atherosclerosis over a 10-year period (Matthews, Owens, Kuller, Sutton-Tyrrell, & Jansen-McWilliams, 1998). Women who said they suppressed their anger had more atherosclerosis 10 years later. Not all evidence supports the view that suppression relates to disease (O'Donnell, Fisher, Rickard, & McConaghy, 2000; Price et al., 2001), but enough support exists to make the idea worth further study.

The flip side of this idea is that releasing threatening thoughts and feelings can have physical benefits. James Pennebaker and his colleagues have been at the forefront of research on disclosure of suppressed thoughts and feelings (Pennebaker, 1989;

Pennebaker & Chung, 2007; see also Smyth, 1998). Participants in this research are asked to describe (with complete anonymity, in most studies) their deepest thoughts and feelings either about a specific nontraumatic event or about "the most upsetting or traumatic experience of your entire life." Ideally, the event the participant is to talk about (or write about) is one that he or she hasn't talked about much with others. Thus, it's more likely to be something that's been repressed, at least partially. The disclosure of thoughts and feelings typically takes place for about 20 minutes at a time on four successive days.

The short-term effect of disclosing trauma is that people feel more distress. In the longer term, however, self-disclosure seems to have health benefits. In one study, students who disclosed about traumatic events were less likely to visit the health center in the next six months than those not asked to disclose (Pennebaker & Beall, 1986). Results of another study suggest that disclosure has an influence on the functioning of the immune system (Pennebaker, Kiecolt-Glaser, & Glaser, 1988). In a study of Holocaust survivors, those who seemed to let go the most during disclosure were least

likely to visit their physicians later (Pennebaker, 1989).

Why might disclosure of painful memories and the thoughts and feelings that accompany them have health benefits? Pennebaker is pursuing the idea that the mechanism lies in the cognitive changes that occur during and after the disclosures. He's found evidence that people who come to organize their experiences into causal narratives benefit more than people who do not (Pennebaker & Graybeal, 2001). Interestingly enough, it apparently isn't *having* a coherent story that helps, but the process of *creating* the story.

Pennebaker (1993) argued that the body expresses itself linguistically and biologically at the same time. As we struggle to create meaning from trauma, we create beneficial changes in our biological functions as well. The result is better biological functioning and ultimately better health. This view of the effects of emotional expression surely will continue to evoke controversy and interest. It is a viewpoint with many important implications. If it continues to be supported by research evidence, it will change the way many people think about therapy and even about such activities as keeping a diary!

---

conflict, because the conflict pertains to someone else. On the other hand, transference can point out the significance of the feelings that are being displaced. When transference occurs, then, its interpretation is an important part of the therapy process.

The goal of psychoanalytic psychology is **insight.** Insight in therapy isn't an intellectual understanding. Rather, this term implies the re-experiencing of the emotional reality of repressed conflicts, memories, or urges, previously unconscious parts of one's personality (see Table 9.2). Intellectual understanding has no power to change the person. For a cognitive reorganization to be useful, it must come in the context of an emotional catharsis. On the other hand, emotional release does not help without reorganization (Kelly, Klusas, von Weiss, & Kenny, 2001).

The development of true insight allows people to see how the conflicts and urges have influenced their functioning for years. The insight provides a basis to

Table 9.2 Three Origins of Problems in Personality and the Goal of Psychoanalysis in Treating Each.

Origin	Goal
Fixation	Relive prior conflict to work through
Repressed trauma	Relive experience for catharsis of feelings
Repressed basic needs	Gain emotional insight into the needs and their acceptability

work from so that they can attain greater acceptance of these previously unacceptable parts of the self. One result is that people can get by with less defense in the future.

DOES PSYCHOANALYTIC THERAPY WORK?

Psychoanalytic therapy is long (literally years) and usually emotionally painful. Given the costs, financial and emotional, an important question is whether it's effective. Even Freud's view changed over the years. Initially, he was optimistic. He believed that patients, particularly those who were bright and well educated, could benefit from the insights they gained. He expected them to become better and ultimately happier people.

During the middle of his career, however, his thinking began to shift. He became more convinced that the real value of his work was in his theory of the mind, not the therapy. By the end of his career, he'd become pessimistic about the effectiveness of psychoanalysis. He'd come to believe that most of what happens to a person is due to biological factors that are beyond anyone's control.

How effective *is* psychoanalytic therapy? Early reviews concluded that therapy in general, including psychoanalysis, isn't much help (Eysenck, 1961; Feldman, 1968; Wolpe, 1981). Other reviews, however, found that therapy works and that analytic therapy does about as well as other techniques (M. L. Smith & Glass, 1977; M. L. Smith, Glass, & Miller, 1980).

A problem in interpreting the studies stems from the fact that there are several ways to define success. Whether therapy is successful depends on how success is defined. It could be defined by a therapist's judgment of improvement. It could be defined by the patient's reports of less distress (symptoms such as anxiety or depression). These are, in fact, the ways in which success is typically defined in outcome research.

Psychoanalysts, however, tend to use different criteria of success. Although it's hard to find complete consensus, success in psychoanalysis is often defined by how much insight patients gain into their conflicts and dynamics. This insight may or may not yield less distress. Some believe, however, that the goal of psychoanalysis should be insight, rather than reduced distress. Given this different goal, it's hard to be sure what negative findings say about the success of psychoanalytic therapy (for detail see Fisher & Greenberg, 1977).

This discussion also makes it more understandable why people continue to seek out and endure the painful effort of psychoanalysis. People who undergo this treatment presumably think that they're getting something out of it, or they wouldn't do it. It seems likely that people will find value in psychoanalysis if they believe the psychoanalytic perspective and believe insight is of value. Perhaps the hope of a better life that this conviction can bring is a sufficient benefit in itself to warrant undertaking the therapy process.

Psychoanalytic Defense: Problems and Prospects

The ideas presented in this chapter extend those in Chapter 8, thus adding complexity to the theory with respect to its problems and it prospects. These ideas also can be evaluated on their own merits. How do they fare in today's personality psychology? What are their implications for the broader usefulness of psychoanalytic theory?

We said at the end of Chapter 8 that one problem with psychoanalysis is that its concepts are hard to test. The ideas in this chapter create an even larger problem in that respect. Specifically, defense mechanisms provide limitless flexibility. They can be used to explain virtually anything that might occur. Flexibility is good, because it lets a theory account for a lot. However, it also makes prediction hard. If a theory is too flexible, you can reconcile *any* finding with it. To the extent that findings contrary to prediction can be explained away, the ideas being tested aren't tested at all.

Suppose, for example, you were interested in the idea that anal fixation relates to neatness. If the data show that neatness and anality relate positively, the idea is supported. But if the data show the opposite, you just add a twist. You assume that the messiness is a reaction formation, protecting these people against the anxiety that's created by their underlying need to be neat.

Given the defense mechanisms of psychoanalytic theory, such a twist can always occur. If a desire is too threatening, it's repressed. It emerges in a disguised or distorted form, even opposite to its original form. If this is too threatening (perhaps because a reversal doesn't hide the threat well enough because it's too obvious), then a different distortion occurs. Thus, the theory can explain any outcome. As a result, its predictions can never be disconfirmed. Unfortunately, if a theory can never be disconfirmed, it can never really be confirmed, either.

Despite these criticisms, the basic idea that humans have defenses and self-protective tendencies has been absorbed deeply into the fabric of today's understanding of personality. This principle has been widely accepted, even by people who accept nothing else of the psychodynamic viewpoint.

Other criticisms of the elements of psychoanalysis introduced in this chapter concern the techniques of assessment and therapy. Assessment in this approach relies largely on projective techniques. These techniques have received serious criticism. It's not clear whether projective tests will ever live up to the psychometric standards set by most personality psychologists.

Regarding psychoanalytic therapy, disagreement about its efficacy reflects disagreement on its goals. A further difficulty in evaluating psychoanalysis as therapy is that information isn't always available to verify insights that emerge during therapy. If someone experiences a sudden realization that she's always resented her mother, who died five years ago, is this a realization or a self-deception? If you free associate long enough, eventually you'll recall bad feelings about someone. But in many cases, it's hard to tell how important the bad feelings actually were.

Given the various problems associated with psychoanalytic theory, why has it been so popular? Indeed, there's been a resurgence of interest in psychoanalytic theory in recent years, after a fallow period. There seem to be at least three reasons for this enduring popularity. One is that Freud's was the first comprehensive theory of personality. Whenever something comes first, its influence persists for a long time. Second, Freud spoke to questions that lie at the heart of personality: How does childhood influence later life? What is mental health? To what extent are people's motives accessible to them? The questions he posed began to stake out the territory of what would become personality psychology.

A final reason for the theory's popularity concerns the intuitive appeal of its major themes. Any metaphor that's incorporated into a language is adopted because it captures an element of reality in a striking and vivid way. Psychoanalytic theory uses many images and metaphors. Apart from their scientific status, notions such as unconscious motivation, psychosexual development, and the intrapsychic tug-of-war of conflicting pressures from id, ego, and superego have an emotional appeal. The ideas are novel, exciting, and interesting. In a word, they are *seductive*. Freud's theory undoubtedly took root in part because it portrayed personality in a way that people found—and continue to find—interesting.

· SUMMARY ·

Anxiety is a warning signal to the ego. *Reality anxiety* is fear of a threat in the world. *Neurotic* anxiety is fear that id impulses will get out of control and get you in trouble. *Moral anxiety* is fear of violating the superego's moral code. The ego deals with anxiety (and sometimes prevents it from arising) by employing defense mechanisms.

The basic defense is *repression*—forcing id impulses and other threatening material out of consciousness. Repression is useful, but it ties up energy. *Denial* is a refusal to acknowledge the reality of something that lies outside the mind. Other defenses, which typically act along with repression, are projection (attributing an unacceptable impulse to someone else), rationalization (developing an acceptable but incorrect explanation for your action), intellectualization (separating your thoughts from your feelings and allowing the thoughts but not the feelings to be in awareness), reaction formation (acting in a way opposite to the initial impulse), regression (returning to a mode of behavior fitting an earlier stage of development), displacement (shifting an impulse from one target to another, usually a safer one), and sublimation (transforming an unacceptable impulse to an acceptable one).

The psychoanalytic orientation holds that the unconscious is the key to personality. Freud believed that the unconscious reveals itself in many ways in day-to-day life. *Parapraxes* are slips of the tongue and pen that occur when unconscious desires cause you to act in a way other than you consciously intend. Similar processes are believed to underlie many accidents. Unconscious processes are also revealed in humor and in dreams. Dreams have manifest content (what's in the dream) and latent content (the determinants of the dream, many of which are unconscious). Manifest content usually is symbolic of latent content, which also may be distorted through other mechanisms such as *dream work*.

The unconscious can also be revealed more formally, through projective assessment techniques such as the Rorschach inkblot test. Projective techniques allow the person's unconscious to release symbolic versions of threatening material while describing ambiguous stimuli. The Rorschach is somewhat controversial in that its reliability and validity have not been strongly supported by research evidence.

In the psychoanalytic view, behavioral problems reflect overuse of defenses. Problems may derive from fixations (unresolved conflicts during psychosexual development), from a general repression of libido, or from repressed traumas. In such cases, too much energy is spent in confining the threatening material in the unconscious. The goal of therapy is to release some of the repression, thereby freeing some of the energy.

Psychoanalytic therapy begins with *free association,* saying whatever comes to mind without censoring it in any way. This approach typically produces an incomplete matrix of symbolic meanings from which other elements can be inferred. People in therapy often display *resistance,* which implies that the ego is trying to defend itself against something the therapy is starting to touch on. Often the person in therapy displays *transference,* displacing onto the therapist the feelings related to the person about whom the conflicts exist. The goal of the therapy is *insight,* an emotional experiencing of previously unconscious parts of personality.

Freud came to believe that psychoanalysis was not as beneficial as he had first thought. This pessimistic view also emerged from early evaluation studies of therapy, although more recent studies have been more encouraging. Even in the absence of strong support for the usefulness of psychoanalytic therapy, many people continue to engage in it because they believe it provides benefits that are not adequately assessed by the measures used in outcome research.

· GLOSSARY ·

Anxiety   A feeling warning the ego that something bad is about to happen.

Current concerns   Preoccupations in one's current waking life.

Defense mechanism   An ego-protective strategy to hide threats from yourself and thereby reduce anxiety.

Denial   A refusal to believe that some real condition exists.

Displacement   The shifting of an impulse from its original target to a different one.

Dream work   Processes that distort latent dream content and transform it into manifest content.

Free association   A therapy procedure of saying without hesitation whatever comes to mind.

Identification   Linking oneself symbolically with someone who has a desired quality that is missing from the self.

Insight   An emotional re-experiencing of earlier conflicts in one's life that occurs during therapy.

Intellectualization   The process of thinking about something clinically and without emotion.

Latent content   The underlying sources of symbolic dream images.

Manifest content   The images that make up the dream experience as it is recalled.

Mechanism of opposites   A process in which an unacceptable element of latent content is expressed manifestly as its opposite.

Moral anxiety   The fear of behaving in conflict with the superego's moral code.

Neurotic anxiety   The fear that your id impulses will get out of control and get you into trouble.

Parapraxis   A slip of the tongue, behavior, or memory.

Projection   Ascribing a threatening urge or quality in yourself to someone else.

Projective techniques   An assessment in which you project from the unconscious onto ambiguous stimuli.

Rationalization   Finding a plausible but incorrect explanation for an unacceptable action or event.

Reaction formation   Doing the opposite of what your impulses are.

Reality anxiety   The fear of danger in the world.

Regression   A return to a mode of coping from an earlier developmental stage.

Repression   The process of keeping an idea or impulse in the unconscious.

Resistance   An attempt to avoid becoming conscious of threatening material in therapy.

Rorschach inkblot test   A projective test that uses inkblots as ambiguous stimuli.

Sublimation   The alteration of an id impulse into a socially acceptable act.

Symbolization   The transformation of unacceptable latent dream content into less threatening symbols.

Transference   The displacement onto your therapist of feelings that are tied to an object of conflict.

The Neoanalytic Perspective

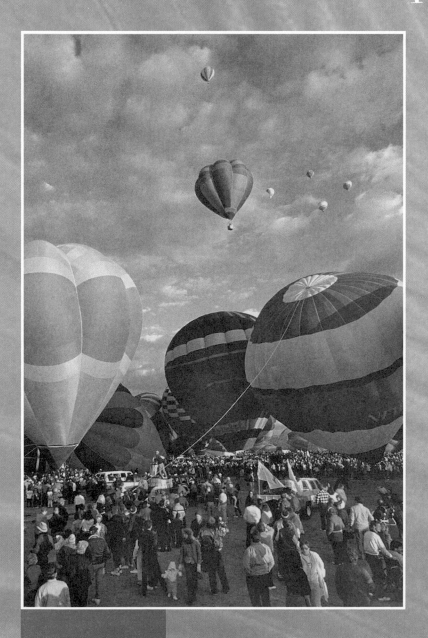

The Neoanalytic Perspective: Major Themes and Underlying Assumptions

As the term *neoanalytic* implies, this perspective on personality derives in part from the psychoanalytic perspective. Sigmund Freud attracted many colleagues and followers. All of them adopted aspects of his viewpoint, but they also differed from him in important ways. They dealt with their ambivalence about psychoanalysis by recasting and extending Freud's ideas in their own terms. In doing so, they de-emphasized aspects of his theory they disliked and expanded those they liked. Their disagreements with Freud are basic enough that their views seem distinctly different from Freud's. For this reason, we've chosen to treat them as a distinct perspective on personality.

These so-called post-Freudian psychodynamic theorists were fairly diverse in their thinking. As a result, there are as many different post-Freudian theories as there were theorists. Treatment of each theory by itself can create a jumble of ideas that's hard to keep straight. On the other hand, there are at least two themes that many of these theories share. As a result, the two chapters on this perspective don't simply discuss each theory in isolation from the others. Rather, they focus on several of the theories that most clearly reflect the two themes that are most salient in post-Freudian psychodynamic thinking. Points made by other theorists that supplement these core ideas are introduced where they seem most relevant.

The theorists who form the neoanalytic group differed from Freud on several grounds. Some neoanalytic theorists were bothered by Freud's emphasis on the importance of sexuality and the idea that sexual issues are important even in infancy. Others took issue with Freud's strong emphasis on the importance of unconscious processes. Perhaps the most frequent criticism among Freud's followers, however, was that he didn't give enough attention to the ego. As a result, many neoanalytic theories focus on the ego and how it functions. As a group, these theories emphasize the existence of certain ego processes and how they come to be. This line of thinking is the focus of Chapter 10.

Theorists who emphasize ego functioning and ego development tend to focus more on how the ego works than on the content of the problems and situations it confronts. However, a second group of neoanalytic theories focuses on the question of what kinds of situations are central in the ego's transactions with the world. In general, the theorists of this second group have held that the ego's primary tasks revolve around the quality of the person's relationships. The theories deriving from this assumption focus on how the ego interacts with, and is affected by, other individuals and the broader social and cultural matrix. The theories with this emphasis on social interaction are described in Chapter 11.

Ego Psychology

Jeremy has an irresistible attraction to computer games. He will sit transfixed for hours at a time in front of any challenging game. When he isn't pumping quarters into an arcade machine, he's parked in front of his computer, trying out whatever new game has just come out. His scores are so high that most of his friends have stopped playing with him. It's just Jeremy and the machine, locked in combat. Why? It's obviously not that he wants to be best in his group or even the best in town (he's long since been that). When asked, Jeremy shrugs and replies, "It's hard to explain—I just want to be as good at it as I can be."

WHY DO people spend large amounts of time becoming good at things that have no practical value? Name an activity, and people somewhere spend countless hours perfecting their skills at it: bowling, golf, cow-chip tossing, ballet, hog calling, and, yes, computer games. Why? Psychoanalysis says there's an explanation for everything. You just need to find the symbolic meaning behind the activity. But how do you feel about the idea that getting good at computer games is, for example, a symbolic reflection of Oedipal urges?

This question raises a more general point. If you're like most people, you had a mixed reaction to psychoanalysis. Most people find aspects of the theory reasonable. For example, many agree that early experience has a big effect on personality. Many agree that conflict is inherent in personality functioning. Most agree that people usually try to gain pleasure and avoid pain. Probably, though, there were aspects of the theory you found less convincing. Maybe you don't agree with Freud's stress on the unconscious. Maybe you're put off by his insistence that so much of human behavior is sexually motivated.

Even Freud's close followers were ambivalent. There were several areas of disagreement, but perhaps the most frequent criticism was that Freud didn't give enough attention to the ego and what it does (see Box 10.1 for another disagreement). Interestingly enough, toward the end of his career, Freud felt the same way. He began to wonder whether the ego might have a more important and autonomous status than he'd earlier believed.

Freud died before he could openly indicate his shifting position on this matter. Even his last publication (Freud, 1949/1940) gives no hint of it. Others knew of his informal statements, though, and found his shifting

BOX 10.1 ANOTHER KIND OF PSYCHODYNAMICS: JUNG'S ANALYTICAL PSYCHOLOGY

This chapter focuses on people who modified Freud's ideas by emphasizing the ego and de-emphasizing the unconscious. We should, however, note another theorist of the time whose ideas moved in the other direction: Carl Jung (e.g., 1960/1926, 1968). Jung was not a follower of Freud but a *contemporary* of Freud (though 20 years younger) who was influenced by many of the same currents of thought as molded Freud's work. Thus, similarities in some of the ideas they advanced seemed initially to give them common ground.

Freud and Jung associated professionally and personally for six years, during which Freud began to view Jung as his "crown prince" and eventual successor (McGuire, 1974). However, two factors drove a wedge between them. The first was a series of theoretical differences. The second was a growing interpersonal difficulty. Freud saw himself as a father figure to Jung, and he began to suspect that Jung wished to usurp his power and authority (note the Oedipal overtones). Jung found this attitude hard to tolerate, and he eventually broke away.

Jung's theory differs from Freud's in many ways. It's a theory of great complexity, and we can make only a couple of points about it here. Jung felt that Freud overemphasized sexuality as a motive but had too limited a view of spirituality. Unlike Freud, for whom spirituality reflected sublimation of sexual drives, Jung considered it a fundamental aspect of human existence.

Jung's thinking was also dominated by the **principle of opposites:** the idea that the human experience consists of polarities, qualities that oppose and tend to balance each other. He proposed a set of dichotomies in human functioning, each of which has some resemblance to what others would view as aspects of ego functioning. Jung believed that people are dominated by one of two attitudes: introversion or extraversion. People dominated by extraversion are absorbed by external experiences and spend their time engaged with the world around them. People dominated by introversion are preoccupied by their inner experiences and tend to be less outgoing. Both tendencies can facilitate adaptation. And even though you're dominated by one of them, the other remains inside you as well, opposing and balancing it.

Jung also assumed two more pairs of opposed functions. The functions in one pair, *thinking* and *feeling,* are both rational, in that each involves a kind of judgment. Thinking is a judgment of which ideas are true; feeling is a judgment about whether you like or dislike something. The functions in the other pair, *sensing* and *intuiting,* are nonrational, in that they don't rely on thought. Both are ways of perceiving—one using senses, the other using the unconscious. Each of these pairs also forms a polarity, with one of each pair tending to dominate the other. Indeed, a further polarization exists between the rational and irrational. Jung believed that combinations of dominance of these functions (plus introversion–extraversion) produce the range of individual differences in personality. Today, these tendencies are measured by an instrument called the Myers-Briggs Type Indicator (Myers & McCaulley, 1985), which is widely used for assessment in settings such as businesses and career counseling (DeVito, 1985).

Although Jung's theory has certain similarities to ego psychology, there are also great differences. For example, instead of de-emphasizing the unconscious, Jung emphasized it even more. Jung believed human beings share a **collective unconscious,** or "racial memory," a set of memories from our human and even prehuman ancestors. He believed that these memories, which aren't recalled consciously, go back for countless generations. They provide the basis for images called **archetypes,** aspects of the world that people have an inherited tendency to notice. Jung described many archetypes, including birth, death, power, magic, unity, God, and the self, which he believed are experienced by everyone. Each of these, in Jung's view, exists in the person because it's been part of the experience of human and prehuman life for millennia.

views more compatible with their own thinking. Encouraged by his change, they began to develop a set of ideas that collectively came to be called **ego psychology.** As the name implies, ego psychology is a psychodynamic framework in which ego functioning has more status than Freud gave it.

The emergence of ego psychology was a subtle and gradual process that began well before Freud's death. Indeed, many would say that some of the ideas in Chapter 9 are just as relevant to ego psychology as to psychoanalysis. It was Anna Freud (1966) who analyzed defenses so carefully, and her ideas weren't identical to those of her father. Recall that the defenses are used *by the ego* to protect itself. Thus, they're easily seen as ego functions and a part of ego psychology.

Principles of Ego Psychology

Anna Freud's analysis of defense mechanisms is a transitional statement. That is, it can be applied either to traditional psychoanalysis or to ego psychology. But other aspects of ego psychology depart more clearly from psychoanalysis. Sigmund Freud emphasized that the ego's primary task was to mediate among the id, the superego, and external reality. From the vantage point of ego psychology, the ego does far more than that. It's involved in the process of *adaptation,* of fitting better into the world. This view holds that adaptation and the conscious processes by which it occurs are more important than is unconscious behavior (Wolberg, 1967).

This isn't the only break from Freud. Ego psychologists widely assumed that the ego exists at birth and has its own energy source. One ego psychologist (Fairbairn, 1952) even went so far as to suggest that there is no id—only ego—and that what were seen as id functions are simply reflections of an ego at a primitive stage of development. All these ideas follow from the core assumption of the ego psychologists: that ego processes are important in their own right.

SHIFTING THE EMPHASIS FROM THE ID TO THE EGO

Because many of the people who became known as ego psychologists began as followers of Freud, they faced a dilemma. They wanted to emphasize the ego, but many also wanted to avoid undermining the core ideas of psychoanalysis. This was a hard problem, because psychoanalysis had given the ego a specific role: to help the impulses of the id gain expression.

Heinz Hartmann (1958/1939, 1964) had a creative and simple solution to this dilemma: He ignored it. He proposed that the ego does two things at once. On the one hand, it reduces conflict between the id and superego and between the id and external reality, just as Freud had said. On the other hand, it acts through its cognitive processes to adapt the person better to the world.

Hartmann held that the ego acts in two different modes to handle these different functions (see Figure 10.1). When it acts to reduce conflict, it's operating in what he called the *conflict sphere* of personality. When it acts to promote adaptation, it's operating in the *conflict-free sphere*. Thus, said Hartmann, Freud's view of the ego was right and so was the emerging view of ego psychology. Each view simply emphasizes different aspects of what the ego does.

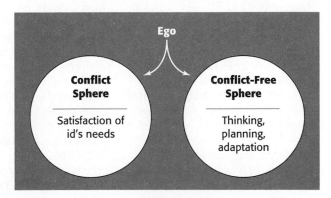

FIGURE 10.1
Hartmann assumed that the ego can operate in either of two modes. In the conflict sphere, it acts to see that the id's impulses are satisfied. In the conflict-free sphere, it engages in activities for its own purposes, aimed at better adaptation.

How can the ego function in two spheres? Hartmann assumed that the ego and the id have the same biological source. Thus, part of the ego stays in contact with the id throughout life. This part of the ego operates in the conflict sphere and tries to satisfy the id's needs. The rest develops more independently and operates in the conflict-free sphere, working for its own purposes. The latter aspect of the ego is what Hartmann and (other ego psychologists) were interested in.

Having said that Freud was partly right (that the ego functions in the conflict sphere), Hartmann then proceeded to ignore that aspect of the ego almost entirely. In that way, he managed to remain connected to psychoanalysis while heading off in a new direction.

ADAPTATION AND AUTONOMY

In Hartmann's view, adaptation to the environment is the ultimate goal of behavior. This became an important theme throughout ego psychology. Adaptation occurs on several levels. *Physically,* people must learn to move their bodies to get where they want to go and do what they want to do. *Psychologically,* people must learn to gain control over their impulses, modifying them and channeling them into appropriate actions.

Hartmann agreed with Freud that sexual and aggressive energies provide the foundation of much of human behavior. He differed, however, in how he viewed people's attempts to deal with their impulses. Freud saw the struggle to inhibit impulses in terms of avoiding anxiety (by avoiding punishment or danger). Hartmann (and others) saw the effort to inhibit impulses as part of a broader process of adaptation. The difference isn't so much in *what* happens as in *why* it happens. To Hartmann, impulse control is rooted in the ego's own goals.

In describing the ego, Hartmann talked about two kinds of autonomy. First, he said that ego processes exist from birth and can function apart from the id; this principle is called **primary ego autonomy.** Thus, people can get satisfaction from using ego processes to think, plan, imagine, integrate information, and so on (see also Box 10.2).

BOX 10.2 THE JOY OF THINKING

Explorations in the Need for Cognition

The idea that ego processes are gratifying in their own right is consistent with a literature on a topic called the **need for cognition.** This is the need to think about and impose meaningful structure on experiences (Cohen, 1957; Cohen, Stotland, & Wolfe, 1955). People high in the need for cognition are likely to evaluate, organize, and elaborate spontaneously on information to which they're exposed. They're less easily bored than people lower in the need (Watt & Blanchard, 1994). They attend more to the details of others' behavior (Lassiter, Briggs, & Bowman, 1991) and think more about its meaning (Lassiter, Briggs, & Slaw, 1991). People high in this need also are flexible and tend to explain events in complex ways (Fletcher, Danilovics, Fernandez, Peterson, & Reeder, 1986). They aren't

necessarily smarter—they just like to think things over (Cacioppo, Petty, Kao, & Rodriguez, 1986; Cacioppo, Petty, & Morris, 1983).

This ego function is reflected in several ways (for a review see Cacioppo, Petty, Feinstein, & Jarvis, 1996). For example, it's known that persuasion affects people in two different ways. When people get a persuasive message, some evaluate it and even *elaborate* on it in their minds. Others just take it at face value. Cacioppo and Petty (1982, 1984) argued that this difference in response rests on the need for cognition. People high in the need for cognition evaluate and elaborate; people low in the need for cognition accept what they're given.

Cacioppo and associates examined this idea by finding people who held the same attitudes on a target issue but differed in their need for cognition (Cacioppo et al., 1983; Cacioppo et al., 1986, Experiment 1). They received an essay trying to persuade them to change

their opinion. Either the essay was full of weak arguments (which people resist), or it was full of strong arguments (which are more persuasive). As you might expect, people with a high cognition need reported thinking harder about the message than those with a lower cognition need. They also remembered more of the arguments in it.

Does thinking harder and remembering more create more persuasion? Not necessarily. Thinking about strong arguments produced more persuasion. Thinking about weak arguments, however, caused people to be more resistant to persuasion. In sum, people high in the need for cognition thought more about the value of what they'd read and used the value as a guide for deciding whether to change their attitudes. This pattern seems much in line with the functions the ego psychologists emphasized as people try to deal effectively and adaptively with external reality.

In this view, being effective is pleasurable in itself. As you exercise your ego, you become more adept, and more efficient (better adapted) in dealing with the world.

The phrase **secondary ego autonomy** refers to the idea that an ego function that was originally done for one purpose may continue to be done long after that purpose has been satisfied. The original purpose may have been to fill another need (even an id need), but the ego function is now gratifying itself. This idea is similar to Allport's (1961) concept of **functional autonomy.** When a behavior that was originally done for one reason continues to occur after that reason no longer applies, the behavior is said to have acquired functional autonomy. It's as though the behavior has now become an end in itself. As an example, think of a person who began an exercise program to lose weight. Even after she's lost the weight, she continues to exercise, because she now finds the exercise itself satisfying.

The idea of an autonomous ego that has the goal of adaptation was widely adopted by other theorists, who extended it in a variety of ways. Among others, Rapaport (1960), Gill (1959), G. S. Klein (1970), and White (1959, 1963) were interested in how the ego goes about fitting itself better to the world.

THE EGO, ADAPTATION, AND COMPETENCE MOTIVATION

Although many ego psychologists view the exercise of ego processes as a source of pleasure and satisfaction, this idea was perhaps elaborated most compellingly by Robert White (1959, 1963). White used two motivational concepts. **Effectance motivation** is the motive *to have an effect* or an impact on one's surroundings. White believed effectance is a basic human motive. During early childhood, it's the major outlet for the ego's energies.

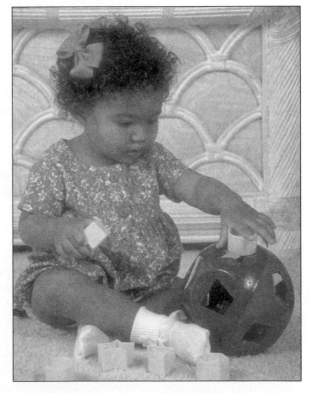

This motive gradually evolves into the more complex **competence motivation.** This is a motive *to be effective* in dealing with the environment. Thus, this motive underlies adaptive ego functioning. Competence motivation can be exercised endlessly. There are always new competencies (and higher levels of competence) to attain. The competence motive thus moves the person toward ever-new masteries (recall Jeremy and his games from the chapter opening).

There are important differences between merely attaining goals and satisfying the competence motive. Attaining a goal satisfies the desire to reach that goal, but the goal itself may or may not pertain to your sense of competence. For instance, if you get a perfect exam score in a course you think is too easy, it won't enhance your sense of competence.

Consider an example of how effectance and competence motives are expressed in behavior and differ from each other. Imagine an infant, surrounded by toys in her crib, who lunges at a dangling mobile and gives it a good whack with her fist. As the mobile jangles and bounces, the child has visible evidence of her impact on the world. This gratifies her desire for effectance. Knocking things over, moving toys around, spreading stewed carrots all over her table tray—each of these actions has an effect on the world around her. Each satisfies the effectance motive. Infants clearly do these things, and they do seem to enjoy them.

Children often seem driven to figure things out on their own. Successful mastery of the environment is important in developing feelings of competence.

Feelings of inferiority can produce strivings for superiority.

But competence motivation is different. Suppose the child is just learning how to stand up. She struggles over and over to pull herself up against the wall of her crib. She does it even though every effort meets with failure. When success finally comes, she giggles and shrieks with pleasure. She has exercised a mastery over the environment, a new competence in dealing with it.

In White's view, effectance and competence motives reflect the way the brain is organized. He held that people inherently seek stimulation from exploring. This urge can be shown in many ways, but its most advanced form is the desire to be competent and feel competent in dealing with the world. This is an adaptive urge. It causes people to engage in effective commerce with their environment to the greatest extent possible.

This theme has had reverberations in other perspectives on personality, not just ego psychology. As you'll see in Chapter 13, some learning theorists came to believe that the sense of personal efficacy is a major determinant of people's actions. It can easily be argued that that line of thought traces to White's emphasis on an intrinsic desire to master the environment. Another theoretical similarity will emerge when you read about humanistic views in Chapter 14.

Is Competence Striving Automatic, or Is It Done to Remedy Inferiority?

White considered the desire for greater competence to be the major force behind people's attempts to be effective. Alfred Adler (1927, 1929, 1931), another ego psychologist, also believed that people strive for greater competence, but for different reasons.

Adler began with an interest in a medical question: Why does one person develop heart trouble, a second respiratory problems, and a third ulcers? Adler proposed that people have an inferiority in some part of the body that makes them vulnerable to illness at that site. He called this weakness an **organ inferiority** (Adler, 1917). He also argued that people try to *compensate* by strengthening the weak organ through exercise and training. He termed this effort a *striving for superiority*. Adler's belief in this principle of compensatory striving was doubtlessly influenced by his own life. He was a sickly child who nearly died in childhood. Through considerable effort, however, he overcame his health problems.

Support for the idea of compensatory striving comes from a study of undersea divers engaged in a demanding task (Helmreich, LeFan, Bakeman, Wilhelm, & Radloff, 1972). This study found that the divers who performed best had had a serious illness during childhood. From Adler's perspective, they were compensating behaviorally for their earlier body inferiority.

Adler went on to expand his thinking to include *all* kinds of inferiority and to extend the principle to personality. He proposed that whenever a person has **feelings of inferiority** (any sense of inadequacy), a compensatory process is activated and the person strives for superiority (Adler, 1927, 1929, 1931). For example, think of a sprinter who feels inferior because she can't run 100 yards in 10 seconds. Because she feels inferior, she trains until she breaks the 10-second barrier. Her satisfaction, however, is relatively short lived. Feelings of inferiority set in again, as she realizes she could be even faster, and the struggle to improve begins anew.

As another example, think of a college freshman who arrives for his first semester knowing no one. He's a little shy, and in a few minutes, he feels a sense of inferiority because people all around him are engaged in conversations. What does he do? He grits his teeth and approaches a group of three people to introduce himself. Within a month, new friendships are sprouting like summer weeds. By now, though, just having friends isn't enough. He feels inferior because the friendships are a little superficial. He thinks he should know some people better than he does. To overcome that, he gets involved in a church group that meets once a week to talk with others about personal reactions to the experience of college life.

There are many ways to respond to a feeling of inferiority. Adler coined the term **lifestyle** to refer both to a person's concerns over inferiority and his or her preferred way of striving for superiority. Having a healthy lifestyle moves the person forward in an adaptive path of development. It allows the person to attain meaningful goals and to get along well with others.

But there are also what Adler called **mistaken lifestyles.** Some people respond to feelings of inferiority by trying to dominate others, or becoming dependent and taking things from others instead of attaining them on their own. Other people respond to feelings of inferiority by trying to avoid situations in which such feelings can arise. They avoid a sense of inferiority by never trying. Other people respond to such feelings by being as useful as they can to others, thereby drawing their own attention away from their inferiorities. These people almost deny the validity of their own ego and their own feelings. Consistent with this view, people who are *excessively* concerned with the needs of others are lower in self-esteem and more likely to neglect their own needs than people whose concern with others is more moderate (Fritz & Helgeson, 1998; Helgeson & Fritz, 1998, 1999).

Adler believed that inferiority feelings and superiority strivings continue to cycle with each other constantly. The result (unless the person has a mistaken lifestyle) is that people keep working to get better, more proficient at what they do. Adler thus viewed the struggle for increased competence to be an important part of healthy ego functioning. He called it the "great upward drive." He believed that healthy people continue to work this way throughout life toward ever-greater integration and perfection.

To Adler, effort toward improvement begins with and stems from feelings of inferiority. He believed everyone has these feelings periodically. These feelings are part of being human. Because the major result of inferiority feelings is an effort to better oneself, the behavior that emerges is exactly the same as the pattern White described. But the two theorists proposed very different mechanisms for it. To White, competence strivings are an intrinsic part of the ego's activity. To Adler, they're a reaction to, and an attempt to replace, feelings of inferiority.

EGO CONTROL AND EGO RESILIENCY

The theorists named thus far all emphasized that the primary goal of the ego is better adaptation to the world. Let's consider this idea a little more closely. *Adaptation* can be seen as having two aspects. One part is learning to *restrain impulses.* This lets you gain better command of your transactions with the world. It prevents mistakes that would arise from acting impulsively. Part of successful adaptation, though, is being *flexible* in dealing with the world. This is knowing when to restrain yourself and when to behave more freely. These issues surrounding restraint of impulses in the service of better adaptation lie at the heart of the work of contemporary ego psychologists Jeanne H. and Jack Block (1980; J. Block, 2002; J. Block & Block, 2006). They and their colleagues examined both aspects of ego functioning.

Block and Block called one aspect **ego control.** This is the extent to which the person tends to inhibit the expression of impulses. At one extreme are people who undercontrol—people who can't delay gratification, who express their feelings and desires immediately. Block and Block described these impulsive people as having many but brief enthusiasms and interests, as being distractible and exploratory. They are nonconforming and unconventional and comfortable with ambiguity and inconsistency. They live impromptu lives.

At the other end are people who overcontrol—people who delay gratification endlessly, who inhibit their actions and feelings, and who insulate themselves from outside distractions. Block and Block describe them as conforming rather than exploratory, as planful and organized. They are uneasy in ambiguous or inconsistent situations, and have narrow and unchanging interests. From their description of what these people are like, it's clear that the Blocks believe great restraint doesn't necessarily mean better adaptation (see Block & Block, 2006).

In the middle of the dimension are people who inhibit and control impulses to a degree but don't overdo it. These people are less organized than those high in ego control, but they're less impromptu and chaotic than those low in ego control. The people in the middle seem better adapted than are those at either extreme.

The other aspect of ego functioning that Block and Block focused on is called **ego resiliency.** This is flexibility. It's the capacity to modify your usual level of ego control—*in either direction*—to adapt to the demands of a given situation. People low in ego resilience can't break out of their usual way of relating to the world, even when it's temporarily good to do so. People who are ego resilient are resourceful and adapt well to changing circumstances. If there's a situational reason to be organized, they can do it without trouble. If there's a reason to be crazy and impulsive, they can be that way too. As Block and Kremen (1996) put it, the ego-resilient person is "as undercontrolled as possible and as overcontrolled as necessary" (p. 351). This means being responsive to what's possible and what's necessary in a given situation.

Not surprisingly, there's evidence that people who are high in ego resilience are better adjusted than people who are low (Klohnen, 1996). For example, in two samples of women, those higher in ego resiliency did better at negotiating menopause than those who were ego brittle. They were more likely to continue their education or career building and had fewer health problems (Klohnen, Vandewater, & Young, 1996). Another project found that children high in ego resilience were faster to develop in their understanding of friendships and moral reasoning than children lower in ego resilience (Hart, Keller, Edelstein, & Hofmann, 1998).

It might be tempting to conclude that people with high ego resilience are just smarter than people with less ego resilience. Thus, they're quicker to recognize what a situation calls for. Although these variables are related, it's not all about intelligence (Block & Kremen, 1996). Pure ego resilience—controlling for effects of IQ—relates to competence in the world of interpersonal interaction.

Ego control and ego resilience have both been related to restraint, in the form of delay of gratification. Funder and Block (1989) conducted a study in which the participants were 14-year-olds being paid four dollars for each of six sessions. After each session, they were given the choice of being paid then or deferring payment until the end. Each time they deferred payment, they'd get a small bonus in "interest." The

Table 10.1 Observer-Rating Items That Distinguished among Three Groups of 18-Year-Olds. Those of one group were total abstainers from drug use, those of the second group were occasional experimenters, and those of the third group were frequent users. *Source:* Adapted from Shedler & Block, 1990.

Items Distinguishing Frequent Users from Occasional Experimenters	Items Distinguishing Total Abstainers from Occasional Experimenters
Is self-indulgent	Is moralistic
Gives up and withdraws in the face of frustration, adversity	Favors conservative values in a variety of areas
Thinks and associates to ideas in unusual ways	Prides self on being objective, rational
Is unpredictable and changeable in behavior, attitudes	Overcontrols needs and impulses; delays gratification unnecessarily
Undercontrols needs and impulses; unable to delay gratification	Is facially and/or gesturally expressive (lower score)
Tends to be rebellious and nonconforming	Is unpredictable and changeable in behavior, attitudes (lower score)
Characteristically pushes and tries to stretch limits	Enjoys sensuous experience (touch, taste, smell, physical contact) (lower score)

question was how often (from five opportunities) they chose to delay. Decisions to delay related to ego control, as expected (controlling for ego resiliency and intelligence). Ego resiliency also played a role. Recall that delay is sometimes a good policy, sometimes not. This situation was set up so that delay produced extra payoff, so delay was good. Flexible people pick up on this and choose to delay, even if that's not their usual style. Thus, ego resiliency related to delay choices (controlling for ego control and intelligence).

These ego qualities have also been related to other kinds of behavior. One program of research found that greater ego control related to longer delays before sexual intercourse (Jessor & Jessor, 1975; Jessor, Costa, Jessor, & Donovan, 1983). Other studies found that ego control has a similar relation to drinking: Undercontrol relates to problem drinking and overcontrol relates to total abstinence (M. C. Jones, 1968, 1971). Shedler and Block (1990) reported similar results with respect to drug use (see Table 10.1).

In theory, ego control and ego resilience are distinct. However, there's evidence that the situation is more complex than that (Eisenberg, Fabes, Guthrie, & Reiser, 2000). It probably is intrinsically harder for someone who's at an extreme in ego control to be resilient, compared with someone with moderate ego control. If so, there would be low ego resilience at both extremes of the ego control dimension.

Several recent studies (Asendorpf & van Aken, 1999; Robins, John, Caspi, Moffitt, & Stouthamer-Loeber, 1996) have found exactly that. These studies found three clusters of people (see Figure 10.2). Overcontrolled people are high in ego control and low in ego resilience. Undercontrolled people are low in ego control and low in ego resilience. Resilient people are moderate in ego control and high in ego resilience. The overcontrolled and undercontrolled groups have the characteristics just described for highs and lows in ego control. The resilient group has the characteristics just described for highs in ego resilience. Future research on this topic may focus more on these three patterns.

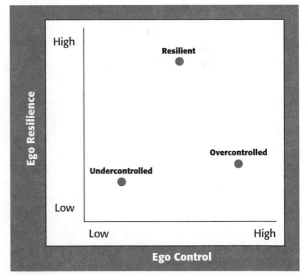

FIGURE 10.2

Approximate locations in two-dimensional space of three clusters of persons. Two clusters are at the extremes in ego control. The third cluster is identified by being high in ego resilience. *Source: Based on information from Robins et al., 1996; Asendorpf & van Aken, 1999.*

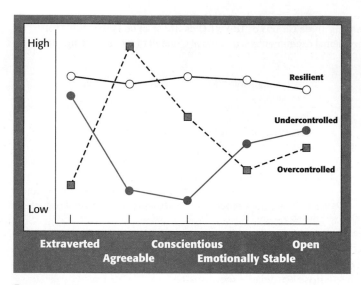

EGO CONTROL, EGO RESILIENCE, AND THE FIVE-FACTOR MODEL

We've noted in earlier chapters that widespread interest in the five-factor model of trait structure (Chapter 4) has led people to ask how other views of personality fit with that model. Several studies have looked at this question regarding ego control and ego resilience (Asendorpf & van Aken, 1999; Robins et al., 1996). The results are very similar across studies. Idealized profiles of three groups of people are shown in Figure 10.3.

The easiest to characterize is the resilient group: They're at the "good" ends of all the scales. The undercontrolled group is as extraverted as the resilients, but they're low in agreeableness and conscientiousness and moderately low in emotional stability and openness. This suggests some-

FIGURE 10.3
Idealized five-factor profiles of people who are resilient, undercontrolled, and over-controlled. *Source: Based on information from Robins et al., 1996; Asendorpf & van Aken, 1999.*

one who's impulsive and cares little about other people's opinions, which fits with other descriptions of these people. In contrast to both of these, the overcontrolled group is introverted, but they are as agreeable as the resilient group. They're also the lowest in emotional stability (i.e., highest in neuroticism) and only moderately open and conscientious. Consistent with the Blocks' portrayal, they seem withdrawn, conforming, and anxious. It seems, then, that there's a fairly easy integration between qualities in the Blocks' model and the five-factor model.

Ego Development

Thus far, we've emphasized the idea that a primary function of the ego is to establish better adaptation to the world. Now we turn to a slightly different viewpoint on this function. Though different, it's fully compatible with the themes emphasized thus far.

Jane Loevinger (1969, 1976) has argued that the ego is primarily a synthesizer and integrator of experience. This function certainly fits the overall goal of enhancing adaptation. In her view, the ego adapts to the world by making sense of the experiences the world presents. She argues that this synthesizing function isn't just one of many things the ego *does*. Rather, this is what the ego *is*. To Loevinger, the process of synthesis and integration is the essence of the ego.

Loevinger has proposed a detailed account of the ego's development (Loevinger, 1966, 1976, 1987; Loevinger & Knoll, 1983). By ego development, she doesn't mean a process by which the ego comes to *exist*. Rather, she means how this synthesizing function evolves across life. Her theory rests on ideas about cognitive development from theorists such as Piaget. A core idea is that as cognitive capabilities grow, people organize and structure their experience in more elaborate ways. As a result, the integrating function that comprises the ego must also act in more elaborate ways.

Loevinger's is a *stage theory*. She believes each shift in the nature of ego functioning derives from, and thus depends on, the nature of ego functioning in the preceding stage. Thus, the person moves through the stages in a particular order. As the person moves to each higher stage, the ego's syntheses become more differentiated and complex but also more integrated.

Why do people move forward into the next stage? It's generally assumed that cognitive development and ego development both emerge because existing functions don't quite fit reality. That is, if an ego function works perfectly, there's no reason to change it. If it doesn't work perfectly, though, there's pressure for it to evolve in ways that work better (Baumeister, 1994; J. Block, 1982). Thus, ego development depends partly on having challenge in one's life (see also Helson & Roberts, 1994).

According to Loevinger, people move through the stages until they can go no further. How far you go is influenced by heredity and by life circumstances (Newman, Tellegen, & Bouchard, 1998). Loevinger does *not* assume that everyone goes through all the stages. It's possible for a person to remain fixed in even a fairly early stage. Such an adult would not be well adapted to certain complexities in life, but would get along adequately in many contexts. Your adult level of ego development is the highest stage you're able to attain as you grow to adulthood.

We should note two differences between this view and Freud's. First, Freud saw personality development as occurring early in life. Loevinger sees ego development as continuing well into adulthood. Second, in Freud's psychoanalytic theory, the ego's basic functioning remains much the same, though the issues it deals with change over the years. Loevinger, however, argues that the nature of the synthesizing process that *defines* the ego actually changes over the course of life.

EARLY EGO DEVELOPMENT

The stages Loevinger identified are summarized in Table 10.2. At first, the ego is primitive. Its major task is to acquire the ability to distinguish self from nonself. This ability emerges during the first stage of ego development, called the *symbiotic* stage.

Table 10.2 Summary of Loevinger's Portrayal of the Stages of Ego Development.
Source: Adapted from Loevinger, 1987.

Stage Name	Behavioral Manifestations
Symbiotic	Working to acquire sense of separation between self and nonself
Impulsive	Assertion of self through impulse expression; relationships with others are exploitive, for own needs
Self-protective	Begins to grasp rules but only as guides to avoid punishment; no moral sense; personal expediency, opportunism
Conformist	Rules adopted because they are accepted by group; concerned with appearing properly to the social group
Self-aware	Realization that rules have exceptions; increased introspection with increased awareness that own behavior isn't perfect
Conscientious	Use of self-evaluated standards rather than group's norm; realization that events have multiple meanings
Individualistic	Clearer sense of individuality; greater tolerance for individual differences
Autonomous	Realization of interdependency among people; awareness of conflicts among one's own needs; recognition of others' need for autonomy
Integrated	Conflicting demands have been resolved; not just tolerance but intense appreciation of others' viewpoints

This name comes from the fact that a young child's tie to the mother is so strong that the child has trouble distinguishing itself from the mother. The process of consolidating a sense of being a separate person is assisted greatly by the emergence of language.

The next period of ego development is the *impulsive* stage. Loevinger says that children of this stage release impulses purposely, as a way to affirm their existence. In effect, the ego is acting to have an impact on the world (note the similarity to effectance motivation). This is a time when phrases such as "by *myself*" emerge often (and often loudly) from the child. The child orients to the present, with little consideration of the future or broad implications of behavior. Children's need for other people is high, because they can't do many things for themselves. But the relationships are exploitive: Others are valued only for what they can give the child.

It's of interest that the behaviors of this period are things that a traditional psychoanalytic view would see as caused by the id. Behavior is impulsive and demanding, and the child doesn't *relate* to other people so much as *use* them. Loevinger argues, though, that the actions reflect not an id, but a poorly developed ego struggling to assert itself. These very different views of the same qualities of behavior illustrate a way in which the ego psychologists' perspective differs from the psychoanalytic perspective.

MIDDLE STAGES OF EGO DEVELOPMENT: CONTROL OF IMPULSES

The intentional releasing of impulses eventually gives way to a different way of relating to the world. The *self-protective* stage marks the first step toward self-control of impulses. During this stage, children start to grasp the idea that there are rules about how to act and that breaking the rules leads to punishment. Children still lack full appreciation of the meaning of rules, however. At this stage, rules simply give information about how the world works—what you have to do to avoid punishment. As Loevinger (1976) put it, the main rule is "Don't get caught." The child's only morality at this stage is expediency.

The self-protective quality of this stage comes from the fact that children use whatever rules they learn mostly for their own advantage. Behavior thus remains exploitive. On the other hand, Loevinger (1987) says this isn't calculated opportunism. It's just an open expression of self-interest. In Loevinger's view, the best indicator of the self-protective mode isn't exploitive behavior but the absence of long-term goals and purposes.

Once again, it seems useful to point to the relation between this theory and Freud's theory. This stage is where the theories bear the greatest resemblance in their views of the ego. Recall that to Freud, the ego is amoral; it acts to satisfy the desires of the id expeditiously, without concern about right or wrong. The behavioral result looks much like what Loevinger describes as happening at the self-protective stage. Yet there's a difference. Loevinger doesn't see this as reflecting the emergence of a new structure in personality. Rather, it reflects a change in how the ego synthesizes and integrates in its efforts to adapt to the world.

The next stage of ego development is called the *conformist* stage. Children attain it by starting to link their own welfare and security to that of a group (family or peers). This is when rules start to be truly internalized. This change requires developing a sense of trust in the group. Rules no longer are seen as ways to avoid punishment. They're used because they reflect social consensus about how to act. Conformists obey rules precisely because the group has them. Little distinction is made between rules that matter and those that don't. Rules are rules. The power of rules comes from their social basis. Thus, the punishments that are most effective during this stage involve social disapproval ("You let us down" or "We don't like what you did").

At this stage, the ego is preoccupied with issues of reputation and social appearance. The appearances are one dimensional, though. Life is seen in stereotypes. People at the conformist level often seem very conventional, but that's not a reliable clue to being at the conformist level. Indeed, real conformists often appear radically different from "most" people. At the same time, though, they're conforming closely to the norms of their own social group. Many adolescents display this pattern, and some people never outgrow it. Control of impulses is regulated by more shame (from looking bad to the group) than in previous stages (Einstein & Lanning, 1998).

The next stage (Loevinger, 1987) seems to be the most common level of ego development among Americans between ages 16 and 26 (Holt, 1980). It's called the *self-aware* level. The name reflects the fact that the person in this stage is seeing—for the first time—multiple possibilities for the self.

Loevinger describes this stage by asking what pressures might move a person beyond conformity. She says that people move on when they come to see they don't fit the "perfect person" stereotype held out to them by conformist thinking. Such a perception seems to depend on developing a greater capacity for (or tendency toward) introspection. During this stage, the person begins to differentiate "what I am" from "what I ought to be." People at this level realize that rules of conduct often have qualifications or exceptions. You can do this "if you're old enough." You can't do this "until you're married." Despite a developing inner complexity, however, people at this stage are still basically conformists in their actions.

One more cognitive change seems to be needed for movement into the *conscientious* stage: an awareness of the fact that events have multiple meanings. This awareness makes it possible to understand and assimilate abstract moral rules. Abstract rules eventually matter more than group-consensus rules. The weakening influence of consensus means that morality now is truly internalized. During this stage and from now on, shame becomes less important in keeping people from breaking moral codes. Loevinger (1987) holds that the distinctive mark of this stage is self-evaluated standards. That is, you approve or disapprove of your conduct because of what you personally believe, not because of the wishes of some social group.

The life of the person at the conscientious stage is richer and more complex than was possible at earlier stages. Instead of seeing other people as just good or bad, you see them as complicated, with good and bad qualities. Achievement is valued for its own sake, rather than as a way to gain advantage over someone else (as in the self-protective stage) or as a way to gain social recognition (as in the conformist stage). Fitting this, there's evidence that women who reach the conscientious stage by middle age also increase in the qualities of *achievement via independence* and *tolerance* during that period (Helson & Roberts, 1994).

ADVANCED STAGES OF EGO DEVELOPMENT: TAKING EVEN MORE INTO ACCOUNT

A transitional level comes between the conscientious stage and the next full stage of development. This transition is called the *individualistic* level. The person at this level has a heightened sense of individuality and lifestyle. There's an emerging tolerance for differences among people concerning these matters. People at the individualistic level also have more appreciation of the fact that a given person is different when in different roles (e.g., wife, mother, daughter, lover, career woman, tennis partner).

These themes are elaborated even more fully as the person moves into the *autonomous* stage. Now the ego is preoccupied with the interdependency among people and the search for self-fulfillment (as opposed to achievement). The person has the capacity to recognize and cope with conflicts among differing needs, differing duties, and combinations of needs and duties. For example, you may need to study all evening for an exam tomorrow, but you also have the duty to "be there" for a friend who's taking the recent death of her father very hard. At the individualist stage, you'd view this conflict as being between your own need and an unyielding environment. In the autonomous stage, you accept the fact that many such conflicts occur intrinsically, even among your own wishes and needs.

The term *autonomous* can be a confusing label for this stage, because the key isn't a desire for one's own autonomy. It's an awareness of *others'* need for autonomy. Along with the ability to deal effectively with your own turmoil comes a greater tolerance for others dealing with their conflicts. Parents who recognize their children's need to learn from their own mistakes display this quality when they let the children make mistakes without stopping them. Loevinger believes that full attainment of this level of ego development (i.e., the ability to use this mode of relating to the world in all of one's interactions) is relatively rare.

The final stage of ego development, which is even more rare (1% of the population), is called *integrated*. Entry into this stage means the person has come to grips with internal conflict and has found a way to satisfy conflicting demands. If necessary, goals that are unattainable or unrealistic are abandoned. In the integrated stage, tolerance for others' viewpoints goes beyond mere tolerance to an intense appreciation of those viewpoints. A conscious attempt is made in this stage to weave the threads of previous stages into an integrated whole.

In summary, Loevinger holds that as the ego passes through these stages of evolution, it acquires greater complexity in its functioning and in its ability to relate and adapt to the world around it. Loevinger also argues that the ego plays the major role in acquiring moral character, impulse control, and internalization of rules of conduct. The ego gradually develops these capabilities over time and experience.

It seems useful to make one last comparison between Loevinger's theory and Freud's. Many qualities that the ego displays in later stages of Loevinger's theory resemble the functions of the superego in Freud's theory. Recall that Loevinger attributes the *lack* of impulse control at an early age to the ego, rather than the id. Similarly, she attributes a moral sense to the ego, rather than superego. From theories such as this, it's clear that ego psychologists elevated the status of the ego partly by ascribing functions to it that Freud had assigned to the id and superego.

RESEARCH ON EGO DEVELOPMENT

Loevinger's analysis of ego development has been studied empirically, but the work is hard to do. One reason is that her model doesn't predict many clear relationships between ego development and overt behavior (Hauser, 1976). Its predictions are more about the mental dynamics that underlie a given behavior. Consequently, much of the research on this theory has been descriptive.

It's known, for example, that older adolescents score higher on a measure of ego development than younger adolescents and that adults score higher than adolescents (Avery & Ryan, 1988). This fits the idea that the characteristics have a developmental progression. Girls seem to develop faster during middle and late childhood, though boys catch up by adulthood (Cohn, 1991). Ego development also relates to development of moral-reasoning capabilities (Lee & Snarey, 1988). This finding establishes convergent validity for both concepts, because there are certain logical similarities between changes in moral reasoning and changes in how the ego deals with reality. In a similar way, ego development has been related to increasing maturity in thinking about interpersonal intimacy (White, Houlihan, Costos, & Speisman, 1990).

Another study obtained evidence on other psychological qualities that should be tied to variations in ego development. Rozsnafszky (1981) studied hospitalized veterans, collecting both self-ratings and observer ratings (made by nurses and therapists) of the participants' traits. These ratings then were related to participants' levels of ego development (Table 10.3). Those at the impulsive or self-protective level showed poor socialization and limited self-awareness. Those at the conformist and self-aware levels were seen as valuing rules, possessions, physical appearance, and social conventions. Those at higher levels displayed greater insight into their own personality and motives. All of these findings are just as would be expected theoretically.

Although studies of behavioral reflections of ego development are somewhat rare, they aren't entirely lacking. There's evidence, for example, that social conformity is greatest among people who are at the conformist and self-aware stage of development. It falls off among people whose development attains higher stages (Hoppe, 1972; Westenberg & Block, 1993). Research has also found that higher ego development relates to higher peer ratings of mature functioning in careers and community involvement (Adams & Shea, 1979). Finally, there's evidence that adolescent inner-city delinquents have lower levels of ego development than nondelinquents (Frank & Quinlan, 1976).

Table 10.3 Observer-Rating Items That Were Found to Distinguish among Three Groups of Male Research Participants. People of one group were at the impulsive or self-protective level of ego development, those of the second group were at the conformist or self-aware level, and those of the third group were at higher levels. *Source:* Adapted from Rozsnafszky, 1981.

Impulsive/Self-Protective
- Exploitive; sees people as sources of supply; *good* seems to mean "good for me"
- Sees what he can get away with; follows rules only to avoid punishment
- Is self-defensive, manipulative, and opportunistic
- Impulsive; when he doesn't get what he wants, he may be self-destructive in an impulsive way

Self-Aware
- Tends to feel guilty if he has not done his duty
- Behaves in a sympathetic, considerate, and helpful manner
- Is concerned with the impression he makes on others
- Compares self to others; wants to be like others (i.e., normal)

More Advanced Stages
- Has insight into own motives and behavior
- Behaves in an ethically consistent manner; is consistent with own behavior
- Is comfortable with uncertainty and complexities; resists seeing the world as black and white
- Values his own and others' individuality and uniqueness

Other research has examined variables that may influence advancement through the stages. It's been found that progress is tied to having a clearer sense of identity (Adams & Shea, 1979) and to being psychologically minded (Helson & Roberts, 1994; Westenberg & Block, 1993). Ego development has also been related to auto-biographical memories that emphasize integrating new meanings in life (Bauer, McAdams, & Sakaeda, 2005). Ego development is related to general intelligence, but they are not the same (Cohn & Westenberg, 2004).

Life challenge (in the form of having a successful career) has predicted progression to higher levels of ego development in adult women (Helson & Roberts, 1994). Indeed, even the successful handling of marital separation and divorce seems to promote ego development (Bursik, 1991). It's also of interest that ego resiliency (flexibility in degree of ego control), discussed earlier in the chapter, relates to attaining higher ego development (Westenberg & Block, 1993).

Ego Development and the Five-Factor Model

Does this view of ego development relate in any way to the five-factor model? The available information suggests that the two do not have a lot in common. Einstein and Lanning (1998) found higher ego development related to greater conscientiousness in men but not women. Higher ego development related to greater openness in women but not men. The authors concluded that the two models are best thought of as complementary, as was also suggested by Loevinger (1993).

However, issues of measurement may play a role. Any of the five traits is likely to be manifested differently at different stages of ego development (Hogansen & Lanning, 2001). The five traits are measured by self-reports that don't permit that diversity to emerge. That is, you get to answer only the items you're given, and the items may or may not relate well to how that trait is reflected at your stage of ego development. Hogansen and Lanning (2001) figured out a way to measure the five factors from the sentence completions used to assess ego development. With the five factors scored this way, level of ego development related strongly to openness ($r = .59$) and more modestly to introversion and emotional stability. Whatever constitutes openness to experience seems to go along well with ego development. For the rest of the traits, the earlier conclusion may be right: These are better thought of as complementary models.

Assessment

Throughout this chapter, we've pointed to ways in which ego psychology differs from Freudian psychoanalysis. It's also useful to consider that issue with respect to assessment. Assessment in ego psychology differs from psychoanalytic assessment in two ways. First, ego psychologists are interested more in the ego than in unconscious conflict. As a result, the techniques they've developed focus on assessing qualities of the ego.

A second difference (which goes hand in hand with the first) is a general difference in technique. Given the de-emphasis on the role of the unconscious, it didn't seem so important to try to ease information from the unconscious by projective techniques. Thus, ego psychology shifted away somewhat from projective tests. Some ego psychologists moved all the way to self-report instruments, although most blend projective and self-report methods.

One similarity does remain, however. Ego psychologists are willing (as was Freud) to draw on a wide range of formal and informal sources to obtain clues about personality.

ASSESSMENT OF LIFESTYLES

Some assessment in ego psychology is highly informal. Recall Adler's belief that people form lifestyles. Your lifestyle leads you to be especially attuned to certain kinds of inferiorities and to deal with them in a characteristic way.

How do you identify a person's lifestyle? Adler believed a lifestyle can be identified by asking the person about his or her earliest memories from childhood or infancy. Adler thought the nature of these memories gives a clue to the themes playing themselves out in the person's life, an idea that has been borne out in research (Bruhn & Schiffman, 1982). In this research, people who saw themselves as having control over events in their lives reported early memories of mastery over the environment. People who saw themselves as having little control tended to recall experiences in which they were passive and events were beyond their control.

Interestingly enough, Adler didn't think it was important that the memories be accurate. What's important is how people view the experiences they recall. It's *how the person looks at the event* that identifies the person's concerns, the inferiority feelings, and the domains in which the person is striving for superiority. Adler believed, in fact, that memories are likely to be distorted by lifestyle (cf. Ross, 1989). For example, if your lifestyle is organized around the idea that others don't give you enough credit, then your memories will tend to reflect that idea. Although any memories can be revealing, Adler felt that a person's earliest memories reveal the most, because they reflect the person's fundamental view of life. "It offers us an opportunity to see at one glance what he has taken as the starting point for his development" (Adler, 1956, p. 351).

Adler collected interesting illustrations of links between early memories and lifestyle. An example is a man whose life was filled with anxiety and jealousy over the possibility that others would be preferred to him. His earliest memory was of being held by his mother and then being put down so she could pick up his younger brother. Adler's own first memories were of illness and death, and his lifestyle oriented around pursuit of a career in medicine (see also Box 10.3). Indeed, Adler found that among a group of medical doctors, memories of serious illness or a death in the family were frequently reported as first memories.

ASSESSMENT OF LEVEL OF EGO DEVELOPMENT

Another aspect of ego functioning that can be useful to assess is level of ego development. Loevinger's analysis of the stages of ego development has been used to create a systematic measure called the Sentence Completion Test for Ego Development (Loevinger & Wessler, 1970; for a more recent manual, see Hy & Loevinger, 1996). It consists of a series of partial sentences to which the person writes an ending. Thus, its format is projective. Unlike most projective tests, though, it has good reliability and validity (Lilienfeld, Wood, & Garb, 2000).

Each response is classified as reflecting one of the stages in Loevinger's model, from the impulsive stage onward (primitive earlier stages can't be measured with this test). Examples of responses reflecting various stages are in Table 10.4. The codings given to each response are entered into a formula, yielding an index of the person's overall ego development. Scorers who've been trained carefully show high interjudge reliability, and there's evidence of high internal consistency and test–retest reliability as well (Redmore & Waldman, 1975). This test was used to assess stage of ego development in the research done on Loevinger's theory discussed earlier in the chapter.

Table 10.4 Examples of Responses to a Sentence-Completion Item and the Stages They Reflect. The item stem, "The thing I like about myself is—," is from the Washington University Sentence Completion Test. *Source:* Adapted from Hy & Loevinger, 1996.

Stage Name	Response	Theme
Presocial	[Not assessed]	
Symbiotic	[Not assessed]	
Impulsive	. . . that I'm nice	Self-gratification
Self-protective	. . . that people like me	Exploitiveness
	. . . my grade in math	
Conformist	. . . that I'm athletic	Stereotypic thinking
	. . . that I don't hate other people	
Self-aware	. . . I'm very considerate of others	Modified stereotype
	. . . that I'm a straightforward person	
Conscientious	. . . that I can forgive and maintain caring feelings	Events in social context
	. . . my ability to look for the good in most things	
Individualistic	. . . that I'm different, but that's OK—I don't want to be like everyone else	Multiple viewpoints
	. . . that I'm really aware of others and how they relate to me	
Autonomous	. . . my personality, my constant striving to become more competent, and yet my ability to be patient	Recognition of mutual autonomy needs
	. . . my outlook on life, the fact that I can take people for who they are, and that I can stand by them while they deal with their problems	
Integrated	. . . the fact that I try to be honest with myself, even though I'm aware that that perception may be delusional	Fully integrated
	. . . that I can think independently and creatively, that I don't judge people I meet, and that I can still be a child when I feel like it	

Problems in Behavior, and Behavior Change

Different ego psychologists have emphasized different aspects of ego functioning, but one theme runs through them all: the key role of the ego's ability to adapt itself to the world. In line with this theme, problems in behavior are seen as reflecting deficiencies in this adaptation.

Ego psychologists view the process of adaptation as never ending. In a sense, then, problems are part of life. People struggle to make themselves better, and difficulties in that struggle are inevitable. Problems become serious only if deficiencies are extreme. Thus, well–being is defined not by whether you confront difficulties but by how well you cope.

INFERIORITY AND SUPERIORITY COMPLEXES

Adler exemplified this view. Recall his belief that inferiority feelings and superiority strivings cycle throughout life. The result usually is that people continue trying to get more proficient at what they do. The issue of inferiority is confronted repeatedly. Problems arise only if feelings of inferiority are so strong as to be overwhelming, pre–venting you from striving. When feelings of inferiority are that strong, the person is said to have an **inferiority complex.**

Box 10.3 The Theorist and the Theory

Adler's Lifestyle and the Ideas to Which It Led

The work of Alfred Adler provides an excellent illustration of how the elements of a theory often stem from the life experiences of the theorist (see Hoffman, 1994). Several themes that Adler contributed to ego psychology drew directly from his own life, as he was well aware (Bottome, 1939). Let's consider a couple of them.

Perhaps the easiest point to make pertains to what we've just said in the main text about early memories. Adler's lifestyle was organized partly around his interest in medicine and the body. His earliest memories were of illness. Adler's lifestyle also reflected personal anxiety and fear of inferiority, and for good reason. As noted, he was seriously ill as a child, and his parents were once told it was futile to try to educate him. Yet he struggled against these obstacles.

This aspect of his lifestyle is deeply symbolized in another of his early memories. He recalled being about 5 years old and being frightened over the fact that the path to school led through a cemetery (Adler, 1927). The other children weren't afraid, which only exaggerated his feelings of inferiority. One day, in an effort to rid himself of his fear, he ran back and forth through the cemetery, over and over. From then on, he was able to walk through it on his way to school without difficulty.

This memory neatly captures Adler's lifelong tendency to combat his fears by deliberately forcing himself to stand up to them. There's something else, though, that makes this example even more interesting. Many years later, Adler met a former schoolmate and asked him something about the cemetery. The man was bewildered by the question, replying that there hadn't *been* a cemetery. After seeking out other former schoolmates and getting the same reply, Adler finally realized that his memory was wrong. This experience doubtlessly played a role in his view that it doesn't matter whether memories are accurate or not—they're still revealing.

As another illustration of how personal experience influenced Adler's views, consider his analysis of birth order. Adler saw the second born as someone who has a constant sense of inferiority by virtue of being developmentally behind the first born. This can work in the second born's favor, because it serves as a constant spur to strivings. But it can also lead to lifelong competitiveness and jealousy. Of considerable interest is the fact that Adler was second born (1870) and throughout his life felt overshadowed by his older brother, who was a wealthy businessman. (His name, ironically, was Sigmund.) It seems likely that this experience led Adler to argue more generally for the impact of birth order on personality.

Finally, and most generally, recall how Adler's theory focuses on how people experience repeated feelings of inferiority and engage in compensatory strivings for superiority. This pervasive theme reflects virtually all of the experiences of Adler's life. His feelings of inferiority in several domains—physical and psychological—led to a great upward drive in his own behavior. This experience, in turn, helped lead Adler to believe that these same processes characterize everyone.

Adler believed an inferiority complex can have either of two sources. One source is neglect or rejection during development. Being neglected may cause a person to feel unworthy and inferior in ways too large to overcome. This person may develop a lifestyle involving dependency or avoidance. Another source is pampering during childhood. Spoiling can undermine the child's desire to strive for superiority, again producing a mistaken lifestyle.

Sometimes an inferiority complex leads to passivity or avoidance. Sometimes, though, strong feelings of inferiority lead a person to *over*compensate, strive for superiority to an exaggerated degree or in inappropriate ways. Inappropriate striving is seen in a lifestyle that involves efforts to dominate others. Sometimes a lifestyle involves a driven way of striving in which the person has to excel at all costs. Such exaggerated striving is sometimes called a **superiority complex.**

Adler also believed that people with problems tend to use certain strategies to protect whatever small sense of superiority they're able to hold onto. These strategies are aimed at diminishing the sense of inferiority. One strategy is to blame others for your shortcomings or failures. People using this strategy may spend all their time seeking revenge instead of making up the failure. Another strategy is to deprecate the accomplishments or qualities of other people. This implies that your own qualities are better than they actually are. This strategy obviously can be applied when competing with others, but it can also apply elsewhere. For example, having very high standards for a mate (you wouldn't consider someone who's not good looking, intelligent, a successful professional, and rich) may mean you're just trying to ease your own sense of inferiority. If no one out there is good enough for you, you must be *really* good.

OVERCONTROL AND UNDERCONTROL

Another way of thinking about problems returns us to the concept of ego control (Eisenberg et al., 2000). Specifically, being extreme on that dimension (and thus having low ego resilience) can create problems (Block, 2002). Both overcontrollers and undercontrollers lack the flexibility that would help them adapt to the world. Overcontrollers are prone to problems such as anxiety and depression (Eisenberg et al., 2004; Robins et al., 1996).

Undercontrollers, as their label suggests, are out of control. They are more likely to have school problems as adolescents and to have symptoms of conduct disorders (Eisenberg et al., 2004; Robins et al., 1996). As noted earlier in the chapter, they are also more prone to socially problematic behavior such as drug use, aggression, and sexual impulsiveness. Other research has similarly found that people with low self-control get worse grades, abuse alcohol, and have impaired social relationships (Tangney, Baumeister, & Boone, 2004).

BEHAVIOR CHANGE

The process of therapeutic change from the viewpoint of ego psychology reflects the overall themes of this line of thought. Therapies practiced by ego psychologists place more emphasis on current problems than on factors in the past that might have led to the problems. The emphasis on current problems fits with a point about assessment in ego psychology. Ego psychologists are more likely than Freudian psychoanalysts to take the person's behavior at face value and not look for symbols and hidden meaning.

The therapist who operates from this viewpoint is more supportive than one who operates from the psychoanalytic viewpoint. On the other hand, the ego psychologist is also clear about where the source of change must lie. That is, problems are viewed as something patients have let emerge in their own lives. The patient thus must take responsibility for dealing with the problems. This tendency to be direct with the patient is another way in which the therapeutic approaches differ.

One consequence of this shift in emphasis is to draw the patient into the therapeutic process as a *collaborator*. This increased emphasis on patient involvement evolves directly from the core idea of ego psychology. That is, the major task of the ego is to promote adaptation to the world. If behavioral problems arise, it's because the ego isn't doing its job. For the ego to alter what it's doing, the patient has to become involved.

Ego Psychology: Problems and Prospects

The group of neoanalysts who came to be known as ego psychologists includes a large number of people. As a group, they proposed a fairly diverse set of ideas. In all cases, however, the ideas reflect the theme that the ego is the most important aspect of personality. This theme is one of two that stand at the forefront of neoanalytic thinking.

Although ego psychology has had its adherents, it's fair to stand back and ask some questions about it. One reasonable question is whether these ideas really have anything at all to do with the psychoanalytic theory from which they evolved. Are these neoanalytic ideas really "analytic"? Or despite the absorption with psychoanalytic traditions, do these ideas actually have more in common with concepts from other areas of personality psychology?

Keep in mind the angle from which the neoanalysts proceeded. Most of them wanted to develop their own ideas, but at the same time, they wanted not to stray too far from Freud. After all, these people were *analysts*. That was their professional identity—to themselves, to one another, and to the world at large. As analysts, they thought of their ideas as amendments to Freud's theory, rather than as separate and distinct theories.

All this orienting toward Freud, however, produced what was in some respects a very narrow view. As a result, the ideas can seem more revolutionary (to analysts) than they are. For example, it's widely believed that Freud created the concept of ego. Ego psychologists certainly saw themselves as building on a Freudian idea. But according to Loevinger (1976), Freud's theory was itself partly a reaction *against an already existing nineteenth-century ego psychology*. She also notes that her own theory of ego development was strongly foreshadowed in the writings of people who came before Freud (e.g., Bain, 1859; Mill, 1962/1859; A. Smith, 1969/1759).

Another comparison is also instructive. Aspects of ego psychology resemble ideas from a group of theorists (discussed later in the book) called *humanistic*. Though the latter group had a starting point very different from that of the neoanalysts, many of their themes resemble themes of ego psychology. Despite this, analytically oriented people tend to ignore humanists. Again, the analytically oriented tend to view their ideas in relation to Freud's theory, rather than in relation to the broader spectrum of ideas in personality psychology.

It's easy to understand why the writings of the ego psychologists disregard nineteenth-century ideas. *Most* psychologists don't know much about nineteenth-century ideas. However, the failure to note other literatures may say something more about ego psychology per se. In particular, psychoanalysis in the United States has long been identified with medicine. Nearly all psychoanalysts begin their training with an MD degree followed by a psychoanalytic specialization. This also was true for early ego psychologists. (Adler and Hartmann, for example, were MDs.) There's a natural tendency to use ideas that are discussed within one's professional circle and to disregard ideas from outside. Because analytically oriented theorists were mostly medical people, they took the ideas of other medical people most seriously.

To some extent, ego psychology began relatively apart from the rest of psychology. It was a branch of psychoanalysis that was growing in the direction of psychology. This changed over the years, as psychologists became more prominent in this group. Theorists such as the Blocks and Jane Loevinger have helped pull ego psychology toward academic personality psychology. This shift has served to integrate neoanalytic ideas more into the mainstream of academic thought. This integration has also yielded an increase in the tolerance and regard that academic psychologists in general have had for psychodynamic conceptualizations.

The evolution of ego psychology appears, however, to carry with it the seeds of a more complete break with traditional psychoanalytic theory. What's unique about psychoanalysis is its emphasis on the dynamics of the unconscious and on the importance of powerful primitive impulses. In large part, ego psychologists have abandoned this conceptual heritage. Although the theories are often still called *psychodynamic,* the dynamics that remain are very, very different from those that Freud asserted. In moving toward greater harmony with the rest of psychology, ego psychology is at the same time leaving Freud behind.

What are the prospects, then, for this view of human behavior? Some of the ideas of this group already have a permanent place in personality psychology—for example, White's ideas about effectance and competence. We are also certain that Loevinger's theory and that of the Blocks will continue to stand as influential views of human development and behavior. If these two theories in particular continue to inspire active research activities, as they do now, ego psychology will continue to remain an essential part of personality psychology.

· SUMMARY ·

Neoanalytic theorists differed from Freud on several points. Many shared a feeling that Freud hadn't given enough emphasis to the ego and its functions. Accordingly, they devised ideas in which the ego plays a more central role. For this reason, they are termed *ego psychologists.*

Hartmann argued that the ego can function to facilitate the id's impulses but can also function autonomously in the service of better adaptation to the environment. He believed that the ego has a separate existence at birth (primary ego autonomy) and that ego functions often continue long after their initial purposes are served (secondary ego autonomy). Others, such as White, emphasized that the ego strives for competence and mastery over the environment. The motive to become more competent serves the goal of better adaptation.

Adler also proposed that people strive for better adaptations, but he assumed a different underlying reason. Adler argued that people repeatedly experience feelings of inferiority in one or another aspect of life and that they respond to those feelings with a compensatory striving for superiority—that is, movement toward greater perfection. Adler used the term *lifestyle* to refer to the person's characteristic constellation of inferiority feelings and preferred way of dealing with them. Some lifestyles are effective, but others (called *mistaken lifestyles*) are not.

Block and Block examined the effects of two other kinds of individual differences: differences in ego control (impulse control) and ego resiliency (flexibility in ego control). Too much ego control is bad; so is too little. Ego resiliency fosters better adaptation. Both qualities relate to behaviors that reflect restraint or impulsiveness, and ego resilience relates to better social development. Evidence suggests that ego control and ego resiliency may combine to form three clusters of persons—overcontrolled, undercontrolled, and resilient. The nature of these clusters converges in an interesting way with the five-factor model from Chapter 4.

Loevinger has examined how the ego's abilities grow and become more complex through a series of stages that extend into adulthood. In early stages, the ego is focused on differentiating itself from others and on affirming its separate existence through expression of impulses. Later, the person begins to learn rules of conduct and to follow them to avoid group censure. Still later, the person begins to appreciate the diversity of viewpoints on existence and experience. People develop through these stages until they exhaust their ability to move further; not everyone goes through all stages. This approach to personality does not connect well at all to the five-factor model, except that ego development seems related to openness to experience.

Assessment in ego psychology partly shifts away from projective techniques toward more objective techniques (though Loevinger's test of ego development is projective). The content of assessment from this viewpoint focuses on the ego and how it's functioning.

From the viewpoint of ego psychology, problems in behavior always are a matter of degree, because no one is perfectly adapted to the world. Struggle is an intrinsic part of life, but serious feelings of inferiority can produce an *inferiority complex* (paralyzing inability to strive) or a *superiority complex* (overcompensatory strivings), either of which is disruptive. Another view of problems is that they derive from being either too high or too low in ego control, both of which represent patterns that are too rigid for successful adaptation.

The approach that ego psychologists take to therapy is similar in some ways to the psychoanalytic approach, but it also differs in important ways. For one, it focuses on the here-and-now problems that the person has, rather than on buried fixations. There is much less of an attempt to probe for deep meanings and a stronger tendency to accept statements at face value. The person seeking treatment is also brought more into the treatment process as a collaborator in the attempt to produce behavior change.

· GLOSSARY ·

Archetypes   Aspects of the world that people have an inherited tendency to notice or perceive.

Collective unconscious   Memories everyone has from human and even prehuman ancestors.

Competence motivation   The motive to be effective or adept in dealing with the environment.

Effectance motivation   The need to have an impact on the environment.

Ego control   The extent to which a person modifies or inhibits impulse expression.

Ego psychology   The neoanalytic theories that give ego functions central importance.

Ego resiliency   The capacity to modify one's usual level of ego control to adapt to new situations.

Feelings of inferiority   The realization that one is deficient in some way, minor or major.

Functional autonomy   The continuance of an act even after its initial purpose no longer exists.

Inferiority complex   Feelings of inferiority bad enough to suggest an inability to solve life's problems.

Lifestyle   A person's pattern of inferiority feelings and manner of striving for superiority.

Mistaken lifestyle   A lifestyle that isn't effective in adapting or attaining superiority.

Need for cognition   A need to think about and impose meaningful structure on experiences.

Organ inferiority   A weakness in an area of the body, making one vulnerable to illness there.

Primary ego autonomy   The idea that the ego exists independently from the id from birth on.

Principle of opposites   The idea that life consists of polarities that oppose and balance each other.

Secondary ego autonomy   The idea that an ego function can become satisfying in its own right.

Superiority complex   Exaggerated striving to excel to compensate for deep inferiority feelings.

Psychosocial Theories

Ever since she was in high school, Christina has had a particular pattern in her love relationships with men. She is close and clingy as the relationship is first being established, wanting almost to be joined to him. Later on, an ambivalent quality emerges. She wants closeness, but at the same time, she does things that drive her lover away: She gets upset with him, gets into arguments over nothing, and isn't satisfied by anything he does to calm her. As he gets more and more irritated by this and their relationship becomes more and more strained, she makes her final move—she breaks up. Even afterward, there's ambivalence. Sometimes she recalls a former lover as being too good for her. Sometimes she thinks of them as no good at all. "Why can't I ever find the right kind of man?" she wonders.

A S THE ego became more prominent in neoanalytic theories and as its functions were examined in more detail, another change was also taking place. There was an increasing emphasis on the idea that personality is inherently social. Theorists began to stress that many issues in personality concern one's relationships with other people.

This is a considerable change of direction. As described in Chapters 8 and 9, Freud's ideas focused within the person. To him, people deal with outside reality only to satisfy impulses better. Even many ego psychologists tended to focus on the internal. They were more interested in how the ego works than in the interplay between it and the social world. This wasn't true of all ego psychologists. For example, though Adler (1930) stressed striving for superiority, he also noted the importance of caring for others, which he saw as necessary to a complete person.

Adler's ideas about the social nature of personality were fairly simple, but others developed more complex ideas on this theme. Those ideas form the basis of this chapter.

Object Relations Theories

We begin with a group of theories that have diverse origins and terminologies but are strikingly similar to one another. This group is referred to by the phrase **object relations** (for overviews, see J. Klein, 1987; Masling & Bornstein, 1994; St. Clair, 1986). In the phrase *object relations,* the object is another *person*. Thus, these theories focus on the individual's relations to others.

The concept of object relations derives from an idea of Freud's (Eagle, 1984). Freud saw an ego cathexis as a bond from the ego to an external object. It forms in order to release id energies effectively. Object relations theories focus on these bonds, but only for people as objects. Here, the point isn't to satisfy the id. Instead, the bond is a *basic ego function*. It's personality's main focus. As in other neoanalytic theories, the emphasis is on the ego (e.g., Fairbairn, 1954).

Object relations theories were developed by several people. They differ in many ways but share two broad themes (J. Klein, 1987; St. Clair, 1986). First, they all emphasize that a person's pattern of relating to others is laid down in early childhood. Second, they all assume that the patterns formed then tend to recur over and over throughout life.

One influential object relations theorist was Margaret Mahler (1968; Mahler, Pine, & Bergman, 1975; see also Blanck & Blanck, 1986). She believed that newborns begin life in a state of psychological fusion with others. In her view, personality development is a process of breaking down this fusion, of becoming an individual who's separate and distinct.

The period when the infant is fused with its mother is called **symbiosis.** Boundaries between mother and self haven't arisen yet (e.g., the infant doesn't distinguish its mother's nipple from its own thumb). At around 6 months of age, the child starts to become aware of its separate existence. Mahler termed this process **separation–individuation.** It involves gradual exploration away from the mother.

The child experiences a built-in conflict between two pressures during this time. The first is a wish to be taken care of by and united with the mother. The second is a fear of being overwhelmed in a merger with her and a desire to establish one's own selfhood. Thus, the child strives for individuation and separation but also wants the earlier sense of union. This conflict is important in adult behavior, as well.

The mother's behavior during this period is important to the child's later adjustment. She should combine emotional availability with a gentle nudge toward independence. If the mother is too present in the child's experience, the child can't establish a separate existence. If the mother pushes too much toward individuation, the child will experience a sense of rejection and loss called *separation anxiety*.

Eventually (at about age 3), the child develops a stable mental representation of its mother. Now, she will be with the child all the time symbolically. The *object relation* is internalized. In the future, the child will use this image in two ways. First, it will be a lens through which the child will view its mother in the future. Second, this internal image will be generalized to other people. In many respects, the child will act toward other people as though they were its mother (and father).

Often, the early years include some stresses—a sense of rejection from a parent or too much smothering fusion. If so, the stresses are carried by your internal object representations into your later life. Because this internalization derives from infant experiences, there can be a lot of distortion. Object representations don't always reflect experiences accurately. What matters, though, isn't what *happens* in childhood but what the child *experiences* as happening.

You may not be very persuaded by the idea that you relate to others as though they were your mother and father. You may think you treat everyone uniquely. An object relations theorist would reply that you think this because you're looking at yourself from *inside* your patterns (Andersen & Chen, 2002). Being inside them, you don't notice them. You notice only variations *within* the patterns. You think the variations are big, but in some ways they're really quite minor.

In this view, the pattern of relating to others that you develop in early childhood forms the core of your way of relating to others for the rest of your life. Indeed, this pattern forms the very core of your personality. You take it for granted, as much as any other aspect of your personality. It's the lens through which you view not just your parents but the entire world.

SELF PSYCHOLOGY

Another important neoanalyst was Heinz Kohut. Because Kohut felt that relationships form the structure of the self, his theory is called **self psychology** (A. Goldberg, 1985). Despite this different label, his theory focuses on experiences that others termed object relations.

Kohut began with the idea that people have narcissistic (self-centered) needs that have to be satisfied through others. He used the term **selfobject** to refer to someone who helps satisfy your needs. In early childhood, selfobjects (parents) are experienced as extensions of the self. Later, the term *selfobject* means any person *as he or she is experienced within the structure of the self.* Even then, selfobjects (other people) exist from the self's point of view and to serve the self's needs.

Kohut thought the child acquires a self through interaction with parents. Parents engage in **mirroring:** responding to the child in an empathic, accepting way. Mirroring gratifies the child's narcissistic needs, because it makes the child temporarily the center of the universe. The child's sense of self is grandiose at first. The illusion of all importance must be sustained to some degree throughout development to create a sense of self-importance to be carried into adulthood. It also must be tempered, though, so the child can deal with difficulties and frustrations later in life.

In a healthy personality, the grandiosity is modified and channeled into realistic activities. It turns into ambition and self-esteem. If there are severe failures of mirroring, though, the child never develops an adequate sense of self. This child will have deeper narcissistic needs than other people later in life, because the needs have been unmet. As a result, he will continue relating to other people immaturely. A delicate balance is required here: The parents must give the child enough mirroring to nurture development but not too much. This is similar in some ways to the balance between forces in Mahler's theory regarding separation–individuation and fusion with the other.

Mirroring continues to be important in relationships throughout life (Tesser, 1991). Later mirroring involves **transference** from parents to other selfobjects. This use of that term means that you *transfer* the orientation you've developed to your parents to other people, using it as a frame of reference for them (Andersen & Chen, 2002). In effect, other people become parent substitutes, and you expect them to mirror you as your parents did. This parallels Mahler's idea that the internal object relation pertaining to a parent is used in forming later relationships.

Kohut's conception of love illustrates adult mirroring. He thought of a love relationship as one in which two people are selfobjects for each other. They mirror each other and enhance each other's self-esteem (Kohut, 1977). Thus, a healthy narcissism in normal adults, which Kohut saw as part of life, is satisfied and nurtured properly through mutual mirroring.

Attachment Theory and Personality

The ideas discussed thus far fit in many ways with ideas proposed by theorists interested in the infant's **attachment** to its mother (e.g., Ainsworth, Blehar, Waters, & Wall, 1978; Bowlby, 1969, 1988; Sroufe & Fleeson, 1986). Attachment is an emotional connection. The need for such a connection is a basic element of the human experience (see Baumeister & Leary, 1995).

The first attachment theorist was John Bowlby. He believed the clinging and following of the infant serve an important biological purpose. They keep the infant close to the mother. That, in turn, increases the infant's chances of survival.

A basic theme in attachment theory is that mothers (and others) who are responsive to the infant create a secure base for the child. The infant needs to know that the major person in his or her life is *dependable*—is there whenever needed. This sense of security gives the child a base from which to explore the world. It also provides a place of comfort (a safe haven) when the child is threatened (see Figure 11.1).

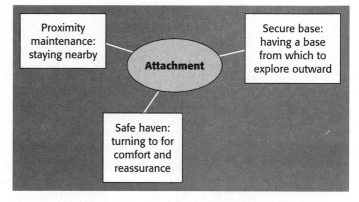

Attachment theorists also believe that the child builds implicit mental "working models" of the self, others, and the nature of relationships. These working models are later used to relate to the world (Bowlby, 1969). This idea resembles both Mahler's beliefs about internalized object representations and Kohut's beliefs about selfobjects.

To assess infant attachment, Mary Ainsworth and her colleagues devised a procedure called the **strange situation** (Ainsworth et al., 1978). This is a series of events involving the infant's mother and a stranger. Of special relevance are two times when the infant is left alone with the stranger and then the mother returns. Assessors observe the infant throughout, paying special attention to its responses to the mother's return.

This procedure has identified several patterns. *Secure attachment* is shown by normal distress when the mother leaves and happy enthusiasm when she returns. There are also two main types of *insecure attachment*. An *ambivalent* (or *resistant*) baby is clingy and becomes very upset when mother leaves. The response to the mother's return mixes approach with rejection and anger. The infant seeks contact with the mother but then angrily resists all efforts to be soothed. In the *avoidant* pattern, the infant stays calm when the mother leaves and responds to her return by ignoring her. It's as though this infant expects to be abandoned and is retaliating in kind.

Observations made in the home suggest a basis for variations in attachment (Ainsworth, 1983; Ainsworth et al., 1978). Mothers of securely attached infants respond quickly to their infants' crying and return their smiles. They also show *synchronous* behavior—making appropriate replies to a variety of infant

FIGURE 11.1
Three defining features of attachment and three functions of attachment. Attachment provides a secure base for exploration, keeps the infant nearby and safe, and provides a source of comfort. *Source: Adapted from Hazan & Shaver, 1994.*

Early attachment patterns can influence the quality of later social relationships.

actions (Isabella, Belsky, & von Eye, 1989). Mothers of ambivalent babies are inconsistent: sometimes responsive and sometimes not. Mothers of avoidant babies are distant, radiating a kind of emotional unavailability and sometimes being outright rejecting or neglectful. Not surprisingly, the personality of the mother relates to how she interacts with the infant (Kochanska, Friesenborg, Lange, & Martel, 2004).

Interestingly enough, it's not always the actions themselves that differ between groups but rather the timing. For example, mothers of secure and avoidant infants don't differ in how much total time they spend holding their babies. Mothers of avoidant babies, however, are less likely to hold their babies *when the babies signal they want to be held*. Timing apparently can be very important.

On the basis of findings such as these, Hazan and Shaver (1994) characterized the secure, ambivalent, and avoidant attachment patterns as reflecting three possible answers to the question, Can I count on my attachment figure to be available and responsive when needed? The possible answers—yes, no, and maybe—correspond to the secure, avoidant, and ambivalent patterns.

In theory, it's possible to get past an insecure attachment by forming a better one with someone later on. This is hard, however, because insecure attachment leads to actions that alienate others. This interferes with creating a new attachment. The clinginess mixed with rejection in the ambivalent pattern can be hard to deal with. (Recall Christina in the chapter opening, who displays an adult version of this.) So can the aloofness and distance of the avoidant pattern. Each of these patterns causes others to react negatively. That, in turn, reconfirms the perceptions that led to the patterns in the first place. Indeed, people with an insecure attachment pattern appear to distort their memory of interactions over time to make them more consistent with their working models (Feeney & Cassidy, 2003). An insecure pattern thus has a self-perpetuating quality.

At the very least, the patterns do seem fairly stable early in life, though they take slightly different form (see Table 11.1). In one study, infant attachment coded at age 1 could be identified by responses to parents at age 6 for 84% of the children (Main & Cassidy, 1988, Study 1). Secure children were still acting secure, avoidant ones were still withdrawn, and ambivalent ones were still being both dependent and sullen.

Table 11.1 Three Forms of Attachment-Related Behavior, Viewed at 1 Year and 6 Years of Age. *Source:* Adapted from Main & Cassidy, 1988.

Name of Pattern at 1 Year	Behavior at 1 Year	Behavior at 6 Years
Secure	Seeks interaction, closeness, contact with returning parent. Readily soothed by parent and returns to play.	Initiates conversation with returning parent or responds to parent's overture. Remains calm throughout.
Avoidant	Actively avoids and ignores returning parent, looks away, remains occupied with toys.	Minimizes opportunity for interaction with returning parent, looking and speaking only briefly, returns to toys.
Ambivalent	Distress over separation isn't soothed by parent. Child wants contact but shows subtle to overt signs of anger.	Posture and voice exaggerate sense of intimacy and dependency. Shows some resistance, subtle signs of hostility.

ATTACHMENT PATTERNS IN ADULTS

Attachment behavior in childhood is interesting, but more relevant to our goals here is how these ideas relate to adult personality. Research on this question began with the idea that the working models of relationships developed in childhood are carried into adulthood (with modifications along the way). These working models influence the adult's social relationships. In that way, they represent the core of personality.

During the past two decades, research on adult attachment patterns has exploded (see Cassidy & Shaver, 1999; Feeney, 2006; Mikulincer & Goodman, 2006; Mikulincer & Shaver, 2007; Rholes & Simpson, 2004). The first study was done by Cindy Hazan and Phillip Shaver (1987). Participants classified themselves from descriptions as being secure, ambivalent, or avoidant. They then described the most important romance of their life (past or current) on several scales (see Figure 11.2).

Secure adults described their most important love relationship as more happy, friendly, and trusting, compared with adults in the other two groups. Their relationships also had lasted longer. Avoidant adults were less likely than the others to report accepting their lovers' imperfections. Ambivalents experienced love as an obsessive preoccupation, with a desire for reciprocation and union, extreme emotional highs and lows, and extremes of both sexual attraction and jealousy. These people were also more likely than others to report that a relationship had been "love at first sight."

Hazan and Shaver also investigated the mental models these people held on the nature of relationships (see Table 11.2). Secure adults said, in effect, that love is real and when it comes, it stays. Avoidants were more cynical, saying that love doesn't last. Ambivalent subjects showed their ambivalence. They said falling in love is easy and happens often to them, but they also agreed that love doesn't last.

Other research suggests that ambivalent college students are most likely to have obsessive and dependent love relationships (Collins & Read, 1990) and also to be most obsessive about lost loves (Davis, Shaver, & Vernon, 2003). Avoidants are the least likely to report being in love either in the present or in the past (Feeney &

FIGURE 11.2
Adults with a secure attachment pattern report higher levels of trust in their romantic partner than do adults, those with an ambivalent pattern report greater obsessive preoccupation, and those with an avoidant pattern report lower levels of acceptance of their partners' imperfections. *Source: Adapted from Hazan & Shaver, 1987.*

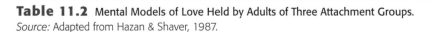

Table 11.2 Mental Models of Love Held by Adults of Three Attachment Groups.
Source: Adapted from Hazan & Shaver, 1987.

Endorsed *more* often by secure adults than others:
   In some relationships, romantic love really lasts; it doesn't fade with time.

Endorsed *less* often by secure adults than others:
   The kind of head-over-heels romantic love depicted in novels and movies doesn't exist in real life.

Endorsed *more* often by avoidant adults than others:
   Intense romantic love is common at the beginning of a relationship, but it rarely lasts forever.
   It's rare to find someone you can really fall in love with.

Endorsed *more* often by ambivalent adults than others:
   It's easy to fall in love.
   I feel myself beginning to fall in love often.

FIGURE 11.3
Combinations of positive and negative views of self and other, yielding four types of attachment patterns. In color are shown the names of the comparable patterns from the three-category model.
Source: Adapted from Bartholomew & Horowitz, 1991.

Noller, 1990), and are the most likely to cope in self-reliant ways after a breakup (Davis et al., 2003). Secures show the most interdependence, commitment, and trust (Mikulincer, 1998; Simpson, 1990). If they experience a breakup, they turn to family and friends as safe havens (Davis et al., 2003). The many ways in which adult attachment affects the course of romantic relationships have become the focus of a great deal of additional research in the past few years (Mikulincer & Goodman, 2006).

HOW MANY PATTERNS?

The proliferation of work on adult attachment has raised many issues, complicating the picture. Early studies used the three main categories from the infancy work, but another approach has also emerged. Bartholomew and Horowitz (1991) started with Bowlby's notion of working models, but focused on models of self and other, rather than models of the relationship. They argued for two dimensions. One is a positive-versus-negative model of self (the self is lovable or not). The other is a positive-versus-negative model of others (others are trustworthy or not). The dimensions are often termed *anxiety* and *avoidance,* respectively (Brennan, Clark, & Shaver, 1998). With this approach, hypotheses often are tested using the two dimensions. Sometimes instead, groups are formed by combining extremes on models of self and other (see Figure 11.3). Two of the groups that result are equivalent to the secures and ambivalents from the three-group approach. However, avoidants from that approach split into two separate groups here, which are called *dismissive* and *fearful,* depending on whether attachment anxiety is also involved.

Each approach has a conceptual strength. The three-category approach nicely conveys the sense that a significant other can be either available, unpredictable, or unavailable. The two-dimensional approach nicely conveys the sense that two separate issues are involved in the attachment response. However, the literature appears to be gradually moving toward the two-dimensional approach.

STABILITY AND SPECIFICITY

Two more questions about this view of personality concern its stability and its generality. If the attachment pattern is part of personality, it should remain fairly stable. Does it? If attachment concerns key figures in one's life, are the same patterns used in casual interactions or groups?

First, let's consider stability. Although findings are mixed, attachment seems moderately stable over fairly long periods of time. Fraley (2002) concluded from a review of studies that a prototype for close relations arises in infancy and doesn't go away, despite new experiences. On the other hand, moderate stability is not total stability. Some people change more than others. Evidence suggests that people who vary in self-portrayal over time are insecure at the core but periodically feel more secure (Davila, Burge, & Hammen, 1997). Research on stability over more extended periods is continuing (Grossmann, Grossmann, & Waters, 2005; Mikulincer & Shaver, 2007).

What about specificity? Does each person have one pattern of relating to others? Or do people have many patterns for different relationships? The answer seems to be many patterns. Even infants sometimes display one pattern to one parent and a different pattern to the other parent. This diversity in relational behavior also appears in adults (Baldwin, Keelan, Fehr, Enns, & Koh-Rangarajoo, 1996; Bartholomew & Horowitz, 1991; Cook,

2000; La Guardia, Ryan, Couchman, & Deci, 2000; Overall, Fletcher, & Friesen, 2003; Pierce & Lydon, 2001). For example, one study had participants define each of their 10 closest relationships in terms of the three categories. Across the 10 descriptions, almost everyone used at least two patterns and nearly half used all three (Baldwin et al., 1996). There's also evidence that people have patterns of attachment to groups, distinct from their patterns for close relationships (Smith, Murphy, & Coats, 1999). There's even evidence that religious beliefs involve yet another pattern of attachment (Kirkpatrick, 1998).

Thus, the ways people relate to others in their lives—even significant others—do seem to have variability. There may be a general orientation for starting new relationships, or a central tendency among the various orientations that a person takes (Crittenden, 1990; Pierce & Lydon, 2001), and it may well derive from early childhood experiences. But adult behavior definitely is more complex than would be the case if each person had just a single way of relating to others.

OTHER REFLECTIONS OF ADULT ATTACHMENT

A surprising range of behaviors has been tied to the attachment patterns that people report for close relationships. Hazan and Shaver (1990) studied relations between attachment and people's orientations to work. Recall that ambivalence involves a sense of insecurity. Consistent with this, ambivalents report unhappiness with the recognition they get at work and their degree of job security. They're also most likely to say their work is motivated by a desire for others' approval. Avoidants report a desire to keep busy with work, and they socialize less during leisure time. Hazan and Shaver suggested that avoidants use work as a way to escape from their lack of relationships.

A good deal of research has looked at how attachment patterns relate to comfort seeking and caregiving in stressful situations (Collins, Ford, Guichard, & Feeney, 2006). In one study (Simpson, Rholes, & Nelligan, 1992), women were told they were going to do a task that creates anxiety. They then waited for five minutes with their boyfriends, who were to do a different task. As anxiety increased, secure women sought support from their partners, talked about being nervous, and so on. Avoidant women did the opposite: The more anxious they got, the *less* they sought support. The men also varied. Among secure men, the more anxiety their partners showed, the more reassuring they were. Among avoidant men, the more anxiety their partners showed, the *less* reassuring they were (see also Kobak & Hazan, 1991). Others have found avoidant men even getting angry when their partners show signs of distress (Rholes, Simpson, & Oriña, 1999). It's interesting in this regard that avoidance predicts greater stress reactivity during discussion of a relationship conflict (Powers, Pietromonaco, Gunlicks, & Sayer, 2006).

This pattern of results has been confirmed and extended in several ways. The tendency to give less support to stressed partners has been shown among avoidant women as well as men (Simpson, Rholes, Oriña, & Grich, 2002). These patterns have also been confirmed by Feeney and Collins (2001) using different methods. They found that avoidance related inversely to a measure of responsive caregiving; avoidance also related inversely to reports of prosocial orientation, trust, and interdependence. Anxiety related to compulsive caregiving and also to higher levels of egoistic motivation and lower levels of trust.

Seeking and supplying support have been looked at in other situations as well. For example, Fraley and Shaver (1998) observed couples at an airport, where one person was leaving on a flight. They found that avoidant women sought contact less, did less caregiving, and displayed more behavioral avoidance than more secure women. Westmaas and Silver (2001) looked at how students reacted to a stranger they thought was being treated for cancer. Avoidants were less supportive in interacting with her than were others. Another study looked at the experience of becoming a new parent (Rholes, Simpson, & Friedman, 2006). Avoidants experienced more stress and found parenting less satisfying compared to people with other attachment patterns.

Additional research suggests that the sense of attachment security makes people more compassionate and responsive to the needs of others in general (Mikulincer & Shaver, 2005). This is true even if the sense of security is increased experimentally, rather than varying naturally (Mikulincer, Shaver, Gillath, & Nitzberg, 2005). The result is that the sense of attachment security promotes altruism for others in need.

Not surprisingly, the motivation for helping others depends on the person's attachment style. Avoidants are more likely to report helping for egotistical reasons (e.g., because they want something in return or because they feel obligated and want to avoid the negative consequences of not helping) and are less likely to report helping because they enjoy helping or have a genuine concern over their partner's well-being (Feeney & Collins, 2003). On the other side, secure persons explain away their partner's unsupportive behavior, whereas insecure persons exaggerate the negative implications of the partner's failure to offer help.

Other research has looked at variation in people's coping responses to stress. One study concerned threats of missile attacks in Israel (Mikulincer, Florian, & Weller, 1993). Avoidants used more "distancing" coping (trying not to think about the situation) than did other people. Ambivalents had higher levels of ineffective emotion-focused reactions (self-criticism, wishing they could change how they felt). Secure people used their social support more than did the other groups.

Recall that one aspect of secure infant attachment is the sense of a secure base. This aspect of attachment has also been examined among adults in several studies. Security relates to an exploratory orientation (Feeney, 2004; Green & Campbell, 2000), perhaps because the sense of security causes people to react more positively to stimuli (Mikulincer, Hirschberger, Nachmias, & Gillath, 2001). Security also reduces the typical negative reactions to outgroups (Mikulincer & Shaver, 2001), suggesting willingness to explore. On the other side of the coin, there's evidence that the avoidant pattern leads people to perceive hostile intent underlying others' behavior (Mikulincer, 1998).

Also of interest is how people with various attachment patterns relate to one another. Not surprisingly, secures are most desired as partners, and they tend to wind up with each other (Collins & Read, 1990). Relationships where the man is avoidant and relationships where the woman is ambivalent are unsatisfying to both partners. On the other hand, there's evidence that avoidant men with ambivalent women tend to be stable pairings (Kirkpatrick & Davis, 1994), despite the dissatisfactions. Why? Avoidant men avoid conflict, which may help the relationship run smoothly. Ambivalent women may work harder at holding things together.

Pairings of avoidants with avoidants and of ambivalents with ambivalents are rare (Kirkpatrick & Davis, 1994). This fits with the idea that people with insecure attachment patterns steer away from partners who would treat them as they were treated in infancy. Avoidants avoid partners who will be emotionally inaccessible, and ambivalents avoid partners who will be inconsistent (Collins & Read, 1990; Kirkpatrick & Davis, 1994; Pietromonaco & Carnelley, 1994; Simpson, 1990).

This pattern of findings also suggests more generally that people are sensitive to the issue that was critical to them earlier. Perhaps in holding the mental model that people will let them down, avoidants consider as partners only people who display more closeness than they'd had earlier. Perhaps in holding the mental model that people are inconsistent, ambivalents consider only people who provide consistency—even if the consistency is consistent distance.

ATTACHMENT PATTERNS AND THE FIVE-FACTOR MODEL

Recall that many people are interested in how various views of personality relate to the five-factor model of trait structure. This has also been examined with attachment patterns in adults. At least two groups have found substantial correlations between measures of adult attachment and two traits from the five-factor model (Carver, 1997a; Shaver & Brennan, 1992). These studies used the three-category view of attachment. They found that avoidants are introverted, secures are extraverted, and ambivalents are high in neuroticism or anxiety proneness.

An even stronger correspondence seems implied by the alternate approach to attachment. As noted earlier, it rests on two dimensions, which are sometimes termed *attachment avoidance* and *attachment anxiety*. Although the focus in each case is on relationships as a context, the dimensions strongly resemble introversion–extraversion and neuroticism. Maybe avoidants are simply not that interested in social connections because they're introverts. That would be consistent with the finding that avoidants encode less when listening to a tape about relationships than do secures (Fraley, Garner, & Shaver, 2000). If we add the twist of viewing extraversion as a desire for social incentives (from Chapter 7) and the idea that neuroticism is essentially anxiety proneness, the fit is even closer. It might even be argued that the attachment patterns represent relationship-focused versions of extraversion and neuroticism.

Do these patterns in personality arise from patterns of parenting (as held by psychosocial theorists)? Or are they manifestations of genetically determined traits, manifestations that simply happen to be social (as held by others)? One study of a very large national adult sample found that reports of interpersonal trauma (e.g., abuse, threat with a weapon, parental violence) related to insecure adult attachment (Mickelson, Kessler, & Shaver, 1997). So did a history of parental depression and anxiety. These findings suggest a social origin to the patterns. Simpson et al. (2002) reported that measures of extraversion and neuroticism did not duplicate the effects of attachment patterns. So even though there is overlap, the attachment dimensions don't seem identical with the "big five" traits.

Erikson's Theory of Psychosocial Development

We turn now to what is probably the most elaborate of psychosocial theories, that of Erik Erikson (1950, 1963, 1968). Erikson adopted Freud's view that personality develops in a series of stages. However, whereas Freud's is a theory of psycho*sexual* development, Erikson's is a theory of psycho*social* development. It describes the impact of social phenomena across life.

Another difference pertains to the age span involved. The stages that Freud described unfold in the first few years of life. In contrast, Erikson believed that personality evolves throughout life, from birth through maturity to death. He also

According to the principle of life-span development, all periods of a person's life are important, infancy through adulthood—even old age.

believed no part of life is more important than any other. Erikson was thus one of the first to propose the idea of **life-span development.** Many consider this to be one of his most important contributions to psychology.

EGO IDENTITY, COMPETENCE, AND THE EXPERIENCE OF CRISIS

The central theme of Erikson's theory is **ego identity** and its development (Erikson, 1968, 1974). *Ego identity* is the consciously experienced sense of self. It derives from transactions with social reality. A person's ego identity changes constantly in response to events in the social world. To Erikson, forming and maintaining a strong sense of ego identity is critical.

A second major theme in Erikson's theory concerns competence and personal adequacy. His stages focus on aspects of mastery. If a stage is managed well, the person emerges with a sense of competence. If not, the person has feelings of inadequacy. This theme in Erikson's theory—that a desire for competence is a motivating force behind people's actions—is similar in many ways to White's ideas about competence, discussed in Chapter 10. One difference is that Erikson's theory was more focused on competence in the social environment.

Erikson viewed development as a series of periods in which some issue is prominent. In his view, people experience a **psychosocial crisis,** or **conflict,** during each stage. The terms *crisis* and *conflict* are interchangeable here. They have a special meaning, though, that differs from the use of either word in day-to-day speech. Here, a crisis is a *turning point:* a period when potential for growth is high but the person is also quite vulnerable. Each crisis is fairly long (none is shorter than about a year), and some are quite long (perhaps 30 years). Thus, Erikson's use of the word conveys the sense of crucial importance more than the sense of time pressure.

The "conflict" in each crisis isn't a confrontation between persons, nor is it a conflict within personality. Rather, it's a struggle between attaining some psychological quality versus failing to attain it. To Erikson, the conflict never ends. Even handling it in the period when it's most intense doesn't mean you've mastered it once and for all. The conflict is always there to some degree, and you confront it repeatedly in different forms throughout life.

Erikson identified eight psychosocial stages. Each focuses on some aspect of transactions with social reality. Each has a conflict, or crisis. Each conflict pits two possibilities against each other, as a pair of opposed psychological qualities. One of the pair is obviously adaptive; the other appears less so. The labels that Erikson gave to the two qualities indicate the nature of the crisis.

People negotiate each stage by developing a balance between the qualities for which the stage is named. The point isn't just to acquire the good quality. In fact, it's important that the ego incorporate *both* sides of the conflict, at least a little. Having too much of the quality that seems good can create problems. For example, if you had only *basic trust* and absolutely no sense of *basic mistrust,* you'd be unable to deal effectively with a world that's sometimes *not* trustworthy.

Nonetheless, successful negotiation of a stage does imply that the balance is weighted more toward the positive value than the negative one. If this occurs, the person emerges from the crisis with a positive orientation toward future events concerning that conflict. Erikson used several terms to refer to this positive orientation: **ego quality, ego strength,** and **virtue** (Erikson, 1964; Stevens, 1983). Once established, these qualities remain a part of your personality.

Erikson was very reluctant to specify age norms for stages. He believed that each person has a unique timetable. Thus, it's hard to say when each stage will begin and end for a person. The ages given here are only rough approximations.

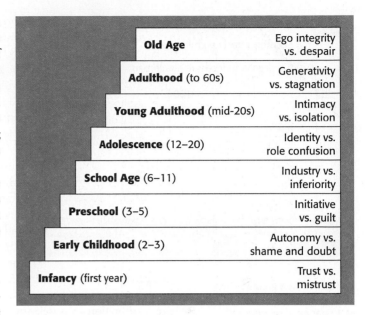

Infancy

The first four stages parallel stages of psychosexual development outlined by Freud. The first stage (see Figure 11.4) is infancy, roughly the first year. The conflict at this stage—the most fundamental crisis of life—is between a sense of *basic trust versus basic mistrust.* In this stage, the infant is totally dependent on others to meet its most basic needs. If the needs are met, the infant develops a sense of security and trust. This is reflected by the infant's feeding easily, sleeping well, and eliminating regularly. Caretakers can leave the infant alone for short periods without causing too much distress, because the infant has learned to trust that they'll return. Mistrust is reflected by fitful sleep, fussiness in feeding, constipation, and greater distress when the infant is left alone.

The sense of trust is extremely important. It provides a basis for believing that the world is predictable, especially relationships. Trust is enhanced by interactions in which caregivers are attentive, affectionate, and responsive. A sense of mistrust is created by inconsistent treatment, emotional unavailability, or rejection. This portrayal closely resembles ideas concerning object relations, basic anxiety, and attachment patterns earlier in this chapter. A predominance of trust over mistrust gives rise to the ego strength of *hope.* Hope is an enduring belief that wishes are attainable. It's a kind of optimism about life.

Early Childhood

The second stage is early childhood (the second and third years of life). Children begin to focus on gaining control over their actions. The crisis of this stage concerns these efforts. It's about creating a sense of *autonomy in actions versus shame and doubt* about being able to act independently.

Erikson followed Freud in assuming that toilet training was an important event here but for different reasons. To Erikson, acquiring control over bladder and bowels is a way to gain feelings of autonomy (self-direction). Achieving control over these functions means you're not at the mercy of your body's impulses. But this is just one way to gain these feelings. When children interact effectively with people and objects, feelings of autonomy and competence emerge. If the efforts lead to failure, ridicule, or criticism—or if parents don't let the children act on their own—the result is feelings of shame and self-doubt. Management of this conflict properly leads to the

FIGURE 11.4
Erikson's eight psychosocial stages, the approximate age range in which each occurs, and the crisis that dominates each stage.

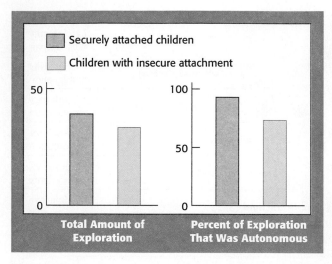

FIGURE 11.5

Children with a greater sense of basic trust and security at 1 year explore more at 2½ years of age than do less securely attached children, and a higher proportion of their exploration is self-initiated, or autonomous. This finding suggests that successful management of the first crisis prepares the child to do better with the second crisis.

Source: Adapted from Hazen & Durrett, 1982.

ego quality of *will:* a determination to exercise free choice.

Much of the research bearing on Erikson's theory focuses on the idea that successful management of one crisis prepares you to deal with the next one. Let's consider how this idea applies to the first two stages. The sense of basic trust is reflected in secure attachment. In one study, attachment was assessed at 1 year; then at 2½ years the children and their mothers came to a laboratory where they could explore a play area (Hazen & Durrett, 1982). Observers coded how many times the child went alone (or led the mother) to a new part of the area—action that reflects autonomy and self-initiation of behavior. They also coded how often the child *was led by* the mother into new parts of the area—action that's *not* autonomous.

As can be seen in Figure 11.5, children who'd been securely attached a year and a half earlier explored more than those who'd been less securely attached. Further, more of the exploration was self-initiated (autonomous) among the securely attached. Conceptually similar results have been reported by several others (e.g., Matas, Arend, & Sroufe, 1978). Thus, a sense of basic trust seems to promote more autonomy later on.

PRESCHOOL

The next period is preschool (from about 3 to 5). Being autonomous and capable of controlling your actions is an important start, but it's only a start. An ability to manipulate objects in the world leads to an increasing desire to exert influence, to make things happen—in short, a desire for *power* (McAdams, 1985). This period corresponds to the stage where Freud saw Oedipal conflicts emerging. As we said earlier, people who are skeptical about the Oedipal conflict tend to treat Freud's depiction as a metaphor for a more extensive power struggle between parents and child, who by now has become willful. Erikson focused on this power struggle.

The conflict at this stage concerns *initiative versus guilt.* Children who take the initiative are seeking to impose their newly developed sense of will on their surroundings. They express and act on their curiosity as they explore and manipulate their world and ask about things going on around them. (This pattern resembles the impulsive stage in Loevinger's theory, described in Chapter 10.)

Acts and words can also be perilous, however. Action that's too powerful can cause others pain. (Grabbing a toy you want can distress another child.) Asking too many questions can become tiresome to adults. If taking the initiative too often leads to disapproval, feelings of guilt will result. Because constantly exerting power does tend to produce some disapproval, initiative eventually must be tempered by restraint. If this crisis is managed well, the child emerges with the ego quality of *purpose:* the courage to pursue valued goals without fear of punishment.

Research has asked whether attaining a sense of basic trust during the first year fosters later initiative. In one study (Lütkenhaus, Grossmann, & Grossmann, 1985), attachment was assessed at age 1 and the children were studied again (at home) at age 3. Those who'd been securely attached were quicker to show initiative in interacting with a stranger than those who'd been insecurely attached. During a game involving a failure, securely attached children responded by increasing their efforts, but the other children decreased their efforts. Thus, the sense of basic trust seems to provide groundwork for the sense of initiative and purpose.

School Age

The next stage corresponds to Freud's latency period (from about 5 to 11). Unlike Freud, Erikson held that this period also has a conflict. He called it *industry versus inferiority*. The term *industry* reflects the fact that the child's life remains focused on doing things that have an impact. But now the nature of those efforts acquires a different shade of meaning. In particular, it's no longer enough just to take the initiative and assert power. Now there's pressure to do things that others judge to be *good,* in two senses. Industriousness isn't just *doing* things; it's doing things that others *value.* It's also doing things in ways that others regard as *appropriate* and *commendable.*

The crisis over this sense of industry begins about when the child enters elementary school. School is aimed at teaching children to become productive and responsible members of society. The school years are also the period when intellectual skills are first tested. Children are urged to do well in school, and the adequacy of their performance is explicitly evaluated.

The school experience also involves learning social roles. Children are beginning to learn about the nature of adult work. They're also being exposed to some of the tools of adult work. In former times, these were tools of farming, carpentry, and homemaking; today, it's more likely to be computers. Another role children are acquiring is that of citizenship. Thus, the child's sense of industry is being judged partly by the acceptability of his or her behavior to the social group.

Children with a strong sense of industry differ in several ways from children with less industry (Kowaz & Marcia, 1991). They tend to prefer reality-based activities over fantasy. They're more able to distinguish the role of effort from that of ability in producing outcomes. They get better grades. And they agree more with statements that are socially desirable.

To emerge from this stage successfully, children must feel they're mastering the tasks set for them in a fashion that's acceptable to those around them. The danger at this stage is developing feelings of inferiority. Such feelings can arise when children are led by others to view their performance as inadequate or morally wrong. Managing the conflict between industry and inferiority results in the ego quality termed *competence:* the sense that one can do things that are valued by others.

Adolescence

Next comes adolescence, a period that begins with the physical changes of puberty and lasts until roughly age 20. This stage is a larger break with the past than any stage up to this point. Part of the sense of separation comes from the physical changes of puberty. Your body doesn't just get larger during this period but also changes in other ways. You have desires you never had before. You're not quite the same person you used to be. But who *are* you?

Part of the break with the past reflects the fact that you're now beginning to think explicitly about yourself and your life in relation to the adult world. You'll have to find your place in that world, and doing so requires you to decide what roles fit your identity. This, in turn, means knowing who you are.

The crisis of this stage is *identity versus role confusion. Identity* reflects an integrated sense of self. It's the answer to the question, Who am I? The phrase *role confusion* reflects the fact that every self has many facets that sometimes seem incompatible. The greater the incompatibility, the harder it is to pull the facets together, and the more confused you are. Worse yet, you can even be in a position where *no* role seems to fit your identity.

To emerge from adolescence with a strong sense of identity requires the person to evolve in two ways. First, you must consolidate the self-conceptions from the previous stages, merging them in a way that's sensible. Second, this integrated self-view must be integrated with the view of you that others hold. This reflects the fact that identity is something you develop in a consensus with the people you relate to. Only by considering both views does a full sense of identity emerge.

Thus, from Erikson's perspective, identity derives from a blending of private and social self-conceptions. The result is a sense of personal continuity or inner congruence. Erikson placed great emphasis on the importance of developing a sense of identity. In many ways, he saw this as each person's major life task (see also Box 11.1).

If the person fails to form a consolidated identity, the result is *role confusion,* an absence of direction in the sense of self. Role confusion is reflected in an inability to select a career (or a college major that will take you toward a career). Role confusion can also lead people to identify with popular heroes or groups (or even antiheroes) to try to fill the void. The virtue associated with successful identity formation is *fidelity*. Fidelity means truthfulness. It's the ability to live up to who you are, despite the contradictions that inevitably occur among the values you hold.

BOX 11.1 THE THEORIST AND THE THEORY

Erikson's Lifelong Search for Identity

Erikson's life had a distinct impact on the form of his theory, particularly his emphasis on the importance of attaining a sense of identity (see Friedman, 1999). Erikson was born in Germany in 1902 to Danish parents. His father abandoned his mother before he was born, and three years later she married Theodor Homburger, a Jewish physician. Erik wasn't told for years that Homburger wasn't his real father. He later referred to that as an act of "loving deceit."

He grew up as Erik Homburger, a Jew with the appearance of a Scandinavian. Jews saw him as a gentile; gentiles saw him as a Jew. For this reason, he wasn't accepted by either group and he began to form an image of himself as an outsider. By adolescence, he'd been told of his adoption, and his identity confusion was further complicated by the realization that his

ancestry was Danish, rather than German.

As he wandered Europe during his early twenties, his feelings of a lack of identity deepened. He worked as a portrait painter but never developed a clear sense of identity as an artist. Eventually, he took a teaching job in Vienna, at a school created for children of Freud's patients and friends. There he became familiar with a number of psychoanalysts, including Anna Freud, with whom he went on to train as an analyst. In 1933, he moved to the United States, where he established a practice as a child analyst. As Erik Homburger, he was also in the research team that Henry Murray brought together, which led to development of the motive approach to personality described in Chapter 5.

In 1939, Homburger became a U.S. citizen. At that time, he took the name *Erikson*. This was an event—and a choice of name—that unquestionably had much personal meaning, symbolizing his full attainment of the sense of identity.

In later years, Erikson spent time studying methods of childrearing and other aspects of cultural life among the Sioux of South Dakota and the Yurok of northern California. These studies were important for two reasons. First, they led to themes that would permeate Erikson's thinking concerning the importance of culture and society in identity. Second, they revealed to him symptoms of dislocation, feelings of having been uprooted and separated from cultural traditions. The members of these tribes appeared to have lost their sense of identity, much as Erikson himself had done earlier in his life. Erikson also saw similar qualities in the lives of veterans of World War II who returned with emotional difficulties.

From all these experiences, Erikson came to believe that the attainment and preservation of a sense of identity—not wholly separate from but rather embedded in one's own society—was the critical task of growing up. This idea was to stand as one of the major themes of his viewpoint on personality.

A good deal of research has evolved from Erikson's ideas about the development of identity during adolescence, much of it by James Marcia (1966, 1976, 1980) and his colleagues. Marcia argued that two things are important in the formation of an identity. The first is the occurrence of an an **identity crisis.** Marcia's use of the word *crisis* here is similar to Erikson's use. An identity crisis is actively exploring different ways of viewing oneself and giving serious thought to the implications of those views. The second is making an **identity commitment.**

Marcia (1966) distinguished four **identity statuses,** each of which is defined by whether a crisis was experienced and whether a commitment was made. *Identity achievement* is the status of a person who's experienced a period of crisis and then made a commitment. *Moratorium* applies to a person who's now in crisis (exploring alternatives) but has no commitment. *Foreclosure* is the status of a person who's made a commitment but with no crisis—for example, a young man planning to be a surgeon because his father and grandfather were surgeons. In *identity diffusion,* there's no crisis and no commitment. Not surprisingly, either achieving or foreclosing on an identity has a benefit. People in these two groups feel better about themselves than people who haven't made commitments (Prager, 1982).

YOUNG ADULTHOOD

The next stage in Erikson's theory is young adulthood (through the mid-20s). The conflict here concerns the desire for *intimacy versus isolation. Intimacy* is a close, warm relationship with someone, with a sense of commitment to that person. Erikson saw intimacy as an issue in relationships of all kinds, nonsexual as well as sexual.

True intimacy requires you to approach relationships in a caring and open way and to be willing to share the most personal aspects of yourself with others. You also must be open and receptive to others' disclosures. Intimacy requires the moral strength to live up to a commitment, even when it requires sacrifice. Erikson believed people are capable of intimacy only if they have a strong sense of identity.

The opposite pole at this stage is *isolation,* feeling apart from others and being unable to make commitments to them. A person can drift into isolation if conditions aren't right for intimacy—if no one's there who fills his or her needs. Sometimes, though, people withdraw into isolation on their own—for instance, if they feel a relationship threatens their sense of separate identity. Withdrawing can have other consequences, however. People can become self-absorbed to the point that they aren't able to establish intimate relationships in the future (Erikson, 1982). The ego quality associated with the ability to be intimate is *love.* This is a mutuality that subdues the antagonisms of separate identities.

The theme that handling one crisis prepares you for the next one continues here. Erikson said people need a strong sense of identity to be able to attain intimacy. Is this true? One study looked at identity strength in college and intimacy in middle age (Kahn, Zimmerman, Csikszentmihalyi, & Getzels, 1985). Intimacy was assessed in terms of whether subjects had married and, if so, whether the marriage had been disrupted by divorce. There was a clear link between a strong identity and a later capacity for intimacy. The effect differed slightly, however, between men and women (see Figure 11.6). Men with stronger identities were more likely to have married

FIGURE 11.6
Percentage of men who had ever been married during the 18-year period after art school and percentage of women who had married and whose marriages remained intact during the same period, as a function of pre-assessed identity formation.
Source: Adapted from Kahn et al., 1985.

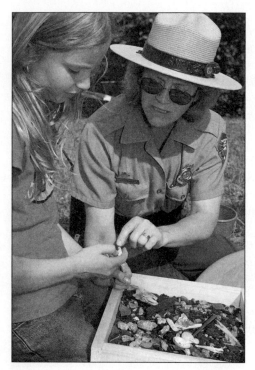

One way in which feelings of generativity are displayed is by helping the next generation learn about life.

during the 18 years. Identity didn't predict whether the women married, but among those who *had* married, those with a strong identity were less likely to divorce. Conceptually similar findings have been reported by others (e.g., Orlofsky, Marcia, & Lesser, 1973; Schiedel & Marcia, 1985; Tesch & Whitbourne, 1982).

The other pole of the conflict of this stage—isolation—has drawn interest in its own right (e.g., Peplau & Perlman, 1982; Shaver & Rubenstein, 1980; Weiss, 1973). Two aspects of it are distinguishable from each other. *Social isolation* is a failure to be integrated into a society. People who stand apart from social groups fail to develop a sense of belonging. In contrast, the failure to have intimacy in your life is termed *emotional isolation*—more simply, loneliness.

Emotional isolation feeds on itself. Recall that to experience intimacy requires self-disclosing, opening oneself to others. Lonely people don't do this (W. H. Jones, Hobbs, & Hockenberg, 1982; Mikulincer & Nachshon, 1991). They're also less responsive, ask fewer questions, and seem less interested in what the other person is saying. As a result, they're hard to get to know and are likely to remain lonely.

ADULTHOOD

Young adulthood is followed by adulthood, the longest of the psychosocial stages, typically lasting into the mid-60s. The crisis of adulthood centers around being able to generate or nurture. For this reason, the central conflict in this stage is termed *generativity versus stagnation*.

The desire for generativity is the desire to create things in the world that will outlive you (Kotre, 1984)—children, for example. By creating a new life tied to yours, you symbolically ensure your continuation into the future. Consistent with this idea, McAdams and de St. Aubin (1992) found that men who'd had children scored higher on a self-report measure of generativity than did childless men. Generativity has also been found to relate to a view of the self as a role model and source of wisdom for one's children (Hart, McAdams, Hirsch, & Bauer, 2001) and to a parenting style that fosters autonomy (Pratt, Danso, Arnold, Norris, & Filyer, 2001).

Although generativity is partly a matter of creating and guiding the growth of the next generation, the concept is broader than that. It includes creating ideas or objects, teaching young people who aren't your own children, and anything that influences the future in a positive way (see Table 11.3). Erikson believed that the desire for

Table 11.3 Aspects of Generativity. *Source:* Adapted from Kotre, 1984, p. 12.

Aspect	Description
Biological	Creating, bearing, and nursing an infant
Parental	Raising, nurturing, shaping, and socializing children, providing them with family traditions
Technical	Teaching the skills that make up the *body* of a culture, training a new generation in techniques for doing things
Cultural	Creating, changing, and maintaining a symbol system that represents the *mind* of a culture, passing it on to the next generation

generativity reflects a shift in focus from one close relationship (intimacy) to a broader concern with society as a whole.

Consistent with this idea, highly generative persons express high levels of commitment to assisting the next generation; they also show an integration between that commitment and a sense of agency (Mansfield & McAdams, 1996; see also de St. Aubin, McAdams, & Kim, 2004; McAdams, Diamond, de St. Aubin, & Mansfield, 1997). Once the quality of generativity emerges, it may continue through the rest of one's life (Zucker, Ostrove, & Stewart, 2002).

Adults who fail to develop this sense of generativity drift into stagnation. *Stagnation* is an inability or unwillingness to give of oneself to the future. These people are preoccupied with their own concerns. They have a self-centered or self-indulgent quality that keeps them from deeper involvement in the world around them. There's also evidence that an absence of generativity is related to poorer psychological well-being (Vandewater, Ostrove, & Stewart, 1997).

If there's a positive balance of generativity, the ego quality that emerges is care. *Care* is a widening concern for whatever you've generated in your life, be it children, something in your work, or something that emerged from your involvement with other people.

OLD AGE

The final stage is maturity, or old age. This is the closing chapter of people's lives. It's a time when people look back and review the choices they made and reflect on their accomplishments (and failures) and on the turns their lives have taken (see also Box 11.2). The crisis here is termed *ego integrity versus despair*. If you emerge from this review feeling that your life has had order and meaning, accepting the choices you made and the things you did, a sense of ego integrity emerges. This is a sense of satisfaction, a feeling that you wouldn't change much about your life.

The opposite pole of this conflict is despair: the feeling that your life was wasted. It's a sense of wishing you'd done things differently but knowing that it's too late. Instead of accepting your life's story as a valuable gift, there's bitterness that things turned out as they did.

Emerging from this life review with a sense of integrity creates the ego quality of *wisdom*. Wisdom involves meaning making and benevolence (Helson & Srivastava, 2002). It is an active concern with life and continued personal growth, even as one confronts the impending reality of death (see also Baltes & Staudinger, 1993; Kunzmann & Baltes, 2003).

THE EPIGENETIC PRINCIPLE

One more issue to address about Erikson's theory is that a given conflict is presumed to exist outside the stage in which it's focal. In the science of embryology, **epigenesis** is the process by which a single cell turns into a complex organism. For this process to occur requires a "blueprint" at the beginning, with instructions for all the changes and their sequencing. Erikson applied this idea to his theory, saying that there's a readiness for each crisis at birth. The core issue of each crisis is especially focal during a particular stage, but all of the issues are always there.

The principle of epigenesis has several implications. For one, as already indicated, it means your orientation to a particular crisis is influenced by the outcomes of earlier ones. It also means that in resolving the core crisis of any stage, you're preparing solutions (in simple form) for the ones coming later. As you deal in adolescence with the conflict between ego identity and role confusion, you're also

BOX 11.2   IS THERE A MIDLIFE CRISIS?

From Erikson's point of view, the last years of life are spent in review, examining choices that were made, values that were pursued, and passions that were abandoned. Erikson saw this review as coming late in life, after the opportunity to make changes has passed.

Others have also talked about a life review (Gould, 1980; Levinson, 1978; Stewart & Vandewater, 1999; Vaillant, 1977) but one that occurs earlier, around age 40 or so. Given its timing, the phenomenon is popularly referred to as the *midlife crisis.* It's a questioning of the decisions you've made over your adult years, the validity and worth of your goals, the adequacy of your life situation—nearly everything about your existence. It's a time of re-evaluation, but it's also a chance to change the way things are before it's too late. If you don't like your life, change it: remake decisions, rearrange your priorities, change careers, change your marriage (or leave it).

The notion of a midlife crisis rests partly on the typical course of life's major events in Western culture. It's common in the United States to finish college and take a job in one's early 20s and to marry and start raising a family in one's 20s and 30s. Depending on when the children are born, they're growing up and leaving home when the parents are in their 40s or early 50s. Around that time, it's also common to experience the death of one or both of one's own parents. Many changes of midlife are profound ones. Is it any wonder that they seem to cry out for a re-evaluation of life?

Another contributor to a crisis is cultural assumptions about the timing of these events. As a result, people do a certain amount of checking to see whether their lives are "on schedule." If you're in your mid-30s, are you making as much money as you're supposed to be? Are you in line for the career advancement you planned on? If you're nearing 40 with no children, you may hear the so-called biological clock ticking, telling you that you'll never have that experience if you don't hurry. Comparing your life against these markers of a "normal" life can produce a lot of soul searching.

Is there a midlife crisis? We're inclined to feel there's some truth to the idea. We know the feelings we've just written about. (We also know why one of us bought a motorcycle some years ago.) People do experience regrets at midlife, and that does cause some people (though not all) to make life changes (Stewart & Vandewater, 1999).

Yet the evidence doesn't indicate that a real midlife crisis is all that common. Two longitudinal studies found little support for the idea in fairly large samples (Clausen, 1981; Haan, 1981). On the other hand, the participants in those studies lived through some very hard times—the Great Depression and World War II—and it's possible that having survived those experiences made them less likely to re-evaluate their choices and goals at midlife. Perhaps the midlife crisis is actually a baby-boomer phenomenon.

Alternatively, it may be that the midlife crisis isn't so much a matter of midlife as it is a reflection of a more consistent tendency to worry. This conclusion would fit with findings obtained by Costa and McCrae (1980) concerning life satisfaction over time. They found that satisfaction was relatively stable across a period of 10 years and that dissatisfaction related to the broad trait of neuroticism. Maybe, then, people who are inclined to worry do so throughout life, and it just happens to be more obvious at midlife.

moving toward handling the crisis of intimacy versus isolation. Finally, this principle means that crises aren't resolved once and for all. Your resolutions of previous conflicts are revisited and reshaped at each new stage of life (Whitbourne, Zuschlag, Elliot, & Waterman, 1992).

IDENTITY AS LIFE STORY

The sense of the epigenetic principle is well conveyed in some of the work of Dan McAdams. His work focuses partly on motivations that underlie personality (discussed in Chapter 5) and partly on the idea that people construct their identities as narratives, or life stories (McAdams, 1985, 1993, 2001). In his view, your story is never completed until the end of your life. It is constantly being written. Indeed, it's constantly under revision, just as your identity is constantly evolving.

As in any good book, the opening chapters of your narrative begin setting the stage for things that happen much later. Sometimes future events are foreshadowed; sometimes things that happen in early chapters create conditions that have to be reacted to later on. As chapters pile up, characters reinterpret events they experienced earlier or understand them in different ways. All the pieces eventually come together into a full and integrated picture, and the picture that results has qualities from everything that's happened throughout the story. McAdams thus sees the broad crisis of identity as one that continues to occupy each person throughout life (McAdams, 2001).

Of interest is how categories of narrative themes show up in many people's lives. McAdams and his colleagues have found that highly generative midlife adults often report life stories in which they had early advantages, became aware of the suffering of others, established a personal belief system that involved prosocial values, and committed themselves to benefiting society. McAdams calls these *commitment stories*. Often these commitment stories also contain *redemption themes,* in which a bad situation somehow is transformed into something good (McAdams, 2006; McAdams, Reynolds, Lewis, Patten, & Bowman, 2001). Indeed, the link from the sense of redemption to the quality of generativity appears quite strong (McAdams, 2006). Adults who are low in generativity sometimes have stories involving *contamination themes,* in which a good situation somehow turns bad.

LINKING ERIKSON'S THEORY TO OTHER PSYCHOSOCIAL THEORIES

Let's look back to the theories discussed earlier in this chapter to make a final point. Those theories represent contributions of their own. Yet in a sense, the fundamental theme of each is the same as that of the first crisis in Erikson's theory: basic trust versus basic mistrust. That's a big part of what security in attachment is about. It seems implicit in object relations theories. This issue is also the core of Erikson's own theory, providing the critical foundation on which the rest of personality is built.

Humans seem to need to be able to trust in the relationships that sustain our lives. In the minds of many theorists, that trust is necessary for adequate functioning. People who are deeply mistrustful of relationships or are constantly frightened about possibly losing relationships have lives that are damaged and distorted. The damage may be slight, or it may be significant. Avoiding such mistrust and doubt (or recognizing and overcoming it, if it's already there) seems a central task in human existence.

Assessment

Let's turn now to assessment from the psychosocial viewpoint. In general, assessment here is similar to that of the ego psychologists. There are two aspects of assessment, however, that are specific to this view.

OBJECT RELATIONS, ATTACHMENT, AND THE FOCUS OF ASSESSMENT

One difference concerns what's being assessed. The psychosocial approach places a greater emphasis than other approaches on assessing the person orientation to relationships.

There are several ways in which a person's mental model of relationships might be assessed. Relevant measures range from some that are open ended in nature (e.g., Blatt, Wein, Chevron, & Quinlan, 1979) to structured self-reports (e.g., Bell, Billington, & Becker, 1986). Some measures assess a range of issues pertaining to relationships (Bell et al., 1986). Others focus specifically on the attachments you have to other people in close relationships (e.g., Bartholomew & Horowitz, 1991; Carver, 1997a; Collins & Read, 1990; Griffin & Bartholomew, 1994; Simpson, 1990).

The object-relations measure of Bell et al. (1986) is a good illustration of content assessed from this viewpoint. It has four scales. The *alienation* scale measures a lack of basic trust and an inability to be close. People high on this scale are suspicious, guarded, and isolated, convinced that others will fail them. This resembles avoidant attachment. Another scale measures *insecure attachment,* which resembles the ambivalent pattern, a sensitivity to rejection and concern about being liked and accepted. The third scale, *egocentricity,* assesses narcissism, a self-protective and exploitive attitude toward relationships and a tendency to view others only in relation to one's own needs and aims. The final scale measures *social incompetence,* shyness and uncertainty about how to engage in even simple social interactions.

A different approach to assessment is the open-ended measure of Blatt et al. (1979). It has a coding system to assess the maturity of people's perceptions of social relations. This measure asks you to describe your mother and father. If you're at a low level of maturity, you tend to focus on how parents acted to satisfy your needs. Higher-level descriptions focus more on parents' values, thoughts, and feelings apart from your needs. At a very high level, the description takes into account internal contradictions in the parent and changes over time. This measure reflects a person's level of separation and individuation from the parent.

PLAY IN ASSESSMENT

Another facet of the psychosocial view on assessment reflects the emphasis on experiences of childhood as determinants of personality. As a result, this view deals with child assessment more than others. The assessment of children tends to emphasize the use of play as a tool. It's often said that children's play reveals their preoccupations (e.g., Axline, 1947, 1964; Erikson, 1963; M. Klein, 1935, 1955a, 1955b). Play lets them express their concerns in ways they can't do in words. Erikson (1963) devised a play situation using a specific set of toys on a table. The child is to imagine that the table is a movie studio and the toys are actors and sets. The child is to create a scene and describe what's happening. Other techniques use less structured settings, but elements almost always include a variety of dolls (e.g., mother, father, older person, children, baby). This permits children to choose characters that relate to their own concerns or preoccupations.

The play situation is projective, because the child imposes a story on ambiguous stimuli. It often has two objective characteristics, however. First is a *behavioral record.* This includes what the child says about the scene and a description of the scene and the sequence of steps taken to create it. Second, the face value of the child's behavior receives more attention than is usual in projectives. It isn't automatically assumed that the child's behavior has deeply hidden meanings.

Children often reveal their feelings through play.

Problems in Behavior, and Behavior Change

Given that psychosocial theorists focus on the nature of people's relationships, it's natural that they see problems as reflecting relationship difficulties. Here are three examples of how this approach applies to problems in behavior.

NARCISSISM AS A DISORDER OF PERSONALITY

One psychosocial view focuses specifically on **narcissism** as a disorder. Indeed, this disorder was the starting point for Kohut's work on the self. Pathological narcissism involves a sense that everyone and everything is an extension of the self or exists to serve the self. There's a grandiose sense of self-importance and need for constant attention. Narcissists show a sense of *entitlement,* of deserving others' adulation. As a result, they often exploit others.

Recall that Kohut said everyone begins life with a grandiose narcissism, which is tempered during development. Some people never escape it, however. To Kohut, inadequate mirroring by parents frustrates the narcissistic needs and prevents formation of an adequate self-structure (Kohut, 1977). Similarly, Kernberg (1976, 1980) said that narcissism arises from parental rejection. The child comes to believe that the only person who can be trusted (and therefore loved) is himself or herself. Fitting this picture, narcissists prefer romantic partners who are admiring over those who offer intimacy (Campbell, 1999). They're also less committed in their relationships, always on the lookout for someone better (Campbell & Foster, 2002).

Unmet narcissistic needs can cause a person to distort reality in several ways in an effort to satisfy those unmet needs. For example, narcissistic people are more likely to inflate their judgments of their own performances in various arenas of life than are less narcissistic people (John & Robins, 1994). If threatened by being told that someone else has outperformed them, they're more likely to put the other person down (Morf & Rhodewalt, 1993).

Narcissists may seem quite agreeable at first, but they wear on other people after a while (Paulhus, 1998). They are very responsive to opportunities for self-enhancement (Wallace & Baumeister, 2002). They love to take credit for successes but respond to failure or criticism with anger (Rhodewalt & Morf, 1998). Indeed, narcissists may erupt in extremes of rage if their desires are thwarted (Bushman & Baumeister, 1998; Stucke & Sporer, 2002) or they experience social rejection (Twenge & Campbell, 2003). This can be a real problem, because they are especially likely to view themselves as victims (McCullough, Emmons, Kilpatrick, & Mooney, 2003).

BASIC ANXIETY, VICIOUS CYCLES, AND NEUROTIC NEEDS

Another way of thinking about problems comes from ideas proposed by Karen Horney (see Box 11.3). Horney (1937, 1945) held that from childhood on, people have a sense of insecurity she called **basic anxiety.** This is a feeling of being abandoned, of being isolated and helpless in a hostile world. It can be minimized by being raised in a home where there's security, trust, love, warmth, and tolerance, but it's there in everyone.

Horney coined the term **vicious cycle** to refer to a pattern that basic anxiety often induces. Feeling insecure increases awareness of the need for love. If the need isn't met through whatever strategies are available (and often it isn't), the result is more anxiety and insecurity. Only if the need for affection is met is the cycle broken.

BOX 11.3 THE THEORIST AND THE THEORY

Karen Horney's Feminism

Karen Horney (pronounced "horn-eye") focused on general themes, such as the role of basic anxiety in behavior, but she also had much to say regarding the psychoanalytic view of women. She was a vocal critic of Freud, believing that he'd managed to get nearly everything wrong.

Recall that Freud believed a woman's life is deeply affected by the fact that she has no penis. According to him, women feel castrated and inferior, and they envy and resent men because of it. Horney came to a very different view (see Quinn, 1987). Her feelings of pleasure and pride in childbirth and motherhood led her to realize how shallow the comparable experiences of men were. Men play a minor role in creating and nurturing new life, and Horney came to think that this causes them to have a deep sense of inferiority. This idea was confirmed in her therapy experiences with men, who gave considerable evidence of envying women's ability to have children.

One result of men's feelings of inferiority is an attempt to compensate through achievement. The world of business is an attempt to *create,* although such creations can never compare to creating a baby. Besides these efforts to compensate, men try to hide their inferiorities by disparaging and devaluing women. By denying women equal rights, men can hide from themselves the fact that they can never be as valuable to human society as women.

Horney argued forcefully that the tendency of women to feel inferior arises not from penis envy but from the cultural context in which they live. If women regard themselves as unworthy, it's because men have treated them that way for so long. It isn't penises that women want but the ability to participate as full members of society. (Horney was born in 1885, so keep in mind that the culture in which she lived was more restrictive than that of today.)

How did Freud feel about all this? He never responded directly to Horney's arguments, but late in life, he wrote something that probably was aimed in her direction: "We shall not be very greatly surprised if a woman analyst who has not been sufficiently convinced of the intensity of her own wish for a penis also fails to attach proper importance to that factor in her patients" (Freud, 1949/1940). To Freud, Horney's theory arose from her own penis envy.

Horney took many positions that anticipated and foreshadowed later developments in psychological theory and in Western culture more broadly. Her feminist stance was no exception. She did much to create the outline of a feminist agenda for the future. She argued that a woman's identity is not to be found in the mere reflection of her husband. Rather, a woman should seek her own identity by developing her abilities and pursuing a career. Truly, Karen Horney was a woman ahead of her time.

People develop strategies to combat basic anxiety. One is to strike back against people who abandon them. Another is trying to win back love by being submissive, never doing anything that could antagonize others. Another is growing an inflated self-concept to compensate for insecurity (as in narcissism). Yet another is seeking power over others to compensate for feelings of loss.

Horney (1942) believed the strategies people use to combat basic anxiety can become a fixed part of personality if they're used too much. She made a list of needs that are acquired by trying to deal with problem relationships (see Table 11.4). She called them **neurotic needs** because they aren't effective solutions to the problem. Instead, they often lead into vicious cycles.

Horney argued that these neurotic needs tend to result in three styles of acting, depending on whether the need moves you *toward* others, *away* from others, or *against* others (Horney, 1945, 1950). Neurotic needs for love and approval move you toward others but in clingy dependency (as in ambivalent attachment). Neurotic needs for independence and self-sufficiency move you away from others (as in the avoidant attachment pattern). Needs such as power and exploitation move you against others. As with all defenses, each can be useful but is problematic if it is used to an extreme. Indeed, extremes of the styles do relate to other measures of personality disorders (Coolidge, Moor, Yamazaki, Stewart, & Segal, 2001).

Table 11.4 Horney's List of Neurotic Needs (and a brief description of each). Each arises from overuse of various strategies of coping with anxiety. *Source:* Adapted from Horney, 1942, 1945.

Neurotic need for affection and approval	Having an indiscriminate wish to please others and live up to their expectations
	Having extreme sensitivity to any sign of rejection or unfriendliness
Neurotic need for a partner who will take over one's life	Feeling extremely afraid of being deserted and left alone
Neurotic need to restrict one's life within narrow borders	Being extremely undemanding, content with little, preferring to remain inconspicuous
Neurotic need for power	Craving power for its own sake, adoring strength and contempt for weakness
	May also be reflected in intellectual exploitation
Neurotic need to exploit others	Using others to your own advantage
Neurotic need for prestige	Basing your self-evaluation on public recognition
Neurotic need for personal admiration	Having an inflated picture of yourself and wishing to be admired for that, not for what you really are
Neurotic ambition for personal achievement	Wanting to be the very best and driving yourself to greater and greater achievements as a result of basic insecurity
Neurotic need for self-sufficiency and independence	Setting yourself apart from others, becoming a loner
	Refusing to be tied down to anyone or anything because of disappointment in attempts to find warm, satisfying relationships with people
Neurotic need for perfection and unassailability	Trying to make yourself impregnable and infallible
	Constantly searching for flaws in yourself so that they can be covered up before becoming obvious to others

Well-adapted people usually adopt one style at a time and shift from one to another flexibly as needed. This flexibility is the hallmark of good adaptation. People with problems rigidly adopt a single orientation, even in situations where one of the other styles might be more useful.

ATTACHMENT AND DEPRESSION

Another window on the nature of problems comes from the idea that an important cause of depression is interpersonal rejection, which has received a good deal of support (Blatt & Zuroff, 1992). Recall that the avoidant attachment pattern is also believed to be a product of neglectful or rejecting parenting, resulting in sadness, despair, and eventual emotional detachment (Carnelley, Pietromonaco, & Jaffe, 1994; Hazan & Shaver, 1994).

The avoidant attachment pattern has also been linked to development of emotional distress when under stress (Berant, Mikulincer, & Florian, 2001). Participants in this study were women who had found out two weeks earlier that their newborns had congenital heart disease. Those with avoidant (and those with anxious) attachment patterns were more distressed. Avoidant patterns also predicted further deterioration in emotional well-being a year later. Other research has also supported the idea that avoidant attachment is a risk factor for depression (Hankin, Kassel, & Abela, 2005).

It's been suggested that both the avoidant attachment pattern and the depression to which it relates can be passed from one generation to another. The argument is based on behavior, rather than genetics. The pattern you acquire as a child is the working model you bring to bear when you have children of your own. If you're an avoidant adult (due to parental rejection), and especially if you're a *depressed* avoidant adult, what kind of parent will you be? An emotionally distant one. You are likely to be experienced as a rejecting parent—not because you dislike your child but because you're so distant. Being emotionally unavailable, you may then create an avoidant child, just like you.

Thus, parents may transfer to the next generation precisely the attachment qualities that made them unhappy themselves. There's support for this line of reasoning on rejection and depression (Besser & Priel, 2005; Whitbeck et al., 1992). There's also evidence of transmission of an erratic pattern of adult behavior that may be tied to the ambivalent attachment pattern (Elder, Caspi, & Downey, 1986).

BEHAVIOR CHANGE

The process of therapeutic behavior change from the viewpoint of psychosocial theories reflects many of the themes we discussed for ego psychology. The techniques tend to focus on the here and now, and the person with the problem is seen as a collaborator in the therapeutic process.

Nevertheless, a few additional techniques were developed by people in the psychosocial tradition. For example, psychologists such as Erikson (1963), Virginia Axline (1947), and Melanie Klein (1955a, 1955b) developed **play therapy** techniques for use with children. These techniques give the child the opportunity to do as he or she wishes, without pressuring, intruding, prodding, or nagging. Under these conditions, children can have distance from others (if they are worried about being smothered by a too ever present parent) or can play out anger or the wish for closeness (if they're feeling rejected or unwanted). The playroom is the child's world. In it, children have the opportunity to bring their feelings to the surface, deal with them, and potentially change their working models of relationships and of the self in positive ways (Landreth, 1991).

Because object relations and self-theories emphasize the role of relationships in problems, they also emphasize relationships as part of the therapeutic process. Therapists try to provide the kind of relationship the patient needs so he or she can reintegrate problematic parts of the self. Healing is brought about by providing a successful experience of narcissism or attachment (almost a kind of re-parenting), replacing the earlier emotional failure.

These therapy techniques can be seen as representing a way of restoring to the person's life a sense of connectedness to others. By modifying the representations of relationships that were built in the past, they permit the developing of more satisfying relationships in the future. The optimism that this approach holds about being able to undo problematic experiences from the past is reflected in the saying "It's never too late to have a happy childhood."

Psychosocial Theories: Problems and Prospects

As was true of ego psychology, the psychosocial neoanalytic approach is home to many theorists. Although they had different starting points, there's a remarkable consistency in the themes behind their work. Each assumes that human relationships are the most important part of human life and that how relationships are managed is a core issue in personality. Each tends to assume that people develop working models of relationships in early experience, which then are used to frame new ones. Also implied is the idea that health requires a balance between being separate and being closely connected to someone (see also Helgeson, 1994, 2003; Helgeson & Fritz, 1999).

A strength of psychosocial theories is that they point us in directions that other theories don't. Thinking about personality in terms of attachment patterns, for example, suggests hypotheses that aren't readily derived from other viewpoints. Work based in attachment theory is leading to a better understanding of how personality plays out in social relations. This picture of this aspect of personality would very likely not have emerged without having the attachment model as a starting point. Furthermore, linking the themes of attachment to models of greater complexity, such as Erikson's, creates a picture of change and evolution across the life span that would be nearly impossible to derive from other viewpoints. The psychosocial viewpoint clearly adds something of great importance to our understanding of personality.

This is not to say that no unresolved issues remain for this approach. One important issue concerns a rather sharp clash between this view and the view of trait psychologists and behavior geneticists. Manifestations of adult attachment patterns correspond well to genetically influenced traits. Avoidants are essentially introverts, secures are extraverts, and anxious–ambivalents are high in neuroticism. Do these patterns result from parenting, or are they genetically determined? There are strong opinions on both sides of this question. It's a question that will surely continue to be examined closely.

Indeed, in considering the prospects of this viewpoint for the future, we should note explicitly that research on psychosocial approaches is continuing full speed. Indeed, adult attachment and related ideas represent one of the most active areas of research in personality psychology today. The recent flood of research on this topic shows no sign of abating (Mikulincer & Shaver, 2007; Rholes & Simpson, 2004). Research on the implications of attachment patterns for the life of the child—and the adult—promises to yield interesting new insights into the human experience. The prospects of this area of work seem very bright, as do the prospects for the approach more generally.

• SUMMARY •

Psychosocial theories emphasize the idea that personality is intrinsically social and that the important issues of personality concern how people relate to others. Several psychosocial theories focus on early life. Mahler's object relations theory proposes that infants begin life merged psychologically with their mothers and that they separate and individuate during the first 3 years of life. How this takes place influences later adjustment.

Kohut's self psychology resembles object relations theory. He said humans have narcissistic needs that are satisfied by other people, represented as *selfobjects*. If the child receives enough mirroring (positive attention) from selfobjects (chiefly the mother), the sense of self develops appropriately. If there's too much mirroring, the child won't be able to deal with frustrations. If there's too little, the development of the self will be stunted.

Some of these ideas are echoed in the work of attachment theorists such as Bowlby and Ainsworth. Secure attachment provides a solid base for exploration. There are also patterns of insecure attachment (ambivalent and avoidant), which stem from inconsistent treatment, neglect, or rejection. There's increasing interest in the idea that infant attachment patterns persist and influence adult personality. There is now a great deal of work on this topic, assessing adult attachment in several ways. Although people do display diverse ways of relating across their social connections, a core tendency seems to exist. Adult attachment patterns influence many aspects of behavior, including how people relate to work activities and how they seek and give emotional support, as well as how they relate to romantic partners.

Another important theory of the psychosocial group is Erikson's theory of psychosocial development. Erikson postulated a series of crises from infancy to late adulthood, giving rise to ego strengths that influence one's ego identity: the consciously experienced sense of self. Erikson assumed that each crisis becomes focal at one stage but that each is present in a less obvious form throughout life.

The first crisis concerns the development of a sense of *basic trust*. The child then becomes concerned with control over its body and the sense of *autonomy* that comes with that. The next issue is *initiative,* as the child seeks to exercise its power. As children enter the school years, they begin to realize that the social environment demands being *industrious*. With adolescence, the child enters a new stage of life and has a crisis over *identity*. In young adulthood, identity issues give way to concern over *intimacy*. In adulthood, the person's concern is over *generativity*. Finally, in the last stage of life, people confront the *integrity* of their lives as a whole.

Assessment techniques from the psychosocial view are similar to those of ego psychology but focus more on relationships. This approach also leads to use of play for assessment with children. The psychosocial view of problems focuses on the idea that problems are rooted in relationship issues. Kohut suggested that pathological narcissism stems from inadequate childhood mirroring. Horney suggested that people suffer from basic anxiety, a feeling of being abandoned, isolated, and alone. People develop strategies to cope with this, but doing so can lead to a vicious cycle of increased anxiety. Strategies for dealing with basic anxiety often involve moving toward, away from, or against other people. Adaptive functioning involves flexibly shifting from one strategy to another as needed. Poor adjustment comes from rigid reliance on one strategy. Insecure attachment seems to create a risk for depression.

These theories approach therapy in ways similar to those of ego psychology, but there are additional variations. One of them is play therapy for children. Object relations and attachment theories also suggest that a relationship with a therapist is critical in permitting reintegration of the sense of self or establishing a sense of secure attachment.

· GLOSSARY ·

Attachment   An emotional connection to someone else.

Basic anxiety   A sense of insecurity, a feeling of being abandoned and isolated.

Ego identity   The overall sense of self that emerges from transactions with social reality.

Ego quality (**ego strength** or **virtue**)   The quality that becomes part of one's personality through successful management of a crisis.

Epigenesis   The idea (adopted from embryology) that an internal plan for future development is present at the beginning of life.

Identity commitment   The adoption of a specific identity.

Identity crisis   A time of intense exploration of alternative ways of viewing oneself.

Identity status   The condition of whether an identity crisis has occurred and whether an identity has been attained.

Life-span development   The idea that developmental processes continue throughout life.

Mirroring   The giving of positive attention and supportiveness to someone.

Narcissism   A sense of grandiose self-importance and entitlement.

Neurotic needs   Maladaptive needs that emerge from overuse of strategies to combat basic anxiety.

Object relations   An individual's symbolized relations to other persons (such as parents).

Play therapy   The use of play as a procedure for conducting therapy with children.

Psychosocial crisis (or **conflict**)   A period when some interpersonal issue is being dealt with and growth potential and vulnerability are both high.

Self psychology   Kohut's theory that relationships create the structure of the self.

Selfobject   The mental symbol of another person who serves functions for oneself.

Separation–individuation   The process of acquiring a distinct identity; separating from fusion with the mother.

Strange situation   A procedure used to assess the attachment pattern of infant to mother.

Symbiosis   A period in which an infant experiences fusion with the mother.

Transference   The viewing of other people through selfobject representations originally developed for parents.

Vicious cycle   A cycle of needing affection, failing to obtain it, and thereby increasing the need.

The Learning Perspective

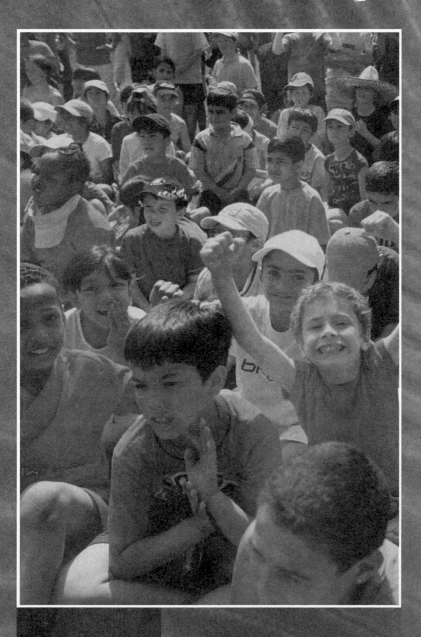

The Learning Perspective:
Major Themes and Underlying Assumptions

The experiences of life change us, and they do so in ways that are lawful and predictable. This is the central assumption of the learning perspective on personality. People have been interested in the processes of learning for a long time. At first, this interest was confined largely to those who studied lower animals. At first, this interest also focused primarily on small bits of behavior.

As knowledge grew, however, a tantalizing possibility began to take shape. The suspicion grew that the principles of learning might constitute the basic building blocks of behavior. All behavior. Not just the actions of rats in laboratory cages, but also the more complex actions of human beings in the world. *Personality,* from this point of view, is an accumulated set of learned tendencies. It's all the tendencies a person has learned over the course of a lifetime's experiences.

It's sometimes said that the basic metaphor of the learning perspective is the person as a white rat. In a sense, this is true, because many who take this perspective on behavior assume that learning processes are *universal,* that is, they are the same in virtually all animals. In that sense, a human being is nothing more than a very complex version of the rats and mice that occupy the attention (and the cages) of many scientists who study the learning process. This metaphor has been accepted by many of the learning theorists who've applied their findings to personality. The principles that they've focused on are discussed in Chapter 12.

Although this metaphor was useful as a starting place, many learning theorists ultimately came to believe that it's too simple. The processes of human learning began to appear more complex than they'd seemed at first. The result was the need for a more elaborated metaphor, along with more elaborate theories of learning. In the new metaphor, the human being is still a learner, but now a more self-directive learner and a learner whose knowledge can accumulate in great leaps, rather than just small increments. The learning is also seen as involving a set of cognitions, which play an important role themselves in behavior. The theories that draw on that expanded metaphor are discussed in Chapter 13.

The learning perspective on personality has also sparked something of a philosophical argument, which evolved and shifted as did the learning approach itself. In simple terms, the argument is about where behavior is *controlled.* Is behavior controlled from *within* the person, or is it controlled by events and processes *outside* the person? The analysis of behavior offered by the earliest learning theorists argued that behavior is shaped by external events, by stimuli and outcomes imposed from the environment. This assumption wasn't viewed with enthusiasm by everyone, perhaps partly because it doesn't offer a very flattering portrayal of human nature. More recently, many learning theorists have backed away from this assumption.

Nevertheless, one theme remains constant within the framework of the learning perspective across its two variants: Changes in behavior occur in predictable ways as a result of experience. By extrapolation, personality must also be susceptible to molding, grinding, and polishing by the events that form the person's unique and individual history.

Conditioning Theories

Lisa has a fondness for pastels. When asked why, she looks sort of blank and says she doesn't know, but she's felt that way at least since her eighth birthday, when she had the most wonderful surprise party, decorated all in pale pink, green, and violet.

Ann works hard at her job at the library. She bustles from meeting to meeting, smoothing disagreements among people she works with and making it easier for them to get their projects done. People express their appreciation in many ways—smiles, thanks, and last month a promotion to staff coordinator. The more signs she gets that she's doing a good job, the more enthusiasm she puts into each new morning.

WHY ARE these people the way they are? Why do people have the preferences they have? What makes one person put a lot of effort into her work when someone else doesn't? One answer is that these aspects of behavior, which contribute so much to the individuality of personality, are acquired through learning.

The beginnings of what would become the *learning perspective* on personality go back a long way. The puzzle of just how learning takes place—what the elements of the process are—intrigued scientists all over the world. The puzzle isn't fully solved even yet. For example, there remain disagreements about whether learning is one process that has several manifestations or whether there are several distinct processes (e.g., Locurto, Terrace, & Gibbon, 1980; Rescorla, 1987; Staats, 1996).

From the learning perspective, personality consists of all the tendencies you've learned during the experiences of your life. If personality is the residue of learning, then it's important to know how learning works. In this part of the chapter, we focus on broad principles of learning (for more see, e.g., B. Schwartz, 1989). For ease in presentation, we'll adopt the view implicitly taken by most people: that there are distinct types of learning that have their own rules. This chapter focuses on forms of learning called *conditioning*. Much of the work on these processes has used animals other than humans. Nonetheless, many people think these processes underlie the human qualities we know as *personality*.

Classical Conditioning

One of the early findings in the effort to understand learning was that responses could be acquired by associating one stimulus with another. This type of learning is called **classical conditioning.** It's sometimes also called *Pavlovian conditioning,* after the Russian scientist Ivan Pavlov, whose work opened the door to understanding it (e.g., Pavlov, 1927, 1955).

BASIC ELEMENTS

Classical conditioning seems to require two things. First, the organism must already respond to some class of stimuli reflexively. That is, the response must occur *reliably and automatically whenever the stimulus occurs.* A **reflex** thus is an existing connection between a stimulus and a response, such that the one causes the other to happen.

Consider some examples of reflexes from day-to-day experience. When you put something dry, acidic, or sour in your mouth (lemonade, tart candy), you start to salivate. When you see an object suddenly increase in size, as though it's approaching rapidly, you reflexively draw back. When skin near sexual organs is rubbed, you feel sexual excitement. When you touch a hot car door, you automatically yank your hand away. When someone smiles warmly at you, you automatically feel good. These reactions happen reflexively for most people. Some are innate and some are learned, but in each case, a stimulus leads directly and reliably to a particular response.

The second condition needed for classical conditioning is that the stimulus in the reflex has to become associated in time and place with another stimulus. The second stimulus is usually (though not always) *neutral* at first. That is, by itself it causes no particular response beyond being noticed. There aren't any special requirements for this stimulus. It can be pretty much anything—a color, a sound, an object, a person.

FIGURE 12.1
The various stages of a typical classical conditioning procedure (time runs left to right in each panel): (A) There is a pre-existing reflexive connection between a stimulus (US) and a response (UR). (B) A neutral stimulus (CS) is then paired repeatedly in time and space with the US. (C) The result is the development of a new response, termed a *conditioned response (CR).* (D) Once conditioning has occurred, presenting the CS by itself will now lead to the CR.

For clarity, people often describe classical conditioning in terms of several stages (see Figure 12.1). The first stage is the situation *before* conditioning happens. At this point, only the reflex exists—a stimulus causing an automatic response. This stimulus is termed the **unconditioned** or **unconditional stimulus (US).** The response it touches off is called the **unconditioned** or **unconditional response (UR).** The word *unconditional* here means there's no special condition required for the response to occur. It's automatic when the stimulus occurs (see Figure 12.1, A).

The second stage is when conditioning takes place. In this stage, the neutral stimulus occurs along with, or slightly before, the US (Figure 12.1, B). The neutral stimulus now gets a technical name: **conditioned** or **conditional stimulus (CS).** We suggest two ways to keep track of what that means. First, this is the stimulus that's becoming *conditioned.* Second, a response occurs in the presence of this stimulus only under a specific condition: that the US be there as well. When the US comes, the UR

Table 12.1 Illustrations of the Elements of Classical Conditioning in Two Common Research Procedures (A and B) in One Common Childhood Experience (C) and in One Common Adult Experience. Note that the elements are arranged here in terms of stimulus and the associated response, not in time sequence.

	US	UR	CS	CR
A.	Lemon juice in mouth	Salivation	Tone	Salivation
B.	Shock to foot	Pain	Light	Fear
C.	Ice cream in mouth	Pleasant taste	Sight of ice cream	Happiness
D.	Romantically enticing partner	Sexual arousal	Mood music	Sexual arousal

follows automatically, reflexively (and remember that it does so *whenever* the US is presented, whether something else is there or not).

When the US and the CS are paired frequently, something gradually starts to change (see Figure 12.1, C). The CS starts to acquire the ability to produce a response *of its own*. This response is termed the **conditioned** or **conditional response (CR)**. The CR is often very similar to the UR. Indeed, in some cases they look identical (Table 12.1, row A), except that the CR is less intense than the UR. In other cases, the two can be distinguished. There is, however, a key similarity: Specifically, if the UR has an unpleasant quality, so will the CR (Table 12.1, row B). If the UR has a pleasant quality, so will the CR (Table 12.1, rows C and D).

How does any of this apply to you? Let's go back to the examples used earlier to illustrate reflexes. Suppose you've started squandering your late evenings at a bar specializing in Italian wines and Sicilian folk music. Every time you take a sip of the very dry Chianti (US), your salivary glands pump like crazy (UR) because of the acidity. This reflexive event is surrounded by the strains of Sicilian folk songs (CS). Eventually, you may come to develop a salivation response (CR) to the music itself.

As another example, suppose that while in that little bar, you meet someone (US) who induces in you an astonishingly high degree of sexual arousal (UR). As you bask in candlelight, surrounded by green wine bottles, crimson wallpaper, and the soft strains of a Sicilian love song (all CSs), you may be acquiring a conditioned sexual response (CR) to those previously neutral features of the setting. Candlelight may never be the same again. The song you're hearing may gain a special place in your heart.

If you know that a US has occurred repeatedly along with a neutral stimulus, how do you know whether conditioning has taken place? To find out, present the CS by itself—without the US (see Figure 12.1, D). If the CS (alone) gets a reaction, conditioning has occurred. If there's no reaction, there's been no conditioning. Generally speaking, the more frequently the CS is paired with the US, the more likely conditioning is to occur. If a US is very strong, however—causing a very intense UR—conditioning may occur with only one pairing. For example, cancer patients undergoing chemotherapy often experience extreme nausea from the medication and develop very strong CRs to surrounding stimuli after only one exposure.

CLASSICAL CONDITIONING AS ANTICIPATORY LEARNING

It has been suggested that CRs represent anticipatory reactions (Rescorla, 1972; Zener, 1937). That is, although CRs are involuntary, they seem to reflect anticipation of, or preparation for, an impending US. Think of the earlier examples. If a tone sounds before lemon juice hits your mouth, the tone is a signal that the lemon will arrive shortly. The CR (salivation) prepares the surface of your mouth for the acidity of the lemon. If a child hears his father's steps coming up the stairs just before he gets a spanking, the steps signal the spanking and the reflexive pain. The CR (fear and perhaps trembling) reflect anticipation of the pain.

Another clue that CRs may involve anticipation comes from studies of timing. We said earlier that conditioning occurs through the more or less simultaneous presentation of the US and the CS. But conditioning is actually most effective if the CS slightly *precedes* the US (as in Figure 12.1). It's less effective if the two come at once. It's even *less* so if the CS comes *after* the US (e.g., Schneiderman & Gormezano, 1964; Spetch, Wilkie, & Pinel, 1981; Spooner & Kellogg, 1947). This also makes it look as though an anticipatory reaction is being developed.

Don't necessarily assume that the anticipatory reaction is a *conscious* anticipation of the US. The tone needn't evoke the image of lemon juice. The sound of steps needn't lead to an inference that a spanking is coming. By one sort of analysis, the CR is connected *to the CS itself,* not to an image of the US that comes to mind. The CS and the reaction to it are assumed to be bound together at this point, so the one reflexively produces the other.

On the other hand, today's learning theorists tend to see things a little differently (Mowrer & Klein, 2001). In particular, many accounts of classical conditioning now emphasize the idea that a link forms between the nervous system's representation of the US and its representation of the CS. (See Box 12.1 for more detail on some of the complexities of this view.) The link may not be represented in consciousness, but it is represented somewhere in the learning system. In this view, networks of links are formed among various stimuli through pairing, as well as from stimuli to responses.

Once conditioning has taken place, the CS–CR combination acts just like any other reflex. That is, once it's solidly there, this combination can serve as US and UR for another instance of conditioning (see Figure 12.2). Once soft candlelight has been conditioned to cause sexual arousal, candlelight itself can be used to condition arousal to other things, such as particular *meals* you eat by candlelight. This process is termed **higher-order conditioning.**

This process means that conditioning can be very pervasive. There are limitations, of course. The most potent USs are those that elicit very intense URs. The farther away you get from biological reflexes, the weaker the reflexes are, and the weaker is the conditioning.

DISCRIMINATION, GENERALIZATION, AND EXTINCTION IN CLASSICAL CONDITIONING

Classical conditioning provides a mechanism for new responses to become attached to neutral stimuli. Yet the CS almost never takes precisely the same form later as it did earlier. On the other hand, you do run across many stimuli later that are somewhat similar to the CS. What happens in these cases?

The answer comes through the concepts **discrimination** and **generalization.** *Discrimination* means telling things apart. More formally, it means responding differently to different stimuli. For example, suppose your experiences in the Sicilian wine bar have led you to associate candlelight, muted crimson wallpaper, and wine bottles (as CSs) with sexual arousal (as CR). If you entered a room that very closely resembled the bar (all other things being equal), you'd begin to feel a mellow glow (your CR). If you walked instead into a room with fluorescent lights and blue walls, that

BOX 12.1 WHAT'S GOING ON IN CLASSICAL CONDITIONING?

Classical conditioning has been part of psychology courses for decades. In most accounts, it's a process that was well mapped out early in the development of learning theory, and there's been little new to add since then. Not everyone agrees with this, however (Mineka & Zinbarg, 2006).

Classical conditioning is usually portrayed as a low-level process in which control over a response gets transferred from one stimulus to another because they occur close together in time. Robert Rescorla (1988) said that's not the way it is. He said conditioning concerns *relations* among events in the world. In his view, organisms use their experiences of relations between parts of the world to represent reality. Rescorla went on to say that the association in time and place isn't what makes conditioning take place. Rather, what's important is the information one stimulus gives about the other. To Rescorla, learning is a process by which the organism's representation of the world is brought into line with the actual state of the world. Organisms learn only when they're "surprised" by something that happens to them.

As a result, two stimuli experienced together sometimes don't become associated (Kamin, 1968). For example, consider two animals. One has had a series of trials in which a light (as a CS) has been paired with a shock (as a US). The other hasn't had this experience. Both then get a series of trials in which both the light and a tone (as *two* CSs) are paired with the shock. The second animal acquires a CR to the tone, but the first one doesn't. Apparently, the earlier experience with the light has made the tone redundant. Because the light already signals that the US is coming, there's no need to condition to the tone, and it doesn't happen.

In the same way, studies have found that cancer patients undergoing chemotherapy can be induced to form conditioned aversions to very specific foods, if an unusual food is given before chemotherapy (Bernstein, 1985). Doing this can make that specific food a scapegoat and prevent the conditioning of aversions to other foods, which otherwise is very common.

Rescorla also challenges other aspects of the traditional view. He argues against the assumption that classical conditioning is a slow process, requiring many pairings of stimuli. He says, in fact, that learning in five to six

trials is common. In summarizing his stance, Rescorla said that classical conditioning "is not a stupid process by which the organism willy-nilly forms associations between any two stimuli that happen to co-occur. Rather, the organism is better seen as an information seeker using logical and perceptual relations among events, along with its own preconceptions, to form a sophisticated representation of the world" (1988, p. 154).

Rescorla is not alone in believing that internal events are more important in conditioning than previously realized. An analysis with somewhat similar characteristics (but even more cognitive in certain respects) was proposed by Holyoak, Koh, and Nisbett (1989). Their model is based in part on ideas from cognitive psychology linked to the term *connectionism* (McClelland & Rumelhart, 1986). The most important characteristic of that model for the issue we're raising here is that it treats classical conditioning as rule learning.

The positions taken by Rescorla and by Holyoak et al. are clearly at odds with the point of view that's expressed in the body of this chapter. The views they express also herald a broad issue that is more prominent in the next chapter: the role of cognition in learning.

---

mellow glow would surely not emerge. You would *discriminate,* in your conditioned reactions, between the two sets of stimuli.

Now a harder question: What would happen if you walked into a room with muted lamplight, walls painted burgundy, and green glass vases? These aren't quite the stimuli that got linked to sexual arousal, but they're close. Here's where the process of *generalization* comes in. In all probability, you'd start to feel the glow, although it might not be as strong as in the first room. As shown in Figure 12.3, generalization from conditioned stimuli definitely takes place. The intensity of the reaction falls off, though, as the stimulus gets further and further removed from the original CS (Hovland, 1937; Moore, 1972). To put it differently, generalization begins to give way to discrimination, as the stimuli become more different from the initial CS. Discrimination and generalization thus are complementary.

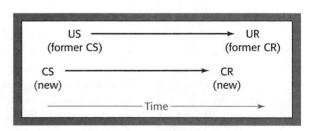

FIGURE 12.2
Once a link has been created between a CS and a CR by classical conditioning, that new reflex can serve as a US–UR pair for additional conditioning, termed *higher-order conditioning.*

FIGURE 12.3
An illustration of generalization of a classically conditioned response to stimuli that are similar to the CS and of discrimination regarding stimuli that are less similar to the CS. The CS is a tone of 1,200 hertz (Hz). Tones that are similar to it (800, 1,600 Hz) elicit CRs—generalization. Tones that are less similar (400, 2,000 Hz) elicit fewer CRs—discrimination. *Source: Data from Moore, 1972, combined across two groups.*

FIGURE 12.4
Extinction in classical conditioning. When a CS appears over and over without the US, the CR becomes progressively weaker and eventually disappears (or nearly does).

Another question: Do conditioned responses go away? Discussions of conditioning don't use words such as *forgetting*. CRs do weaken, however, by a process called **extinction.** This occurs when a CS comes repeatedly without the US (Pavlov, 1927). At first, the CS leads reliably to the CR (see Figure 12.4). Gradually, over repeated presentations, the CR grows weaker. The CR doesn't actually disappear, however. Even when a response stops in a given session, there's a spontaneous recovery the next day (Wagner, Siegel, Thomas, & Ellison, 1964). It is now believed that classical conditioning leaves a permanent record in the nervous system and that its effects can be muted but not erased (see Bouton, 1994, 2000).

EMOTIONAL CONDITIONING

As you may have realized already, a lot of the classical conditioning in humans involves responses with emotional qualities. That is, stimuli that most clearly cause reflexive reactions are those that elicit positive feelings (hope, delight, excitement) or bad feelings (fear, anger, pain). The term **emotional conditioning** is sometimes used to refer to classical conditioning in which the CRs are emotional reactions.

Conditioning of emotional responses is important to the learning view on personality. It's argued that the likes and dislikes—all the preferences that help define personality—arise through this process (De Houwer, Thomas, & Baeyens, 2001). Linking a neutral stimulus to a pleasant event creates a like (Razran, 1940; Staats & Staats, 1958). Linking a stimulus to an upsetting event creates a dislike (J. B. Watson & Raynor, 1920; see also Cacioppo & Sandman, 1981; Riordan & Tedeschi, 1983; Staats, Staats, & Crawford, 1962). In fact, just hearing someone describe a good or bad trait in someone else can link that trait in your mind to the person who's doing the describing (Skowronski, Carlston, Mae, & Crawford, 1998).

Different people experience different bits of the world and thus have different patterns of emotional arousal. Different people also experience the same event from the perspective of their unique "histories." As noted in Chapter 6, children from the same family experience the family differently (Daniels & Plomin, 1985). As a result, people can wind up with remarkably different patterns of likes and dislikes (see Box 12.2). Thus, emotional conditioning can play a major role in creating the uniqueness of personality (Staats & Burns, 1982).

Instrumental Conditioning

A second form of conditioning is called **instrumental conditioning.** (This phrase is often used interchangeably with *operant conditioning,* despite slight differences in meaning.) Instrumental conditioning differs in several ways from classical conditioning. For one, classical conditioning is *passive.* When a reflex occurs, conditioning doesn't require you to *do* anything—just to be there and be aware of other stimuli. Instrumental conditioning is *active* (Skinner, 1938). The events that define it begin with a behavior on your part (even if the behavior is the act of remaining still).

THE LAW OF EFFECT

Instrumental conditioning is a simple process, although its ramifications are widespread. The process goes like this: If a behavior is followed by a better or more satisfying state of affairs, the behavior is more likely to be done again later in a similar situation (see Figure 12.5, A). If a behavior is followed by a worse or less satisfying state of affairs, the behavior is less likely to be done again later (see Figure 12.5, B).

This simple description—linking an action, an outcome, and a change in the likelihood of future action—is the *law of effect* deduced by Thorndike a century ago (Thorndike, 1898, 1905). The law of effect is simple but profound. It provides a way to account for regularities in behavior. That is, any situation permits many potential acts (see Figure 12.5, C). Some acts come to occur with great regularity; others happen once and disappear, never to return. Others turn up occasionally but only occasionally. Why? Because some have been followed by satisfying outcomes, and others haven't.

All the actions a person might do in a given situation can be seen as a **habit hierarchy,** a list of response potentials (N. E. Miller & Dollard, 1941). The order derives

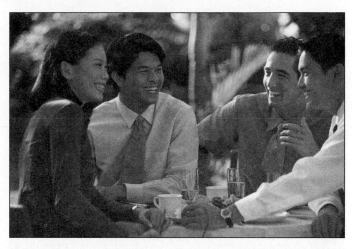

One purpose of the business lunch is to associate your company and its products (as CSs) with the positive feelings produced by a good meal in a nice restaurant (as USs).

BOX 12.2 CLASSICAL CONDITIONING AND ATTITUDES

Where do attitudes come from? The answer provided in this chapter is that you develop attitudes by classical conditioning. A neutral stimulus (CS) begins to produce an emotional reaction (CR) after it's paired with a stimulus (US) that already creates an emotional reaction (UR). This approach holds that people acquire emotional responses to attitude objects (classes of things, people, ideas, or events) in exactly that way. If the attitude object is paired with an emotion-arousing stimulus, it comes to evoke the emotion itself. This response, then, is the basis for an attitude.

A good deal of evidence fits this depiction. Over 65 years ago, Razran (1940) presented several political slogans to people and had them rate how much they approved of each. Later, he presented the slogans again under one of three conditions: while the people were eating a free lunch, while they

were inhaling noxious odors, or while they were sitting in a neutral setting. Later on, they rated their approval of the slogans a second time. Slogans paired with a free lunch were now rated more positively than before. Slogans paired with unpleasant odors were now rated more negatively than before.

Many other studies have found similar results (De Houwer et al., 2001). Attitudes toward people can form the same way. Walther (2002) found that pairing photos of neutral persons with liked or disliked persons led to positive and negative attitudes, respectively, toward the neutral persons. These attitudes were also found to be resistant to extinction.

There's also the potential for higher-order conditioning here. Negative attitudes formed by associating a neutral person with a disliked person can produce further conditioning from that one to another neutral person (Walther, 2002). And think about the fact that words such as *good* and *bad* are tied

in most people's experience to positive and negative events (Staats & Staats, 1957, 1958) and thus probably cause emotional responses themselves. People use such words all the time around others, creating opportunities for higher-order conditioning.

A large number of studies have shown that classical conditioning *can* be involved in development of attitudes. They don't tell us whether attitudes *are* usually acquired this way. But events that arouse emotions are common in day-to-day life, which provides opportunities for conditioning to take place. For example, the business lunch is remarkably similar to Razran's experimental manipulation. It seems not at all unreasonable that classical conditioning may underlie many of people's preferences for persons, events, things, places, and ideas. Given that these preferences are important aspects of personality, conditioning would appear to represent an important contributor to personality.

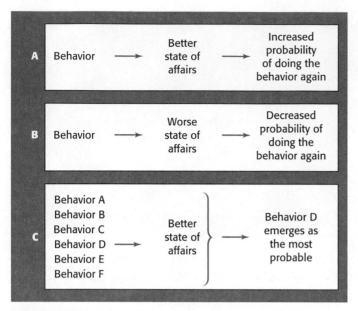

FIGURE 12.5
Instrumental conditioning: (A) Behavior that is followed by a more satisfying state of affairs is more likely to be done again. (B) Behavior that is followed by a less satisfying state of affairs is less likely to be done again. (C) This principle accounts for the fact that (over time and experiences) some behaviors emerge from the many possible behaviors as habitual responses that occur in specific situations.

from prior conditioning. Some responses are very likely, because they've often been followed by more satisfying states of affairs. Others are less likely, and others even less so. For example, in the cafeteria at noon, getting and eating lunch are very likely, working on coursework is less likely (though maybe not too far down the list), but taking off your clothes and reciting Shakespeare are very *un*likely. As another example, if you need to ask your parents for money, there are some tactics you'll use because they've worked in the past and others you've given up because they haven't worked. Habit hierarchies continually evolve, as the various actions you try are followed by either more or less satisfying states of affairs.

REINFORCEMENT AND PUNISHMENT

The term **reinforcer** has now replaced the phrase *satisfying state of affairs.* The term conveys the sense that it *strengthens* the tendency to do whatever act came before it. A *reinforcer* is anything that strengthens a behavioral tendency. Reinforcers can reduce biological needs (e.g., food or water) or satisfy social desires (e.g., smiles and acceptance). Some get their reinforcing quality indirectly (e.g., money). There's even evidence that visual sensations (seeing something you like) can act as reinforcers (Hayes, Rincover, & Volosin, 1980).

Different kinds of reinforcers have different names. A *primary reinforcer* is one that diminishes a biological need. A *secondary reinforcer* has acquired reinforcing properties by association with a primary reinforcer (through classical conditioning) or by virtue of the fact that it can be used to *get* primary reinforcers (Wolfe, 1936; Zimmerman, 1957).

The term **punisher** refers to unpleasant outcomes. Punishers reduce the tendency to do the behavior that came before them, although there's been controversy about how effective they are (Rachman & Teasdale, 1969; Solomon, 1964; Thorndike, 1933). Punishment can also be primary or secondary. That is, some events are intrinsically aversive (e.g., pain). Others are aversive because of associations with primary punishers.

Another distinction is also important, but a little tricky. When you think of reinforcement, what probably comes to mind are things you like—gifts, money, trips to fun places, CDs, and so on. When you think of punishment, you probably think of pain—being yelled at, slapped, or frowned at. In reality, however, both concepts are broader and more subtle than that.

Reinforcement always implies moving the person's "state of affairs" in a positive direction. But this can happen in two ways. The more obvious way is receiving the good things that come to mind as reinforcers (gifts, money). Receiving these things is termed **positive reinforcement.** *Positive* implies *adding* something good. When positive reinforcement occurs, the behavior that preceded it becomes more likely.

There's also a second kind of reinforcement called **negative reinforcement.** Negative reinforcement occurs when something *unpleasant* is *removed.* For instance, when your roommate stops playing his annoying *Polka Favorites* CD over and over, that might be a negative reinforcer for you. Removing something unpleasant moves the state of affairs in a positive direction—from unpleasant to neutral. It thus is reinforcing. Negative reinforcement can be just as potent as positive reinforcement. Whatever you did before your roommate's music stopped will become more likely in the future.

Punishment also comes in two forms. Most people think of punishment as adding pain, moving the state of affairs from neutral to negative. But sometimes punishment involves removing something good, changing from a positive to a neutral (thus less satisfying) state of affairs. This principle—punishing by withdrawing something good—underlies a tactic that's widely used to discourage unwanted behavior in children. It's called a **timeout,** short for "time out from positive reinforcement" (Drabman & Spitalnik, 1973; Risley, 1968). A timeout takes the child from whatever activity is going on to a place where there's nothing fun to do. Many find this practice appealing because it seems more humane than painful punishments such as spanking. In principle, however, a timeout creates a less satisfying state of affairs for the child and thus should have the same effect on behavior as any other punishment.

A final issue here is that it's hard to specify how *satisfying* an outcome is (and thus how reinforcing it is). An outcome's value is determined partly by your situation. If you're starving, being handed a box of stale cheese puffs is a good outcome. If you've just had a great meal, the cheese puffs won't seem so good. In the same way, a truly starving man may not be impressed by a beautiful woman's overtures of sex, which in other circumstances would seem to him an *extremely* satisfying state of affairs.

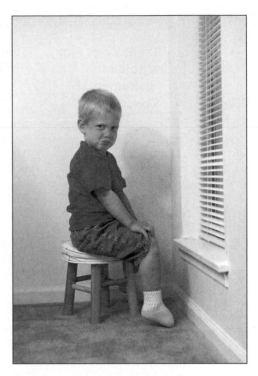

Timeout is an effective way of discouraging unwanted behavior in children.

This issue has led many people (though not all) to think of instrumental conditioning as a process that occurs primarily when the person has a motive to which the reinforcer relates (see Box 12.3). Indeed, many people use the term *instrumental* more broadly, going beyond the conditioning process per se. This broader use of the word implies *goal directed,* conveying the sense that the behavior is the instrument or tool by which a desired outcome is obtained.

DISCRIMINATION, GENERALIZATION, AND EXTINCTION IN INSTRUMENTAL CONDITIONING

Several ideas introduced in discussing classical conditioning also apply to instrumental conditioning, with slight differences in connotation. For example, *discrimination* still means responding differently in the presence of different stimuli. Here, however, the difference in response results from variations in prior reinforcement.

To understand how this kind of discrimination develops, imagine that when a stimulus is present, a particular action is always followed by a reinforcer. When the stimulus is absent, that action is *never* followed by a reinforcer. Gradually, the presence or absence of the stimulus gains an influence over whether the behavior takes place. It becomes a **discriminative stimulus,** a stimulus that turns the behavior on and off. You use the stimulus to discriminate among situations and thus among responses. Miller and Dollard (1941) called this a *cue function.* Behavior that's cued by discriminative stimuli is said to be *under stimulus control.*

Here's an illustration of discriminative stimuli that may be familiar. Imagine a high school class whose teacher is stiff and formal and doesn't tolerate play in class. The

BOX 12.3   THEORETICAL CONTROVERSY

Do Motives Play a Role in Instrumental Conditioning?

As pointed out in the main text, you have to know an organism's present state to know what's reinforcing to it. There are, however, several ways to think about this.

Neal Miller and John Dollard (1941; Dollard & Miller, 1950), the first theorists to try to portray the full breadth of personality in terms of learning, held that the nature of reinforcement is intimately tied to motivation. Their view relied on Clark Hull's (1943) theory of motivation. Hull said that when an organism is deprived of a needed substance (e.g., food or water), it experiences an increase in **drive.** When drive goes up, it increases the tendency to emit behaviors high in the habit hierarchy. Sooner or later, you get what you've been deprived of. That causes drive to go back down. According to Miller and Dollard, *drive reduction constitutes reinforcement.*

In this view, to know what will reinforce a person, you need to know the person's needs or motives.

Not all conditioning theorists have agreed that motivational concepts are helpful here. An alternative view was posed by B. F. Skinner (e.g., 1953, 1974), who argued that the effort to explain behavior doesn't benefit from guessing about what's going on inside the organism. He was quite outspoken about his belief that concepts like motive, wish, desire—not to mention cognition—serve more to confuse the picture than to clarify it.

Skinner argued that use of terms such as *motive* and *wish* is often circular. That is, we often infer that people are motivated to do something by whether they do it. Skinner asked, Why not forget about the motive and simply analyze the acts? Indeed, Skinner felt that terms such as *drive* and *motive* are actually misleading, because they create the impression of an explanation while not really explaining anything.

Rather than talk about drives or needs, Skinner said, you should simply describe the stimulus conditions of deprivation versus satiation. *Deprivation* is a period of the absence of a consummatory behavior (for example, eating or drinking). *Satiation* is the end of a period of intense consummatory behavior. Both events are observable. Along with knowledge of prior reinforcement contingencies, they provide all the information necessary to predict behavior. This theoretical position is often called **radical behaviorism** because it represents a strict (thus radical) application of the idea that one shouldn't invent imaginary mechanisms when behavior can be accounted for by observable events (Baum, 2005; O'Donohue & Kitchener, 1999).

In sum, these two theoretical models agree in one respect and disagree in another. Both assume it's important to take the organism's present condition into account. But they take very different views on how to think about the organism's present condition.

---

teacher sometimes misses class due to illness. The substitute is relaxed and easygoing. In truth, he'd rather have a good time with the class than stick to the lesson plan. When he's there, cutting up is followed by reinforcement more often than when the regular teacher's there. The predictable result is that quiet prevails for the regular teacher, but the class turns into a party when the substitute's there. Because the shift occurs as a function of the teacher (the discriminative stimuli), the students' behavior is under stimulus control.

Earlier in this section, we mentioned the idea of a *habit hierarchy* (an ordering of the likelihood of doing various behaviors). We said that the hierarchy shifts constantly because of the ongoing flow of reinforcing (and nonreinforcing) events. It shifts constantly for another reason as well: Every change in situation means a change in cues (discriminative stimuli). The cues suggest what behaviors are reinforced in that situation. Thus, the shift in cues rearranges the list of behavior probabilities. Changing contextual cues can disrupt even very strong habits (Wood, Tam, & Guerrero Witt, 2005).

The concept of discriminative stimulus is important to reinforcement views of personality. It accounts for complexity in behavior. Very slight changes in the stimulus field dramatically alter behavior. As a traffic light turns green, people drive forward;

as the light turns red, they stop. As the clock reads 12:00, people leave their desks and go to lunch; as the clock reads 1:00, the same people return and start to work again. These differences in behavior are large in scope, but they're caused by extremely small changes in the surrounding array of stimuli.

The principle of generalization is also important here. It contributes a sense of continuity in behavior. As you enter a new setting and see objects and people you've never seen before, you respond easily and automatically. There are similarities between the new setting and previous discriminative stimuli. You generalize behaviors from the one to the other, and action flows smoothly forward. You may never have seen a particular style of spoon before, but you won't hesitate to use it on the soup. You may never have driven a particular make of car before, but if that's what the rental agency gives you, you'll probably be able to handle it.

The principle of generalization gives conditioning theorists a way to talk about traitlike qualities. A person should behave consistently across time and circumstances if discriminative stimuli stay fairly similar across the times and circumstances. Because key stimulus qualities often *do* stay the same across settings (even if other qualities differ greatly), the person's action tendency also stays the same across the settings. The result is that, to an outside observer, the person appears to have a set of internal traits. In this view, however, consistency of behavior depends on similarities of environments (an idea that's not too different from the discussion of consistency late in Chapter 4).

Extinction in instrumental conditioning occurs when a behavior that once led to a reinforcer no longer does so. As the behavior is done over and over—with no reinforcer—its probability drops. Eventually, it's barely there at all (though just as in classical conditioning there's a tendency for spontaneous recovery, causing some to believe that it hasn't gone away; Bouton, 1994; Rescorla, 1997, 1998). Thus, extinction is a way in which behavioral tendencies fade.

ALTERING THE SHAPE OF BEHAVIOR

The concepts of reward and punishment provide a way of talking about how behaviors become more or less likely to occur. Thus far, however, we haven't dealt with how a behavior changes in its form. Still missing is the concept of **shaping.**

Let's look first at shaping in the laboratory. Many times it's not practical to wait for a desired act and then reinforce it. Instead, reinforcement is first given for a rough *approximation* of the behavior, which then begins to occur more often. Gradually, you reinforce only closer and closer approximations of the desired act. This method is called **successive approximation.** Through it, the behavior of the organism comes to be very specific. That is, behavior is *shaped* in a particular direction. To characterize the process differently, the organism is learning a continually changing discrimination.

One might think of this as simply a convenient laboratory tactic, but much the same thing happens all the time outside the lab. Whether by chance or by design, general tendencies (e.g., going to school) are reinforced at first. These general tendencies then are channeled into more specific tendencies (e.g., studying political science) by shifts in patterns of reinforcement. This shaping can ultimately result in specific and highly specialized tendencies (attending law school, becoming a state representative). Shaping, then, provides a way to understand how behavior (indeed, personality) evolves continuously, with changing reinforcement patterns.

FIGURE 12.6
Behavioral tendencies created by four different types of reinforcement schedules, in which the total reinforcement across a long span of time is equivalent. Behavior is portrayed as *cumulative frequencies* of response, or responses summed across time. Each small mark on the line represents the occurrence of a reinforcer. As you can see, some reinforcement schedules produce higher and more consistent rates of behavior than others.

Source: Adapted from Reese, 1966.

SCHEDULES OF REINFORCEMENT

The issue of whether behavior tendencies stay or disappear is important in thinking about personality. Extinction helps us understand which behaviors persist and which do not, but it's not the only principle that matters. The persistence of an action tendency is also influenced by the *pattern* with which it's been reinforced in the past.

In reading about instrumental conditioning, people often assume that a reinforcement occurs every time the behavior occurs. But common sense and your own experience should tell you life's not like that. Sometimes reinforcements are frequent, but sometimes not. Variations in frequency and pattern are called *schedules of reinforcement*. A simple variation in schedules is between continuous and partial (or intermittent) reinforcement. In **continuous reinforcement,** the behavior is followed by a reinforcer *every single time.* In **partial reinforcement,** the behavior is followed by a reinforcer *less often than every time.*

There are many patterns of partial reinforcement. The reinforcer can come after a certain *number of occurrences* of the behavior (your teacher smiles and says "good" every fifth time you contribute to class discussion). This pattern is called a *ratio schedule.* The number involved can be large (every tenth time) or small (every second time). The numbers can be *fixed* (every fifth time exactly) or *variable* (randomly varying, but every fifth time on the average). The reinforcer may depend on the passage of some time as well as the occurrence of the behavior (a week has to pass since your teacher last smiled and said "good," but then he does it the very next time you contribute in class). This pattern is called an *interval schedule.* Intervals can also be fixed (exactly one week has to pass before your next contribution is rewarded) or variable (on the average, one week has to pass before your next contribution is rewarded).

Different schedules of reinforcement lead to different behavior tendencies across time. Figure 12.6 shows the tendencies associated with each type of schedule just described (adapted from Reese, 1966). The tendencies are described there in terms of cumulative frequencies of response—responses added up across time. Each small mark on the line represents the occurrence of a reinforcer.

A *fixed ratio schedule* causes a high rate of responding, with a brief pause immediately after reinforcement. This schedule is reflected in so-called piecework, in which a person is paid a fixed amount per unit of work (object assembled, basket of vegetables picked, and so on). A *variable ratio schedule* creates an even higher rate of response, without pauses after reinforcement. An example of a variable ratio is gambling, which pays off occasionally but unpredictably.

The *fixed interval schedule* produces a pronounced and reliable *scalloping* of the curve, a complete absence of behavior just after reinforcement, followed by a gradual renewal, which accelerates until the next reinforcer occurs. A good illustration of this schedule is the study behavior of students whose psychology course has exams at predictable intervals. They study most just before exams. This pattern also describes the behavior of the U.S. Congress, which passes most of its bills just before it adjourns (Weisberg & Waldrop, 1972).

Scalloping isn't apparent at all in the last schedule, the *variable interval schedule.* This one is characterized by consistent activity, as with the variable ratio schedule, but (in general) at a lower level of activity. An example of this schedule is the behavior of students whose instructor gives pop quizzes unexpectedly, rather than tests at predictable intervals.

THE PARTIAL REINFORCEMENT EFFECT

As you can see, reinforcement patterns can get complicated. What's most important, though, is that infrequent and unpredictable reinforcement affects behavior differently than reinforcement that's frequent and predictable. There are two differences. The first is that you acquire a new behavior faster when reinforcement is frequent than when it's not. Eventually, even infrequent reinforcement results in high rates of the behavior, but it may take a while.

The other effect is less intuitive but more important. It's often called the **partial reinforcement effect**. It shows up when reinforcement stops (see Figure 12.7). Take away the reinforcer, and a behavior built in by continuous reinforcement will go away quickly. A behavior built in by partial (less frequent) reinforcement will remain longer. It's more *resistant to extinction* (Amsel, 1967; Humphreys, 1939).

This effect isn't simply a matter of how easy or hard it is to tell when the extinction period is starting (Jenkins, 1962; Theios, 1962). Rather, there seems to be a subtle difference in what's conditioned in the first place (Amsel, 1967). In intermittent reinforcement, a nonreinforcement is actually becoming a discriminative stimulus that cues *persistence* (because if you keep trying, you eventually get a reinforcement). Nonreinforcement continues to act as a discriminative stimulus for a long time, even when the reinforcer's gone for good. When you start with continuous reinforcement, though, the link between nonreinforcement and persistence is never made. When the reinforcer goes away, nothing remains to keep the behavior going.

In the same vein, it has been argued that people learn to be industrious by receiving patterns of reinforcement that cause sensations of effort to become a cue for persistence (Eisenberger, 1992). Thus, instead of finding the experience of effort aversive, people find it rewarding. One can imagine a situation in which even a very aversive experience, such as fear, can become a discriminative stimulus for persistence. Such a case would represent a kind of "conditioned courage."

The partial reinforcement effect carries an important message: If you want a behavior to remain relatively persistent in someone, don't reinforce it all the time. In fact, the lower the rate of reinforcement (if it's enough to sustain the behavior), the stronger the link between the cue of nonreinforcement and persistence. Ironically, although this view emphasizes the importance of reinforcement in producing behavior, it also emphasizes the importance of *non*reinforcement during conditioning in *sustaining* behavior.

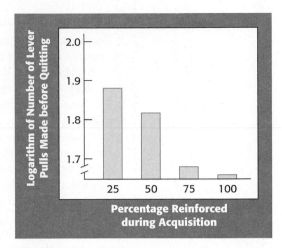

FIGURE 12.7

Effect of partial reinforcement and continuous reinforcement on persistence. Participants first played on a slot machine that paid off 25%, 50%, 75%, or 100% of the time. Then they were allowed to continue playing for as long as they liked, but they never again won. As can be seen, partial reinforcement leads to greater resistance to extinction. That is, the groups initially rewarded less than 100% of the time persist longer when all reward is removed. Moreover, the lower the percentage of partial reinforcement initially given, the greater the persistence. *Source: Adapted from Lewis & Duncan, 1956.*

Many personal superstitions are learned through a schedule of random partial reinforcement.

LEARNING "IRRATIONAL" BEHAVIOR

People who use conditioning principles often emphasize that the behavior need not *cause* the reinforcer for conditioning to occur. The behavior needs only to be *followed* by the reinforcer. Whatever behavior preceded the reinforcer is strengthened by the reinforcer's occurrence.

This relationship can lead to rather strange effects, as Skinner (1948) pointed out in a study of pigeons. Picture a bird in a cage, which gets a reinforcer (a bit of food) at a regular interval, regardless of what it's doing. Every reinforcer strengthens the behavior that preceded it. At first, because behavior is somewhat random, several behaviors are strengthened. Eventually, though, one action is reinforced often enough that it starts to predominate. Because it's more common, it now gets reinforced even more. The result is that the bird is now doing an entirely arbitrary behavior quite regularly.

Because the pigeon acts as though these specific actions are causing the reinforcer, Skinner called this *superstitious behavior.* He argued that seemingly irrational or senseless behaviors in people develop exactly the same way. Reinforcers occurred for reasons unrelated to the behavior, and they built the behavior in and shaped it into its present form. By the way, Skinner didn't assume that the pigeon was thinking about what caused the reinforcement, only that its behavior gave that outward appearance (see Box 12.4).

There's no difference between the process by which superstitious behaviors are acquired and the process by which any other behaviors are acquired. To call a behavior *irrational* (versus *adaptive*) is an observer's value judgment. To the conditioning

---

BOX 12.4 BEHAVIORISTS' VIEW OF THE ROLE OF THOUGHT IN CONDITIONING

Conditioning theorists hold that behavior tendencies are determined by reinforcement patterns. Most of them treat thought processes as irrelevant to this process (Rachlin, 1977). Although Skinner's pigeons may have *acted as though* they thought a particular action was producing the reinforcer, the appearance is illusory. Even if pigeons could think (which is questionable), their thoughts aren't behind the behavior. The reinforcement pattern is behind the behavior.

It's undeniable that people (unlike pigeons) talk and think. To conditioning theorists, however, these tendencies among humans simply reflect the fact that verbal behaviors (both overt speech and covert thought) become conditioned in particular ways (e.g., Miller & Dollard, 1941). That is, people are conditioned to think in particular patterns and to talk in certain ways. But the real causes of all three phenomena—the behavior, the talk, and the thoughts—are the patterns of reinforcement.

Behaviorists try to avoid as much as possible using words such as *intention, thought, cognition,* and *consciousness* because they see them as unnecessary in explaining how people act (Baum, 2005; Skinner, 1987). Many behaviorists see the mental events that occur along with behavior and reinforcement as **epiphenomena,** phenomena with no causal role. They just happen alongside the behavior, or may even be caused by the behavior as subjective offshoots (cf. Rachlin, 1977). Skinner (1989) pointed out, in this regard, that

many words now used to describe mental states had their origins in descriptions of behavior. This history fits his contention that the behavior is what really matters.

This point of view has been more than a little controversial over the years. It hasn't been well received at all by people outside the behaviorist camp (see Catania & Harnad, 1988, for a wide-ranging discussion). Critics of the behaviorist position point out that a conditioning view has difficulty in accounting for a number of phenomena, including the emergence of language in children (Chomsky, 1959). This criticism has led some people to regard the conditioning view as incorrect. It led others more sympathetic to the learning perspective to modify the theories, a response that is taken up in the next chapter.

theorist, all behavior is acquired the same way—through reinforcement. On the other hand, there's a big difference between the situation just described and situations people normally encounter. Skinner had full control over the birds' environment. He could easily present reinforcers in a completely arbitrary pattern. In contrast, people's reinforcers more often follow particular behaviors for nonarbitrary reasons. These contingencies shape most human behavior into orderly patterns that only more rarely appear to be superstitious or irrational.

REINFORCEMENT OF QUALITIES OF BEHAVIOR

One final point about learning through instrumental conditioning: It's most intuitive to think that the reinforcer makes a particular *act* more likely in the future. However, there's evidence that what becomes more likely isn't always an act, but some *quality* of action (Eisenberger & Selbst, 1994). For example, reinforcing *effort* in one setting can increase *effortfulness* in other settings (Mueller & Dweck, 1998). Reinforcing accuracy on one task increases accuracy on other tasks. Reinforcing speed on one task increases speed elsewhere. Reinforcing creativity yields more creativity (Eisenberger & Rhoades, 2001). Reinforcing focused thought produces more focused thinking elsewhere (Eisenberger, Armeli, & Pretz, 1998). Reinforcing variability produces greater variability in behavior (Neuringer, 2004). Indeed, reinforcement can influence the process of selective attention (Libera & Chelazzi, 2006).

Thus, reinforcement can change not just particular behaviors but whole dimensions of behavior. This idea broadens considerably the ways in which reinforcement principles may act on human beings. It suggests that reinforcers act at many levels of abstraction. Indeed, perhaps many aspects of behavior at many different levels are reinforced *simultaneously* when a person experiences a more satisfying state of affairs. This possibility creates a far more complex picture of change through conditioning than was apparent in earlier parts of the chapter.

Assessment

From the view of conditioning theories, personality is the accumulation of a person's conditioned tendencies (Ciminero, Calhoun, & Adams, 1977; Hersen & Bellack, 1976; Staats, 1996). By adulthood, you have a wide range of emotional responses to various stimuli, which you experience as attitudes and preferences. You also have tendencies to engage in various kinds of actions in various kinds of settings. These tendencies differ from person to person in probability, resistance to extinction, and what discriminative stimuli cue them.

This view has at least three implications for personality assessment. Most simply, it suggests that assessment should focus on behavioral qualities, rather than cognitions. The assessment procedures suggested by this approach focus on observable aspects of emotional reactions or action tendencies, rather than on trying to obtain a general sense of what the person is like (Kanfer & Saslow, 1965).

A second implication stems from the idea that emotional responses are linked to specific CSs and that actions depend on discriminative stimuli (stimuli associated with reinforcement of the actions). This means that feelings and actions are tied to specific classes of situations or to cues within those situations. Thus, assessment should focus on specific classes of situations and specific responses, rather than on creating broad generalizations about the person.

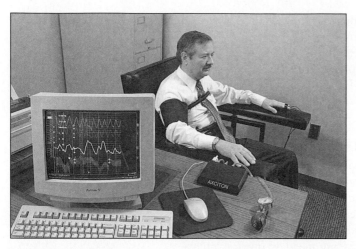

Physiological responses provide one index of the intensity of emotional reactions.

A final implication is that there's no better form of assessment than observation. People can give self-reports of feelings and self-reports of act tendencies, but these may not be reliable or accurate. A better way to assess people's responses is to observe. Put the person in the situation you're interested in and let the person do or feel what comes naturally. Then measure what happens, as directly as possible, with as little interpretation as possible.

TECHNIQUES

This view of personality relates to two kinds of assessment techniques. One focuses on assessment of emotional responses; the other is broader in scope. The first, sometimes called **physiological assessment,** relies on the fact that emotional responses have several components. Besides subjective qualities, emotions also have physiological aspects (Cacioppo & Petty, 1983; Greenfield & Sternbach, 1972). When you experience an emotion (especially if it's intense), changes take place in your body: changes in muscle tension, heartrate, blood pressure, brain waves, sweat gland activity, and more. The changes can be thought of as internal behaviors.

These responses can be measured by devices called *physiographs.* The reactions thus are observable aspects of emotional experiences. More specifically, the degree of response can be taken as an index of the *intensity* of an emotional reaction. To illustrate, imagine yourself wired to a physiograph, which is collecting your body's responses. As you sit there, you are shown a series of stimuli that are possible sources of fear reactions: snakes, spiders, a view downward from the top of a tall building, and so on. Your body's responses reflect the intensity of any fear you have. An observer could conclude, for example, that you're scared of heights but not by snakes. All this can be assessed without a word from you. Your internal behavior gives all the information. Some think these procedures are quite useful in assessing problems such as posttraumatic stress disorder (Keane et al., 1998; Orr et al., 1998).

Physiological assessment is direct and objective, but it's also elaborate and technical. It tends to be used more in research than in clinical applications. A second technique can also be used to assess emotional responses, called **behavioral assessment** (Barlow, 1981; Haynes & O'Brien, 2000; Staats, 1996). It entails observing the person's overt behavior in situations of interest. Emotions such as fear can be assessed by behavioral indicators—trembling, paleness, avoidance, and so on. This technique can also be applied more broadly. It can be used to assess what kinds of activities people undertake, for how long, and in what patterns.

Behavioral assessment varies widely in how it's actually done. Sometimes the observer simply counts acts of specific types, checks possibilities from a prearranged list, or watches how far into a sequence of action a person goes before stopping (Lang & Lazovik, 1963; O'Leary & Becker, 1967; Paul, 1966). In other cases, the procedure is more elaborate, using automated devices to record how long the person being assessed engages in various behaviors.

For example, behavioral assessment of children often uses recorders with separate channels to keep track of the frequency and duration of activities such as talking, running, and sitting alone (Lovaas, Freitag, Gold, & Kassorla, 1965). The observer pushes a separate button that corresponds to each behavior category and continues holding for as long as that kind of behavior is being performed by the child whose behavior is being assessed.

These various techniques are useful but they have their drawbacks. Most obviously, they're elaborate and thus hard to use. Another problem is that different techniques don't always give the same results. The amount of behavioral avoidance in a situation—an index one might expect to be highly correlated with fear—doesn't always correspond well with self-reports of fear (Bernstein, 1973). Physiograph records may not fit well with either of these measures. Given this kind of disagreement, it's hard to know which measure represents the "real" fear level.

Problems in Behavior, and Behavior Change

If personality derives from classical and instrumental conditioning, then so does maladaptive behavior. People sometimes learn things that interfere with their lives. They sometimes fail to learn things that make life easier. This view suggests a basis for several kinds of personality problems along with ways of treating such problems. As a group, the treatment techniques are termed **behavior modification** or **behavior therapy** (Craighead, Kazdin, & Mahoney, 1981). These terms reflect the fact that the emphasis is on changing the person's actual *behavior*.

CLASSICAL CONDITIONING OF EMOTIONAL RESPONSES

One class of problems is emotional reactions that interfere with effective functioning. For example, people sometimes have intensely unpleasant anxiety when exposed to specific kinds of stimuli. Sometimes the anxiety is also inappropriate, because the same stimuli don't provoke comparable anxiety in other people.

Intense irrational fears are called **phobias.** The phobic person experiences fear whenever a particular stimulus is present and often becomes anxious just from thinking of it. Although a phobic reaction can become tied to virtually any stimulus, some phobias are more common than others. Common focal points for phobias are animals such as dogs, snakes, and spiders; closed-in spaces such as elevators; open or exposed spaces such as railings on high balconies; and germs and the possibility of infection.

The conditioning view assumes that phobic reactions are classically conditioned (though see Box 12.5). In this view, the person at some point must have experienced intense fear while in the presence of what's now the phobic stimulus (cf. Watson & Raynor, 1920). The previously neutral stimulus thereby took on the ability to provoke anxiety. The same principle presumably applies no matter what the feared stimulus is.

As an example, consider the plight of Allison, who nearly drowned in a boating accident three years ago. The intense fear she experienced became linked to a wide range of stimuli that had been neutral (even positive) for her—stimuli such as her father's boat, the lake she was on, and other aspects of the surroundings. Since this experience, Allison has been unable to walk out on a dock or step onto a boat without trembling violently and turning ghostly pale. She can't even drive near the lake without getting upset.

The conditioning view also leads to suggestions about how to treat phobias. Two ideas are important. The first is *extinction*. The anxiety reaction should weaken if the CS (the phobic stimulus) is presented repeatedly or for a long time without the US

BOX 12.5 ANOTHER VIEW ON PHOBIAS AND RESPONSES TO ANXIETY

A somewhat different view on the development of phobic behavior was suggested by Miller and Dollard. Their view used *instrumental conditioning* along with classical conditioning. Miller and Dollard assumed that people acquire new drives by classical conditioning from biologically built-in drives (N. E. Miller, 1948, 1951). Fear was seen as a learned drive that develops from pain. Once a fear drive is acquired, cues that arouse fear engage a drive to escape the fear. Remember that Miller and Dollard equated drive reduction with reinforcement. If you avoid or escape from whatever has cued fear, the drive goes down. This reinforces the avoidance or escape behavior, making the same behavior more likely next time.

Consider an example: Imagine there are two ways to get to class in the morning. The shorter, faster route requires you to go over a high, scary bridge, which makes you anxious. As you approach the bridge, fear mounts—and so does the drive to escape the fear. One day you decide to go the long way and avoid the bridge. As you head away from the bridge, your drive level goes down. The avoidance behavior is reinforced. As a result, you're more likely to avoid the shorter route in the future. If this occurs often, you'll have a phobia concerning the bridge.

Some stimuli that cause anxiety can't be avoided through overt behavior because the stimuli are internal—your thoughts. How can you reduce the fear if your own thoughts are creating it? The answer is simple: *Just don't think of whatever it is that's threatening you.* Successful "not-thinking" gets rid of the fear. It thereby causes a reduction in the drive, which reinforces the not-thinking tendency. In this way, Miller and Dollard accounted in conditioning terms for the psychoanalytic phenomenon of repression. Repression is not-thinking. It occurs because doing it reduces the fear drive. Eventually, not-thinking happens before the threatening thought even comes to mind. Thus, the thought never becomes conscious.

The fact that Miller and Dollard's theory was able to deal with this psychoanalytic phenomenon wasn't just a curious sidelight. In fact, their theory was intended more generally as an explicit attempt to address psychoanalytic concepts through the principles of learning. This analysis of phobic behavior and repression is just one example of their efforts in that direction (see also J. S. Brown, 1948, 1957; N. E. Miller, 1944). As suggested by this example, it proved to be possible to use the language of learning to understand events that Freud and others had viewed in very different terms.

(whatever induced fear during conditioning). Oddly enough, by actively avoiding the phobic stimulus in their day-to-day activities, people such as Allison are actually preventing extinction from taking place.

The second important idea is that a *different* emotion can become conditioned to the *same* stimulus. If the new emotion is incompatible with fear, it will gradually come to predominate in place of the fear (a process termed **counterconditioning**). Although these ideas—extinction and counterconditioning—differ slightly from each other, in practice they lead to the same general sorts of therapeutic procedures.

One technique is **systematic desensitization**. People are first taught to relax thoroughly. This relaxation response is the *emotion* that's intended to take over for the anxiety. The therapist and the phobic person create an anxiety hierarchy—a list of situations with the feared stimulus, ranked by how much anxiety each creates (see Table 12.2). This hierarchy varies from person to person in what situations create the greatest fear.

In the desensitization process, you relax as fully as you can and then visualize a scene from the least threatening end of the hierarchy. The anxiety aroused by this image is allowed to dissipate. Then, while you continue to relax, you imagine the scene again. Do this sequence repeatedly, until the scene provokes no anxiety at all. Then move to the next level. Gradually, you're able to imagine increasingly threatening scenes without anxiety. Eventually, the imagined scenes are replaced by the actual feared stimulus. As the anxiety is countered by relaxation, you're able to interact more and more effectively with the stimulus that previously produced intense fear.

Table 12.2 An Anxiety Hierarchy Such as Might Be Used in Systematic Desensitization for One Type of Acrophobia (fear of heights). Each scene is carefully visualized while the person relaxes completely, working from the least threatening scene (at the bottom) to those that produce greater anxiety (toward the top).

Looking down from the top of the Empire State Building
Walking around the top floor of the Empire State Building
Looking out the window of a 12-story building
Looking over the balcony rail of a 4-story building
Looking out the window of a 4-story building
Looking up at a 30-story building from across a small park
Reading a story about the construction of a skyscraper
Reading a story that mentions being on top of the Statue of Liberty
Hearing a news story that mentions the tall buildings of a city
Seeing a TV news story in which tall buildings appear in the background

Systematic desensitization has proven very effective in reducing fear reactions, particularly fears that focus on a specific stimulus (e.g., Brady, 1972; Davison & Wilson, 1973). It works far more quickly than do many other therapies and thus is less expensive. The technique has been of enormous benefit to people with debilitating anxieties. How disruptive a phobia is, of course, depends on its focus. A fear of elephants wouldn't have too big an impact on most people's lives, but anxiety over entering stores with crowds of people can cripple your existence.

More recently, desensitization has been taken in a different direction. Many clinical researchers now use treatments in which the person is exposed to a more intense dose of the feared stimulus and endures it—while anxiety rises then gradually falls. The person is kept exposed to the feared stimulus well after the physical aspects of the anxiety have subsided. It seems that extinction occurs more quickly when the person is in a state of rest after the anxiety has fallen off. Such **exposure treatments** for phobias can sometimes be done in as little as one session (Öst, Ferebee, & Furmark, 1997). This sort of treatment has also proven to be superior for severe posttraumatic disorders (Foa & Meadows, 1997).

ADDITIONAL BENEFITS

Procedures such as these have secondary benefits. First, they've gone a long way to minimize the shame that people feel when their emotions hamper their actions. The learning perspective teaches people that having fear is no reason to be ashamed. Fear isn't a sign of a diseased personality. To the contrary, even irrational fears can result from ordinary events of life through the mechanism of classical conditioning.

Additional benefit can also come from learning techniques such as relaxation. These techniques are tools that people can apply more broadly any time they feel anxious or upset (Goldfried, 1971; Goldfried & Merbaum, 1973). The techniques thus promote effective functioning far beyond the therapy setting in which they're first learned.

Although the treatment of phobias provides a clear example of how the concepts of classical conditioning can be applied to problems, there are other examples. People often have conditioned responses of other emotions that they don't want to have, such as anger. Such undesired responses can be treated in the same way as fear: by extinguishing or counterconditioning the response.

It's hard to emphasize strongly enough how much the conditioning approach to phobias differs from approaches suggested by some other theoretical perspectives. For example, a psychoanalytic therapist (Chapter 9) wouldn't look for an instance of classical conditioning, but would try to uncover hidden conflicts from childhood. To the psychoanalyst, if it mattered at all what stimuli now elicit anxiety (and it might not), it would only be to suggest in a symbolic way what the real problem is. These approaches are quite different.

CLASSICAL CONDITIONING OF AVERSION

Classical conditioning in therapy is usually aimed at getting rid of conditioned responses. Sometimes, however, people want to *acquire* conditioned responses. These are cases in which people now have positive responses to stimuli they want to dislike and avoid. This would be a way to describe people who are trying to stop smoking or drinking (Cannon, Baker, Gino, & Nathan, 1986; Hackett & Horan, 1979). Stimuli related to those behaviors (liquor, cigarettes, and so on) are now tied to pleasant emotions. They would be easier to stay away from if they provoked *un*pleasant emotions.

Application of conditioning to this kind of situation is called **aversion therapy** (Rachman & Teasdale, 1969). The logic is much the same as that of counterconditioning, but the goal now is to condition a *negative* emotional response instead of a positive response. Doing this requires presenting the stimulus as a CS along with a US that produces a negative reaction. For example, nausea-inducing drugs are sometimes used as a US to be linked to the taste of liquor and cues for drinking (Cannon et al., 1986). Electric shock is used as a US to be linked to the touch of a cigarette (Powell & Azrin, 1968).

Aversive conditioning isn't as widely used as other behavior therapies, for several reasons. Some find the procedures objectionable, and some have raised questions about whether it's as effective as other procedures (Lichtenstein & Danaher, 1976; Powell & Azrin, 1968).

CONDITIONING AND CONTEXT

The point of using procedures based on extinction and counterconditioning is to replace an undesired response with a neutral response or a response opposite to the original one. However, there are some issues that complicate things. As noted earlier, it's now believed that extinction doesn't remove the original conditioning (Bouton, 1994, 2000). Rather, it creates a second conditioned response that dominates over the original one. Sometimes, though, the original response comes back. How might that be made less likely?

An important role is played by context. That is, the context of the original conditioning often differs from the context of the therapy. In effect, each context is a set of discriminative stimuli. People acquire a neutral response (via extinction) to the target stimulus in the therapy room. But when they return to the setting where the response was learned, the old response may reappear (Bouton, 2000). Why? Because the stimuli of the original setting *weren't there during the extinction*. As a result, they still link to CRs and serve as cues for behavior.

For the new response to predominate in the person's experience, one of two things must happen. First, the person can acquire the new response in a setting that resembles the setting where the old response was acquired. This will cause the new response to generalize to the original setting. Alternatively, the person can avoid the original setting. That's why many approaches to avoiding relapse emphasize staying away from settings resembling those where the original response was acquired.

As a concrete example, consider work on smoking relapse. Withdrawal from nicotine isn't the sole problem in quitting (Perkins, 1999). Relapse rates are as high as 60%, even if smokers get nicotine other ways (Kenford, Flore, Jorenby, & Smith, 1994). Many who quit smoking return to it well after the end of nicotine withdrawal (Brandon et al., 1990). Why? The smoking is linked by conditioning to particular contexts (after meals, after sex, or when drinking at social gatherings). The context itself remains a discriminative stimulus for smoking long after the craving for nicotine is gone (Carter & Tiffany, 1999).

Programs to quit smoking now emphasize efforts to extinguish responses to the cues linked to smoking. The contextual cues are presented alone, with no smoking. The hope is that the nonsmoking response will condition to those cues, and the person will thereby become resistant to relapse. Such programs have had only limited success (Conklin & Tiffany, 2002). Perhaps that's because they've used normative smoking cues, rather than personalized ones. Because everyone has a unique smoking history, individualizing the cues may promote better success (Conklin & Tiffany, 2001).

INSTRUMENTAL CONDITIONING AND MALADAPTIVE BEHAVIORS

Another set of problems in behavior relates to the principles of instrumental conditioning. The reasoning here stems from the idea that behavioral tendencies are built in by reinforcement. Indeed, tendencies can be acquired in ways that make them resistant to extinction.

How might this reasoning be applied to problems? Imagine that a certain behavior or class of behavior—throwing tantrums when you don't get your way—was reinforced at one period of your life because your parents gave in to them. The reinforcement strengthened the tendency to repeat the tantrums. If reinforced often enough and in the right pattern of partial reinforcement, the behavior will become both frequent and persistent.

Later, when you grow older, the behavior will become less appropriate. It won't be reinforced as often, although people may give in to it occasionally. (It's surprising how often people reinforce the exact behaviors they wish would stop.) Although the reinforcement will be rare, the behavior will continue (thanks to the partial reinforcement effect). The behavior will seem irrational to observers, but from the conditioning view, it will just be showing resistance to extinction.

The principles of instrumental conditioning suggest that the way to change undesired behavior is to change the patterns of reinforcement. The best approach would be to increase reinforcements after a desired (alternative) action. At the same time, reduce even further (if possible) any reinforcement of the undesired action. This should shape behavior toward greater adaptiveness or suitability. This approach is sometimes called **contingency management.**

An example comes from the literature of health psychology. Childhood obesity is a risk factor for serious health problems later on. It stems partly from habits such as watching TV instead of being active and partly from poor diet. Research has shown that reinforcing less sedentary activities causes both an increase in those activities and a decrease in the sedentary activities (L. H. Epstein, Saelens, Myers, & Vito, 1997). Similarly, reinforcing the choice of fruits and vegetables over snack foods causes an increase in the tendency to choose those healthy foods (Goldfield & Epstein, 2002).

Contingency management programs have also been used in efforts to keep people from drug and alcohol abuse. It can be used to shape undesired behavior in the direction of abstinence over time before quitting (Preston, Umbricht, Wong, & Epstein, 2001). It also can be useful in treating alcohol dependence (Petry, Martin, Cooney, & Kranzler, 2000) and in supporting abstinence from cocaine use (Higgins, Wong, Badger, Haug Ogden, & Dantona, 2000).

All of this is straightforward when it is easy to control the reinforcement. But sometimes reinforcement occurs in unexpected ways and places. For example, consider video games. People have the potential to learn a lot when they play video games. Why? Because the game often incorporates reinforcement for particular kinds of behavior in the game. It's been shown that playing games that reinforce violence in the game result in more violence and hostility outside the game (Carnagey & Anderson, 2005).

INSTRUMENTAL CONDITIONING OF CONFLICT

Another potential contributor to problems in personality is inconsistency in reinforcement. That is, a given act can be reinforced at some times and punished at other times. If the reinforcement and punishment occur in different settings, the person will learn a discrimination. But if they occur in the same setting (or if the cues for discrimination are hard to tell apart), the result is **conflict** (Dollard & Miller, 1950; N. E. Miller, 1944). That is, the reinforcement causes a tendency to do the behavior, and the punishment causes a tendency to not do it.

Whichever tendency is stronger is the one that will dominate. The fact that the other tendency is there, however, means there will be discomfort as the behavior is being done (or not done). If the situation is conflicted enough, the person may even learn to treat punishment as a discriminative stimulus for *doing* the behavior (if persistence is eventually followed by reinforcement). This person's behavior will appear especially irrational and can even be self-destructive, but it's a predictable result of inconsistent outcomes.

This issue is of special concern in childrearing, because parents can easily fall into the pattern of mixing reinforcement and punishment for the same behavior (e.g., sometimes punishing tantrums and sometimes giving in to them). It's interesting that many of the transitions of childhood that can be difficult for this reason are the transitions noted by Freud many years ago: weaning, toilet training, establishing power relationships between parent and child. Freud saw these situations as conflicted due to sexual pressures. But they also seem open to analysis in terms of inconsistent treatment by the parents.

INSTRUMENTAL CONDITIONING AND BIOFEEDBACK

Another use of instrumental conditioning concepts in therapy focuses on changing internal behaviors. The behaviors are usually small in scale—for example, muscle tensing that creates headaches or influences blood pressure, muscle cramping that produces pain in one's neck or lower back, and small muscle movements in areas that are paralyzed. As these examples imply, this therapy deals primarily with problems of pain or other conditions of ill health.

It was long thought that most internal behaviors of this type are outside voluntary control. Eventually, however, it was discovered that people could learn to control the internal actions through procedures thought to involve instrumental conditioning. The procedures as a group are called **biofeedback.**

Biofeedback training requires an internal behavior that's specific in one sense but vague in another. For example, you might be asked to raise the temperature of your hand, reduce muscle tension in your forehead, or lower your pulse rate. You aren't told *how* to do this, just to do it. While you try, you're attached to a machine that continuously tells you whether you're successful, by a signal light or tone. The light or tone (the biofeedback) acts as a reinforcer for whatever you did just before. The result is that people can learn to do very subtle internal behaviors through such training. Presumably, once the behavior is well learned, it will continue to occur even without the biofeedback.

This technique has been proposed as a way to treat physical problems that involve subtle muscle activity (Blanchard & Epstein, 1978). Many people, for example, can change their blood pressure during biofeedback, although this particular effect doesn't generalize well outside the training setting (Shapiro & Surwit, 1979). Biofeedback is also used as a treatment for many kinds of pain (Elmore & Tursky, 1981).

Conditioning Theories: Problems and Prospects

The conditioning view on personality has been particularly influential among two groups of psychologists: researchers who are actively involved in the experimental analysis of behavior in the laboratory and clinicians who received their training when behavior therapies were at their height of popularity. The conditioning view is attractive to these two groups for two different reasons, which in turn represent two strengths of this view of personality.

First, the conditioning viewpoint emerged—as had no other perspective before it—from the crucible of experimental research. The ideas that form this approach to behavior were intended to be subjected to close scrutiny, to be either upheld or disconfirmed through research. Many of the ideas have been tested thoroughly, and the evidence that supports them is substantial. This empirical base is important. Having a viewpoint on the nature of personality that can be verified by careful, objective observation is very satisfying to the researcher.

The second reason for the impact of conditioning ideas is the effectiveness of behavioral therapy techniques. Clinical psychologists found that many of people's problems in life can be treated with fairly simple procedures. With this realization, the clinicians began to look carefully at the principles behind the procedures. The learning perspective has taken on an aura of importance and credibility among this group of psychologists because of its good fit with these effective techniques of behavior change.

Although many psychologists find this viewpoint congenial, it also has its share of problems and criticisms. Some of the criticisms derive from a virtue we just named: the emphasis on research. More specifically, conditioning theorists have emphasized the study of laboratory animals. If the laws of learning are the same across different species, it makes no difference which animal they study. Many people, however, are wary of the assumption that underlies that strategy—that learning is the same across species. Indeed, skepticism on this point helped foster the development of a second generation of learning theories, discussed in Chapter 13.

A more subtle criticism concerns the researchers' tendency to simplify the situation under study. Simplification ensures experimental control. Having control helps clarify cause and effect. But it sometimes results in experimental situations that offer extremely few options for behavior. There's sometimes a nagging suspicion that the behavior occurred because there were so many pressures in its direction and so little chance to do anything *else*. What happens to behavior when the person leaves the laboratory? With more options, will the regularities still hold up?

This question turns out to be a very important one. Breland and Breland (1961) tried to use operant procedures to train animals. They were distressed to discover that reinforcers often were less powerful than animals' natural tendencies. For example, they tried to train a raccoon to pick up coins and put them into a "bank," but found it had a strong tendency to hold the coins and rub them together. The raccoon looked like a miser, but it was only trying to do what it would do with crayfish in its normal environment: rub them together to remove their shells. In the same way, pigs being trained to deposit wooden coins into a bank preferred to drop the coins, root them along the ground, and toss them into the air. The Brelands eventually questioned whether lab studies of conditioning really provide an accurate picture of behavior in normal environments. Perhaps the picture that's being conveyed is actually quite distorted.

Another problem with this view is that it isn't really so much a theory of personality as a view of the determinants of behavior. Some people think this view is too simplistic to provide a meaningful view of personality. The processes of learning presumably operate continuously in a piecemeal and haphazard fashion. The human experience, on the other hand, seems highly complex and orderly. How do the haphazard learning processes yield such an orderly product?

To put it another way, conditioning theories tell us a lot about how a specific behavior becomes more probable or less probable, but it doesn't tell us so much about the person who is doing the behavior. The processes in the theories are cold and mechanistic. There seems to be little place here for the subjective sense of personhood, little focus on the continuity and coherence that characterize the sense of self. In sum, to many people, this analysis of personality doesn't convey the subjective experience of what it means to *have* a personality. Perhaps the greatest challenge to the conditioning approach, then, is to convince skeptics that it accounts for the subjective qualities that seem so important to personality.

· SUMMARY ·

The conditioning approach to personality emphasizes two types of learning. In classical conditioning, a neutral stimulus (CS) is presented along with another stimulus (US) that already elicits a reflexive response (UR). After repeated pairings, the CS itself comes to elicit a response (CR) that's similar to the UR. The CR appears to be an anticipatory response that prepares for the US.

This basic phenomenon is modified by discrimination (different stimuli leading to different responses) and extended by generalization (different stimuli leading to similar responses). CRs fade if the CS is presented repeatedly without the US, a process termed *extinction*. Classical conditioning is important to personality primarily when the responses being conditioned are emotional reactions (emotional conditioning). Classical conditioning thus provides a basis for understanding people's unique preferences and aversions, and it provides a way of analyzing certain psychological problems, such as phobias.

In instrumental conditioning (a more active process), a behavior is followed by an outcome that's either positively valued or aversive. If the outcome is positively valued, the tendency to perform the behavior is strengthened. Thus, the outcome is called a *reinforcer*. If the outcome is aversive (a *punisher*), the tendency to perform the behavior is reduced. *Discrimination* in instrumental conditioning is responding in different ways to different situational cues; *generalization* is responding in a similar way to different cues; and *extinction* is the reduction of a behavioral tendency through non-reinforcement of the behavior. Behavior is shaped in new directions by reinforcing successively better approximations of the behavior you want eventually to occur. Reinforcers can occur in many patterns, termed *schedules*. The most important effect of variations in reinforcement schedules is that behavior learned by intermittent (partial) reinforcement is more persistent (under later conditions of nonreinforcement) than is a behavior learned by continuous reinforcement.

The conditioning approach holds that personality is the sum of the person's conditioned tendencies. Assessment, from this point of view, emphasizes the observation of various aspects of behavior tendencies as they occur in specific situations. Assessment can focus on people's physiological responses, their overt behaviors, or their reports of emotional reactions in response to different kinds of stimuli.

The conditioning approach assumes that problems in behavior are the result of the same kinds of conditioning processes as result in normal behavior. Classical conditioning can produce intense and irrational fears, called *phobias*; instrumental conditioning can produce behavior tendencies that persist even when they are no longer adaptive. These various problems can be treated by means of conditioning procedures, which collectively are termed *behavior therapy* or *behavior modification*. Systematic desensitization counterconditions fear reactions with relaxation. Other kinds of exposure treatments keep people focused on distressing situations until long after the burst of anxiety calms down. Aversion therapy conditions negative reactions in the place of positive reactions. The principles of instrumental conditioning underlie a variety of therapy techniques. In biofeedback training, people learn to engage in certain kinds of internal behavior for such goals as controlling pain.

· GLOSSARY ·

Aversion therapy   The conditioning of an aversive reaction to what's now a positive stimulus.

Behavior modification (or **behavior therapy**)   The changing of behavior therapeutically through conditioning processes.

Behavioral assessment   An assessment made by observing a person's overt behavior.

Biofeedback   The technique of learning to control an internal activity by instrumental conditioning.

Classical conditioning   The pairing of a neutral stimulus with an unconditioned stimulus.

Conditioned (or **conditional**) **response (CR)**   A response to the CS that's acquired by classical conditioning.

Conditioned (or **conditional**) **stimulus (CS)**   A neutral stimulus that's paired with a US to become conditioned.

Conflict   The simultaneous arousal of two incompatible behavioral tendencies.

Contingency management   Programs in which reinforcement is increased for desired behaviors and withheld after undesired behaviors.

Continuous reinforcement   A schedule in which reinforcement follows each instance of the behavior.

Counterconditioning   The linking of an emotion to a stimulus that differs from the emotion the stimulus now causes.

Discrimination   Responding in a different manner to different stimuli.

Discriminative stimulus   A cue that controls the occurrence of behavior.

Drive   A motivational state that increases behaviors that are high in the habit hierarchy.

Emotional conditioning   Classical conditioning in which the CR is an emotional reaction.

Epiphenomena   Phenomena that occur along with behavior but have no causal role in behavior.

Exposure treatments   Treatments in which people stay focused on the distressing topic until well after their anxiety reaction dissipates.

Extinction   In classical conditioning, the reduction of a CR by repeating the CS without the US; in instrumental conditioning, the reduction of a behavioral tendency by removing reinforcement.

Generalization   Responding in a similar manner to somewhat different stimuli.

Habit hierarchy   The ordering of a person's potential responses by their likelihood.

Higher-order conditioning   Event in which a former CS now acts as a US in a new instance of conditioning.

Instrumental conditioning   Conditioning in which a behavior becomes more likely because it is followed by a desirable event or less likely because it is followed by an undesirable event.

Negative reinforcement   The removal of an aversive stimulus.

Partial reinforcement   A schedule in which the behavior is reinforced less often than every time it occurs.

Partial reinforcement effect   The fact that a behavior acquired through partial reinforcement is resistant to extinction.

Phobia   An inappropriately intense fear of some specific class of stimuli.

Physiological assessment   The measuring of physiological aspects of emotional reactions.

Positive reinforcement   A reinforcement involving addition of a desired stimulus.

Punisher   An undesired event that weakens the behavior that came before it.

Radical behaviorism   The position that behavior should be explained solely on the basis of observable events.

Reflex   An event in which a stimulus produces an automatic response.

Reinforcer   An event that strengthens the behavior that came before it.

Shaping   Changing the nature of ongoing behavior by reinforcing a specific aspect of the behavior.

Successive approximation   Shaping by reinforcing closer approximations of the desired behavior.

Systematic desensitization   A therapeutic procedure intended to extinguish fear.

Timeout   A punishment in which a child is temporarily removed from an enjoyable activity.

Unconditioned (or **unconditional**) **response (UR)**   A reflexive response to an unconditioned stimulus.

Unconditioned (or **unconditional**) **stimulus (US)**   A stimulus that causes a reflexive (unconditioned) response.

CHAPTER 13

Social-Cognitive Learning Theories

"I was watching my 2-year-old the other day in the kitchen when he reached in and popped open the childproof latch on one of the cabinet doors, just like that, and reached in for a pan. I was so surprised I thought my teeth were gonna fall out. How do you suppose he figured out how to do that? Must've been from watching me, I guess."

"My job has changed a lot in the last year. The business has expanded really fast. In fact, the boss hasn't always had time to create new procedures for everything we do. We've had to make our own guesses about what would work. It hasn't been too bad, though. We seem to be guessing right most of the time. Sometimes you don't know if a decision was right until way later on, but that just makes it more interesting."

A S YOU saw in Chapter 12, the concepts of learning are powerful tools for analyzing behavior. The principles of conditioning account well for two large parts of human experience. They explain how attitudes and preferences seem to derive from emotional reactions. They also explain how behavior tendencies strengthen and fade as a result of good and bad outcomes.

Powerful as those theories are, however, they weren't completely accepted, even by everyone who believes learning is the key to personality. Some became disenchanted with conditioning theories because they ignore aspects of behavior that seem obvious outside the lab. For example, people often learn by watching one another. People often decide whether to do something by thinking about what would happen if they did it.

How can conditioning theories account for a baby's suddenly doing something complex that he'd never done before? How can they deal with the decision processes of a person trying to guess what to do in a specific situation at work? The conditioning theories don't seem wrong, exactly, but they seem incomplete. They explain some things well, but they don't cover it all.

From these dissatisfactions—and from the work to which they led—came what might be seen as another generation of learning theories. They provide a view of personality based in learning, but they emphasize mental events more than do the earlier theories. For this reason, they're often

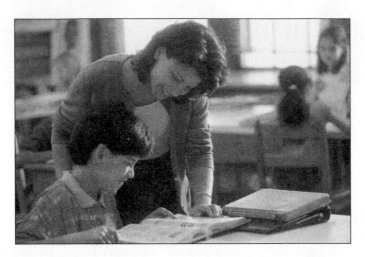

Many of the important reinforcers affecting human behavior are social in nature.

called *cognitive* learning theories. They also emphasize social aspects of learning more than was done before. Thus, they're often called *social* learning theories.

Elaborations on Conditioning Processes

Theorists of the newer learning approach didn't abandon conditioning principles. Instead, they began by elaborating on them. The easiest way to start a discussion of the newer theories is with those elaborations.

SOCIAL REINFORCEMENT

As social learning theory began to evolve, its theorists began to rethink the usefulness of studying lower animals. Can human behavior be analyzed by studying laboratory rats, or is it wiser to focus on people? What variables matter most in *human* learning? Asking these questions led to a different view of *reinforcement*.

Many came to believe that reinforcement in human experience (beyond infancy, at least) has little or nothing to do with physical needs. Rather, people are most affected by **social reinforcers**: acceptance, smiles, hugs, praise, approval, interest, and attention from others (Bandura, 1978; Kanfer & Marston, 1963; Rotter, 1954, 1982). The idea that the important reinforcers for people are social is one of several senses in which these learning theories are social (Brokaw & McLemore, 1983; A. H. Buss, 1983; Turner, Foa, & Foa, 1971).

Here's an example of the power of social reinforcement. Hall, Lund, and Jackson (1968) examined children who spent little time studying. After assessing baselines, the researchers gave social reinforcement in the form of attention and praise whenever a child engaged in studying. Figure 13.1 shows the impact of this procedure on one child. This child studied more than twice as much when social reinforcement was given than when it was not.

Emphasizing social reinforcement has a second theoretical implication. In particular, social learning theorists see no need to refer to *drives* in order to discuss reinforcement (e.g., Bandura, 1977a; Rotter, 1954, 1982). They say social reinforcers don't act via physical need states. It isn't usually necessary, for example, that the person being reinforced be in a state of deprivation.

A description of social reinforcement should also mention **self-reinforcement**. This term has two meanings. The first is that people may give themselves reinforcers after doing something they've set out to do

FIGURE 13.1
The effect of social reinforcement. This third-grade boy, whose baseline level of studying in class was quite low (Period 1), was systematically given attention and approval for studying. This greatly increased his study behavior (Period 2). To see whether the effect depended on social reinforcement, attention was removed, which caused a decrease in studying (Period 3). Reinstituting the social reinforcement (Period 4) caused a return to a high rate of studying. *Source: Adapted from Hall et al., 1968.*

(Bandura, 1976; Goldiamond, 1976; Heiby, 1982). For example, you might reward yourself with a pizza for studying six straight hours, or you may get yourself a new piece of stereo equipment after a semester of good grades.

The second meaning of self-reinforcement derives more directly from the concept of social reinforcement. It's the idea that you react to your own behavior with approval or disapproval, much as you react to someone else's behavior. In responding to your actions with approval, you reinforce yourself. In responding with disapproval, you punish yourself. This sort of internal self-reinforcement and self-punishment plays an important role in social–cognitive learning theories of behavior and behavior change (Bandura 1977a, 1986; Kanfer, 1977; Kanfer & Hagerman, 1981; Mischel, 1973, 1979).

VICARIOUS EMOTIONAL AROUSAL

Another elaboration on conditioning comes from the fact that people can experience events vicariously—through someone else. Vicarious processes represent a second sense in which human learning is social. That is, vicarious processes involve two people: one to experience something directly, another to experience it indirectly.

One type of vicarious experience is **vicarious emotional arousal,** or empathy. This occurs when you observe someone feeling an intense emotion and you experience the same feeling yourself (usually less intensely). *Empathy* isn't the same as *sympathy,* a feeling of concern for someone else who's suffering (Gruen & Mendelsohn, 1986; Wispé, 1986). In empathy, you feel the same feeling, good or bad, as the other person (Stotland, 1969). Everyone can have this experience, but people differ in its intensity (Eisenberg et al., 1994; Levenson & Ruef, 1992; Marangoni, Garcia, Ickes, & Teng, 1995).

Examples of empathy are easy to point to (see also Box 13.1). When something wonderful happens to a friend, putting her in ecstasy, you feel happy yourself. Being

BOX 13.1   EMPATHY AND ALTRUISM

In this part of the chapter, we focus on the idea that vicarious processes influence learning. While we're talking about empathy, though, we'd like to point to another aspect of human behavior to which empathy is relevant: *altruism,* or helping. One general view on helping is that when you see someone else suffering, your empathy causes you to help. There are, however, different theories about *why* this happens.

A theory developed by Robert Cialdini and his colleagues (e.g., Cialdini, Schaller, Houlihan, Arps, Fultz, & Beaman, 1987) holds that empathy in this situation causes you to experience distress. One way to escape from the feelings is to do something to reduce the other person's suffering. In this view, empathy leads to helping as a way to reduce your *own* distress; the benefit to the other person is a side effect. A competing theory by Daniel Batson and his colleagues (Batson, 1990, 1991; Batson et al., 1988) holds that empathy creates a desire to relieve the suffering of the other person, plain and simple.

Which is right? The answer actually may be that *both* are right. There's evidence that exposure to someone else's distress provokes several different emotions, not just one (Batson, Fultz, & Schoenrade, 1987; Fultz, Schaller, & Cialdini, 1988). The feelings include distress, sadness, and sympathy for the other person. These different feeling qualities may well lead to very different motivations.

Despite some contradictory evidence (Batson, Bolen, Cross, & Neuringer-Benefiel, 1986; K. O. Smith, Keating, & Stotland, 1989), the data seem to suggest that empathic concern for someone else arouses a desire to ease that person's suffering and that this desire is separate from a desire to reduce one's own distress (Batson, 1990). The desire to reduce one's own distress also plays an important role, though, and may turn out to be the most important one (Maner, Luce, Neuberg, Cialdini, Brown, & Sagarin, 2002). No matter which pathway predominates, it's clear that empathy plays an important role in bringing people to each other's aid.

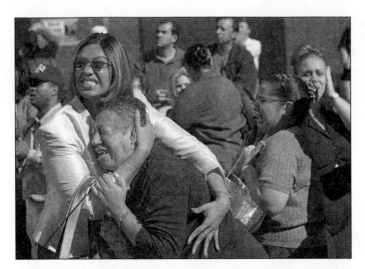

Empathy causes us to experience other's emotions. Others' grief elicits sadness from us and happiness elicits joy. As you look at this picture, you are probably beginning to feel the same emotions that the people in the picture are experiencing.

around someone who's frightened makes most people feel jumpy. Laughter is often contagious, even when you don't know what the other person is laughing at. There's even evidence that being around someone who's embarrassed can make you feel embarrassed too (R. S. Miller, 1987).

Experiencing vicarious emotional arousal doesn't *constitute* learning, but it creates an *opportunity* for learning. Recall the discussion of emotional conditioning from Chapter 12. Feeling an emotion in the presence of a neutral stimulus can cause that stimulus to become capable of evoking a similar emotion. It doesn't matter how the emotion is created. It's only necessary that it be *present*. The emotion can be caused by something you experience directly, but it can also arise vicariously. Thus, vicarious emotional arousal creates a possibility for classical conditioning. Such an event is called **vicarious classical conditioning.**

For example, in one procedure, participants simply watched a second person. A tone sounded (a neutral stimulus), and then the second person received an electric shock and grimaced. After a series of pairings of tone and shock, the observers began to react emotionally when the tone was sounded by itself (Berger, 1962; see also Bandura & Rosenthal, 1966; Vaughan & Lanzetta, 1980). This was true even though the observers never experienced pain directly. This appears to represent vicarious classical conditioning.

VICARIOUS REINFORCEMENT

Another vicarious process may be even more important. This one, called **vicarious reinforcement,** is very simple: If you observe someone do something that's followed by reinforcement, you become more likely to do the same thing yourself (Kanfer & Marston, 1963; Liebert & Fernandez, 1970). If you see a person punished after doing something, you're less likely to do it. The reinforcer or punishment went to the other person, not to you. But your own behavior is affected as though you'd received it yourself (see Figure 13.2).

This process is very important. It permits a lot of the trial and error of instrumental conditioning to take place secondhand. You don't have to "behave" all the time—just watch others behave and see what follows. Learning this way lets you learn about a lot of situations that other people are in, including some you'd rather not experience firsthand. Taking advantage of this can also save wear and tear on self-esteem, because you learn from other people's mistakes as well as their successes. Sometimes vicarious reinforcement even produces better learning than direct reinforcement does. Apparently, the vicarious situation lets you give "learning" some of the attention you'd normally devote to "behaving" (Berger, 1961; Hillix & Marx, 1960).

How do vicarious reinforcement and punishment influence people? Presumably, seeing someone be reinforced after a behavior leads you to infer you'd get the same reinforcer if you acted the same way (Bandura, 1971). If someone else is punished, you conclude the same thing would happen to you if you acted that way (Bandura, 1973; Walters & Parke, 1964). Often the inferences are more extensive. For example, you may limit your conclusion to situations that resemble the one you observed. To put it differently, you may learn *discriminations* vicariously. For instance, you may learn from observing others that talking in class leads to a scolding, but only in certain classes.

Note that the effect of vicarious reinforcement appears to involve developing an implicit (or even explicit) expectancy—that is, a mental model of links between acts and reinforcers. This is one case of a more general theme in the social–cognitive learning approach: the involvement of expectancies in learning. This theme comes up again later in the chapter.

SEMANTIC GENERALIZATION

We said the newer theories are more social and more cognitive than the earlier ones. So far, we've mostly focused on ways they're more social. Now let's consider ways they're more cognitive.

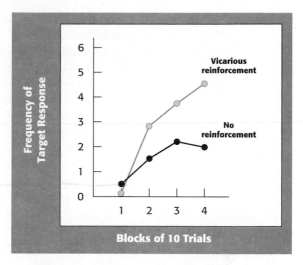

Another elaboration on the principles of conditioning came from looking more closely at the phenomenon of *generalization*—responding in a similar way to stimuli that are similar to (but not the same as) those for which conditioning has already taken place. Most animals generalize in response to varying lights or tones, but people can generalize in more interesting ways. They can do **semantic generalization,** which is generalization along a dimension of *meaning*. It's something people do often and take completely for granted.

Semantic generalization, just as any other generalization, can occur in both classical conditioning and instrumental conditioning (Diven, 1936; Maltzman, 1968). As an illustration of how it happens in classical conditioning, imagine a person who's been through a nasty divorce and now has negative emotional reactions to the mere mention of the word *divorce*. This person might well generalize this emotional reaction to semantically related words, such as *courtroom, lawyer, alimony,* and *breakup*.

Semantic generalization is explained by assuming that conditioning doesn't take place to a stimulus itself. Rather, it occurs toward cognitive elements that represent aspects of the stimulus. Semantic generalization occurs when there are mental associations to other words with related meanings. The theories discussed in this chapter assume this kind of elaborate mental structure. This is one of several senses in which they are *cognitive* learning theories.

RULE-BASED LEARNING

Another elaboration on conditioning is suggested by the idea that people can use instrumental learning to learn *rules,* rather than just to learn behaviors. Conditioning principles suggest that behavior tendencies build incrementally. Each reinforcer strengthens the tendency slightly. The longer the history of reinforcement, the stronger the tendency to behave in a certain way.

There are cases, though, that don't fit this picture. Perhaps the easiest illustration of how rules are used in human behavior comes from language acquisition. Language uses a large set of rules. For example, there are rules that specify how parts of a sentence are ordered and rules concerning how to create verb tenses and noun forms.

Early in life, children don't pay much attention to rules. They're focused on learning what specific words mean. As they get older and say things that are more

FIGURE 13.2

Effect of vicarious reinforcement. Participants were asked to say any word at random into a microphone whenever a signal was given. They also heard someone they thought was a co-participant say words periodically. In one condition, the experimenter reinforced the other voice by saying "good" every time it said a human noun. The measure of interest was how often the real participant said human nouns. As can be seen here, the reinforcement given to the other person caused a steady increase in the participants' tendency to do the same, despite the fact that they were never reinforced themselves. *Source: Adapted from Kanfer & Marston, 1963.*

complicated, they begin to use new word forms (e.g., new verb tenses), which they acquire word by word. At some point, though, children seem to realize that there are regularities to language, and they begin to use those regularities in their speech. A child may not be able to tell what the rule is, but the rule gets used when the child speaks. How do you know the child has learned a rule? You know because at this stage, the child sometimes *overregularizes*—uses the rule even where it doesn't apply (Marcus, 1996).

Consider the English rule for specifying past tense, which is to add *-ed* at the end (e.g., *cook* becomes *cooked*). There are many exceptions to this rule—verbs for which past tense is created a different way. For instance, *go* becomes *went, take* becomes *took, and break* becomes *broke*. Children use these irregular verb forms perfectly well when they first learn them. Apparently they memorize the words (which may involve an incremental conditioning process). The words are used correctly right up to the point where the rule starts to be used. At that point, the child applies the rule to every verb, even the irregular ones. As a result, the child now begins to make errors. A child who said "I went into the backyard" only a few weeks ago will now sometimes say "I goed into the backyard." This suggests that the child is acquiring a rule.

Once rule-based learning begins to take place, it becomes a pervasive feature of human learning. Past infancy, humans seem to respond to outcomes by learning implicit rules and conceptual principles. When you learn how to study for a psychology test, you're learning principles of preparing for tests in general. When you learn to drive, you're learning not just a set of movements, but a set of rules for creating forward motion, stopping, distancing from other cars, and so on. Whenever you've learned a rule, you can apply it to widely divergent new situations (e.g., preparing for an exam in a new course or driving in unfamiliar territory).

What, then, is the role of incremental conditioning in behavior? Perhaps incremental learning influences how a rule first emerges. That is, reinforcement processes may nudge you a little bit at a time in the right direction until you begin to identify a rule. When the rule comes into focus, concept learning takes over and the rate of learning increases.

EXPECTANCIES CONCERNING OUTCOMES

The learning theories in this chapter include a facet that can be viewed in either of two ways. It might be an elaboration on conditioning theories, or a step away from conditioning. This facet provides another sense in which these theories are cognitive. Specifically, the theories assume that people hold *expectancies* about whether given behaviors will lead to desired outcomes (Rotter, 1954). This expectancy, then, is an important determinant of what the person does.

This concept is often discussed along with a view on motivation termed *expectancy–incentive theory*. (We touched on this view in Chapter 5.) **Incentives** are values that goals have for the person. Incentives don't necessarily depend on deprivation. The concept thus differs from the concept of drive. **Expectancies,** here, are implicit judgments about the likelihood that a given behavior will attain the goal. Predicting behavior, from this view, requires you to take into account both incentives and expectancies (Feather, 1982).

The idea that people hold expectancies and that expectancies influence action wasn't new when it was absorbed into social learning theory (e.g., Brunswik, 1951; Lewin, 1951b; Postman, 1951; Tolman, 1932). But an emphasis on expectancies (in one form or other) is a cornerstone of this approach to personality (Rotter, 1954; see also Bandura, 1977a, 1986; Kanfer, 1977; Mischel, 1973).

Box 13.2 Theoretical Controversy: How Does Learning Take Place?

We've treated the principles of social–cognitive learning theories as elaborations on conditioning theories. Our aim has been to show how the various changes can be inserted into the picture of the learning process that was drawn in Chapter 12. Some of the modifications, however, raise questions about the concepts that they seem at first to embellish. This box briefly explores two such questions (see also Brewer, 1974).

The Role of Awareness

The first concerns the role of *awareness* in conditioning. It's long been assumed that conditioning is automatic (cf. Skinner, 1953). There's reason to suspect, though, that it involves cognition. For example, several studies seem to indicate that people show little or no classical conditioning from repeated pairings of stimuli unless they realize the stimuli are correlated (Chatterjee & Eriksen, 1962; Dawson & Furedy, 1976; Grings, 1973). On the other side of the coin, sometimes just expecting an aversive event (as a US) can produce conditioned responses to other stimuli

(Bridger & Mandel, 1964; Spacapan & Cohen, 1983). There's also evidence that people change their behavior in response to reinforcers only when they've become aware of what's being reinforced (Dulany, 1968; Spielberger & DeNike, 1966).

Extinction may also involve cognition. After classical conditioning of a fear response, a statement that the painful US will no longer be given sometimes eliminates fear of the CS (Bandura, 1969; Grings, 1973). Classical conditioning is supposed to be automatic, independent of thought. It's supposed to link stimuli directly with responses. But effects such as these suggest that expectations may play an important role (Bandura, 1986).

The Concept of Reinforcement

The second issue concerns the concept of *reinforcement*—and, by implication, the very nature of instrumental conditioning. Conditioning theorists say *reinforcers* are events that strengthen the tendency to do the behavior that preceded them. Yet Bandura (1976, 1977a), a prominent social learning theorist, explicitly rejected this sense of the reinforcement concept, while continuing to use the term *reinforcement*

(see also Bolles, 1972; Brewer, 1974; Rotter, 1954).

If reinforcers don't strengthen action tendencies, what do they do? Bandura said they do two things: In providing information about outcomes, they lead to hypotheses (expectancies) about what actions work in what settings. They also provide the potential for future motivational states through mental anticipation of the reinforcer in the future. In the same way, Henderlong and Lepper (2002) argued that praise enhances motivation by linking outcomes to causes that are controllable. Many people would agree that these various functions are important. But do the functions really constitute *reinforcement* in any meaningful sense? If not, do they actually belong in the process of instrumental conditioning?

The two issues addressed here—the nature of reinforcement and the role of awareness in conditioning—raise a far broader question: If reinforcement doesn't strengthen response tendencies and if conditioning isn't really conditioning, then just how strong a conceptual connection remains between the social–cognitive learning theories and the conditioning theories from which they grew?

Let's be sure we're clear about how this view differs from the conditioning approach (see also Box 13.2). Conditioning views assume that reinforcement has a direct effect on the probability of the behavior. They *don't* assume that mental representations (expectancies) matter. In the social–cognitive theories, people think over the available evidence—past outcomes, the situation they now confront—and judge the likelihood of the desired outcome. These expectancy judgments then influence behavioral choices (e.g., Kirsch, 1985).

Theorists disagree about exactly what kinds of expectancies matter. Major theories have been proposed concerning two specific types of expectancies. These ideas are described, in the order they were developed, in the next two sections.

Locus-of-Control Expectancies

The first idea was developed by Julian Rotter (1954, 1966) from his observations of people in therapy. Rotter's observations led him to this conclusion: Given the same event, different people learn different things. More specifically, some people learn from reinforcement, just as the principle of instrumental conditioning says. Others seem not to learn anything at all.

As an illustration, imagine two college freshmen, Bert and Ernie, who are shy and have trouble making conversation with women. Each goes to the university guidance center for help. The therapist provides suggestions for topics of conversation, ways to make the conversation move along, and so on. After some practice, the therapist asks each young man to go out and have a conversation with an attractive young woman who works in the next office.

In each case, the woman's response is pleasant and positive. Bert returns to the therapist and says, "I did what you suggested, and she seemed to like me. I'm going to remember those suggestions from now on, because they really seem useful." Ernie returns and says, "I did what you suggested. She acted friendly. Why? I don't know." Bert's response looks like instrumental learning: If something works well enough to be reinforced, it tends to be done again. But what sense does Ernie's response make?

Rotter became convinced that people differ from each other in the extent to which they see a cause-and-effect link between their behaviors and the reinforcers that follow. Rotter believed, as do most social learning theorists, that instrumental learning requires seeing that connection. Because some people (like Bert) see a link between behavior and reinforcer, the reinforcer affects their behavior. People who don't see a link (like Ernie) react haphazardly to reinforcers. Instrumental conditioning, for these people, isn't straightforward at all.

The phrase used in discussing this idea is **locus of control** (Rotter, Seeman, & Liverant, 1962; Rotter, 1966, 1990). *Locus* means "place." People termed *internals* (internal locus of control) see reinforcers as controlled from within, by their own actions. People termed *externals* (external locus of control) see reinforcers as controlled by things outside themselves, things other than their own actions. Although locus of control is a continuous dimension, it's often described by its endpoints. Because the terms *internal* and *external* are so commonly used to refer to the two orientations, the concept is referred to with the letters *I–E*.

This dimension has been studied both in experiments and in individual-difference research. In experiments, temporary locus of control is created by telling some people that task outcomes are caused by skill (internal) and telling other people that they're caused by chance (external). In one early study, Phares (1957) found that people with skill instructions used their outcomes as a guide to likely future outcomes. This is just what should occur from instrumental conditioning. It didn't occur, though, among those who were told their outcomes were based on luck (see also Holden & Rotter, 1962; Walls & Cox, 1971).

A huge body of evidence has also accumulated on individual differences in locus of control (Lefcourt, 1976; Phares, 1976). People with an internal locus of control adjust their expectancies upward after success and downward after failure. Externals often shift their expectancies in the direction *opposite* to the prior outcome. These differences in how people learn have important implications for other more elaborate behaviors, including such areas as academic achievement (Findley & Cooper, 1983).

Most research on this topic has used Rotter's measure (1966) of locus of control, but this scale has been criticized on several grounds. For one, it measures only generalized expectancies, not specific ones. It also mixes perceptions of control over personal outcomes with perceptions of control over government and so on (cf. Gurin, Gurin, Lao, & Beattie, 1969; Mirels, 1970). Finally, there is more diversity among externals than internals, because there are many different ways to have an external control orientation (Hersch & Scheibe, 1967).

These criticisms led to new measures (Lefcourt, 1981). Several people created measures that focus selectively on one domain of behavior at a time (Lefcourt, Martin, Fick, & Saleh, 1985; Lefcourt, Von Baeyer, Ware, & Cox, 1979; Paulhus, 1983; Paulhus & Christie, 1981; Wallston & Wallston, 1978, 1981). Another effort has been to separate causal influences from one another. For example, Levenson's (1973, 1981) scale distinguishes between chance factors and powerful others as external causes of outcomes.

Although the locus-of-control concept has been influential, a theoretical question has been raised about it. Recall the underlying rationale: Instrumental learning requires seeing a link between action and outcome. Rotter (1966) assumed that this link requires an internal locus of control. Others, however (e.g., Weiner, Heckhausen, Meyer, & Cook, 1972), challenged that view, noting that much of the relevant evidence confounds two qualities.

Consider the experiments described earlier, in which task outcomes were said to be based on either luck or skill. These two labels differ in the locus of the cause, but they also differ in other ways. Skill is a *stable* causal force, whereas chance is more *variable*. Which dimension influences change in expectancy: locus or stability? Research tends to favor stability (e.g., Diener & Dweck, 1978; McMahan, 1973; Meyer, 1980; Weiner et al., 1972; Weiner, Nierenberg, & Goldstein, 1976).

This raises broader questions about the meaning of the locus-of-control literature more generally. For example, does the I–E personality scale similarly confound locus with stability? This question hasn't been answered. It's been suggested, though, that the I–E scale confounds locus of causality with confidence about the outcomes, with internals being more confident than externals (Carver, 1997b). This would suggest that expectancies about good outcomes in the future may be what matters, rather than the perceived locus of cause.

EFFICACY EXPECTANCIES

A second variation on the theme of expectancies also derives partly from clinical experience. Albert Bandura (1977b) argued that people with problems generally know exactly what actions are needed to reach the outcomes they want. Just knowing what to do, however, isn't enough. You also have to be confident of your ability to *do* the behavior. This confidence about having the ability to carry out a desired action is what Bandura terms **efficacy expectancy,** or **self-efficacy.** To Bandura, when therapy works, it's because the therapy has restored the person's sense of efficacy, or confidence in the ability to carry out actions that earlier were troublesome.

The concept of efficacy expectancy draws conceptually on a variety of earlier sources, including White's discussion (1959) of competence motivation (outlined in Chapter 10). White believed the competence motive is central to human behavior. Bandura argues more specifically that a sense of personal efficacy is needed for people to strive consistently (see also Box 13.3).

Efficacy expectancy differs from internal locus of control, despite superficial similarities. In principle, people with internal locus of control see both good and bad outcomes as depending on their own actions. In principle, they don't necessarily feel they have the competence to act in effective ways. In theory, they're just as likely to view bad outcomes as showing they're bad at what they're trying to do. For example, Joe has an internal locus of control. He believes that getting good grades relates

Box 13.3 THE THEORIST AND THE THEORY

Bandura Stresses Personal Agency but Also Appreciates the Role of Chance

Albert Bandura has made many contributions to the learning perspective on personality, having done pioneering work on observational learning and the effects of social reward. More recently, he has argued forcefully for the importance of feelings of personal efficacy. Yet this theorist who places such emphasis on personal agency has also been outspoken in pointing to the role of chance encounters in people's lives, including his own.

Bandura was born in 1925 in a small town in northern Alberta, Canada, the son of wheat farmers of Polish descent. His town's school had only two teachers and a handful of students, but it gave him a good enough start to send him to college at the

University of British Columbia. There, sharing a ride to class with several other students, he had a chance encounter that would change his life. His friends, mostly pre-med and engineering students, had very early classes. Lacking anything better to do at that early hour, Bandura decided to kill time by taking a psychology course. He liked it so much that he decided to make psychology his career (Evans, 1989).

A similar chance encounter gave Bandura a special interest in *clinical* psychology. During a summer spent as a laborer, filling potholes in the Alaskan highway in the Yukon, he found himself in the company of an odd assortment of characters, people who had fled to the remote North for a variety of unsavory reasons. This chance exposure to a range of bizarre individuals caused Bandura to develop an appreciation for the minor "psychopathology of everyday life," which

continued to spark his interest for years thereafter.

A third chance encounter is especially notable (Bandura, 1982b). While a graduate student, he went one day to play golf with a friend. By chance, they found themselves playing behind two attractive young women. The two twosomes became a foursome for the rest of the round, and one of the women later became Bandura's wife. As Bandura (1982b) wrote, without this chance encounter "it is exceedingly unlikely" the two of them would ever have met.

Surely this story isn't unique. Many lifelong relationships begin with improbable and unforeseen encounters. Indeed, Bandura's point was how often life is influenced in dramatic and critical ways by chance events. It's somewhat ironic, though, that chance encounters played such an important role in determining the life goals of this theorist whose belief in human self-agency came to be so strong.

---

directly to his preparing for exams. He also believes he doesn't know how to prepare for exams. Thus, it's possible for someone with an internal locus of control to have low expectancies of personal efficacy.

What about the person with an external locus of control? This one is a little trickier. In a sense, the concept of self-efficacy seems less relevant to these people at all. If their outcomes depend on the whims of fate or powerful people around them, efficacy isn't much of an issue. One might argue that the absence of a sense of personal control implies a low sense of personal efficacy. On the other hand, Bandura sometimes treats a belief in the efficacy of external agents (such as medications) as equivalent to belief in one's own personal efficacy. This suggests that even externals can have high efficacy expectancies if they see themselves as lucky or well connected.

Research on Bandura's concept began by focusing on changes associated with therapy and quickly expanded to examine a wide range of other topics (Bandura, 1986, 1997). Here are some examples: Brown and Inouye (1978) found that people with high self-efficacy were more persistent on problems than people with lower efficacy perceptions. Wood and Bandura (1989) found that self-efficacy influenced how business students performed in a management task. Manning and Wright (1983) found that efficacy perceptions predicted the ability to control pain during childbirth (see also Litt, 1988). Cozzarelli (1993) found that efficacy perceptions predicted adjustment to the experience of abortion. Bauer and Bonano (2001) found that efficacy perceptions predicted less grief over time among persons adapting to bereavement. Efficacy expectancies have also been shown to predict whether drug users stay clean during the year after treatment (Ilgen, McKellar, & Tiet, 2005). There's even evidence that acquiring a sense of efficacy can have a positive influence on immune function (Wiedenfeld, O'Leary, Bandura, Brown, Levine, & Raska, 1990).

Beyond these direct associations, perceptions of efficacy may underlie the positive effects found for other variables. For example, efficacy perceptions may be a pathway by which social support gives people a sense of well-being (Major et al., 1990). There's also evidence that self-esteem and optimism operate through perceptions of efficacy (Major, Richards, Cooper, Cozzarelli, & Zubek, 1998).

Observational Learning

As we said earlier, many aspects of social learning theory can be viewed as elaborations on the concepts of classical and instrumental conditioning. There is, however, at least one part of social learning theory that leaves the conditioning concepts behind, suggesting a completely different basis for learning. This part is called **observational learning.** Two people are involved in this process, providing yet another basis for the term *social learning theory*.

Observational learning takes place when one person performs an action and another person observes the act and thereby acquires the ability to repeat it (Bandura, 1986; Flanders, 1968). For such an event to represent observational learning unambiguously, the behavior should be one the observer doesn't already know. At a minimum, the behavior should be one the observer hadn't previously associated with the context in which it's now occurring.

Observational learning allows people to pack huge amounts of information into their minds quickly. This makes it very important. Observational learning occurs as early as the first year of life (Meltzoff, 1985). What's most remarkable about it is how simple it is. It seems to require little more than the observer's noticing and understanding what's going on.

This last statement requires several qualifications, which help to give a better sense of what observational learning is (see Table 13.1). First, observational learning requires the observer to *pay attention* to the model (the person being observed). If attention isn't given to the right aspect of the model's behavior, the behavior won't be encoded well enough to be remembered.

This principle has several implications. For one, it means that observational learning will be better with some models than others. Models that draw attention for some reason—from their power or attractiveness—are most likely to be effective. The role of attention also means that some *acts* are more likely to be encoded than others. Acts that are especially noticeable have more impact than acts that aren't (cf. McArthur, 1981; Taylor & Fiske, 1978). Other variables that matter here are the observer's capabilities, intentions, and concentration. For instance, if an observer is distracted by music while viewing a model, he may miss entirely what she's doing.

A second important set of processes in observational learning concern *retention* of what's observed. In one way or another, what's been observed has to be represented in memory (which makes this a cognitive as well as a social sort of learning).

Two strategies of coding predominate. One is *imaginal coding,* or creating a mental picture of what you're seeing. The other is *verbal coding,* or creating a description to

Table 13.1 Four Categories of Variables (and specific examples of each) That Influence Observational Learning and Performance. *Source:* Adapted from Bandura, 1977a, 1986.

Attention for Encoding	Characteristics of the model:
	    Is the model attractive or powerful or an expert?
	Characteristics of the behavior:
	    Is the behavior distinctive, clear, and simple?
	Characteristics of the observer:
	    Is the observer motivated to attend and capable of attending?

Retention	Use of imagery as an encoding strategy Use of language as an encoding strategy Use of mental rehearsal to keep in memory
Production	Observer's capacity to produce necessary responses Observer's prior experience with overall behavior Observer's prior experience with components of behavior

Performance	Consequences to the model:
	    Is the model rewarded or punished, or are there no consequences?
	Consequences to the observer:
	    Is the observer rewarded or punished, or are there no
	    consequences?

yourself of what you're seeing. Either strategy can produce a memory that can later be used to repeat the behavior (Bandura & Jeffery, 1973; Bandura, Jeffery, & Bachicha, 1974; Gerst, 1971). Mental rehearsal (repeating the mental picture or description) also helps retention (Jeffery, 1976).

Once an action's in memory, one more thing is needed for the act to occur. Specifically, you have to translate what you observed into a form you can *produce* in your own actions. How successful you are depends partly on whether you already know some of the components of the act. It's easier to reproduce a behavior if you have the skills that underlie it or know some of the action involved in it. That's why it's often so easy for experienced athletes to pick up a new sport. They often already know movements similar to those used in the new sport.

The importance of having components available also applies to the encoding process (see W. Johnson & Kieras, 1983). For example, if you already know names (or have good images) for components of the modeled activity, you have to put less into memory. If you have to remember every little thing, it gets harder to keep straight. Think of the difference in complexity between the label *Sauté one onion* (or *Remove the brake pad assembly*) and the set of physical acts the label refers to. Now think about how much easier it is to remember the label than the sequence of acts. Using the label as mental shorthand simplifies the task for memory. But you can do this only if you know what the label refers to (see the cartoon).

SHOE by Jeff MacNelly

Having readily available summary labels for action sequences greatly simplified the task of storing things in memory. *Reprinted by permission: Tribune Media Services.*

ACQUISITION VERSUS PERFORMANCE

Observational learning permits fast learning of complicated behaviors. Given what we've just discussed, it also seems to be a case of "the more you already know, the easier it is to learn." An important distinction needs to be made, however, between the *acquisition* of a behavioral potential and the *performance* of the behavior. People don't always repeat the actions they see. In fact, people learn a great deal of actions that they never do.

To know whether observational learning will result in behavior, we need to know something else. We need to know what reinforcement or punishment the person expects the behavior to lead to (Bandura, 1977a, 1986). A good illustration of the distinction between acquisition and performance comes from an early study of children by Bandura (1965). Children saw a five-minute film in which an adult model performed a series of distinctive aggressive acts toward an inflated doll. The model accompanied each act with verbalizations, each associated with one aggressive behavior. For example, as he pounded the doll on the head with a mallet, he said, "Sockeroo—stay down."

At this point, three experimental conditions were created using three versions of the film. In one condition, another adult entered the picture, praised the model as a "strong champion," and said his excellent performance deserved a special treat. He then gave the model some candy, making it clear that it and the social approval were both consequences of the aggressive acts. In a second condition (the no-consequence control group), this final scene was simply omitted. In a third condition, this scene was replaced by one in which the second adult came in and punished the model for the aggressive actions. In this condition, the model was called a "big bully" and was spanked by the other person, who made it clear that the punishment resulted from the aggressive acts.

After seeing one of these three films, each child in the study was taken to an observation room that held a wide range of toys. Among the toys was an inflated doll identical to the one in the film. The child was left alone for 10 minutes. Hidden assistants noted whether the child did any of the previously modeled aggressive acts. The number of acts the child did was the measure of spontaneous *performance*.

Ten minutes later, the experimenter returned. At this point, the child was offered an incentive (fruit juice and picture stickers) to show the experimenter as many of the previously viewed aggressive acts as the child could remember. The number of behaviors correctly shown was the measure of *acquisition*.

The results of this study are very instructive. The top line in Figure 13.3 shows how many acts children

Many complex behaviors are acquired by children through observational learning.

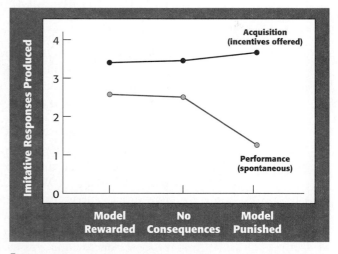

FIGURE 13.3

Acquisition and performance. Participants observed a model display a series of aggressive acts that led to reward, no consequences, or punishment. Participants then had an opportunity to imitate the model spontaneously (performance). Finally, they were asked to demonstrate what they could remember of the model's behavior (acquisition). The study showed that reinforcement of the model played no role in acquisition but did influence spontaneous performance. *Source: Adapted from Bandura & Walters, 1963.*

reproduced correctly in the three experimental conditions, when given an incentive to do so (the measure of acquisition). It's obvious there isn't a trace of difference in acquisition. Reinforcement or punishment for the model had no impact here.

Spontaneous performance, though, shows a different picture. The outcome for the model influenced what the observers did spontaneously. As in many studies (Thelen & Rennie, 1972), the effect of punishment was greater than the effect of reward, although other evidence shows that both can be effective in this sort of situation (e.g., Kanfer & Marston, 1963; Liebert & Fernandez, 1970; Rosekrans, 1967).

In conclusion, vicarious reinforcement influences whether people spontaneously do behaviors they've acquired by observation. This effect is the same as in any instance of vicarious reinforcement. It thus reflects vicarious instrumental learning. In contrast, reinforcement to the model has no influence on acquisition of the behavioral potential. Thus, observational learning and instrumental learning are distinct processes.

Observational learning is a powerful process in human learning (and in the learning of some other animals; Zentall, Sutton, & Sherburne, 1996). Its power and its value to personality development lie in the fact that it allows huge amounts of information to be added to a person's behavioral repertoire quickly. It's much faster than shaping through instrumental conditioning or even vicarious instrumental conditioning. On the other hand, observational learning doesn't determine which acts occur in which situations (motivational and reinforcement variables seem to do that). Rather, it's a way for behavior potentials to be acquired for use. To paraphrase Bandura (1977a), once the ability to engage in observational learning emerges (in infancy), it's virtually impossible to prevent people from learning what they see.

Manifestations of Cognitive and Social Learning

The processes described thus far provide a set of tools for analyzing behavior. To indicate how broadly they can be used, the next sections describe two areas in which the processes play central roles (see also Box 13.4). The various processes get tangled up with one another in both areas. Nevertheless, they can be distinguished conceptually, and we'll do so as we go along.

MODELING AND SEX-ROLE ACQUISITION

Sex roles are behavior patterns that people in a given culture see as more appropriate in one sex than the other (cf. Bussey & Bandura, 1999; Deaux & Lewis, 1984; Eagly, 1987; Eagly & Wood, 1999). As with all roles, sex roles are expectations about how to act. American society has a fairly stereotyped set of sex roles, though their content is always evolving somewhat.

Children learn about sex roles early in life. This knowledge is acquired by several processes discussed in this chapter. Some information comes from explicitly stated rules ("Little girls don't play tackle football" or "Little boys don't wear dresses"). Observational learning also plays a role (Sears, Rau, & Alpert, 1965). Sons who watch their fathers shaving and working with wrenches encode how to do those things. Daughters who watch their mothers do housework and cook encode how to do those things.

But wait a minute. Don't children watch both parents? Shouldn't boys and girls learn the same things by observational learning? Yes and no. Certainly, both boys and girls do encode a lot of information about activities of both sexes. But there's some

BOX 13.4 MODELING AND DELAY OF GRATIFICATION

Social–cognitive learning theories emphasize that people's acts are determined by cognitions about potential outcomes of their behavior (Kirsch, 1985). This emphasis returns us to the concept of **self-control,** the idea that people sometimes restrain their own actions.

Self-control is an idea we considered at length in Chapter 10. As noted there, people often face the choice of getting a desired outcome immediately or getting a better outcome later on. The latter choice—delay of gratification—isn't all that easy to make. Imagine that after saving for four months, you have enough money to go to an oceanside resort for two weeks. You know that if you saved for another 10 months, you could take the trip to Europe you've always wanted. One event is closer in time. The other is better, but getting it requires more

self-control. Ten more months with no vacation is a long time.

As we noted earlier, many variables influence people's ability to delay. Especially relevant to this chapter is the role played by *modeling* (Mischel, 1974). Consider a study by Bandura and Mischel (1965) of fourth- and fifth-graders who (according to a pretest) preferred either immediate or delayed reward. Children of each preference were put into one of three conditions. In one, the child saw an adult model make a series of choices between desirable items that had to be delayed and less desirable ones that could be had immediately. The model consistently chose the opposite of the child's preference. Children in the second condition read about the model's choices. In the third condition (a control group), there was no modeling.

All the children were given a series of delay-of-gratification choices just afterward and again a month later. Seeing a model who chose immediate rewards

made delay-preferring children more likely to choose immediate reward. In the same manner, seeing a model who chose delayed rewards made immediate-preferring children more likely to delay. These effects were maintained a month later. Similar effects were shown among 18- to 20-year-old prison inmates who'd had only weak tendencies to delay gratification before being exposed to models showing strong preference for delay (Stumphauzer, 1972).

How do models exert this influence on self-control? Presumably through vicarious reinforcement. In the Bandura and Mischel (1965) study, for example, the model vocalized reasons for preferring one choice over the other. The statements imply that the model felt reinforced by his choices (see also Bandura, Grusec, & Menlove, 1967; Mischel & Liebert, 1966; Parke, 1969). Thus, people obtain information from seeing how others react to experiences and use that information to guide their own actions.

---

evidence that a discrimination is made even in encoding. Why? There's evidence that children prefer and identify more with same-sex adults (Maccoby & Wilson, 1957; Mischel, 1970; Stevenson, Hale, Hill, & Moely, 1967). People also presumably attend more to models they like than to models they don't like, which means more encoding.

A far greater contributor to sex-role behavior, however, is the subtle web of social reinforcement, both direct and vicarious. Children are rewarded for attending to, and acting like, adults and children of their own sex. Little Tommy gets more approval when watching Daddy change the oil in the car than when watching Mommy put on her makeup. Little Suzy is treated the opposite way. Given these patterns of reinforcement, Tommy and Suzy spend more time watching the activities of one adult than the other. They also probably see those activities differently in terms of relevance to themselves.

Even if they prefer models of their own sex, children undoubtedly learn a lot of opposite sex-role behavior. But remember the acquisition–performance distinction. At an early age, children see which actions are gender appropriate and spontaneously perform mostly those appropriate to their gender (Bussey & Bandura, 1984). Why? They've been led to anticipate certain reward and punishment contingencies (Fagot, 1977; Raskin & Israel, 1981). Suzy may be praised and cuddled after putting on makeup, but Tommy won't (nor will the message be lost on Mikey, if he happens to be observing).

There's one question about gender roles that's been debated, even argued over: Why is the content of the roles what it is? The evolutionary view (discussed in Chapter 6) gave one answer. Another answer is that the qualities of the roles depend on cultural contexts. Wood and Eagly (2002) summarized evidence that where cultures differ in pressures, the nature of gender roles also differs across cultures.

Though live models are important in the acquisition of sex roles (and other behavior), in the modern world, **symbolic models** are also important. Indeed, their influence is pervasive. Symbolic models are figures on TV, in movies, magazines, books, and so on. The actions they portray—and the patterns of reinforcement around those actions—can have a big impact on both acquisition and performance of observers. If TV portrays women as weak and silly, then observers learn that weakness is feminine behavior. If TV portrays men as hiding their emotions, then observers learn that masculinity means not showing feelings.

In the social learning view, there's nothing magic about what behaviors define sex roles. Indeed, this point of view would see all roles as a little arbitrary. Given that there's something of value in each sex role, many wonder whether there may be virtue in encouraging people to have the positive qualities of both roles. Having both so-called masculine qualities (e.g., assertiveness) and feminine qualities (e.g., gentleness, sympathy) has been called **androgyny** (S. L. Bem, 1974, 1975; Kaplan & Bean, 1976; Kaplan & Sedney, 1980). It's been suggested that such diversity makes people more adaptable and flexible (Taylor & Hall, 1982).

MODELING OF AGGRESSION AND THE ISSUE OF MEDIA VIOLENCE

Another topic to which social–cognitive learning theories have been applied is symbolic models in aggression. This topic is particularly sensitive, given the level of violence in TV programs and movies. All the ways models influence observers are implicated here, to one degree or another (C. A. Anderson et al., 2003). At least three processes have been proposed, and there is a lot of support for all of them.

First, people who observe innovative aggressive techniques (live or on film) can and do acquire the techniques as behavior potentials by observational learning. That is, observational learning *does* occur wherever it *can* occur (Geen, 1998; Heller & Polsky, 1975). This principle looms large as producers strive to make movies seem new and different every year. A common source of novelty is new methods for inflicting pain on others.

Second, observing violence that is permitted, condoned, or even rewarded helps promote the belief that aggression is an appropriate way to deal with conflict or disagreement. Vicarious reinforcement thus increases the likelihood that viewers will use such tactics themselves. (By implication, this is also why some people worry about the level of sex on TV and in movies.)

When it's suggested that violence is reinforced in the media, a common reply is that the "bad guys" in TV and movie stories get punished. Note two things, though. First, the punishment usually comes late in the story, after aggression has produced a lot of short-term reinforcement. As a result, aggression is linked more closely to reinforcement than to punishment. Second, the actions of the heroes usually are also aggressive, and these actions are highly reinforced. From that, there's a clear message that aggression is a good way to deal with problems.

Does viewing "acceptable" aggression make people more likely to use aggression in their own lives when they're annoyed? The overwhelming majority of the evidence says yes. Whether the model is live (e.g., Baron & Kempner, 1970) or symbolic (e.g., Bandura, 1965; Liebert & Baron, 1972), exposure to aggressive models increases the aggression of observers.

The final point to be made here is more diffuse. It's that repeated exposure to violence *desensitizes* observers to human suffering. The shock and upset that most people would associate with acts of extreme violence are extinguished by repeated exposure to violence. The police chief of Washington, DC, was quoted in 1991 as saying, "When I talk to young people involved with violence, there's no remorse, . . . no sense that this is morally wrong." Exposure to violence in video games can produce a similar desensitizing effect (Bartholow, Sestir, & Davis, 2005).

Evidence of desensitization comes from several sources (e.g., Cline, Croft, & Courrier, 1973; Geen, 1981; Thomas, Horton, Lippincott, & Drabman, 1977). The results of one study are shown in Figure 13.4 (Thomas et al., 1977, Experiment 1). Participants were attached to a machine that measured emotional reactions as "bumps" of arousal. They first watched a videotape of either an exciting volleyball championship or a violent program. As can be seen in Figure 13.4, A, the tapes (overall) were equally arousing. Later, participants briefly viewed what they thought was a real confrontation resulting in physical violence. As Figure 13.4, B, shows, those who'd seen the violent TV show reacted less to this than did the other group. Watching the TV violence apparently made them less sensitive to real-life violence.

This process has long-term consequences that are profoundly worrisome. As people's emotional reactions to violence become extinguished, being victimized (and also victimizing others) is seen as an ordinary part of life. It's hard to study the impact of this process in its full scope. The effects are pervasive enough, however, that they represent a real threat to society.

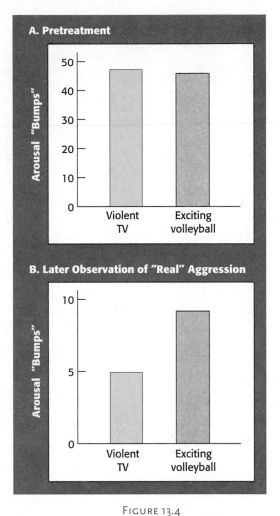

FIGURE 13.4
Habituation to aggression by viewing aggression. (A) Participants watched a videotape of either an exciting volleyball championship or a violent TV program, which were equally arousing (as measured by arousal bumps). (B) When seeing an apparently real confrontation that resulted in physical violence, participants who had watched the violent TV reacted less to this aggression than did the other group. Presumably watching the TV violence made them less sensitive to later real-life violence. *Source: Adapted from Thomas, Horton, Lippincott, & Drabman, 1977, Experiment 1.*

Assessment

Let's turn now to assessment. This section addresses the social–cognitive learning view on assessment in very general terms. The goal is to make explicit some of the logical threads that underlie it.

Three issues are important. The first is that self-report devices are widely used to assess personality from this view, as opposed to behavioral observation. Recall that the cognitive view of learning emphasizes the role of thoughts in behavior. Given that, it's only natural to take people's reports of their tendencies to act in various ways and to experience various kinds of thoughts and feelings as being appropriate and useful sources of information.

The second issue concerns what variables are measured. Given the assumption that cognitive processes influence behavior, assessment from this view tends to focus on *experiential* variables. That is, instead of charting actions, assessments frequently ask people how they feel in certain situations or what kinds of thoughts go through their minds in those situations (see Table 13.2). Particularly important are people's

Table 13.2 Assessing People's Psychological Experiences in Difficult Exam Situations. The first set of items (answered on scales ranging from "Strong agreement" to "Strong disagreement" examines emotional reactions to the exam; the second set examines cognitions that can interfere with test performance. *Source:* Items from Morris, Davis, & Hutchings, 1981. Copyright 1981 by the American Psychological Association. Adapted by permission of the author.

Emotionality	I feel my heart beating fast.
	I am so tense that my stomach is upset.
	I have an uneasy, upset feeling.
	I am nervous.
	I feel panicky.
Worry	I feel regretful.
	I am afraid that I should have studied more for this test.
	I feel that others will be disappointed in me.
	I feel I may not do as well on this test as I could.
	I do not feel very confident about my performance on this test.

expectancies: expectancies of control, expectancies of coping, and expectancies of personal efficacy. This emphasis should be no surprise, because expectations are regarded as so important in this view of behavior.

A third issue is also implicit in the last paragraph. Assessment in the social–cognitive learning view tends to emphasize responses to *specific* categories of situations. This emphasis actually applies throughout the learning perspective on personality. It reflects the fact that behavior can vary greatly from one situation to another. The social–cognitive learning view differs from the conditioning view, however, in its emphasis on *personal views* of situations, rather than *objective definitions* of situations (e.g., Mischel, 1973). One person sees a philosophy class as a chance to learn something new; another person sees the same class as a threat to his grade-point average. This approach says it's people's representations that determine how they act. This must be taken into account in assessment.

Problems in Behavior, and Behavior Change

Let's now turn to problems in behavior from the social–cognitive learning view and some of the treatment procedures that derive from this view. Again, the discussion combines concepts from conditioning theories with concepts that are more cognitive and social in nature.

CONCEPTUALIZING BEHAVIORAL PROBLEMS

As noted in Chapter 12, principles of conditioning suggest that inappropriate emotions such as fear result from classical conditioning. Similarly, inappropriate behavioral tendencies result from reinforcement patterns. The social–cognitive learning approach suggests further contributors, using three key principles: vicarious conditioning, expectancies, and observational learning.

Thinking about vicarious processes suggests two changes to earlier analyses. First, you don't have to have direct experience with a stimulus to develop an emotional response (such as fear) toward it. You can acquire emotional responses vicariously. Second, your patterns of action can be influenced by watching outcomes that other people experience. Vicarious reinforcement can build in a behavior, even if the behavior isn't desirable. Vicarious punishment can reduce your tendency to do a behavior, even if the behavior is actually adaptive.

All these effects may be viewed as mediated in part by expectancies (see Bandura, 1986). If you *expect* to experience strong fear in high places, you'll avoid high places. If you *expect* to get social approval for bullying someone else, you may do it. If you *expect* to be rejected by someone, or to do badly on an exam, or even to do badly at "life" (Scheier & Carver, 1992), you may not try. These expectations can develop from direct experience, from vicarious experience, from things that other people tell you, or from putting two and two together in your own head.

No matter how expectations are acquired, they can have powerful effects on your actions and feelings. Negative expectations can cause you to stop trying, thereby making success impossible. The conviction that success won't come leads to a pattern of low motivation and reduced effort that's sometimes called **learned helplessness** (see Box 13.5).

A final source of behavior problems, in the social learning view, is more specific. Problems sometimes reflect **skill deficits**. A person with a skill deficit is literally unable to do something that's necessary or desirable. Some skill deficits reflect deficits in observational learning. That is, in some cases, people never had good models to learn from. Without being able to learn how to do important things (such as cooking, taking notes in class, dancing, and many others), people can have gaps in the ability to function.

Note that having a skill deficit can influence the development of expectations. People who know they lack particular skills come to anticipate bad outcomes when the skills are relevant. (For example, people who see themselves as lacking social skills come to expect the worst in social situations.) People who do have the relevant skills may come to view the situations as being under their personal control (Lefcourt et al., 1985).

MODELING-BASED THERAPY FOR SKILL DEFICITS

It will be no surprise to discover that *modeling* plays an important role in the therapy techniques identified with the social–cognitive learning viewpoint. Techniques involving modeling have been used in two areas: skill deficits and emotion-based problems.

When people lack specific types of adaptive behaviors, they can often add the skills by observing good models. The model is put in the situation for which the skill is lacking and makes an action appropriate to the situation. The observer (the person in therapy) is then encouraged to repeat the action. This repetition can be overt (action), or it can be covert (mentally practicing the action). Indeed, the modeling can also be covert, with the subject being told to imagine someone else doing a particular behavior within a particular scenario (Kazdin, 1975).

In principle, modeling can be used to supply missing skills any place there are deficits. Research on this subject, however, commonly focuses on such areas as basic social skills (e.g., La Greca & Santogrossi, 1980; La Greca, Stone, & Bell, 1983; Ross, Ross, & Evans, 1971) and assertiveness (Goldfried & Davison, 1976; Kazdin, 1974, 1975; McFall & Twentyman, 1973; Rosenthal & Reese, 1976). *Assertiveness* is acting to make sure your rights aren't violated while also not violating someone else's rights. It can be hard to know just how to respond to a problem situation in a manner that's

BOX 13.5 HELPLESSNESS: CASE STUDY OF A THEORY

The concept of learned helplessness originated in the finding that exposure to painful and unavoidable shocks made it harder for dogs to learn an avoidance or escape response when that response became possible (Overmier & Seligman, 1967; Seligman & Maier, 1967). This finding led to a flood of research on humans. The typical procedure looks at effects of prolonged failure on later performances. Extensive failure often has an adverse—sometimes devastating—impact on later performance (e.g., Hiroto & Seligman, 1975; I. W. Miller & Norman, 1979; Roth, 1980). This has implications for analyzing problems such as depression (Abramson, Metalsky, & Alloy, 1989; Abramson, Seligman, & Teasdale, 1978).

The evolution of theories of helplessness makes an interesting case study. It's particularly interesting when taken in combination with the issue discussed in Box 13.2—the relationship between conditioning and social–cognitive learning theories. The first explanation for the effect was based, somewhat loosely, on conditioning principles. Exposure to unavoidable shock results in learning that an outcome (removal of pain) isn't contingent on behavior (avoidance effort). The result is a reduction in effort, to the point where the animal no longer tries at all.

Indeed, the term *learned helplessness* was coined because the animal looked as though it had learned it was helpless to avoid the shocks. In conditioning terms, the pretreatment extinguished the attempt to escape. Thus, the animal doesn't do any escape behavior when it actually would work.

As analogous research was done on people, however, the theory became progressively more cognitive. Explanations of helplessness in humans typically rely on expectations of future noncontingency (Abramson et al., 1978) or expectations of being unable to control outcomes (Wortman & Brehm, 1975). In simple terms, the person develops (temporarily) the idea that good outcomes can't be obtained because they're not related to his or her actions.

More recent analyses of helplessness have included additional cognitive processes. Several analyses have emphasized attributional variables as a way of discussing how the expectation of bad outcomes develops (Abramson et al., 1978; I. W. Miller & Norman, 1979; Roth, 1980). Vicarious and verbal–symbolic processes also appear to play an important role here. For example, watching someone else experience noncontingency (particularly someone you think has the same ability as you) can produce behavioral impairments in you (Brown & Inouye, 1978; DeVellis, DeVellis, & McCauley,

1978). These various effects appear to indicate that the *cognition* of uncontrollability is critical to helplessness, rather than actual uncontrollability.

As if these weren't cognitive enough, another approach added yet another layer of thought processes. This approach (Frankel & Snyder, 1978; M. L. Snyder, Stephan, & Rosenfield, 1978) holds that people do poorly after prolonged failure because the failure threatens their self-esteem. That is, rather than risk further confirmation that they can't do the task, they stop trying. The withdrawal of effort creates a face-saving attribution while at the same time (ironically) causing the poor outcome they'd been afraid of in the first place (Frankel & Snyder, 1978).

Thus, a phenomenon identified in the animal conditioning lab was extended to human behavior. In doing this, however, theorists who pursued the phenomenon have increasingly invoked cognitive processes as a way of accounting for it. Doing so raises several questions: Do the same processes apply to human helplessness as apply to helplessness in other species? One probably wouldn't want to argue that dogs stop trying to escape because they're concerned about their self-esteem. But what about the other processes—expectancies and attributions? At the moment, there's no clear answer to this question.

---

properly assertive. But observing a model who illustrates appropriate responses (combined with a little practice, to make sure you can do the same thing) can make a big difference.

In therapies dealing with skill deficits, observational learning is often intermingled with vicarious reinforcement. There are cases, though, in which one or the other seems most relevant. In some cases, people literally don't know what to do in a given situation. Observational learning is most relevant here, because it provides new responses. In other cases, it's not so much that people don't know what to do, but that they have doubts about whether doing it will work. In these cases, vicarious reinforcement seems to play a larger role.

MODELING AND RESPONSES TO FEAR

In discussing modeling and fear-related behavior problems, a distinction is made between two kinds of models: those who exhibit mastery and those who exhibit coping (e.g., Meichenbaum, 1971). A **mastery model** seems to be completely without fear regarding what the person in therapy fears. This model presumably creates vicarious extinction of the conditioned fear, as the observer sees that the model experiences no distress.

In contrast, a **coping model** is one who initially displays fear, but overcomes the fear and eventually handles the situation. The effect of this model presumably depends on the fact that the model is in the *same situation* as the observer but is (noticeably) able to overcome the fear by active effort. This effect seems more cognitive than that of the mastery model. Although the evidence isn't entirely consistent, coping models seem more effective than mastery models in therapy for reducing fears (Kornhaber & Schroeder, 1975; Meichenbaum, 1971). This effectiveness attests to the powerful role that cognitive processes can play in coping with fear.

Seeing someone else cope successfully with something that you fear can help you develop the ability to cope successfully yourself.

Another distinction to be made here is between modeling in which the observer just observes and **participant modeling,** in which the model (often the therapist) performs the behavior in front of the other person, who then repeats it. Participant modeling usually involves a lot of verbalization, instruction, and personalized assurance from the model. It takes more of the therapist's time, but it's more powerful as a behavior change technique (e.g., Bandura, 1982a; Bandura, Adams, & Beyer, 1977).

In a typical case of modeling therapy for a specific fear, a model approaches, engages, and deals with the feared stimulus. While doing so, the model describes the feelings that develop and the mental strategies that are being used to cope. Then the observer tries to do the same thing—first with the therapist's help and then alone. This procedure is effective at reducing fears and increasing coping in a variety of domains. These include fears aroused by animals such as dogs and snakes (Bandura et al., 1977; Bandura, Grusec, & Menlove, 1967; Bandura & Menlove, 1968); by surgery, injections, and dental work (Melamed & Siegel, 1975; Melamed, Weinstein, Hawes, & Katin-Borland, 1975; Vernon, 1974); and by test taking (Cooley & Spiegler, 1980; Malec, Park, & Watkins, 1976; Sarason, 1975).

THERAPEUTIC CHANGES IN EFFICACY EXPECTANCY

The research just outlined indicates that models who display an ability to cope with difficulties can help people to overcome their own fears. But how does it happen? Bandura (1977b) says these effects illustrate a broader principle behind behavior change. He says that when therapy is effective (through whatever technique), it works by increasing the person's sense of efficacy for a given class of situations. In his view, when a model shows an ability to overcome a fear, it helps give observers a sense that they can also overcome their fears. This enhanced perception of personal efficacy, then, results in greater effort and persistence.

A. Approach Behavior

Participant modeling
Modeling only
No treatment

Percent of Desired Performance

100
90
80
70
60
50
40
30
0

Before
treatment

Posttest

B. Efficacy Judgments

Percent of Desired Performance

100
90
80
70
60
50
40
30
0

Before
treatment

Before
posttest

After
posttest

After treatment

FIGURE 13.5
(A) Level of approach toward a feared stimulus and (B) self-efficacy judgments. Both behavior and efficacy perceptions were assessed before therapy (left side of each panel) and afterward (right side of each panel). Efficacy perceptions were assessed both before and immediately after the behavioral posttest.
Source: Adapted from Bandura, Adams, & Beyer, 1977.

These ideas, which were introduced earlier in the chapter, have been tested in many studies of the therapy process (e.g., Avia & Kanfer, 1980; Bandura et al., 1977; Bandura, Adams, Hardy, & Howells, 1980; Bandura & Schunk, 1981; DiClemente, 1981; Gauthier & Ladouceur, 1981). As an illustration, consider an early experiment by Bandura et al. (1977), in which people with an intense fear of snakes received one of three treatments. In a participant-modeling condition, they saw a therapist perform a series of increasingly scary actions with a live snake. Then, with the therapist's assistance, they tried the same actions. In a modeling-only condition, participants saw a model but didn't practice the activities. Those in a control condition had no therapy at all.

Participants were tested both before and after therapy on a behavioral avoidance test. This required trying a range of actions with the snake without assistance. Participants also rated their expectations for being able to perform each of the acts in the avoidance test. They made these ratings at three times: after the behavioral pretest and both before and after the behavioral posttest. This self-report constituted a measure of perceived self-efficacy.

Figure 13.5, A, shows that participant modeling had a better impact on behavior than did modeling without practice, which had a better impact than no treatment. These differences in behavior were paralleled by differences in efficacy statements (see Figure 13.5, B). Moreover, both approach outcomes generalized (particularly for the participant-modeling group) to a snake that looked distinctly different from the snake used during treatment.

In Bandura's view, results such as these make several points (Bandura, 1986, 1997). The broadest is that change in efficacy expectancy can mediate behavior change. That is, the behavior changes *because* of a change in the expectancy. Two other points concern factors that determine efficacy perceptions. Notice that the expectancy ratings in this study changed most among people who had an opportunity to show themselves that they could cope (the participant-modeling group). This fits with Bandura's belief that *performance accomplishments* are the strongest influence on efficacy perceptions.

The study also demonstrates a second influence on efficacy perceptions, however: *vicarious experiences*. That is, the modeling-only group outperformed the control group and also reported greater efficacy. Vicarious consequences don't have as strong an impact as personal outcomes, but they definitely play a role. Bandura (1977b) also holds that *verbal persuasion* and *emotional arousal* can influence efficacy perceptions.

Although Bandura's view is very influential, it's also had some criticism. (Commentaries, both pro and con, can be found in Rachman [1978].) Most of the discussion bears on whether efficacy perceptions are causes or consequences of behavior, but there are also other issues. For example, increasing efficacy perceptions is not useful for everyone. Some prefer to place responsibility for changing their behavior elsewhere (Burger, 1989; Chambliss & Murray, 1979). This leads to the question of which is critical: perceptions of personal efficacy, or expectations that desired out-comes will occur (Carver & Scheier, 1986, 1998).

SELF-INSTRUCTIONS AND COGNITIVE–BEHAVIORAL MODIFICATION

One last approach to therapy we'll note here is called **cognitive–behavioral modification** (Meichenbaum, 1971, 1972, 1977; Meichenbaum & Goodman, 1971). This approach assumes that problems stem from ineffective and disruptive cognitions that slip into people's minds. People often tell themselves that problems are bigger or less resolvable than they really are—or even that they can't cope. The expectation of a bad outcome causes them not to try. The goal of cognitive–behavioral therapies is to get the person to recognize cases of maladaptive thinking and make suitable adjustments.

This process involves teaching the person to identify stimuli that bring out negative cognitions. Then the therapist and client develop substitute cognitions designed to be adaptive (see Table 13.3). These cognitions emphasize three strategies: (1) break the problem situation into concrete components, each of which can be mastered by itself; (2) acknowledge that problem emotions (e.g., anxiety or anger) may exist, but be determined not to let them overwhelm you; and (3) redirect yourself to the actions that have to be done to manage the situation effectively, instead of worrying about how well you'll do.

One more set of self-statements is used after the coping attempt is done. These statements emphasize that progress is incremental: If you didn't do as well as you hoped this time, you'll do better next time. This sort of self-statement helps prevent people from becoming discouraged (from developing negative expectations). Once these mental statements are laid out and learned, the person practices using them when confronting the problem that's being dealt with.

Cognitive–behavioral therapies often focus on specific problems, such as test anxiety (Meichenbaum, 1972), anger (Novaco, 1978), physical pain (Turk, 1978), and

---

Table 13.3 Examples of Coping Statements Used in Cognitive Therapy. The purpose of the therapy is to train people to engage in effective self-instructions such as these, rather than fill their minds with negative thoughts when engaged in a stressful or fear-inducing activity. *Source:* From Meichenbaum, 1974.

Preparing for the Stressor
What exactly do you have to do?
You can develop a plan to deal with it.
Don't worry—worry won't help anything.
No negative self-statements—just think rationally.

Confronting and Coping with the Stressor
One step at a time—you can handle the situation.
This anxiety is what the doctor said you would feel. It's a reminder to use your coping exercises.
Don't try to eliminate fear totally—just keep it manageable.
When fear comes, just pause.
Keep the focus on the present—what is it you have to do?

After the Coping Attempt
It's getting better each time you use the procedures.
You can be pleased with the progress you're making.

---

children's impulsiveness (Meichenbaum & Goodman, 1971). It should be obvious, though, that it's easy to generalize to other kinds of stressful experiences. For example, one study found that teaching coping skills to handle test anxiety resulted in lowered anxiety, improved academic performance, and higher levels of a generalized sense of self-efficacy (R. E. Smith, 1989). The term **stress inoculation** is sometimes used to refer to the process of training people to use these techniques not just for one problem but for a broad range of stressful events (Meichenbaum, 1985).

Social-Cognitive Learning Theories: Problems and Prospects

The social–cognitive learning view on personality has been influential in personality psychology over a period of several decades. Some of the reasons for its influence are the same as those noted earlier for the conditioning view. That is, the concepts of this approach have been tested extensively in research and have generally been supported. Similarly, cognitive–behavioral therapy techniques have been shown to be very effective for many kinds of problems.

The social–cognitive learning approach also gains extra benefits from having addressed problems confronted by the conditioning approach. A criticism of the conditioning approach mentioned in Chapter 12 is that research on conditioning usually involves drastically simplified laboratory situations. This criticism is far less applicable to the social–cognitive learning approach. People working from it have examined behavior in very diverse settings and contexts.

Another criticism of the conditioning view is that it seems to have little place for the sense of *personhood,* the continuity and coherence that characterize the sense of self. This criticism is also less applicable to the social–cognitive learning theories. Concepts such as the sense of personal efficacy have a great deal to do with that sense of personhood, even if the focus is on only a limited part of the person at any given time. The idea of evaluating oneself with respect to the attainment of desired incentives also evokes the sense of personhood.

A problem remaining for both learning viewpoints concerns the relationship between the two. The two approaches to learning that are described in Chapters 12 and 13 are split by a disagreement so fundamental that it's hard to know how a single perspective can be welded from the pieces. We minimized this issue while presenting the theoretical principles, but it deserves examination.

The problem is this: In explaining behavior, the conditioning approach restricts itself to events that are observable. Behavioral tendencies are explained from patterns of prior experiences and present cues. Nothing else is needed. If cognitions exist, they are irrelevant—foam on the stream of behavior, shaped by the same forces as shape behavior, but not important in causing behavior. The social–cognitive learning approach is in direct opposition to this view. Expectations cause behavior. Actions follow from thinking, rather than occur in parallel with thinking.

This latter characterization fits more with the introspections that most people have about their own lives. As noted earlier, however, treating cognitions as causes of behavior may mean rejecting some of the most fundamental tenets of the conditioning approach. In the more cognitive view, classical and instrumental conditioning aren't necessarily incremental processes occurring outside awareness; they depend on expectancies and mental models. Reinforcement is seen as providing information about future incentives, instead of acting directly to strengthen behavioral tendencies.

The emphasis on expectancies and other cognitions isn't the only area of conflict between approaches. Social–cognitive learning theorists agree with conditioning theorists that reinforcement is necessary to maintain behavior (despite holding a view of reinforcement that differs drastically from that of conditioning theorists). But sometimes a behavior occurs with no obvious reinforcer. In such a case, theorists may assert that the behavior is being supported by self-reinforcement. The appeal to self-reinforcement is far from satisfying, both to conditioning theorists and to people who stand outside the learning perspective. If self-reinforcement accounts for behavior *sometimes,* why not *all the time*? Why is external reinforcement *ever* necessary? How do you decide when it's needed and when it isn't?

One challenge for the evolution of the thinking of the social–cognitive learning theorists is to determine how—or whether—their ideas can be reconciled with the principles of conditioning. Are the newer theories extrapolations from the previous theories, or are they fundamentally different? Can they be merged, or are they competitors for the same theoretical niche? That is, some people would say the newer version of the learning perspective should simply *replace* the conditioning version—that the conditioning view was wrong, that human learning simply doesn't occur that way.

Some people have abandoned the effort at integration and simply stepped away from the issue altogether. For example, in recent years, Bandura has dropped the word *learning* from the phrase he uses to characterize his theory. He now calls it *social–cognitive theory* (Bandura, 1986). This raises the question of whether his current ideas (as opposed to his earlier ideas) should be seen as belonging to the learning perspective on personality at all.

Bandura's change of label reflects a more general trend among people who started out within the social learning framework. Many of these people have been influenced in the past 30 years by the ideas of cognitive psychology. Many people who used to call their orientation to personality a *social learning view* now would hedge. Some of them would now give their orientation a different label, one that would be more likely to include terms such as *cognitive* and *self-regulation*. There has been a gradual fraying of the edge of the social learning approach, which blends with the cognitive self-regulation theories. This overlap will become more apparent in later chapters.

This blurring and shifting between bodies of thought raises a final question for the social–cognitive learning approach: Will this approach retain its identity as an active area of work in the years to come, or will it disperse and have its themes absorbed by other viewpoints?

· SUMMARY ·

Dissatisfactions with the conditioning approach led to development of another generation of learning theories. They're called *cognitive* because they emphasize the role of thought processes in behavior, and *social* because they emphasize the idea that people often learn from one another. Several aspects of these theories can be thought of as *elaborations* on conditioning principles, although close examination of the elaborations raises questions about the validity of those conditioning principles.

These elaborations include an emphasis on the role of social reinforcement (rather than other sorts of reinforcement) in shaping behavior. Social reinforcers such as acceptance and approval can also be applied to oneself. Because humans have the capability for empathy (vicariously aroused emotions), we can experience classical conditioning vicariously. We can also experience reinforcement and punishment vicariously, causing shifts in action tendencies on the basis of someone else's outcomes. Functions such as *discrimination* and *generalization* are broadened in these theories to include such phenomena as semantic generalization. This view also holds that human learning is not always incremental. That is, we often learn rules and then apply them to new situations.

A fundamental principle that seems to underlie many aspects of human learning is that expectancies concerning upcoming events and outcomes play an important part in determining our responses. Specific theorists have also focused on two additional kinds of expectancy. Rotter holds that people who expect their outcomes to be determined by their actions (*internals*) learn from reinforcers but that people who expect their outcomes to be unrelated to their actions (*externals*) do not. Bandura holds that perceptions of personal efficacy or competence determine whether a person will persist when in stressful circumstances.

One portion of this approach to personality stands as completely distinct from conditioning principles: the process of acquiring behavior potentials through *observational learning*. This process requires only that an observer attend to a model (who is displaying a behavior), retain some memory of what was done (usually a visual or verbal memory), and have the component skills to be able to reproduce what was modeled. This process of acquisition is not directly influenced by reinforcement contingencies, although reinforcement can have an indirect effect by influencing how much attention is paid to the model. On the other hand, spontaneous performance of the acquired behavior is very much influenced by perceptions of reinforcement contingencies. It's easy to see the importance of the various processes of social–cognitive learning in many domains, including the acquisition of sex-role behavior, the tendency to be aggressive, and strategies that are used to delay gratification.

Personality assessment within this framework emphasizes the use of self-report devices. Many of these instruments are designed to measure subjective qualities such as feelings, cognitions, and expectancies (consistent with the emphasis placed on these qualities as determinants of behavior). There is also a growing emphasis on assessment within the context of the person's own definitions of situations.

Problems in behavior can develop through both vicarious and direct learning. Problems also result when people haven't had the opportunity to learn needed behaviors from models. Therapy techniques based on the social–cognitive learning approach often involve modeling procedures, whether as an attempt to remedy skill deficits through observational learning or as an attempt to show the utility of coping skills through vicarious reinforcement. Such techniques seem most effective when subjects overtly engage in the behaviors under the therapist's guidance, which led Bandura to suggest that improvement is mediated by a growing sense of efficacy. Other therapies emphasize the idea that people often hurt themselves by saying things to themselves that are negativistic. These therapies teach people to stop these negative self-statements and substitute self-statements that emphasize active, effective coping.

· GLOSSARY ·

Androgyny   The condition of having both masculine and feminine qualities.

Cognitive–behavioral modification   A therapeutic technique that attempts to change behaviors by changing thought patterns.

Coping model   A model that displays fear but ultimately handles it.

Efficacy expectancy   Confidence of being able to do something successfully.

Expectancy   Judgment about how likely a specific behavior is to attain a goal.

Incentive   The desirability of an outcome.

Learned helplessness   A state of low motivation and effort following extensive exposure to lack of control.

Locus of control   A dimension of believing that one's outcomes are caused by oneself or by external forces.

Mastery model   A model that displays no fear.

Observational learning   Acquiring the ability to do a new behavior by watching someone else do it.

Participant modeling   The act of practicing a behavior that's hard for oneself while using the therapist as model.

Self-control   The regulation and sometimes restraint of one's own activities.

Self-efficacy   Confidence of being able to do something successfully.

Self-reinforcement   The approval one gives to oneself for one's own behavior.

Semantic generalization   Generalization along a dimension of meaning.

Sex role   The behaviors associated more with members of one sex than the other.

Skill deficit   The absence or insufficiency of a needed behavior or skill.

Social reinforcer   Praise, liking, acceptance, or approval received from someone else.

Stress inoculation   A therapy to develop the ability to cope with a broad range of stressors.

Symbolic models   Models in print, movies, TV, and so on.

Vicarious classical conditioning   Conditioning in which the unconditioned response occurs via empathy.

Vicarious emotional arousal   The tendency to feel someone else's feelings along with them; also called *empathy*.

Vicarious reinforcement   An event in which a reinforcement experienced by someone else has a reinforcing effect on one's own behavior.

The Phenomenological Perspective

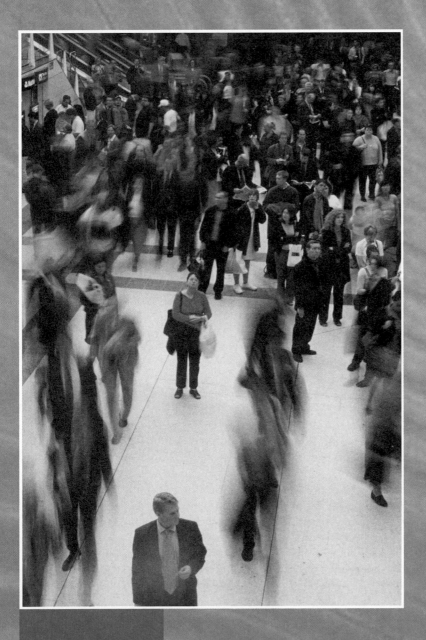

The Phenomenological Perspective: Major Themes and Underlying Assumptions

Every person who ever lived has been unique. No two people have ever had quite the same orientation to life. In fact, no two people ever experience any event precisely the same way. This is true whether the event is *perceptual* (seeing or hearing something), *cognitive* (thinking about something or coming to a conclusion), or *behavioral* (acting in one way or another). Each of us has a slightly different physical perspective on every event we witness. Each of us also has a unique psychological view, causing us to interpret in slightly personalized ways all the information we take in from the world.

The phenomenological perspective on personality has its roots in the uniqueness of each person's frame of reference. One major theme underlying this perspective is that the subjective experience of reality is extremely important. The personal frame of reference that makes each of us different from everyone else has a very powerful influence on every bit of our lives. Indeed, the word *phenomenology* literally means "the subjective experiences of an individual." Pressed to its logical extreme, this emphasis on the subjective and personal implies that so-called *objective* reality is unimportant. All that really matters is the subjective frame of reference that the individual takes toward the *experience* of reality.

Another theme of the phenomenological perspective is that people can determine for themselves (indeed, *must* determine for themselves) what their lives are to be like. Self-determination—free will—is part of human nature, to be exercised by each person who chooses to do so. Unfortunately, some people let themselves slip into thinking they don't have this capacity. Some people let regrets over the past or worries about the future blind them to opportunities of the present. In the phenomenological view, this happens only when people lose sight of the freedom of self-determination that's actually theirs.

A final assumption that underlies much of this perspective on personality is that human beings are intrinsically good and self-perfecting. According to this view, it's human nature to be drawn consistently toward greater health, self-sufficiency, and maturity, unless there are strong pressures to the contrary. The theories that make up this perspective thus are optimistic ones, focused on possibilities and potentials, rather than on constraints and limitations. If there's a metaphor that characterizes the phenomenological perspective, it may be the human being as an opening flower or growing tree, evolving naturally toward greater beauty and completeness.

The phenomenological perspective on personality is represented by theories of two types. They are treated separately from each other, based on which of these themes they emphasize. Some contributors to this perspective place greatest emphasis on self-determination and the intrinsically positive nature of the human being. This aspect of the approach is discussed in Chapter 14. Another theorist who's contributed to this perspective emphasized more strongly the subjective nature of people's perceptions and cognitions. He argued that we literally create for ourselves a unique and personal world of experience. This aspect of the phenomenological perspective is discussed in Chapter 15.

Humanistic Psychology: Self-Actualization and Self-Determination

Julia spends most of her waking hours doing things for others. She talks often with her mother, whose life never goes smoothly and who always wants more from Julia than she can give. Julia sometimes feels as though she's being drawn into quicksand, but she never complains. Then there's Eric, a guy she used to date. Eric's life is a mess, and he often calls her late at night for advice. Although she needs her sleep, she never refuses him a sympathetic ear. Julia always seems to be setting her own life aside for the benefit of others. It's as though she thinks she's unworthy as a person unless she does so. Deep inside, a small voice says she's wrong about that (but she's usually too busy to hear). And sometimes, just sometimes, she has the feeling that a different destiny awaits her, if she could only free herself to find it.

THE EXPERIENCE of being human is mysterious and challenging. You have events, feelings, thoughts, and choices that are different from those of any other person who ever has lived or ever will live. You are continuously "becoming," evolving from a simpler version of yourself into a more complex version. It's sometimes mystifying, because you don't always understand why you feel what you're feeling. But the fact that the life you're living is your own—a set of sensations that belongs to you and nobody else—makes the experience also vivid and compelling.

How does your self know *how* to "become"? As you evolve over your lifetime, how do you still remain yourself? Why do you sometimes feel as though part of you wants to grow in one direction and another part wants to grow in another direction? Why do you still have the sense of being an integrated person even when things pull in different ways inside you? What makes this experience of being human so special? These are among the questions asked by theorists whose ideas form the phenomenological perspective on personality. In this chapter, we examine some of the answers they've given.

The subject of this chapter is sometimes referred to with the phrase **humanistic psychology,** or the *human potential movement* (Schneider, Bugental, & Pierson, 2001). These terms reflect the idea that everyone has the potential for growth and development. *No one* is inherently bad or unworthy. A goal of humanistic psychology is to help people realize this about themselves, so they'll have the chance to grow.

Self-Actualization

An important figure in humanistic psychology was Carl Rogers. His ideas provide a way to talk about how potential is realized and how that can fail to happen. In Rogers's view, the potential for positive, healthy growth expresses itself in everyone if there are no strong opposing influences. This growth is termed **actualization.** Actualization is a tendency to develop capabilities in ways that *maintain or enhance the organism* (Rogers, 1959).

In part, the actualizing tendency is reflected physically. For example, your body actualizes as your immune system kills disease organisms. Your body actualizes when it grows bigger and stronger. The actualizing principle also applies to personality. When it promotes maintenance or enhancement of the self, it's called **self-actualization.** Self-actualization moves you toward more autonomy and self-sufficiency. It enriches your life experiences and enhances creativity. It promotes **congruence,** *wholeness or integration* within the person, and it minimizes disorganization or incongruence.

Rogers believed that the actualizing tendency is part of human nature. This is also reflected in another term he used: the **organismic valuing process.** This phrase refers to the idea that the organism automatically evaluates its experiences to tell whether they are enhancing actualization. If they aren't, the organismic valuing process creates a nagging sense that something isn't right.

Rogers used the phrase **fully functioning person** to describe someone who is self-actualizing. Such people are open to experiencing their feelings and are not threatened by them, no matter what the feelings are. Fully functioning people trust the feelings. They are also open to experiencing the world. Rather than hide from it, they immerse themselves in it. The result is that the fully functioning person lives a life filled with meaning, challenge, and excitement but also a willingness to risk pain. The fully functioning person isn't a particular *kind of person*. It's a *way of functioning* that can be adopted by anyone who chooses to live that way (see Box 14.1).

THE NEED FOR POSITIVE REGARD

Self-actualization isn't the only big influence on human behavior, however. People also are motivated to be accepted and to have the love, friendship, and affection of others—particularly others who matter to them (called *significant others*). Rogers referred to this acceptance with the term **positive regard.**

We all have a strong need to experience positive regards from others, to feel wanted, appreciated, and respected.

BOX 14.1 THE THEORIST AND THE THEORY

Carl Rogers as a Fully Functioning Person

Although Carl Rogers apparently didn't consciously draw on his own life in developing his theory, his life certainly embodied all the theory's principles. Rogers lived a life characterized by a willingness to change and an openness to experience. Several times, he left the security of the familiar and moved in new directions, using only his intuitions and feelings as guides. Rogers was very much the fully functioning, self-actualizing person his theory describes.

Rogers was born in Oak Park, Illinois, in 1902, the middle child in a large family. His parents were conservative and devoutly Christian. During college, he decided to pursue a life in the ministry. At the same time, he also

participated in a six-month-long religious conference in China. This trip had a profound effect on him. The exposure to religious leaders from different cultures changed his thinking about religious issues. He began to entertain the possibility that all he had believed might be wrong. Rogers wrote to his parents, announcing his independence from their religious views, fully realizing the emotional cost that such an act would incur.

Rogers took his degree in history and then continued pursuing his remaining interest in religion, while also taking courses in psychology. After a while, though, he abandoned the path of religion forever to focus on psychology. After earning his doctorate, he took his first job in Rochester, New York. There, two experiences greatly influenced his thinking. First, clinical experience made it apparent that psychoanalytic therapy,

which dominated the group in which he worked, was often ineffective. Second, he recognized vast disagreements among his senior colleagues about how to deal with specific cases. In short, conventional wisdom didn't seem to be working, and the authorities couldn't agree about what to do. To Rogers, it was time to go it alone and develop his own way of treating problems.

In 1939, Rogers published the first of his books on the therapeutic technique he'd developed. This led to a series of academic appointments at several universities. In his later years, he left the familiar confines of academia and set out once again to make a change. The latter part of his career took place at the Western Behavioral Sciences Institute in California, where he pursued a developing interest in group therapies, and at the Center for Studies of the Person.

Positive regard can come in two ways, and the difference is important. Affection given without special conditions—with "no strings attached"—is called **unconditional positive regard.** Sometimes, though, affection is given only if certain conditions are satisfied. The conditions vary from case to case, but the principle is the same: I'll like you and accept you, but only if you act in a particular way. This is called **conditional positive regard.** Much of the affection that people get in their day-to-day lives is conditional.

Another phrase used here is **conditions of worth.** These are the conditions under which the person is judged to be worthy of positive regard. When people act to conform to a condition of worth, they're doing so not because the act is *intrinsically* desirable, but to get positive regard from other people (see the cartoon at right).

Rogers argued that after years of having conditions of worth applied to us by people around us, we start to apply

People sometimes attempt to impose conditions of worth on other people.
Reprinted by permission: Tribune Media Services.

them to *ourselves* (Sheldon & Elliot, 1998). We give ourselves affection and acceptance only when we satisfy those conditions. This pattern of self-acceptance (and self-rejection) is called **conditional self-regard.** Conditional self-regard makes you behave so as to fit the conditions of worth you're applying to yourself (Crocker & Wolfe, 2001).

Conditions of worth and conditional regard have an important effect: *Changing your behavior, values, or goals to gain acceptance can interfere with self-actualization.* Because self-actualizing is more important than fulfilling conditions of worth, it should get first priority. But the need for positive regard is so salient that its influence is often felt more keenly.

Let's consider a couple of examples to see how these motives can conflict with each other. Joel is a young man who's decided to give up a possible career in music because his father needs help in the family business. In doing this, Joel is responding to conditions of worth imposed by his family. Bowing to those conditions of worth, however, may mean denying something that's important inside him, something that's truly a part of who he is.

The same kind of conflict is experienced by Julia, the woman described in the chapter opening. Recall that Julia spends much of her time and energy giving of herself to others. Her actions, however, seem driven by a need to prove she's worthy as a human being. She seems to be applying conditions of worth to herself. By trying to live up to them, Julia prevents herself from hearing the voice of self-actualization and from growing in her own way.

Finally, Mary feels a strong desire for a career, but her parents want her to marry and raise a family. If her parents won't fully accept her unless she bends to their wishes, they're creating a condition of worth for her. Accepting this condition may interfere with her self-actualization. Remember, though, that conditions of worth aren't always imposed from outside. It's possible that Mary's desire for a career may itself be a condition of worth, a self-imposed condition (just like Julia's need to prove her worthiness by giving to others). Mary may have decided she won't accept herself as a complete person unless she has a career.

It can be very hard to distinguish a true desire from a condition of worth (janoff-Bulman & Leggatt, 2002). What defines a condition of worth is that it's a *precondition for acceptance,* either self-acceptance or acceptance by others. A condition of worth is always coercive: It pushes you into doing things. Whenever such conditions are applied, they can prevent self-actualization. There's also evidence that when parents place such conditions on their children, the result is resentment and lower well-being (Assor, Roth, & Deci, 2004).

CONTINGENT SELF-WORTH

Jennifer Crocker and her colleagues have conducted a good deal of research on the idea that people place such conditions of worth on themselves (Crocker & Knight, 2005; Crocker & Park, 2004; Crocker & Wolfe, 2001). People who use their performance in some domain of life as a precondition for self-acceptance are said to have contingent self-worth (which means essentially the same as conditional self-regard). Conditions of worth come in many forms. Some people are demanding about their academic performance and others about their appearance.

Contingencies can be motivating, in some ways. People who impose an academic condition of worth study more than other people; people who impose an appearance-based condition of worth exercise more and shop for clothes more than other people (Crocker, Luhtanen, Cooper, & Bouvrette, 2003). When a failure happens in some domain, though, it's more upsetting for those who have a contingency in that domain than for those who do not. And the failure can then result in loss of motivation for those who failed to meet the contingency.

Consistent with the view expressed by Rogers, holding oneself to these conditions has costs. It is stressful and disrupts relationships (Crocker & Knight, 2005).

Perhaps most important, it keeps you focused on that particular condition of worth instead of letting you grow freely in self-actualization.

Self-Determination

The ideas of Rogers are echoed in a more recent theory of **self-determination** proposed by Ed Deci (Deci, 1975) and developed by Deci and Richard Ryan (1980, 1985, 1991, 2000; Ryan, 1993; Ryan & Deci, 2001; see also Vallerand, 1997). Deci and Ryan believe that having a life of growth, integrity, and well-being means satisfying three needs. The needs are for autonomy (self-determination), competence, and relatedness. Research confirms that people in general do see these needs as being most important (Sheldon, Elliot, Kim, & Kasser, 2001).

This theory began with the idea that behavior can reflect several underlying dynamics. Some actions are *self-determined,* done because the actions have intrinsic interest or value to you. Other actions are *controlled,* done to gain payment or to satisfy some pressure. A behavior can be controlled even if the control occurs entirely inside your own mind. If you do something because you know you'd feel guilty if you didn't do it, you're engaging in controlled behavior.

Whether behavior is controlled or self-determined can have several consequences. One of them concerns how long you'll stay interested in the activity. People stay interested longer when their actions are self-determined. There's a lot of evidence that promising rewards for working on activities can undermine people's interest in them (Deci, Koestner, & Ryan, 1999). The effect has been found in children as well as adults. In children, it's been called "turning play into work" (Lepper & Greene, 1975, 1978).

It's not the reward itself that does this. What matters is whether people see their actions as self-determined. Telling people they're going to be paid for something often seems to make them infer that their behavior isn't self-determined. As a result, they lose interest.

Sometimes, though, the presence of reward increases motivation instead of undermining it (Elliot & Harackiewicz, 1994; Harackiewicz, 1979; Henderlong & Lepper, 2002). Why? Because reward has two aspects (Deci, 1975). It has a *controlling* aspect, telling you your actions aren't self-determined. It can also have an *informational* aspect, telling you something about yourself. If a reward tells you you're competent, it increases your motivation (Eisenberger & Rhoades, 2001; Koestner, Zuckerman, & Koestner, 1987). It's even possible for a reward to promote a sense of autonomy, under the right conditions (Henderlong & Lepper, 2002). If the reward implies a condition of worth, however, or if it implies you're acting only for the reward, then the controlling aspect stands out and your motivation falls off.

Deci and Ryan believe that people want to feel a sense of autonomy in everything they do. In this view, accomplishments such as doing well in your courses are satisfying only if you feel a sense of self-determination in them. If you feel forced or pressured to do those things, then you'll be less satisfied (Flink, Boggiano, & Barrett, 1990; Grolnick & Ryan, 1989). Indeed, pressuring *yourself* to do well can also reduce motivation (Ryan, 1982). This fits the idea that people can impose conditions of worth on themselves.

INTROJECTION AND IDENTIFICATION

Deci and Ryan and their colleagues have used several more terms in describing controlled and self-determined behavior. *Introjected regulation* happens when a person treats a behavior as a "should" or an "ought." That is, the person does the behavior to avoid guilt or to gain self-approval. You've taken the behavior up but not really accepted it as your own. If you try to do well in a class so you won't feel guilty about wasting your parents' money, that's introjected behavior. Introjected behavior is controlled, but the control is being exerted from inside. If you try to do well so your parents won't look down on you, that's also controlled, but it's not introjected because the control is outside you.

In *identified regulation,* the person has come to hold the behavior as personally meaningful and valuable. If you try to do well in a class because you believe learning the information is important to your growth, that's identified regulation. Identified regulation is self-determined. It's not quite as self-determined as intrinsically motivated behavior (for which the interest is naturally there), but it's close. In general, as people mature, they regulate less by introjected values and more by identified (autonomous) values (Sheldon, 2005).

These ideas have many applications. For example, think about what you want out of life. There's evidence that wanting financial success (which generally reflects controlled behavior) relates to poorer mental health, whereas wanting community involvement relates to better mental health (Kasser, 2002; Kasser & Ryan, 1993). Of course, *why* the person has the aspiration is also important (Carver & Baird, 1998). Wanting community involvement for controlling reasons (e.g., because it will make people like you) is bad. Wanting financial success for truly self-determined reasons (because the process itself is intrinsically enjoyable) can be good.

The pressures that lead to introjected regulation stem from the desire to be accepted by others or to avoid a sense of guilt over doing things you think others won't like. This fits with Rogers's belief that the desire for positive regard can disrupt self-actualization. A lot depends on whether significant others place conditions of worth on you. Restrictive parenting produces adults who value conformity instead of self-direction (Kassner, Koestner, & Lekes, 2002).

Having a sense of autonomy also seems to foster further autonomy. In one research project, medical students who thought their professors were supportive of their own autonomy became even more autonomous in their learning over time (Williams & Deci, 1996). They also felt more competent in the skills they were learning, and they acted toward others in ways that supported the others' autonomy.

NEED FOR RELATEDNESS

Deci and Ryan also hold that people have an intrinsic need for relatedness (Baumeister & Leary, 1995). At first glance, it might seem that the need for relatedness should conflict with the need for autonomy. However, Deci and Ryan's definition of *autonomy* doesn't mean being separate from others and thus low in relatedness. It means having the sense of free self-determination (Deci & Ryan, 1991, 2000). Real relatedness doesn't conflict with this.

Several studies have confirmed that autonomy and relatedness can exist side by side. One project found across several studies that autonomy and relatedness were complementary: Each related independently to well-being (Bettencourt & Sheldon, 2001). Another study found that a measure of behaving autonomously was tied to *more* relatedness, in the form of having open and positive communication with significant others. People who regulated their lives in a controlled way were the ones who interacted defensively with others (Hodgins, Koestner, & Duncan, 1996). Yet other research has found that being autonomous promotes the use of relationship-maintaining coping strategies and positive responses in discussing the relationships

(Knee, Patrick, Vietor, Nanayakkara, & Neighbors, 2002). The result is less defensive-ness and more understanding responses to conflict (Knee, Lonsbary, Canevello, & Patrick, 2005).

Support for autonomy is a powerful force. When relationship partners are sup-portive of autonomy, the relationship is experienced as being better and richer (Deci, La Guardia, Moller, Scheiner, & Ryan, 2006). The relationship also feels better to you when you support your *partner's* autonomy (Deci et al., 2006).

Still, the need for relatedness has some resemblance to the need for positive regard. Why, then, doesn't it interfere with self-actualization? The answer seems to be that Deci and Ryan's conception of relatedness implies a genuine connection to others, an unconditional acceptance rather than a connection based on pressure and demand. It might be more accurate to equate this need to a need for *unconditional* regard.

SELF-CONCORDANCE

Self-determination theory has important implications for thinking about the goals people pursue in their lives. Elsewhere in this book, you will read about personality being expressed in the goals people take up (for example, Chapter 17). But goals are not equal in what they're about or in their contributions to well-being. The key is that it's good to pursue goals that are **self-concordant**, or consistent with your core values (Sheldon & Elliot, 1999). You care more about such goals. You'll also benefit more from attaining them than from attaining goals that don't connect to your core values. Support for this reasoning comes from several sources (Brunstein, Schultheiss, & Grässmann, 1998; Sheldon & Elliot, 1999; Sheldon & Kasser, 1998).

There's even evidence that pursuit of self-concordant goals can create a longer-term spiral of benefit (Sheldon & Houser-Marko, 2001). When you try to reach self-concordant goals, you try harder, you have more satisfying experiences, and you attain better well-being. This experience promotes greater motivation for the next self-concordant goal, and the cycle continues.

FREE WILL

Humanistic psychologists emphasize the idea that people have freedom to decide for themselves how to act, what to become. Rogers believed that people are free to choose whether to act in self-actualizing ways or to accept conditions of worth. Deci and Ryan believe that people are exerting their will when they choose to act in self-determined ways.

The concept of *free will* is interesting and controversial. It's nearly impossible to know for sure whether we have free will, but people cer-tainly seem to *think* they do. One reflection of this belief is called **reactance** (Brehm, 1966; Brehm & Brehm, 1981). Reactance happens when you expect to have a particular freedom and you see the freedom as being threatened. The result is an attempt to regain or reassert that freedom. There are lots of examples. Young children who've been told they can't do something want to do it all the more. In the same way, "playing hard to get" can create more attraction. The best illustration of

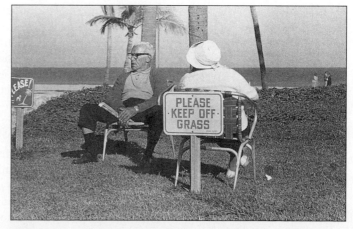

When we are prevented from doing something that we want to do, our desire to do that activity increases even more.

reactance, however, may be what's often said when one person is pressuring another: "Don't tell me what to do!" A substantial literature supports the idea that reactance leads to reassertion of freedom (Brehm & Brehm, 1981).

Although people think they have free will, research raises questions about it. Wegner and Wheatley (1999) set up a situation in which pairs of people together moved a computer mouse (as if using a Ouija board). One person (who was actually part of the experiment) caused the mouse to stop at particular moments, so the cursor fell on specific objects on the computer screen. Through complicated procedures, the researchers caused the true participant to think of the object on which the cursor stopped, either just before or after the stop occurred. If the thought about the object came just before the stop (which, remember, was caused by the other person), the participant reported having stopped there intentionally. This and other evidence led Wegner (2002) to suggest that free will is an illusion. This issue, of course, will continue to be debated.

The Self and Processes of Defense

Let us now turn to the concept of *self*. Rogers is sometimes called a *self theorist,* because he stressed the importance of the self. As did many theorists, he assumed that the self doesn't exist at birth but that infants gradually differentiate self from nonself. As the person grows, the self becomes more elaborate and complex. It never reaches an end state but continues to evolve.

Rogers used the term *self* in several ways. Sometimes, he used it to refer to the subjective awareness of being (Rogers, 1965). At other times, he used it interchangeably with *self-concept.* The self-concept is the set of qualities a person views as being part of himself or herself (much like the concept of *ego identity;* Chapter 11). Many distinctions can be made among the elements of the self-concept. One of them is between the actual (or real) self and the ideal self. The **ideal self** is an image of the kind of person you want to be. The **actual self** is what you think you're really like.

Recall that self-actualizing is supposed to promote congruence. *Congruence* means "fitting closely together." One kind of congruence is between the actual and ideal selves. In particular, as self-actualization takes place, it creates a closer fit between the actual and the ideal. It leads you to become more like the self you want to be.

A second kind of congruence that's also important is between the actual self and experience. That is, the experiences you have in life should fit with the kind of person you think you are. For example, if you think you're a kind person and you find yourself doing something that's insensitive and unkind, there's an incongruity between self and experience. If you think you're a smart person but find yourself doing poorly in a course, there's an incongruity between self and experience. Self-actualization should tend to promote a closer congruence here, as well.

INCONGRUITY, DISORGANIZATION, AND DEFENSE

Incongruence is disorganization, a fraying of the unitary sense of self. You don't always know it consciously, but the organismic valuing process notes it automatically. Rogers said that incongruence—either a perceived gap between real and ideal or experiencing something that doesn't fit your self-image—leads to anxiety.

The experience of incongruence can also make people vulnerable to yet further problems. Low self-esteem (incongruity between actual and ideal self) leads people to underestimate how much their significant others care for them (Murray, Holmes, & Griffin, 2000; Murray, Holmes, Griffin, Bellavia, & Rose, 2001). This misperception can cause them to react poorly to their partners. They feel pessimistic about the relationship and may act in ways that are not genuine. Ultimately, the relationship is less likely to flourish.

It isn't always possible to have complete congruence. Rogers assumed, though, that people defend themselves against even the *perception* of incongruence to avoid the anxiety it creates. Defenses against perceptions of incongruity form two categories, which aren't so different from some of the defenses addressed by psychoanalytic theory (Chapter 9).

One kind of defense involves *distortion of experience*. Rationalization is such a distortion, creating a plausible but untrue explanation for why something is the way it is. Another distortion occurs when you see an event as being different from the way it really is. For instance, if you say something that makes someone else feel bad, you may protect yourself by believing that the other person wasn't really bothered.

The second kind of defense involves *preventing threatening experiences from reaching awareness*. Denial—refusing to admit to yourself that a situation exists or an experience took place—serves this function. A woman who ignores overwhelming evidence that her boyfriend is unfaithful to her is engaging in denial.

You can also prevent an experience from reaching awareness indirectly, by not letting yourself be in a situation where the experience would be *possible*. By taking steps to prevent it from occurring, you prevent its access to consciousness. This is a subtle defense. For example, a person whose self-image is threatened by sexual feelings among attractive strangers may avoid going to the beach or to a nightclub, thereby preventing the experience from occurring.

SELF-ESTEEM MAINTENANCE AND ENHANCEMENT

Defenses act to maintain and enhance the congruity or integrity of the self. Another way to put it is that defenses protect and enhance self-esteem (though see Box 14.2). The idea that people go out of their way to protect self-esteem has been around for a long time. It's been an active area of study under several labels, including self-evaluation maintenance, self-affirmation, ego defensiveness, and egotism (e.g., Darley & Goethals, 1980; M. L. Snyder, Stephan, & Rosenfield, 1976, 1978; Steele, 1988; Tesser, 1986, 1988; Tesser & Campbell, 1983).

It's often said that two conditions are required for concerns to arise about maintaining (or enhancing) self-esteem (Snyder et al., 1978). First, an event must take place that's attributable to you. An event that's outside your control is not relevant to you. Second, the event must be good or bad, thereby having a potential connotation for self-esteem.

What happens when there's a threat to self-esteem? Just as Rogers argued, people either distort perceptions or keep them out of awareness. If self-esteem is threatened, people minimize the negativity of the event, thus distorting their perceptions. Alternatively, they try to prevent the event from being attributed to permanent qualities of the self, thereby denying its relevance.

Let's consider a couple of examples. A common threat to self-esteem is failure. Failure (academic, social, or in another domain) can make most of us feel inadequate. What do people do when they fail? They make excuses (C. R. Snyder & Higgins, 1988). They blame the failure on things beyond their control. They attribute the failure to task difficulty, to chance, to other people, or (in a bind) to a lack of effort

Box 14.2 How Can You Manage Two Kinds of Congruence Simultaneously?

This section of the chapter discusses how people protect or enhance their self-image to defend against perception of incongruence between the actual self and the ideal self. Don't forget, though, that another kind of incongruence—between the self and experience—is also distressing. Unfortunately, there are circumstances when the desire to avoid one kind of incongruity can plunge you right into the other.

What kind of circumstance would do that? An example is suggested by the work of William Swann and his colleagues on what they call *self-verification* (e.g., Swann, 1987, 1990). The principle behind this research is that once people have an idea of what they're like, they want to have that self-concept confirmed by other people's reactions to them. That is, people want their experience to be congruent with their self-concept. For example, if you think you're a good athlete, you want others to think so too. If you think you're shy, you want others to realize it. It may seem odd, but the desire to verify beliefs about yourself extends even to beliefs that are unflattering

(Swann, Wenzlaff, & Tafarodi, 1992). If you think you're homely, you'd rather have someone else agree than say the opposite.

But there's a problem. For the person who holds a negative self-view, there's a built-in conflict between self-verification and self-protection. *Self-verification* is trying not to have incongruity between one's self and one's experience. *Self-protection* is trying not to be aware of incongruity between one's desired self and actual self. Attempts to diminish the two incongruities can pull a person in opposite directions.

Swann and his colleagues argue that both of these forces operate in everyone. Which one dominates at a given moment depends on your options. Keep in mind that most people's self-concept contains both positive and negative qualities (Swann, Pelham, & Krull, 1989). Suppose, then, you had the chance to obtain information about yourself (from another person or from a personality test). Would you prefer to get information about what you view as your best quality or about what you view as your worst? Given this option, most people

prefer to learn about something they view as desirable. This fits the self-protection tendency.

But suppose you know that the quality about which you can get information is one you think is negative. Would you rather get information that says you're good in that quality or that says you're bad? The answer obtained by Swann, Pelham, and Krull (1989) is that if the information is about a quality people perceive as negative, they tend to seek unfavorable information.

In sum, the self-protection and self-enhancement tendency seems to influence where people look (and don't look) when they consider relations between their actual and desired selves. We prefer to look at favorable self-aspects. Once we're looking at some self-aspect in particular, though, the self-verification tendency influences the kind of information we focus on. We want information that confirms our view of who we are—that fits our experienced self to our actual self. In each case, the effect is to enhance perceptions of congruence, consistent with the ideas proposed by Rogers.

(e.g., Bradley, 1978; Snyder et al., 1976, 1978). This happens whether the event is as trivial as failure on a laboratory task or as profound as the experience of divorce (Gray & Silver, 1990). Blaming something else creates distance between the failure and you. Given enough distance, the failure doesn't threaten your self-esteem.

When you experience success, on the other hand, you have the chance to *enhance* your self-esteem. You can do this by ascribing the success to your abilities (Agostinelli, Sherman, Presson, & Chassin, 1992; Bradley, 1978; Snyder et al., 1976, 1978; Taylor & Brown, 1988). Indeed, there's even evidence that people think that their positive personal qualities are under their own control, allowing them to claim credit for being the way they are (Alicke, 1985).

A person can also protect self-esteem after a failure by distorting perceptions another way. As we said earlier, an event is relevant to self-esteem only if it has an impact that's either good or bad. You can be self-protective, then, by minimizing the event's impact. Making a bad impression on someone isn't a problem if that person isn't worth bothering with. Doing poorly on a test doesn't matter if the test isn't important or valid. People who are told they did poorly on a test say exactly that: It's not so important and not so valid (Greenberg, Pyszczynski, & Solomon, 1982).

SELF-HANDICAPPING

Distorting perceptions of bad outcomes maintains self-esteem. But so does denial to awareness. One way to deny access to awareness is called self-handicapping (e.g., Arkin & Baumgardner, 1985; Higgins, Snyder, & Berglas, 1990; Jones & Berglas, 1978; Jones & Pittman, 1982). Self-handicapping is acting to create the very conditions that tend to produce a failure. If you have a test tomorrow, it's self-handicapping to party all night instead of studying. If you want to make a good impression on someone, it's self-handicapping to show up drunk or drenched in sweat.

Why would you do this to yourself? If you want to reach a goal, why create conditions that make it harder? The theory is that failing to attain a goal is a threat to self-esteem. You can't really fail, though, if success is prevented by circumstances beyond your control. If such conditions exist, the stigma of failing goes away. If you fail the test or make a poor impression, well, *no one* could do well under those conditions. So it wasn't really a failure. Thus, you've prevented the awareness of failing. Note that for this strategy to be successful, you need to be *unaware of using it*. If you realize you're setting up barriers for yourself, the barriers won't have the same psychological meaning.

Self-handicapping may be common, but it's not a good strategy. People who tend to self-handicap cope poorly with stress (Zuckerman, Kieffer, & Knee, 1998). Indeed, self-handicapping and maladjustment reinforce each other (Zuckerman & Tsai, 2005). In addition, if people think you're self-handicapping, they will react negatively to you (Hirt, McCrea, & Boris, 2003). And don't forget that self-handicapping helps create the very failure it was intended to protect against.

STEREOTYPE THREAT

A concept that has similarities to the ideas we've been discussing is called stereotype threat. It was first proposed and studied by Claude Steele and his colleagues (Pronin, Steele, & Ross, 2004; Steele, 1997; Steele & Aronson, 1995). It begins with the fact that some social groups are stereotyped in ways that lead to expectations of poor performances of some sort. For example, the negative stereotype of African Americans includes an expectation that they will perform poorly on intellectual tasks. The negative stereotype of women includes an expectation that they will perform poorly on math tests. The negative stereotype of elderly people includes an expectation that they will perform poorly on memory tasks. Members of these groups can be threatened by being viewed through the stereotype, rather than as individuals. This sense of being prejudged occupies the person's mind and promotes negative thinking (Cadinu, Maass, Rosabianca, & Kiesner, 2005). All of this can interfere with performance, thus confirming the stereotype.

What may be even worse, however, is what may occur if this happens frequently. Steele (1997) argued that the person begins to disidentify with the behavioral domain in which the threat is occurring, or stops caring about it. This protects self-esteem by denying that the experience is relevant to the self. Failure doesn't matter if the test isn't important. But disidentification also has bad consequences. As does self-handicapping, it makes poor performance more likely (due to withdrawal of effort). Further, disidentification ultimately causes people to stop caring about

BOX 14.3 THE THEORIST AND THE THEORY

Abraham Maslow's Focus on the Positive

Abraham Maslow focused his work almost exclusively on the positive side of human experience. He was interested in what caused some people to achieve greatness in their lives and to succeed where others failed. He cared about issues of personal growth and the realization of human potential. It's clear that these interests were influenced by events in his own life.

Maslow was born in 1908 in Brooklyn, New York, the oldest of seven children of Russian–Jewish immigrants. His home life definitely did not foster personal growth. His father thought little of him and even publicly ridiculed his appearance. This led young Maslow to seek out empty cars whenever he rode the subway, sparing others the sight of him. If Maslow's father treated him badly, his mother was worse. Because the family was

poor, she kept a lock on the refrigerator to keep the children out, feeding them only when she saw fit. Maslow once characterized her as a "cruel, ignorant, and hostile figure, one so unloving as to nearly induce madness in her children" (Hoffman, 1988, p. 7).

Maslow later said that his focus on the positive side of personality was a direct consequence of his mother's treatment of him. It was a "reaction formation" to the things his mother did and the qualities she represented (Maslow, 1979, p. 958). Thus, from a life begun in hardship came a determination to understand the best in human experience.

Maslow entered college intending a career in law, but he quickly became disenchanted because law focuses so much on evil and so little on good. He turned to psychology. According to Maslow, that was when his life really started. His doctoral work, done under the direction of well-known primate researcher Harry Harlow, focused on how dominance is established among

monkeys. Thus, even while conducting animal research, Maslow was interested in what sets exceptional individuals off from others who are less special.

Maslow shifted this research interest to humans during the period surrounding World War II. New York in the 1930s and 1940s was a gathering place for some of the greatest intellectuals of Europe who were escaping from Nazi Germany. Maslow was quite taken with several of these individuals and tried to find out everything he could about them. In this search to understand how these people came to be exceptional, Maslow was sowing the seeds of more formal work he would conduct later on.

Maslow was deeply moved by the suffering and anguish caused by World War II. He vowed to devote his life to proving that humans were capable of something better than war, prejudice, and hatred. He proceeded to do just that, by studying the process of self-actualization.

important areas of endeavor in which they may actually have considerable skill (Bergeron, Block, & Echtenkamp, 2006).

Self-Actualization and Maslow's Hierarchy of Motives

Another theorist who emphasized the importance of self-actualization was Abraham Maslow (1962, 1970). He was interested in the qualities of people who seem to get the most out of life—the most fully functioning of persons, the healthiest and best adjusted. He spent most of his career trying to understand how they were able to be so complete and so well adapted (see Box 14.3).

As part of this effort, Maslow eventually came to examine motivation and how diverse motives are organized. His view of motivation was very different from the view discussed in Chapter 5. Maslow came to view human needs as forming a hierarchy (Maslow, 1970), which is often portrayed as a pyramid (see Figure 14.1). He pointed out that needs vary in their immediacy and power. Some are extremely primitive, basic, and demanding. Because they're so fundamental, they form the base of the pyramid. These needs are *physiological*—pertaining to air, water, food, and so on—things obviously necessary for survival.

The qualities at the next higher level are also necessary for survival but are less demanding. These are *safety and* (physical) *security* needs—shelter from the weather, protection against predators, and so on. Maslow considered this second class of needs to be less basic than the first class because they require satisfaction less frequently. You need to get oxygen every few seconds, water every few hours, food once or twice a day. But once you've found an apartment, you have physical shelter for quite a while (as long as you pay the rent). If both your apartment and your air supply became inaccessible, you'd surely try to regain the air first and worry about the apartment later.

At the next level of the hierarchy, the needs begin to have more social qualities. The level immediately above safety needs is the category of *love and belongingness*. Here the needs are for companionship, affection, and acceptance from others (much like the need for positive regard). Needs of this type are satisfied through interaction with other people.

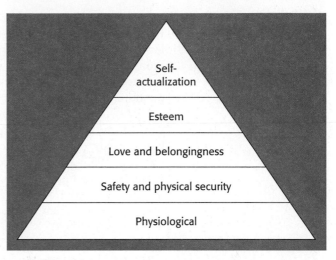

FIGURE 14.1
Maslow's theoretical hierarchy of needs. Needs lower on the hierarchy are more demanding and animalistic. Needs higher on the hierarchy are more subtle, but more distinctly human. *Source: Based on Maslow, 1970.*

Higher yet on the pyramid are *esteem* needs: needs bearing on evaluation (and self-evaluation). Esteem needs include the need for a sense of mastery and power and a sense of appreciation from others (Leary & Baumeister, 2000). Notice that this differs from acceptance and affection in the last paragraph. *Acceptance* may not be evaluative. *Appreciation* is. You're appreciated and esteemed for some quality or qualities that you possess. The need for appreciation thus is more elaborate than the need for acceptance.

At the top of the hierarchy stands *self-actualization*. Maslow used this term much as Rogers did to mean the tendency to become whatever you're capable of becoming—to extend yourself to the limits of your capacities. This, to Maslow, is the highest of human motives.

The pyramid is a visual analogue for Maslow's core assumptions. He assumed that low-level needs are more primitive and more demanding than needs higher on the hierarchy. As noted earlier, the need for air is more demanding than the need for shelter. Maslow's assumption was broader than that, however. He also assumed that the need for physical shelter is more demanding than the need to have a sense of being accepted, and that the need for a sense of belonging is more demanding than the need to be appreciated or powerful. Maslow thus held that the power of the motive force weakens as you move up the pyramid. On the other hand, as you move up, the needs are also more distinctly human and less animalistic.

Thus, Maslow saw a trade-off between the constraints of biology and the uniqueness of being human. We have needs that make us different from other creatures. Self-actualization is the highest and most important. But we can't escape the motives we share with other creatures. Those needs are more powerful when they're unsatisfied than the needs that make us special.

In general, people must deal with the needs they have at lower levels of the pyramid before they can attend to higher needs. Two implications follow. First, if a need begins to develop at a lower level while you're trying to satisfy a higher one, the lower-level need can cause you to be pulled away from the higher-level one. Your attention, in effect, is pulled downward, and you're forced to do something about the lower need (see Wicker, Brown, Wiehe, Hagen, & Reed, 1993).

The second implication concerns how people move up through this set of needs. It may be precisely the freeing of your mind from the demands of low-level needs that lets you be attuned to the very quiet voice of self-actualization. Remember, the further up the pyramid you go, the more subtle and less survival related is the motive. Self-actualization, the highest motive, is the last to be taken into account. Only when the other needs are quieted can this one be attended to.

The steps on the hierarchy also differ from each other in one more sense. Maslow said that motives low on the pyramid are **deficiency-based motives,** whereas those high on the pyramid (particularly self-actualization) are **growth-based motives** (Maslow, 1955). That is, lower needs arise from deprivation. Satisfying such needs means escaping unpleasant conditions. Self-actualization, in contrast, is more like the distant call of your still-unrealized potential as a person. Satisfying this need isn't a matter of avoiding an unpleasant state. Rather, it's the seeking of growth (see also Sheldon et al., 2001).

Finally, compare Maslow's ideas to those of Rogers. Recall that Rogers emphasized two motives: the self-actualizing tendency and the need for positive regard (affection and acceptance). It's possible to see a similarity between those ideas and Maslow's more elaborate structure (see Figure 14.1). The bottom two levels of Maslow's pyramid refer to needs that Rogers ignored. Rogers focused on social needs, which for Maslow begin at the third level. Maslow assumed, as did Rogers, that the need for acceptance could be more demanding than the need for self-actualization. The structure of the pyramid clearly implies that people can be distracted from self-actualization by the need for positive regard.

The intermediate level of Maslow's pyramid—esteem needs—can be viewed as an elaboration on the need for positive regard. Esteem needs seem similar in many ways to Rogers's conditions of worth. The two theorists differed in how they saw this motive. To Rogers, bowing to conditions of worth is bad. To Maslow, esteem needs are part of being human, although less important than the need to self-actualize. The two agreed, however, that this need can get in the way of self-actualization. In sum, despite the fact that each theorist had unique ideas about personality, their theoretical views also have much in common.

CHARACTERISTICS OF FREQUENT SELF-ACTUALIZERS

The concept of self-actualization is, in many ways, the most engaging and intriguing of the ideas of these theorists. Although Maslow painted a broad picture of human motives, self-actualization most fully absorbed his interest and imagination. He devoted much of his career to studying it.

According to Maslow, everyone has the potential to self-actualize, and everyone has an intrinsic desire to become more and more the person that he or she is capable of being. Because self-actualization is so diffuse a quality, it can appear in virtually any kind of behavior. It isn't just the painter, musician, writer, or actor who can be self-actualizing. It's any person who's in the process of becoming more congruent, more integrated, more complete as a person.

Despite the belief that every person has this potential, Maslow also recognized that some people self-actualize more than others. To better understand the process, he sought out people who displayed self-actualizing properties often. He worked hard to describe these people, in part because self-actualization is such a hard concept to grasp. By describing them, he hoped to help others recognize self-actualizing experiences in their own lives.

Table 14.1 Characteristics of Self-Actualizers. *Source:* Based on Maslow, 1968.

Self-actualizing people . . .

- are *efficient* and accurate *in perceiving* reality
- are *accepting* of themselves, of other people, and of nature
- are *spontaneous* in thought and emotion, natural rather than artificial
- are *problem centered*, or concerned with eternal philosophical questions
- are *independent* and *autonomous* when it comes to satisfactions
- have a continued *freshness of appreciation* of ordinary events
- often experience so-called *oceanic feelings*, a sense of oneness with nature that transcends time and space
- *identify with* all of *humanity* and are democratic and respectful of others
- form *deep ties* but *with only a few persons*
- *appreciate*, for its own sake, the *process* of doing things
- have a *philosophical*, thoughtful, nonhostile *sense of humor*
- have a childlike and fresh *creativity and inventiveness*
- maintain an inner *detachment from* the *culture* in which they live
- are sufficiently *strong*, independent, and guided by their own inner visions that they sometimes appear *temperamental* and even *ruthless*

Maslow came to believe that frequent self-actualizers share several characteristics (Maslow, 1962, 1968). Here are a few of them (for a more complete list, see Table 14.1): Self-actualizers are *efficient* in their perception of reality. That is, their experience is in extra-sharp focus. Self-actualizers can spot the confused perceptions of others and cut through tangles. People who frequently engage in self-actualization are also *accepting*. They accept both themselves and others. Their self-acceptance isn't smug self-promotion. Self-actualizers realize they're not perfect. They accept themselves *as they are,* imperfections and all. They also accept the frailties of people around them, as a part of who those people are.

Another characteristic of the self-actualizer is a mental *spontaneity*. This is reflected in a creativity without artificiality. This is often linked to a fresh appreciation of life, an excitement in the process of living. The idea that creativity relates to self-actualization has received research support. In one study (Amabile, 1985), writers were led to think about the act of creation either from the view of extrinsic incentives (thus lower on Maslow's hierarchy) or from qualities intrinsic to the act itself (by implication, self-actualization). They then wrote poems. Judges later rated the creativity of the poems. Those written after thinking about external incentives were lower in creativity than those written from the self-actualizing orientation.

The self-actualizing person is often said to be *problem centered,* but this phrase is a little misleading. The word *problem* here refers to enduring questions of philosophy or ethics. Self-actualizers take a wide view, consider universal issues. Along with this goes an independence from their own culture and immediate environment. The self-actualizer lives in the universe, and only secondarily in this apartment, city, or country. Frequent self-actualizers know relationships require effort. They have deep ties because relationships matter to them, but the ties are often limited to a very few others.

Toward the end of his life, Maslow made a distinction between these people and another kind of self-actualizers (Maslow, 1971), whom he called **transcendent self-actualizers.** These people are so invested in self-actualization that it becomes the most precious aspect of their life. They are more consciously motivated by universal

BOX 14.4 SELF-ACTUALIZATION AND *YOUR* LIFE

By now you've read a lot about the concept of self-actualization, and it may all sound pretty abstract. To get a more concrete feel for the idea, try spending a few minutes thinking about how it applies to your own life.

For example, think about how Maslow's hierarchy of needs pertains to your current existence. Which level of the hierarchy dominates your day-to-day experiences? Are you mostly concerned with having a sense of belonging to a social group (or perhaps a sense of acceptance and closeness with a particular person)? Is the need to feel valued and respected what you're currently focused on? Or are you actively trying to grow as close as possible to the blueprint hidden inside you that holds the secret of your possibilities?

Now think back to your junior year of high school and what your life was like back then. What were your needs and concerns during that period? Since then, has your focus moved upward on the hierarchy or downward, or are you focused at about the same level?

Here's another question: Think about your current mission in life, the goal that gives your life focus and provides it meaning. Where did it come from? Did it get passed down to you by your parents (or someone else)? Or does it come from deep inside you? How *sure* are you that your goal is your own and not someone else's assignment for you, a condition of worth? How sure are you that it isn't an assignment you've given *yourself*? What would it feel like to spend the rest of your life doing "assignments"?

Another question: You can't always do what you want. Everyone knows that. Sometimes you *have* to do things. But how much of the time? How much of your time—how much of your *self*—should be used up doing your duty, being obedient to conditions of worth, before you turn to your other needs? How dangerous is it to say to yourself that you'll do these assignments—these duties—for a while, just for a little while, and that after a few weeks or months or years, you'll turn to the things you

really want? How sure are you that you won't get in a rut and come to see the assignments as the only reality in life? How sure are you that you'll be able to make the decision to turn to your own self-actualization, years down the road, when it's become such a habit to focus on fulfilling conditions of worth?

Not every experience in life is self-actualizing. Even people who self-actualize extensively get stalled sometimes and have trouble with it. When *you* find yourself unable to self-actualize, what's preventing it? What barriers to growth do you confront from time to time? Are they the demands of other needs? Do they stem from your relationships with your parents and family? With your friends? Or are they barriers you place in front of yourself?

Obviously, these questions aren't easy to answer. You can't expect to answer them in just a few minutes. People spend a lifetime trying to answer them. But these questions are important, and thinking about them for a little while should give you a more vivid sense of the issues raised by the phenomenological approach.

---

values or goals outside themselves (such as beauty, truth, and unity). They're more holistic about the world, seeing the integration of all its elements. There's a transcendence of the self, so that self-actualization almost becomes "universe-actualization." All of experience seems sacred to these people. They see themselves as the tools by which capabilities are expressed, rather than the owners of the capabilities. From this characterization comes the term *transpersonal* ("beyond the person"). This term is sometimes used to refer to this way of viewing human potential (see also Box 14.4).

PEAK EXPERIENCES

In trying to describe the process of self-actualization, Maslow also focused on moments in which self-actualization was clearly occurring. Remember, not every act involves self-actualization, even for a person who self-actualizes a great deal. Maslow used the term **peak experiences** to refer to moments of intense self-actualization.

In peak experiences, people have a sense of being connected with the elements of their surroundings. Colors and sounds seem crisper. There's a sharper clarity in perceptions (see Privette & Landsman, 1983). There's also a loss of the sense of time as the experience flows by. The feelings associated with the peak experience are often those of awe, wonder, or even ecstasy. The peak experience tends to take you outside yourself. You aren't thinking about yourself but rather are experiencing whatever you're experiencing as fully as possible.

Peak experiences *can* occur in a passive way (for instance, in examining a great work of art). Usually, though, they occur when people are engaged in action (Czikszentmihalyi, 1975; Privette & Landsman, 1983). Indeed, there's evidence that they happen more during work than during leisure (Czikszentmihalyi & LeFevre, 1989). The person having a peak experience is so immersed in an activity that the activity seems to "become" the person. The term **flow** is also used for such experiences (Czikszentmihalyi, 1990; Czikszentmihalyi & Czikszentmihalyi, 1988).

We should re-emphasize that it's not necessary that the activity involve artistic creation or any such thing. What's important isn't *what's* being done but rather *how* it takes place. If you're completely immersed in it, if it's stretching you as a human being, it can be a peak experience.

Peak experiences occur when a person is deeply engaged in a demanding activity and fully caught up in the moment. Imagine how this football player feels while scoring this touchdown.

Existential Psychology: Being and Death

So far, we've focused on several ideas: that people have a natural tendency toward growth, that people can exert free will to change the course of their lives, that people defend against perceptions of incongruence and try to prevent them from arising, and that the motive to grow is at the peak of a hierarchy of motives. However, there's another side to growth and human potential: The possibilities of self-actualization have a cost. They bring responsibilities.

This is one message of another group of phenomenological psychologists called **existential psychologists**. The term *existential* is related to the word *existence*. It pertains to a philosophical view which holds that existence is all anyone has. Each person is alone in an unfathomable universe. This view stresses that each person must take responsibility for his or her choices in life. This view fits the phenomenological orientation in emphasizing the importance of the individual's experience of reality.

THE EXISTENTIAL DILEMMA

A concept that's central to the existentialist view is **dasein.** This German word is often translated as "being in the world." This phrase is used to imply the totality of a person's experience of the self as an autonomous, separate, and evolving entity (Binswanger, 1963; Boss, 1963; May, 1958). The term *dasein* also emphasizes that humans have no existence apart from the world and that the world has no meaning apart from the people in it.

To the existentialists, the basic issue in life is that life inevitably ends in death, which can come at any time (Becker, 1973). Death is the one event no one escapes, no matter how self-actualizing his or her experiences are. Awareness of the inevitability of death provokes *angst*—dread, anguish far deeper than the anxiety experienced over incongruity. There exist only being and not-being, and we constantly face the polarity between them.

How should you respond to this realization? To the existentialists, this is the key question in life. The choice is to retreat into nothingness or to have the courage to *be*. At its extreme, the choice is whether or not to commit suicide, thus avoiding the absurdity of a life that will end in death anyway. To kill oneself is to choose nothingness. But nothingness can also be chosen in less extreme ways. People can choose not to act authentically, not to commit themselves to the responsibilities and goals that are part of who they are. They can drift, go along with some crowd. When people fail to take responsibility for their lives, they're choosing nothingness.

What's involved in the choice to be? To the existentialists, life has no meaning unless you create it. Each person with the courage to do so must assign meaning to his or her existence. You assign meaning to your life by acting authentically, by being who you are. The very recognition of the existential dilemma is an important step to doing this. As May (1958, p. 47) put it, "To grasp what it means to exist, one needs to grasp the fact that he might not exist."

Exercising this freedom isn't easy. It can be hard to find the way to knowing who you are, and it can be hard to stare death in the face. It's often easier to let other people decide what's right and just go along. Existential psychologists believe, though, that all persons are responsible for making the most of every moment of their existence and fulfilling that existence to the best of their ability (Boss, 1963; Frankl, 1969; May, 1969). This responsibility is inescapable, and it's not to be taken lightly.

Although people are responsible for their choices, even honest choices aren't always good ones. You won't always deal perfectly with the people you care about. You'll sometimes lose track of your connection to nature. Even if your choices are wise, you'll still have **existential guilt** over failing to fulfill your possibilities. This guilt is strongest when a person who's free to choose fails to choose. But people who are aware are never completely free of existential guilt, because it's impossible to fulfill every possibility. In realizing some of your capabilities, you prevent others from being expressed. Thus, existential guilt is inescapable. It's part of the cost of being.

EMPTINESS

The existentialists also focus on the problem of emptiness in life. They are concerned that people have lost faith in values (May, 1953). Many people no longer have a sense of worth and dignity. This is partly because they've found themselves powerless to influence forces such as government and big business. The planet warms, and we do nothing to stop it. Businesses need multibillion dollar bailouts, and we're stuck with the bill. The leaders of our country commit us to wars without justifying them, or even declaring them as wars, and we bear the consequences.

When people lose their commitment to a set of values, they experience a sense of emptiness and meaninglessness. When people feel this way, they turn to others for answers. The answers aren't there, however, because the problem is really within the person. This illustrates once again the existentialist theme that you must be responsible for your own actions and that truth can come only from within and from your actions.

TERROR MANAGEMENT

Some of the ideas of existential psychology are reflected in *terror management theory* (Greenberg, Pyszczynski, & Solomon, 1986). This theory begins with the idea that an awareness of one's eventual death creates existential angst, or terror (Becker, 1973). People respond to the terror by trying to live lives of meaning and value. This much matches what we said about existential psychology.

Terror management theory goes on to suggest, however, that people often don't define the meaning of life on their own. Rather, they use a process of social and cultural consensus. This means that group identity plays an important role in how people affirm the value of their lives. Reminders of mortality lead people to be more protective of their own cultural values (Greenberg, Solomon, & Pyszczynski, 1997). By weaving themselves into a meaningful cultural fabric, a fabric that will last long after they're gone, they affirm their own value as human beings.

People respond to reminders of mortality by holding more closely to their social fabric.

This theory has led to a great deal of research over the past two decades (Greenberg et al., 1997). Some of these studies have shown that making people aware of their mortality causes them to become more favorable toward those who uphold their worldview and more negative toward those who don't. This *mortality salience* also makes people adhere more to cultural norms themselves. Americans become more patriotic; jihadists become more devoted to their cause (Pyszczynski, Solomon, & Greenberg, 2002). Mortality salience can make people act more altruistically—for instance, by supporting charities (jonas, Schimel, Greenberg, & Pyszczynski, 2002)—but only if the charities connect to their own culture.

Much of the research on this topic examines how people affirm their cultural worldview after being reminded of their mortality. However, at least one study has looked at how people affirm values of the self (McGregor, Zanna, Holmes, & Spencer, 2001, Study 4). After a mortality salience manipulation, participants completed a measure of identity seeking and an assessment of their goals for the immediate future. Those whose mortality had been brought to mind stood higher on the measure of identity seeking than others. They also reported intending to work at projects that were more self-consistent than were the projects reported by others.

Terror management theory leads to a number of other interesting ideas. One is that terror management is the reason people view themselves as separate from other animals. To think of yourself as an animal is to be reminded of your death, because all animals die. Consistent with this idea, making mortality salient causes people to have more disgust in response to animals and to favor more strongly the idea that humans are distinct from other animals (Goldenberg, Pyszczynski, Greenberg, Solomon, Kluck, & Cornwell, 2001).

This view also has implications for sexuality (Goldenberg, Pyszczynski, Greenberg, & Solomon, 2000). Sex is one more reminder of your animal nature. That may be one reason many people are nervous about sex: It reminds them of their mortality. People sidestep this reminder in many ways. They ascribe aesthetic value to the sex act. They create romance around it to distract themselves from its animal qualities (Florian, Mikulincer, & Hirschberger, 2002). They create cultural standards of beauty that are idealized and symbolic. In doing so, the *animal* is transformed to the *spiritual*.

People struggle against existential terror in many ways. According to terror management theory, propping up self-esteem can establish a sense of one's value and stave off existential angst (Pyszczynski, Greenberg, Solomon, Arndt, & Schimel, 2004). Recent research has added the idea that confronting mortality motivates people to form close relationships (Mikulincer, Florian, & Hirschberger, 2003). In fact, the push toward affiliation may be even more important than the affirmation of cultural values (Wisman & Koole, 2003).

As we said, this theory has prompted a great deal of research, extending in many directions. For present purposes, however, let's link it back to existentialism. The research makes it clear that reminding people of their eventual death makes them try to affirm the value of their lives. People do this mostly (though not entirely) by embracing the values of the culture in which they live. Only a little evidence indicates that people try to create their own personal meanings. Does this mean that for most people, the response to existential angst is to let other people decide what's right and just go along? Surely this would dismay the existential psychologists. It may simply mean, though, that values are naturally defined more by groups than the existentialists realized.

Assessment

A basic issue in personality assessment is how to go about it. Various views suggest different approaches to the process. This view suggests yet another one.

INTERVIEWS IN ASSESSMENT

Phenomenological psychologists are less tied than other psychologists to the structure of specific measuring instruments. To them, assessment isn't a process of having a person respond to a set of stimuli. It's a process of finding out *what the person is like*. Given this view, they are very much at home with interviewing as an assessment technique. The interview offers maximum flexibility. It lets the person being assessed say whatever comes up. It lets the interviewer follow stray thoughts and ask questions that might not otherwise occur. It lets the interviewer get a subjective sense of what that person is like from *interacting* with him or her.

Finding out what a person is like in this way requires empathy. After all, the interviewer is trying to enter the other person's private world. Empathy isn't automatic. It requires sensitivity to small changes. As an interviewer, you must repeatedly check the accuracy of your sensing to make sure you haven't taken a wrong turn. (Empathy isn't important just for interviewing, by the way. Rogers saw it as important to doing therapy and to being a fully functioning person.)

An extensive interview produces a lot of information. One way to evaluate this information is called **content analysis.** This involves grouping the person's statements in some way and seeing how many statements are in each group. For example, in an interview Susan said two things about herself expressing self-approval, eighteen expressing self-disapproval, and fifteen that were ambivalent. One might infer from this that Susan isn't very satisfied with herself.

This tactic can also be used to assess progress in therapy. For example, in a second interview after three months of therapy, Susan made five statements that expressed approval of herself, five that expressed disapproval, and eight that were ambivalent. One implication might be that Susan is now less negative about herself than before.

The flexibility that makes interviews useful also creates problems. Unless an interview is highly structured, it's hard to compare one with another. If Jane expresses more self-disapproval than Sally, is it because Jane dislikes herself more than Sally? Or did the interviewer just happen to follow up a particularly bothersome aspect of Jane's self-image? If Susan expresses less self-disapproval after therapy than before, is it because she's become more satisfied with herself or because the interviewer failed to get into self-critical areas in the second interview?

It's also clear that what a person says in an interview can vary as a function of other things. For example, people are more self-disclosing to an interviewer who has good rapport with them (Jourard, 1974). In fact, small differences in an interviewer's verbal behavior can produce large differences in what people say. Thus, many see the interview as primarily a tool for getting informal impressions, rather than for conducting a full assessment.

MEASURING THE SELF-CONCEPT BY Q-SORT

The other core issue in assessment is what qualities to assess. Theorists discussed in this chapter suggest several answers. One answer is to assess the self-concept.

A technique Rogers preferred for assessing self-concept is called the **Q-sort** (e.g., J. H. Block, 1961; Rogers & Dymond, 1954). There are many variations on this procedure, but the basic process is the same. It always involves giving the person a large set of items printed on cards. The items often are self-evaluative statements, as in Table 14.2, but they can be phrases, words, or other things. The person doing the Q-sort is asked to sort the cards into piles (see Figure 14.2). At one end are just a few cards with statements that are *most like you,* at the other end are just a few cards with statements that are *least like you*. Piles in between represent gradations between the extremes, and have larger numbers of cards.

There are rules about how many cards can go in a given pile (Figure 14.2). Usually, people start by sorting very generally (like me, not like me, neither) and then sorting further. By the time you're done, you've had to look hard at the statements and decide which one or two are most and least descriptive. By comparing qualities, the person is forced into self-evaluation. The Q-sort differs in this respect from rating scales in which each response is separate. These scales let the person say that all the descriptors apply equally well. This can't possibly happen in a Q-sort.

In the most basic Q-sort, you sort the statements according to how you think you *actually are*. Q-sorts can also be used, though, to get more complex information. Sometimes people sort the statements again according to what they were like earlier in their lives. It's then possible to look at how well the two match. Differences

Table 14.2 Statements Commonly Used in Q-Sort Procedures.

I am intelligent.	I am ambitious.
I often feel guilty.	I am an impulsive person.
I am optimistic.	I get anxious easily.
I express my emotions freely.	I make strong demands on myself.
I understand myself.	I get along easily with others.
I am lazy.	I often feel driven.
I am generally happy.	I am self-reliant.
I am moody.	I am responsible for my troubles.

Most
like me   Least
                                                                like me

(1)   (2)   (3)   (4)   (5)   (4)   (3)   (2)   (1)

FIGURE 14.2
In the Q-sort procedure, you sort a set of cards containing descriptive statements into a row of piles. At one end of the row might be the card containing the single statement that's most like you, at the other end the card containing the single statement that's least like you. The other piles of cards represent gradations between these two points. As you can see from the numbers in parentheses in this example, the piles toward the middle are permitted to have more cards in them than the piles closer to the end points. Thus, you're forced to decide which items really are very much like and unlike yourself.

between the two reflect changes in self-concept over time. It's also possible to sort for the ideal self (the kind of person you want to be). Then you can look to see how much difference or similarity there is between the ideal and the actual. Similarity reflects *congruence,* the closeness between your ideal self and your perceived self.

MEASURING SELF-ACTUALIZATION

A second content for personality assessment is suggested by the emphasis on self-actualization. Given this emphasis, it would seem desirable to measure the degree to which people have characteristics of frequent self-actualization.

The Personal Orientation Inventory (POI) was developed for this purpose (Shostrom, 1964, 1974; see also Knapp, 1976). The POI consists of paired statements. People choose the one from each pair they agree with more. The POI has two major scales. One, called *time competence,* reflects in part the degree to which the person lives in the present, as opposed to being distracted by the past and future. As the word *competence* hints, though, it also has a more complex meaning. Time-competent people are able to effectively tie the past and future with the present. They sense continuity among these three aspects of time.

The second scale assesses a tendency to be *inner directed* in the search for values and meaning. Self-actualizers are believed to have a stronger tendency toward inner direction in determining their values than people who are less self-actualizing. It's been found that scores on the POI improve after group therapy (Dosamantes-Alperson & Merrill, 1980).

Jones and Crandall (1986) developed another measure of self-actualization. Their scale has four factors, reflecting self-direction, self-acceptance, acceptance of emotions, and trust and responsibility in interpersonal relations. As with the POI, there's evidence that scores on this scale change after group therapy (Crandall, McCown, & Robb, 1988).

MEASURING AUTONOMY AND CONTROL

Yet another quality that's important to the viewpoints presented in this chapter is the extent to which a person's actions tend to be *autonomous* versus *controlled.* A number of self-report measures exist to assess this difference among people. One measure assesses the extent to which people generally tend to function in a self-determined way in their lives (Sheldon, Ryan, & Reis, 1996). This measure of general self-determination can give a broad sense of a person's behavior across multiple domains. It's been used, for example, to show that people high in general self-determination have harmony between their needs and goals (e.g., Thrash & Elliot, 2002).

Several other measures focus on how people behave in some specific domain of life. For example, Ryan and Connell (1989) developed a measure of children's academic behavior and prosocial behavior. The items ask children why they do various things and provide potential reasons that had been chosen to reflect controlled or autonomous motivation. In another project, Black and Deci (2000) developed a measure to ask college students their reasons for learning things in their courses. Again, options are provided for reasons that are controlled and reasons that are autonomous. Another such measure was devised to assess the motives underlying religious behavior (Ryan, Rigby, & King, 1993).

Problems in Behavior, and Behavior Change

How are problems in living conceptualized in this view? Recall that fully functioning people are attuned to the actualizing tendency and experience a sense of coherence and consistency. They're not trying to live up to conditions of worth. They're being who they are. To Rogers (and others), lack of congruity within the self creates psychological problems. (For supporting evidence of various kinds, see Deci and Ryan [1991]; Higgins [1990]; and Ryan, Sheldon, Kasser, and Deci [1996].)

To Rogers, incongruity (between experience and self-concept or within the self-concept) is experienced as anxiety (though see Box 14.5 for a more complex view). Anxiety is a signal from the organismic valuing process that the self is disorganized. Although we have ways to protect the self from such threats (discussed earlier in the chapter), anxiety can occur. This is especially likely if the person focuses too much on conditions of worth and acts in ways that interfere with self-actualization. If incongruities get large, the person will act in ways that are labeled *neurotic*. If they get extreme enough, the person will act in ways that are labeled as *psychotic*.

When the holistic self is threatened by uncertainty, the person becomes not just more distressed but more rigid (McGregor et al., 2001). This seems to be an effort to hold onto the self that existed before. People faced by an incongruity in one self-aspect

BOX 14.5 SELF-DISCREPANCIES AND EMOTIONS

Rogers believed that incongruity of any sort creates anxiety. This belief is challenged by work done by Tory Higgins (1987) and his colleagues, who say the situation is more complicated.

Higgins says that three aspects of self need to be taken into account, not just two: the *actual*, the *ideal*, and the *ought* selves. To Higgins, the ideal self is what you wish for yourself, the self to which you aspire. The ought self is defined by duty or obligation. An *ought* is something you feel compelled to be, rather than desire to be. An ought sounds very much like a condition of worth. Higgins refers to ideals and oughts as **self-guides,** because they serve as comparison points for the actual self and as guides for behavior.

Higgins assumes, as did Rogers, that incongruities between the self-guides and the actual self produce negative feelings. Unlike Rogers, however,

Higgins distinguishes between two feelings, which come from two different kinds of incongruities. Specifically, Higgins holds that discrepancies between the actual and *ideal* selves cause feelings of sadness and dejection. Discrepancies between the actual and *ought* selves cause feelings of anxiety.

Studies have consistently supported this reasoning (e.g., Higgins, Bond, Klein, & Strauman, 1986; Strauman, 1989; Strauman & Higgins, 1987). In most studies, self-concept is assessed by having people list 10 attributes they think contribute to their actual selves, 10 they think contribute to their ideal selves, and 10 they think contribute to their ought selves. The extent of discrepancy between the actual and ideal is computed by counting the number of matches on the two lists and the number of opposites. A similar procedure is used to assess discrepancy between the actual and ought selves. Either in the same session or at another time, subjects also report their

moods, including feelings of depression and feelings of anxiety.

The usual finding is that the extent of actual–ideal discrepancy relates uniquely to depression but not anxiety. The extent of actual–ought discrepancy relates uniquely to anxiety but not depression. These results are especially impressive in light of the fact that depression and anxiety tend to occur together. In fact, many psychologists have viewed them as different facets of the same thing. Being able to distinguish between them is no small feat.

It's also of interest that the ought self seems to be linked conceptually to the notion of conditions of worth. That is, an ought is an obligation, a duty. The ideal self, in contrast, isn't tied to conditions of worth. This body of research, then, suggests a variation on the position taken by Rogers. Incongruities that derive from failures to meet conditions of worth lead to anxiety. Incongruities that derive from a failure to self-actualize are reflected in dejection.

stress their certainty about other things, apparently trying to compensate for what's been threatened. They become more zealous or extreme in their beliefs and personal values. In fact, McGregor et al. (2001) suggested that this is what happens in the terror management responses discussed earlier in the chapter.

The process of therapy, to Rogers, is essentially the process of reintegrating a partially disorganized self. This involves reversing the processes of defense to confront the discrepancies between the elements of the person's experience. Doing so isn't easy, however.

Rogers believed that an important condition must be met before such changes can occur. Specifically, the conditions of worth that distorted the person's behavior in the past must be taken away. The person still needs positive regard, but it must be *unconditional*. Only then will the person feel able to confront the discrepancies. Removing the conditions of worth will allow the person to focus more fully on the organismic valuing process, the quiet inner voice that knows what's good and what's bad for you. This, in turn, allows a reintegration of the self. Consistent with this is evidence that people are less defensive when they're accepted for who they are than when they're accepted in an evaluative, conditional way (Arndt, Schimel, Greenberg, & Pyszczynski, 2002; Schimel, Arndt, Pyszczynski, & Greenberg, 2001).

Unconditional positive regard, then, is a key to therapy. But it's a complex key. For unconditional regard to be effective, it must be given *from the person's own frame of reference*. That is, it means acceptance for who *you* think you are. Someone who knows nothing about you or your feelings can't give meaningful acceptance. This is a second reason it's important for a therapist to be empathic. The first was that empathy is necessary to get an adequate sense of what the client is like. The second is that it's necessary if the therapist is to show unconditional positive regard for the client in a way that will facilitate reintegration of the client's personality.

There's one more potential problem here. Sometimes people undertake therapy to satisfy someone's conditions of worth for them. It stands to reason that people who are trying to make changes for autonomous reasons will do better than people trying to make similar changes to satisfy conditions of worth. In at least one domain of change—weight loss—there's evidence that this is so. In one study, people who lost weight for autonomous reasons lost more and kept it off longer than those who did it for less autonomous reasons (Williams, Grow, Freedman, Ryan, & Deci, 1996).

CLIENT-CENTERED THERAPY

There are several humanistic approaches to therapy (Cain & Seeman, 2002). The one that's best known, developed by Rogers (1951, 1961; Rogers & Stevens, 1967), is called **client-centered therapy,** or **person-centered therapy.** As the phrase implies, the client takes responsibility for his or her own improvement. Recall Rogers's belief that the tendency toward actualizing is intrinsic. If people with problems can be put in a situation in which conditions of worth are removed, they should naturally reintegrate themselves. This is a bit like the rationale for putting a bandage on a wound. The bandage doesn't heal the wound, but by maintaining a sterile environment, it helps the natural healing process take place.

In person-centered therapy, the therapist displays empathy and unconditional positive regard. This lets the client escape temporarily from conditions of worth and begin exploring aspects of experience that are incongruent with the self. Throughout, the therapist remains nondirective and nonevaluative, showing no emotion and giving no advice. The therapist's role is to *remove* the pressure of conditions of worth. By avoiding evaluative comments (e.g., saying that something is good or bad), the effective therapist avoids imposing additional conditions of worth.

Rather than be evaluative, the therapist tries to help clients gain a clear perspective on their own feelings and experiences. In general, this means reflecting back to the client, in slightly different ways, things the client is saying so the client can re-examine them from a different angle. There are two variations on this procedure.

The first is called **clarification of feelings.** Part of what the client does in the therapy session is emotional, expressing feelings about things, either directly in words or indirectly in other ways. As feelings are expressed, the therapist repeats those expressions in different words. The purpose here is to make the client more aware of what his or her true feelings are. Simply being reminded of the feelings can help this to happen.

A moment's reflection should confirm the usefulness of this technique. Feelings are often fleeting. When people express feelings in their words or actions, they often fail to notice them. Moments later, they may be unaware of having had them. If the feelings are threatening, people actively defend against recognizing them. The process of reflecting feelings back to the client allows the nature and the intensity of the feelings to become more obvious to the client. This puts the client into closer touch with the experience.

The second kind of reflection in person-centered therapy is more intellectual and less emotional. It's called **restatement of content**. This is equivalent to what was just described but in terms of the *ideas* in the client's statements—the cognitive content of what the client says.

Is client-centered therapy effective? It can be (M. L. Smith & Glass, 1977). Studies of this technique have focused primarily on changes in self-image. There's evidence that people do change their pictures of themselves after client-centered therapy, so that their perceived self becomes more congruent with their ideals (e.g., Butler & Haigh, 1954; Truax & Mitchell, 1971).

BEYOND THERAPY TO PERSONAL GROWTH

To humanistic psychologists, therapy isn't a special process of fixing something that's wrong and then forgetting about it. Rather, it's on a continuum with other life experiences. In this view, a person who's living life to the fullest should always engage in more or less the same processes as occur in therapy. These processes provide a way for people who have average lives—or even very good lives—to further enrich their experiences and to self-actualize even more completely.

Rogers's view of the ideal way of life is captured in the phrase *fully functioning person*. He believed that personal growth throughout life should be a goal for everyone. Growth requires the same conditions as those needed for effective therapy. Growth requires that the people with whom you interact be genuine and open, with no holding back and no putting up false fronts. It requires empathic understanding together with unconditional positive regard. This view on growth is similar to Maslow's view on self-actualization: Growth isn't a goal that's reached once and cast aside. It's a way of living to be pursued throughout your lifetime.

Humanistic Theories: Problems and Prospects

The humanistic view is regarded by many as an intuitively *accessible* approach to personality. The intuitive appeal of this view derives partly from its emphasis on the uniqueness and validity of each person's experience. Indeed, this view treats each person's subjective experience as being of primary importance. This emphasis on personal experience fits well with what many people bring to mind when they think of the word *personality,* especially when they think of their *own* personality. For this reason, this viewpoint feels comfortable and commonsensical to many people.

This viewpoint also has at least two other virtues. First, it represents an optimistic and positive view of human nature. Humanistic psychologists such as Rogers, Maslow, Deci, and Ryan have argued strenuously that people are intrinsically good—naturally motivated to be the best they can be. According to this view, that motive will be expressed in everyone, as long as other circumstances don't interfere too much.

This optimistic outlook on humanity is also reflected in a practical virtue of the humanistic view. This view emphasizes the importance of fully experiencing and appreciating your own reality and maintaining close contact with your own feelings. This emphasis provides a strategy for living that many people have used to enrich their lives. The benefits sometimes have come through formal therapy. But remember that many phenomenologists assume there's no real distinction between therapy and the more ordinary "course corrections" that are part of normal living. Thus, the move toward personal enrichment has come for many people in informal ways. It's been sort of a self-guided exploration of how to make one's life better.

Although humanistic psychology certainly has virtues, it has had problems as well. One problem in the past was a lack of precision. It was hard to generate research from the theories. For example, consider self-actualization. To study self-actualization, you need to know the areas of life to which the actualizing tendency is relevant for each person you're studying. But actualization occurs in different ways within different people. In theory, it might be necessary to study as many types of behavior as there are people being studied.

This difficulty was a serious one. However, more recent humanists have taken many steps to overcome it. Deci and Ryan and their co-workers, who share many orienting assumptions with earlier humanists, have devised hypotheses that can be tested readily and in a straightforward manner. Findings from research on topics such as self-determination provide powerful support for many assumptions of the humanistic viewpoint.

A second set of criticisms of humanistic psychology aims at a quality that was just described as a virtue: its optimistic, positive view of human nature. This view is sometimes criticized as arbitrary, naïve, sentimental, and romantic. Some believe it has no basis other than the theorists' belief that people are inherently good. Not everyone believes that all people are inherently good (Baumeister & Campbell, 1999).

The idea that everyone's self-actualization should be encouraged is also criticized. Some say that if this principle were carried to its extreme, it would require that everyone be encouraged to live life to the fullest, regardless of the consequences for anyone else. The result of such unrestrained self-expression would be chaos. Such a way of life would create serious conflict whenever one person's self-actualization somehow interfered with someone else's self-actualization, which certainly would happen.

It's also worth noting that the optimistic overtones that permeate so much of humanistic psychology are largely missing from the writings of the existentialists. Whereas humanists such as Rogers and Maslow emphasized the fulfilling quality that can come from making your own way in the world, the existentialists emphasize that doing this is hard and can be very painful. Living honestly means confronting harsh realities and absurdities and rising above them. This picture is very different from the one painted by Rogers and Maslow. It can be difficult to reconcile the warm and glowing optimism of the one view with the angst of the other.

Another point of contention about this view on personality concerns the concept of free will. Humanists tend to assume that people can decide for themselves what to do at any point in their lives. Others regard this conception of free will as a convenient fiction, an illusion that is misleading at best. Surely people act as though they *think* they have free will. But how to demonstrate the *existence* of free will has never been an easy problem to solve. Indeed, as noted earlier, there's now evidence for the position that the perception of will is illusory (Bargh & Ferguson, 2000; Wegner, 2002).

What, then, are the prospects for this approach to personality? Although many questions remain to be answered, the future of this way of thinking seems a great deal brighter than it did two decades ago. Several areas of vigorous and enthusiastic research activity have opened up seams of knowledge bearing on assumptions made years earlier by the pioneers of humanism. Topics such as self-determination, stereotype threat, terror management, and self-discrepancies are all being actively explored. The development and exploration of these sorts of ideas are a source of considerable encouragement for the future prospects of this approach.

· SUMMARY ·

The theorists of this chapter emphasize that people have an intrinsic tendency toward self-actualization. *Self-actualization* is the tendency to develop your capabilities in ways that maintain or enhance the self. This tendency promotes a sense of congruence, or integration, within the person. Its effectiveness is monitored by the organismic valuing process.

People also have a need for *positive regard,* acceptance and affection from others. Positive regard may be unconditional, or it may be conditional on your acting in certain ways. These conditions of worth mean that the person is held worthy only if he or she is acting in a desired manner. Conditions of worth, which can be self-imposed as well as imposed by others, can cause you to act in ways that oppose self-actualization.

Self-determination theory focuses on the difference between behavior that's self-determined and behavior that's controlled in some fashion. People enjoy activities more if they feel they're doing them from intrinsic interest instead of extrinsic reward. People whose lives are dominated by activities that are controlled are less healthy than people whose lives are self-determined.

Many theorists of this group assume that people have free will. This is a very hard idea to test, but people do seem to think they have free will. Studies of reactance have shown that people resist threats to freedoms they expect to have. Other research has questioned whether free will is illusory, though.

Behavior that opposes the actualizing tendency creates *disorganization* in the sense of self. Disorganization can be reduced by two kinds of defenses. You can distort perceptions of reality to reduce the threat, or you can act in ways that prevent threatening experiences from reaching awareness (for example, by ignoring them). Use of these defenses is seen in the fact that people blame their failures on factors outside themselves but take credit for their successes. People also engage in self-handicapping strategies, creating esteem-protective explanations for the possibility of failure before it even happens. Use of self-handicapping is paradoxical because it increases the like-lihood of failure.

Maslow elaborated on the idea of self-actualization by proposing a hierarchy of motives, ranging from physical needs (most basic) to self-actualization (at the top). Basic needs are more demanding than higher needs, which (being more subtle) can affect you only when the lower needs are relatively satisfied. Maslow's intermediate levels appear to relate to the need for positive regard, suggesting why it can be hard to ignore the desire for acceptance from others.

Existential psychologists point out that with freedom comes the responsibility to choose for yourself what meaning your life has. The basic choice is to invest your life with meaning or to retreat into nothingness. When people are reminded of their own mortality, they try harder to connect to cultural values. Even if people try to find meaning, they can't escape existential guilt. No life can reflect all the possibilities it holds, because each choice rules out other possibilities.

This view on personality uses many assessment techniques, including both interviews and self-reports. Regarding content, it emphasizes the self-concept, self-actualization, and self-determination. One way to assess self-concept is the *Q-sort,* in which a set of items is sorted into piles according to how much they apply to oneself. Different "sorts" can be compared with each other for additional information.

From this perspective, problems derive from *incongruity.* Large incongruity is reflected as neurosis; when even more extreme, the result is psychosis. Therapy is a process of reintegrating a partly disorganized self. For reintegration to occur, the client must feel a sense of unconditional positive regard. In *client-centered therapy,* people are led to refocus on their feelings about their problems. The (nonevaluative) therapist simply helps clients to clarify their feelings. In this viewpoint, the processes of therapy blend into those of ordinary living, with the goal of experiencing continued personal growth.

· GLOSSARY ·

Actual self   One's self as one presently views it.

Actualization   The tendency to grow in ways that maintain or enhance the organism.

Clarification of feelings   The procedure in which a therapist restates a client's expressed feelings.

Client-centered therapy (also called **person-centered therapy**)   A type of therapy that removes conditions of worth and has clients examine their feelings.

Conditional positive regard   Affection that's given only under certain conditions.

Conditional self-regard   Self acceptance that's given only under certain conditions.

Conditions of worth   Contingencies placed on positive regard.

Congruence   An integration within the self and a coherence between the self and one's experiences.

Content analysis   The grouping and counting of various categories of statements in an interview.

Contingent self-worth   Self-acceptance that's based on performance in some domain of life.

Dasein   "Being in the world"; the totality of one's autonomous personal existence.

Deficiency-based motive   A motive reflecting a lack within the person that needs to be filled.

Existential guilt   A sense of guilt over failing to fulfill all of one's possibilities.

Existential psychology   The view that people are responsible for investing their lives with meaning.

Flow   The experience of being immersed completely in an activity.

Fully functioning person   A person who's open to the experiences of life and who's self-actualizing.

Growth-based motive   A motive reflecting the desire to extend and elaborate oneself.

Humanistic psychology   A branch of psychology emphasizing the universal capacity for personal growth.

Ideal self   The personal values to which one aspires.

Organismic valuing process   The internal signal that tells whether self-actualization is occurring.

Peak experience   A subjective experience of intense self-actualization.

Positive regard   Acceptance and affection.

Q-sort   An assessment technique in which descriptors are sorted according to how much they apply to oneself.

Reactance   A motive to regain or reassert a freedom that's been threatened.

Restatement of content   A procedure in which a therapist rephrases the ideas expressed by a client.

Self-actualization   A process of growing in ways that maintain or enhance the self.

Self-concordance   Pursuing goals that are consistent with one's core values.

Self-determination   Deciding for oneself what to do.

Self-guides   Qualities of the self one desires to be (ideal) or feels compelled to be (ought).

Self-handicapping   Creating situations that make it hard to succeed, thus enabling avoidance of self-blame for failure.

Stereotype threat   Having a negative perception of the self because of feeling prejudged.

Transcendent self-actualizers   People whose actualization goes beyond the self to become more universal.

Unconditional positive regard   Acceptance and affection with "no strings attached."

CHAPTER 15

Personal Constructs

Rachel and Jerry are sitting in the lounge taking a break from studying. They're talking about a new movie they've both just seen, and they're disagreeing loudly about how good it was (or wasn't). Rachel thinks the plot was subtly intricate and that there was a delicate tension throughout. Jerry thinks there wasn't any plot at all and that the film could not possibly have moved more slowly. At this point, Susan joins them and chimes in with her opinion. She didn't see the nuances of plot that Rachel saw, but she points out that the film had a lot of symbolism. Jerry just shakes his head in disbelief.

THE SAME physical world exists for everyone. An oak tree growing across the street is the same object when *you* look at it as when *anyone else* looks at it. A building stands there—brick and mortar—and no matter who's looking at it, its nature doesn't change. Physical reality is, after all, physical reality.

But people's experience of the world isn't based entirely on physical reality. Rachel, Jerry, and Susan saw the same film, but their experiences weren't even remotely the same. That's potentially true of all experiences. For example, consider again that oak across the street. You might look at it and sense a graceful product of nature's mysteries. Someone else may glance at the same tree and see a source of shade on a hot day. Another person might see a nuisance, a tall thing covered with leaves that soon will have to be raked. A fourth person may see a source of hardwood for furniture. The physical reality is the same for all, but the *experience* of it can vary widely from person to person.

This is also true in experiencing ourselves, the people around us, the actions we engage in, and the events of our lives. Consider John, a student who works extra hard at his courses, spending weekends in the library instead of partying. John sees his actions as an effort to learn as much as he can, about as many things as he can, while he has the chance. John's father sees these actions as an effort to establish a good record, thereby getting a good start toward a high-paying job. To one of John's professors, the pattern is an effort to compensate for feelings of inferiority. Dan, a casual friend, sees mindless compulsiveness. Susan, an even more casual friend, thinks it's silly to study so much and sees John as an incredibly dull person.

How is it that people have such different experiences when exposed to the same reality? Where do these differences in interpretation come from? Some psychologists answer these questions by saying that *physical reality* isn't the same as *human experience*. It's merely the raw material. No one can examine all the raw material available—no one has the time. No one can deal with *just* raw material, either. You have to impose organization on it, create order from the chaos. So each person *samples* the raw material and constructs a personal vision of how reality is organized. These mental representations then provide the basis for future perceptions, interpretations, and actions (Jussim, 1991).

It might even be said that *personality* consists of the organization of mental structures through which the person views reality (or which the person imposes on reality). This is essentially the position taken by George Kelly, whose ideas are the subject of this chapter (Kelly, 1955; for reviews, see Adams-Webber, 1979; Bannister, 1970, 1985; Bonarius, Holland, & Rosenberg, 1980; Mancuso & Adams-Webber, 1982).

Kelly is considered part of the phenomenological perspective because he emphasized the uniqueness of each person's subjective worldview. As you read about his ideas, you'll see some similarity to themes of Chapter 14, such as the idea that people choose for themselves how to think and act. But in many ways, Kelly's ideas also foreshadow a cognitive view that began to form nearly two decades later (discussed in Chapter 16). It may be useful to think of Kelly's theory as a bridge between the phenomenological perspective and a newer perspective that hadn't yet come into being.

Personal Constructs and Personality

Kelly argued that the best way to understand personality is to think of people as *scientists*. This view was also being promoted at about the same time by Fritz Heider (1958), an early cognitive theorist in social psychology. Just as scientists do, all of us have a need to predict events and to understand things that happen around us. Just as scientists, all of us develop theories of reality.

The need for prediction is basic to life. It shows up in every aspect of behavior. Think about it. You're making a prediction about the nature of the world every time you turn on a faucet and expect water to come out. You test a prediction whenever you turn a doorknob (expecting the door to open) or eat (expecting not to get sick). In truth, it's hard to think of any action that doesn't involve an implicit prediction about how reality is organized. Most of these predictions are made automatically and unconsciously, but they're predictions nonetheless.

Because so much of human life is social, the desire for predictability is especially important in social events. Every time you look at someone's expression and use it as a guide to his or her feelings, you're predicting social reality. Virtually all social encounters—even those as simple as buying something at a store—involve many implicit assumptions and predictions. In order to choose our own actions, we need to interpret other people's actions.

Each person responds to this need to predict by constructing a personal view of the world and how it works. This personal view, or theory, is a guide to predicting and interpreting future events. In Kelly's terms, people generate a set of **personal constructs** and impose them on reality. In his view, people don't experience the world directly. Rather, they know the world through the lens of their constructs. This is the essence of Kelly's "fundamental postulate" of human behavior: that people's behavior, thoughts, and feelings are determined by the constructs they use to anticipate or predict events.

BOX 15.1 APPRAISAL AND STRESS

Kelly's assertion that personal constructs determine how people see the world is echoed in a number of other theories. An example is a theory of psychological stress developed by Richard Lazarus, Susan Folkman, and their colleagues (e.g., Lazarus, 1966; Lazarus & Folkman, 1984). You certainly have an intuitive understanding of what the word *stress* means. However, the precise nature of stress has been hard to agree on. Lazarus took a very cognitive view of it, which fits nicely with many of the ideas discussed in this chapter.

Lazarus argues that the experience of stress involves three processes. The first, **primary appraisal,** is the process of perceiving an impending threat. The next, **secondary appraisal,** is the process of determining what to do (of the many things that might be done) to deal with the threat. The third element,

coping, is doing whatever's been chosen. It should be obvious that this analysis relies extensively on the concept of appraisal. *Appraisal* is weighing and evaluating the meaning of the raw material of one's perceptions. The word *appraisal,* in fact, is similar in meaning to the word *construal.*

Lazarus has always emphasized that the two appraisal processes rely heavily on the person's representation of reality. As a result, many kinds of stress can easily be said to be in the mind of the beholder, rather than in the outside world. That is, perceiving a threat (versus no threat) is largely a matter of how people construe the situations they're in. A bustling city street may seem absolutely harmless to one person, enticing to another, and fraught with peril to someone else.

Similarly, how people choose to respond to a threat will depend partly on how they construe various actions. For one person, walking away from a threat means losing face or looking

foolish. For another person, the same response means being efficient and not wasting energy. In both cases, personal interpretations are crucial determinants of what people experience and how they act in response to a given event.

It's also assumed that people often *reinterpret* the meanings of events, either while they are taking place or after they occur. These reappraisals can be induced by changes in the situation or by changes in the constructs the person brings to bear on the situation. In some cases, called **defensive reappraisal,** the act of reappraising seems calculated to produce the best possible construal, even if it's unrealistic. In other cases, however, the reappraisal seems to be more a matter of finding an interpretation that fits the event well. This emphasis on people's ability to reorganize their interpretations of stressors is similar to the philosophical orientation that Kelly called *constructive alternativism.*

Kelly saw constructs as important because he believed all events in life are open to multiple interpretations (see also Box 15.1). Kelly used the term **constructive alternativism** as a label for this idea and for the further assumption that people decide for themselves what constructs to apply to events. Kelly held that people can always alter their experiences, even looking back on them, by construing them in different ways.

We should perhaps say something about the meaning of the word *event* before going on. Kelly used this word to refer broadly to virtually anything in a person's experience. We'll use it the same way here. *Event* can refer to objects, people, feelings, experiences, or physical events. We should also say something about the word *construe.* This word refers to mental processes that range from perception to understanding and interpretation. It's a broader word than any of these, encompassing all of them. It's also a more specific word, in the sense that it implies actively taking a point of view.

USING CONSTRUCTS

Applying a construct to an event is slightly more complex than it might seem at first. The process is similar to the way a scientist uses a theory. That is, when you apply a construct, you *hypothesize* (implicitly) that it will fit an event. Then you *test* the hypothesis by applying the construct and predicting something. If your prediction is *confirmed,* the construct applies and you retain it as useful. If your prediction is *disconfirmed,* you may rethink when to apply the construct, you may revise the construct, or you may even abandon it. Constructs that predict events most of the time have a high degree of **predictive efficiency.**

To illustrate, Ann believes that some men see women as unique individuals, with their own distinct qualities, whereas other men see women as stereotypes. When meeting and first talking with Jim, she construes him as a man who views women as individuals. She's about to test this construal by making the implicit prediction that he'll be interested in her weekend activity: motocross racing. If Jim is interested or impressed, her prediction will be confirmed. If he recoils in horror, her prediction will be disconfirmed. If the latter occurs, something about how Ann applies the construct, or something about the construct itself, may require revision.

Kelly's starting point was that people use their constructs to predict and anticipate events. He expanded on this basic idea by making a set of more focused statements, called *corollaries,* about constructs and how they're used. Here are several of them.

CONSTRUCTS ARE BIPOLAR

Kelly assumed that constructs are bipolar. That is, a construct consists of a pair of opposing characteristics. Examples are *friendly versus unfriendly* and *stable versus changeable.* The pole you're applying to the event you're construing is the **emergent pole.** If you view a person as friendly, you're applying your friendliness construct, with *friendly* as the emergent pole.

The end of the construct that's *not* being actively applied to the event is the **implicit pole.** The implicit pole is just as important as the emergent pole in defining the construct's nature. It's meaningless to think of someone as *friendly* unless you have an implicit recognition that it's possible for people to be *unfriendly.* Thus, both ends are involved in defining the construct, even though it's easy to lose track of that.

Kelly believed that constructs are *dichotomous* as well as *bipolar.* That is, he believed that people use constructs in a yes-or-no manner, not as varying on a continuum. Kelly admitted that people see gradations, but he had a way to deal with that (Kelly, 1955). He assumed that gradations arise from an array of interrelated dichotomous constructs. The array makes finer and finer distinctions, as one dichotomous decision leads to another one, at a lower level (see Figure 15.1).

For example, consider the construct *long versus short.* You can use it as a dichotomy, then repeat the process over and over again. It's as though you decide how long something is in a quick series of steps. First you decide if it's basically long or short. Assume you decide it's long. That throws out half the scale (the right half of Figure 15.1). Then you decide whether it's long or not among the generally long. That decision then reduces the range by half again, and you make another decision within whichever part is left. If you do this often enough, the decisions become so fine grained that the result is equivalent to a continuum.

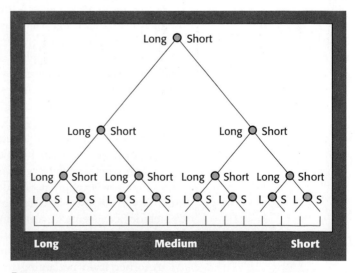

FIGURE 15.1

A dichotomous decision, repeated several times across ever-finer units, creates a set of possibilities that duplicates the range of variation along a continuum. The simple set of decisions illustrated here yields 16 gradations. Given a few more decisions, the result would be indistinguishable from a continuously varying scale.

Consistent with Kelly's general view, there's evidence that people tend to polarize their perceptions—particularly social perceptions—seeing the world in black-and-white terms. For example, when people are in different groups, they tend to think of the two groups in terms of *us versus them* (Tajfel & Turner, 1986). In the same way, people who are very committed to a partner in a close relationship tend to polarize their perceptions by devaluing potential alternative partners (D. J. Johnson & Rusbult, 1989).

THE ROLE OF RECURRENCES

Constructs reflect qualities that *recur* in a person's experience, that show up repeatedly. It's rare for a construct to emerge on the basis of a single event. Constructs evolve over time and across repeated experiences. Developing a construct from a series of events is complicated by the fact that no two events are exactly alike, even if they're from the same family of events. Think, for instance, of filling your car at a gas station. The experience is somewhat the same each time, but it's not identical from one time to another.

The fact that constructs are based on recurring elements makes good sense from the view we began with—that people try to anticipate events according to a personal theory. The kind of theory that's most sensible to invent would be one that's been useful in construing *many* events, not just a few. It follows, then, that constructs should be based on *recurring* themes or qualities.

RANGE AND FOCUS OF CONVENIENCE

Although recurrences are important, it's also important to recognize that most constructs won't be useful *everywhere*. A few can be used widely, for instance, *good versus bad*. But most are more limited in scope, and some apply only narrowly. For example, *friendly versus unfriendly* can be applied to fewer events than *good versus bad. Supportive versus not supportive* can be applied to even fewer. *Willing to lend class notes versus unwilling to lend class notes* applies to still fewer. The set of events for which a construct is useful is called its **range of convenience**. This range is wide for some constructs, narrow for others.

When people try to apply a construct to events outside its range of convenience, predictive efficiency usually drops. For example, the range of convenience of the construct *happy versus sad* includes people, some animals, songs, many social events, and maybe such things as skies and flowers. It would be harder to apply that construct to events such as stones or spaghetti. The result of *trying* to apply it to such events will likely be a lack of predictive efficiency. In general, it's not too often that people try to apply a construct to events that fall outside its range of convenience.

A construct's range of convenience isn't permanently fixed, however, because sometimes you *do* apply it outside its range of convenience and it works. The **permeability** of a construct is the degree to which its range of convenience can be spread to include new events. A construct that's permeable lets new types of events be added into its range of convenience fairly easily. One that's impermeable is more rigid and less likely to absorb new events into its range of convenience.

Another term pertaining to a construct's applicability is its **focus of convenience**: the events for which the construct is *most* predictive. A construct's focus of convenience is some narrower *portion* of its range of convenience.

For example, consider the constructs *sociable versus unsociable* and *polite versus impolite,* and situations where you might apply them. If you wanted to guess how many people Jane will talk to at a party, you'd probably be better off using the construct of *sociability* than *politeness*. This event falls within the range of convenience of both, but talking to people at a party is almost the essence of sociability. It's clearly in its focus of convenience. If you wanted to predict how Jane would reply to a surly store clerk, the *sociability* construct might work. But you'd probably do better predicting from *politeness*. Its focus of convenience is events that involve role-based behavior and specific social conventions. Both the party and the store clerk interaction are within the *range* of convenience of each construct. But differences in *focus* of convenience make one construct more useful than the other for each type of event.

ELABORATION AND CHANGE IN CONSTRUCT SYSTEMS

As indicated earlier, people's constructs evolve across time and experience. Change can come in several ways. If a construct continues to predict events well, it becomes more refined. If it predicts in new and interesting ways, it grows.

Kelly gave names to these two kinds of changes. **Definition** occurs during ordinary use of a construct. It involves applying the construct in a familiar way to an event it's very likely to fit. Applying it this way allows it to become more explicit or possibly more refined and precise. For example, people often squeeze avocados to tell whether they're ripe. The construal *ripe* implies a prediction of what you'll find when you cut the avocado open. Repeated application of this technique lets you refine your sense of how much softness implies perfect ripeness.

The other kind of elaboration, called **extension,** involves using the construct to predict or construe an event it hasn't been applied to before. This use has more potential for error, given the unfamiliarity, but it also provides the potential for elaboration. If the construct predicts well in unfamiliar territory, it thereby proves more broadly useful than was obvious before. This outcome adds more information than does definition. As an example, a person who's familiar with avocados but not cantaloupes may apply the squeeze technique to decide whether a cantaloupe is ripe. If the prediction made this way is accurate, the *ripeness* construct has been extended.

The idea of extension relates to two ideas we just discussed: permeability and range of convenience. Constructs that are *permeable* can be applied to new events more easily than those that are less permeable. Thus, they're more capable of change by the extension process.

Both extension and definition are important processes. Indeed, both are necessary. They differ in important ways, though. In general terms, definition is the *safer* of the two, whereas extension is potentially the more *informative* of the two.

Which process is more likely to occur depends on several factors. Some people are chronically more likely than others to go out on a limb and apply a construct in new ways, as extension requires. Indeed, some people make a habit of seeking out opportunities to engage in extension (see also Box 15.2). On the other hand, people don't normally do this throughout their construct systems at once. That is, doing definition in some domains is a way of creating a sense of security. You then can risk trying extension in some other domain.

Temporary factors probably also influence whether definition or extension occurs. For instance, being upset or anxious (maybe because of a wrong prediction) may inhibit extension. Having been made uncertain about one thing, you may want to be very certain about other things (McGregor, Zanna, Holmes, & Spencer, 2001). In contrast, boredom may lead to extension (Sechrest, 1977). Knowing which will occur at any moment may require knowing whether the person is motivated toward security or adventure at that moment.

BOX 15.2 THE THEORIST AND THE THEORY

George Kelly, Conceptual Pioneer

Just as individuals must elaborate and extend their construct systems, so must theorists. George Kelly was a theorist who was always willing to shift his construct system in directions that felt right to him, no matter what anyone else thought. His ideas moved along paths not yet traveled by personality theorists. He displayed a true pioneering spirit in his work, a pioneering spirit that had a counterpart in his personal history.

Kelly was born in 1905 on a farm in Kansas. When he was 4, his parents uprooted the family to move to Colorado to homestead a parcel of land (Thompson, 1968). Homesteading was a risky life in the best of circumstances, and the circumstances the Kellys confronted weren't the best. The land they'd claimed had no water. As a

result, they soon moved back to Kansas. Still, their westward migration reflected considerable independence of spirit. This spirit is also shown in Kelly's theoretical independence.

Two other experiences in Kelly's life also appear to be reflected directly in the theory he developed. The first occurred while he was teaching at a junior college in Iowa. His duties there included being drama coach. The fact that Kelly held this role is interesting for two reasons. First, it may well have helped sensitize him to the elusive nature of objective reality and the importance of the person's private understanding in creating a personal reality. Second, Kelly later developed a form of therapy in which the client is asked to enact a role, as if in a play. It seems likely that the idea for this technique, which is described later in the chapter, derived in part from Kelly's experiences with acting.

The other noteworthy experience occurred when Kelly was on the faculty

at Fort Hays State College in Kansas. While there, he developed a traveling clinic to serve public schools by helping teachers deal with problem children. Kelly made two observations during this period that influenced his later thinking. First, he discovered that inventing an unusual explanation for a client's problem often caused improvement. It didn't seem to matter what the explanation was, as long as it had two qualities: It had to account for the facts as the client understood them, and it had to suggest the usefulness of looking at the situation in a different way. If people could be made to look at their situation differently, they seemed to improve. Second, Kelly discovered that the problems teachers were reporting often said more about the teachers than the students. That is, what defined the problem was the way the teacher was construing the child's behavior, not the child's actual behavior. Both observations were strongly reflected in Kelly's theory.

Evolution of a construct system through definition and extension is growth. By implication, at least, both stem from people's choices about how to use constructs. Sometimes, though, circumstances *force* changes on people. Such changes can be disruptive. If you encounter a very unusual event, you don't have constructs readily available to interpret it. If an existing construct is used and fails badly, or if the person feels an absence of *any* construct to apply, the result can be abrupt change in the construct system. We'll consider the question of forced change later in the chapter when we take up the question of how to think about problems in adjustment.

ORGANIZATION AMONG CONSTRUCTS

The personal construct is the basic unit of analysis in this theory. But constructs don't rattle around loose in people's minds, to be applied piecemeal. Kelly assumed that each person's constructs are interrelated in an organized fashion. He argued that constructs form a hierarchy. Some are at low (*subordinate*) levels of abstraction, and others at higher (*superordinate*) levels, subsuming or taking in the more basic ones (see also Epstein, 1983). For example, *good versus bad* may subsume *generous versus stingy, friendly versus unfriendly,* and *broken versus unbroken. Good versus bad* thus is superordinate to the others.

Earlier in the chapter, we described how a hierarchy of constructs could create a sense of continuous variability on a dimension. In the example we used to illustrate that idea (construal of length), the same fundamental quality was dichotomized at each decision point. What we're talking about now is a little different. The qualities at the different levels relate to one another, but they aren't the same.

Is the hierarchical arrangement that you have among your constructs permanent? No. The organization is retained only if it has predictive efficiency. One common change is in what specific subordinate constructs a specific superordinate construct includes. For example, Alice's *friendly versus unfriendly* construct used to subsume *polite versus impolite*. She eventually grew to see these two as not being related. In her new organization, *politeness* relates instead to constructs such as *manipulative versus not manipulative*.

Organizations among constructs can be even more fluid than that. In principle, it's possible for two constructs to *reverse* places, so that the subordinate one becomes superordinate and vice versa. For instance, Judy's *loving versus not loving* used to be a broad construct that encompassed a number of others, such as *accepting versus rejecting*, which was more specific. Over time and experience, though, she came to see the sense of *acceptance* as broader. Her viewpoint shifted so that *loving* was encompassed by *acceptance*. She now has a different organization, in which the relationship between constructs has reversed (see Figure 15.2).

Organizations among constructs play a role in individual differences in personality. Assume for a moment that two people have similar sets of constructs but different *organizations* among them (see Figure 15.2). These two people would be quite different from each other in how they view and relate to the world.

There's one last point to make about these hierarchies: At any given moment, the organization constrains your construals and actions. In particular, using a given superordinate construct dictates which subordinate constructs you're most likely to use in more fine-grained construals of the event. That is, any superordinate construct subsumes *some* lower-level ones but not others. Using a superordinate construct channels you toward subordinate constructs that fall under it and away from those that don't. This, in turn, greatly influences the character of your subsequent impressions.

For example, Julie walks up to David after class, converses for a few minutes, and then asks whether he wants to study with her for their upcoming test. If David initially construes Julie as a *student,* he's likely to apply constructs that are under *student* in his hierarchy as he further construes her behavior. He may filter her conversation to judge how much she knows and decide from that whether the proposed study session would be useful. However, if David initially construes Julie as an *attractive woman,* he'll apply different constructs to the same aspects of her behavior. He may see her conversation as a sign of interest, the offer to study together as a ploy to get to know him better, and the study session as a step toward intimacy.

INDIVIDUALITY OF CONSTRUCTS

Thus far, our discussion of constructs and their organization has largely disregarded the word *personal*. However, that word was every bit as important to Kelly as the word

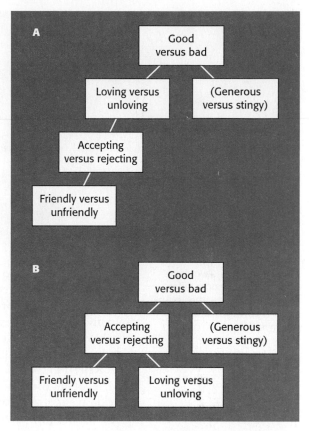

FIGURE 15.2
Two potential hierarchies of constructs held by one person at two different times (or by two different people), incorporating the same constructs but organized differently. In organization A, *loving versus unloving* subsumes *accepting versus rejecting,* which in turn subsumes *friendly versus unfriendly.* In B, *accepting versus rejecting* subsumes both *friendly versus unfriendly* and *loving versus unloving.* Someone with organization B would hold *acceptance* as fundamental and as implicit both in *friendliness* and in *loving,* which are distinct. Someone with organization A would treat *loving* as fundamental and as implicit in *acceptance,* which in turn is implicit in *friendliness.*

People have a need to understand and predict events around them. People differ greatly from each other, however, in how they interpret any given event.

construct. Kelly emphasized that each person's understanding of reality is separate from everyone else's. Each person's construct system is unique.

It's easy to be misled on this point by the fact that people usually can find words for their constructs and different people even use the same words. However, words don't always mean precisely the same thing to one person as to another. Perhaps the easiest illustration is the deceptively simple statement *I love you.* This sentence can have a vast number of meanings, depending on who's saying it to whom and the psychological context in which it's being said.

Indeed, even when two people think they agree about the meaning of a single word, it's impossible to be sure they do. For example, you say something is *red,* and I agree with you: It's red. But is your experience of redness, your construal of it, exactly the same as mine or even close to mine? Who can know? In principle, the same problem occurs in all experience. And that is precisely Kelly's point about people's constructs. Even if the words are the same, the constructs are probably not. Indeed, Kelly emphasized that constructs are *preverbal.* People can have a hard time representing their constructs, even to themselves, except as raw experience (Kelly, 1969; see also Riedel, 1970).

If all of our constructs are potentially so different, how do we ever communicate? How do we ever get along with one another? The answer, in part, is that your constructs don't *totally* diverge from those of other people. Remember, constructs are retained only if they have predictive efficiency. If they fail to predict adequately, you modify or discard them and form new ones. By the time you're an adult, you've tested your constructs quite a bit. So has everyone else. There has to be *some* similarity between your construct system and the systems of other people, or they wouldn't have been maintained for so long.

Nevertheless, construct systems do differ enough that there's plenty of potential for disagreement. How then do people find a sense of harmony with each other? How do they even get to know each other? In Kelly's view, the process of getting to know other people is partly (perhaps largely) a matter of testing your constructs against theirs. If you find you agree about what constructs apply to various events, you feel comfortable with each other. To put it another way, people with similar construct systems see the same things when they look at the world. That similarity of views is reassuring and forms the basis of a friendship. From this view, you form relationships with other people by jointly assessing similarities in construct systems (see Duck, 1973, 1977; Duck & Allison, 1978; Klion & Leitner, 1991; Tesser, 1971).

Both the use of constructs in forming impressions of other people and the fact that different people use different constructs are nicely illustrated in research by Higgins, King, and Mavin (1982). Participants were asked to write down the traits of several specific friends (Study 1) or the traits of several specific types of people (Study 2). The traits that a given person wrote down frequently (Study 1) or wrote down first (Study 2) were taken as representing important constructs for that person, because they were so accessible in memory.

Several days later, in what was portrayed as a separate study, each participant read a description of a target person written especially for him or her. The description included some of the participant's important (accessible) constructs and some that were less important (less accessible). After doing another task (to interfere with memory), the participants wrote their impressions of the target person. Then they tried to recall the description they'd read. As expected, the participants' impressions were influenced by the constructs that were important to them personally, and they tended to disregard the other ones (see Figure 15.3). Indeed, they had a harder time even recalling the unimportant ones. Apparently, then, different people do rely on different mental dimensions in construing others.

SIMILARITIES AND DIFFERENCES BETWEEN PEOPLE

In Kelly's view, people are psychologically similar to each other if their systems of constructs are similar. Two people need not have gone through the same events to have similar constructs. Nor will two people who do experience the same events necessarily have similar constructs. A given construct can emerge from a thousand different events, and any event can be construed in many different ways. What makes people resemble each other is similarity in their *patterns of construals*—however the patterns arise— not similarity in their "learning histories" (see also Gilovich, 1990).

To Kelly, this principle applies to differences and similarities between persons and also to those between cultures. People from a given culture typically share a physical environment and manner of upbringing, but Kelly thought this was of secondary importance. To him, the essence of a culture is a similarity in how people construe experiences (Kelly, 1962).

Research appears to support the idea that cultural differences relate to variations in people's constructs (Triandis et al., 1984). Participants in this research made judgments about what kinds of behavioral elements occur in different kinds of social interactions. Analyzing the judgments made by each participant revealed something of the constructs applied by that person to social situations. Comparisons from one person to another indicated that people from the same culture shared elements of their construct systems. These similarities were *not* shared as widely across the different cultures.

ROLE TAKING

Much of life involves social interaction. If people have different construct systems, how do they interact? According to this theory, a social interaction entails an elaborate set of processes. It involves an attempt by each person to construe some part of the construct system held by the other. In other words, to really interact with someone else requires you to try to understand and anticipate how that person is understanding and anticipating reality. This is what Kelly meant by **role taking** with respect to another person.

When in a role, you're especially interested in understanding how the other person views *your* role. What does the person expect of you? What constructs is the person using to predict your behavior? If you can answer these questions in your own mind, you can act in ways that the other person can interpret within his or her construct system.

Is it possible to take roles effectively if your construct system differs from those of the other people involved? Yes and no. Role taking is more complete and effective if you construe the other person's construct system in more or less the way it actually

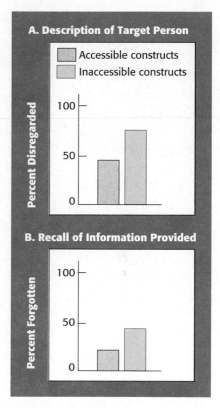

FIGURE 15.3
Each participant received a description of a target person that was made up of several accessible constructs (ones that the participant used spontaneously) and several inaccessible constructs (ones that the participant didn't use spontaneously). (A) In writing impressions of their target people later on, participants gave a lot of weight to the accessible constructs that had been mentioned and tended to disregard the others. (B) Indeed, participants were even less able to remember the inaccessible constructs when asked to recall the initial descriptions of their target people. *Source: Adapted from Higgins, King, & Mavin, 1982, Experiment 1.*

exists. But it's not the entire construct system that matters. The effectiveness of your role taking depends mainly on how accurately you construe the other person's construal of *your* role.

Evidence that people work to get pictures of each other's roles when interacting comes from research on how people try to establish common ground in a conversation. For example, an expert has to use different terms when talking with a novice than when talking with another expert. The expert also must decide how much detail to convey. But this decision isn't made just once. The expert has to continue to judge whether the novice is following the expert, and adjust further, if necessary. This continued adjustment does occur in people's conversations (Isaacs & Clark, 1987). Furthermore, it's an interactive process between those conversing. People who overhear the conversation don't grasp the common ground as clearly as the people in it (Schober & Clark, 1989).

We enact many roles in the course of our lives. Not all are important or have more than superficial impact. The role of store customer, for instance, matters little to most of us most of the time. Other roles, however, are extremely important, even central to our lives. These roles, which Kelly termed **core roles,** are major determinants of our sense of identity. Examples are occupational and professional roles, the roles of parent and child, close friend, lover, and so on. Whether any of these actually *is* a core role depends on the person, of course.

Because core roles are important, failing to perform them adequately can have adverse consequences. Kelly said that failing to enact a core role in the way it's construed by another person produces guilt. **Guilt** thus is an awareness of a disparity between your actions and the actions you see as fitting the other's expectations for your role. This definition of guilt is similar in some respects to Rogers's discussion of *conditions of worth* (Chapter 14), in which people feel uncomfortable when they fail to live up to others' expectations for them.

PERSONAL CONSTRUCTS AND BEHAVIORAL CONSISTENCY

Back in Chapter 4, we addressed in some detail the issue of behavioral consistency. We noted there that people are apparently less consistent in their actions than seemed implied by early trait views of personality. This evidence led to the emergence of an *interactionist* position, in which personality and situational forces are seen as joint determinants of behavior.

The personal construct viewpoint allows us to address this issue in a way that's very similar to the context-dependent view of traits presented toward the end of Chapter 4 (and also discussed in Chapter 16). It says that to predict a person's behavior in any given situation, we need to know how the person *construes* the situation. An individual will act in a consistent way across situations to the degree that the situations are construed in similar ways.

This idea sounds a little like the principle of generalization from the learning perspective. Where it differs from generalization is its emphasis on the personal. It doesn't matter whether the situations look the same or different to an outside *objective* observer. What matters is whether the person who's behaving

An effective communicator presents ideas in terms the listener can understand.

perceives the situations as similar. Similar construals of situations should yield cross-situational consistency. Divergent construals should yield less consistency.

Research by Lord (1982) found support for this idea. Participants described what characteristics would go into being *conscientious* in each of six common situations (e.g., keeping good lecture notes, keeping an orderly closet). These descriptions were done using a variation on the Q-sort method described in Chapter 14. These Q-sorts produced profiles of how the participant viewed the characteristics of each situation. The profiles were then compared with one another (for each participant) to assess their similarity.

Participants' actual conscientiousness was rated by an observer later in six situations corresponding closely to those the participant had rated. Participants' level of conscientiousness proved to be most consistent across the situations that they'd construed in similar terms. Behavior was less consistent across situations that they'd construed in divergent terms.

Assessment

We've focused in this chapter on the idea that personality is defined by the constructs that a person uses in dealing with the world. Personality assessment from this viewpoint likewise emphasizes assessment of the constructs the person uses.

KELLY'S ROLE CONSTRUCT REPERTORY TEST

In thinking about how to get an accurate view of another person's system of constructs, Kelly confronted a dilemma: It's useless to do behavioral observation, because a given behavior might stem from the use of any of several constructs. But asking people to describe their constructs isn't satisfactory either, for several reasons.

First, although we've given names to constructs throughout the chapter, constructs aren't always easy to label. As noted earlier, many are intuitive or preverbal. They exist in a private experiential form that can't be expressed. Second, people aren't used to describing their constructs. As a result, they may not do a good job at communicating what they mean, even if they can pin it down. Finally, the words that people choose to describe constructs are often so open to interpretation that it's hard to get clear, specific meanings from what's being said.

Faced with these problems, Kelly tried to devise a strategy for getting at people's constructs indirectly. Rather than have people verbalize their constructs, he had them engage in construals. Across repeated construals, the nature of the construct system should begin to reveal itself. Kelly called his procedure the Role Construct Repertory Test, a name that's usually shortened to **Rep Test.** As implied by the longer title, this test often (although not always) focuses on constructs used to perceive aspects of people and their roles.

The Rep Test involves the use of a printed grid (see Figure 15.4). In this grid, significant people in your life (who have different roles) are listed at the heads of columns. The rows are used to specify a set of comparisons and construals to make. In taking the test, you begin by reading a definition for each role that's being used and deciding who in your life best fits that definition. Then you write that person's name on the grid next to the role label, not using any person's name twice.

Then you start with the construals. For each row, you're asked to think about the people listed in three specific columns (marked by circles in the figure). More

	Yourself	Mother	Father	Spouse	Pal	Rejecting person	Pitied person	Attractive person	Emergent Pole	Implicit Pole
Sort no.	1	2	3	4	5	6	7	8	Emergent Pole	Implicit Pole
1						○	○	○		
2	○			○	○					
3	○						○	○		
4				○	○		○			
5	○	○	○							
6		○	○				○			
...										
n		○		○		○				

FIGURE 15.4

Example of the sort of grid used in the Rep Test. You begin by filling in the names of the people who play various roles in your life in the slanted sections across the top. Then you conduct a series of comparisons among sets of three people at a time, deciding how two of them are similar to each other in a way that makes them different from the third. (See the text for a more complete description.)

Source: From Kelly, 1955. Reproduced with permission of Gladys Kelly.

precisely, you are to think of an important characteristic that makes two of those three people similar to each other and different from the third. Once you've decided, you mark the two that are similar and write a word or phrase in the column headed "Emergent Pole" to indicate how the two are alike. In the column headed "Implicit Pole," you indicate how the third person is different. Next you look at the people (roles) in the other columns, decide whether they fit the emergent pole of the construct or the implicit pole, and mark each accordingly. When you've done one row, you go to the next, repeating the whole process row by row.

As you go through the rows, you're generating a list of constructs. These aren't the only constructs you have. But since the people listed across the top are people who play important roles in your life, the constructs that come up are probably important in your construals of people. Several of the comparisons in the Rep Test are of interest in their own right. Consider line 3 in Figure 15.4, where you're asked to think about yourself, an attractive person, and a pitied person. Which of the two will you see as more like yourself and why? This comparison reveals something about your feelings toward yourself and also what aspect of yourself comes easily to mind.

The roles listed in Figure 15.4 represent only a few of the roles in the full Rep Test. Furthermore, people doing this test also usually do many construals, thus providing a much larger base of information. This procedure has also been adapted to assess construals of other sorts of events, such as social issues (Epting, 1972), occupations (Shubsachs, 1975), and situations (Krieger, Epting, & Leitner, 1974; Neimeyer & Neimeyer, 1981).

Though the Rep Test is useful, it also has limitations. As noted earlier, people's constructs can't always be verbalized. The Rep Test tries to get around this by asking people to actively construe people and to use whatever construct naturally comes to mind to say what makes people similar or different. This strategy only partly handles the problem, though, because the person still has to provide a label for the construct.

This requirement creates two potential problems. The first is the ordinary problem of whether the word used to identify the construct means the same thing to one person as to another. The second problem is that being asked repeatedly to label your constructs may create a bias in what constructs you use while doing the test. Specifically, you may be inclined to report only constructs that are easy to verbalize, even if those aren't the most important constructs in your mind (cf. Shubsachs, 1975). Thus, even the Rep Test may be susceptible to the problems inherent in just asking people to describe their construct systems.

Problems in Behavior, and Behavior Change

The importance of personal constructs in personality is also stressed in considering the nature of problems and what's involved in the process of therapy (see also Neimeyer, 1985).

Personal Constructs and Psychological Distress

In Kelly's view, normal human functioning involves successfully anticipating and interpreting events. Problems in behavior thus involve problems in interpreting or predicting events.

Such difficulties can arise for several reasons. One possibility is confronting events that differ drastically from any previously experienced. Because of this lack of experience, you may not have constructs that seem relevant. The event, in effect, is beyond your ability to grasp it. Another possibility is that you may be trying to construe the event with a construct with poor predictive efficiency for that situation.

Kelly said that when people don't have adequate constructs, they feel uncertain and helpless. He labeled this experience **anxiety.** If the event is outside the available construct system, people sometimes even have trouble grasping why they're experiencing anxiety.

How often do people experience events that differ greatly from their prior experiences?

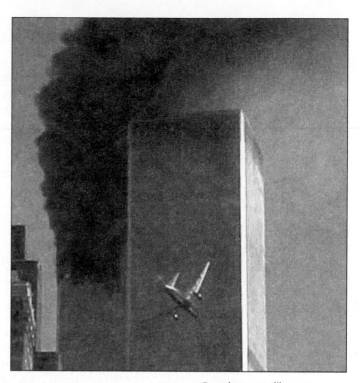

Experiences unlike any you have had before are hard to absorb, because you lack constructs for them.

Perhaps more often than you might imagine. Think back to your first week at college, for example. That period is often filled with experiences that differ enough from what people knew before to make them wonder what's going on. Perhaps you even felt concern or apprehension. The same feelings can occur for someone entering a new job (Van Maanen, 1973, 1975), being hospitalized for an illness, or having her first child (Deutsch, Ruble, Fleming, Brooks-Gunn, & Stangor, 1988). In fact, anytime you do *anything* for the very first time, it can be unsettling, just because it's the first time and you don't know exactly what to expect.

As more extreme cases, consider the experiences of people involved in disasters, such as hurricanes, fires, and earthquakes. It's often said that such experiences are traumatic precisely because they are so unlike anything the people have ever gone through before. Consequently, the people have no constructs to interpret the events or anticipate their consequences. Think about people in the midst of divorce, victims of crime, and those who win huge sums of money. These people are suddenly experiencing things that prior events in their lives haven't prepared them for. Part of the difficulty in living through these events is the very lack of constructs available for use in anticipating their consequences and implications.

It's unpleasant to discover that your constructs are inadequate to deal with events. Even worse, however, are events that suggest that important aspects of your construct system may be completely *wrong* and that major change is necessary (cf. Leitner & Cado, 1982). The more central the construct that's challenged, the more extensive the change that's necessary and the greater the problem. The sense of an imminent major change in one's fundamental construct system is termed **threat.** The experience of threat is much the same as that of anxiety but more extreme. Both arise from poor prediction from the construct system. In threat, however, the failure is more massive and fundamental.

DEALING WITH ANXIETY AND THREAT

Reducing anxiety (or threat) is straightforward in principle, though it can be more difficult in practice. One way is to generate a new construct. This response to poor prediction may be the major source of new constructs across a person's lifetime (see also Box 15.3). The other way to deal with threat or anxiety is to modify an existing construct so the experience can be successfully construed through it. If the event can then be construed with predictive efficiency, the anxiety or threat should evaporate.

As noted earlier in the chapter, sometimes you can modify a construct by extending its range of convenience. Doing this means saying, in effect, that the new experience really isn't totally new. It has similarities to other experiences you've had; you just didn't notice it before.

Sometimes this doesn't work, though, and you have to change the construct in a bigger way. Making one change may even require more changes. Why? Recall that

---

BOX 15.3 RECONSTRUCTING YOUR WORLD AFTER A TRAUMATIC EVENT

Minor adversity strikes everyone on occasion—getting a test score that's a point short of the grade you wanted, finding a ticket on your car window after shopping just a little too long, or coming down with the flu the day before spring break. Most people's constructs allow them to interpret and understand such minor inconveniences (e.g., "Stuff happens"). But what about a traumatic event—being diagnosed with a life-threatening illness, being raped or beaten, or hearing that members of your family were just killed in a car accident?

Traumatic events are harder to integrate into one's world view than minor events, for many reasons. For one, traumatic events often are sudden and unexpected. Moreover, traumatic events often create irreversible, long-lasting problems for the future. By their very nature, traumatic events suggest a world that's unpredictable and uncontrollable (Tedeschi & Calhoun, 1995). They can undermine the most basic assumptions people hold about themselves and their world (e.g., Horowitz, 1986; Janoff-Bulman, 1992).

Kelly's theory suggests that people who experience a traumatic event will struggle to create new constructs for interpreting it. That's also what more recent theorists say. Tedeschi and Calhoun (1995) argue that a traumatic event partly destroys the person's worldview. They also say that the event thereby initiates a potential for growth. The shattering of one worldview prompts an effort to construct a new more meaningful one. Others have taken similar positions (e.g., Davis, Nolen-Hoeksema, & Larson, 1998; Taylor, 1983; Thompson & Janigian, 1988).

Research has even begun to show that making sense of traumatic events can help people adjust and move forward. For example, Thompson (1985) studied people whose homes were severely damaged by fire. Those who found a positive meaning in the event coped best with it. Thompson found similar effects among people who suffered a stroke (Thompson, 1991). Other research has shown that finding positive aspects of having cancer seems to help people cope with it (Andrykowski, Brady, & Hunt, 1993; Stanton et al., 2002; Taylor, Lichtman, & Wood, 1984; Tomich & Helgeson, 2002), though the data are not com-

pletely consistent (Tomich & Helgeson, 2004).

These and other studies have begun to establish a link between psychological well-being and the capacity to understand and find meaning in traumatic events (for review, see Helgeson, Reynolds, & Tomich, 2006). It's even possible that finding meaning may promote physical health. Bower, Kemeny, Taylor, and Fahey (1998) examined immune functioning and mortality among HIV-positive gay men who had recently experienced the AIDS-related death of a partner or close friend. Men who found meaning in the death showed better immune functioning during the months afterward compared to those less able to find meaning. Those who found meaning also had a lower rate of AIDS-related mortality during that period. Conceptually similar results have been reported by Tomich and Helgeson (2002) in a study of physical functioning among breast cancer patients. Although there are inconsistencies in the literature (Helgeson et al., 2006), it may be that finding meaning not only enhances well-being after a traumatic event, but it also helps keep people alive.

your construct system forms a hierarchy. Subordinate constructs contribute to and help define high-level ones. When you change your sense of what one construct means to you, you're rearranging some of the connections in your hierarchy, maybe even a lot of connections.

Sometimes the problem isn't that you don't have a construct to use but that you're continuing to use a construct that's outlived its usefulness. Sometimes you're treating a construct as though it has a broader range of convenience than it actually has. The result in each of these cases is unsuccessful anticipation of new events. Again, the solution is to reorganize your construct system. In the latter case, the reorganization means restricting the construct's range of convenience. If your construct has really outlived its usefulness, though, you're back to having to come up with a new one.

From the personal construct view on personality, the distress that goes with poor prediction of events is the primary symptom of problems. This is what leads a person to seek help. Keep in mind that the construct system is the essence of personality from this point of view. The process of therapy is one of assisting people in elaborating or altering their construct system to improve its predictive efficiency (see Epting, 1980; Fransella, 1972). Better prediction will result in less anxiety, distress, and dissatisfaction.

FIXED-ROLE THERAPY

What kinds of therapeutic procedures help attain this goal? Keep in mind that there's no perfect construct system that people should adopt to be adjusted to reality. Everyone has a personal view of the world. Each person must evolve an arrangement of constructs that will be functional from his or her personal viewpoint. The goal of therapy is to facilitate evolution of the construct system in its own way.

Kelly believed the best way to promote evolution of the construct system is to have the person change outward behavior. This will force the person to generate unusual construals of events that result. The procedure Kelly developed for doing this is called **fixed-role therapy.** In this procedure, the client enacts the role of a hypothetical person. This person is carefully crafted to have certain characteristics that the client wants. This fixed-role character is even given a name, to provide a sense of identity to the role.

The therapeutic process begins with an assessment in which the client completes a self-characterization or self-description. On the basis of this, the therapist develops a role for the client to enact. The role is a composite of some of the client's positive characteristics and of some characteristics the client feels are lacking.

The use of a composite role has several benefits. Building in some familiar characteristics helps make the role easier to adopt because it keeps the role from being entirely alien. Building pre-existing *positive* qualities into it helps to create a sense of confidence in your ability to enact the role, and it strengthens the use of constructs that contribute to those positive qualities.

When the fixed role has been established, you're asked to enact it for a while. The idea is not to adopt the role as a permanent part of your personality but just to enact it for some period. This instruction means there's little risk involved, which takes some of the pressure off. If you aren't happy with how something goes, you can look at the experience as just a bit of acting that needs more polishing, not as a failure. It often happens, however, that after a while, the client stops thinking of the role as a role and starts to think of it as a natural part of himself or herself (Collier & Callero, 2005).

Enacting this fixed role forces the client to construe events in ways that differ from those used previously. For example, Luke sees himself as shy and passive and interpersonally inadequate. Luke might be asked to take on the role of a person who's quiet but "deep," a person whom others find interesting and stimulating but who doesn't always show those characteristics openly because he's more interested in learning something from others than in showing his own strengths. He's a person who has a pronounced but subtle influence on others, so that people don't always realize they're being influenced until later on.

Notice that this role (which is adapted from Kelly, 1955, p. 121) is a composite of Luke's self-image and characteristics that he sees himself as lacking. The role incorporates quietness (which Luke now has) but recasts it within a general effectiveness in interpersonal interaction. In order to enact this role, Luke must construe his behavior in ways that differ from his previous view of himself. He must construe his quietness as a positive act of benefiting from others, rather than as a sign of passivity and inadequacy. In this way, he's rearranging his system of constructs. As he enacts this role over time, he should gradually reorganize his construct system, modifying constructs at some points and perhaps developing new ones at other points. The result should be a system with a high degree of predictive efficiency that permits him to live a more satisfying life than he did before.

Personal Construct Theory: Problems and Prospects

Personal construct theory shares a couple of strengths with the humanistic theories described in Chapter 14. Its emphasis on the uniqueness and validity of each person's experience fits with the emphasis those theories place on the importance of subjective experiences. Similarly, the principle of constructive alternativism suggests a basis for assuming that people tend toward being better over time. That is, people can always reconstrue events in more and more functional ways.

The personal construct view places less of an emphasis on will than does the humanistic orientation. Although in principle you're free to determine for yourself how to construe the present, past experiences have a big influence on present construals. When people make drastic reorganizations of how they view the world, they don't do so easily or without strain. It remains an open question, then, how free people actually are from their past.

Perhaps the greatest strength of this view on personality is one that was wholly unanticipated by its author. As you'll see in the next chapter, Kelly's intuitions foreshadowed several themes that would re-emerge later on from very different sources. These ideas came from cognitive psychology, not personality, and returned to personality only through a circuitous path. Kelly's view, however, was much more idiographic than the newer cognitive view (recall his emphasis on the idea that constructs are personal). This idiographic emphasis humanizes the ideas in a way that the newer views don't usually do.

One historic problem of personal construct psychology is that it's not terribly conducive to research. There is a cadre of personality psychologists who are devoted to personal construct psychology, and there are journals devoted to personal construct psychology. But the group who takes this view is relatively small in number.

What are the prospects for this view on personality? We've continued to include it in this book largely because of its status as a forerunner of cognitive theories. The extent to which this is true is quite remarkable. In some ways, it is this convergence of lines of thought that provides a continuing basis for interest in personal construct psychology. Lacking an active research literature of its own, however, personal construct psychology is beginning to acquire the patina of ideas that are primarily of historical interest. It appears to be on its way to fading from the scene, perhaps becoming a footnote in the discussion of newer cognitive models.

· SUMMARY ·

Kelly believed that people have a fundamental need to predict the events that they experience. They do so by developing a system of personal constructs, which they use to interpret or construe new events. *Constructs* are derived from recurring elements in one's experience, but because they're developed separately by each person, each person's system of constructs is unique. *Constructive alternativism* is the idea that any event, for any person, is open to multiple interpretations and that people decide for themselves how to construe each event.

People implicitly evaluate their constructs over time in terms of *predictive efficiency,* or the degree to which the constructs allow the person to interact successfully with the world. Kelly treated constructs as bipolar and dichotomous. Each construct under use has an *emergent pole,* the end of the conceptual dimension that is being applied to the event being construed. The *implicit pole* of the construct is the end not being applied. A construct's *range of convenience* is the range of events to which it can be applied meaningfully. Its *focus of convenience* is the range of events for which it is optimally predictive.

Constructs can be refined by actively using them in familiar ways (a process called *definition*) and can be elaborated by using them in unfamiliar ways (a process called *extension*). Changes in one's construct system can also be induced by situations in which one finds oneself without adequate constructs to interpret an event. Constructs are organized in a hierarchical system of inclusiveness. This organization is not permanent, however, just as the constructs themselves are not permanent. How long any aspect of the construct system remains stable depends on its predictive efficiency.

Kelly held that constructs are unique to each person, despite the fact that they're often illustrated by familiar words. The fact that each person's constructs are potentially different from those of other people raises questions about how people can interact effectively. In Kelly's view, getting to know other people means testing one's own constructs against theirs. People are similar to the extent their construct systems are similar. Interpersonal interaction in this viewpoint involves the taking of a role with respect to some other person. *Role taking* entails construing how the other person is construing you in your role. *Core roles* are those roles that are particularly important to one's sense of identity.

Assessment from Kelly's viewpoint is done by the Rep Test, which assesses the constructs that people use in construing their role relations and other aspects of their experience. Kelly's viewpoint on problems in self-management was that people experience *anxiety* when events fall outside the range of convenience of their construct systems, and they experience *threat* when they anticipate a major reorganization of important aspects of their construct systems because of poor predictive efficiency. Kelly developed *fixed-role therapy* as a way of getting people to engage in behaviors that they would not ordinarily engage in, for the purpose of developing different ways of construing events in their lives.

· GLOSSARY ·

Anxiety   The response to inability to impose a construct adequately on an event one is experiencing.

Constructive alternativism   The idea that any event can be construed in many ways.

Coping   The effort to handle a threat by executing whatever response has been chosen.

Core roles   The roles that are central to one's life, contributing to one's identity.

Defensive reappraisal   The process of defining a threat out of existence.

Definition   The applying of a construct in a familiar way, causing its refinement.

Emergent pole   The end of a construct that's being applied to the event being construed.

Extension   The applying of a construct to an unfamiliar event in an attempt to increase its range of convenience.

Fixed-role therapy   A therapy in which the client enacts a role that differs somewhat from his or her current self-perception.

Focus of convenience   The range of applicable events for which a construct has the best prediction.

Guilt   The sensing of a discrepancy between one's acts and another's role expectations for oneself.

Implicit pole   The end of the construct that isn't being applied to the event being construed.

Permeability   The degree to which a construct extends to events to which it hasn't yet been applied.

Personal construct   A mental representation used to interpret events.

Predictive efficiency   The degree to which a construct can be applied successfully to events.

Primary appraisal   The process of perceiving a threat in the environment.

Range of convenience   The range of events for which a construct is useful.

Rep Test   A test used to identify a person's major constructs.

Role taking   The process of construing how another person construes oneself.

Secondary appraisal   The process of determining how to respond to a threat.

Threat   The perception of an impending reorganization of one's construct system.

The Cognitive Self-Regulation Perspective

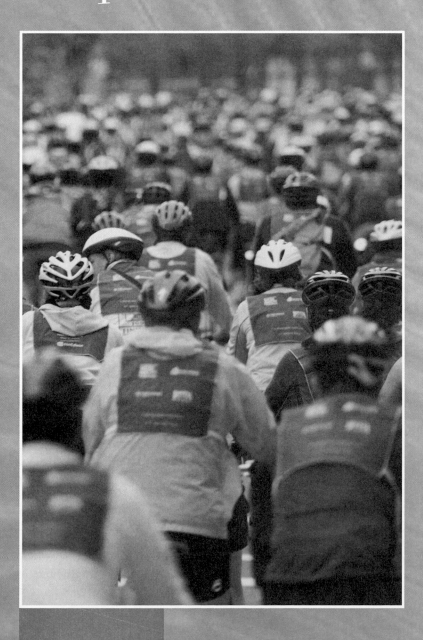

The Cognitive Self-Regulation Perspective: Major Themes and Underlying Assumptions

The human nervous system is a vast and elaborate network of tiny cells that communicate continuously with each other. These cells relay information from one place to another throughout your life, whether you're awake or asleep. This network has been compared to many things over the decades, including a network of telephone lines, a paper-shuffling bureaucracy, and a computer. As computer functions were extended to control autonomous agents, some came to think that a *robot* metaphor is better than a *computer* metaphor, because human lives are filled with actions aimed at reaching goals. To some psychologists, it doesn't seem outlandish to ask whether human beings pursuing those goals are not perhaps the ultimate "guided missiles."

Theories that relate these metaphors to personality aren't as well developed as theories with longer histories. Nonetheless, this way of thinking does seem to have at least a few implications for personality. Those implications are described in Chapters 16 and 17.

The ideas presented in these chapters rest implicitly on three assumptions. The first is that understanding behavior means understanding how people deal with the information that surrounds them. *Information* is a pretty vague term, but its meaning is fairly intuitive. Look around the room. You're surrounded by sights and sounds and maybe by other people doing things. Each of these is a source of information. The information comes in tiny bits, but you don't experience it that way. You see *walls,* not just patches of color. You hear a *song,* not unconnected bits of noise. You have an *impression* of your roommate, not just a collection of facts. To have these broader experiences, you integrate and organize the bits of information the world provides you.

A second assumption is that the flow of life consists of an elaborate web of decisions. Some of them are conscious, but far more occur outside your awareness. Your personality is reflected partly in the flow of decision making in your mind. It's reflected in the biases that follow from the sort of mental organization you have and how you use it. The flow of implicit decisions is more unpredictable than people used to think. The realization of this has led to some reworking of theories about cognitive processes. This, in turn, also has implications for thinking about personality. Despite these changes, some theorists think that human thought is a continuing stream of implicit decisions at many levels.

These two assumptions underlie some of the ideas presented in Chapter 16. There, we describe theories about how the mind is organized and how personality is thus structured. The ideas described there focus on how events are represented in memory and how memories guide your experience of the world. How all this complexity is organized and used is an important issue from the cognitive vantage point.

A third assumption behind this perspective on personality is that human behavior is goal directed. This idea represents a view of motivation, albeit somewhat different from the motive view that was considered in Chapter 5. The idea that goals underlie behavior is consistent with the robotics metaphor. A robot has a purpose (or several) that it's trying to fulfill. It often has some kind of representation of its goal, and it tries to move toward that representation.

A self-regulation view on personality assumes that people do much the same—take up (or create) goals and try to move toward them. To be sure they're moving in the right direction, people monitor their progress. From this idea comes the term *self-regulation*. In this view, human action is continually aimed at attaining some goal or other. Life is a never-ending stream of sensing, checking, and adjusting—an ever-continuing process of moving within a network of self-defined goals. This idea provides part of the basis of Chapter 17.

These two chapters are more interconnected than were the pairs of chapters on any other perspective besides psychoanalysis. The ideas in these two chapters aren't so much *alternative* views as *interrelated* views. One set of ideas tends to flow into the other. Chapter 16 focuses on the person's mental world; Chapter 17 focuses on how this mental world is reflected in actions.

Contemporary Cognitive Views

Don and Sandy have been shopping for a house. Some options were easy to discard: one was way too much money, one was right next to a gas station, one was ugly. Others were harder. They're getting to be good at noticing things they care about. They've started making a brief list of the pros and cons of each, sure that by doing that they'll make a rational choice. Last month, though, they went to a house on Forest Hills Drive. It's smaller than they wanted, needs more work than they wanted, doesn't have the pool they wanted. But something about it seemed exactly right. Almost at once they decided to buy it, and now it's their home.

ONE TOPIC in cognitive psychology is how people represent their experiences mentally. Another is how people make decisions. Hundreds of studies have examined these processes, and many theories have been proposed to account for them. The picture of how such processes work has also influenced how theorists think about personality.

Aspects of the picture are startlingly similar to ideas proposed much earlier by George Kelly, described in Chapter 15. Kelly never saw himself as a cognitive theorist. In fact, he actively distanced himself from that idea (Neimeyer & Neimeyer, 1981). Study of cognitive processes in personality stemmed mostly from other lines of thought (Bruner, 1957; Heider, 1958; Koffka, 1935; Köhler, 1947; Lewin, 1951a). In fact, in what came to be called the "cognitive revolution" in psychology, Kelly was pretty thoroughly ignored. Yet aspects of today's cognitive view of personality greatly resemble his ideas.

For example, cognitive theorists view people as implicit scientists who try to predict the world, as did Kelly. But there's a different slant on *why*. Today's view is that you're surrounded by more information than you can use. You can't check every bit, so you don't try (Gigerenzer & Goldstein, 1996). Instead, you impose an organization. You use partial information to make inferences about the rest (J. R. Anderson, 1991; Nisbett & Ross, 1980). This saves mental resources (Macrae, Milne, & Bodenhausen, 1994). That's important, because you usually have several things on your mind at once, and you *need* those resources. You can save resources this way, though, only if you can predict events fairly well.

Representing Your Experience of the World

Cognitive theorists are interested partly in how people organize, store, and retrieve memories of their experiences. How do we do these things?

SCHEMAS AND THEIR DEVELOPMENT

People impose order from recurrences of similar qualities across repeated events. In doing so, they form **schemas,** mental organizations of information (also called *knowledge structures*). Schemas are (roughly) categories. Sometimes the sense of category is explicit, but sometimes it's only implicit. Schemas can include many kinds of elements, including perceptual images, abstract knowledge, feeling qualities, and information about time sequence (Schwarz, 1990).

Most views assume that schemas include information about specific cases, or **exemplars,** and also information about the more general sense of what the category is. Thus, for any given category (e.g., football players), you can bring to mind specific examples. You can also bring to mind a sense of the category as a whole (a typical football player). This sense of the category as a whole is captured in an idealized best member of the category, often called its **prototype.** In some theories, this is the best *actual* member you've found so far. In other theories, it's an *idealized* member, an average of those you've found so far.

The word *category* tends to imply that there's a definition for what the schema does and does not include, but that's not always so. Features of the category all contribute to its nature, but often they aren't necessary. For example, your *bird* schema probably includes the idea that birds fly. But some birds don't fly (e.g., chickens and penguins). This means flying can't be a defining feature of birds, though flying does make an animal more likely to be a bird. The term **fuzzy set** has been used to convey the sense that the schema is defined in a fuzzy way by a set of criteria that are relevant but not necessary (Lakoff, 1987; Medin, 1989). The more criteria that are met by an exemplar, the more likely it will be seen as a category member. But if there's no *required* criterion, members can vary a lot in the attributes they do and don't have.

Theories about schemas differ, but all of them treat schemas as having an organizing quality. They integrate meaning. An *event* is a collection of people, movements, objects in use, and so on. But unless you have a sense of what the event's *about,* it might just as well all be random. In the same way, the attributes of an *object* are just a collection of bits unless you have an overriding sense of what the object *is.* The schema, in effect, is the glue that holds the bits of information together.

Once schemas are developed, they're used to recognize new experiences. You identify new events by quickly (and mostly unconsciously) comparing them to existing schemas (J. R. Anderson, 1976, 1985; Medin, 1989; Rosch & Mervis, 1975; E. E. Smith, Shoben, & Rips, 1974). If the features of the new event resemble an existing schema, the new stimulus is recognized as "one of those." This is how we recognize objects and events. Each new perception is based partly on incoming information and partly on what you've got as schemas (Jussim, 1991).

EFFECTS OF SCHEMAS

Schemas have several effects. First, they make it easy to put new information into memory. It's as though the schema were made of Velcro. Once a schema's been evoked, new information sticks to it easily. But what information sticks depends on what schema you use. The schema tells where in the experience to look for information. Specifically, you look for information that relates to the schema. A change in schemas changes what you look for. As a result, you notice different things. Having different goals in mind can change what schema is used. For example, Don and Sandy in the chapter opening looked at houses as potential buyers. They noticed and remembered things about appliances and room layouts. If they'd looked at houses as potential burglars, they'd instead have noticed such things as jewelry, TVs, and stereos (R. C. Anderson & Pichert, 1978).

These schema-based biases can be self-perpetuating. That is, schemas tell you more than where to look. They also suggest what you're going to find. You're more likely to remember what *confirms* your expectation than what doesn't. This can make the schema more solid in the future and thus more resistant to change (Hill, Lewicki, Czyzewska, & Boss, 1989).

Another effect of schemas follows from the fact that information is often missing from events. If a schema is evoked, it gives you additional information from *memory*. You assume that what's in the schema is true of the new (schema-related) event, because it's been true in the past. For example, if you hear about Joe doing laundry, you're likely to assume he put soap in the washer, even if that's not mentioned. In fact, you may even believe later you'd been told that when you hadn't (Cantor & Mischel, 1977). Something you assume is true unless you're told otherwise is called a **default.** A second effect of schemas, then, is to bring default information from memory to fill gaps.

SEMANTIC MEMORY, EPISODIC MEMORY, AND SCRIPTS

Schemas are organizations among memories. But memories are organized in several ways (Tulving, 1972). **Semantic memory** is organized by meaning. It comprises categories of objects and concepts. For example, most people have a schema for *boats,* with images of what boats look like and words that describe their nature. This schema often incorporates feeling qualities as well, if the person thinks of boats as a source of either fun or danger.

A second type of organization, **episodic memory,** is memory for events, or *episodes.* It comprises memory for your experiences in space and time (Tulving, 1993). In episodic memory, elements of an event are strung together as they happened (Freyd, 1987). Some episodes are long and elaborate—for example, going to high school. Others are brief—for example, a screech of tires on pavement, followed by crashing metal and tinkling glass. A brief event can be stored both by itself and as a part of a longer event (e.g., a car crash may have been a vivid episode in your experience of high school).

Scripts refer to well-defined sequences of behavior that tell us what to expect and what to do in certain situations, such as going to a wedding.

If you experience enough episodes of a given type, a schema for that class of episodes starts to form. This kind of schema is often called a **script** (Schank & Abelson, 1977). Scripts are prototypes of event categories. They're used partly to perceive and interpret common events, such as going to the hardware store, mowing the lawn, and so on. A script provides a perception with a sense of duration and a sense of flow and change through the event. As with all schemas, scripts have defaults, things you assume to be true.

For example, read this description: "John went to a new Thai restaurant last night. He had chicken curry, spicy. After paying his bill, he went home." You understood this description by using your *dining out* script. Your defaults added a lot of details to what you read. You probably assumed John drove to the restaurant (although you might have assumed he walked). You probably assumed he ordered the chicken before he ate it, rather than snatching it off someone else's table. And you probably assumed that the bill he paid was for his dinner, not for broken dishes. In all these cases, you supplied information to fill in gaps in the story. Scripts allow a lot of diversity, but each has a basic structure. Thus, when you encounter a new variation on it, you easily understand what's going on.

It's easy to distinguish between semantic and episodic memory, but most experience is coded both ways at once. For example, conceptual categories (semantic) develop through repeated exposure to regularities in experiences (episodic). If a young child tries to play with several animals and has varying degrees of success, it may help lead the child to discover that dogs and cats are two different categories of animals.

In recent years, theorists have become more aware of the important role that feelings play in schemas. The involvement of feelings has many implications. For example, having a feeling can evoke particular schemas (Niedenthal, Halberstadt, & Innes-Ker, 1999). Feeling qualities seem especially likely to be part of schemas when the feeling is one of threat (Crawford & Cacioppo, 2002). Presumably, this is because sensing threat is so important for survival that we preferentially code information about it.

SOCIALLY RELEVANT SCHEMAS

Soon after cognitive psychologists began to study categories, personality and social psychologists began to study how these processes apply to socially meaningful stimuli. This came to be called **social cognition** (Fiske & Taylor, 1984; Higgins & Bargh, 1987; Kunda, 1999; Macrae & Bodenhausen, 2000; Schneider, 1991; Wyer & Srull, 1986). People form categories of all sorts of socially meaningful things—for example, people, gender roles, environments, social situations, types of social relations, emotions, and the structure of music.

People differ in how readily they develop schemas (Moskowitz, 1993; Neuberg & Newsom, 1993). People also differ in the content and complexity of their schemas. This comes partly from the fact that people have different amounts of experience in a given domain. For example, some people have elaborate mental representations of the diversity among wines; others know only that some wine is red and some is white.

SELF-SCHEMAS

A particularly important schema is the one you form about yourself (Greenwald & Pratkanis, 1984; Markus, 1977; Markus & Wurf, 1987; T. B. Rogers, 1981), called the **self-schema.** This term is a little like *self-concept,* but it's also a little different. The self-schema, like any schema, makes it easier to remember things that fit it. It provides you with a lot of default information. It also tells you where to look for new information. Your self-schema can even bias your recall, twisting your recollections so they fit better with how you see yourself now (Ross, 1989).

Does the self-schema differ from other schemas? Well, it seems to be larger and more complex (Rogers, Kuiper, & Kirker, 1977). This makes sense, because you've probably spent more time noticing things about yourself than about anything else in the world. It incorporates both trait labels and information about concrete behaviors (Fekken & Holden, 1992; Schell, Klein, & Babey, 1996), and it has more emotional elements than other schemas (Markus & Sentis, 1982). There are questions, though, about whether the self-schema is truly special. Features that seem special in it are also present in other well-developed schemas (Greenwald & Banaji, 1989; Karylowski, 1990). Perhaps it seems special only because it's so well developed.

The self-schema is more complex than other schemas, and individuals' self-schemas differ in complexity (Linville, 1987). Some people keep their different self-aspects distinct from each other. Each role these people play, each goal they have, each activity they do has its own place in their self-image. These people are high in **self-complexity.** Other people's self-aspects are less distinct. Everything blends together. These people are low in self-complexity.

This difference has interesting implications. For people low in self-complexity, feelings relating to a bad event in one aspect of life tend to spill over into other aspects of the sense of self (Linville, 1987). Having trouble in a course may make you also feel bad about your social life. This doesn't happen as much for people higher in self-complexity, apparently because the separations and boundaries they have between self-aspects prevent it (see also Niedenthal, Setterlund, & Wherry, 1992; Showers & Ryff, 1996).

In the same way, thinking of oneself in a contextualized way—even temporarily—can dampen emotional reactions to a specific failure. In one study (Mendoza-Denton, Ayduk, Mischel, Shoda, & Testa, 2001), people who had been led to think of themselves in terms of particular classes of situations ("I am _____ when _____") were less affected emotionally by bad outcomes than those who were led to think of themselves in broader terms ("I am _____").

How do people acquire (or fail to acquire) complexity in the self-schema? It may be partly a matter of how much you think about yourself. Nasby (1985) found that people who say they think about themselves a lot have self-schemas with more complexity and detail than people who say they think about themselves less. Presumably, the very process of thinking about yourself causes more growth and articulation of the self-schema.

Another way of viewing self-complexity is to think of the self as a *family* of self-schemas, rather than one (e.g., Markus & Nurius, 1986). In a sense, you're a different person when you're in different contexts (Andersen & Chen, 2002; Swann, Bosson, & Pelham, 2002). You make different assumptions about yourself. You attend to different aspects of what's going on. When you go from your friends at college to your parents at home, it's as though you're putting aside one schema about yourself and taking up another one.

Self-schemas also vary in other ways. Markus and her colleagues (e.g., Markus & Nurius, 1986) suggest that people have diverse images of themselves. People have selves they expect to become, selves they'd like to become (Hewitt & Genest, 1990), and selves they're afraid of becoming (Carver, Lawrence, & Scheier, 1999). People have disliked selves (Ogilvie, 1987) and selves they think they ought to be (Higgins, 1987, 1990). These various **possible selves** can be brought to bear as motivators because they provide goals to approach or to avoid.

ENTITY VERSUS INCREMENTAL SCHEMAS

Another variation in self-schemas is in how much stability people assume. An easy example of this is how people think of their abilities (Dweck & Leggett, 1988).

To some people, an ability is an *entity*. It's something you have more of or less of, but it doesn't change. To other people, an ability is something you can *increment,* or increase through experience. (Once you establish one or the other of these views, you tend to maintain it [Robins & Pals, 2002].)

Both views reflect coherent schemas about ability, but the two views lead to different experiences. When people have an entity view, performing a task is about *proving* their ability. If they do poorly, they're distressed and want to quit. When people have an incremental view, performing a task is about *extending* their ability. If they do poorly, they see it as a chance to increase the ability.

Are these views really schemas? They do seem to act in ways schemas do. For example, they guide people's search for new information (Plaks, Stroessner, Dweck, & Sherman, 2001). When people hold an entity view, they attend to (and remember) cues of consistency. When people hold an incremental view, they attend to (and remember) cues of change.

People who hold an incremental view of ability treat setbacks as challenges for future improvements.

ATTRIBUTION

An important aspect of experiencing events is judging their causes. Inferring a cause tells you whether it was intentional or accidental. It also tells you something about how likely it is to occur again. Inferring the cause of an event is called **attribution** (Heider, 1944, 1958). People do this spontaneously, without even knowing they're doing it (Hassin, Bargh, & Uleman, 2002). Attribution has been studied extensively, and several principles have been identified.

One principle is that people tend to judge events they experience (as actors) differently from events they see or hear about (as observers). *Observers* tend to assume that other people's behavior reflects their personality (Jones & Nisbett, 1971). *Actors,* however, tend to see the same acts as caused by the situation. Thus, the same action can be seen in very different ways by two people. For example, if *you* are late for an appointment, *I* may think it's because you're irresponsible. If *I* am late, I may think it's because things out of my control slowed me down.

The process of making attributions relies partly on schemas about the nature of social situations (Read, 1987). Default values from those schemas help you make inferences beyond the information that's present (Carlston & Skowronski, 1994). And (as in other contexts) using different schemas causes people to make different inferences about the causes of events.

Another important aspect of attribution is the interpretations that people make for good and bad outcomes—successes and failures. Success and failure can have many causes, but work has focused on four causes: ability, effort, task difficulty, and luck or chance factors. The best-known analysis of this kind of attribution is that of Bernie Weiner (1979, 1986, 1990).

Weiner points out that these causes can be placed on a dimension of *locus of causality:* Either the cause is *internal,* part of yourself (ability, effort), or it's *external,* outside

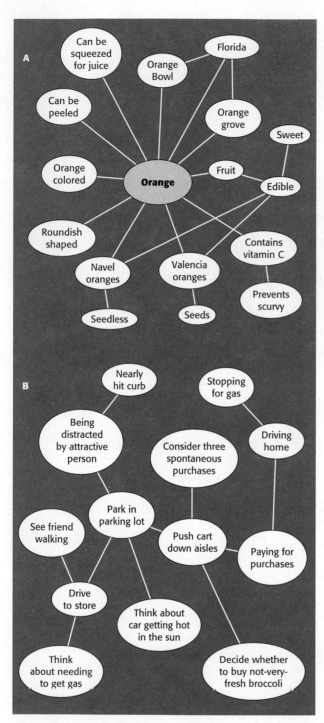

FIGURE 16.1

(A) Part of the network of semantic associations surrounding the concept *orange*. (B) Part of the network of episodic memories surrounding the event *going to the grocery store for broccoli, strawberries, and beer.*

yourself (chance factors, task difficulty, powerful others). Causes also vary in *stability*. Some seem fairly stable (ability), whereas others vary from one time to another (effort). In general, people tend to interpret their successes as having internal stable causes—specifically, their ability. (Note that this enhances self-esteem, as suggested in Chapter 14.) People generally tend to see their failures as caused by relatively *unstable* influences, such as bad luck or too little effort.

On the other hand, there are also individual differences in attributional tendencies, which can have big effects. If you see failure as caused by unstable factors, there's no need to worry about the future. That is, since the cause is unstable, the situation probably won't be the same next time. If the cause is stable, though, the picture is quite different. If you failed because you don't have ability or because the world is permanently against you, you're going to face that same situation next time and every time. Your future will hold only more failure. Your behavior, thoughts, and feelings can be deeply affected by that. Seeing stable and permanent reasons for bad life outcomes relates to depression (e.g., Abramson, Alloy, & Metalsky, 1995; Abramson, Metalsky, & Alloy, 1989; Abramson, Seligman, & Teasdale, 1978; Weiner & Litman-Adizes, 1980) and even sickness and death (e.g., Buchanan, 1995; Peterson, 1995).

Activation of Memories

We've talked about schemas from several angles now. Do schemas just pile up on top of each other in memory? Certainly not. One view is that memories form a vast network (see Figure 16.1). **Nodes,** or areas of storage, are linked if they have some logical connection. Some connections are semantic, linking attributes that contribute to a category (Figure 16.1, A). Others are episodic, linking attributes that form an event (Figure 16.1, B). Bits of information that have a lot to do with each other are strongly linked. Bits of information that don't have much to do with each other are not as strongly linked. In this view, knowledge is an elaborate web of associations of different strengths among a huge number of nodes of information. (Don't think about distance between nodes, by the way, only strength of association; distance isn't part of this picture.)

When a memory node is activated, the information it contains appears in consciousness. A node can be activated by an intentional search (e.g., think of your phone number) or in other ways. As one node becomes active, *partial* activation spreads to other nodes that are related to it. The stronger the relation, the greater the spread. Partial activation makes it easier for the related area to come all the way to consciousness. That is, because it's already partly activated, it takes less of a boost to make it fully active.

To use the examples in Figure 16.1, thinking of an orange partially activates related semantic nodes. Thinking of an orange tends to remind you of navel oranges, the color and flavor of oranges, orange trees, maybe the Orange Bowl. Since orange groves and the Orange Bowl are both in Florida, you may be slightly reminded of Florida, as well. In the same way, thinking about a bit of an episode partially activates related nodes. Thinking about being in the parking lot tends to remind you vaguely of the person you saw there, which in turn may remind you of the fact that you almost lost control over your driving and ran up over the curb.

These examples involve *partial* activation. The memory may not make it all the way to consciousness without another boost from somewhere. But it's more likely to get there than it was before. An extra boost sometimes comes from another source (e.g., seeing someone who looks a little like the person in the parking lot or hearing the song that was on the radio while you were parking). Given that extra boost, the node becomes active enough for its content (the image of the person) to pop into awareness. If the node hadn't already been partially active, the boost wouldn't have been enough.

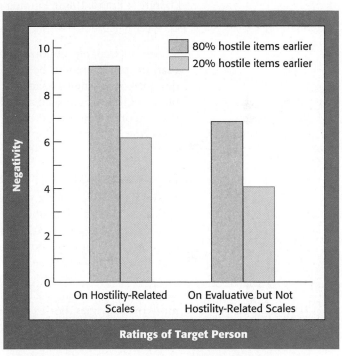

PRIMING AND THE USE OF INFORMATION

The idea that partial activation causes easier access to memories has led to a technique called **priming**. Priming is activating a node of information in a task that comes before the task of interest starts. This technique was first used to study two questions. One is whether the same information is more accessible later on. That is, after priming, it takes a while for the activation to fade. This would leave the node more accessible than before, until the activation is gone. The other is whether *related* information becomes more accessible after the priming.

The answer to both questions is yes. For example, Srull and Wyer (1979) had people do a task in which they read words related to hostility. Later, in what was presented as a different study, they were more likely to see an ambiguously portrayed person as hostile (see Figure 16.2). They rated the person more negatively on other evaluative terms, as well, suggesting a spread of activation to related areas of memory.

These effects occur only if the primed information can plausibly be applied to the later event (Higgins & Brendl, 1995). If you prime *dishonest,* it won't influence your judgments of *athletic* ability. On the other hand, priming seems to activate the

FIGURE 16.2
Effects of priming. Participants read a set of items, 80% of which (or 20% of which) contained words related to *hostility.* Later, in what they thought was a different experiment, they read an ambiguous portrayal of a target person and rated him on two sets of scales: some pertaining to hostility and others evaluative but not directly related to hostility. Reading a larger number of hostile words caused the target person to be seen as more hostile and as less pleasant. *Source: Adapted from Srull & Wyer, 1979, Experiment 1, immediate condition.*

full dimension, not just the end that's primed (Park, Yoon, Kim, & Wyer, 2001). If you prime *honest* and then present a target that might be *dishonest,* people are more likely to see dishonesty. (This fits Kelly's idea, discussed in Chapter 15, that constructs are bipolar dichotomies.)

The technique of priming makes use of the fact that events can make information more accessible. But people also differ in what categories are usually accessible for them (Bargh, Lombardi, & Higgins, 1988; Higgins, King, & Mavin, 1982; Lau, 1989). The most accessible categories are the ones they *use* the most. Thus, *chronic* accessibility reflects people's readiness to use particular schemas in seeing the world (Bargh & Pratto, 1986). Finding out about what schemas are chronically accessible in a particular person, then, can provide information about how that person sees the world.

As an example, children who grow up in poor neighborhoods are more likely than other children to be exposed to violence. This exposure may lead them to develop social schemas with violent themes. These schemas should be very accessible for children from such neighborhoods and thus likely to be used. Consistent with this, children from low-income neighborhoods see more hostile intent in ambiguous actions than do other children (Brady & Matthews, 2006; Chen & Matthews, 2001).

NONCONSCIOUS INFLUENCES ON BEHAVIOR

We've been talking about ways in which information moves from memory to consciousness and is then used in various ways. However, a line of research by John Bargh and his colleagues (e.g., Chartrand & Bargh, 1996; Fitzsimons & Bargh, 2004) has made it very clear that information does not have to reach consciousness in order to influence what happens next.

In this work, research participants receive **subliminal** primes—that is, primes outside their awareness. These subliminal primes often have the same effect as do more overt primes. For example, people who have the goal of forming an impression pay attention to different things than people who have the goal of memorizing. Activating these goals subliminally has the same effect as activating them overtly (Chartrand & Bargh, 1996). As another example, goals are often linked to particular relationships (e.g., your father may be linked in your mind with doing well on your exams). It appears that priming the relationships outside awareness activates the related goal, which you then set about pursuing unconsciously (Fitzsimons & Bargh, 2003). There's also evidence that subliminally priming an emotion causes judgments of subsequent stimuli to take on that emotional quality (Ferguson, Bargh, & Nayak, 2005).

The findings of this work are fascinating. They represent an important reason for a renewed interest in the processes of the unconscious (Hassin, Uleman, & Bargh, 2005). This view of the unconscious is very different from that of Freud (described in Chapter 8). Yet it holds (as did Freud) that the impact of forces that operate outside awareness can be quite pronounced.

When you think carefully about what priming is, you realize that it happens constantly in life (Carver & Scheier, 2002). Whenever you hear something, read something, think something, or watch something, it makes the corresponding parts of your memories active. This, in turn, causes partial activation in related areas and will leave residual activation in the areas that are now active. That can have a wide range of subtle effects on behavior (see also Box 16.1).

Box 16.1 What's in a Name?

Priming is a funny process. It happens all the time, though people don't realize it. And it can have some very unexpected effects on people's behavior. For example, consider your name. Your name is part of your self-schema. For most of us, our name marks family ties. But does your name have a broader impact on your life? Beyond the fact that some people are teased for having unusual names, most people would probably say no.

Studies have shown, however, that people's names may be involved with important life decisions. Pelham, Mirenberg, and Jones (2002) reported 10 studies of people's names and how they related to where the people lived and what their businesses were. Five studies found that people were more likely to live in places whose names resembled their own than would

happen by chance. For example, men named *Jack* live in Jacksonville in a greater proportion than in, say, Philadelphia. There are more than *twice* as many men named *Louis* in Louisiana than would be expected by chance. Women named *Virginia* are extra likely to move to Virginia but not to Georgia, whereas the reverse is true of women named *Georgia*.

It's not just where people live. It's also what they do. People tend to have jobs that have the same first initial as their own names. *Sheri's* odds of owning a *salon* are greater than chance but not *Carol's. Carol* is more likely to own a *candle* shop. People named *Thompson* have a greater than chance involvement in the *travel* business.

Pelham and his colleagues have also examined these effects in other areas of life (see Pelham et al. [2002]). In the 2000 presidential campaign, people whose last names start with *B*

were more likely to give to the *Bush* campaign, and those whose last names start with *G* were more likely to give to *Gore*. People are also more likely to marry other people whose names resemble their own (J. T. Jones, Pelham, Carvallo, & Mirenberg, 2004).

Why do these things happen? The explanation is that most people have positive feelings about themselves as part of the self-schema. The positive feelings are evoked by anything that reminds them of themselves. This happens even if the reminding is very slight and even if it's unconscious. In effect, if you're named *Ken* and you live in Kentucky, you're surrounded by primes to your self-schema. People may gravitate slightly to anything that evokes that warm sense of self. We don't know if there's a *Ken* in Kentucky who owns a *kennel* and is married to a woman named *Karen*. But if there is, we'd bet he's a very contented man.

Connectionist Views of Mental Organization

For the most part, the way we've been discussing cognition thus far reflects a view in which cognition concerns symbol processing. That view dominated cognitive psychology for many years. In the mid–1980s, however, another view emerged, which is now having an impact on how we think about personality. This other view of cognitive processes has several labels, including *parallel distributed processing* (McClelland, Rumelhart, & PDP Research Group, 1986), *neural networks* (Anderson, 1995; Levine & Leven, 1992), and, perhaps most common, **connectionism** (J. L. McClelland, 1999).

This view uses neuronal processes, rather than computer processes, as a metaphor for cognitive processes. Because the nervous system processes information simultaneously along many pathways, parallel processing is one of its key features. This view also holds that representations aren't centralized in specific nodes. Rather, a representation exists only in a pattern of activation of an entire network of neurons.

Connectionists describe cognition in terms of networks of simple neuronlike units, in which *processing* means passing activations from one unit to another (see Figure 16.3). Each activation can be either excitatory or inhibitory. Thus, it either adds to or subtracts from the total of the unit to which it serves as input. Each unit sums its inputs (pluses and minuses) and passes the total onward. Energy passes in only one direction for each connection, as in neurons. But connections are often assumed in which activation goes from a "later" unit back to an "earlier" one, which is also true

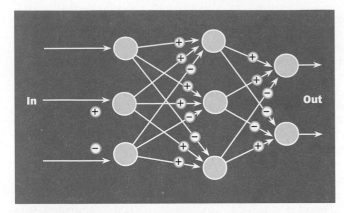

FIGURE 16.3

Example of a connectionist network. The network consists of units that receive and send activation, with two connections (printed in color) that feed activation back to "earlier" units. A given activation can be either excitatory (+) or inhibitory (–). Each unit receives activation from all the units that project to it and sends activation to all the units that it projects to.

Source: Adapted from Carver & Scheier, 1998.

of neurons. The network reacts to an input with a pattern of activity. This activity goes through the network's layers starting on the input side, through whatever elaborate connections exist, to the output side. The pattern that emerges on the output side is the response to the input.

The pattern of activations in the network is updated repeatedly—potentially very often. Gradually, the system "settles" into a configuration and further updates yield no more change. A common way to view this is that the system *simultaneously satisfies multiple constraints* that the units place on each other (Thagard, 1989). For example, if there are two units that inhibit each other, they can't both be highly active at the same time. Each is trying to constrain the other's activity. One of them eventually inhibits the other enough to keep it from being active. Diverse constraints settle out during the repeated updating of activations. The process is complicated, but here's the bottom line: The parallel constraint satisfaction process creates the greatest organization and coherence it can across the network, given the constraints.

The literature of connectionism in cognitive psychology is large and growing rapidly (e.g., J. A. Anderson, 1995; Dawson, 2005; Elman, 2005; Seidenberg, 2005; Smolensky, Mozer, & Rumelhart, 1996; Wendelken & Shastri, 2005). Several authors have also tried to indicate why these ideas are useful for other areas of psychology, including personality (Caspar, Rothenfluh, & Segal, 1992; Kunda & Thagard, 1996; Overwalle & Siebler, 2005; Read & Miller, 1998, 2002; Read, Vanman, & Miller, 1997; Schultz & Lepper, 1996; Smith, 1996).

One interesting application is to social perception and decision making (Read et al., 1997; Thagard & Millgram, 1995). These phenomena involve selecting one possibility from among two or more. When you view an ambiguous figure (see Figure 16.4), you perceive one or the other possibility, not a blend of the two. The perception of one or the other pops into mind. In the same way, when you make a decision, you pick one option. You don't usually get to blend options. Again, even if you're trying to be rational, it's often the case that an answer seems to pop into your mind. Think back to Don and Sandy in the chapter opening, who were trying to find a house they liked. They were being rational and orderly, but a decision just suddenly appeared.

How would connectionists analyze such an experience? They would say the experience is being constructed from bits of input. The bits activate units in the network, and the units place constraints on each other. Activations get transferred from unit to unit, around and around. As the activation pattern is updated over and over, some constraints get stronger over cycles, and some get weaker. The network as a whole settles into a pattern. The pattern is the perception or the decision. Although there may be many cycles, the time involved can be very short. Subjectively, the pattern (perception or decision) emerges as a final product, sometimes abruptly.

These processes can create influences in multiple directions. That is, decisions are made from fitting bits of evidence together despite their constraints on one another. Once a decision has been reached, however, there's also an influence back on your evaluation of the evidence, making it more coherent with the decision (Simon, Snow, & Read, 2004).

Something that's interesting about these networks is that it can be very hard to tell ahead of time how they will settle out. The pattern of constraints can be intricate. Constraints may relate to each other in ways that aren't obvious. The network doesn't care about the "big picture." That's not how it works. Each unit just keeps sending out activations as a function of how active *it* is. In the pushing and pulling, perceptions and decisions can emerge that seem irrational. And they aren't rational, in a sense. The decision about buying a house isn't the algebraic sum of the ratings of the good and bad points of each house. It's more interwoven. This aspect of the connectionist approach in particular makes it feel very different from the symbolic approach.

Another thing that's interesting is that often these networks are very stable, but sometimes they reorganize abruptly (Read & Miller, 2002). In many cases, if you change one part of the input, nothing much changes. Reverberations from the change are dampened in the network. Sometimes, though, change in one part of the input is critical. If the effects of that small change are amplified instead of dampened, there can be profound reverberations over cycles, producing a drastic reorganization. Thus, if you're looking at a figure such as the one in Figure 16.4, it can suddenly reorganize and become the alternate image. These ideas have been used to discuss how the self-concept is sometimes resistant to and sometimes responsive to information from outside (Nowak, Vallacher, Tesser, & Borkowski, 2000).

FIGURE 16.4
An example of an ambiguous figure. This image can be seen either as a young woman turning aside or as an old woman with a protruding nose and chin. Although your perception can easily shift from one to the other, you don't see a blend of images.
Source: Adapted from Boring, 1930.

DUAL-PROCESS MODELS

Cognitive psychologists wrestled for some time with differences between the symbol-processing approach and the connectionist approach. In the end, several turned to the idea that cognition involves two kinds of thought, rather than one. Smolensky (1988) argued that a *conscious processor* is used for effortful reasoning and following of programs of instructions and that an *intuitive processor* manages intuitive problem solving, heuristic strategies, and skilled or automatic activities using connectionist processes. This view has also been expressed in several other **dual-mode models** in cognitive psychology (De Neys, 2006; Holyoak & Spellman, 1993; Sloman, 1996).

When doing controlled processing, the mind in effect says, "Find a rule, apply it to the situation, carry out its logical steps of inference and action, and make decisions as needed. If no rule is available, use whatever's closest." When the mind is in connectionist mode, the settling process goes on until the elements shake out and a pattern emerges. The activity of this mode fits the experience of insight: A pattern appears suddenly where none was before.

The idea that people experience the world through two different modes of processing also appears in the literature of personality. Depictions of two modes of processing bear a very strong resemblance to an argument made some time ago by Seymour Epstein (1985, 1990, 1994). Epstein's *cognitive–experiential self-theory* assumes we experience reality through two systems. The *rational system* operates mostly consciously, uses logical rules, and is fairly slow. This is the symbolic processor that we think of as our rational mind. The *experiential system* is intuitive. It's a "quick and dirty" way of assessing and responding to reality. It relies on shortcuts and information that's readily available. It functions automatically and quickly.

Epstein believes that both systems are always at work and that they jointly determine behavior. Each can also be engaged to a greater degree by circumstances. For example, asking people to give strictly logical responses to hypothetical events tends to place them in the rational mode. Asking them how they would respond if the events happened to them tends to place them in the experiential mode (Epstein, Lipson, Holstein, & Huh, 1992). The more emotionally charged a situation is, the more thinking is dominated by the experiential system.

In Epstein's view, the experiential system resulted from eons of evolution. It dominates when speed is needed (as when the situation is emotionally charged). You can't be thorough when you need to act fast (for example, to avoid danger). Maybe you can't even wait to form an intention. The rational system is more recent in origin. It provides a more cautious, analytic, planful way of proceeding. That also has advantages, of course, when there is enough time and freedom from pressure to think things through.

More recently, the dual-process idea has emerged several more times in forms that are very similar to this (for review see Carver, 2005). Metcalfe and Mischel (1999) proposed there is a "hot" system that's emotional, impulsive, and reflexive. It operates in a connectionist manner. There is also a "cool" system that is strategic, flexible, slower, and unemotional. This line of thought was derived in part from a long line of research on delay of gratification (see Box 16.2). But it obviously applies more broadly.

A different application of this idea is to the anger that arises in response to rejection. In a study by Ayduk, Mischel, and Downey (2002), students recalled a situation in which they had been rejected or excluded. After bringing that situation to mind,

Box 16.2 Delay of Gratification

The Role of Cognitive Strategies

Several previous chapters have discussed the ability to delay gratification —to wait a while for something good. From a psychoanalytic view (Chapter 8), this is a matter of the ego holding the id in check until the time is right to fulfill its desires. From the view of ego psychology (Chapter 10), traits of ego control and ego resiliency determine self-restraint. From the view of the learning perspective (Chapter 13), whether a person delays or not depends on the reward structure of the situation and the behavior of salient models.

The cognitive point of view suggests yet another angle on the process of delaying gratification. Specifically, an important influence on delay of gratification is the mental strategies people use (Kanfer, Karoly, & Newman, 1975; Mischel, 1974, 1979). *What* people think about—and *how* they think about it—can make delays easier or harder.

Early work showed that preschoolers would wait 10 times longer for a desired food if it wasn't visible than if it was (Mischel & Ebbesen, 1970). On the other hand, delays were easier to tolerate if pictures of the rewards were present (Mischel & Moore, 1973). Later research showed these effects could be changed by varying how children *thought* about the desired object. Thinking about consummatory aspects of a food, such as its taste, made it nearly impossible for children to delay (Mischel & Baker, 1975). In contrast, attending to qualities of the food that weren't related to eating made it possible for children to tolerate delay quite ble for children to tolerate delay quite easily (see also Kanfer et al., 1975; Moore, Mischel, & Zeiss, 1976; Toner & Smith, 1977).

Research on how these self-control strategies evolve shows that there's a natural progression over time (Mischel, 1979). At first, children attend to aspects of the reward that are most appealing (such as taste), which doesn't help (Yates & Mischel, 1979). Eventually, they begin to generate cognitive strategies to keep these thoughts from their awareness. The result is increased self-restraint. As Mischel (1990) pointed out, it's not what's in front of the children that matters but what's going on in their heads. The same is true for adults (Trope & Fishbach, 2000, 2005). This research thus reinforces one of Mischel's major theoretical points: the importance of people's mental strategies in determining their behavior.

some were told to focus on the feelings and sensations they'd experienced, and others were told to focus on the arrangement of people, objects, and lighting in the event. Then they wrote down what they had thought and felt while recalling the experience. Those who had taken a "cool" stance on the situation reported less anger and hurt than did the others.

The dual-process idea has also emerged in a number of other places. For example, Lieberman, Gaunt, Gilbert, and Trope (2002) looked at attributions that are relatively effortful versus those that are automatic (because they'd been made over and over). As did Epstein, they assume that the reflexive system is attuned to pressured and emotional demands of the world and that it acts very quickly. The other system uses symbolic logic and is slower. As did Epstein, they believe that both systems are always at work and that each can be induced to dominate by variations in the situation. After reviewing findings from several sources, Lieberman et al. (2002) concluded that the consciously controlled and automatic versions of attribution are managed by different parts of the brain.

These dual-process models resemble some ideas from Chapter 7. We said there that behavior sometimes reflects automatic impulses and sometimes the oversight of a temperament of constraint or effortful control. Controlled behavior seems restrained and socialized. Behavior dominated by automatic processing can be impulsive and may seem unsocialized. Those ideas resemble the dual-process models described here. The focus here is a little different, however: the idea that personality may have two cognitive modes with different "feels." One mode is clearly recognizable as *thinking.* The other is more like intuitive *reacting* (see also Kuhl, 2000).

Many people have believed thinking is more important and more a part of personality. But intuitive reacting may be a far more potent influence on behavior than most people realize (see also Toates, 2006). The dual-mode theories outlined here all assume that it's harder for the effortful process to dominate over the automatic process when the person's mind is relatively full (e.g., when you're trying to do two things at once). Similarly, the automatic process tends to take over when the situation is emotional or pressured. Being cognitively busy and being pressured or emotionally aroused applies to a good proportion of most people's lives.

EXPLICIT AND IMPLICIT KNOWLEDGE

Another body of research on mental representations also seems to fit a dual-mode view of cognition. This research examines the idea that people have both **explicit knowledge** (which is accessible on demand) and **implicit knowledge** (which isn't). To put it differently, implicit knowledge is the existence of automatic mental associations we aren't really aware of.

A topic that helped lead to the emergence of this line of thought concerns prejudices and how they're represented in the mind. Many people believe they aren't prejudiced against minorities—that they treat all people equally well. It turns out, though, that many of these same people have stronger mental links from these minorities to the semantic quality *bad* than from the minorities to *good* (Greenwald, McGhee, & Schwartz, 1998). These links are called *implicit associations,* because they are measured quite indirectly (usually through a set of reaction-time trials) and because people are unaware of the links.

The discovery of implicit attitudes has led to a much larger exploration of explicit knowledge of various kinds, including implicit theories of the self (Beer, 2002) and implicit self-esteem (DeHart, Pelham, & Tennen, 2006; Greenwald, Banaji, Rudman,

Farnham, Nosek, & Mellott, 2002). Implicit self-esteem has been found to relate to negative feeling states in day-to-day life, independent of any role of explicit self-esteem (Conner & Barrett, 2005). It is of considerable interest that *implicit* self-esteem is not very highly correlated with *explicit* self-esteem (the self-esteem that's reported on self-report scales). The same is often true of attitudes. There's evidence that both implicit and explicit attitudes of various types relate to behavior, but often to different aspects of behavior (Asendorpf, Banse, & Mücke, 2002).

Why aren't these two aspects of knowledge closely related? One possibility follows from the view that much of implicit knowledge comes from simple association learning—classical and instrumental conditioning—whereas explicit knowledge comes from verbal, conceptual learning. Perhaps the experiences that provide associative and verbal knowledge about the self (or anything else) are more separate than people have often assumed. For example, a child may be harshly treated by parents but told verbally that he is a wonderful boy. These two sources of experience don't agree well with each other. Over time, this would lead to different knowledge at the implicit (associative) and explicit (verbal) levels.

It might follow from this that the implicit knowledge starts forming earlier in life than explicit knowledge. That is, conditioning begins very early. Conceptual and verbal learning develop somewhat later. Consistent with this line of thought, negative implicit attitudes toward minorities are displayed as early as age 6; egalitarian explicit attitudes emerge at about age 10, but the implicit attitudes remain as they were (Baron & Banaji, 2006).

In introducing this topic, we said that implicit and explicit attitudes may relate to dual-mode models of cognition. It seems possible that what we are referring to here as *implicit knowledge* is the same sort of associative system that others have termed an *experiential* or *reflexive* or *intuitive system*. The *explicit knowledge* would seem to be more related to a *rational, deliberative system*. Fitting that picture, there is evidence that controlled processes are what help people override automatic tendencies to stereotype others (Payne, 2005) and react to cues of stigma (Pryor, Reeder, Yeadon, & Hesson-McInnis, 2004).

Broader Views on Cognition and Personality

Much of the cognitive view of personality concerns specific mental processes that underlie personality. This work tends to be tightly focused on particular issues. As a result, the cognitive approach is very fragmented (Funder, 2001). Attempts have been made, however, to make more integrative statements about cognition and personality. Two of the most influential statements were made by Walter Mischel, a theorist with a huge influence on today's cognitive view (see also Box 16.3). Interestingly, these statements were made nearly a quarter century apart.

COGNITIVE PERSON VARIABLES

As is true of many who now hold a cognitive view on personality, Mischel earlier was identified with the *cognitive–social learning* view. The theoretical statement he made in 1973 represents a transition between Mischel the learning theorist and Mischel the cognitive theorist. He proposed that an adequate theory of personality must take into account five classes of cognitive variables in the person, all of which are influenced by learning. Given these criteria, Mischel gave them the long name of *cognitive–social learning person variables*. He intended them to take the place of traits (Mischel, 1990).

Box 16.3 The Theorist and the Theory

Mischel and His Mentors

Professional mentors influence their students in many ways. Most obviously, they impart a set of skills and a way of looking at the world, which the students then apply to domains of their own choosing. Sometimes, however, there's more to it than that. Sometimes an imprint on the mind of a student reverberates for a long time in his or her work. The student absorbs the essence of the mentor's view and recasts it in a new and more elaborated form. This seems to be the case in the career of Walter Mischel.

Mischel was born in Vienna in 1930 and lived within walking distance of Sigmund Freud's house. When he was 9, his family fled to New York to escape Nazism. Mischel grew up in New York and became a social worker, using Freud's theory of personality. His enthusiasm for psychoanalysis waned, however, when he tried to apply it to juvenile offenders in New York's Lower East Side. After a time, Mischel set off to continue his studies at Ohio State University.

There, he came under the influence of two psychologists who were already making a mark on personality psychology: George Kelly and Julian Rotter. Kelly's ideas (described in Chapter 15) emphasized the importance of personal constructs. Rotter's ideas (described in Chapter 13) concerned the importance of people's expectations in determining their behavior. Both Kelly and Rotter were also skeptical about a purely dispositional approach to personality.

Mischel's work has incorporated all three of these themes, although he has also taken each theme in directions of his own. For example, as discussed in Chapter 4, Mischel (1968) sparked a huge controversy in personality psychology over the question of whether behavior has enough cross-situational consistency to warrant believing in dispositions. He spent much of his career focusing on issues in the cognitive–social learning perspective, including the role played by various kinds of expectancies. In the past three decades, his views have become increasingly cognitive, leading to what some see as a resolution of the controversy he sparked in 1968. As we noted at the start of this chapter, the emergence of today's cognitive view on personality has roots in several places other than Kelly's ideas. Surely, however, one reason for the emergence of this cognitive view is the impact that Kelly the mentor had on the young Walter Mischel.

One class of variables is the person's *competencies*, the skills that one develops over life. Just as people develop skills for manipulating the physical world, they develop social skills and problem-solving strategies, tools for analyzing the social world. These competencies are much like what was discussed in Chapter 10 in the context of the idea that the ego functions to promote better adaptation.

Different people have different patterns of competencies, of course. Some people have the ability to empathize with others, some have the skill to fix brakes, some have the ability to make people laugh, and some have the ability to make people follow them into danger. Situations also vary in what competencies they call for (Shoda, Mischel, & Wright, 1993). Thus, different situations provide opportunities for different persons to take advantage of.

The second class of variables is *encoding strategies and personal constructs*. This covers schemas, as well as what Kelly said about the unique worldview that each person develops. You construe events and people differently, depending on the schema you're using. (You look at the house one way if you're a potential buyer, another way if you're a potential burglar.) It's not the objective situation that determines how you react, but how you construe it. Two people react to a situation differently because they literally experience it differently.

Encoding strategies are ways of seeing the world. But to know what people will *do* in that world, you also need to know their *expectancies*. One type of expectancy is the anticipation that one event typically is followed by another. For example, hearing a siren is often followed by seeing an emergency vehicle. Seeing dark clouds and hearing thunder are often followed by rain. Expectancies about what's connected to what provide continuity in experience. A second type of expectancy is *behavior-outcome expectancy,* the belief that particular acts typically lead to particular outcomes. These are much like the outcome expectancies in Bandura's social–cognitive learning theory (discussed in Chapter 13). Entering a restaurant (behavior) usually is followed by being greeted by a host or waiter (outcome). Being friendly to others (behavior) is usually followed by friendly responses (outcome). Typing the right codes into an ATM (behavior) usually leads to receiving money (outcome). If the expectancies you have match reality, your actions will be effective. If you've learned a set of behavior-outcome expectancies that don't fit the world, you'll be less effective.

Expectancies begin to specify what people do: People do what they think will produce outcomes. The fourth part of the puzzle is knowing what outcomes the person wants to produce, the person's *subjective values.* These values are what cause people to use their expectancies in action. If the available outcome isn't one the person cares about, the expectancies won't matter.

The fifth set of variables Mischel (1973) discussed is what he called *self-regulatory systems and plans.* People set goals, make plans, and do the various things that need to be done to see that the plans are realized in action. This covers a lot of ground. Since Mischel proposed his five categories, this category has taken on something of a life of its own. In part for this reason, we'll talk about it separately in Chapter 17.

PERSONALITY AS A COGNITIVE–AFFECTIVE PROCESSING SYSTEM

Mischel and Shoda (1995) proposed a model that extends and elaborates Mischel's earlier statement. (We discussed the Mischel and Shoda model briefly in Chapter 4.) They described what they called a *cognitive–affective processing system.* The linking of *cognitive* to *affective* in this label reflects the recognition that emotion plays a key role in much of cognitive experience.

Mischel and Shoda said that people develop organizations of information about the nature of situations, other people, and the self. These schemas are more complex in one sense than what we've described thus far. Specifically, Mischel and Shoda said that they have a kind of *if . . . then* property, a conditional quality. Saying someone is aggressive doesn't mean you think the person is aggressive every moment. It means you think he or she is more likely than most people to be aggressive in a certain class of situations.

Evidence from several sources supports this view. For example, in describing others, we often use *hedges,* conditions under which we think the others act a particular way (Wright & Mischel, 1988). This suggests that people normally think in conditional terms about each other. In fact, the better you know someone, the more likely you are to think in conditional terms about him or her (Chen, 2003).

Mischel and Shoda said that people also think conditionally about themselves. That is, each person's behavior also follows an *if . . . then* principle. Schemas to construe situations include information about appropriate actions in those situations (Carver & Scheier, 1981). Norms are mentally represented as links between settings and the behaviors that relate to those settings (Aarts & Dijksterhuis, 2003). If a situation is identified that's linked to a particular behavior, then that behavior will tend to occur (*if . . . then*).

In this view, individuality arises from two sources. First, people differ in the accessibility of their various schemas and the cues that evoke the schemas. Thus, different schemas are likely to pop up for different people in a given setting. People literally perceive different things in the same situation. Second, people differ in their *if . . . then* profiles. When a schema is active, the person will act in ways that fit it. But that may mean different actions for different people.

For example, some people will view an ambiguous remark made by another person as a rejection, some as a provocation, some as an indication that a "power play" is underway, and some as an indication that the other person was out too late last night and is hung over. If Marty sees a power play—even if no one else in the room does—he erupts in bluster and bravado. If he doesn't see it that way, he doesn't do that. Ed is also sensitive to power plays, but he has a different *if . . . then* link: If Ed sees a power play, he gets very quiet and starts looking for cues about who's likely to win. Thus, even if Ed and Marty identify the same situation—a power play—they will act quite differently from each other.

To predict consistency of action, then, you need to know two things. First, you need to know how the person construes the situation (which depends on the person's schemas and their accessibility). Second, you need to know the person's *if . . . then* profile. In this view, the unique profile of *if . . . then* relations is seen as a *behavioral signature* for a person's personality (Shoda, Mischel, & Wright, 1994). Indeed, these profiles of *if . . . then* relations may in some sense *define* personality (Mischel, Shoda, & Mendoza-Denton, 2002). These profiles are relatively stable over time (Shoda et al., 1994) and thus account for temporal consistency in behavior. Consistency over time, of course, is a key element in conceptions of personality.

This line of thought has been applied by Andersen and Chen (2002) to the core social relationships in a person's life. They argue that we develop schematic knowledge of people who are significant to us early in life. When we encounter new people who resemble one of those significant people enough to activate that schema, it evokes the *if . . . then* profile associated with that significant person. You act more like the version of yourself that you displayed to that significant other.

This general viewpoint on behavior suggests that schemas are deeply interconnected to one another. Schemas about what people are like relate to schemas about the nature of situations. Both of these are tied to schemas for acting. Although you may focus on one of these at a time, the use of one implicitly involves the use of the others as well (Shoda et al., 1989).

Consistent with this line of thought, there's evidence that some of the same brain structures are involved in perception–cognition and related actions. For instance, certain neurons that are active when a monkey *does* an action are also active when the monkey *sees* the same action being done (Gallese, 2001; Rizzolatti, Fogassi, & Gallese, 2002). They are often called **mirror neurons.** Similar evidence has also been found in humans (Buccino et al., 2001). Later work extended the finding to sound. Neurons that are active when the monkey does or sees the action are also active when the monkey *hears* sounds associated with that action (Kohler, Keysers, Umiltà, Fogassi, Gallese, & Rizzolatti, 2002). Such findings have led to the idea that perceptual memories may actually be organized in terms of potentials for action (Fadiga, Fogassi, Gallese, & Rizzolatti, 2000).

Assessment

From the cognitive viewpoint, personality assessment emphasizes assessing people's mental structures. There are many ways to assess mental pictures of reality (e.g., Merluzzi, Glass, & Genest, 1981) called **cognitive assessment** techniques. They range from interviews and self-reports to *think-aloud protocols,* in which people say what comes into their minds while doing an activity. A variation on this is *experience sampling,* which is more intermittent.

THINK-ALOUD, EXPERIENCE SAMPLING, AND SELF-MONITORING

The technique used is often determined by the nature of the event of interest. For example, think-aloud approaches are used to assess cognition during problem solving (Ericsson & Simon, 1993). They're aimed at finding out what thoughts occur at various stages of problem solving. The intent is to examine such questions as which strategies are effective and which aren't and how the strategies of experts and novices differ (Simon & Simon, 1978).

Experience sampling (or thought sampling) typically has somewhat different purposes. This technique has people report at certain times what they've been thinking and doing. Sometimes the reports are made at scheduled times, and sometimes people are randomly paged and asked to report (e.g., Gable, Reis, & Elliot, 2000; Hormuth, 1990; Laurenceau, Barrett, & Pietromonaco, 1998; Pietromonaco & Barrett, 1997). This procedure lets you sample across a wide range of events in the person's day. That way, you can find out what cognitions and emotions go along with which kinds of events. The result is a clearer picture of what various events feel like to the people who are taking part in them.

For example, Csikszentmihalyi and Csikszentmihalyi (1988) paged people at irregular intervals and had them record their activities, thoughts, and feelings. As noted in Chapter 14, a focus of that work was on optimal experience. There were several interesting findings: Positive feelings relate mostly to *voluntary* actions, not things people *have* to do. Satisfaction, freedom, alertness, and creativity relate to events in which people's attention is tightly focused on what they're doing (Csikszentmihalyi, 1978). Interestingly, positive feelings of immersion are very likely during work (see also Table 16.1).

More recent research has extended experience sampling methodology into many new domains. Further, it's now common to collect people's reports of their thoughts and feelings on hand-held computers (Gable et al., 2000; Laurenceau et al., 1998; Pietromonaco & Barrett, 1997). This makes collecting these sorts of cognitive assessments extremely easy. This technique is now being used to study ideas from a wide variety of theoretical perspectives.

Table 16.1 Activities Producing Positive Feelings of Immersion. Positive feelings of being deeply and pleasantly involved in one's activities are tied to a wide range of activities. People were given descriptions that expressed such feelings and were asked to indicate one context in which they themselves had had similar experiences in their own lives. *Source:* Adapted from Csikszentmihalyi, 1982.

Activity Named	Percentage of People Naming It
Work activities (working, being involved in challenging problems at work)	31
Hobbies and home activities (cooking, singing, photography, sewing, etc.)	22
Sports and outdoor activities (golf, dancing, swimming, etc.)	18
Social activities (spending time with spouse or children, parties, vacationing)	16
Passive attending activities (listening to music, reading, watching TV)	13

Another technique, termed *event recording* or *self-monitoring,* focuses not on particular moments of the day but on particular classes of events. This technique has you record instances of specific event types (Ewart, 1978; Mahoney, 1977; Nelson, 1977). You note the particular behavior, emotion, or thought pattern, and record information about what was going on at the time (e.g., the time of day, whether you were with others or alone, what the situation was). Doing this lets you see regularities in the contexts that surround particular thoughts and emotions. You get a better understanding of what schemas you're automatically using.

CONTEXTUALIZED ASSESSMENT

Another aspect of the cognitive view on assessment is the idea that personality should be assessed for specific classes of contexts. This element is shared with the cognitive–social learning view. Several studies indicate that doing this adds important information.

Research on this issue by Wright and his colleagues has focused on assessment of children with problems. In one study (Wright, Lindgren, & Zakriski, 2001), teachers rated boys on two measures. One was a commonly used measure of problem behaviors (aggression and social withdrawal) that didn't identify the context in which they happen. The other measure assessed how often the behaviors occur *in response to specific situations.* The broad measure was able to distinguish aggressive children from others but didn't distinguish between two groups of boys whose aggression occurred in very different contexts. Thus, the contextualized measure provided fine-grained information that the other did not.

In another study (Wright, Zakriski, & Drinkwater, 1999), children were observed in a residential setting over a six-week period. Elaborate recordings were made of their behaviors and the contexts in which they occurred. Each child was also rated on the measure of problem behaviors that ignores context. Each child was classified by the latter measure as being an *externalizer* (displaying behaviors such as aggression), an *internalizer* (displaying behaviors such as social withdrawal), a *mixed case,* or *not a clinical case* (i.e., not fitting a diagnosis).

The behavioral signatures of these groups differed in ways that could not have been predicted by the global ratings. When teased or threatened by a peer, externalizers tended to hit and boss, whereas internalizers whined and withdrew. Outside these specific situations, these groups of children didn't differ behaviorally from children who had no problem diagnosis. The mixed cases didn't do any of these things in response to teasing, but they did tend to both hit and withdraw socially when a peer simply talked to them. Again, contextualized assessment gave much more information about those being assessed (see also Wright & Zakriski, 2003).

DIAGNOSTIC CATEGORIES AS FUZZY SETS

The cognitive approach has one more implication concerning assessment that differs completely from anything we've said thus far. This point isn't about assessment methods but about the result of some assessments. In particular, it concerns how clinicians organize their knowledge about the nature of people's problems.

People with psychological problems aren't just one big group. They fit into several diagnostic categories based on symptoms. Categories once had defining characteristics. If a person had all of a specific set of qualities, he or she was in that category. Otherwise, he or she wasn't. An alternative strategy is suggested by a view on the nature of categories discussed earlier, in which categories don't have explicit definitions. Rather, the category is a fuzzy set, made up of a set of features that category members often have but sometimes don't. In the same way, a diagnostic category may be a collection of features that are *often* present in exemplars of that category *but not always* (Cantor, Smith, French, & Mezzich, 1980).

Using the old strategy, if a person generally fits a diagnostic category but lacks a specific feature, the psychologist would hesitate to place the person in that category. With the newer strategy, the psychologist may be more willing to do so. Under this strategy, fit to the category is determined by the *proportion* of features that fit that category. This approach emphasizes the idea that diagnosis is probabilistic, rather than exact (Cantor et al., 1980).

Problems in Behavior, and Behavior Change

The focus on cognitive structure that's been so apparent throughout this chapter is also involved in how this view conceptualizes psychological problems and therapeutic behavioral change.

INFORMATION-PROCESSING DEFICITS

One implication of the cognitive view is that some problems reflect deficits in basic cognitive or memory functions: attending, extracting and organizing information, and so on. For example, people with schizophrenia need more time than other people to recognize stimuli such as letters (Miller, Saccuzzo, & Braff, 1979; Steronko & Woods, 1978). It isn't clear whether this implies a deeper problem or whether it bears only on perceiving. Just by itself, however, this problem would account for some of the difficulty a schizophrenic person has in life.

Another simple idea is that there's a limit on attentional capacity. If you pay too much attention to things other than what you're trying to do, you become less efficient at what you're trying to do. Using attention elsewhere can also make it hard to learn. For example, anxiety takes up attention. For that reason alone, being anxious can make it harder to process other things (Newman et al., 1993; Sorg & Whitney, 1992). People with test anxiety or social anxiety thus become less efficient when their anxiety is aroused. A related argument has been used to explore deficits related to depression (Conway & Giannopoulos, 1993; Kuhl & Helle, 1986).

Some styles of *deploying* attention may also create problems (Crick & Dodge, 1994). For example, children who are overly aggressive don't attend to cues of other children's intentions (Dodge, 1986; Dodge & Crick, 1990). As a result, they often misjudge others' intentions and act aggressively. Indeed, they often strike out preemptively (Hubbard, Dodge, Cillessen, Coie, & Schwartz, 2001). This may also be true of violent adults (Holtzworth-Munroe, 1992).

Why do people deploy their attention in ineffective ways? Their *schemas* lead them to do so. Recall that one effect of schemas is to tell you where to look for information in a new event: You look for information that fits the schema. Thus, a biased or faulty schema can bias the search for cues, which can lead to misinferences and inappropriate actions.

DEPRESSIVE SELF-SCHEMAS

A broad implication of the cognitive view is that many problems stem from schemas that interfere with effective functioning in more complex ways. This reasoning has been applied to several problems, most notably depression. Theorists hold that people sometimes develop ideas about the world that are inaccurate or distorted, which lead to adverse effects (e.g., Beck, 1976; Ellis, 1987; Meichenbaum, 1977; Young & Klosko, 1993). Aaron Beck (1972, 1976; Beck, Rush, Shaw, & Emery, 1979) is one theorist who thinks that depression and other problems follow from such distortions. In effect, people with these problems use faulty schemas to interpret events. They rely on negative preconceptions (their schemas) and ignore information that's available in the environment (though see Box 16.4).

In Beck's view, the inaccurate schemas are used quickly and spontaneously. They produce a stream of what he calls **automatic thoughts.** These automatic thoughts (e.g., "I can't do this," "What's the point of trying?," "Everything's going to turn out wrong") influence feelings and behaviors. The pattern has a run-on quality, because the negative feelings lead to more use of negative schemas, which in turn leads to more negative affect (cf. Nolen-Hoeksema, Morrow, & Frederickson, 1993; Wenzlaff, Wegner, & Roper, 1988). Indeed, just expecting emotional distress makes distress more likely (Kirsch, 1990; Kirsch, Mearns, & Catanzaro, 1990).

People who are prone to depression or anxiety seem to rely too much on information in memory and rely too little on the reality of the situation. This creates problems because the self-schemas of these people are negative (Kuiper & Derry, 1981; Segal, 1988). When people use the negative schemas, they naturally expect bad outcomes. They don't look at the situation with an open mind but attend to and encode the worst side of what's happening (Gotlib, 1983).

Box 16.4 Theoretical Controversy

Whose Perceptions Are Distorted, Anyway?

Beck's theory of depression is based on the premise that people who get depressed make a variety of cognitive distortions. He sees these distortions as leading to depressed feelings and to other symptoms of depression. However, research has raised questions about who's doing more distorting: people who are depressed or people who aren't.

In one research program bearing on this question (Alloy & Abramson, 1988), participants were presented a series of problems. For some, there was a connection between their responses and the outcome of the problem. For others, there was no relation between response and outcome. The measure of interest was participants' estimates of the degree to which their responses had controlled the outcomes.

The results were surprising. The researchers found that depressed persons were in fact fairly *accurate* in their judgments. People who weren't depressed, on the other hand, tended to overestimate the control they'd had over good outcomes that in reality were random. No one was surprised that the depressed and nondepressed groups differed. What was surprising was that the *depressed* persons apparently had the better grip on reality.

Another study made a similar case, using very different procedures (Lewinsohn, Mischel, Chaplin, & Barton, 1980). Participants were observed in social interaction and were rated on several dimensions by observers. The participants also rated themselves. The results revealed that people who weren't depressed saw themselves in a better light than the observers did. People who were depressed saw themselves pretty much as the observers saw them. Again, the depressed participants had a better grasp on reality than did the nondepressed.

What are the implications of these findings for Beck's theory of depression? In answering this question, it's important to keep in mind that depressed people *did* differ from nondepressed people in the expected direction. Thus, Beck's argument that depression involves distortion—*in comparison with other people*—still holds. What was startling was that this distortion resulted in greater, rather than less, accuracy. Thus, if Beck's theory about depression is correct, it seems to need one additional assumption: that the perceptions of nondepressed people incorporate a rosy and unrealistic glow of optimism. A number of people have, in fact, come to precisely that conclusion (Taylor & Brown, 1988; Weinstein, 1989).

Beck uses the term **cognitive triad** to refer to negative thinking about the self, the world, and the future. Depressed people also use other distortions. They *overgeneralize* in a negative way from a single bad outcome to their overall sense of self-worth (Carver, 1998; Carver, La Voie, Kuhl, & Ganellen 1988; Hayes, Harris, & Carver, 2004). They make *arbitrary inferences,* jumping to negative conclusions when there isn't evidence for them (Cook & Peterson, 1986). They *catastrophize,* anticipating that every problem will have a terrible outcome. And they interpret bad outcomes as *permanent* (Abramson et al., 1978; Abramson et al., 1989). The result of all this is a low sense of self-worth and hopelessness for the future (Haaga, Dyck, & Ernst, 1991; J. E. Roberts, Gotlib, & Kassel, 1996; J. E. Roberts & Monroe, 1994).

A few paragraphs back, we said that Beck views the use of negative mental structures as automatic. This argument has taken on new overtones in recent years in light of the emerging idea that implicit and explicit aspects of the self compete for influence on behavior (described earlier in the chapter). This emerging idea suggests that the negative mental structures are in a part of the brain that's different from the part guiding conscious, effortful action. The negative patterns may have come from conditioning or just become automatic over the years. Regardless, in the dual-mode view they influence behavior unless overridden by a more effortful process.

This is much the argument that Beevers (2005) has made about vulnerability to depression. Specifically, a person with negative associations in the implicit self is likely to often be subject to negative feelings. This person needs to make an effortful corrective process to counter those negative associations in the implicit self. If that effortful process doesn't occur, the implicit self maintains control over the person's experiences and depression is more likely.

COGNITIVE THERAPY

In Beck's view, therapy should get the person to put faulty schemas aside and build new ones. People must learn to recognize automatic self-defeating thoughts and substitute other self-talk for them. This is termed **cognitive restructuring** or **reframing.** They should also try to focus on the information in the situation and rely less on preconceptions. To put it differently, these people should become more *controlled* in processing what's going on and less *automatic* (cf. Barber & DeRubeis, 1989; Kanfer & Busemeyer, 1982).

The procedures used for changing faulty schemas and their consequences are known broadly as **cognitive therapies** (Beck, 1976, 1991; Beck et al., 1979; DeRubeis, Tang, & Beck, 2001). There are several different techniques. A surprising one is getting people to go ahead and do things they expect (unrealistically) to have bad consequences. If the bad outcome doesn't happen, the people are thereby led to reexamine—and perhaps change—their expectations.

More generally, people are encouraged to view their thought patterns as hypotheses to be tested, instead of as certainties. They're also encouraged to go ahead and test the hypotheses. For example, if you're a person who thinks a single failure means you can't do anything right, you might be told to examine your skills in other domains immediately after a failure. If you're a person who thinks everyone will despise you if you do anything wrong, you might be told to test this assumption by being with friends the next time you do something wrong.

Even a small amount of this sort of "reality testing" can have a large impact on how people view themselves. In one study (Haemmerlie & Montgomery, 1984), students with strong social anxiety were given a simple treatment for it. The treatment was having a conversation with a member of the opposite sex who'd been told to initiate conversation topics, use the pronoun *you* fairly often, and avoid being negative. These *biased interactions* were held twice, a week apart, for about an hour each time. The result was a large reduction in signs of anxiety (see Figure 16.5).

Contemporary Cognitive Theories: Problems and Prospects

Some psychologists find the cognitive view on personality exciting. Others find it less so. It's seen by many as disorganized and not yet mature (Funder, 2001). Those who find it interesting acknowledge that it has many loose ends. Some critics of this view, on the other hand, think it's a passing fad, a misguided effort to graft a very different part of psychology someplace it just doesn't belong.

One criticism of the cognitive view has been that some who use it took the *computer* metaphor too literally. Knowing how a computer does something doesn't necessarily tell us anything about how people do the same thing. There may be dozens of ways to get a computer to do something, but there's no assurance that any of them is even remotely the same as the way a person does it. One response to this is that the computer metaphor has been a useful tool, even if it's hard to know how far to press the analogy. When the metaphor is taken in its general form, rather than as a precise blueprint, it yields interesting suggestions about human thought. Many of these suggestions have been supported in research.

Another criticism of the cognitive view is that it's nothing more than a transplantation of cognitive psychology into the subject of personality. What's gained by knowing that a person's knowledge is schematically organized? What does it tell you about personality to know that these knowledge structures can be brought into use by priming them?

One answer is that these aspects of the mind's functioning do seem to have important implications for the kinds of day-to-day behaviors we usually think of in terms of personality. People absorb new experiences in terms of their current understanding of the world. Thus, it's useful to know what biases are created by their current understanding (i.e., schemas). How people interpret their experiences is also influenced by the goals they have in mind. Because different people have different goals, they experience events in very different ways.

The fact that people's construals can be influenced by priming is of special interest, partly because it relates to an idea of Freud's but with a very different spin. The idea is that people do things for reasons they're unaware of. Priming studies show that this definitely does happen, but the reason need not reside in the psychoanalytic unconscious. The process may be far more superficial (and for that reason less ominous). But because it's superficial, it may also be far more common than previously realized (Bargh & Chartrand, 1999; Carver & Scheier, 2002; Hassin et al., 2005).

The broadest answer to criticisms of the cognitive view, however, may be this: The cognitive viewpoint on personality is part of a broad attempt to understand the

FIGURE 16.5
Scores before and after on three measures among socially anxious men who engaged in unpressured positive conversations with a woman on two different occasions compared with scores of men who did not do so. The measures are (A) self-rated general social anxiety, (B) self-rated state anxiety (taken while in the presence of an attractive woman), and (C) distance from the woman while engaged in a cooperative task. The pleasant experiences improved participants' scores on all these variables. *Source: Adapted from Haemmerlie & Montgomery, 1984.*

operating characteristics of the mind. A better understanding of those characteristics can't help but illuminate important aspects of personality. From this view, the intrapersonal functioning of personality is a reflection of the complexities of the mind and its workings. It's not possible to fully understand the former without understanding the latter.

· SUMMARY ·

The cognitive orientation to personality considers how people attend to, process, organize, encode, store, and retrieve information. *Schemas* are mental organizations of information that develop over experience and are used to identify new events. Some think schemas organize around prototypes (best members); some say that schemas have fuzzy, or inexact, definitions. Schemas make new events easy to remember. They also provide default information to fill in the gaps of events. Schemas can represent concepts (in semantic memory) and events (in episodic memory). Each aspect of memory holds *exemplars* and *generalities.* Stereotypic event categories are called *scripts.*

Social cognition refers to cognitive processes bearing on stimuli relevant to social behavior. People develop schematic representations of many kinds of socially relevant categories. People also develop *self-schemas,* representations of themselves. The self-schema is more elaborate than other schemas, but it seems to follow the same principles. The self-schema may have several facets (e.g., possible selves). Some social schemas imply permanence (entity); some imply potential for change (incremental).

Many psychologists view *memory* as a vast set of content nodes, linked to each other by various associations. Activating one node in memory causes partial activation of related nodes (*priming*), causing that information to become more accessible. Priming can even happen outside awareness. Connectionist models view memory in terms of patterns in overall networks. A given pattern reflects the satisfaction of many constraints simultaneously. This view applies nicely to social perception and decision making. Some theorists believe there are two distinct kinds of thought processes: one quick, intuitive, and connectionist, the other slower, rational, and linear. Research on implicit attitudes suggests that people have knowledge at two levels, which may correspond to the two modes of thought processes.

Broad statements on cognitive views of personality emphasize the importance of people's schemas, encoding strategies, personal competencies, expectancies about how things are related in the world, values or incentives, and self-regulatory systems. People's behavior is seen as following *if . . . then* contingencies, in which the *if* describes a situation and the *then* describes a behavioral response. In this view, personality is a profile of these contingencies, forming a unique "behavioral signature" for each person.

Assessment from this viewpoint is the process of determining the person's cognitive tendencies and contents of consciousness. Cognitive assessment techniques include think-aloud procedures, thought sampling, and monitoring of the occurrence of particular categories of events. These procedures give a clearer idea of what sorts of thoughts are coming to mind in various kinds of situations, typically situations that are problematic. Also important is the idea that assessment be contextualized, to capture the person's *if . . . then* contingencies.

Problems in behavior can come from information-processing deficits (e.g., difficulty encoding, ineffective allocation of attention). Problems can also arise from development of negative self-schemas. In this view, depression results from various kinds of cognitive distortions, all of which cause events to seem more unpleasant or as having more negative implications than is actually true. *Cognitive therapy* involves, in part, attempting to get people to stop engaging in these cognitive distortions and to develop more adaptive views of the events that they experience. This may entail correcting automatic, intuitive processes through oversight from consciousness, effortful processes.

· GLOSSARY ·

Attribution   The process of making a judgment about the cause (or causes) of an event.

Automatic thoughts   Self-related internal dialogue that often interferes with behavior.

Cognitive assessment   Procedures used to assess cognitive processes and contents of consciousness.

Cognitive restructuring or **reframing**   The process of taking a different and more positive view of one's experience.

Cognitive therapy   Procedures aimed at reducing cognitive distortions and the resulting distress.

Cognitive triad   Negative patterns of thinking about the self, the world, and the future.

Connectionism   An approach to understanding cognition based on the metaphor of interconnected neurons.

Default   Something assumed to be true until one learns otherwise.

Dual-mode models   Models assuming two different modes of cognition—one effortful, one automatic.

Episodic memory   Memory organized according to sequences of events.

Exemplar   A specific example of a category member.

Fuzzy set   A category defined by a set of attributes that aren't absolutely necessary for membership.

Implicit knowledge   Associations between things in memory that are not directly accessible.

Mirror neurons   Neurons that are active both when perceiving an action and when doing the action.

Node   An area of memory that stores some element of information.

Possible self   An image of oneself in the future (expected, desired, feared, etc.).

Priming   The process of activating an element in memory by using the information contained in it.

Prototype   The representation of a category in terms of a best member of the category.

Schema   An organization of knowledge in memory.

Script   A memory structure used to represent a highly stereotyped category of events.

Self-complexity   The degree to which one's self-schema is differentiated and compartmentalized.

Self-schema   The schematic representation of the self.

Semantic memory   Memory organized according to meaning.

Social cognition   Cognitive processes focusing on socially meaningful stimuli.

Subliminal   Occurring too fast to be consciously recognized.

CHAPTER 17

Self-Regulation

As Susan awakes, thoughts come to mind about the presentation she's to give this morning. While dressing, she rehearses the points she intends to make. She catches herself skipping too quickly from one to another and makes a mental note to slow down in the middle section so she doesn't leave anything out. For the twentieth time, she retraces her logic, looking for flaws. She wants this to be perfect—to nail down the recommendation for law school she's going to ask her professor for next week. She has planned what to wear to make the impression she wants to make, and just before leaving, she checks her appearance in the hall mirror. A little poking and rearranging of her hair, and she turns to go. As she opens the door, she runs a mental checklist of what she needs to have with her—notes for her presentation, money, purse, keys, and—oh, yeah—the photos she said she'd show Carolyn. Grab the photos. Check to see that the door's locked. Check to be sure there's enough gas in the car. Check to see if there's enough time to take the scenic route to campus. And she's off. "Good," Susan thinks. "Things are going just the way I want them to. Everything's right on track."

P EOPLE SHIFT from one task to another as the day proceeds, yet there's usually coherence and continuity as well. Your days are usually planful (despite disruptions and impulsive side trips) and include many activities. How do you move so easily from one thing to another, keep it all organized, and make it all happen? These are some of the questions behind this chapter.

The approach to personality discussed here uses several metaphors. One of them is *person as robot* (also know by the more formidable label *autonomous artificial agent*). The growth of robotics has influenced the way some people think about human nature (Brooks, 2002; Dawson, 2004; Fellous & Arbib, 2005). As more has been learned about how to get machines to do things, the suspicion has arisen that some of the ideas involved may help us understand how people do things.

The easiest way to start exploring these ideas is to think of them as a view of *motivation*. Much of this chapter focuses on how people adopt, prioritize, and attain goals. In some ways, these functions resemble what was discussed in Chapter 5 as *motives*.

From Cognition to Behavior

As we continue, it will also help to keep in mind the cognitive view of personality discussed in Chapter 16. The general view that people have an organized network of memories is assumed here, too. Now, though, the focus is on how the cognitions and memories result in behavior.

SCHEMAS AND ACTIONS

As noted in Chapter 16, the schemas people use to understand events often include information about behavior. You use this information to recognize what other people are doing. But you also use information from memory to guide the *making of behavior*. Information in schemas helps you decide what to do in the class of situation the schema represents (Burroughs & Drews, 1991; Dodge, 1986). For example, just as the *dining out* script lets you understand someone else's evening, it also reminds you what actions to take if *you* are dining out—order before you're served and pay the bill before you leave.

What's the relation between the information used to recognize acts and the information used to do acts? It's not clear whether one schema serves two purposes or whether there are two parallel forms—one for understanding and one for doing (Petri & Mishkin, 1994). However, there does at least seem to be overlap. As noted in Chapter 16, it's been found that certain neurons (so-called *mirror neurons*) are active both when an action is being watched and when the same action is being done (Gallese, 2001; Rizzolatti, Fogassi, & Gallese, 2002). This suggests a very strong link between thinking and doing.

INTENTIONS

Sometimes a situation evokes a schema that provides guidelines for action. Often, though, actions follow from intentions. An important question, then, is, How are intentions formed? Icek Ajzen and Martin Fishbein (Ajzen, 1985, 1988; Ajzen & Fishbein, 1980) say the process uses a kind of mental algebra creating an action probability. If the probability is high enough, an intention is formed to do the act.

According to Ajzen and Fishbein, when people are deciding whether to do something, they weigh several kinds of information (see Figure 17.1). They think about the action's likely outcome and how much they want it. For example, you might think that spending money on a Caribbean trip over spring break would result in a lot of fun, and you really want that fun. The outcome and its desirability merge to form an **attitude** about the behavior. Because it stems from your own wants, your attitude is your *personal orientation* to the act.

Two other kinds of information pertain to the act's *social* meaning to you. One kind of information is whether people who matter to you want you to do the action. You might think about your parents, who don't want you to take the trip (they want

FIGURE 17.1

Foundations of intentions. The belief that an act will produce a particular outcome and the personal desirability of the outcome merge to form an *attitude* (a personal orientation to the act). The belief that other people want you to do the act and the desire to go along with their wishes merge to form a subjective *norm* (a social orientation to the act). The attitude and the subjective norm are weighted in forming the *intention*. The intention then influences the *behavior*. *Source: Adapted from Ajzen, 1988.*

you to come home instead). Or you might think about your friends, who think the trip is a great idea. The other element is how much you want to please the people you're thinking about. How much do you want to please your parents, or at least stay on their good side? How much do you want to go along with your friends' wishes? What the other people in your mind want you to do and how much that matters to you merge to form a **subjective norm** about the action.

The intention derives from both the attitude and the subjective norm. If both favor the behavior, you'll form a strong intention to do it. If both oppose the behavior, you'll form a strong intention *not* to do it. Things are more complex when the attitude and subjective norm conflict. Sometimes you want an outcome, but you know your parents (or your friends) don't want you to do the behavior. In this case, which intention you form depends on which matters more: satisfying yourself or satisfying your parents (or friends).

GOALS

Underlying what we've said so far is the idea that behavior is directed toward *goals*. Schemas suggest behaviors to do. Forming an intention means setting up a goal to attain. The idea that human experience is organized around goals has been discussed a lot in the past two decades (e.g., Austin & Vancouver, 1996; E. S. Elliott & Dweck, 1988; Freund & Baltes, 2002; Pervin, 1983, 1989). Diverse terms have been used, including *life tasks* (Cantor & Kihlstrom, 1987), *personal strivings* (Emmons, 1986), *current concerns* (Klinger, 1987), and *personal projects* (Little, 1989), but the core theme is much the same. The theme is that people's goals energize their activities, direct their movements, and even provide meaning for their lives (Baumeister, 1989).

FIGURE 17.2
Circumplex formed by relationships among diverse goals, across 15 cultures. Goals vary along the dimension of intrinsic versus extrinsic and separately along the dimension of concerning the physical self versus transcending the self. *Source: Based on Grouzet et al., 2005.*

All these constructs assume both overall goals and subgoals. That is, any life task can be achieved in many ways. The way you choose depends on other aspects of your life. Strategies that are used to pursue life tasks also differ from one person to another (Langston & Cantor, 1989). For example, someone who's relatively shy will have different strategies for making friends than a person who's more outgoing.

In this view, the self is made up partly of goals and organizations among them. Indeed, there's evidence that traits derive their meaning from the goals to which they relate (Read, Jones, & Miller, 1990; B. W. Roberts & Robins, 2000). Goals and aspirations certainly vary from person to person. Yet there is evidence that goals have a coherent set of relations to each other among persons from diverse cultures. That is, goals come together in a two-dimensional circumplex in which some are compatible with each other and some are in conflict (Grouzet et al., 2005). One dimension ranges from intrinsic to extrinsic goals (see Figure 17.2); the other ranges from goals pertaining to the physical self to goals involving self-transcendence. (Both dimensions are consistent with ideas discussed in Chapter 14.)

GOAL SETTING

Many goals specify intended and desired actions but don't imply any standard of excellence. The goal of going water skiing on a hot afternoon doesn't necessarily imply a goal of excellence (though it might). Forming an intention to go to the grocery store creates a guide for behavior, but it's not really very challenging.

On the other hand, performance level is clearly an issue in some areas. In many activities, the goal isn't just to perform; it's to do *well*. An example is taking a college course. For many people, the goal isn't just completing the course, it's getting a good grade. Another example is business performance. The goal isn't just to survive, but to thrive. One question that arises in such contexts is this: Does setting a particular goal level influence how well you do?

Yes. Setting higher goals leads to higher performance (Locke & Latham, 1990). This is true when high goals are compared to easy goals, and it's also true when they're compared to the goal of "Do your best." Apparently, most people don't take "Do your best" literally. It's taken as "Try to do reasonably well." Thus, it leads to poorer performance than does setting a specific high goal.

Why do higher goals lead to better performance? There are three interrelated reasons. First, setting a higher goal causes you to *try* harder. For example, you know you won't solve 50 problems in 10 minutes unless you push yourself. So you start out pushing yourself. Second, you're more *persistent*. A brief spurt of effort won't do; you'll have to push yourself the entire time. Third, high goals make you *concentrate* more, making you less susceptible to distractions. In all these respects, setting a lower goal causes people to ease back a little.

The positive effect of setting high goals is well documented, but it has a very important limitation. In particular, if you're given a goal that's totally unrealistic, you won't adopt it. You won't try for it. If you don't adopt it, it's as if the goal doesn't exist. The key, then, is taking up a goal that's high enough to sustain strong effort but not so high that it's rejected instead of adopted.

IMPLEMENTATION INTENTIONS AND THE IMPORTANCE OF STRATEGIES

In describing goals, we noted that typically there are *subgoals,* or strategies related to them. Peter Gollwitzer and his colleagues (Brandstätter, Lengfelder, & Gollwitzer, 2001; Gollwitzer, 1999; Gollwitzer & Brandstätter, 1997) have made a similar distinction between two kinds of intentions. A **goal intention** is the intent to reach a particular outcome. An **implementation intention** concerns the how, when, and where of the process. It's the intention to take specific actions when encountering specific circumstances. This linking of context to action is what we described as *if . . . then* links in Chapter 16 (Mischel & Shoda, 1995). Some *if . . . then* links are habitual and well learned (Brandstätter & Frank, 2002). Sometimes, though, they need to be formed consciously for specific intended paths of behavior.

Implementation intentions are more concrete than goal intentions. They serve the goal intentions. They're important because they help stop problems that can arise in getting the behavior done. Often people fail to fulfill goal intentions because they haven't decided how to go about doing so. An implementation intention, being concrete and specific, takes care of that. Sometimes people fail to act because they're distracted and brief opportunities pass them by. Having an implementation intention helps you recognize the opportunity quickly and act on it (Brandstätter et al., 2001). Sometimes people fail to act because they're worn out. Having an implementation intention helps you overcome the lack of energy (Webb & Sheeran, 2003). Forming an implementation intention to do something hard (e.g., writing an assigned paper over Christmas break) greatly increases the likelihood of actually doing it (Gollwitzer & Brandstätter, 1997).

On the other hand, the implementation intention by itself doesn't seem to be enough. You also have to have a strong and active goal intention (Sheeran, Webb, &

Gollwitzer, 2005). In fact, implementation intentions help more if the goal fits with your sense of self than if it doesn't (Koestner, Lekes, Powers, & Chicoine, 2002).

Implementation intentions make a link between a situational cue and a strategy for moving toward the goal. Another body of work also shows the importance of having such links. It derives from the concept of *possible self*. As described in Chapter 16, possible selves are broad images of the person you think you might become. For a desired possible self to influence behavior, you also have to have strategies to attain it (Oyserman, Bybee, & Terry, 2006; Oyserman, Bybee, Terry, & Hart-Johnson, 2004). If the strategies are not already there to be used, effort needs to be spent in creating them.

DELIBERATIVE AND IMPLEMENTAL MINDSETS

Goal intentions and implementation intentions matter. But forming intentions and doing the actions they entail are different processes. People do them with different mindsets (Heckhausen & Gollwitzer, 1987). Forming an intention requires weighing possibilities, thinking of pros and cons, and juggling options. This is called a **deliberative mindset** because the person is deliberating the decision to act. It is relatively unbiased, careful, and cautious in the service of making the best choice (Taylor & Gollwitzer, 1995).

Once the intention has been formed, actually doing the behavior entails a different mindset. People no longer deliberate. Now it's all about doing. This is called an **implemental mindset** because it focuses on implementing the intention to act. This mindset is optimistic and minimizes potential problems in the service of trying as hard as possible to carry out the action (Taylor & Gollwitzer, 1995). Generally, it fosters persistence (Brandstätter & Frank, 2002).

There's evidence that these two mindsets may use different areas of the brain. Lengfelder and Gollwitzer (2001) studied patients with frontal-lobe damage and patients with damage in other areas. They found those with frontal damage were impaired in deliberating. However, if they were provided with *if . . . then* implementation intentions, they weren't impaired at acting. This suggests that the planning is done in the frontal cortex, whereas the handling of the action is done elsewhere.

Self-Regulation and Feedback Control

We've discussed behavioral schemas, intentions, the use of goals, the impact of lofty goals, and the importance of having strategies. But once a goal is set and an intention formed, what ensures that the behavior you *actually do* is the one you *set out to do*? This question brings us to the concept of *feedback control* (Carver & Scheier, 1981, 1998; MacKay, 1963, 1966; Miller, Galanter, & Pribram, 1960; Powers, 1973; Scheier & Carver, 1988; Wiener, 1948).

FEEDBACK CONTROL

A **feedback loop** has four parts (see Figure 17.3). The first is a value to self-regulate toward: a *goal, standard of comparison,* or *reference value* for behavior. (All of these mean the same thing here.) These can come from many places and can exist at many levels of abstraction. For example, they can be plans, intentions, possible selves, or strategies.

The second element is a perception of your present behavior and its effects. This just means noting what you're doing and the effect it's having. Often this is just a flicker of awareness, sensing in a vague way what you're doing. Sometimes it means thinking carefully about what you've been doing over a longer period. Sometimes people literally watch what they're doing (e.g., at dance studios). Although it's easiest to talk about it in terms of *thinking,* this function (as a function) doesn't require consciousness (Bargh & Ferguson, 2000).

These perceptions are compared with the goal by an element termed a **comparator.** If you're doing what's intended, there's no discrepancy between the two, and you continue as before. If your behavior *differs* from what you intended, though, a final process kicks in. This process changes the behavior, adjusts it to bring it more in line with your intention. (For a subtle theoretical issue pertaining to this viewpoint, see Box 17.1.)

The word *feedback* is used because when you adjust the action, the result is "fed back" in the form of a new perception, which is rechecked against the reference value. This loop is also called a *control system,* partly because each event in the loop depends on the result of a previous one. Thus, each prior event controls the next one.

The feedback idea has several implications. For one, it assumes that behavior is purposeful (as do the goal concepts discussed earlier). In this view, virtually all behavior involves trying to conform to some reference value. Life is a process of forming goals and intentions (broad and narrow, short term and long term) and adjusting behavior to match them, using feedback perceptions to tell whether you're doing as you've intended.

According to this logic, self-regulation is continuous and never ending. Every change in output changes current conditions. The new condition has to be checked against the goal. In addition, goals are often dynamic—evolving over time. For example, think of the goal of doing well in school, or making a particular impression on someone (and maintaining it), or taking a vacation trip. You do well in school not by going to a particular end point but by doing well at many tasks over time. You take a vacation trip not by leaving and coming back but by doing activities that constitute vacationing. There's a continuous interplay between adjusting your action and moving forward to the next phase of an evolving goal.

As we said about goals, referring to something as a *standard* here means only it's the value used as a guide. It doesn't necessarily mean a standard of excellence (though it can). Think of a student who's regulating study behavior around the goal of making a C in a course by looking over class notes the night before the exam but not much more. The *structure* of this behavior (setting a goal, checking, and adjusting as needed) is exactly the same as that of a student who's trying to make an A. They're just using two different comparison values.

FIGURE 17.3
Diagram of a discrepancy-reducing feedback loop, which shows the basic processes presumed to underlie self-corrective behavioral self-regulation in both artificial and living systems.

In order for feedback control to occur, people need to monitor what they are currently doing.

Box 17.1 Theoretical Issue

Feedback versus Reinforcement

It's long been known that people doing tasks benefit from knowing the results of their last efforts (Locke & Latham, 1990; Schmidt, 1988). But this evidence is interpreted differently by different people. According to the view under discussion, knowledge of results is *feedback*, which people can use to adjust their behavior. It's sometimes argued, however, that the feedback is actually a *reinforcer* (Kulhavy & Stock, 1989). That's a rather different view of what's going on.

What's the role of reward and punishment in the self-regulation view? People whose work is discussed in this chapter don't entirely agree. Some see reward, particularly self-reward, as

important. For example, Bandura (1986) holds that the self-reward or self-praise that a person engages in after attaining a desired goal is a crucial aspect of self-regulation.

On the other side of the disagreement, we've argued that this concept isn't needed (Carver & Scheier, 1981, 1990). In our view, it doesn't add anything to say that the person engages in self-praise after goal attainment. Although self-praise may occur, it's only a reaction to an event; the *event* is what matters. The crucial events, in this view, are the goal attainment and the person's realization of how the goal was reached.

The concept of reinforcement comes from learning theory. In thinking about this issue, it's of interest that learning theorists have long argued about the role of reinforcement in learning. Tolman (1932) believed that

reward—even to a laboratory rat—doesn't stamp anything in but just provides information that the animal can learn from. Specifically, the animal learns what leads to what, by experiencing the events in association with one another. Tolman said rewards and punishments aren't necessary for learning, but they can draw attention to aspects of the learning situation that are particularly relevant.

It's also been found that a simple social reinforcer such as saying "good" has more impact if you've been led to believe that the person saying "good" does so only rarely (Babad, 1973). Presumably, this is because events that are rare provide more information than events that are common. That finding joins with Tolman in suggesting that it may be the *informational value* of the reinforcer that matters, not the reinforcer itself.

SELF-DIRECTED ATTENTION AND THE ACTION OF THE COMPARATOR

Does human behavior follow the pattern of feedback control? One source of evidence is studies of the effects of self-directed attention. It's been argued that when you have a goal or intention in mind, directing your attention toward yourself engages the comparator of the loop that's managing your behavior (Carver & Scheier, 1981, 1998).

In some studies of self-directed attention, participants are exposed to things that remind them of themselves (e.g., an audience, a TV camera, or a mirror that shows their image). In other studies, researchers measure the strength of people's natural tendency to be self-reflective (Fenigstein, Scheier, & Buss, 1975; Trapnell & Campbell, 1999).

The idea that self-directed attention engages a comparator leads to two kinds of predictions. First, self-focus should increase the tendency to compare goals with current behavior. It's hard to study that, but here's an indirect way. Create a situation in which people can't make a mental comparison between a goal and behavior without getting some concrete information. Put people in that situation, then measure how much they seek the information. Presumably, more seeking of the information implies more comparison. In several studies based on this reasoning, self-focused persons sought comparison-relevant information more than less self-focused persons (Scheier & Carver, 1983).

If self-directed attention engages a comparator, something else should happen as well: Behavior should be regulated more closely to the goal. It does. As an illustration, people in one project (Carver, 1975) said they either opposed or favored the use of punishment as a teaching tool. Later, all of them had to punish someone for errors in learning. All were told to use their own judgment about how much punishment to use. Only those who were self-aware actually did so. Many other studies also show that self-focus leads to goal matching, ranging quite widely in the standards of comparison evoked for use.

HIERARCHICAL ORGANIZATION

These studies suggest that feedback processes might be involved in behavior. But a feedback loop is pretty simple. How do you actually get behavior out of it? One answer is that feedback loops may exist in layers. William Powers (1973) argued that this type of organization is what makes physical action possible. Others have made related arguments (e.g., Broadbent, 1977; Gallistel, 1980; Rosenbaum, 1987, 1990; Toates, 2006; Vallacher & Wegner, 1987).

The notion of a **feedback hierarchy** assumes there are both high-level and low-level goals that relate to each other. You have the goal of being a particular possible self, but you may also have the goal of having clean clothes to wear and the goal of making it to your psychology class on time. How do these things fit together? Recall the structure of the feedback loop from Figure 17.3. Powers says that in a hierarchy, the *behavioral output* of a high-level loop consists of setting a goal for a lower-level loop (see Figure 17.4). High-level loops don't "behave" by physical actions but by providing guides to the loops below them. Only the very lowest loops actually create physical acts, by controlling muscle groups (Rosenbaum, 1987, 1990, 2005). Each layer receives feedback appropriate to its level of abstraction.

The levels proposed by Powers that are most relevant to personality are shown in Figure 17.4. At the top are very abstract qualities he called **system concepts.** An example is the broad sense of ideal self people try to maintain. Richard, the person whose behavior is outlined in Figure 17.4, is trying to live up to his desired self-image. Doing this resembles the experience of self-actualization (Chapter 14). It promotes the sense of personal wholeness and integration.

People don't just go out and *be* their ideal selves, though. Trying to attain that ideal self means trying to live in accord with the **principles** it specifies. Thus, Powers called the next level *principle control.* Principles are broad guidelines. They specify broad qualities of behavior, which can be displayed in many ways. When they're active, principles help you decide what activities to start and what choices to make as you do them (Verplanken & Holland, 2002). Principles tend to correspond to traits.

As Figure 17.4 shows, Richard's ideal self includes a principle corresponding to *thoughtfulness.* This principle can be used as a guide for many kinds of action, including taking this opportunity to buy flowers. As another example, the principle of *honesty* would lead a person to ignore an opportunity to cheat on an exam. The principle of

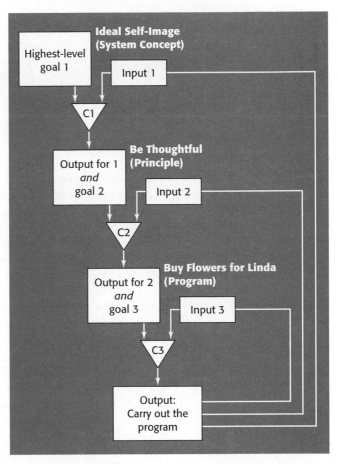

FIGURE 17.4
Diagram of a three-level hierarchy of feedback systems. This diagram shows the "cascade" of control that flows from higher-level loops to lower-level ones. High-level loops set the goals for the loops directly below them. The levels of control illustrated here are those at the top of the hierarchy proposed by Powers (1973). The diagram shows a cross-section of the behavior of a man who is actively attempting to (1) match his self-perceptions to his idealized self by (2) following the principle of *thoughtfulness,* which is being manifested (3) in the programmatic activity of buying flowers for his wife.

Calvin and Hobbes

by Bill Watterson

Though principles often have overtones of goodness and morality, that need not be the case. Principles can also be self-serving. What's necessary is that a principle must be abstract enough to apply to many kinds of behavior.

Calvin and Hobbes copyright Watterson. Distributed by Universal Press Syndicate. Reprinted with permission. All rights reserved.

frugality would lead a person to choose a moderately priced restaurant over an expensive one.

What defines something as a *principle* is its abstractness and broad applicability, not its social appropriateness. Thus, expedience is a principle, even though it's not socially desirable (see the cartoon). Knowing only that something is a principle doesn't tell what direction it pulls behavior. For example, it's been shown that different principles can lead people either to support affirmative action or to oppose it (Reyna, Henry, Korfmacher, & Tucker, 2005).

Just as people don't go out and *be* their ideal selves, they don't just go out and *do* principles. Principles act by specifying **programs** (or by specifying decisions within programs; see Figure 17.4). A program resembles a script (Schank & Abelson, 1977). It specifies a general course of action but with many details left out. Enacting a program (or script) thus requires you to make choices within a larger set of possibilities. Programs, in effect, are strategies.

The principle of *thoughtfulness* led Richard to enter the program of buying flowers. This program is partly specified: Stop at the florist, pick out flowers, and pay for them. But which flowers he gets will depend on what's available; he can pay with cash or a credit card; and he may or may not have to put money into a parking meter.

Two more things about this example: Both stem from the fact that there are several ways to conform to this principle. First, Richard might have chosen another program—making Linda a special dinner or washing her car. Entering any of these programs would conform to the same principle. Second, matching the principle of *thoughtfulness* didn't require *entering* a program; the principle might have come into play *during* a program. For example, if Linda had told him to buy flowers on his way home, he'd be buying flowers anyway. The *thoughtfulness* principle might have become active in the midst of the buying-flowers program, leading him to decide to buy Linda's favorite flower, even though it's out of season and therefore expensive.

Much of what people do in their day-to-day lives seems programlike, or scriptlike. Most of the intentions you form in an average day involve programs. Doing the laundry, going to a store or the movies, studying for an exam, fixing lunch, trying to get noticed by that person in class—all of these are programs. They all have general courses of predictable acts and subgoals, but exactly what you do at a given point can vary, depending on the situation.

Most likely, there are well-learned links between many principles and the programs to which they pertain. Connections between programs and lower levels of control are probably

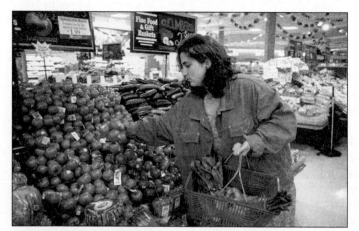

Much of what we do in our day-to-day lives, such as grocery shopping, has a programlike or scriptlike character.

even stronger. For example, there's evidence that when a person has a goal in mind that concerns travel, it automatically activates information about a plausible and common way to get there (Aarts & Dijksterhuis, 2000).

ISSUES CONCERNING HIERARCHICAL ORGANIZATION

Several questions come up when people think about hierarchies. For example, are all the levels active all the time? Not necessarily. People can go for a very long time without thinking about their ideal selves. Behavior often is guided for long periods by programs. To put it differently, lower levels may sometimes be *functionally superordinate.*

That's probably what happens when people do the routine "maintenance" activities of life: buying groceries, washing dishes, driving to school. At such times, people may often lose all sight of higher-order goals. Note also that programs inherently require decisions. That in itself may cause them to be attended to more often than other levels. It's interesting that when people describe themselves, they tend to describe things they *do,* rather than what they *are* (McGuire & McGuire, 1986). This suggests that the program level may be especially salient to people.

When low levels are functionally superordinate, it's almost as though the higher layers were disconnected. But the disconnect is rarely permanent. Goals at high levels can be affected by things that happen while lower levels are in charge. The effect can be either good or bad. A program (buying shoes on sale) can help you match a principle (frugality), even if that's not why you're doing it (you just liked the shoes). A program can also create a problem, if it violates the principle. For example, many health-conscious people have a principle of eating lowfat foods. But if they get caught up in the action at a party (with lower levels in charge), they may eat lots of greasy food, which they will later regret.

We said earlier that goals can be achieved in diverse ways. Any specific act can also be done in the service of diverse principles. For example, Richard in Figure 17.4 could have been buying flowers not to be thoughtful but to be manipulative—to get on Linda's good side. The same motions would occur, but they'd be aimed at a very different higher-order goal.

Another point is that people often try to match several values at once—at the *same level.* Sometimes the values are compatible (being frugal while being conscientious). In other cases they're less so (being frugal while dressing well; getting good grades while having a very active social life). In such cases, matching one value creates a problem for the other (Emmons & King, 1988; Emmons, King, & Sheldon, 1993). This defines **goal conflict.**

EVIDENCE OF HIERARCHIES

Is behavior organized hierarchically? Work by Robin Vallacher and Dan Wegner suggests that it is (Vallacher & Wegner, 1985, 1987). They began by asking how people view their actions, a process called **action identification.** Any behavior can be identified in a wide variety of ways. For example, taking class notes can be identified as "sitting in a room and making marks on paper with a pen," "taking notes in a class," "trying to do well in a course," or "getting an education." Some identities are concrete; others more abstract. How you think about your actions presumably says something about the goals you're using in your behavior.

Vallacher and Wegner held that people generally tend to see their actions in as high level a way as they can. Thus, you're more likely to see your student behavior as "attending classes," "getting an education," or "listening to a lecture" than as "walking into a building, sitting down, and listening to someone talk." But if a person starts to struggle in regulating an act at the high level, he or she retreats to a lower-level identity for the action. In terms of the previous section, difficulty at a high level causes a lower level to become functionally superordinate. Using that lower-level identity, the person irons out the problem. As the problem is resolved, the person tends to drift again to a higher-level identification.

For example, if you're in class taking notes and having trouble understanding the lecture, you may stop thinking of your behavior as "taking helpful notes" and start thinking of it as "writing down as much as I possibly can so I can try to figure it out later." If the lecture gets easier to follow after a while, you may be able to start thinking of your behavior in more abstract terms again.

EMOTIONS

How does the self-regulation view treat emotions? Long ago, Herb Simon (1967) argued that emotions are *crucial*. People often have several goals in place at the same time, which they have to pursue sequentially (e.g., you go to a gas station, then stop for lunch, then drive to the beach, where you study for an exam while getting some sun, and then you go home and do some laundry if there's time). The order of doing things is partly a matter of priorities—how important each goal is to you at the time.

Priorities are subject to rearrangement. Simon argued that emotions are an internal call to rearrange. *Anxiety* is a signal that you're not paying enough attention to personal well-being (an important goal) and you need to do so. *Anger* may be a signal that your autonomy (another goal that people value) needs to have a higher priority.

Implicit in this analysis is that progress toward many goals is monitored outside awareness, as you focus on one goal at a time. If a problem arises for some goal, emotion pertaining to it arises. If the problem gets big enough, the emotion becomes intense enough to interrupt what you're doing. For example, look back at the goals described two paragraphs earlier. If you had decided to put off buying gas until after doing the other things, you might start to feel anxious about maybe being stranded at the beach with an empty gas tank. If the anxiety got strong enough, you'd change your mind (reprioritize) and stop for the gas after all.

Simon's theory fits the idea that emotions are produced by a system that monitors "how well things are going" toward attaining goals (Carver & Scheier, 1990, 1998). When progress is going well, you feel good. When it's going *really* well, you feel joy, even ecstasy. When things are going poorly, on the other hand, negative feelings arise: frustration, anxiety, or sadness. If you're actually losing ground, the negative feelings intensify. In all these cases, the emotion is a subjective readout of how well you're doing regarding that goal.

Evidence fitting this comes from several studies. For example, Hsee and Abelson (1991, Experiment 2) put people in hypothetical situations where they'd bet money on sports events. Each viewed a display showing progress toward winning—at different rates—and indicated how satisfied he or she would be with each event. Of special interest are events in which the starting and ending points were identical but the rate of change differed. Participants liked the faster change better than the slower one.

Feelings have implications for action. As suggested by Simon (1967), when something is going badly and negative feelings arise, you engage more effort toward the goal the feeling relates to. If you're behind at something and feeling frustrated, you try harder. If you're scared of something, you try harder to get away from it. How positive feelings affect action is less clear. It's been argued, though, that they also affect priorities (Carver, 2003). When you feel good about some goal, you can "coast" a little on that one and check to see if anything else needs your attention. This would allow the priority of another goal to rise.

EFFECTS OF EXPECTANCIES: EFFORT VERSUS DISENGAGEMENT

Until the last section, the focus of this chapter has been mostly on behavior when no major difficulties arise. However, things don't always work so well. People often encounter obstacles when they try to carry out their intentions and attain their goals. What happens then?

As we just said, obstacles cause negative feelings. If the obstacles are serious, they also tend to disrupt effort—sometimes briefly, sometimes longer. This can occur before you start (if you anticipate trouble) or while you're acting (if snags arise along the way). The interruptions remove you temporarily from the action and lead you to judge how likely you are to reach your goal, given the situation you're in.

Expectancy of success is a concept idea that's come up in other chapters. We discussed it in the motive viewpoint (Chapter 5). We also discussed it in social learning theory (Chapter 13) and in Mischel's cognitive view (Chapter 16). The expectancy concept actually provides a major link between learning models and cognitive self-regulation models.

The way expectancies function in self-regulation models is essentially the same as in the other theories. Confidence of overcoming obstacles leads people back into self-regulatory effort. With enough doubt, however, people are more likely to **disengage,** or reduce their effort toward goal attainment. Perhaps they will even abandon the goal altogether, temporarily or permanently (Klinger, 1975; Kukla, 1972; R. A. Wright, 1996).

Effort is a continuum. It can be useful, though, to think of variations in effort as forming a rough dichotomy (see Figure 17.5). Think of it as the question of whether you keep trying or quit. In many cases, people have only those two options. This view of the impact of expectancies lets the person who's walked into a corner back out of it and take up another goal (Wrosch, Dunne, Scheier, & Schulz, 2006; Wrosch, Scheier, Carver, & Schulz, 2003).

Different people emphasize different facets of expectancies. We've focused on confidence versus doubt of attaining desired outcomes, rather than the *reasons* the confidence or doubt exists (Carver & Scheier, 1998). Bandura, in contrast (described in Chapter 13), stresses self-efficacy expectancy: believing one has the personal capability of doing the action that needs to be done. Whatever variation you prefer, there's evidence that expectancies play an important role in determining how hard people try and how well they do. People who are confident about reaching their goals (or who hold perceptions of high efficacy) are more persistent and perform better than doubtful people. They do better in many ways (see also Box 17.2).

For example, consider a study of women who were learning to protect themselves against sexual assault (Ozer & Bandura, 1990). They learned skills for self-defense and verbal techniques to deal with dangerous situations. At several points, they rated their confidence that they could do both the physical maneuvers and the verbal tactics. They also rated their confidence that they could turn off thoughts about sexual

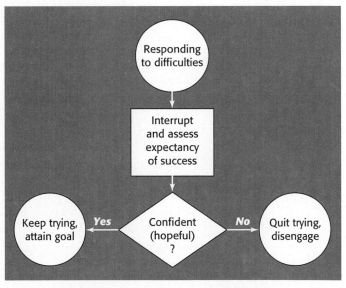

FIGURE 17.5
When people confront difficulties in moving toward their goals, they sometimes interrupt their efforts to assess the likelihood of succeeding. Sufficient confidence leads to renewed efforts; sufficient doubt leads to giving up. All responses seem ultimately to fall into one of these two classes.

Box 17.2   Confidence about Life

Effects of Generalized Optimism

In the main text, we say that expectancies are an important determinant of people's behavior. The expectancies considered there are mostly specific ones: confidence versus doubt about making a desired impression, achieving an academic goal, or carrying out a specific strategy. However, just as people have both specific and general goals, people also have both specific and generalized expectancies. What's been known for centuries as *optimism* is generalized confidence; what's been known as *pessimism* is generalized doubt—not about one specific outcome but about life in general (Scheier & Carver, 1992; Scheier, Carver, & Bridges, 2001). This generalized confidence is very traitlike. It's quite stable over time and seems genetically influenced (Plomin et al., 1992).

Optimism, as a dimension of personality, has been studied for a long while, and a lot is known about it (Scheier et al., 2001). People who are optimistic about life are better liked than pessimists (Carver, Kus, & Scheier, 1994). Probably for that reason, they're better at forming social networks when they go to a new environment (Brissette, Scheier, & Carver, 2002). They are also better in relationships, because they are more supportive of their partners in resolving conflicts (Srivastava, McGonigal, Richards, Butler, & Gross, 2006).

Much of the research on optimism deals with its influences on how people deal with stressful situations (Scheier et al., 2001). Optimists deal better with adversity than pessimists, whether experiencing a missile attack (Zeidner & Hammer, 1992) or confronting cancer (Carver et al., 1993; Stanton & Snider, 1993) or heart disease (Scheier et al., 1989). They have less distress, are more focused on moving forward, and are less likely to withdraw from their usual activities (Carver, Lehman, & Antoni, 2003). They seem more prepared to accept the reality of the stressful experience (Carver et al., 1993). They don't stick their heads in the sand and ignore threats to their well-being. They attend to risks in their lives but only if the risk concerns a serious problem and also pertains to them (Aspinwall & Brunhart, 1996).

Most of what is known about optimism concerns people's actions and their subjective emotional experiences. At least a little research has gone beyond that, however, looking at people's physical responses to adversity. For example, Scheier et al. (1999) found that after major heart surgery, pessimists were more likely than optimists to require rehospitalization. Optimists literally healed better. Other recent studies have related optimism to lower risk of cancer death (Allison, Guichard, Fung, & Gilain, 2003) and cardiovascular death (Giltay, Kamphuis, Kalmijn, Zitman, & Kromhout, 2006). The idea that this personality trait may have pervasive health benefits is now being actively investigated.

---

assault. The key outcome was ratings of the extent to which they took part in (or avoided) activities outside the home.

The results were complex, but a broad theme runs through them. The sense of confidence was very important. The women's confidence that they could use their new coping skills related to perceptions of less vulnerability and ultimately to behavior. In sum, confidence in diverse areas helped the women cope more effectively with their social world.

Partial Disengagement

We've distinguished sharply here between effort and giving up. Sometimes, though, the line blurs. Sometimes a goal can't be attained, but another one can be substituted for it (Freund & Baltes, 2002; Wrosch et al., 2003). For example, a man who enjoys sports becomes wheelchair bound. He can't play football, but he can turn to sports that don't require using his legs.

Sometimes disengagement involves only scaling back from a lofty goal in a given domain to a less demanding one. This is disengagement in the sense that the person is giving up the first goal while adopting the lesser one. It's more limited in the sense that it doesn't entail leaving the domain. This partial disengagement keeps you engaged in the domain you had wanted to quit. By scaling back, giving up in a small way, you keep trying to move ahead, thus *not* giving up in a larger way.

We should stress that whether giving up is bad or good depends on the context (Wrosch et al., 2006; Wrosch et al., 2003). In some cases, disengagement is bad. It's a poor way of coping with the difficulties of life. These are cases where being persistent would pay off in success. In such cases, the goal shouldn't be abandoned so easily.

On the other hand, it's often necessary to give up or defer goals when circumstances make it hard or impossible to reach them. For example, it's senseless to hold onto a lost love who will never return. Giving up sometimes is the right response. But when it *is* the right response, it sometimes doesn't happen. In this case, the failure to disengage leads to continuing distress. We return to this point later on, when we consider problems in behavior.

Further Themes in Self-Regulation

The chapter thus far has presented a relatively straightforward picture in which people form intentions and then shift to a mode of implementing the intentions and which may go well or poorly. We've talked a little about the fact that people have goals at various levels of abstraction and the fact that people have many goals at once (and thus many semi-autonomous feedback loops going at the same time). Here, we bring up three complications to this picture.

APPROACH AND AVOIDANCE

The chapter to this point has been based on the idea that self-regulation involves moving toward goals. An issue that came up in other chapters also comes up here. Specifically, not all actions involve *approach*. Some involve *avoidance*. By this, we don't mean disengaging from a desired (approach) goal. We mean actively trying to get away (or stay away) from a threat. Because no word seems quite parallel to *goal* for the thing you try to avoid, we've sometimes called it an *antigoal* (Carver & Scheier, 1998).

Discussion of the motivation view on personality (Chapter 5) noted that two opposite motives can underlie the same action. As an example, you can try to perform well at a task (action) either to approach success or to avoid failure. Those motives aren't the same (and sometimes the behavior isn't quite the same either). Virtually anything you think about doing can be viewed in terms of either *making* one thing happen or *preventing* something else from happening (E. T. Higgins, 1997). The same issue arises in this chapter.

As it happens, there is a category of feedback processes that enlarges discrepancies, rather than reducing them. That seems to provide a basis for a self-regulatory model of avoidance. It is clear, as well, that emotions are involved both when trying to approach and trying to avoid. In either case, you can be doing well or doing poorly. Thus, the self-regulatory model has a place for both kinds of processes, approach and avoidance. In the interest of minimizing confusion, though, we will not talk much more about the avoidance function here (see Carver & Scheier, 2007).

INTENTION-BASED AND STIMULUS-BASED ACTION

The chapter thus far has also focused mostly on behavior that is intentional: behavior that starts with the setting of goals. However, there is a good deal of evidence that not all behavioral self-regulation happens that way. Some behavior—maybe a lot of it—is cued by stimulus qualities that the person encounters.

Early hints of this phenomenon came from studies intended to show that interpretive schemas were closely linked to specifications for action. These studies used

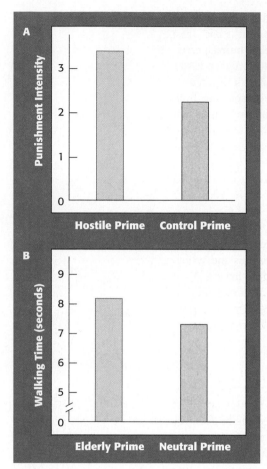

FIGURE 17.6
Effects of priming an interpretive schema on behavior related to that schema. (A) People who had been exposed to hostile content in a sentence-formation task gave punishments of greater intensity in a later task than people exposed to less hostile content. (B) People who had been exposed to elements of the elderly stereotype in a sentence-formation task took longer to walk to the elevator when leaving the experiment than people exposed to neutral words. *Sources: Panel A is based on data from Carver et al., 1983, Study 2; Panel B is based on data from Bargh et al., 1996, Experiment 2.*

priming techniques to activate schemas and found influences on overt behavior. In one case, people had to form sentences from scrambled sets of words (Carver, Ganellen, Froming, & Chambers, 1983). For some people but not others, the word sets had hostile content. Later, all had to punish someone else while teaching a concept. Those who'd read the words with hostile content gave stronger punishment than did the others (see Figure 17.6, A).

Another study used a similar task to prime the stereotype of the elderly (Bargh, Chen, & Burrows, 1996). Some people read many words pertaining to the stereotype; some did not. All then received credit for participation. The question of interest was how long it took them to walk down the corridor on their way out. Those exposed to the stereotype of the elderly walked more slowly, as though they themselves were old (see Figure 17.6, B).

The interpretation of these effects goes like this: To form sentences from the words, you have to understand the words. Understanding the words requires activating nodes of meaning in memory. This activation spreads to nodes bearing on *behavior.* This quality then emerges in the person's own behavior (Bargh, 1997). In fact, the link goes both ways: Acting in a way that fits a stereotype brings that stereotype to mind for use in later perception (Mussweiler, 2006).

Findings such as these are part of a large and growing literature on automaticity (some of which was mentioned in Chapter 16; see also Moors & De Houwer, 2006). Much of this work has been done by John Bargh and his colleagues (Bargh, 1997; Bargh & Chartrand, 1999; Bargh & Ferguson, 2000; Dijksterhuis & Bargh, 2001). Many studies now show clearly that goals can be activated (and people pursue them) with no knowledge that it's happening (for review see Bargh & Williams, 2006). Indeed, some of the studies show that goals can be activated by subliminal stimuli.

Although it's impressive to see how people's minds can be tricked by various sorts of priming, the more important message is that automaticity is important in behavior. Indeed, it's been argued that habitual actions occur in much the same way as the priming effects: Situations activate goals that are associated with them, and behavior follows the goals automatically (Aarts & Dijksterhuis, 2000). Similarly, categories of people activate specific responses that are well learned to that group, and behavior follows automatically (Jonas & Sassenberg, 2006).

Nonetheless, the idea that behavioral qualities can be activated and slide into the ongoing flow of behavior without your awareness is, in some ways, startling. Your actions can be affected by things you hear on the radio or read in the paper, by conversations you have, by random stimuli you encounter—and *you don't even know it.* This idea provides an interpretation of modeling effects (Chapter 13), in which people repeat things they observe others do (Carver et al., 1983). People mimic, without realizing it, the postures and gestures of their partners in interactions (Chartrand & Bargh, 1999). The pervasiveness of such effects leads some people to ask whether behavior is best seen as *directed* or as *self-organizing* (Carver & Scheier, 2002; Vallacher & Nowak, 1997; Vallacher, Read, & Nowak, 2002).

Can both be right? Certainly. In Chapter 16, we described dual-mode models of cognition. One mode is said to use connectionist, associationist processes and the other, symbolic processes. The first mode is characterized as *intuitive,* whereas the second is characterized as *rational.* It seems reasonable to suggest that the dual-process models can also help reconcile how intentions and automaticity both influence action (Bargh & Williams, 2006; Kuhl, 2000; Rothbart, Ellis, Rueda, & Posner, 2003; Strack & Deutsch, 2004).

The interpretation goes like this. The intuitive system functions automatically. When a stimulus happens to cue an action quality, that action quality slips into the behavioral stream. It seems likely that the action quality has to be either simple or well learned for this to happen. That is, the intuitive system is capable of handling fairly complicated events (Kuhl, 2000), but its capacities derive from associations. It's good at being impulsive and quickly responsive, but it's not good at thinking things through.

The rational system, in contrast, is brought into play when you form an intention, or set a goal purposefully. When this system is in charge, behavior is self-regulated in an effortful, top-down manner. It is effortful, planful (Eisenberg et al., 2004). Its purpose is to handle situations that *have* to be thought through, because no automatic cue-driven response is ready to go. Being organized to think things through, however, makes it slower to act (Keller, Wascher, Prinz, Waszak, Koch, & Rosenbaum, 2006).

In talking about the cognitive view in Chapter 16, we noted that people have a natural tendency to conserve mental resources while thinking, because they have many things on their minds at once. The same principle is true here. Being able to do something with little thought is extremely useful, because it lets you think about other things at the same time as you're doing whatever you're doing (Wood, Quinn, & Kashy, 2002).

SELF-REGULATION AS SELF-CONTROL

Another issue that should receive attention is that acts of *self-regulation* sometimes (though not always) entail *self-control.* That is, sometimes people act to restrain behavior aimed at one goal to make it possible to attain another goal. Self-control always represents a case of conflict, because the goals are incompatible.

Situations entailing self-control arise in a great many circumstances, and the conflicts in question apply to very important practical problems (see Part VI in Baumeister & Vohs, 2004). This situation exists, for example, in the context of dieting. The dieter is motivated by hunger to eat and is motivated to restrain eating. The same conflict arises in circumstances surrounding substance abuse and domestic violence. People who are effective at self-control employ a variety of strategies to counteract temptations that keep them from gaining the long-term goal (Trope & Fishbach, 2000, 2005).

Discussions of self-control failure (Baumeister & Heatherton, 1996) tend to portray the situations as involving a relatively automatic tendency to act in one way that is opposed by a planful and effortful tendency to restrain the act. The action that is being inhibited is often characterized as an *impulse,* a desire that would automatically be translated into action unless it is controlled (perhaps in part because this action is habitual, perhaps in part because it is more primal). Once again, this seems to have overtones of the two-mode models. Consistent with this, there is evidence that identifying an action in high-level terms makes it easier to disregard immediate outcomes in favor of delayed outcomes (Fujita, Trope, Liberman, & Levin-Sagi, 2006).

Assessment

The self-regulation view on personality is fairly new. It's been far more theoretical than applied. Nevertheless, it offers a few suggestions concerning personality assessment.

ASSESSMENT OF SELF-REGULATORY QUALITIES

The view described in this chapter emphasizes the existence of several processes in human experience. This emphasis suggests it may be useful to measure individual differences in self-regulatory processes (Williams, Moore, Pettibone, & Thomas, 1992).

For example, *private self-consciousness* (Fenigstein et al., 1975) is a tendency to be self-reflective—to think about your feelings, motives, actions, and so on. (The term *self-conscious* here doesn't mean "embarrassment," just "self-focus.") It may follow that people high in self-consciousness are careful and thorough self-regulators (maybe even obsessive–compulsive ones). They notice it if their actions don't match their intentions, and they adjust accordingly. People with less self-consciousness are more random and less guided in their behavior (see also Box 17.3). Consistent with this, self-consciousness relates to conscientiousness from the five-factor model (Trapnell & Campbell, 1999). There's even evidence that those high in self-consciousness are more prone to engage in self-regulation that's automatic and nonconscious (Hull, Slone, Meteyer, & Matthews, 2002).

BOX 17.3   REDUCTION OF SELF-REGULATION

Deindividuation and Alcohol

Elsewhere in the chapter, we described how self-focused attention causes better self-regulation toward salient standards. If greater self-focus makes behavior *better* regulated, it follows that reduced self-focus causes behavior to be *more poorly* regulated. But what does this mean? It doesn't mean the person stops behaving altogether. It means the behavior is more likely to fluctuate, to become less carefully thought out and more responsive to cues of the moment.

Two bodies of research have studied the effects of reduced self-awareness. Their origins are different, but the effects are strikingly similar. One set of studies concerns deindividuation. The other concerns alcohol.

Deindividuation is an experience people have when they become immersed in a group. In so doing, they can lose their sense of personal identity. They are more likely to use obscenities (Festinger, Pepitone, & Newcomb, 1952), to be aggressive (Prentice-Dunn & Rogers, 1980, 1982), and to engage in childish and uninhibited acts. There's evidence that deindividuation involves loss of self-focus (Diener, 1979; Mullen, 1986; Prentice-Dunn & Rogers, 1982, 1989). It's easy to see the effects as reflecting poor self-regulation regarding programs and principles that normally guide behavior. Thus, there's a tendency to act impulsively, to respond to cues of the moment rather than to use well-thought-out plans. Behavior becomes a string of spontaneous sequences, rather than a pattern guided by higher-order values.

These effects of deindividuation are remarkably similar to some of the effects of alcohol. People who've been drinking are often inappropriately aggressive and overly responsive to cues of the moment. Alcohol is widely regarded as a releaser of inhibitions, and it's sometimes used intentionally for that purpose. As a group, the behavioral effects of alcohol seem to reflect a loss of careful self-regulation. As with deindividuation, the result seems to be a string of sequences of spontaneous acts, rather than carefully planned activity.

Furthermore, the behavioral effects of alcohol and deindividuation seem to have at least one process in common. Alcohol appears to act (at least partly) by reducing self-awareness (Hull, 1981; Hull & Rielly, 1986) and executive function (Giancola, 2004). As this happens, you stop monitoring your values and intentions. Your behavior becomes more disorganized, impulsive, and fragmented. Thus, two distinct sets of phenomena—deindividuation and alcohol intoxication—can be interpreted by a single principle. Both seem to involve interference with a process that underlies the normal self-regulation of behavior.

Note that self-focus by itself is relatively content free. That is, its self-regulatory effect is largely unrelated to the goal being used. Thus, an athlete who's self-conscious should be sure to work out. A self-conscious biology major should be sure she's up to date in her biology reading. A self-conscious musician should focus closely on moving toward the music-related goals he's set for himself.

Trapnell and Campbell (1999) distinguished two aspects of self-consciousness. They think two motives underlie it: curiosity (which is a growth-oriented motive) and the desire to probe negative feeling states (which ultimately is a safety-seeking motive, if the source of the feelings can be isolated). They created a measure called the Rumination–Reflection Questionnaire, to focus separately on these motives. *Rumination* items refer to being unable to put something behind you. *Reflection* items refer to being fascinated and inquisitive. Not surprisingly, reflection relates to openness to experience, and rumination relates to neuroticism.

Another self-regulatory function that might be useful to assess is whether people tend to view their behavior in high-level or lower-level terms. Vallacher and Wegner (1989) developed a measure called the Behavior Identification Form for that purpose. They argued that people with similar traits can differ greatly from each other if they think of their goals at different levels. People who identify their actions at high levels tend to look at the "big picture," whether they're socializing, studying, or making music. People who identify their actions at lower levels tend to focus more on the "nuts and bolts" of what's going on, no matter the domain.

ASSESSMENT OF GOALS

We don't mean to imply that the content of behavior doesn't matter to this viewpoint. As we said earlier, the self-regulation view emphasizes *goals*. It would seem useful, from this view, to assess people's goals and how they're organized (Emmons, 1986; Pervin, 1983). One might even want to assess what sort of "possible selves" the person has in mind (Markus & Nurius, 1986). Knowing what goals are salient to a person might be more informative than knowing other aspects of what the person is "like."

An example of this is the technique Emmons (1986) used to assess personal striving. He asked people to describe their recurring personal goals in four areas: work/school, home/family, social relationships, and leisure/recreation. People were to think about their own intentions and goals and not to compare themselves with other people. Within these guidelines, they were free to write down any striving that seemed important to them. This produced an individualized picture of the goal values that occupied the person's mind over a given span of time.

Problems in Behavior and Behavior Change

Given how new the self-regulation point of view is, one might expect it to have had little or no impact on understanding either problems or therapy. This isn't so, however (see J. C. Hamilton, Greenberg, Pyszczynski, & Cather, 1993; Ingram, 1986; Merluzzi, Rudy, & Glass, 1981). Self-regulation models have made a number of suggestions about those topics (see also Box 17.4).

PROBLEMS AS CONFLICTS AMONG GOALS AND LACK OF STRATEGY SPECIFICATIONS

The hierarchical model suggests several ways for problems to arise (Carver & Scheier, 1990, 1998). The simplest way stems from the idea of a deeply rooted conflict between

Box 17.4 Regulating with the Wrong Feedback

A central theme of this chapter is that people act and then check to see whether they're doing what they intended to do. Just how fundamental is this principle? Research from health psychology suggests that feedback matters so much that people will seek it out and rely on it even when it doesn't tell them anything. They'll rely on it even when they're *told* it doesn't tell them anything. They'll rely on it even though relying on it creates *problems.*

Consider people being treated for hypertension, or high blood pressure (Baumann & Leventhal, 1985; Meyer, Leventhal, & Gutmann, 1985). People with hypertension have no reliable symptoms, yet most quickly come to believe they can isolate symptoms of it. Indeed, the longer they're in treatment, the more likely they are to think so. In one study, more than 90% of those in treatment for more than three months claimed to be able to tell (Meyer et al., 1985).

Can they? By and large, no. In another study (Baumann & Leventhal, 1985), self-reports of elevated blood pressure were well correlated with self-reports of symptoms and self-reported moods. But they were virtually unrelated to actual elevation.

Unfortunately, people with hypertension use their symptoms as a guide to whether their blood pressure's up. They then make important decisions on the basis of those symptoms. In particular, they use the symptom to tell them whether to take their medication. If they think their blood pressure isn't up (because the symptom isn't there), they don't take the medication. If they feel no symptoms, they often drop out of treatment altogether. This can lead to serious medical problems—all because the people are relying on faulty feedback to guide their actions.

This example concerns a physical problem, rather than a psychological one. But the same pattern can also be seen in cases where people misinterpret others' reactions to them or rely on the wrong kinds of cues. If you take someone's frown as a sign of rejection when really he's remembering he forgot to put the cat out, you may behave in ways that create problems for you, rather than help you attain your desired ends.

These examples also illustrate how much people rely on feedback to guide behavior. If the people with hypertension perceive a present state (symptom) that is discrepant from their standard (no symptoms), they act to reduce the discrepancy (take their medication). They're using feedback, just as the self-regulation approach says people do all the time. One view of such phenomena is that people *need* feedback. The natural tendency to use feedback is so strong that people will continue to do so even when the feedback they're using is actually unrelated to what they're trying to control.

---

goals. Conflict occurs when a person is committed to two goals that can't be attained easily at the same time (being a successful attorney while being a good wife and mother; having a close relationship while being emotionally independent). You may alternate between the goals, but this can be exhausting and distressing (Emmons & King, 1988). It requires a lot of effort to keep the conflict from re-emerging. Another solution is to decide that one goal contributes more to your higher-order values than the other and trim back investment in the other one.

A second idea suggested by the hierarchical model is that people sometimes want abstract goals but lack the know-how to reach them. If specifications from level to level are missing, self-regulation falls apart. Thus, many people want to be "fulfilled," "successful," or "well liked"; many even have more specific goals, such as "not arguing with my wife" or "being more assertive," but don't know strategies to attain them. They can't specify the concrete behavior that would move them in the right direction, so they can't make progress and are distressed. For things to be better, the strategies need to be built in (Oyserman et al., 2006).

Problems from an Inability to Disengage

A third source of problems stems from the idea that people who expect failure quit trying. As noted earlier, sometimes this is the right response. (When you realize you've forgotten your money, you quit shopping.) Sometimes, though, it can't be done easily. Some goals are very hard to give up, even if you have grave doubts about reaching them. Examples are doing well in your chosen work and having a fulfilling relationship with another person. Why is it so hard to give them up? The hierarchical view says it's because these goals are high in your hierarchy (thus, central to your self) or represent paths to those higher goals. Sometimes abandoning a concrete goal means giving up on the person you want to be.

When people have serious doubts about attaining important goals, they show a predictable pattern. They stop trying, but soon confront that goal again. For example, having decided to give up on having a fulfilling relationship, you see a movie about relationships, which reminds you that you want one. Having given up trying to get along with a co-worker, you find you're assigned to work on a project together. Having given up on your calculus assignment, you see it's time for calculus class. Deep doubt about reaching an important goal can lead to a repeated cycle of sporadic effort, doubt, distress, disengagement, and reconfronting the goal.

Generally, when people fail at something, they want to ignore it, put it behind them, and move on. After a failure, most people avoid self-focus; after a success, they seek it out. Seeking self-focus here presumably means focusing on the *success*. Avoidance of self-focus presumably means trying to avoid thinking about the *failure*. Pyszczynski and Greenberg (1985, 1987) found, however, that people who are depressed show the *opposite* pattern: They are more likely to self-focus after a *failure* than after a success. What's going on? Apparently, depressed people have trouble giving up goals. Given a failure, they hang onto the goal, even if it wasn't important. They also let success slide by without enjoying it.

It's not always bad to keep thinking about a failure. It can motivate you to try harder next time (if there is a next time). Sometimes it leads to ideas about how to do things differently next time (Martin & Tesser, 1996). But Pyszczynski and Greenberg (1985, 1987) argued that it's dangerous to do this when the failure can't be undone (see also Wrosch et al., 2003). When people lose a big source of self-worth and focus too long on trying to regain it, major distress results. Doing this too often turns it into a habit. Focusing on failure and ignoring success not only maintains depressive symptoms, but it also makes the pattern self-perpetuating.

A similar point was made by Susan Nolen-Hoeksema and her colleagues, who argued that people who are prone to depression focus much of their attention on their sad feelings. This rumination acts to prolong the depressed state (Nolen-Hoeksema, Morrow, & Frederickson, 1993; Nolen-Hoeksema, Parker, & Larson, 1994).

SELF-REGULATION AND THE PROCESS OF THERAPY

Control-process ideas have also been used by several theorists in addressing therapy issues. Fred Kanfer and his colleagues (e.g., Kanfer & Busemeyer, 1982; Kanfer & Hagerman, 1985; Kanfer & Schefft, 1988; see also Semmer & Frese, 1985) have depicted therapy in a way that's quite compatible with the self-regulatory ideas presented throughout this chapter, as well as with the cognitive principles discussed in Chapter 16.

One point these researchers have made is that much of human behavior isn't well monitored consciously but is cued automatically and habitually. This is a point that was made early in this chapter and has been made by many cognitive theorists as well (e.g., Beck, 1972, 1976; Dodge, 1986; Semmer & Frese, 1985). Therapy is partly an effort to break down the automaticity. The person must engage in more controlled or monitored processing of what's going on. Doing this should yield responses that are more carefully thought out.

Does this mean that people dealing with problems must spend the rest of their lives carefully monitoring their actions? Some think so (Kirschenbaum, 1987). To avoid lifelong monitoring, therapy must provide a way to make the desired responses automatic in place of the problem responses. How do you do that? Presumably, it's an issue of how thoroughly coded the links are in memory. New responses become automatic by building them into memory very redundantly. This makes them more likely to be used later, when the person is on "automatic pilot." Techniques that are in widespread use—such as imagery, role-play, and practicing therapeutic changes in real-life situations—probably do exactly this.

Another point made by Kanfer and Busemeyer (1982) is that the process of therapy is itself a dynamic feedback system. It's a series of stages in which clients repeatedly use feedback, both from therapy sessions and from actions outside therapy, to adjust their movement through a long-term plan of change. The goals and issues that guide the process of changing behavior also keep changing. As you proceed, you must keep checking to make sure the concrete goals you're working toward support your higher-order goals.

THERAPY IS TRAINING IN PROBLEM SOLVING

A point that's been made by many people is that therapy is not just for the present. It should make the person a better problem solver, more equipped to deal with problems in the future (Nezu, 1987; Schefft & Lehr, 1985). Being able to generate choices and select the best ones are important skills, whether you get them through therapy or on your own.

A useful way to create choices is called **means–end analysis** (Newell & Simon, 1972). You start by noting the difference between your present state and your desired state (the *end*). Then you think of an action that would reduce the difference (a *means*). At first, the things that come to mind are abstract, involving large-scale goals. You then examine each large step and break it into subgoals. If you keep breaking things down long enough, the means–end path becomes complete and concrete enough to get you from here to there. You've created a strategy.

This line of thought has been used in a program designed to help low-income, African American middle school students develop an academic identity (Oyserman, Terry, & Bybee, 2002). Students in this program had trouble creating possible selves that involved school as a pathway to adulthood. Oyserman et al. developed a small-group intervention to do that. They gave students the experience of developing academic possible selves. Moreover, it tied those possible selves to strategies for achieving desired short-term goals and extended them to adult self-images. The program emphasized the solving of everyday problems, breaking them down by means–end analysis. The result was that the students bonded more strongly to school.

It's good to have goals broken down enough to be concrete and specified. On the other hand, it's also possible to specify things too much. In particular, following too rigid a timetable can cause you to lose motivation. People seem to do best when they have flexibility. By being able to choose when to try to move forward, they can recognize better when certain kinds of efforts are counterproductive. They're also able to be "opportunistic," or take advantage of unexpected opportunities (Hayes-Roth & Hayes-Roth, 1979).

Finally, it's important to seek accurate feedback about the effects of your actions. If you get accurate feedback, you don't have to make perfect choices. If you make continual adjustments from the feedback you get, you keep moving in the right direction. This principle, which is basic to the self-regulation approach, yields an important kind of freedom—the freedom from having to be right the first time.

Self-Regulation Theories: Problems and Prospects

As is true of the cognitive view, there have been mixed reactions to the self-regulation view on personality. It shares loose ends and unanswered questions with the cognitive view, and it has some of its own. It remains unclear whether these are fatal problems or just gaps to be filled.

One criticism of this view derives from the *robotics* metaphor. Critics say that artificial systems can't possibly be good models for human behavior. Humans have free will and make their own decisions. Robots have to rely on the programs they've been given.

One response to this criticism is that it rests on the assumption that people have free will, and not everyone shares that assumption (Bargh & Ferguson, 2000; Wegner, 2002). Further, the behavior of so-called *intelligent* artificial systems moves further every year in the direction of what looks suspiciously like self-determination (Brooks, 2002). It seems clear that how humans and artificial systems resemble and differ from each other will continue to be debated well into the future. But as the behavior of artifacts becomes more and more personlike, the debate will likely focus on increasingly subtle points.

Another response is that the robotics metaphor isn't the only one applicable to this line of thought. Electronic examples are often used to illustrate the principle of feedback control, but the feedback concept wasn't invented by engineers. It was devised to account for functions of the body (Cannon, 1932). The robotics metaphor may not always feel appropriate to living systems, but the feedback principle itself was devised precisely *for* living systems.

Another criticism sometimes made of this approach (even within the physiological metaphor) is that a model based on feedback principles is merely a model of **homeostasis** (literally, "steady state"). Homeostatic mechanisms exist to control body temperature, the levels of various elements in the blood, and many other physical parameters of the body. But how much sense does it make to think this way about something we know is always *changing*? Human behavior isn't about steady states. Doesn't the self-regulation view imply that people should be immobile and stable, or just do the same thing over and over?

Actually, no. People do regulate some things in a recurrently homeostatic way—for example, the amount of affiliation they engage in across time (O'Connor & Rosenblood, 1996)—but not always. As we noted earlier, many goals are dynamic (e.g., going on a vacation trip, having an interesting conversation with someone). Being dynamic doesn't make them any less goal-like. It just means that the whole process of matching the behavior to the goal must be dynamic as well. If the goal is to create a flow of experiences, rather than a state, then the qualities of behavior being monitored will also have this changing quality. So there's no contradiction between the fact that humans keep changing what they're doing and the idea that behavior occurs within a system of feedback control.

Greater difficulty is posed by another criticism aimed at the hierarchical model—that it fails to deal effectively with the homunculus problem. *Homunculus,* a term once used to explain how people act, refers to a hypothetical tiny man who sits inside your head and tells you what to do. That explains *your* behavior. But who tells the *little man* what to do? If people are just fancy robots, what tells the person what to do? Where do the highest goals come from, the ones that specify all the lower goals?

One response is that cognitive models typically assume an executive system that coordinates other activities, makes decisions, and so on. The executive is manifest in subjective experience as consciousness. The executive presumably has control over many other systems and thus in some ways is the analogue of the homunculus. This reasoning is plausible, but it isn't altogether satisfying.

Another response is that people have built-in goals of survival, personal coherence, and so on. These goals are vague enough that they rarely appear in consciousness, but they're pervasive enough that they constantly influence in subtle ways people's decisions about what goals to take up. Thus, behavior is being guided by values that are built into the organism but that aren't always apparent to the person. This line of reasoning is plausible too, but it's also less than fully satisfying. The homunculus problem thus remains a real one.

Another criticism of the self-regulation view (as well as the cognitive view of Chapter 16) is similar to a criticism made of the learning perspective: All this seems too much a description from the outside looking in. There's too little feel of what it means to *have* a personality. This view describes the "self-regulation of behavior," but what does it really say about personality? This approach emphasizes structure and process, rather than content. For this reason, some see the ideas as dealing with an empty shell, programmed in ways that aren't well specified, for purposes and goals that are largely arbitrary (e.g., Deci & Ryan, 2000).

There is some merit to this criticism. We note, however, that these ideas weren't devised to focus directly on *personality.* Rather, they were intended to focus on issues that stand at a slight tangent from personality. Although the ideas don't form a full theory of personality, they provide a window on the nature of human experience that seems to have some implications for personality. Will these ideas evolve into a more complete picture of personality? It's too early to know.

Despite these criticisms, the self-regulation view on personality has proven to have merit. It's had heuristic value, suggesting new places to look for information about how things work. Indeed, it makes some predictions that aren't intuitively suggested by other views. This value alone makes it likely that it will be around for a while. Only the test of time and further study will tell whether this approach will continue to emerge as a viable perspective on personality.

· SUMMARY ·

In self-regulation models, behavior is sometimes specified by interpretive schemas, if an interpretation is closely tied to an action quality. Sometimes actions follow from intentions. *Intentions* are products of a mental algebra in which personally desired outcomes and social considerations are weighed to yield an intent to act or not act.

Theory concerning self-regulation emphasizes *goals.* The goals underlying behavior have a variety of labels, including *life tasks, personal strivings, personal projects,* and *current concerns.* This view treats the structure of the self as an organization among goals. Some goals are fairly neutral, but others imply a standard of excellence. In the latter case, setting higher goals results in higher performances. This is because committing oneself to a more demanding goal focuses one's efforts more fully. If the goal is too high, though, people don't adopt it.

Some intentions concern attaining end goals; others are about implementing action plans to reach those end goals. The latter are important for ensuring that behavior actually gets done. Implementation intentions constitute linking of strategies to the contexts in which the person wants to engage them. Intentions are formed in a deliberative mindset, but once the person starts to pursue them, the person is in an implementational mindset.

Once a goal for behavior has been evoked, *self-regulation* reflects a process of feedback control. A reference value (or goal) is compared against present behavior. If the two differ, behavior is adjusted, leading to a new perception and comparison. Given that many goals are dynamic and evolving, this view emphasizes that self-regulation is a never-ending process. A single feedback loop is too simple to account for the diversity in people's actions alone, but complexity is provided by the fact that feedback systems can be organized in a hierarchy, in which one system acts by providing reference values to the system directly below it. The concept of hierarchy accounts for the fact that a goal can be attained by many kinds of actions, and also the fact that the same action can occur in service to diverse goals.

Emotions have been viewed within this framework as calls for reprioritizing one's goals. Emotions are also viewed as giving a subjective reading of how well you're progressing toward a goal. Emotions thus convey important information that has a strong influence on behavior.

When a person encounters obstacles in his or her efforts, self-regulation is interrupted and the person considers whether success or failure is likely. If the expectancies are positive enough, the person will keep trying; if not, the person may disengage from the effort and give up. Disengagement is sometimes the adaptive response, but people sometimes give up too quickly. Sometimes disengagement is only partial—goal substitution or scaling back. This keeps the person engaged, in one way, while disengaging in another.

Although much of this chapter concerns conformity to goals, self-regulation models also include discussions of avoidance. *Avoidance* means creating distance instead of conformity. Another issue is that some behavior occurs via intentions but some actions are triggered fairly automatically, even without the person's awareness. This difference between sources of influence is sometimes dealt with by dual-process models resembling those discussed in Chapter 16. An *intuitive* system promotes behaviors that are triggered by cues of the moment; a *rational* system promotes behaviors that are thought out and intentional. Self-regulation sometimes entails self-control: the prevention of behavior with one goal in service to another more important goal.

Assessment, from this view, is partly a matter of assessing individual differences in self-regulatory functions, such as self-reflectiveness or the level of abstraction at which people view their goals. This view also suggests the value of assessing goals themselves. There are several ways to conceptualize problems from this view. One possibility focuses on conflict between incompatible goals; another points to a lack of specification of midlevel behavioral reference values to guide behavior. Another emphasizes that people sometimes are unable to disengage from behaviors that are necessary for the attainment of higher-order goals. There's evidence that people who are depressed display an exaggerated inability to disengage.

Just as behavior can be construed in terms of self-regulatory systems, so can the process of behavior change induced by therapy. People in therapy use feedback from decisions they've put into practice to make further decisions. They monitor the effects of changes in behavior to determine whether the changes have produced the desired effects. One long-term goal of therapy is to make people better problem solvers through techniques such as *means–end analysis,* so that they can make their own adjustments when confronting new problems.

· GLOSSARY ·

Action identification   The way one thinks of or labels whatever action he or she is performing.

Attitude   A personal evaluation of the desirability of an action.

Comparator   A mechanism that compares two values to each other.

Deliberative mindset   A careful mindset that is used while deciding whether to take an action.

Disengage   To cease and put aside self-regulation with regard to some goal.

Feedback hierarchy   An organization of feedback loops, in which superordinate loops act by providing reference values to subordinate loops.

Feedback loop   A self-regulating system that maintains conformity to some comparison value.

Goal conflict   An attempt to self-regulate toward two incompatible goals at the same time.

Goal intention   The intention to attain some particular outcome.

Homeostasis   Regulation around a constant steady state.

Implemental mindset   A positively biased mindset used while implementing an intention to act.

Implementation intention   The intention to take specific actions in specific contexts.

Means–end analysis   The process of creating a plan to attain an overall goal (end) by breaking it into successively more concrete goals (means).

Principle   A broad, abstract action quality that could be displayed in any of several programs.

Program   A guideline for the actions that take place in some category of events (as a script).

Subjective norm   A person's impression of how other people value an action.

Subliminal stimuli   Stimuli presented too quickly to be consciously recognized.

System concept   A very abstract guide for behavior, such as an ideal sense of self.

Personality in Perspective

Overlap and Integration

Six blind men from Indostan heard of a creature called an *elephant*. They went to determine its nature. One of them bumped into the elephant's side and concluded that elephants resemble walls. A second encountered a tusk and decided elephants are like spears. The third, grasping the wriggling trunk, decided that elephants are similar to snakes. Wrapping his arms around one of its legs, the fourth concluded that elephants resemble trees. The fifth felt a floppy ear and surmised that an elephant is a type of fan. Coming upon its tail, the sixth decided that elephants are like ropes.

Each of these men was sure his investigation had led him to the truth. And, indeed, each man was partly right. But each was partly wrong, as well.

—Hindu fable

IN THE preceding chapters, you encountered a series of viewpoints on the nature of personality. Each was rooted in its own assumptions about how best to view human nature. Each had its own way of thinking about how people function. Each had its own view of the sources of individual differences, as well as their meaning and importance. Each approach also had its drawbacks, places where things were left unexplained or even unexamined.

In writing about these perspectives on personality, we tried to give you a sense of what each was like from inside that perspective. In so doing, we tended to emphasize what makes each approach special, distinct from other approaches. The views do differ in important ways, and some points of conflict seem hard to resolve. For example, how can you reconcile the belief that people have free will (from the phenomenological perspective) with the belief that behavior is determined by patterns of prior outcomes (from the learning perspective) or the belief that behavior is determined by internal forces (from the psychoanalytic perspective)?

Our emphasis on the uniqueness of each theory may have led you to see the theories as being quite different from one another. The diversity may even have led you to wonder whether the theorists were describing the same *creature* (as would be true for anyone listening to the blind men describe the elephant). The diversity of ideas in earlier chapters raises questions: Do the various perspectives have anything in common? Is one perspective right, or better than the others? If so, which one? In this chapter, we consider these questions.

Do the theories you've read about have anything in common? Yes. The first part of this chapter describes several commonalities we think are interesting. You certainly noticed some of them already, but others are more subtle and harder to spot. We also consider a couple of key issues that many different theories address, albeit from different angles.

The question of which view is *best* or *right* is harder to answer. One answer is that even big differences among theories may not mean that one is right and the others are wrong. It often happens that some issue, or some element of personality, seems very important from the view of one theory but is less important or even irrelevant from the view of another theory. As with the blind men, one theory grapples closely with an issue, but another theory doesn't even touch on it. To borrow Kelly's phrase, each theory has a *focus of convenience* that differs from that of any other theory.

Perhaps, then, various perspectives on personality are facets of a bigger picture. From this point of view, the perspectives would complement, rather than contradict, each other. Each may have some truth, but none by itself has the whole truth. The idea that the perspectives are facets of a broader picture is developed more fully in the last part of the chapter.

Similarities among Perspectives

Let's first consider some specific similarities among the views described earlier in the book. We won't point to every similarity. Rather, we will simply give you a sense of some of the connections that can be made.

We begin with commonalities between psychoanalysis and other views. Psychoanalysis is a natural starting point. It's been around for a very long time. Some people regard it as the only really comprehensive theory of personality ever devised. For both of these reasons, it's a natural comparison point for every other approach.

On the other hand, psychoanalysis is also a particularly *unusual* theory. This suggests it may be hard to find similarities between it and other approaches. As we noted earlier in the book, even neoanalytic theories, which *derive* from psychoanalysis, don't seem to share a lot with it. Nonetheless, there are several similarities worth noting. In fact, parallels have been suggested between psychoanalysis and at least three other perspectives: the biological, learning, and cognitive self-regulation perspectives.

PSYCHOANALYSIS AND BIOLOGY: EVOLUTIONARY PSYCHOLOGY AND THE STRUCTURAL MODEL

How does psychoanalysis relate to the biological approach? Freud was strongly influenced by Darwin's view of evolution, a fact that's often overlooked. Psychoanalytic theory is about beings that are deeply concerned with biological necessities: survival and reproduction. Attaining these goals is critical, because that's what biological life is all about. It should be no surprise, then, that the core of personality focuses on them. On the other hand, because humans live in a dangerous world, it's necessary to deal with complexities imposed by reality. Because we live in groups, it's eventually important to deal with another issue as well: the fact that people other than us also have needs.

This is the general line of thought that lies behind an attempt by Leak and Christopher (1982) to interpret some of Freud's ideas from the framework of evolutionary psychology. They noted that the evolutionary view sees behavior as self-serving (with one exception, to which we turn momentarily). This self-serving quality in the biological view resembles the selfish nature of Freud's concept of the id. The id is primitive and single minded about its desires. It represents the self-interested animal that our genes make us as those genes try to continue their existence.

The id isn't rational; nor are the genes. Freud tied rationality to the ego, a mechanism to mediate between id and reality. Leak and Christopher (1982) suggested that the genes also need some help in dealing with some of the complexities of reality. They argued that the cortex of the brain evolved to serve this purpose. Evolution of the cortex in the species would parallel evolution of the ego in the person. Both structures—cortex and ego—permit greater planfulness and care in decision making. Both are adaptations that foster survival.

What about the superego? This is the trickiest part of Leak and Christopher's (1982) argument. To view the superego in evolutionary terms requires one more idea. Specifically, survival isn't only an individual matter. Humans evolved as highly social beings, living and surviving in groups. Because we're so interdependent, we sometimes do better in the long run by letting group needs override personal needs in the short run. As noted in Chapter 6, it's been argued that people in groups evolved mechanisms for inducing, even forcing, reciprocal altruism (Trivers, 1971). A genetic mechanism to do this would enhance the adaptive success of the group.

In psychological terms, evolving such a mechanism looks like developing a capacity to have a superego. Thus, having a superego confers an evolutionary advantage. People who adopt the values of their social group and conform to those values will be accepted as members of the group. They will be more likely to get the benefits that follow from group membership (for example, having other members take care of you if you're sick). These benefits have survival value.

In sum, Leak and Christopher (1982) suggested that the ego (conscious rationality) is a behavioral management system, for which the id and the superego provide motivation. There are two types of motivation—selfish and group related—with adaptive value. The id adapts to the physical environment, where competition for resources is intense and selfish. The superego is the tendencies that evolved in response to pressures from group living.

PSYCHOANALYSIS AND EVOLUTIONARY PSYCHOLOGY: FIXATIONS AND MATING PATTERNS

We see one more similarity between psychoanalytic and evolutionary views, one that's quite different from the points made by Leak and Christopher. Think back to the Oedipal conflict and the fixations that can emerge from it. Fixation in the phallic stage for a male is said to cause an exaggerated attempt to show that he hasn't been castrated. He does this by having sex with as many women as possible and by seeking power and status. Female fixation in this stage involves a seductiveness that doesn't necessarily lead to sex.

These effects look remarkably similar to the mating strategies that evolutionary psychologists argue are part of our species. Recall from Chapter 6 the idea that men and women have different reproductive strategies due to differing investment in offspring (Trivers, 1972). The male mating tactic is to create the appearance of power and status and to mate as frequently as possible. The female tactic is to appear highly desirable but to hold out for the best mate available. These tactics have strong echoes in the fixations just described. We can't help but wonder whether Freud noticed a phenomenon that's biologically based, and ascribed psychodynamic properties to it in order to fit it better into his theory.

PSYCHOANALYSIS AND CONDITIONING

Now consider psychoanalysis and the learning perspective. We noted a relationship in Chapter 12, in passing, while discussing Miller and Dollard's (1941) effort to describe personality in terms of conditioning. In doing that, they were trying to translate psychoanalytic concepts into the ideas of learning. Thus, there's a built-in link between aspects of Freud's theory and Miller and Dollard's theory.

Of particular relevance is Miller and Dollard's (1941) analysis of repression. This concept is important in psychoanalysis and it therefore was something of a focus for Miller and Dollard. They saw *repression* as a conditioned tendency not to think about things that are distressing. By not thinking about them, you avoid the pain. Escaping the pain reinforces the tendency not to think. It thereby builds this tendency in more completely. In this way, Miller and Dollard accounted for a phenomenon that's central to the psychodynamic view, using very different language.

Though it may not be obvious, development of the not-thinking tendency also is a special case of extinction. That is, learning *not to think* means that the tendency *to think* is getting weaker. If you're learning not to think about a distressing topic, whatever stimulus formerly cued the thought no longer does so. Thus, the conditioned response (thinking) is extinguishing. It's only one more step to suggest that there may be a connection between *all* instances of extinction and repression, or *anticathexis.*

Freud said an anticathexis uses energy to keep an impulse or thought out of consciousness. If the restraining force isn't strong enough, the response leaks out. Recall that in Chapter 12, we described a phenomenon called *spontaneous recovery after extinction.* This recovery means that the behavioral tendency is still there. This in turn suggests that, at some level, extinction may involve creating an active restraint. Because a restraint presumably requires energy, it may be the same as an anticathexis.

Thinking about *anticathexes* in conditioning terms leads us to consider *cathexes* as well. We noted in Chapter 8 that psychoanalytic theory distinguishes between id cathexes and ego cathexes. An *id cathexis* is binding energy in an activity or object that satisfies a need. An *ego cathexis* doesn't satisfy a need directly. Rather, it binds energy in an object or activity that's *associated* with the satisfying of a need.

There's a similarity between these ideas and conditioning concepts. *Primary reinforcers* in operant conditioning are things that directly satisfy a need (e.g., food or water). Obtaining a primary reinforcer might be equivalent to having an id cathexis. *Secondary reinforcers* are stimuli *associated* with primary reinforcers or which provide a way to *get* primary reinforcers. Getting (or anticipating) a secondary reinforcer seems similar to forming an ego cathexis.

A final similarity between conditioning and psychoanalytic views concerns the role of the unconscious in determining behavior. To behaviorists, behavior stems from prior conditioning. Conditioning occurs outside consciousness. In effect, this says that behavior results from unconscious influences. In this particular learning view, people do things for reasons they may not be aware of. This is consistent with one of Freud's beliefs. Obviously, Freud had different dynamics in mind. Nonetheless, it's a potentially important link between the views.

PSYCHOANALYSIS AND SELF-REGULATION: HIERARCHY AND THE STRUCTURAL MODEL

The psychoanalytic approach to personality also has certain similarities to the cognitive self-regulation approach. One similarity derives from the notion of a self-regulatory hierarchy. The behavioral qualities involved range from very limited movements through organized sequences to abstract higher-level qualities. As pointed out in Chapter 17, attention can be diverted from the higher levels. When this happens, behavior is more spontaneous and responsive to cues of the moment. It's as though low-level action sequences, once triggered, run off by themselves. In contrast to this impulsive style of behavior, actions being regulated according to higher-order values (programs or principles) have a more carefully managed character.

Aspects of this description hint at similarities to Freud's three-part view of personality. Consider the spontaneity and responsiveness to situational cues in the self-regulation model when high-level control isn't being exerted. This resembles certain aspects of id functioning. An obvious difference is Freud's assumption that id impulses are primarily sexual or aggressive. The self-regulation model, in contrast, makes no such assumption. It's worth noting, though, that alcohol intoxication and deindividuation, which seem to reduce control at high levels (Chapter 17), often lead to sexual and/or destructive activity.

The link between id processes and low-level control is a bit tenuous. In contrast, there's quite a strong resemblance between program control in the self-regulation approach and ego functioning in the psychoanalytic approach. Program control involves planning, decision making, and behavior that's pragmatic, as opposed to either impulsive or principled. These qualities also characterize the ego's functioning.

Levels higher than program control resemble, in some ways, the functioning of the superego. Principle control, in some cases at least, induces people to conform to moral principles. Control at the highest level involves an effort to conform to your idealized sense of self. These efforts resemble, in some respects, the attempt to fit your behavior to the principles of the ego ideal and to avoid a guilty conscience for violating these principles.

The fit between models at this high level isn't perfect, partly because not all principles are moralistic. Yet here's a question: Why did Freud focus on morality and ignore other kinds of ideals? Was it perhaps because morality was so prominent an issue in his society at that time? Maybe the superego is really the capacity to follow rules *in general,* rather than just moral rules. If this were so—if the superego actually pushed behavior toward *other* principles as well as moral ones—the similarity between models would be even greater.

PSYCHOANALYSIS AND COGNITIVE PROCESSES

Several links exist between psychoanalytic themes and ideas from cognitive psychology (e.g., Westen, 1998). Matthew Erdelyi (1985) has even suggested that Freud's theory was largely a theory of cognition. Indeed, he said that Freud was straining toward an analogy between mind and computer but never got there because the computer didn't exist yet.

Erdelyi (1985) argued that cognitive psychologists essentially reinvented many psychodynamic concepts. For example, Freud assumed a process that keeps threats out of awareness. This is similar in some ways to the filtering process by which the mind preattentively selects information to process more fully. Freud's concept of ego becomes executive control processes. The strength of a cathexis is the amount of

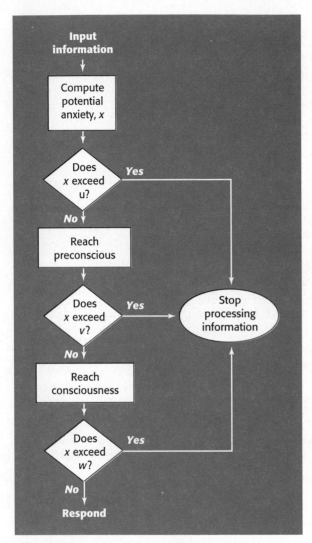

FIGURE 18.1

An information-processing picture of repression and denial. Input information (top)—whether perceptual or from a suppressed memory—is judged preattentively for its anxiety-inducing value. Then come a series of implicit decisions. First, does the anxiety the information would create (x) exceed a criterion of *unbearability* (u)? If so, processing stops; if not, the material goes to a memory area corresponding to the preconscious. Next, does the predicted anxiety exceed a *serious discomfort* criterion (v)? If so, processing ceases and the information stays in memory; if not, the information moves to consciousness. The final decision is whether to acknowledge openly the information that's now conscious, depending on whether the anxiety from doing so will exceed a final criterion (w). This sequence provides for information never to be stored in memory, to be stored but not reach consciousness, to reach consciousness but be suppressed, or to be acknowledged openly. *Source: Adapted from Erdelyi, 1985.*

attention devoted to something. The topography of the mind becomes a matter of levels of processing, and distortions become biases in processing.

As an example of Erdelyi's (1985) approach, consider repression and denial (see also Paulhus & Suedfeld, 1988). When ideas, desires, or perceptions arise that are threatening, repression and denial prevent them from reaching consciousness. This reaction can occur before a threatening stimulus is even experienced, a phenomenon termed **perceptual defense,** or it can involve forgetting an event after it's been experienced. Erdelyi argued that these reflect a sequence of information-processing decisions (see Figure 18.1).

Information is partially analyzed preattentively. This may yield an implicit estimate of how much anxiety would arise if the information reached awareness. If the estimate exceeds a threshold, processing stops and the information never goes further. If the estimate is lower than the threshold, the information goes to a memory area corresponding to the preconscious. Similar decisions are made at other stages, with lower and lower criteria for moving to the next level of processing. This model treats repression, response suppression, and self-deception more generally as reflecting checks at several stages of information processing.

As implied by this description, today's cognitive view assumes that much of the mind is unconscious. Indeed, the study of unconscious processes is a very active area of work (Bargh, 1997; Hassin, Uleman, & Bargh, 2005). Today's cognitive view tends to equate *consciousness* with *attention.* Events that are unconscious are those that get little or no attention.

There are several reasons an event might get little attention. It may be tagged preattentively as having too much potential for anxiety. Or it might occur in a part of the nervous system that attentional processes can't reach. Many cognitive scientists think of the nervous system as a set of special-purpose components, only some of which can be examined consciously (Gardner, 1985). Thus, the basic "wiring" of the system renders some aspects of experience inaccessible.

Sometimes events are unconscious because some behaviors are highly preprogrammed and automatic. Acts that are automatic require little or no monitoring. Highly automated sequences can be triggered by stimuli that are noted by the nervous system at some level but never reach consciousness (Bargh, 1997; Norman, 1981). Even elaborate actions drop mostly out of awareness as they become routine (which all experienced drivers discover at one time or other, as they arrive at home with no memory of how they got there).

These descriptions obviously differ in important ways from Freud's treatment of the unconscious. Only Erdelyi's (1985) example involving preattentive estimates of anxiety implies the sort of process that Freud assumed. All these ideas, however, suggest ways in which information can fail to reach consciousness.

Another body of work has linked cognitive processes to the psychoanalytic concept of *transference*. Transference occurs when a person in therapy displaces emotional reactions onto the therapist. Presumably, these reactions were initially stimulated by significant others in the person's earlier life. Recent studies provide a cognitive explanation for such a turn of events (Andersen, Glassman, Chen, & Cole, 1995; Glassman & Andersen, 1999).

Specifically, the schemas people have of significant others seem chronically to be partially active (thus accessible). As with other instances of partial activation, this makes it easier for the schema to emerge and be used in perceiving and interpreting other stimuli. As a result, you may view many people through the lens of that schema and not even realize it. If someone does something that reminds you vaguely of your mother's way of inducing guilt, you may use your *mother* schema and perceive that person as like your mother.

Indeed, when such schemas pop up, self-aspects relating to those significant others emerge as well (Hinkley & Andersen, 1996). Thus, if someone tends to induce guilt as your mother did, you may react just as you did to your mother (e.g., by becoming irrationally angry), even if the reaction isn't appropriate to the present situation. All this can happen in therapy, or anywhere.

Highly programmed acts, such as walking, can occur with little awareness. This suggests a possible point of contact between cognitive self-regulation ideas and psychodynamic theory.

SOCIAL LEARNING AND COGNITIVE SELF-REGULATION VIEWS

As newer theories were created over the years, personality psychologists were often influenced by ideas that were being used in other areas of psychology. Indeed, this cross-fertilization has been very common. Among the sources of ideas for personality psychologists during the past several decades were learning psychology and cognitive psychology. To a considerable extent, people who sampled from these sources sampled from both, rather than just one.

One result of this pattern is a set of similarities between the social–cognitive learning approach (Chapter 13) and the cognitive self-regulation approaches (Chapters 16 and 17). One of these similarities is also shared with Kelly's personal construct theory (Chapter 15). These approaches have diverse histories, but their central concepts resemble one another more than just a little. Indeed, as you may have noticed, the work of several people pertains not just to one of these views but to two or more of them.

One area of overlap concerns the importance these approaches ascribe to cognitive processes in creating representations of the world and the self. Differences among theories on this issue stem largely from the fact that each has different *reasons* for emphasizing cognition. In discussing cognition from the social learning approach, Mischel (1973) said that if we want to understand learning, we have to look at people's mental representations of stimuli, not the stimuli themselves. People learn from what *they* think is there, not what an outsider sees. The way the stimuli are mentally represented and transformed determines how people will respond to them (see also Bandura, 1977a, 1986).

From the learning perspective, these statements emphasize that human learning is more complicated than it seems. An event doesn't lead automatically to conditioning that's the same for everyone. From the learning perspective, such statements are qualifications on theories of learning. They say to other learning theorists that the *person* has to be considered in analyzing learning. That's the point of such statements—*when they're made from the learning perspective.*

When embedded in Kelly's theory of personal constructs or today's cognitive view on personality, however, ideas about the role of cognition take on a broader life. From these views, cognitive processes are central to understanding *everything* about personality. When Mischel (1973) takes the cognitive view on personality, he focuses not on the subtleties of learning but on how people organize their understanding. Note the difference of emphasis. In the cognitive view, the idea that people *organize* their experience is a key principle regarding the essence of personality. Learning per se is more peripheral, and it may even be disregarded altogether. Cognitive processes are also critical to the self-regulation view on personality, although once again there's a slight difference of emphasis. The focus in the self-regulation approach is mostly on the role cognitions play in *creating behavior.*

Another similarity between the social learning and cognitive self-regulation views concerns expectancies. (Indeed, expectancies also appear in the need-and-motive approach, and they're implicit in ego psychology.) All these approaches see expectancies as determinants of how hard people try to do things. Many people—Rotter (1954, 1966), Bandura (1977a, 1986), Kanfer (1977), Kirsch (1985, 1990), Mischel (1973, 1979), Carver and Scheier (1981, 1990, 1998), and others—have argued that people hold expectancies about the effects their actions are likely to have and whether they can do things they want to do. These expectations can influence how hard a person tries and what the person learns from an event.

The social learning and cognitive self-regulation approaches also resemble each other in the structure they assume underlies behavior. (Kelly's theory becomes less relevant here, because Kelly didn't say much about behaving, as opposed to construing.) The social learning view says people have *incentives,* which draw them forward into action. Incentives function the same as *goals,* a concept that plays a key role in the self-regulation perspective. Indeed, other perspectives also have constructs that serve a comparable role (see Table 18.1).

There is, however, one important difference of emphasis here between the learning and self-regulation views. It concerns the concept of *reinforcement.* The social learning view uses this concept explicitly. The concept is basic to the principle of instrumental learning. As we noted in Chapter 13, however, one social learning theorist—Bandura—has consistently used the concept differently than did earlier theorists. To Bandura, reinforcers create mental representations of future incentives.

Table 18.1 Comparable Behavioral Concepts Taken from Four Perspectives on Personality.

Concept	Theoretical Perspective
Incentive	Social learning
Goal, reference value	Self-regulation
Motive	Need and motive
Ego cathexis	Psychoanalytic

They cause people to learn expectancies about what actions are useful in what situations. But reinforcers don't directly increase the tendency to do the acts that preceded them. The way Bandura used this concept raises questions about whether its meaning is compatible with that assumed by other learning theorists.

Keep in mind, though, that Bandura stands with one foot in the learning perspective and one in the cognitive self-regulation perspective. His view on reinforcement may reflect Bandura the self-regulation theorist more than Bandura the learning theorist. As we noted in Chapter 17, self-regulation theorists are divided on reinforcement as a concept. Some say that people self-reinforce after success. Others see the concept of self-reinforcement as less useful.

This may be a point where theorists' personal histories influenced how their theories were constructed. Most self-regulation theorists who assume a role for self-reinforcement began their work in the learning perspective. Only gradually did they identify with the emerging cognitive self-regulation view. Perhaps they retained a role for self-reinforcement from a psychological inertia, because it represented a comfortable tie to the past. It's also of interest that those theorists are more likely to talk about *self-reinforcement* than *external reinforcement* (e.g., Kanfer, 1977). It's the person's own goal representations that matter, after all. Only *you* can decide whether your goal's been met. Thus, self-reinforcement, rather than external reinforcement, is at the heart of these discussions.

To others, introducing self-reinforcement as a concept simply raises questions. Certainly, people often feel pride after success and sadness after failure. But do these reactions create the learning? Or are they just emotional reactions to informational events, with the latter being what really matters? This is an issue that's not been settled in the self-regulation perspective (or, to some extent, even in the learning perspective; see Timberlake, 1993; Viken & McFall, 1994).

NEOANALYTIC AND COGNITIVE SELF-REGULATION PERSPECTIVES

The learning and cognitive self-regulation perspectives arose in academic psychology, with an emphasis on controlled research. Early neoanalytic psychology, in contrast, derived mostly from the clinical experiences of the theorists. Despite this difference, there's a surprising convergence among these views (cf. Westen, 1991).

Consider, for example, a series of conceptual similarities between self-regulation ideas and Adler's ideas. Recall that Adler saw people as motivated by feelings of inferiority, which make them strive for superiority. He referred to the continual struggle for greater competence as a great upward drive. As we said in Chapter 10, he believed that feelings of inferiority cause healthy people to work throughout life toward greater integration and perfection.

Adler also believed that people establish long-term goals for their lives. He called this the principle of *fictional finalism*. This term conveys the sense that people are motivated by views of their final outcomes and that those views are invented, or fictional. Future goals are always fictional in the sense that they aren't yet real. People act, however, as though they're headed toward these end points and use them as guides for their efforts. To Adler, these future-oriented goals (which he also called *guiding self-ideals*) are more important determinants of behavior than are events in the person's past.

These ideas resemble ideas from the cognitive self-regulation perspective in two ways. First, Adler's thinking placed considerable emphasis on goals, which are also a cornerstone of the self-regulation view of personality. Indeed, Adler's fictional life plans seem quite similar to the possible selves discussed by Markus and her colleagues.

The other similarity relates to the structure of people's strivings. Adler's account resembles the self-regulation approach in one way here, while differing from it in another. The similarity is Adler's belief that changes in behavior are prompted by discrepancies between where you are and where you want to be. When a person notices an *inferiority* (as Adler called it), he or she tries to overcome it. The structure of this process is very similar to that of the feedback loop described in Chapter 17. The difference is that Adler emphasized the role of subjective feelings of inferiority. The self-regulation model doesn't assume such feelings. It simply assumes that when goals have been set, the person tries to meet them.

MASLOW'S HIERARCHY AND HIERARCHIES OF SELF-REGULATION

There are also similarities between elements of the phenomenological perspective and the cognitive self-regulation perspective. We noted earlier a strong thematic resemblance between Kelly's theory of personal constructs and today's cognitive theories. But this isn't the only similarity. Consider Maslow's hierarchy of motives (Chapter 14). There are at least two similarities between that hierarchy and the self-regulation hierarchy.

First, Maslow conceived of the motive qualities at the top of the hierarchy as more abstract and subtle, but also as more integrative, than those at lower levels. The levels of the hierarchy of control also have this character. Second, Maslow saw the lower motives as more demanding than the higher ones, in the sense that a deficit or a problem lower in the hierarchy draws the person's attention to it and forces him or her to deal with it. Similarly, in at least one version of the control hierarchy, if a problem develops at a low level, attention is brought to that level in an attempt to resolve the problem.

There are, however, differences between these views as well. The biggest difference concerns the *content* of the hierarchies. Maslow's analysis was explicitly an analysis of *motives* intended to incorporate both biological needs and psychological motives. The control hierarchy, in contrast, focuses on the structure of *action* with goals that relate to qualities of behavior. This difference means that the two hierarchies are very different at their low levels. Maslow's hierarchy points to survival needs; the other hierarchy points to muscle movements.

At higher levels, though, the two hierarchies are more similar. The highest level of control in the self-regulation view seems roughly equivalent to the concept of self-actualization used by Maslow and Rogers. There's still one difference, however. Woven through the writings of Maslow and Rogers on this topic is the sense that self-actualization is something that happens *to* you, if you can free yourself from the demands of motives at lower levels and just let yourself sense what your body is saying is right for you. It shouldn't involve an effort. If you're *trying* to self-actualize, you probably *aren't* self-actualizing.

The nature of self-regulation in the control hierarchy is ambiguous in that regard. It's by no means clear that such high-level self-regulation is free of effort. On the other hand, the nature of the goal at the highest level—an ideal self that relates to the many principles in force at the next lower level—is quite diffuse. It's so diffuse, in fact, that it isn't too hard to imagine that self-regulation toward it might also feel diffuse. Thus, the subjective experience of self-regulation at the highest level might *not* feel effortful in the same way as does self-regulation at lower levels.

SELF-ACTUALIZATION AND SELF-REGULATION

Two other similarities between the self-actualization view and the self-regulation view of personality go beyond Maslow's hierarchy. One similarity is that both viewpoints use concepts corresponding to idealized and experienced qualities of self. The labels *real self* and *ideal self* are explicit in the phenomenological view of Rogers. The sense of an idealized self is also one value at the top of the control hierarchy, as is the experienced actual self that's compared with it.

The comparison process itself is also similar between the approaches. Rogers emphasized that people compare their current selves with their ideal selves and that they experience anxiety when there's incongruity between them. The comparison between a sensed condition and a standard, or reference point, is also intimately involved in the self-regulation perspective, not only with respect to an ideal self but at all levels of the hierarchy.

DISPOSITIONS AND THEIR EQUIVALENTS IN OTHER MODELS

Another resemblance among theories brings us full circle to an idea with which we began this book. We started with the concept of *dispositions,* and we now return to it. As we noted in Chapter 1, a major theme of personality psychology is how people differ from one another, not just temporarily but in an enduring way. This theme is the basis for the dispositional perspective on personality. Dispositions take a variety of forms: traits, enduring motive qualities, and (in a biological extension of this view) inherited temperaments.

The essence of dispositions, if not the concept itself, is also prominent in at least two more views on personality. The psychoanalytic view assumes that people derive stable personality qualities from childhood psychosexual crises. The neoanalytic view holds that early experiences influence personality in other ways. Erikson assumed that childhood psychosocial crises shape adult personality, and object relations and attachment theories make similar assumptions.

These theories differ regarding the source of dispositions. Yet the theories share two assumptions: that something is stamped or etched into the individual early in life and that this characteristic continues to influence the person from then on. The disposition has been viewed as a biological temperament, a transformation of sexual drives, a reflection of a psychosocial crisis, a learned motive quality, and simply a trait. Yet all these theories treat the disposition as having an enduring impact on the person's life experiences. This similarity among approaches, which is often overlooked, is not a trivial one.

Indeed, the disposition concept also has a place in other views. For example, one version of the learning approach assumes that people differ in locus of control, which helps determine how and what people learn. One aspect of the self-regulation approach assumes that people vary in the disposition to be self-reflective and thus carefully self-regulated. In both of these cases (and others as well), it's assumed that individual differences are stable dispositions that influence a broad range of the person's experiences.

Recurrent Themes, Viewed from Different Angles

Our emphasis in the preceding section was on the notion that certain ideas in one theoretical perspective resemble ideas from another perspective. We also want to note another kind of similarity across perspectives: a similarity in the issues the theories consider. We said earlier in this chapter that different theories often address different issues. That's true. But at least a couple of issues recur across a surprisingly wide range of perspectives.

IMPULSE AND RESTRAINT

One of these issues concerns what seems to be a basic distinction between *impulse* and *restraint*. This issue has been part of personality psychology for a long time, but it has become even more prominent in recent years. The issue is often introduced in the context of delay of gratification, where a choice must be made between a small reward now and a larger reward later. We've discussed the phenomenon of delay of gratification from several viewpoints: psychoanalysis (where we said the ego restrains the id's impulses), ego psychology (where we described variations in ego control and ego resiliency), social learning theory (where we considered effects of models), and the cognitive view (where the focus was on mental images that can foster restraint).

But the issue of impulse versus restraint is far broader than that. In some ways, it's fundamental to personality. As a result, its broader manifestations emerge in many views of personality:

- It's there in trait psychology, in which a trait of conscientiousness is assumed to be defined partly by self-discipline and deliberation (McCrae & Costa, 1987). Indeed, another trait theory treats constraint as a basic dimension of personality (Tellegen, 1985).
- It comes up in temperament theories, where some argue that constraint is in fact a basic temperament (Clark & Watson, 1999) and others argue for a similar temperament that's been called *effortful control* (Rothbart et al., 2003).
- It's found in biological process models, where an argument is made that approach and avoidance systems are joined by a system that concerns restraint versus impulsiveness (Carver & Miller, 2006; Depue & Spoont, 1986; Eysenck & Eysenck, 1976; Zuckerman, 2005).
- It's a core issue in psychoanalysis concerning the balance between the id's desires in many domains and the ego's restraint over how and when those desires are met.
- It emerges in neoanalytic theories, where ego control (ranging from overcontrol to undercontrol) is a key dimension of personality (J. H. Block & J. Block, 1980).
- It's there in cognitive theories, in the form of a contrast between rational and experiential systems (Epstein, 1994) and in a contrast between "hot," incentive-related cognition and "cool," restrained cognition (Metcalfe & Mischel, 1999).
- It also appears in self-regulation theories, in the distinction between deliberative and implemental mindsets (Heckhausen & Gollwitzer, 1987).

Impulse versus restraint has emerged in the past decade as a key issue in several areas of personality psychology (Carver, 2005). Indeed, this issue is one influence that's led a number of people to think about cognitive processing as occurring in two modes (as described in Chapter 16). In these theories, the management of behavior is seen as subject to two layers of influence, which may use two different parts of the brain. One system provides an automatic, intuitive, superficial, and fast way of interacting with the world. It's believed to have evolved earlier. The other system provides a rational, deliberative, but slower way of interacting with the world. It's believed to be of more recent origin.

The question of how and why a person chooses to act quickly versus hold back from acting is basic. It's no wonder that many theories say something about this question. This issue undoubtedly will remain a focus of interest for many people in the years ahead.

INDIVIDUAL VERSUS GROUP NEEDS

Another fundamental issue concerns the competing pressure of individualistic self-interest versus the needs arising from being involved in groups (or couples). In many specific cases, this issue is tangled up with the issue of action versus restraint. This is because the needs of other people are often what urges restraint on one's own impulses. Conceptually, however, it's a separate issue.

Earlier in this chapter, we noted that psychoanalytic theory and evolutionary psychology both confront the contrast between these pressures. In psychoanalysis, the ego deals with the immediate demands of both social and physical reality and the superego deals with other, more complex, aspects of social needs. In evolutionary psychology, people have individualistic needs—survival, competition for mates. But they also have group-based needs—cooperation with one's mate and with the larger society.

This distinction between individualistic and social goals also appears in other approaches. In trait psychology, it emerges in two places. One is the trait of *agreeableness,* which concerns maintaining positive relations with others. People high on this dimension are attuned to mutual well-being; those lower on the dimension are unconcerned with others' interests. The distinction also emerges in the trait of *extraversion.* Extraverts want to have social impact. Introverts are less concerned with group involvement and follow more individualistic paths.

In the motive approach, this issue shows up in the motives to achieve and exert power versus to affiliate and attain intimacy. The issue is also in the biological process approach in unsocialized sensation seeking, with its disregard of others' needs. It's in the social version of the neoanalytic approach, in the issue of separation–individuation versus merger. And it's in the self-actualization approach in the balance between the self-actualizing tendency and the need for positive regard from other people.

In all these cases, people confront the need to balance the two competing pressures. Both pressures are important but in different ways. Given all this attention from theorists of so many different perspectives, this issue appears to be critically important in human experience.

Combining Perspectives

As should now be apparent, similarities do exist between seemingly unrelated approaches to personality. These similarities may, in time, allow integration of the approaches. It's probably safe to say, though, that most personality psychologists view that as a distant goal. One reason is the sheer size and complexity of the job.

Theorists do sometimes try to integrate across boundaries. For example, Cattell (1985) tried to merge psychoanalytic elements of the id, ego, and superego with physiological qualities of temperament and cognitive variables such as expectancy, all in a factor-analytic framework. It's hard, however, to fit all the pieces together in a way that people can use easily.

Theorists such as Eysenck and Zuckerman have tried to integrate across two or three perspectives. In describing Eysenck's work in earlier chapters, we treated it as two sets of ideas with separate focuses of convenience. Some of them are biological, dealing with brain function (and to some extent the heritability of differences). Others form a hierarchical model of relations among acts, habits, traits, and supertraits. Though we presented the ideas as separate, Eysenck viewed them as an integrated model with multiple facets. Zuckerman (1991, 1994, 2005) has made a similar kind of statement, binding together—in a single model—trait, inheritance, and biological-process views.

ECLECTICISM

Another option, exercised by many psychologists, is to take an *eclectic approach* to personality. This involves drawing useful ideas from many theories, rather than being tied to just one or two. Essentially, it means saying that different ideas are useful for different purposes and that there may be no approach that's best for all purposes. To understand a phenomenon, you may need to look at it from the angle of a theory that focuses on it, rather than a theory that doesn't. As Scarr (1985, p. 511) put it, "There is no need to choose a single lens for psychology when we can enjoy a kaleidoscope of perspectives."

This sort of approach suggests that views of personality from the various perspectives may be mutually supportive. It may not be necessary to integrate them into a single set of constructs or principles. As we said earlier, the focus of convenience of one theory differs from that of any other theory. By taking bits of theory across several focuses of convenience, perhaps we can obtain a more well-rounded picture of what personality really is.

Thus, many personality psychologists today accept the idea that personality was shaped by evolutionary pressures. Most assume there are inherited temperaments and that the processes by which personality is reflected are biological. Several ideas from psychoanalytic theory are also widely accepted—for example, that determinants of behavior are sometimes outside awareness and that mechanisms exist within the mind that protect us from things we don't want to deal with. Many personality psychologists accept the idea that early experiences have a big impact on what people are like. (Indeed, there's even evidence from the learning lab that associations conditioned first to a stimulus are more permanent than associations conditioned later; Bouton, [1994].) Obviously, learning has an impact on personality. People do seem to organize records of the experiences of their lives in idiosyncratic ways. We may well have an inner voice of self-actualization. Behavior may even reflect the operation of feedback loops.

All of these ideas may be true or only some of them. All of them may be useful or only some of them. Many psychologists pick and choose bits from various perspectives and use them where they seem reasonable. The choice among the available elements is an individual one.

AN EXAMPLE: BIOLOGY AND LEARNING AS COMPLEMENTARY INFLUENCES ON PERSONALITY

Perhaps the simplest illustration of an eclectic approach is that psychologists almost universally acknowledge the importance to personality of both biology and learning. Everyone does this: people who focus on biology, people who focus on learning, and people who focus on some other part of personality. Early learning theorists claimed the mind is a "blank slate," on which any kind of personality can be sketched. It's clear, though, that this isn't true. There are biological constraints on learning.

A key point is that some associations are learned more easily than others. A term used to describe this is **preparedness.** This term implies that organisms are prepared to condition certain links more easily than others (Öhman & Mineka, 2001; Seligman & Hager, 1972). Preparedness isn't all or nothing. It's a dimension of ease versus difficulty in learning connections. Presumably, this is biologically influenced.

For example, if you get sick to your stomach, you could, in theory, develop a conditioned aversive response toward any number of stimuli. If conditioning depended only on association between stimuli, you should condition aversions to *all* neutral stimuli that are present. However, in reality, you're more likely to develop an aversion to a *flavor* experienced just before getting sick than to other stimuli (Garcia & Koelling, 1966). Apparently the links are just easier to create in the nervous system for some pairs of events than others.

Both biological and learning principles are needed to understand fully the phenomenon of preparedness—such as the biological readiness that chimps and people show in learning to use tools.

Preparedness also seems to be involved in instrumental learning. That is, some kinds of actions are easier for animals to learn than others, even if the same reward follows both. Rats learn more quickly to avoid a foot shock by jumping than by pressing a bar (Wickelgren, 1977). Pigeons quickly learn to peck a spot to obtain food, but it's hard to get them to learn to *refrain* from pecking to get food.

Just as it's clear the mind is not a blank slate, it's also clear that the expression of most biological tendencies depends on experience. Earlier in the book, we talked about *diathesis-stress models,* in which a particular kind of stress produces a problem only if the person also has a particular vulnerability (which might be biological, though it doesn't have to be). Such models are widely accepted. One reason for this acceptance is that twin studies of disorders show two things at once: that serious disorders such as schizophrenia are genetically influenced and that genes aren't everything. That is, if you are the monozygotic twin of someone with schizophrenia, your chances of being schizophrenic are elevated but still less than 100%. If genes were all that mattered, the figure would be 100%.

Thus, an eclectic acceptance of both biology and learning as important influences on personality seems well founded. Perhaps other combinations will prove in the future to be similarly well founded.

Which Theory Is Best?

As we said just earlier, one answer to the question of which theory is best is that *no* theory is perfect, and you may benefit from using bits and pieces of many theories. We should point out, though, that this question is sometimes answered another way. This answer returns us to a point we made in the book's opening chapter. We think it provides a fitting way to end, as well.

Over a century ago, William James wrote that a theory must account reasonably well for the phenomena that people experience as real, but to be successful, a theory must do more than that. James wrote (1890, p. 312) that people will believe those theories which "are most interesting, those which appeal most urgently to our aesthetic, emotional, and active needs." Put more simply, the theory that's best is the one you *like* best. The one that's best—for you—is the one that appeals to you most, the one you find most interesting and engaging. Edward Tolman (1959, p. 152) also put it pretty simply: "I have liked to think about psychology in ways that have proved congenial to me. . . . In the end, the only sure criterion is to have fun. And I have had fun."

· SUMMARY ·

Although various perspectives on personality differ from one another in important ways, they also resemble one another in important ways. The psychoanalytic perspective is similar to at least three alternative views. First, ideas about biological evolution in the species parallel Freud's ideas about the evolution of personality in the individual. That is, in each case, a primitive force (the genes, the id) needs another force to help it deal with reality (the cortex, the ego), and eventually it also needs a force to keep it in contact with the social world (inherited sensitivity to social influence, the superego). Second, one branch of the conditioning view was devised to create a link between psychoanalytic concepts and the language of learning. Third, the psychoanalytic view and the cognitive self-regulation view resemble each other in two ways. The notion of a hierarchy of control echoes psychoanalytic theory's three components of personality. Work on cognition has also developed concepts that resemble, in some ways, those postulated years earlier by Freud.

A substantial overlap exists between the social learning and the cognitive self-regulation viewpoints. They share an emphasis on mental representations of the world (as does Kelly's theory of personal constructs), although the theories have somewhat different rationales for the emphasis. They also have similar views of the importance of people's expectancies and similar views on the basic structure of behavior.

A similarity also exists between self-regulation ideas and Adler's neoanalytic theory. Both assume that behavior is aimed at reducing discrepancies, and both emphasize the importance of people's long-term goals. The notion of a hierarchy in self-regulation also suggests a similarity between that view and the phenomenological view, especially Maslow's. Although the lower levels of Maslow's motive hierarchy deal with motives that are ignored in the control hierarchy, at their upper levels, the models resemble each other more closely. The principle of self-actualization also resembles the self-regulation model in the concepts of ideal and actual self and the desire for congruity between them.

Another similarity among approaches concerns the concept of disposition. Obviously, this construct is central to the dispositional perspective. It's also important in the psychoanalytic and neoanalytic views. In all these cases (and by implication in others as well), the assumption is made that people have qualities that endure over time and circumstances and that influence their behaviors, thoughts, and feelings.

Although the various theories differ in their focus, certain issues do seem to recur across many of them. This represents another kind of similarity among the theories. One issue that many different theories address is the polarity between impulse versus restraint. Indeed, this issue has become increasingly prominent in recent years. Another is the competing pressures of individual self-interest and communal interest.

Thus, there are areas of overlap among theories. Yet the theories also differ. Which theory, then, is right? One answer is that *all* the perspectives seem to have something of value to offer. Many psychologists prefer an *eclectic position,* taking elements and ideas from several views, rather than just one. At a minimum, people who operate within the framework of a given theory must take into account the limitations imposed by other views. For example, temperament theorists believe much of personality is determined by genetics, but they also assume that temperaments are modified by learning. Learning theorists believe that personality is a product of a learning history, but it's clear that some kinds of learning are easier than others. Perhaps the future will see greater emphasis on this eclecticism, the sharing of ideas from one perspective to another.

· GLOSSARY ·

Perceptual defense   Responding to screen out a threatening stimulus before it enters awareness.

Preparedness   The idea that some conditioning is easy because the animal is biologically prepared for it to happen.

Aarts, H., & Dijksterhuis, A. (2000). Habits as knowledge structures: Automaticity in goal-directed behavior. *Journal of Personality and Social Psychology, 78,* 53–63.

Aarts, H., & Dijksterhuis, A. (2003). The silence of the library: Environment, situational norm, and social behavior. *Journal of Personality and Social Psychology, 84,* 18–28.

Abramson, L. Y., Alloy, L. B., & Metalsky, G. I. (1995). Hopelessness depression. In G. M. Buchanan & M. E. P. Seligman (Eds.), *Explanatory style* (pp. 113–134). Hillsdale, NJ: Erlbaum.

Abramson, L. Y., Metalsky, G. I., & Alloy, L. B. (1989). Hopelessness depression: A theory-based subtype of depression. *Psychological Review, 96,* 358–372.

Abramson, L. Y., Seligman, M. E. P., & Teasdale, J. D. (1978). Learned helplessness in humans: Critique and reformulation. *Journal of Abnormal Psychology, 87,* 49–74.

Adams, G. D., & Fastnow, C. (2000, November 10). *A note on the voting irregularities in Palm Beach, Florida.* Retrieved from http://madison.hss.cmu.edu

Adams, G. R., & Shea, J. A. (1979). The relationship between identity status, locus of control, and ego development. *Journal of Youth and Adolescence, 8,* 81–89.

Adams-Webber, J. R. (1979). *Personal construct theory: Concepts and applications.* New York: Wiley.

Adler, A. (1917). *Study of organ inferiority and its psychical compensation.* New York: Nervous and Mental Diseases Publishing.

Adler, A. (1927). *Practice and theory of individual psychology.* New York: Harcourt, Brace, & World.

Adler, A. (1929). *The science of living.* New York: Greenberg.

Adler, A. (1930). Individual psychology. In C. Murchison (Ed.), *Psychologies of 1930.* Worcester, MA: Clark University Press.

Adler, A. (1931). *What life should mean to you.* Boston: Little, Brown.

Adler, A. (1956). *The individual psychology of Alfred Adler: A systematic presentation of selections from his writings.* H. L. Ansbacher & R. R. Ansbacher (Eds.). New York: Basic Books.

Adler, A. (1958). *What life should mean to you.* New York: Capricorn Books. (Originally published, 1931)

Adler, A. (1964). *Social interest: A challenge to mankind.* New York: Capricorn Books. (Originally published, 1933)

Agostinelli, G., Sherman, S. J., Presson, C. C., & Chassin, L. (1992). Self-protection and self-enhancement biases in estimates of population prevalence. *Personality and Social Psychology Bulletin, 18,* 631–642.

Ahadi, S., & Diener, E. (1989). Multiple determinants and effect size. *Journal of Personality and Social Psychology, 56,* 398–406.

Ainsworth, M. D. S. (1983). Patterns of infant–mother attachment as related to maternal care. In D. Magnusson & V. Allen (Eds.), *Human development: An interactional perspective.* New York: Academic.

Ainsworth, M. D. S., Blehar, M. C., Waters, E., & Wall, T. (1978). *Patterns of attachment.* Hillsdale, NJ: Erlbaum.

Ajzen, I. (1985). From intentions to actions: A theory of planned behavior. In J. Kuhl & J. Beckmann (Eds.), *Action control: From cognition to behavior.* New York: Springer-Verlag.

Ajzen, I. (1988). *Attitudes, personality, and behavior.* Chicago: Dorsey.

Ajzen, I., & Fishbein, M. (1980). *Understanding attitudes and predicting social behavior.* Englewood Cliffs, NJ: Prentice-Hall.

Alexander, R. (1979). *Darwinism and human affairs.* Seattle: University of Washington Press.

Alicke, M. D. (1985). Global self-evaluation as determined by the desirability and controllability of trait adjectives. *Journal of Personality and Social Psychology, 49,* 1621–1630.

Allen, J. J., Iacono, W. G., Depue, R. A., & Arbisi, P. (1993). Regional electroencephalographic asymmetries in bipolar seasonal affective disorder before and after exposure to bright light. *Biological Psychiatry, 33,* 642–646.

Allen, L. S., & Gorski, R. A. (1992). Sexual orientation and the size of the anterior commissure in the human brain. *Proceedings of the National Academy of Sciences of the U.S.A., 89,* 7199–7202.

Allison, P. J., Guichard, C., Fung, K., & Gilain, L. (2003). Dispositional optimism predicts survival status 1 year after diagnosis in head and neck cancer patients. *Journal of Clinical Oncology, 21*(3), 543–548.

Alloy, L. B., & Abramson, L. Y. (1988). Depressive realism: Four theoretical perspectives. In L. B. Alloy (Ed.), *Cognitive processes in depression* (pp. 223–265). New York: Guilford.

Allport, G. W. (1937). *Personality: A psychological interpretation.* New York: Holt.

Allport, G. W. (1961). *Pattern and growth in personality.* New York: Holt, Rinehart, & Winston.

Almagor, M., Tellegen, A., & Waller, N. G. (1995). The Big Seven model: A cross-cultural replication and further exploration of the basic dimensions of natural language trait descriptors. *Journal of Personality and Social Psychology, 69,* 300–307.

Amabile, T. M. (1985). Motivation and creativity: Effects of motivational orientation on creative writers. *Journal of Personality and Social Psychology, 48,* 393–399.

Amsel, A. (1967). Partial reinforcement effects on vigor and persistence: Advances in frustration theory derived from a variety of within-subject experiments. In K. W. Spence & J. T. Spence (Eds.), *The psychology of learning and motivation* (Vol. 1). New York: Academic.

Anastasi, A. (1988). *Psychological testing* (6th ed.). New York: Macmillan.

Andersen, S. M., & Chen, S. (2002). The relational self: An interpersonal social-cognitive theory. *Psychological Review, 109,* 619–645.

Andersen, S. M., Glassman, N. S., Chen, S., & Cole, S. W. (1995). Transference in social perception: The role of chronic accessibility in significant-other representations. *Journal of Personality and Social Psychology, 69,* 41–57.

Anderson, C., John, O. P., Keltner, D., & Kring, A. M. (2001). Who attains social status? Effects of personality and physical attractiveness in social groups. *Journal of Personality and Social Psychology, 81,* 116–132.

Anderson, C. A., Berkowitz, L., Donnerstein, E., Huesmann, L. R., Johnson, J. D., Linz, D., Malamuth, N. M., & Wartella, E. (2003). The influence of media violence on youth. *Psychological Science in the Public Interest, 4,* 81–110.

Anderson, J. A. (1995). *An introduction to neural networks.* Cambridge, MA: MIT Press.

Anderson, J. R. (1976). *Language, memory and thought.* Hillsdale, NJ: Erlbaum.

Anderson, J. R. (1985). *Cognitive psychology and its implications* (2nd ed.). New York: Freeman.

Anderson, J. R. (1991). The adaptive nature of human categorization. *Psychological Review, 98,* 409–429.

Anderson, J. W. (1988). Henry Murray's early career: A psychobiographical exploration. *Journal of Personality, 56,* 138–171.

Anderson, R. C., & Pichert, J. W. (1978). Recall of previously unrecallable information following a shift in perspective. *Journal of Verbal Learning and Verbal Behavior, 17,* 1–12.

Andrykowski, M. A., Brady, M. J., & Hunt, J. W. (1993). Positive psychosocial adjustment in potential bone marrow transplant recipients: Cancer as a psychosocial transition. *Psycho-oncology, 2,* 261–276.

Andrzejewski, M. E., Spencer, R. C., & Kelley, A. E. (2006). Dissociating ventral and dorsal subicular dopamine D_1 receptor involvement in instrumental learning, spontaneous motor behavior, and motivation. *Behavioral Neuroscience, 120,* 542–553.

Archer, J. (2006). Testosterone and human aggression: An evaluation of the challenge hypothesis. *Neuroscience and Biobehavioral Reviews, 30,* 319–345.

Archer, J., & Coyne, S. M. (2005). An integrated review of indirect, relational, and social aggression. *Personality and Social Psychology Review, 9,* 212–230.

Ardrey, R. (1966). *The territorial imperative.* New York: Dell.

Arkin, R. M., & Baumgardner, A. H. (1985). Self-handicapping. In J. H. Harvey & G. Weary (Eds.), *Attribution: Basic issues and applications.* New York: Academic.

Arndt, J., Schimel, J., Greenberg, J., & Pyszczynski, T. (2002). The intrinsic self and defensiveness: Evidence that activating the intrinsic self reduces self-handicapping and conformity. *Personality and Social Psychology Bulletin, 28,* 671–685.

Arnett, P. A., Smith, S. S., & Newman, J. P. (1997). Approach and avoidance motivation in psychopathic criminal offenders during passive avoidance. *Journal of Personality and Social Psychology, 72,* 1413–1428.

Asendorpf, J. B., Banse, R., & Mücke, D. (2002). Double dissociation between implicit and explicit personality self-concept: The case of shy behavior. *Journal of Personality and Social Psychology, 83,* 380–393.

Asendorpf, J. B., & van Aken, M. A. G. (1999). Resilient, overcontrolled, and undercontrolled personality prototypes in childhood: Replicability, predictive power, and the trait-type issue. *Journal of Personality and Social Psychology, 77,* 815–832.

Asendorpf, J. B., & Wilpers, S. (1998). Personality effects on social relationships. *Journal of Personality and Social Psychology, 74,* 1531–1544.

Aserinsky, E., & Kleitman, N. (1953). Regularly occurring periods of eye motility, and concomitant phenomena during sleep. *Science, 118,* 273.

Ashton, M. C., Lee, K., & Goldberg, L. R. (2004). A hierarchical analysis of 1,710 English personality-descriptive adjectives. *Journal of Personality and Social Psychology, 87,* 707–721.

Ashton, M. C., Lee, K., Perugini, M., Szarota, P., de Vries, R. E., Di Blas, L., Boies, K., & De Raad, B. (2004). A six-factor structure of personality-descriptive adjectives: Solutions from psycholexical studies in seven languages. *Journal of Personality and Social Psychology, 86,* 356–366.

Ashton, M. C., Lee, K., & Son, C. (2000). Honesty as the sixth factor of personality: Correlations with Machiavellianism, primary psychopathy, and social adroitness. *European Journal of Personality, 14,* 359–368.

Aspinwall, L. G., & Brunhart, S. N. (1996). Distinguishing optimism from denial: Optimistic beliefs predict attention to health threats. *Personality and Social Psychology Bulletin, 22,* 993–1003.

Assor, A., Roth, G., & Deci, E. L. (2004). The emotional costs of parents' conditional regard: A self-determination theory analysis. *Journal of Personality, 72,* 47–88.

Atkinson, J. W. (1957). Motivational determinants of risk-taking behavior. *Psychological Review, 64,* 359–372.

Atkinson, J. W., & Birch, D. (1970). *The dynamics of action.* New York: Wiley.

Atkinson, J. W., Heyns, R. W., & Veroff, J. (1954). The effect of experimental arousal of the affiliation motive on thematic apperception. *Journal of Abnormal and Social Psychology, 49,* 405–410.

Atkinson, J. W., & McClelland, D. C. (1948). The projective expression of needs II. The effect of different intensities of the hunger drive on thematic apperception. *Journal of Experimental Psychology, 38,* 643–658.

Atkinson, J. W., & Raynor, J. O. (Eds.). (1974). *Motivation and achievement.* Washington, DC: V. H. Winston.

Austin, J. T., & Vancouver, J. B. (1996). Goal constructs in psychology: Structure, process, and content. *Psychological Bulletin, 120,* 338–375.

Avery, R. R., & Ryan, R. M. (1988). Object relations and ego development: Comparison and correlates in middle childhood. *Journal of Personality, 56,* 547–569.

Avia, M. D., & Kanfer, F. H. (1980). Coping with aversive stimulation: The effects of training in a self-management context. *Cognitive Therapy and Research, 4,* 73–81.

Avila, C. (2001). Distinguishing BIS-mediated and BAS-mediated disinhibition mechanisms: A comparison of disinhibition models of Gray (1981, 1987) and of Patterson and Newman (1993). *Journal of Personality and Social Psychology, 80,* 311–324.

Axelrod, R., & Hamilton, W. D. (1981). The evolution of cooperation. *Science, 211,* 1390–1396.

Axline, V. M. (1947). *Play therapy.* Boston: Houghton Mifflin.

Axline, V. M. (1964). *Dibs: In search of self.* Boston: Houghton Mifflin.

Ayduk, O., Mischel, W., & Downey, G. (2002). Attentional mechanisms linking rejection to hostile reactivity: The role of "hot" versus "cool" focus. *Psychological Science, 13,* 443–448.

Babad, E. Y. (1973). Effects of informational input on the "social deprivation-satisfaction effect." *Journal of Personality and Social Psychology, 27,* 1–5.

Badner, J. A., & Gershon, E. S. (2002). Meta-analysis of whole-genome linkage scans of bipolar disorder and schizophrenia. *Molecular Psychiatry, 7,* 405–411.

Bailey, J. E., Argyropoulos, S. V., Lightman, S. L., & Nutt, D. J. (2003). Does the brain noradrenaline network mediate the effects of the CO_2 challenge? *Journal of Psychopharmacology, 17,* 252–259.

Bailey, J. M., Dunne, M. P., & Martin, N. G. (2000). Genetic and environmental influences on sexual orientation and its correlates in an Australian twin sample. *Journal of Personality and Social Psychology, 78,* 524–536.

Bailey, J. M., Gaulin, S., Agyei, Y., & Gladue, B. A. (1994). Effects of gender and sexual orientation on evolutionarily relevant aspects of human mating psychology. *Journal of Personality and Social Psychology, 66,* 1081–1093.

Bailey, J. M., & Pillard, R. C. (1991). A genetic study of male sexual orientation. *Archives of General Psychiatry, 48,* 1089–1096.

Bailey, J. M., Pillard, R. C., Neale, M. C., & Agyei, Y. (1993). Heritable factors influence sexual orientation in women. *Archives of General Psychiatry, 50,* 217–223.

Bain, A. (1859). *The emotions and the will.* London, England: Longman.

Baldwin, M. W., Keelan, J. P. R., Fehr, B., Enns, V., & Koh-Rangarajoo, E. (1996). Social-cognitive conceptualization of attachment working models: Availability and accessibility effects. *Journal of Personality and Social Psychology, 71,* 94–109.

Balmary, M. (1979). *Psychoanalyzing psychoanalysis: Freud and the hidden fault of his father.* Baltimore, MD: Johns Hopkins University Press.

Baltes, P. B., & Staudinger, U. M. (1993). The search for a psychology of wisdom. *Current Directions in Psychological Science, 2,* 75–80.

Bandura, A. (1965). Influence of models' reinforcement contingencies on the acquisition of imitative response. *Journal of Personality and Social Psychology, 1,* 589–595.

Bandura, A. (1969). *Principles of behavior modification.* New York: Holt, Rinehart, & Winston.

Bandura, A. (1971). Vicarious and self-reinforcement processes. In R. Glaser (Ed.), *The nature of reinforcement.* New York: Academic.

Bandura, A. (1973). *Aggression: A social learning analysis.* Englewood Cliffs, NJ: Prentice-Hall.

Bandura, A. (1976). Self-reinforcement: Theoretical and methodological considerations. *Behaviorism, 4,* 135–155.

Bandura, A. (1977a). Self-efficacy: Toward a unifying theory of behavioral change. *Psychological Review, 84,* 191–215.

Bandura, A. (1977b). *Social learning theory.* Englewood Cliffs, NJ: Prentice-Hall.

Bandura, A. (1978). The self system in reciprocal determinism. *American Psychologist, 33,* 344–358.

Bandura, A. (1982a). The psychology of chance encounters and life paths. *American Psychologist, 37,* 747–755.

Bandura, A. (1982b). Self-efficacy mechanism in human agency. *American Psychologist, 37,* 122–147.

Bandura, A. (1986). *Social foundations of thought and action: A social cognitive theory.* Englewood Cliffs, NJ: Prentice-Hall.

Bandura, A. (1997). *Self-efficacy: The exercise of control.* New York: Freeman.

Bandura, A., Adams, N. E., & Beyer, J. (1977). Cognitive processes mediating behavioral change. *Journal of Personality and Social Psychology, 35,* 125–139.

Bandura, A., Adams, N. E., Hardy, A. B., & Howells, G. N. (1980). Tests of the generality of self-efficacy theory. *Cognitive Therapy and Research, 4,* 39–66.

Bandura, A., Grusec, J. E., & Menlove, F. L. (1967). Vicarious extinction of avoidance behavior. *Journal of Personality and Social Psychology, 5,* 16–23.

Bandura, A., & Jeffery, R. W. (1973). Role of symbolic coding and rehearsal processes in observational learning. *Journal of Personality and Social Psychology, 26,* 122–130.

Bandura, A., Jeffery, R., & Bachicha, D. L. (1974). Analysis of memory codes and cumulative rehearsal in observational learning. *Journal of Research in Personality, 7,* 295–305.

Bandura, A., & Menlove, F. L. (1968). Factors determining vicarious extinction of avoidance behavior through symbolic modeling. *Journal of Personality and Social Psychology, 8,* 99–108.

Bandura, A., & Mischel, W. (1965). Modification of self-imposed delay of reward through exposure to live and symbolic models. *Journal of Personality and Social Psychology, 2,* 698–705.

Bandura, A., & Rosenthal, T. L. (1966). Vicarious classical conditioning as a function of arousal level. *Journal of Personality and Social Psychology, 3,* 54–62.

Bandura, A., & Schunk, D. H. (1981). Cultivating competence, self-efficacy, and intrinsic interest through proximal self-motivation. *Journal of Personality and Social Psychology, 41,* 586–598.

Bandura, A., & Walters, R. (1963). *Social learning and personality development.* New York: Holt, Rinehart, & Winston.

Bannister, D. (Ed.). (1970). *Perspectives in personal construct theory.* London, England: Academic.

Bannister, D. (1985). *Issues and approaches in personal construct theory.* London, England: Academic.

Barash, D. P. (1977). *Sociobiology and human behavior.* New York: Elsevier.

Barash, D. P. (1986). *The hare and the tortoise: Culture, biology, and human nature.* New York: Penguin.

Barash, D. P. (2001). *Revolutionary biology: The new, gene-centered view of life.* London, England: Transaction.

Barber, J. P., & DeRubeis, R. J. (1989). On second thought: Where the action is in cognitive therapy for depression. *Cognitive Therapy and Research, 13,* 441–457.

Barch, D. M. (2004). Pharmacological manipulation of human working memory. *Psychopharmacology, 174,* 126–135.

Bargh, J. A. (1997). The automaticity of everyday life. In R. S. Wyer, Jr. (Ed.), *Advances in social cognition* (Vol. 10, pp. 1–61). Mahwah, NJ: Erlbaum.

Bargh, J. A., & Chartrand, T. L. (1999). The unbearable automaticity of being. *American Psychologist, 54,* 462–479.

Bargh, J. A., Chen, M., & Burrows, L. (1996). Automaticity of social behavior: Direct effects of trait construct and stereotype activation on action. *Journal of Personality and Social Psychology, 71,* 230–244.

Bargh, J. A., & Ferguson, M. J. (2000). Beyond behaviorism: On the automaticity of higher mental processes. *Psychological Bulletin, 126,* 925–945.

Bargh, J. A., Gollwitzer, P. M., Lee-Chai, A., Barndollar, K., & Trötschel, R. (2001). The automated will: Nonconscious activation and pursuit of behavioral goals. *Journal of Personality and Social Psychology, 81,* 1014–1027.

Bargh, J. A., Lombardi, W. J., & Higgins, E. T. (1988). Automaticity of chronically accessible constructs in person X situation effects on person perception: It's just a matter of time. *Journal of Personality and Social Psychology, 55,* 599–605.

Bargh, J. A., & Pratto, F. (1986). Individual construct accessibility and perceptual selection. *Journal of Experimental Social Psychology, 22,* 293–311.

Bargh, J. A., & Williams, E. L. (2006). The automaticity of social life. *Current Directions in Psychological Science, 15,* 1–4.

Barkow, J. H., Cosmides, L., & Tooby, J. (1992). *The adapted mind: Evolutionary psychology and the generation of culture.* New York: Oxford University Press.

Barlow, D. H. (Ed.). (1981). *Behavioral assessment of adult disorders.* New York: Guilford.

Barnier, A. J., Levin, K., & Maher, A. (2004). Suppressing thoughts of past events: Are repressive copers good suppressors? *Cognition and Emotion, 18,* 513–531.

Baron, A. S., & Banaji, M. R. (2006). The development of implicit attitudes: Evidence of race evaluations from ages 6 and 10 and adulthood. *Psychological Science, 17,* 53–58.

Baron, R. A. (1974a). The aggression-inhibiting influence of heightened sexual arousal. *Journal of Personality and Social Psychology, 30,* 318–322.

Baron, R. A. (1974b). Sexual arousal and physical aggression: The inhibiting influence of "cheesecake" and nudes. *Bulletin of the Psychonomic Society, 3,* 337–339.

Baron, R. A. (1979). Heightened sexual arousal and physical aggression: An extension to females. *Journal of Research in Personality, 13,* 91–102.

Baron, R. A., & Bell, P. A. (1977). Sexual arousal and aggression by males: Effects of type of erotic stimuli and prior provocation. *Journal of Personality and Social Psychology, 35,* 79–87.

Baron, R. A., & Kempner, C. R. (1970). Model's behavior and attraction toward the model as determinants of adult aggressive behavior. *Journal of Personality and Social Psychology, 14,* 335–344.

Baron, R. A., & Richardson, D. R. (1994). *Human aggression* (2nd ed.). New York: Plenum.

Barrett, L. F., Williams, N. L., & Fong, G. T. (2002). Defensive verbal behavior assessment. *Personality and Social Psychology Bulletin, 28,* 776–788.

Barron, F. (1953). An ego-strength scale which predicts response to psychotherapy. *Journal of Consulting Psychology, 17,* 327–333.

Bartholomew, K., & Horowitz, L. M. (1991). Attachment styles among young adults: A test of a four-category model. *Journal of Personality and Social Psychology, 61,* 226–244.

Bartholow, B. D., & Anderson, C. A. (2001). Effects of violent video games on aggressive behavior: Potential sex differences. *Journal of Experimental Social Psychology, 38,* 283–290.

Bartholow, B. D., Sestir, M. A., & Davis, E. B. (2005). Correlates and consequences of exposure to video game violence: Hostile personality, empathy, and aggressive behavior. *Personality and Social Psychology Bulletin, 31,* 1573–1586.

Batson, C. D. (1990). How social an animal? The human capacity for caring. *American Psychologist, 45,* 336–346.

Batson, C. D. (1991). *The altruism question: Toward a social-psychological answer.* Hillsdale, NJ: Erlbaum.

Batson, C. D., Bolen, M. H., Cross, J. A., & Neuringer-Benefiel, H. E. (1986). Where is the altruism in the altruistic personality? *Journal of Personality and Social Psychology, 50,* 212–220.

Batson, C. D., Dyck, J. L., Brandt, J. R., Batson, J. G., Powell, A. L., McMaster, M. R., & Griffitt, C. (1988). Five studies testing two new egoistic alternatives to the empathy–altruism hypothesis. *Journal of Personality and Social Psychology, 55,* 52–77.

Batson, C. D., Fultz, J., & Schoenrade, P. A. (1987). Distress and empathy: Two qualitatively distinct vicarious emotions with different motivational consequences. *Journal of Personality, 55,* 19–39.

Bauer, J. J., & Bonanno, G. A. (2001). I can, I do, I am: The narrative differentiation of self-efficacy and other self-evaluations while adapting to bereavement. *Journal of Research in Personality, 35,* 424–448.

Bauer, J. J., McAdams, D. P., & Sakaeda, A. R. (2005). Interpreting the good life: Growth memories in the lives of mature, happy people. *Journal of Personality and Social Psychology, 88,* 203–217.

Baum, W. M. (2005). *Understanding behaviorism: Behavior, culture, and evolution.* Oxford, England: Blackwell.

Baumann, L. J., & Leventhal, H. (1985). "I can tell when my blood pressure is up, can't I?" *Health Psychology, 4,* 203–218.

Baumann, N., Kaschel, R., & Kuhl, J. (2005). Striving for unwanted goals: Stress-dependent discrepancies between explicit and implicit achievement motives reduce subjective well-being and increase psychosomatic symptoms. *Journal of Personality and Social Psychology, 89,* 781–799.

Baumeister, R. F. (1989). The problem of life's meaning. In D. M. Buss & N. Cantor (Eds.), *Personality psychology: Recent trends and emerging directions* (pp. 138–148). New York: Springer-Verlag.

Baumeister, R. F. (1994). The crystallization of discontent in the process of major life changes. In T. F. Heatherton & J. L. Weinberger (Eds.), *Can personality change?* (pp. 281–297). Washington, DC: American Psychological Association.

Baumeister, R. F. (2002). Ego depletion and self-control failure: An energy model of the self's executive function. *Self and Identity, 1,* 129–136.

Baumeister, R. F., Bratslavsky, E., Muraven, M., & Tice, D. M. (1998). Ego depletion: Is the active self a limited resource? *Journal of Personality and Social Psychology, 74,* 1252–1265.

Baumeister, R. F., & Campbell, W. K. (1999). The intrinsic appeal of evil: Sadism, sensational thrills, and threatened egotism. *Personality and Social Psychology Review, 3,* 210–221.

Baumeister, R. F., & Heatherton, T. F. (1996). Self-regulation failure: An overview. *Psychological Inquiry, 7,* 1–15.

Baumeister, R. F., & Leary, M. R. (1995). The need to belong: Desire for interpersonal attachments as a fundamental human motivation. *Psychological Bulletin, 117,* 497–529.

Baumeister, R. F., & Vohs, K. D. (Eds.). (2004). *Handbook of self-regulation: Research, theory, and applications.* New York: Guilford.

Beck, A. T. (1972). *Depression: Causes and treatments.* Philadelphia: University of Pennsylvania Press.

Beck, A. T. (1976). *Cognitive therapy and the emotional disorders.* New York: International Universities Press.

Beck, A. T. (1991). Cognitive therapy: A 30-year retrospective. *American Psychologist, 46,* 368–375.

Beck, A. T., Rush, A. J., Shaw, B. F., & Emery, G. (1979). *Cognitive therapy of depression: A treatment manual.* New York: Guilford.

Becker, E. (1973). *The denial of death.* New York: Free Press.

Beer, J. S. (2002). Implicit self-theories of shyness. *Journal of Personality and Social Psychology, 83,* 1009–1024.

Beevers, C. G. (2005). Cognitive vulnerability to depression: A dual process model. *Clinical Psychology Review, 25,* 975–1002.

Bell, M., Billington, R., & Becker, B. (1986). A scale for the assessment of object relations: Reliability, validity, and factorial invariance. *Journal of Clinical Psychology, 42,* 733–741.

Belmont, L., & Marolla, F. A. (1973). Birth order, family size, and intelligence. *Science, 182,* 1096–1101.

Bem, D. J., & Allen, A. (1974). On predicting some of the people some of the time: The search for cross-situational consistencies in behavior. *Psychological Review, 81,* 506–520.

Bem, S. L. (1974). The measurement of psychological androgyny. *Journal of Consulting and Clinical Psychology, 42,* 155–162.

Bem, S. L. (1975). Sex role adaptability: One consequence of psychological androgyny. *Journal of Personality and Social Psychology, 31,* 634–643.

Benet, V., & Waller, N. G. (1995). The Big Seven factor model of personality description: Evidence for its cross-cultural generality in a Spanish sample. *Journal of Personality and Social Psychology, 69,* 701–718.

Benet-Martínez, V., & John, O. P. (1998). Los Cinco Grandes across cultures and ethnic groups: Multitrait multimethod analyses of the Big Five in Spanish and English. *Journal of Personality and Social Psychology, 75,* 729–750.

Benjamin, J., Li, L., Patterson, C., Greenberg, B. D., Murphy, D. L., & Hamer, D. H. (1996). Population and familial association between the D4 dopamine receptor gene and measures of novelty seeking. *Nature Genetics, 12,* 81–84.

Bentler, P. M. (1990). Comparative fit indexes in structural models. *Psychological Bulletin, 107,* 238–246.

Berant, E., Mikulincer, M., & Florian, V. (2001). Attachment style and mental health: A 1-year follow-up study of mothers of infants with congenital heart disease. *Personality and Social Psychology Bulletin, 27,* 956–968.

Berenbaum, S. A., & Hines, M. (1992). Early androgens are related to childhood sex-typed toy preferences. *Psychological Science, 3,* 203–206.

Berg, I. A. (Ed.). (1967). *Response set in personality assessment.* Chicago: Aldine.

Bergeman, C. S., Chipuer, H. M., Plomin, R., Pedersen, N. L., McClearn, G. E., Nesselrode, J. R., Costa, P. T., Jr., & McCrae, R. R. (1993). Genetic and environmental effects on openness to experience, agreeableness, and conscientiousness: An adoption/twin study. *Journal of Personality, 61,* 159–179.

Berger, S. M. (1961). Incidental learning through vicarious reinforcement. *Psychological Reports, 9,* 477–491.

Berger, S. M. (1962). Conditioning through vicarious instigation. *Psychological Review, 69,* 450–466.

Bergeron, D. M., Block, C. J., & Echtenkamp, B. A. (2006). Disabling the able: Stereotype threat and women's work performance. *Human Performance, 19,* 133–158.

Bergmann, M. S. (1980). Symposium on object relations theory and love: On the intrapsychic function of falling in love. *Psychoanalytic Quarterly, 49,* 56–77.

Berkowitz, L., & Alioto, J. T. (1973). The meaning of an observed event as a determinant of its aggressive consequences. *Journal of Personality and Social Psychology, 28,* 206–217.

Bernhardt, P. C., Dabbs, J. M., Jr., Fielden, J., & Lutter, C. (1998). Testosterone changes during vicarious experiences of winning and losing among fans at sporting events. *Physiology and Behavior, 65,* 59–62.

Bernstein, A., Newman, J. P., Wallace, J. F., & Luh, K. E. (2000). Left-hemisphere activation and deficient response modulation in psychopaths. *Psychological Science, 11,* 414–418.

Bernstein, D. A. (1973). Situational factors in behavioral fear assessment: A progress report. *Behavior Therapy, 4,* 41–48.

Bernstein, I. L. (1985). Learning food aversions in the progression of cancer and its treatment. *Annals of the New York Academy of Sciences, 443,* 365–380.

Berry, D. S., & Miller, K. M. (2001). When boy meets girl: Attractiveness and the five-factor model in opposite-sex interactions. *Journal of Research in Personality, 35,* 62–77.

Bertrand, S., & Masling, J. M. (1969). Oral imagery and alcoholism. *Journal of Abnormal Psychology, 74,* 50–53.

Besser, A., & Priel, B. (2005). The apple does not fall far from the tree: Attachment styles and personality vulnerabilities to depression in three generations of women. *Personality and Social Psychology Bulletin, 31,* 1052–1073.

Bettelheim, B. (1982). Reflections: Freud and the soul. *New Yorker, 58,* 52–93.

Bettencourt, B. A., & Sheldon, K. (2001). Social roles as mechanisms for psychological need satisfaction within social groups. *Journal of Personality and Social Psychology, 81,* 1131–1143.

Binswanger, L. (1963). *Being-in-the-world: Selected papers of Ludwig Binswanger.* New York: Basic Books.

Bjork, J. M., Dougherty, D. M., Moeller, F. G., & Swann, A. C. (2000). Differential behavioral effects of plasma tryptophan depletion and loading in aggressive and nonaggressive men. *Neuropsychopharmacology, 22,* 357–369.

Bjorklund, D. F., & Pellegrini, A. D. (2002). *Origins of human nature: Evolutionary developmental psychology.* Washington, DC: American Psychological Association.

Black, A. E., & Deci, E. L. (2000). The effects of instructors' autonomy support and students' autonomous motivation on learning organic chemistry: A self-determination theory perspective. *Science Education, 84,* 740–756.

Blackburn, R. (1968a). Emotionality, extraversion and aggression in paranoid and non-paranoid schizophrenic offenders. *British Journal of Psychiatry, 115,* 1301–1302.

Blackburn, R. (1968b). Personality in relation to extreme aggression in psychiatry offenders. *British Journal of Psychiatry, 114,* 821–828.

Blanchard, E. B., & Epstein, L. H. (1978). *A biofeedback primer.* Reading, MA: Addison-Wesley.

Blanchard, R. (2004). Quantitative and theoretical analyses of the relation between older brothers and homosexuality in men. *Journal of Theoretical Biology, 230,* 173–187.

Blanchard, R., Cantor, J. M., Bogaert, A. F., Breedlove, S. M., & Ellis, L. (2006). Interaction of fraternal birth order and handedness in the development of male homosexuality. *Hormones and Behavior, 49,* 405–414.

Blanck, R., & Blanck, G. (1986). *Beyond ego psychology: Developmental object relations theory.* New York: Columbia University Press.

Blatt, S. J., Wein, S. J., Chevron, E., & Quinlan, D. M. (1979). Parental representations and depression in normal young adults. *Journal of Abnormal Psychology, 88,* 388–397.

Blatt, S. J., & Zuroff, D. C. (1992). Interpersonal relatedness and self-definition: Two prototypes for depression. *Clinical Psychology Review, 12,* 527–562.

Block, J. (1977). Advancing the science of personality: Paradigmatic shift or improving the quality of research? In D. Magnusson & N. S. Endler (Eds.), *Personality at the crossroads: Current issues in interactional psychology* (pp. 37–63). Hillsdale, NJ: Erlbaum.

Block, J. (1982). Assimilation, accommodation, and the dynamics of personality development. *Child Development, 53,* 281–295.

Block, J. (1995). A contrarian view of the five-factor approach to personality assessment. *Psychological Bulletin, 117,* 187–215.

Block, J. (2001). Millennial contrarianism: The five-factor approach to personality description 5 years later. *Journal of Research in Personality, 35,* 98–107.

Block, J. (2002). *Personality as an affect-processing system: Toward an integrative theory.* Mahwah, NJ: Erlbaum.

Block, J., & Block, J. H. (2006). Venturing a 30-year longitudinal study. *American Psychologist, 61,* 315–327.

Block, J., & Kremen, A. M. (1996). IQ and ego-resiliency: Conceptual and empirical connections and separateness. *Journal of Personality and Social Psychology, 70,* 349–361.

Block, J., von der Lippe, A., & Block, J. H. (1973). Sex-role and socialization patterns: Some personality concomitants and environmental antecedents. *Journal of Consulting and Clinical Psychology, 41,* 321–341.

Block, J. H. (1961). *The Q-sort method in personality assessment and psychiatric research.* Springfield, IL: Charles C. Thomas.

Block, J. H. (1973). Conceptions of sex role: Some cross-cultural and longitudinal perspectives. *American Psychologist, 28,* 512–526.

Block, J. H. (1979). Another look at sex differentiation in the socialization behaviors of mothers and fathers. In F. L. Denmark & J. Sherman (Eds.), *Psychology of women: Future directions for research.* New York: Psychological Dimensions.

Block, J. H., & Block, J. (1980). The role of ego-control and ego-resiliency in the organization of behavior. In W. A. Collins (Ed.), *Development of cognition, affect, and social relations* (Minnesota symposia on child psychology, Vol. 13, pp. 39–101). Hillsdale, NJ: Erlbaum.

Bocklandt, S., Horvath, S., Vilain, E., & Hamer, D. H. (2006). Extreme skewing of X chromosome inactivation in mothers of homosexual men. *Human Genetics, 118,* 691–694.

Bogg, T., & Roberts, B. W. (2004). Conscientiousness and health-related behaviors: A meta-analysis of the leading behavioral contributors to mortality. *Psychological Bulletin, 130,* 887–919.

Bolger, N., & Zuckerman, A. (1995). A framework for studying personality in the stress process. *Journal of Personality and Social Psychology, 69,* 890–902.

Bolles, R. C. (1972). Reinforcement, expectancy, and learning. *Psychological Review, 79,* 394–409.

Bonarius, H., Holland, R., & Rosenberg, S. (Eds.). (1980). *Personal construct theory: Recent advances in theory and practice.* London, England: Macmillan.

Booth, A., & Dabbs, J. M., Jr. (1993). Testosterone and men's marriages. *Social Forces, 72,* 463–477.

Borgatta, E. F. (1964). The structure of personality characteristics. *Behavioral Science, 12,* 8–17.

Boring, E. G. (1930). A new ambiguous figure. *American Journal of Psychology, 42,* 444–445.

Borkenau, P., Riemann, R., Angleitner, A., & Spinath, F. M. (2001). Genetic and environmental influences on observed personality: Evidence from the German observational study of adult twins. *Journal of Personality and Social Psychology, 80,* 655–668.

Borkenau, P., Riemann, R., Angleitner, A., & Spinath, F. M. (2002). Similarity of childhood experiences and personality resemblance in monozygotic and dizygotic twins: A test of the equal environments assumption. *Personality and Individual Differences, 33,* 261–269.

Bornstein, R. F., & Masling, J. (1985). Orality and latency of volunteering to serve as experimental subjects: A replication. *Journal of Personality Assessment, 49,* 306–310.

Borsboom, D., Mellenbergh, G. J., & van Heerden, J. (2004). The concept of validity. *Psychological Review, 111,* 1061–1071.

Boss, M. (1963). *Psychoanalysis and Daseinsanalysis.* New York: Basic Books.

Bottome, P. (1939). *Alfred Adler: A biography.* New York: Putnam's.

Botwin, M. D., & Buss, D. M. (1989). Structure of act-report data: Is the five-factor model of personality recaptured? *Journal of Personality and Social Psychology, 56,* 988–1001.

Bouchard, T. J. (2004). Genetic influence on human psychological traits. *Current Directions in Psychological Science, 13,* 148–151.

Bouchard, T. J., Jr., Lykken, D. T., McGue, M., Segal, N. L., & Tellegen, A. (1990). Sources of human psychological differences: The Minnesota study of twins reared apart. *Science, 250,* 223–228.

Bouton, M. E. (1994). Context, ambiguity, and classical conditioning. *Current Directions in Psychological Science, 3,* 49–53.

Bouton, M. E. (2000). A learning theory perspective on lapse, relapse, and the maintenance of behavior change. *Health Psychology, 19,* 57–63.

Bower, J. E., Kemeny, M. E., Taylor, S. E., & Fahey, J. L. (1998). Cognitive processing, discovery of meaning, CD4 decline, and AIDS-related mortality among bereaved HIV seropositive men. *Journal of Consulting and Clinical Psychology, 66,* 979–986.

Bowlby, J. (1969). *Attachment and loss: Vol. 1, Attachment.* New York: Basic Books.

Bowlby, J. (1988). *A secure base: Parent–child attachment and healthy human development.* New York: Basic Books.

Boyatzis, R. E. (1973). Affiliation motivation. In D. C. McClelland & R. S. Steele (Eds.), *Human motivation: A book of readings.* Morristown, NJ: General Learning Press.

Bradburn, N. M., & Berlew, D. E. (1961). Need for achievement and English industrial growth. *Economic Development and Cultural Change, 10,* 8–20.

Bradley, G. W. (1978). Self-serving biases in the attribution process: A reexamination of the fact or fiction question. *Journal of Personality and Social Psychology, 36,* 56–71.

Brady, J. P. (1972). Systematic desensitization. In W. S. Agras (Ed.), *Behavior modification: Principles and clinical applications.* Boston: Little, Brown.

Brady, S. S., & Matthews, K. A. (2006). Effects of media violence on health-related outcomes among young men. *Archives of Pediatric Adolescent Medicine, 160,* 341–347.

Bramel, D., Taub, B., & Blum, B. (1968). An observer's reaction to the suffering of his enemy. *Journal of Personality and Social Psychology, 8,* 384–392.

Brandon, T. H., Tiffany, S. T., Obremski, K. M., & Baker, T. B. (1990). Postcessation cigarette use: The process of relapse. *Addictive Behaviors, 15,* 105–114.

Brandstätter, H. (1983). Emotional responses to other persons in everyday life situations. *Journal of Personality and Social Psychology, 45,* 871–883.

Brandstätter, V., & Frank, E. (2002). Effects of deliberative and implemental mindsets on persistence in goal-directed behavior. *Personality and Social Psychology Bulletin, 28,* 1366–1378.

Brandstätter, V., Lengfelder, A., & Gollwitzer, P. M. (2001). Implementation intentions and efficient action initiation. *Journal of Personality and Social Psychology, 81,* 946–960.

Branje, S. J. T., van Lieshout, C. F. M., & van Aken, M. A. G. (2004). Relations between big five personality characteristics and perceived support in adolescents' families. *Journal of Personality and Social Psychology, 86,* 615–628.

Breedlove, S. M. (1992). Sexual dimorphism in the vertebrate nervous system. *Journal of Neuroscience, 12,* 4133–4142.

Breedlove, S. M. (1994). Sexual differentiation of the human nervous system. *Annual Review of Psychology, 45,* 389–418.

Brehm, J. W. (1966). *A theory of psychological reactance.* New York: Academic.

Brehm, S. S., & Brehm, J. W. (1981). *Psychological reactance: A theory of freedom and control.* New York: Academic.

Breland, H. M. (1974). Birth order, family constellation, and verbal achievement. *Child Development, 45,* 1011–1019.

Breland, K., & Breland, M. (1961). The misbehavior of organisms. *American Psychologist, 16,* 681–684.

Brennan, K. A., Clark, C. L., & Shaver, P. R. (1998). Self-report measurement of adult attachment: An integrative overview. In J. A. Simpson & W. S. Rholes (Eds.), *Attachment theory and close relationships* (pp. 46–76). New York: Guilford.

Brenner, C. (1957). *An elementary textbook of psychoanalysis.* Garden City, NY: Doubleday.

Brewer, W. F. (1974). There is no convincing evidence for operant or classical conditioning in adult humans. In W. B. Weimer & D. S. Palermo (Eds.), *Cognition and the symbolic processes.* Hillsdale, NJ: Erlbaum.

Bridger, W. H., & Mandel, I. J. (1964). A comparison of GSR fear responses produced by threat and electric shock. *Journal of Psychiatric Research, 2,* 31–40.

Briggs, S. R. (1989). The optimal level of measurement for personality constructs. In D. M. Buss & N. Cantor (Eds.), *Personality psychology: Recent trends and emerging directions* (pp. 246–260). New York: Springer-Verlag.

Brissette, I., Scheier, M. F., & Carver, C. S. (2002). The role of optimism in social network development, coping, and psychological adjustment during a life transition. *Journal of Personality and Social Psychology, 82,* 102–111.

Britt, T. W., & Shepperd, J. A. (1999). Trait relevance and trait assessment. *Personality and Social Psychology Review, 3,* 108–122.

Broadbent, D. E. (1977). Levels, hierarchies, and the locus of control. *Quarterly Journal of Experimental Psychology, 29,* 181–201.

Broadbent, E., Petrie, K. J., Alley, P. G., & Booth, R. J. (2003). Psychological stress impairs early wound repair following surgery. *Psychosomatic Medicine, 65,* 865–869.

Brody, N. (Ed.). (1987). Special issue on the unconscious. *Personality and Social Psychology Bulletin, 13,* 293–429.

Brokaw, D. W., & McLemore, C. W. (1983). Toward a more rigorous definition of social reinforcement: Some interpersonal clarifications. *Journal of Personality and Social Psychology, 44,* 1014–1020.

Brooks, R. A. (2002). *Flesh and machines: How robots will change us.* New York: Pantheon.

Brown, I., Jr., & Inouye, D. K. (1978). Learned helplessness through modeling: The role of perceived similarity in competence. *Journal of Personality and Social Psychology, 36,* 900–908.

Brown, J. S. (1948). Gradients of approach and avoidance responses and their relation to level of motivation. *Journal of Comparative and Physiological Psychology, 41,* 450–465.

Brown, J. S. (1957). Principles of intrapersonal conflict. *Journal of Conflict Resolution, 1,* 135–154.

Bruhn, A. R., & Schiffman, H. (1982). Prediction of locus of control stance from the earliest childhood memory. *Journal of Personality Assessment, 46,* 380–390.

Bruner, J. S. (1957). On perceptual readiness. *Psychological Review, 64,* 123–152.

Brunstein, J. C., & Maier, G. W. (2005). Implicit and self-attributed motives to achieve: Two separate but interacting needs. *Journal of Personality and Social Psychology, 89,* 205–222.

Brunstein, J. C., Schultheiss, O. C., & Grässmann, R. (1998). Personal goals and emotional well-being: The moderating role of motive dispositions. *Journal of Personality and Social Psychology, 75,* 494–508.

Brunswik, E. (1951). The probability point of view. In M. H. Marx (Ed.), *Psychological theory.* New York: Macmillan.

Buccino, G., Binkofski, F., Fink, G. R., Fadiga, L., Fogassi, L., Gallese, V., Seitz, R. J., Zilles, K., Rizzolatti, G., & Freund,

H. J. (2001). Action observation activates premotor and parietal areas in somatotopic manner: An fMRI study. *European Journal of Neuroscience, 13,* 400–404.

Buchanan, A., Brock, D. W., Daniels, N., & Wikler, D. (2000). *From chance to choice: Genetics and justice.* New York: Cambridge University Press.

Buchanan, G. M. (1995). Explanatory style and coronary heart disease. In G. M. Buchanan & M. E. P. Seligman (Eds.), *Explanatory style* (pp. 225–232). Hillsdale, NJ: Erlbaum.

Buller, D. J. (2005a). *Adapting minds: Evolutionary psychology and the persistent quest for human nature.* Cambridge, MA: MIT Press.

Buller, D. J. (2005b). Evolutionary psychology: The emperor's new paradigm. *Trends in Cognitive Sciences, 9,* 277–283.

Burger, J. M. (1989). Negative reactions to increases in perceived personal control. *Journal of Personality and Social Psychology, 56,* 246–256.

Burnstein, E., Crandall, C., & Kitayama, S. (1994). Some neo-Darwinian decision rules for altruism: Weighing cues for inclusive fitness as a function of the biological importance of the decision. *Journal of Personality and Social Psychology, 67,* 773–789.

Burroughs, W. J., & Drews, D. R. (1991). Rule structure in the psychological representation of physical settings. *Journal of Experimental Social Psychology, 27,* 217–238.

Bursik, K. (1991). Adaptation to divorce and ego development in adult women. *Journal of Personality and Social Psychology, 60,* 300–306.

Bushman, B. J. (2002). Does venting anger feed or extinguish the flame? Catharsis, rumination, distraction, anger, and aggressive responding. *Personality and Social Psychology Bulletin, 28,* 724–731.

Bushman, B. J., & Baumeister, R. F. (1998). Threatened egotism, narcissism, self-esteem, and direct and displaced aggression: Does self-love or self-hate lead to violence? *Journal of Personality and Social Psychology, 75,* 219–229.

Bushman, B. J., Baumeister, R. F., & Phillips, C. M. (2001). Do people aggress to improve their mood? Catharsis beliefs, affect regulation opportunity, and aggressive responding. *Journal of Personality and Social Psychology, 81,* 17–32.

Buss, A. H. (1983). Social rewards and personality. *Journal of Personality and Social Psychology, 44,* 553–563.

Buss, A. H., & Plomin, R. (1975). *A temperament theory of personality development.* New York: Wiley-Interscience.

Buss, A. H., & Plomin, R. (1984). *Temperament: Early developing personality traits.* Hillsdale, NJ: Erlbaum.

Buss, D. M. (1984). Toward a psychology of person-environment correlation: The role of spouse selection. *Journal of Personality and Social Psychology, 47,* 361–377.

Buss, D. M. (1985). Human mate selection. *American Scientist, 73,* 47–51.

Buss, D. M. (1988). The evolution of human intrasexual competition: Tactics of mate attraction. *Journal of Personality and Social Psychology, 54,* 616–628.

Buss, D. M. (1989). Sex differences in human mate preferences: Evolutionary hypotheses tested in 37 cultures. *Behavioral and Brain Sciences, 12,* 1–49.

Buss, D. M. (1991). Evolutionary personality psychology. *Annual Review of Psychology, 42,* 459–491.

Buss, D. M. (1994a). *The evolution of desire: Strategies of human mating.* New York: Basic Books.

Buss, D. M. (1994b). The strategies of human mating. *American Scientist, 82,* 238–249.

Buss, D. M. (1995). Evolutionary psychology: A new paradigm for psychological science. *Psychological Inquiry, 6,* 1–30.

Buss, D. M. (2001). Cognitive biases and emotional wisdom in the evolution of conflict between the sexes. *Current Directions in Psychological Science, 10,* 219–223.

Buss, D. M. (Ed.). (2005a). *The handbook of evolutionary psychology.* New York: Wiley.

Buss, D. M. (2005b). *The murderer next door: Why the mind is designed to kill.* New York, Penguin.

Buss, D. M., Gomes, M., Higgins, D. S., & Lauterbach, K. (1987). Tactics of manipulation. *Journal of Personality and Social Psychology, 52,* 1219–1229.

Buss, D. M., Larsen, R. J., Westen, D., & Semmelroth, J. (1992). Sex differences in jealousy: Evolution, physiology, and psychology. *Psychological Science, 3,* 251–255.

Buss, D. M., & Schmitt, D. P. (1993). Sexual strategies theory: An evolutionary perspective on human mating. *Psychological Review, 100,* 204–232.

Buss, D. M., & Shackelford, T. K. (1997). From vigilance to violence: Mate retention tactics in married couples. *Journal of Personality and Social Psychology, 72,* 346–361.

Bussey, K., & Bandura, A. (1984). Influence of gender constancy and social power on sex-linked modeling. *Journal of Personality and Social Psychology, 47,* 1292–1302.

Bussey, K., & Bandura, A. (1999). Social cognitive theory of gender development and differentiation. *Psychological Review, 106,* 676–713.

Butcher, J. N. (Ed.). (1996). *International adaptations of the MMPI-2: Research and clinical applications.* Minneapolis: University of Minnesota Press.

Butcher, J. N., Dahlstrom, W., Graham, J., Tellegen, A., & Kaemmer, B. (1989). *Manual for administering and scoring the MMPI-2.* Minneapolis: University of Minnesota Press.

Butler, J. M., & Haigh, G. V. (1954). Changes in the relation between self-concepts and ideal concepts consequent upon client-centered counseling. In C. R. Rogers & R. F. Dymond (Eds.), *Psychotherapy and personality change: Coordinated research studies in the client-centered approach.* Chicago: University of Chicago Press.

Byrne, D., McDonald, R. D., & Mikawa, J. (1963). Approach and avoidance affiliation motives. *Journal of Personality, 31,* 21–37.

Cacioppo, J. T., Gardner, W. L., & Berntson, G. G. (1999). The affect system has parallel and integrative processing components: Form follows function. *Journal of Personality and Social Psychology, 76,* 839–855.

Cacioppo, J. T., & Petty, R. E. (1980). The effects of orienting task on differential hemispheric EEG activation. *Neuropsychologia, 18,* 675–683.

Cacioppo, J. T., & Petty, R. E. (1982). The need for cognition. *Journal of Personality and Social Psychology, 42,* 116–131.

Cacioppo, J. T., & Petty, R. E. (1983). *Social psychophysiology.* New York: Guilford.

Cacioppo, J. T., & Petty, R. E. (1984). The need for cognition: Relationship to attitudinal processes. In R. P. McGlynn, J. E. Maddux, C. Stoltenberg, & J. H. Harvey (Eds.), *Social perception in clinical and counseling psychology.* Lubbock: Texas Tech Press.

Cacioppo, J. T., Petty, R. E., Feinstein, J. A., & Jarvis, W. B. G. (1996). Dispositional differences in cognitive motivation: The life and times of individuals varying in need for cognition. *Psychological Bulletin, 119,* 197–253.

Cacioppo, J. T., Petty, R. E., Kao, C. F., & Rodriguez, R. (1986). Central and peripheral routes to persuasion: An individual difference perspective. *Journal of Personality and Social Psychology, 51,* 1032–1043.

Cacioppo, J. T., Petty, R. E., & Morris, K. J. (1983). Effects of need for cognition on message evaluation, recall, and persuasion. *Journal of Personality and Social Psychology, 45,* 805–818.

Cacioppo, J. T., & Sandman, C. A. (1981). Psychophysiological functioning, cognitive responding, and attitudes. In R. E. Petty, T. M. Ostrom, & T. C. Brock (Eds.), *Cognitive responses in persuasion.* Hillsdale, NJ: Erlbaum.

Cadinu, M., Maass, A., Rosabianca, A., & Kiesner, J. (2005). Why do women underperform under stereotype threat? Evidence for the role of negative thinking. *Psychological Science, 16,* 572–578.

Cain, D. J., & Seeman, J. (Eds.). (2002). *Humanistic psychotherapies: Handbook of research and practice.* Washington, DC: American Psychological Association.

Cameron, O. G., Abelson, J. L., & Young, E. A. (2004). Anxious and depressive disorders and their comorbidity: Effect on central nervous system noradrenergic function. *Biological Psychiatry, 56,* 875–883.

Campbell, D. T. (1960). Recommendations for the APA test standards regarding construct, trait, and discriminant validity. *American Psychologist, 15,* 546–553.

Campbell, D. T., & Fiske, D. W. (1959). Convergent and discriminant validation by the multitrait–multimethod matrix. *Psychological Bulletin, 56,* 81–105.

Campbell, W. K. (1999). Narcissism and romantic attraction. *Journal of Personality and Social Psychology, 77,* 1254–1270.

Campbell, W. K., & Foster, C. A. (2002). Narcissism and commitment in romantic relationships: An investment model analysis. *Personality and Social Psychology Bulletin, 28,* 484–495.

Cannon, D. S., Baker, T. B., Gino, A., & Nathan, P. E. (1986). Alcohol-aversion therapy: Relation between strength of aversion and abstinence. *Journal of Consulting and Clinical Psychology, 54,* 825–830.

Cannon, W. B. (1932). *The wisdom of the body.* New York: Norton.

Cantor, N., & Kihlstrom, J. F. (1987). *Personality and social intelligence.* Englewood Cliffs, NJ: Prentice-Hall.

Cantor, N., & Mischel, W. (1977). Traits as prototypes: Effects on recognition memory. *Journal of Personality and Social Psychology, 35,* 38–48.

Cantor, N., Smith, E. E., French, R., & Mezzich, J. (1980). Psychiatric diagnosis as prototype categorization. *Journal of Abnormal Psychology, 89,* 181–193.

Caporeal, L. R. (2001). Evolutionary psychology: Toward a unifying theory and a hybrid science. *Annual Review of Psychology, 52,* 607–628.

Carey, G. (2003). *Human genetics for the social sciences.* Thousand Oaks, CA: Sage.

Carey, G., Goldsmith, H. H., Tellegen, A., & Gottesman, I. I. (1978). Genetics and personality inventories: The limits of replication with twin data. *Behavior Genetics, 8,* 299–313.

Carlston, D. E., & Skowronski, J. J. (1994). Savings in the relearning of trait information as evidence for spontaneous inference generation. *Journal of Personality and Social Psychology, 66,* 840–856.

Carnagey, N. L., & Anderson, C. A. (2005). The effects of reward and punishment in violent video games on aggressive affect, cognition, and behavior. *Psychological Science, 16,* 882–889.

Carnelley, K. B., Pietromonaco, P. R., & Jaffe, K. (1994). Depression, working models of others, and relationship functioning. *Journal of Personality and Social Psychology, 66,* 127–140.

Carroll, L. (1987). A study of narcissism, affiliation, intimacy, and power motives among students in business administration. *Psychological Reports, 61,* 355–358.

Carter, B. L., & Tiffany, S. T. (1999). Meta-analysis of cue reactivity in addiction research. *Addiction, 94,* 327–340.

Carter, C. S. (1998). Neuroendocrine perspectives on social attachment and love. *Psychoneuroimmunology, 23,* 779–818.

Carver, C. S. (1975). Physical aggression as a function of objective self-awareness and attitudes toward punishment. *Journal of Experimental Social Psychology, 11,* 510–519.

Carver, C. S. (1997a). Adult attachment and personality: Converging evidence and a new measure. *Personality and Social Psychology Bulletin, 23,* 865–883.

Carver, C. S. (1997b). The Internal–External scale confounds internal locus of control with expectancies of positive outcomes. *Personality and Social Psychology Bulletin, 23,* 580–585.

Carver, C. S. (1998). Generalization, adverse events, and development of depressive symptoms. *Journal of Personality, 66,* 609–620.

Carver, C. S. (2003). Pleasure as a sign you can attend to something else: Placing positive feelings within a general model of affect. *Cognition and Emotion, 17,* 241–261.

Carver, C. S. (2004). Negative affects deriving from the behavioral approach system. *Emotion, 4,* 3–22.

Carver, C. S. (2005). Impulse and constraint: Perspectives from personality psychology, convergence with theory in other areas, and potential for integration. *Personality and Social Psychology Review, 9,* 312–333.

Carver, C. S., & Baird, E. (1998). The American dream revisited: Is it *what* you want or *why* you want it that matters? *Psychological Science, 9,* 289–292.

Carver, C. S., Ganellen, R. J., Froming, W. J., & Chambers, W. (1983). Modeling: An analysis in terms of category accessibility. *Journal of Experimental Social Psychology, 19,* 403–421.

Carver, C. S., Kus, L. A., & Scheier, M. F. (1994). Effects of good versus bad mood and optimistic versus pessimistic outlook on social acceptance versus rejection. *Journal of Social and Clinical Psychology, 13,* 138–151.

Carver, C. S., LaVoie, L., Kuhl, J., & Ganellen, R. J. (1988). Cognitive concomitants of depression: A further examination of the roles of generalization, high standards, and self-criticism. *Journal of Social and Clinical Psychology, 7,* 350–365.

Carver, C. S., Lawrence, J. W., & Scheier, M. F. (1999). Self-discrepancies and affect: Incorporating the role of feared selves. *Personality and Social Psychology Bulletin, 25,* 783–792.

Carver, C. S., Lehman, J. M., & Antoni, M. H. (2003). Dispositional pessimism predicts illness-related disruption of social and recreational activities among breast cancer patients. *Journal of Personality and Social Psychology, 84,* 813–821.

Carver, C. S., & Miller, C. J. (2006). Relations of serotonin function to personality: Current views and a key methodological issue. *Psychiatry Research, 144,* 1–15.

Carver, C. S., Pozo, C., Harris, S. D., Noriega, V., Scheier, M. F., Robinson, D. S., Ketcham, A. S., Moffat, F. L., & Clark, K. C. (1993). How coping mediates the effect of optimism on distress: A study of women with early stage breast cancer. *Journal of Personality and Social Psychology, 65,* 375–390.

Carver, C. S., & Scheier, M. F. (1981). *Attention and self-regulation: A control-theory approach to human behavior.* New York: Springer-Verlag.

Carver, C. S., & Scheier, M. F. (1986). Functional and dysfunctional responses to anxiety: The interaction between expectancies and self-focused attention. In R. Schwarzer (Ed.), *Self-related cognitions in anxiety and motivation.* Hillsdale, NJ: Erlbaum.

Carver, C. S., & Scheier, M. F. (1990). Principles of self-regulation: Action and emotion. In E. T. Higgins & R. M.

Sorrentino (Eds.), *Handbook of motivation and cognition: Foundations of social behavior* (Vol. 2, pp. 3–52). New York: Guilford.

Carver, C. S., & Scheier, M. F. (1998). *On the self-regulation of behavior.* New York: Cambridge University Press.

Carver, C. S., & Scheier, M. F. (2002). Control processes and self-organization as complementary principles underlying behavior. *Personality and Social Psychology Review, 6,* 304–315.

Carver, C. S., & Scheier, M. F. (2007). Feedback processes in the simultaneous regulation of action and affect. In J. Y. Shah & W. L. Gardner (Eds.), *Handbook of motivation science.* New York: Guilford.

Carver, C. S., & White, T. L. (1994). Behavioral inhibition, behavioral activation, and affective responses to impending reward and punishment: The BIS/BAS scales. *Journal of Personality and Social Psychology, 67,* 319–333.

Caspar, F., Rothenfluh, T., & Segal, Z. (1992). The appeal of connectionism to clinical psychology. *Clinical Psychology Review, 12,* 719–762.

Caspi, A., Elder, G. H., Jr., & Bem, D. J. (1987). Moving against the world: Life-course patterns of explosive children. *Developmental Psychology, 23,* 308–313.

Caspi, A., Elder, G. H., Jr., & Bem, D. J. (1988). Moving away from the world: Life-course patterns of shy children. *Developmental Psychology, 24,* 824–831.

Caspi, A., & Herbener, E. S. (1990). Continuity and change: Assortative marriage and the consistency of personality in adulthood. *Journal of Personality and Social Psychology, 58,* 250–258.

Caspi, A., McClay, J., Moffitt, T. E., Mill, J., Martin, J., Craig, I. W., Taylor, A., & Poulton, R. (2002). Role of genotype in the cycle of violence in maltreated children. *Science, 297,* 851–854.

Caspi, A., Roberts, B. W., & Shiner, R. L. (2005). Personality development: Stability and change. *Annual Review of Psychology, 56,* 453–484.

Cassidy, J., & Shaver, P. R. (Eds.). (1999). *Handbook of attachment: Theory, research, and clinical applications.* New York: Guilford.

Catania, A. C., & Harnad, S. (Eds.). (1988). *The operant behaviorism of B. F. Skinner: Comments and consequences.* New York: Cambridge University Press.

Cattell, H. E. P. (1993). Comment on Goldberg. *American Psychologist, 48,* 1302–1303.

Cattell, R. B. (1947). Confirmation and clarification of primary personality factors. *Psychometrica, 12,* 197–220.

Cattell, R. B. (1965). *The scientific analysis of personality.* Baltimore: Penguin.

Cattell, R. B. (1978). *The scientific use of factor analysis.* New York: Plenum.

Cattell, R. B. (1979). *Personality and learning theory, Volume 1. The structure of personality in its environment.* New York: Springer-Verlag.

Cattell, R. B. (1985). *Human motivation and the dynamic calculus.* New York: Praeger.

Cattell, R. B., Eber, H. W., & Tatsuoka, M. M. (1977). *Handbook for the 16 personality factor questionnaire.* Champaign, IL: IPAT.

Cattell, R. B., & Kline, P. (1977). *The scientific analysis of personality and motivation.* New York: Academic.

Cervone, D. (1997). Social-cognitive mechanisms and personality coherence: Self-knowledge, situational beliefs, and cross-situational coherence in perceived self-efficacy. *Psychological Science, 8,* 43–50.

Cervone, D. (2004). The architecture of personality. *Psychological Review, 111,* 183–204.

Chambliss, C. A., & Murray, E. J. (1979). Efficacy attribution, locus of control, and weight loss. *Cognitive Therapy and Research, 3,* 349–354.

Chamorro-Premuzic, T., & Furnham, A. (2003). Personality predicts academic performance: Evidence from two longitudinal university samples. *Journal of Research in Personality, 37,* 319–338.

Chance, S. E., Brown, R. T., Dabbs, J. M., Jr., & Casey, R. (2000). Testosterone, intelligence and behavior disorders in young boys. *Personality and Individual Differences, 28,* 437–445.

Chaplin, W. F., Phillips, J. B., Brown, J. D., Clanton, N. R., & Stein, J. L. (2000). Handshaking, gender, personality, and first impressions. *Journal of Personality and Social Psychology, 79,* 110–117.

Chapman, L. J. (1967). Illusory correlations in observational report. *Journal of Verbal Learning and Verbal Behavior, 6,* 151–155.

Chartrand, T. L., & Bargh, J. A. (1996). Automatic activation of impression formation and memorization goals: Nonconscious goal priming reproduces effects of explicit task instructions. *Journal of Personality and Social Psychology, 71,* 464–478.

Chartrand, T. L., & Bargh, J. A. (1999). The chameleon effect: The perception–behavior link and social interaction. *Journal of Personality and Social Psychology, 76,* 893–910.

Chassin, L., Flora, D. B., & King, K. M. (2004). Trajectories of alcohol and drug use and dependence from adolescence to adulthood: The effects of familial alcoholism and personality. *Journal of Abnormal Psychology, 113,* 483–498.

Chatterjee, B. B., & Eriksen, C. W. (1962). Cognitive factors in heart rate conditioning. *Journal of Experimental Psychology, 64,* 272–279.

Chen, E., & Matthews, K. A. (2001). Cognitive appraisal biases: An approach to understanding the relation between socioeconomic status and cardiovascular reactivity in children. *Annals of Behavioral Medicine, 23,* 101–111.

Chen, S. (2003). Psychological-state theories about significant others: Implications for the content and structure of significant-other representations. *Personality and Social Psychology Bulletin, 29,* 1285–1302.

Chomsky, N. (1959). Review of *Verbal behavior* by B. F. Skinner. *Language, 35,* 26–58.

Christensen, A. J., Ehlers, S. L., Wiebe, J. S., Moran, P. J., Raichle, K., Ferneyhough, K., & Lawton, W. J. (2002). Patient personality and mortality: A 4-year prospective examination of chronic renal insufficiency. *Health Psychology, 21,* 315–320.

Church, A. T. (Ed.). (2001). Introduction: Culture and personality [Special issue]. *Journal of Personality, 69,* 787–801.

Church, A. T., & Burke, P. J. (1994). Exploratory and confirmatory tests of the big five and Tellegen's three- and four-dimensional models. *Journal of Personality and Social Psychology, 66,* 93–114.

Cialdini, R. B., Schaller, M., Houlihan, D., Arps, K., Fultz, J., & Beaman, A. L. (1987). Empathy-based helping: Is it selflessly or selfishly motivated? *Journal of Personality and Social Psychology, 52,* 749–758.

Ciminero, A. R., Calhoun, K. S., & Adams, H. E. (Eds.). (1977). *Handbook of behavioral assessment.* New York: Wiley.

Claridge, G. S. (1967). *Personality and arousal.* New York: Pergamon.

Clark, L. A., Kochanska, G., & Ready, R. (2000). Mothers' personality and its interaction with child temperament as predictors of parenting behavior. *Journal of Personality and Social Psychology, 79,* 274–285.

Clark, L. A., & Watson, D. (1999). Temperament: A new paradigm for trait psychology. In L. A. Pervin & O. P. John (Eds.), *Handbook of personality: Theory and research* (2nd ed., pp. 399–423). New York: Guilford.

Clark, R. A., & McClelland, D. C. (1956). A factor-analytic integration of imaginative and performance measures of the need for achievement. *Journal of General Psychology, 55,* 73–83.

Clark, R. D., & Hatfield, E. (1989). Gender differences in receptivity to sexual offers. *Journal of Psychology and Human Sexuality, 2,* 39–55.

Clark, W. R. (1996). *Sex and the origins of death.* New York: Oxford University Press.

Clausen, J. A. (1981). Men's occupational careers in the middle years. In D. H. Eichorn, J. A. Clausen, N. Haan, M. P. Honzik, & P. H. Mussen (Eds.), *Present and past in middle life* (pp. 321–351). New York: Academic.

Cleare, A. J., & Bond, A. J. (1995). The effect of tryptophan depletion and enhancement on subjective and behavioural aggression in normal male subjects. *Psychopharmacology, 118,* 72–81.

Cleare, A. J., & Bond, A. J. (1997). Does central serotonergic function correlate inversely with aggression? A study using D-fenfluramine in healthy subjects. *Psychiatry Research, 69,* 89–95.

Cline, V. B., Croft, R. G., & Courrier, S. (1973). Desensitization of children to television violence. *Journal of Personality and Social Psychology, 27,* 360–365.

Cloninger, C. R. (1987). A systematic method of clinical description and classification of personality variants: A proposal. *Archives of General Psychiatry, 44,* 573–588.

Cloninger, C. R. (1988). A unified biosocial theory of personality and its role in the development of anxiety states: A reply to commentaries. *Psychiatric Developments, 2,* 83–120.

Clower, C. E., & Bothwell, R. K. (2001). An exploratory study of the relationship between the Big Five and inmate recidivism. *Journal of Research in Personality, 35,* 231–237.

Coccaro, E. F., Kavoussi, R. J., Cooper, T. B., & Hauger, R. L. (1997). Central serotonin activity and aggression: Inverse relationship with prolactin response to *d*-fenfluramine, but not CSF 5-HIAA concentration, in human subjects. *American Journal of Psychiatry, 154,* 1430–1435.

Cohen, A. R. (1957). Need for cognition and order of communication as determinants of opinion change. In C. I. Hovland (Ed.), *The order of presentation in persuasion.* New Haven, CT: Yale University Press.

Cohen, A. R., Stotland, E., & Wolfe, D. M. (1955). An experimental investigation of need for cognition. *Journal of Abnormal and Social Psychology, 51,* 291–294.

Cohen, D., Nisbett, R. E., Bowdle, B. F., & Schwarz, N. (1996). Insult, aggression, and the Southern culture of honor: An "experimental ethnology." *Journal of Personality and Social Psychology, 70,* 945–960.

Cohen, S. (2005). The Pittsburgh common cold studies: Psychosocial predictors of susceptibility to respiratory infectious illness. *International Journal of Behavioral Medicine, 12,* 123–131.

Cohen, S., Doyle, W. J., Turner, R. B., Alper, C. M., & Skoner, D. P. (2003). Emotional style and susceptibility to the common cold. *Psychosomatic Medicine, 65,* 652–657.

Cohen-Bendahan, C. C. C., van de Beek, C., & Berenbaum, S. A. (2005). Prenatal sex hormone effects on child and adult sex-typed behavior: Methods and findings. *Neuroscience and Biobehavioral Reviews, 29,* 353–384.

Cohn, L. D. (1991). Sex differences in the course of personality development: A meta-analysis. *Psychological Bulletin, 109,* 252–266.

Cohn, L. D., & Westenberg, P. M. (2004). Intelligence and maturity: Meta-analytic evidence for the incremental and discriminant validity of Loevinger's Measure of Ego Development. *Journal of Personality and Social Psychology, 86,* 760–772.

Collier, P. J., & Callero, P. J. (2005). Role theory and social cognition: Learning to think like a recycler. *Self and Identity, 4,* 45–58.

Collins, N. L., Ford, M. B., Guichard, A. C., Feeney, B. C. (2006). Responding to need in intimate relationships: Normative processes and individual differences. In M. Mikulincer & G. Goodman (Eds.), *The dynamics of love: Attachment, caregiving, and sex* (pp. 149–189). New York: Guilford.

Collins, N. L., & Read, S. J. (1990). Adult attachment, working models, and relationship quality in dating couples. *Journal of Personality and Social Psychology, 58,* 644–663.

Conklin, C. A., & Tiffany, S. T. (2001). The impact of imagining personalized versus standardized urge scenarios on cigarette craving and autonomic reactivity. *Experimental and Clinical Psychopharmacology, 9,* 399–408.

Conklin, C. A., & Tiffany, S. T. (2002). Applying extinction research and theory to cue-exposure addiction treatments. *Addiction, 97,* 155–167.

Conley, J. J. (1985). Longitudinal stability of personality traits: A multitrait-multimethod-multioccasion analysis. *Journal of Personality and Social Psychology, 49,* 1266–1282.

Conner, T., & Barrett, L. (2005). Implicit self-attitudes predict spontaneous affect in daily life. *Emotion, 5,* 476–488.

Constantian, C. A. (1981). *Attitudes, beliefs, and behavior in regard to spending time alone.* Unpublished doctoral dissertation, Harvard University, Cambridge, MA.

Converse, J., & Presser, S. (1986). *Survey questions: Handcrafting the standardized questionnaire.* Newbury Park, CA: Sage.

Conway, M., & Giannopoulos, C. (1993). Dysphoria and decision making: Limited information use for evaluations of multiattribute targets. *Journal of Personality and Social Psychology, 64,* 613–623.

Cook, M. L., & Peterson, C. (1986). Depressive irrationality. *Cognitive Therapy and Research, 10,* 293–298.

Cook, W. L. (2000). Understanding attachment security in a family context. *Journal of Personality and Social Psychology, 78,* 285–294.

Cooley, E. J., & Spiegler, M. D. (1980). Cognitive versus emotional coping responses as alternatives to test anxiety. *Cognitive Therapy and Research, 4,* 159–166.

Coolidge, F. L., Moor, C. J., Yamazaki, T. G., Stewart, S. E., & Segal, D. L. (2001). On the relationship between Karen Horney's tripartite neurotic type theory and personality disorder features. *Personality and Individual Differences, 30,* 1387–1400.

Cooper, M. L., Shapiro, C. M., & Powers, A. M. (1998). Motivations for sex and risky sexual behavior among adolescents and young adults: A functional perspective. *Journal of Personality and Social Psychology, 75,* 1528–1558.

Corr, P. J., Pickering, A. D., & Gray, J. A. (1997). Personality, punishment, and procedural learning: A test of J. A. Gray's anxiety theory. *Journal of Personality and Social Psychology, 73,* 337–344.

Cortes, J. B., & Gatti, F. M. (1965). Physique and self-descriptions of temperament. *Journal of Consulting Psychology, 29,* 432–439.

Costa, P. T., Jr., & McCrae, R. R. (1980). Influence of extraversion and neuroticism on subjective well-being: Happy and unhappy people. *Journal of Personality and Social Psychology, 38,* 668–678.

Costa, P. T., Jr., & McCrae, R. R. (1985). *The NEO Personality Inventory manual.* Odessa, FL: Psychological Assessment Resources.

Costa, P. T., Jr., & McCrae, R. R. (1988a). From catalog to classification: Murray's needs and the five-factor model. *Journal of Personality and Social Psychology, 55,* 258–265.

Costa, P. T., Jr., & McCrae, R. R. (1988b). Personality in adulthood: A six-year longitudinal study of self-reports and spouse ratings on the NEO personality inventory. *Journal of Personality and Social Psychology, 54,* 853–863.

Costa, P. T., Jr., & McCrae, R. R. (1989). Personality continuity and the changes of adult life. In M. Storandt & G. R. VandenBos (Eds.), *The adult years: Continuity and change* (pp. 45–77). Washington, DC: American Psychological Association.

Costa, P. T., Jr., & McCrae, R. R. (1992). *Revised NEO Personality Inventory (NEO-PI-R) and NEO Five-Factor Inventory (NEO-FFI) professional manual.* Odessa, FL: Psychological Assessment Resources.

Costa, P. T., Jr., & McCrae, R. R. (1995). Domains and facets: Hierarchical personality assessment using the revised NEO Pesonality Inventory. *Journal of Personality Assessment, 64,* 21–50.

Costa, P. T., Jr., & Widiger, T. A. (Eds.). (2002). *Personality disorders and the five-factor model of personality* (2nd ed.). Washington, DC: American Psychological Association.

Couch, A., & Keniston, K. (1960). Yeasayers and naysayers: Agreeing response set as a personality variable. *Journal of Abnormal and Social Psychology, 60,* 151–174.

Cozzarelli, C. (1993). Personality and self-efficacy as predictors of coping with abortion. *Journal of Personality and Social Psychology, 65,* 1224–1236.

Craig, K. D., & Weinstein, M. S. (1965). Conditioning vicarious affective arousal. *Psychological Reports, 17,* 955–963.

Craighead, W. E., Kazdin, A. E., & Mahoney, M. J. (1981). *Behavior modification: Principles, issues, and applications.* Boston: Houghton Mifflin.

Cramer, P. (2000). Defense mechanisms in psychology today: Further processes for adaptation. *American Psychologist, 55,* 637–646.

Cramer, P., & Tracy, A. (2005). The pathway from child personality to adult adjustment: The road is not straight. *Journal of Research in Personality, 39,* 369–394.

Crandall, R., McCown, D. A., & Robb, Z. (1988). The effects of assertiveness training on self-actualization. *Small Group Behavior, 19,* 134–145.

Crawford, C. B. (1989). The theory of evolution: Of what value to psychology? *Journal of Comparative Psychology, 103,* 4–22.

Crawford, C. B., Smith, M. S., & Krebs, D. (Eds.). (1987). *Sociobiology and psychology: Ideas, issues and applications.* Hillsdale, NJ: Erlbaum.

Crawford, L. E., & Cacioppo, J. T. (2002). Learning where to look for danger: Integrating affective and spatial information. *Psychological Science, 13,* 449–453.

Crews, F. (1996). The verdict on Freud. *Psychological Science, 7,* 63.

Crick, N. R., & Dodge, K. A. (1994). A review and reformulation of social information-processing mechanisms in children's social adjustment. *Psychological Bulletin, 115,* 74–101.

Cristóbal-Azkarate, J., Chavira, R., Boeck, L., Rodríguez-Luna, E., & Veàl, J. J. (2006). Testosterone levels of free-ranging resident mantled howler monkey males in relation to the number and density of solitary males: A test of the challenge hypothesis. *Hormones and Behavior, 49,* 261–267.

Crittenden, P. M. (1990). Internal representational models of attachment relationships. *Infant Mental Health Journal, 11,* 259–277.

Crocker, J. (1981). Judgment of covariation by social perceivers. *Psychological Bulletin, 90,* 272–292.

Crocker, J., & Knight, K. M. (2005). Contingencies of self-worth. *Current Directions in Psychological Science, 14,* 200–203.

Crocker, J., Luhtanen, R. K., Cooper, M. L., & Bouvrette, A. (2003). Contingencies of self-worth in college students: Theory and measurement. *Journal of Personality and Social Psychology, 85,* 894–908.

Crocker, J., & Park, L. E. (2004). The costly pursuit of self-esteem. *Psychological Bulletin, 130,* 392–414.

Crocker, J., & Wolfe, C. T. (2001). Contingencies of self-worth. *Psychological Review, 108,* 593–623.

Cronbach, L. J., & Meehl, P. E. (1955). Construct validity in psychological tests. *Psychological Bulletin, 52,* 281–302.

Crouse, B. B., & Mehrabian, A. (1977). Affiliation of opposite-sexed strangers. *Journal of Research in Personality, 11,* 38–47.

Crowne, D. P., & Marlowe, D. (1964). *The approval motive: Studies in evaluative dependence.* New York: Wiley.

Csikszentmihalyi, M. (1975). *Beyond boredom and anxiety.* San Francisco: Jossey-Bass.

Csikszentmihalyi, M. (1978). Attention and the holistic approach to behavior. In K. S. Pope & J. L. Singer (Eds.), *The stream of consciousness: Scientific investigations into the flow of human experience.* New York: Plenum.

Csikszentmihalyi, M. (1982). Toward a psychology of optimal experience. In L. Wheeler (Ed.), *Review of personality and social psychology* (Vol. 3, pp. 13–36). Beverly Hills, CA: Sage.

Csikszentmihalyi, M. (1990). *Flow: The psychology of optimal experience.* New York: Harper & Row.

Csikszentmihalyi, M., & Csikszentmihalyi, I. S. (Eds.). (1988). *Optimal experience: Psychological studies of flow in consciousness.* New York: Cambridge University Press.

Csikszentmihalyi, M., & LeFevre, J. (1989). Optimal experience in work and leisure. *Journal of Personality and Social Psychology, 56,* 815–822.

Cunningham, M. R., Barbee, A. P., & Pike, C. L. (1990). What do women want? Facialmetric assessment of multiple motives in the perception of male facial physical attractiveness. *Journal of Personality and Social Psychology, 59,* 61–72.

Cutter, H. S. G., Boyatzis, R. E., & Clancy, D. D. (1977). The effectiveness of power motivation training in rehabilitating alcoholics. *Journal of Studies on Alcohol, 38,* 131–141.

Dabbs, J. M., Jr. (1992a). Testosterone and occupational achievement. *Social Forces, 70,* 813–824.

Dabbs, J. M., Jr. (1992b). Testosterone measurements in social and clinical psychology. *Journal of Social and Clinical Psychology, 11,* 302–321.

Dabbs, J. M., Jr. (1997). Testosterone, smiling, and facial appearance. *Journal of Nonverbal Behavior, 21,* 45–55.

Dabbs, J. M., Jr. (1998). Testosterone and the concept of dominance. *Behavioral and Brain Sciences, 21,* 370–371.

Dabbs, J. M., Jr., Alford, E. C., & Fielden, J. A. (1998). Trial lawyers: Blue collar talent in a white collar world. *Journal of Applied Social Psychology, 28,* 84–94.

Dabbs, J. M., Jr., Bernieri, F. J., Strong, R. K., Campo, R., & Milun, R. (2001). Going on stage: Testosterone in greetings and meetings. *Journal of Research in Personality, 35,* 27–40.

Dabbs, J. M., Jr., & Dabbs, M. G. (2000). *Heroes, rogues and lovers: Testosterone and behavior.* New York: McGraw-Hill.

Dabbs, J. M., Jr., de La Rue, D., & Williams, P. M. (1990). Testosterone and occupational choice: Actors, ministers, and other men. *Journal of Personality and Social Psychology, 59,* 1261–1265.

Dabbs, J. M., Jr., Frady, R. L., Carr, T. S., & Besch, N. F. (1987). Saliva testosterone and criminal violence in young adult prison inmates. *Psychosomatic Medicine, 49,* 174–182.

Dabbs, J. M., Jr., Hargrove, M. F., & Heusel, C. (1996). Testosterone differences among college fraternities: Well-behaved vs. rambunctious. *Personality and Individual Differences, 290,* 157–161.

Dabbs, J. M., Jr., & Mallinger, A. (1999). High testosterone levels predict low voice pitch among men. *Personality and Individual Differences, 27,* 801–804.

Dabbs, J. M., Jr., & Mohammed, S. (1992). Male and female salivary testosterone concentrations before and after sexual activity. *Physiology and Behavior, 52,* 195–197.

Dabbs, J. M., Jr., & Morris, R. (1990). Testosterone, social class, and antisocial behavior in a sample of 4,462 men. *Psychological Science, 1,* 209–211.

Dabbs, J. M., Jr., Riad, J. K., & Chance, S. E. (2001). Testosterone and ruthless homicide. *Personality and Individual Differences, 31,* 599–603.

Dabbs, J. M., Jr., Ruback, R. B., Frady, R. L., Hopper, C. H., & Sgoutas, D. S. (1988). Saliva testosterone and criminal violence among women. *Personality and Individual Differences, 9,* 269–275.

Daitzman, R., & Zuckerman, M. (1980). Disinhibitory sensation seeking, personality and gonadal hormones. *Personality and Individual Differences, 1,* 103–110.

Daly, M., & Wilson, M. I. (1988). *Homicide.* New York: Aldine de Gruyter.

Daly, M., & Wilson, M. I. (1990). Killing the competition: Female/female and male/male homicide. *Human Nature, 1,* 81–107.

Daly, M., & Wilson, M. I. (1996). Violence against stepchildren. *Current Directions in Psychological Science, 5,* 77–81.

Daniels, D. (1986). Differential experiences of siblings in the same family as predictors of adolescent sibling personality differences. *Journal of Personality and Social Psychology, 51,* 339–346.

Daniels, D., & Plomin, R. (1985). Differential experience of siblings in the same family. *Developmental Psychology, 21,* 747–760.

Darley, J. M., & Goethals, G. R. (1980). People's analyses of the causes of ability-linked performances. In L. Berkowitz (Ed.), *Advances in experimental social psychology* (Vol. 13). New York: Academic.

Davidson, M. A., McInnes, R. G., & Parnell, R. W. (1957). The distribution of personality traits in seven-year-old children: A combined psychological, psychiatric, and somatotype study. *British Journal of Educational Psychology, 27,* 48–61.

Davidson, R. J. (1988). EEG measures of cerebral asymmetry: Conceptual and methodological issues. *International Journal of Neuroscience, 39,* 71–89.

Davidson, R. J. (1992). Prolegomenon to the structure of emotion: Gleanings from neuropsychology. *Cognition and Emotion, 6,* 245–268.

Davidson, R. J. (1995). Cerebral asymmetry, emotion, and affective style. In R. J. Davidson & K. Hugdahl (Eds.), *Brain asymmetry* (pp. 361–387). Cambridge, MA: MIT Press.

Davidson, R. J., Ekman, P., Saron, C. D., Senulis, J. A., & Friesen, W. V. (1990). Approach–withdrawal and cerebral asymmetry: Emotional expression and brain physiology I. *Journal of Personality and Social Psychology, 58,* 330–341.

Davidson, R. J., Jackson, D.C., & Kalin, N. H. (2000). Emotion, plasticity, context, and regulation: Perspectives from affective neuroscience. *Psychological Bulletin, 126,* 890–909.

Davidson, R. J., Pizzagalli, D., Nitschke, J. B., & Putnam, K. (2002). Depression: Perspectives from affective neuroscience. *Annual Review of Psychology, 53,* 545–574.

Davidson, R. J., & Sutton, S. K. (1995). Affective neuroscience: The emergence of a discipline. *Current Opinion in Neurobiology, 5,* 217–224.

Davila, J., Burge, D., & Hammen, C. (1997). Why does attachment style change? *Journal of Personality and Social Psychology, 73,* 826–838.

Davis, C. G., Nolen-Hoeksema, S., & Larson, J. (1998). Making sense of loss and benefiting from the experience:

Two construals of meaning. *Journal of Personality and Social Psychology, 75,* 561–574.

Davis, D., Shaver, P. R., & Vernon, M. L. (2003). Physical, emotional, and behavioral reactions to breaking up: The roles of gender, age, emotional involvement, and attachment style. *Personality and Social Psychology Bulletin, 29,* 871–884.

Davis, P. J. (1987). Repression and the inaccessibility of affective memories. *Journal of Personality and Social Psychology, 53,* 585–593.

Davis, P. J., & Schwartz, G. E. (1987). Repression and the inaccessibility of affective memories. *Journal of Personality and Social Psychology, 52,* 155–162.

Davison, G. C., & Wilson, G. T. (1973). Processes of fear reduction in systematic desensitization: Cognitive and social reinforcement factors in humans. *Behavior Therapy, 4,* 1–21.

Dawkins, R. (1976). *The selfish gene.* New York: Oxford University Press.

Dawson, M. E., & Furedy, J. J. (1976). The role of awareness in human differential autonomic classical conditioning: The necessary-gate hypothesis. *Psychophysiology, 13,* 50–53.

Dawson, M. R. W. (2004). *Minds and machines.* Malden, MA: Blackwell.

Dawson, M. R. W. (2005). *Connectionism: A hands-on approach.* Malden, MA: Blackwell.

Deaux, K., & Lewis, L. L. (1984). Structure of gender stereotypes: Interrelationships among components and gender label. *Journal of Personality and Social Psychology, 46,* 991–1004.

Deci, E. L. (1975). *Intrinsic motivation.* New York: Plenum.

Deci, E. L., Koestner, R., & Ryan, R. M. (1999). A meta-analytic review of experiments examining the effects of extrinsic rewards on intrinsic motivation. *Psychological Bulletin, 125,* 627–668.

Deci, E. L., La Guardia, J. G., Moller, A. C., Scheiner, M. J., & Ryan, R. M. (2006). On the benefits of giving as well as receiving autonomy support: Mutuality in close friendships. *Personality and Social Psychology Bulletin, 32,* 313–327.

Deci, E. L., & Ryan, R. M. (1980). The empirical exploration of intrinsic motivational processes. In L. Berkowitz (Ed.), *Advances in experimental social psychology* (Vol. 13). New York: Academic.

Deci, E. L., & Ryan, R. M. (1985). *Intrinsic motivation and self-determination in human behavior.* New York: Plenum.

Deci, E. L., & Ryan, R. M. (1991). A motivational approach to self: Integration in personality. In R. Dienstbier (Ed.), *Nebraska symposium on motivation: Perspectives on motivation* (Vol. 38, pp. 237–288). Lincoln: University of Nebraska Press.

Deci, E. L., & Ryan, R. M. (2000). The "what" and "why" of goal pursuits: Human needs and the self-determination of behavior. *Psychological Inquiry, 11,* 227–268.

DeHart, T., Pelham, B. W., & Tennen, H. (2006). What lies beneath: Parenting style and implicit self-esteem. *Journal of Experimental Social Psychology, 42,* 1–17.

De Houwer, J., Thomas, S., & Baeyens, F. (2001). Associative learning of likes and dislikes: A review of 25 years of research on human evaluative conditioning. *Psychological Bulletin, 127,* 853–869.

DeLisi, L. E., Shaw, S. H., Crow, T. J., et al. (2002). A genome-wide scan for linkage to chromosomal regions in 382 sibling pairs with schizophrenia or schizoaffective disorder. *American Journal of Psychiatry, 159,* 803–812.

Della Libera, C., & Chelazzi, L. (2006). Visual selective attention and the effects of monetary rewards. *Psychological Science, 17,* 222–227.

Deluty, R. H. (1985). Consistency of assertive, aggressive, and submissive behavior for children. *Journal of Personality and Social Psychology, 49,* 1054–1065.

Demorest, A. (2005). *Psychology's grand theories: How personal experiences shaped professional ideas.* Mahwah, NJ: Erlbaum.

De Neys, W. (2006). Dual processing in reasoning: Two systems but one reasoner. *Psychological Science, 17,* 428–433.

Depue, R. A. (1979). *The psychobiology of the depressive disorders: Implications for the effect of stress.* New York: Academic.

Depue, R. A. (1995). Neurobiological factors in personality and depression. *European Journal of Personality, 9,* 413–439.

Depue, R. A., & Collins, P. F. (1999). Neurobiology of the structure of personality: Dopamine, facilitation of incentive motivation, and extraversion. *Behavioral and Brain Sciences, 22,* 491–517.

Depue, R. A., & Iacono, W. G. (1989). Neurobehavioral aspects of affective disorders. *Annual Review of Psychology, 40,* 457–492.

Depue, R. A., Krauss, S. P., & Spoont, M. R. (1987). A two-dimensional threshold model of seasonal bipolar affective disorder. In D. Magnusson & A. Öhman (Eds.), *Psychopathology: An interactional perspective* (pp. 95–123). Orlando, FL: Academic.

Depue, R. A., Luciana, M., Arbisi, P., Collins, P., & Leon, A. (1994). Dopamine and the structure of personality: Relation of agonist-induced dopamine activity to positive emotionality. *Journal of Personality and Social Psychology, 67,* 485–498.

Depue, R. A., & Morrone-Strupinksy, J. V. (2005). A neurobehavioral model of affiliative bonding: Implications for conceptualizing a human trait of affiliation. *Behavioral and Brain Sciences, 28,* 313–395.

Depue, R. A., & Spoont, M. R. (1986). Conceptualizing a serotonin trait: A behavioral dimension of constraint. *Annals of the New York Academy of Sciences, 487,* 47–62.

Derryberry, D., & Rothbart, M. K. (1997). Reactive and effortful processes in the organization of temperament. *Development and Psychopathology, 9,* 633–652.

DeRubeis, R. J., Tang, T. Z., & Beck, A. T. (2001). Cognitive therapy. In Dobson, K. S. (Ed.), *Handbook of cognitive-behavioral therapies* (2nd ed., pp. 349–392). New York: Guilford.

de St. Aubin, E., McAdams, D. P., & Kim, T. (2004). *The generative society: Caring for future generations.* Washington DC: American Psychological Association.

DeSteno, D., Bartlett, M. Y., Braverman, J., & Salovey, P. (2002). Sex differences in jealousy: Evolutionary mechanism or artifact of measurement? *Journal of Personality and Social Psychology, 83,* 1103–1116.

Detera-Wadleigh, S. D., Berrettini, W. H., Goldin, L. R., Boorman, D., Anderson, S., & Gershon, E. S. (1987). Close linkage of c-harvey-ras-1 and the insulin gene to affective disorder is ruled out in three North American pedigrees. *Nature, 325,* 806–808.

Deutsch, F. M., Ruble, D. N., Fleming, A., Brooks-Gunn, J., & Stangor, C. (1988). Information-seeking and maternal self-definition during the transition to motherhood. *Journal of Personality and Social Psychology, 55,* 420–431.

DeVellis, R. F., DeVellis, B. M., & McCauley, C. (1978). Vicarious acquisition of learned helplessness. *Journal of Personality and Social Psychology, 36,* 894–899.

DeVito, A. J. (1985). Review of Myers–Briggs Type Indicator. In J. V. Mitchell (Ed.), *The ninth mental measurements yearbook* (pp. 1029–1032). Lincoln, NE: Buros Institute of Mental Measurements.

Di Blas, L., & Forzi, M. (1999). Refining a descriptive structure of personality attibutes in the Italian language: The abridged big three circumplex structure. *Journal of Personality and Social Psychology, 76,* 451–481.

Dick, D. M., & Rose, R. J. (2002). Behavior genetics: What's new? What's next? *Current Directions in Psychological Science, 11,* 70–74.

Dickens, W. T., & Flynn, J. R. (2001). Heritability estimates versus large environmental effects: The IQ paradox resolved. *Psychological Review, 108,* 346–369.

Dickerson, S. S., & Kemeny, M. E. (2004). Acute stressors and cortisol responses: A theoretical integration and synthesis of laboratory research. *Psychological Bulletin, 130,* 355–391.

DiClemente, C. C. (1981). Self-efficacy and smoking cessation. *Cognitive Therapy and Research, 5,* 175–187.

Diener, C. I., & Dweck, C. S. (1978). An analysis of learned helplessness: Continuous changes in performance, strategy, and achievement cognitions following failure. *Journal of Personality and Social Psychology, 36,* 451–462.

Diener, E. (1979). Deindividuation, self-awareness, and disinhibition. *Journal of Personality and Social Psychology, 37,* 1160–1171.

Digman, J. M. (1990). Personality structure: Emergence of the five-factor model. *Annual Review of Psychology, 41,* 417–440.

Digman, J. M. (1997). Higher-order factors of the Big Five. *Journal of Personality and Social Psychology, 73,* 1246–1256.

Digman, J. M., & Inouye, J. (1986). Further specification of the five robust factors of personality. *Journal of Personality and Social Psychology, 50,* 116–123.

Digman, J. M., & Shmelyov, A. G. (1996). The structure of temperament and personality in Russian children. *Journal of Personality and Social Psychology, 71,* 341–351.

Digman, J. M., & Takemoto-Chock, N. K. (1981). Factors in the natural language of personality: Re-analysis, comparison, and interpretation of six major studies. *Multivariate Behavioral Research, 16,* 149–170.

Dijksterhuis, A., & Bargh, J. A. (2001). The perception–behavior expressway. In M. P. Zanna (Ed.), *Advances in experimental social psychology* (Vol. 33, pp. 1–40). San Diego: Academic.

Dijkstra, P., & Buunk, B. P. (1998). Jealousy as a function of rival characteristics: An evolutionary perspective. *Personality and Social Psychology Bulletin, 24,* 1158–1166.

DiLalla, L. F., & Gottesman, I. I. (1991). Biological and genetic contributors to violence—Widom's untold tale. *Psychological Bulletin, 109,* 125–129.

Diven, K. (1936). Certain determinants in the conditioning of anxiety reactions. *Journal of Psychology, 3,* 291–308.

Dixon, N. F. (1981). *Preconscious processing.* Chichester, England: Wiley.

Dodge, K. A. (1986). A social information-processing model of social competence in children. In M. Perlmutter (Ed.), *Minnesota symposium on child psychology* (Vol. 18). Hillsdale, NJ: Erlbaum.

Dodge, K. A., & Crick, N. R. (1990). Social information-processing bases of aggressive behavior in children. *Personality and Social Psychology Bulletin, 16,* 8–22.

Dollard, J., & Miller, N. E. (1950). *Personality and psychotherapy: An analysis in terms of learning, thinking, and culture.* New York: McGraw-Hill.

Dollinger, S. J., & Orf, L. A. (1991). Personality and performance in "personality": Conscientiousness and openness. *Journal of Research in Personality, 25,* 276–284.

Domhoff, G. W. (2003). *The scientific study of dreams: Neural networks, cognitive development, and content analysis.* Washington, DC: American Psychological Association.

Donnellan, M. B., Conger, R. D., & Bryant, C. M. (2004). The big five and enduring marriages. *Journal of Research in Personality, 38,* 481–504.

Donnerstein, E. (1980). Aggressive erotica and violence against women. *Journal of Personality and Social Psychology, 39,* 269–277.

Donnerstein, E. (1983). Erotica and human aggression. In R. G. Geen & E. Donnerstein (Eds.), *Aggression: Theoretical and empirical reviews.* New York: Academic.

Donnerstein, E., Donnerstein, M., & Evans, R. (1975). Erotic stimuli and aggression: Facilitation or inhibition? *Journal of Personality and Social Psychology, 32,* 237–244.

Donnerstein, E., & Hallam, J. (1978). The facilitating effects of erotica on aggression toward females. *Journal of Personality and Social Psychology, 36,* 1270–1277.

Doob, A. N. (1970). Catharsis and aggression: The effect of hurting one's enemy. *Journal of Experimental Research in Personality, 4,* 291–296.

Dosamantes-Alperson, E., & Merrill, N. (1980). Growth effects of experiential movement psychotherapy. *Psychotherapy: Theory, Research, and Practice, 17,* 63–68.

Douglas, C. (1993). *Translate this darkness: The life of Christiana Morgan.* New York: Simon & Schuster.

Drabman, R. S., & Spitalnik, R. (1973). Training a retarded child as a behavioral teaching assistant. *Journal of Behavior Therapy and Experimental Psychiatry, 4,* 269–272.

Dreisbach, G., & Goschke, T. (2004). How positive affect modulates cognitive control: Reduced perseveration at the cost of increased distractibility. *Journal of Experimental Psychology: Learning, Memory, and Cognition, 30,* 343–353.

Duck, S. W. (1973). *Personal relationships and personal constructs.* London, England: Wiley.

Duck, S. W. (1977). Inquiry, hypothesis, and the quest for validation: Personal construct systems in the development of acquaintance. In S. W. Duck (Ed.), *Theories of interpersonal attraction.* London, England: Academic.

Duck, S. W., & Allison, D. (1978). I liked you but I can't live with you: A study of lapsed friendships. *Social Behavior and Personality, 8,* 43–47.

Dulany, D. E. (1968). Awareness, rules and propositional control: A confrontation with S-R behavior theory. In T. R. Dixon & D. L. Horton (Eds.), *Verbal behavior and general behavior theory.* Englewood Cliffs, NJ: Prentice-Hall.

Dunn, J., & Plomin, R. (1990). *Separate lives: Why siblings are so different.* New York: Basic Books.

Dunning, D., & McElwee, R. O. (1995). Idiosyncratic trait definitions: Implications for self-description and social judgment. *Journal of Personality and Social Psychology, 68,* 936–946.

Dweck, C. S., & Leggett, E. L. (1988). A social-cognitive approach to motivation and personality. *Psychological Review, 95,* 256–273.

Eagle, M. N. (1984). *Recent developments in psychoanalysis: A critical evaluation.* New York: McGraw-Hill.

Eagly, A. H. (1987). *Sex differences in social behavior: A social-role interpretation.* Hillsdale, NJ: Erlbaum.

Eagly, A. H., & Wood, W. (1999). The origins of sex differences in human behavior: Evolved dispositions versus social roles. *American Psychologist, 54,* 408–423.

Eaves, L. J., Eysenck, H. J., & Martin, N. G. (1989). *Genes, culture, and personality: An empirical approach.* San Diego: Academic.

Ebbesen, E. B., Duncan, B., & Konecni, V. J. (1975). Effects of content of verbal aggression on future verbal aggression: A field experiment. *Journal of Experimental Social Psychology, 11,* 192–204.

Ebrecht, M., Hextall, J., Kirtley, L., Taylor, A., Dyson, M., & Weinman, J. (2004). Perceived stress and cortisol levels predict speed of wound healing in healthy male adults. *Psychoneuroendocrinology, 29,* 798–809.

Ebstein, R. P. (2006). The molecular genetic architecture of human personality: Beyond self-report questionnaires. *Molecular Psychiatry, 11,* 427–445.

Ebstein, R. P., Novick, O., Umansky, R., Priel, B., Osher, Y., Blaine, D., Bennett, E. R., Nemanov, L., Katz, M., & Belmaker, R. H. (1996). Dopamine D4 receptor (D4DR) exon III polymorphism associated with the human personality trait of novelty seeking. *Nature Genetics, 12,* 78–80.

Edwards, A. L. (1957). *The social desirability variable in personality assessment and research.* New York: Dryden.

Edwards, A. L. (1959). *Edwards Personal Preference Schedule manual.* New York: Psychological Corporation.

Egeland, J. A., Gerhard, D. S., Pauls, D. L., Sussex, J. N., & Kidd, K. K. (1987). Bipolar affective disorders linked to DNA markers on chromosome 11. *Nature, 325,* 783–787.

Einstein, D., & Lanning, K. (1998). Shame, guilt, ego development, and the five-factor model of personality. *Journal of Personality, 66,* 555–582.

Eisenberg, N. (2002). Emotion-related regulation and its relation to quality of social functioning, In W. W. Hartup & R. A. Weinberg (Eds.), *Child psychology in retrospect and prospect: The Minnesota symposium on child psychology* (Vol. 32, pp. 133–171). Mahwah, NJ: Erlbaum.

Eisenberg, N., Fabes, R. A., Guthrie, I. K., & Reiser, M. (2000). Dispositional emotionality and regulation: Their role in predicting quality of social functioning. *Journal of Personality and Social Psychology, 78,* 136–157.

Eisenberg, N., Fabes, R. A., Murphy, B., Karbon, M., Maszk, P., Smith, M., O'Boyle, C., & Suh, K. (1994). The relations of emotionality and regulation to dispositional and situational empathy-related responding. *Journal of Personality and Social Psychology, 66,* 776–797.

Eisenberg, N., Spinrad, T. L., Fabes, R. A., Reiser, M., Cumberland, A., Shepard, S. A., Valiente, C., Losoya, S. H., Guthrie, I. K., & Thompson, M. (2004). The relations of effortful control and impulsivity to children's resiliency and adjustment. *Child Development, 75,* 25–46.

Eisenberger, R. (1992). Learned industriousness. *Psychological Review, 99,* 248–267.

Eisenberger, R., Armeli, S., & Pretz, J. (1998). Can the promise of reward increase creativity? *Journal of Personality and Social Psychology, 74,* 704–714.

Eisenberger, R., & Rhoades, L. (2001). Incremental effects of reward on creativity. *Journal of Personality and Social Psychology, 81,* 728–741.

Eisenberger, R., & Selbst, M. (1994). Does reward increase or decrease creativity? *Journal of Personality and Social Psychology, 66,* 1116–1127.

Ekehammer, B. (1974). Interactionism in personality from a historical perspective. *Psychological Bulletin, 81,* 1026–1048.

Elder, G. H., Jr., Caspi, A., & Downey, G. (1986). Problem behavior and family relationships: Life course and intergenerational themes. In A. B. Sorenson, F. Weinert, & L. R. Sherrod (Eds.), *Human development and the life course: Multidisciplinary perspectives* (pp. 293–340). Hillsdale, NJ: Erlbaum.

Elder, G. H., Jr., & MacInnis, D. J. (1983). Achievement imagery in women's lives from adolescence to adulthood. *Journal of Personality and Social Psychology, 45,* 394–404.

Ellenberger, H. F. (1970). *The discovery of the unconscious.* New York: Basic Books.

Elliot, A. J. (2005). A conceptual history of the achievement goal construct. In A. J. Elliot & C. S. Dweck (Eds.), *Handbook of competence and motivation* (pp. 52–72). New York: Guilford.

Elliot, A. J., Gable, S. L., & Mapes, R. R. (2006). Approach and avoidance motivation in the social domain. *Personality and Social Psychology Bulletin, 32,* 378–391.

Elliot, A. J., & Harackiewicz, J. M. (1994). Goal setting, achievement orientation, and intrinsic motivation: A mediational analysis. *Journal of Personality and Social Psychology, 66,* 968–980.

Elliot, A. J., & Harackiewicz, J. M. (1996). Approach and avoidance achievement goals and intrinsic motivation: A mediational analysis. *Journal of Personality and Social Psychology, 70,* 461–475.

Elliot, A. J., & McGregor, H. A. (2001). A 2 × 2 achievement goal framework. *Journal of Personality and Social Psychology, 80,* 501–519.

Elliot, A. J., & Sheldon, K. M. (1997). Avoidance achievement motivation: A personal goals analysis. *Journal of Personality and Social Psychology, 73,* 171–185.

Elliot, A. J., & Thrash, T. M. (2002). Approach–avoidance motivation in personality: Approach and avoidance temperaments and goals. *Journal of Personality and Social Psychology, 82,* 804–818.

Elliott, E. S., & Dweck, C. S. (1988). Goals: An approach to motivation and achievement. *Journal of Personality and Social Psychology, 54,* 5–12.

Ellis, A. E. (1987). The impossibility of achieving consistently good mental health. *American Psychologist, 42,* 364–375.

Elman, J. L. (2005). Connectionist models of cognitive development: Where next? *Trends in Cognitive Sciences, 9,* 112–117.

Elmore, A. M., & Tursky, B. (1981). A comparison of two psychophysiological approaches to the treatment of migraine. *Headache, 21,* 93–101.

Emmons, R. A. (1986). Personal strivings: An approach to personality and subjective well-being. *Journal of Personality and Social Psychology, 51,* 1058–1068.

Emmons, R. A., & Diener, E. (1986). Situation selection as a moderator of response consistency and stability. *Journal of Personality and Social Psychology, 51,* 1013–1019.

Emmons, R. A., Diener, E., & Larsen, R. J. (1986). Choice and avoidance of everyday situations and affect congruence: Two models of reciprocal interactionism. *Journal of Personality and Social Psychology, 51,* 815–826.

Emmons, R. A., & King, L. A. (1988). Conflict among personal strivings: Immediate and long-term implications for psychological and physical well-being. *Journal of Personality and Social Psychology, 54,* 1040–1048.

Emmons, R. A., King, L. A., & Sheldon, K. (1993). Goal conflict and the self-regulation of action. In D. M. Wegner & J. W. Pennebaker (Eds.), *Handbook of mental control* (pp. 528–551). Englewood Cliffs, NJ: Prentice-Hall.

Endler, N. S., & Magnusson, D. (1976). *Interactional psychology and personality.* Washington, DC: Hemisphere.

Entwisle, D. R. (1972). To dispel fantasies about fantasy-based measures of achievement motivation. *Psychological Bulletin, 77,* 377–391.

Epstein, L. H., Saelens, B. E., Myers, M. D., & Vito, D. (1997). Effects of decreasing sedentary behaviors on activity choice in obese children. *Health Psychology, 16,* 107–113.

Epstein, S. (1983). The unconscious, the preconscious, and the self-concept. In J. Suls & A. G. Greenwald (Eds.), *Psychological perspectives on the self* (Vol. 2). Hillsdale, NJ: Erlbaum.

Epstein, S. (1985). The implications of cognitive-experiential self theory for research in social psychology and personality. *Journal for the Theory of Social Behavior, 15,* 283–310.

Epstein, S. (1990). Cognitive–experiential self-theory. In L. Pervin (Ed.), *Handbook of personality: Theory and research* (pp. 165–192). New York: Guilford.

Epstein, S. (1994). Integration of the cognitive and the psychodynamic unconscious. *American Psychologist, 49,* 709–724.

Epstein, S., Lipson, A., Holstein, C., & Huh, E. (1992). Irrational reactions to negative outcomes: Evidence for two conceptual systems. *Journal of Personality and Social Psychology, 62,* 328–339.

Epting, F. R. (1972). The stability of cognitive complexity in construing social issues. *British Journal of Social and Clinical Psychology, 11,* 122–125.

Epting, F. R. (1980). *Personal construct theory psychotherapy.* New York: Wiley.

Erdelyi, M. H. (1985). *Psychoanalysis: Freud's cognitive psychology.* New York: Freeman.

Erdelyi, M. H. (in press). The unified theory of repression. *Behavioral and Brain Science.*

Ericsson, K. A., & Simon, H. A. (1993). *Protocol analysis: Verbal reports as data* (Rev. ed.). Cambridge, MA: MIT Press.

Erikson, E. H. (1950). *Childhood and society.* New York: Norton.

Erikson, E. H. (1963). *Childhood and society* (2nd ed.). New York: Norton.

Erikson, E. H. (1964). *Insight and responsibility.* New York: Norton.

Erikson, E. H. (1968). *Identity: Youth and crisis.* New York: Norton.

Erikson, E. H. (1974). *Dimensions of a new identity.* New York: Norton.

Erikson, E. H. (1982). *The life cycle completed: A review.* New York: Norton.

Ernst, C., & Angst, J. (1983). *Birth order: Its influence on personality.* Berlin, Germany: Springer-Verlag.

Esterson, A. (1993). *Seductive mirage: An exploration of the work of Sigmund Freud.* Chicago: Open Court.

Esterson, A. (1998). Jeffrey Masson and Freud's seduction theory: A new fable based on old myths. *History of the Human Sciences, 11,* 1–21.

Esterson, A. (2001). The mythologizing of psychoanalytic history: Deception and self-deception in Freud's accounts of the seduction theory episode. *History of Psychiatry, 12,* 329–352.

Esterson, A. (2002). The myth of Freud's ostracism by the medical community in 1896–1905: Jeffrey Masson's assault on truth. *History of Psychology, 5,* 115–134.

Evans, R. I. (1989). *Albert Bandura: The man and his ideas—A dialogue.* New York: Praeger.

Ewart, C. K. (1978). Self-observation in natural environments: Reactive effects of behavior desirability and goal-setting. *Cognitive Therapy and Research, 2,* 39–56.

Exner, J. E., Jr. (1974). *The Rorschach systems.* New York: Grune & Stratton.

Exner, J. E., Jr. (1993). *The Rorschach: A comprehensive system: Vol. 1. Basic foundations* (3rd ed.). New York: Wiley.

Exner, J. E., Jr. (1996). A comment on "The comprehensive system for the Rorschach: A critical examination." *Psychological Science, 7,* 11–13.

Eysenck, H. J. (1952). *The scientific study of personality.* New York: Macmillan.

Eysenck, H. J. (1961). The effects of psychotherapy. In H. J. Eysenck (Ed.), *Handbook of abnormal psychology.* New York: Basic Books.

Eysenck, H. J. (1964a). *Crime and personality.* Boston: Houghton Mifflin.

Eysenck, H. J. (1964b). Involuntary rest pauses in tapping as a function of drive and personality. *Perceptual and Motor Skills, 18,* 173–174.

Eysenck, H. J. (1967). *The biological basis of personality.* Springfield, IL: Charles C. Thomas.

Eysenck, H. J. (1970). *The structure of human personality* (3rd ed.). London, England: Methuen.

Eysenck, H. J. (1975). *The inequality of man.* San Diego: EdITS.

Eysenck, H. J. (Ed.). (1981). *A model for personality.* Berlin: Springer-Verlag.

Eysenck, H. J. (1983). Psychopharmacology and personality. In W. Janke (Ed.), *Response variability to psychotropic drugs.* London, England: Pergamon.

Eysenck, H. J. (1986). Models and paradigms in personality research. In A. Angleitner, A. Furnham, & G. Van Heck (Eds.), *Personality psychology in Europe, Vol. 2: Current trends and controversies* (pp. 213–223). Lisse, Holland: Swets & Zeitlinger.

Eysenck, H. J. (1992). Four ways five factors are *not* basic. *Personality and Individual Differences, 13,* 667–673.

Eysenck, H. J. (1993). Comment on Goldberg. *American Psychologist, 48,* 1299–1300.

Eysenck, H. J., & Eysenck, M. W. (1985). *Personality and individual differences: A natural science approach.* New York: Plenum.

Eysenck, H. J., & Eysenck, S. B. G. (1975). *Manual of the Eysenck Personality Questionnaire.* San Diego: EdITS.

Eysenck, H. J., & Eysenck, S. B. G. (1976). *Psychoticism as a dimension of personality.* London, England: Hodder & Stoughton.

Fadiga, L., Fogassi, L., Gallese, V., & Rizzolatti, G. (2000). Visuomotor neurons: Ambiguity of the discharge or "motor" perception? *International Journal of Psychophysiology, 35,* 165–177.

Fagot, B. I. (1977). Consequences of moderate cross-gender behavior in preschool children. *Child Development, 48,* 902–907.

Fairbairn, W. R. D. (1952). *Psycho-analytic studies of the personality.* New York: Basic Books.

Fairbairn, W. R. D. (1954). *An object relations theory of personality.* New York: Basic Books.

Fairbanks, L. A. (2001). Individual differences in response to a stranger: Social impulsivity as a dimension of temperament in vervet monkeys (*Cercopithecus aethiops sabaeus*). *Journal of Comparative Psychology, 115,* 22–28.

Falbo, T. (1981). Relationships between birth category, achievement, and interpersonal orientation. *Journal of Personality and Social Psychology, 41,* 121–131.

Faraone, S. V., Taylor, L., & Tsuang, M. (2002). The molecular genetics of schizophrenia: An emerging consensus. *Expert reviews in molecular medicine, 23.* Retrieved from http://www.expertreviews.org/02004751h.htm

Feather, N. T. (1961). The relationship of persistence at a task to expectations of success and achievement-related motivation. *Journal of Abnormal and Social Psychology, 63,* 552–561.

Feather, N. T. (Ed.). (1982). *Expectations and actions: Expectancy–value models in psychology.* Hillsdale, NJ: Erlbaum.

Feeney, B. C. (2004). A secure base: Responsive support of goal strivings and exploration in adult intimate relationships. *Journal of Personality and Social Psychology, 87,* 631–648.

Feeney, B. C. (2006). An attachment theory perspective on the interplay between intrapersonal and interpersonal processes. In K. D. Vohs & E. J. Finkel (Eds.), *Self and relationships* (pp. 133–159). New York: Guilford.

Feeney, B. C., & Cassidy, J. A. (2003). Reconstructive memory related to adolescent-parent conflict interactions: The influence of attachment-related representations on immediate perceptions and changes in perceptions over time. *Journal of Personality and Social Psychology, 85,* 945–955.

Feeney, B. C., & Collins, N. C. (2003). Motivations for caregiving in adult intimate relationships: Influences on caregiving behavior and relationship functioning. *Personality and Social Psychology Bulletin, 29,* 950–968.

Feeney, B. C., & Collins, N. L. (2001). Predictors of caregiving in adult intimate relationships: An attachment theoretical perspective. *Journal of Personality and Social Psychology, 80,* 972–994.

Feeney, J. A., & Noller, P. (1990). Attachment style as a predictor of adult romantic relationships. *Journal of Personality and Social Psychology, 58,* 281–291.

Fehr, E., & Gächter, S. (2002). Altruistic punishment in humans. *Nature, 415,* 137–140.

Feingold, A. (1992). Gender differences in mate selection preferences: A test of the parental investment model. *Psychological Bulletin, 112,* 125–139.

Fekken, G. C., & Holden, R. R. (1992). Response latency evidence for viewing personality traits as schema indicators. *Journal of Research in Personality, 26,* 103–120.

Feldman, F. (1968). Results of psychoanalysis in clinic case assignments. *Journal of the American Psychoanalytic Association, 16,* 274–300.

Fellous, J. -M., & Arbib, M. A. (Eds.). (2005). *Who needs emotions? The brain meets the robot.* New York: Oxford University Press.

Fenichel, O. (1945). *The psychoanalytic theory of neurosis.* New York: Norton.

Fenigstein, A., & Buss, A. H. (1974). Association and affect as determinants of displaced aggression. *Journal of Research in Personality, 7,* 306–313.

Fenigstein, A., Scheier, M. F., & Buss, A. H. (1975). Public and private self-consciousness: Assessment and theory. *Journal of Consulting and Clinical Psychology, 43,* 522–527.

Ferguson, M. J., Bargh, J. A., & Nayak, D. A. (2005). Afteraffects: How automatic evaluations influence the interpretation of subsequent, unrelated stimuli. *Journal of Experimental Social Psychology, 41,* 182–191.

Festinger, L., Pepitone, A., & Newcomb, T. (1952). Some consequences of deindividuation in a group. *Journal of Abnormal and Social Psychology, 47,* 382–389.

Findley, M. J., & Cooper, H. M. (1983). Locus of control and academic achievement: A literature review. *Journal of Personality and Social Psychology, 44,* 419–427.

Finkel, E. J., & Campbell, W. K. (2001). Self-control and accommodation in close relationships: An interdependence analysis. *Journal of Personality and Social Psychology, 81,* 263–277.

Fisher, S. (1973). *The female orgasm.* New York: Basic Books.

Fisher, S., & Greenberg, R. P. (1977). *The scientific credibility of Freud's theories and therapy.* New York: Basic Books.

Fiske, D. W. (1949). Consistency of the factorial structures of personality ratings from different sources. *Journal of Abnormal and Social Psychology, 44,* 329–344.

Fiske, S. T., & Taylor, S. E. (1984). *Social cognition.* Reading, MA: Addison-Wesley.

Fitzsimons, G. M., & Bargh, J. A. (2003). Thinking of you: Nonconscious pursuit of interpersonal goals associated with relationship partners. *Journal of Personality and Social Psychology, 84,* 148–164.

Fitzsimons, G. M., & Bargh, J. A. (2004). Automatic self-regulation. In R. F. Baumeister & K. D. Vohs (Eds.), *Handbook of self-regulation: Research, theory, and applications* (pp. 151–170). New York: Guilford.

Flanders, J. P. (1968). A review of research on imitative behavior. *Psychological Bulletin, 69,* 316–337.

Fleeson, W. (2001). Toward a structure- and process-integrated view of personality: Traits as density distributions of states. *Journal of Personality and Social Psychology, 80,* 1011–1027.

Fleeson, W. (2004). Moving personality beyond the person-situation debate. *Current Directions in Psychological Science, 13,* 83–87.

Fleeson, W., Leicht, C. (2006). On delineating and integrating the study of variability and stability in personality psychology: Interpersonal trust as illustration. *Journal of Research in Personality, 40,* 5–20.

Fleeson, W., Malanos, A. B., & Achille, N. M. (2002). An intraindividual process approach to the relationship between extraversion and positive affect: Is acting extraverted as "good" as being extraverted? *Journal of Personality and Social Psychology, 83,* 1409–1422.

Fletcher, G. J. O., Danilovics, P., Fernandez, G., Peterson, D., & Reeder, G. D. (1986). Attributional complexity: An individual differences measure. *Journal of Personality and Social Psychology, 51,* 875–884.

Flink, C., Boggiano, A. K., & Barrett, M. (1990). Controlling teaching strategies: Undermining children's self-determination and performance. *Journal of Personality and Social Psychology, 59,* 916–924.

Florian, V., Mikulincer, M., & Hirschberger, G. (2002). The anxiety-buffering function of close relationships: Evidence that relationship commitment acts as a terror management mechanism. *Journal of Personality and Social Psychology, 82,* 527–542.

Flory, J. D., Matthews, K. A., & Owens, J. F. (1998). A social information processing approach to dispositional hostility: Relationships with negative mood and blood pressure elevations at work. *Journal of Social and Clinical Psychology, 17,* 491–504.

Flynn, F. J. (2005). Having an open mind: The impact of openness to experience on interracial attitudes and impression formation. *Journal of Personality and Social Psychology, 88,* 816–826.

Foa, E. B., & Meadows, E. A. (1997). Psychosocial treatments for posttraumatic stress disorder: A critical review. *Annual Review of Psychology, 48,* 449–480.

Fodor, E. M. (1984). The power motive and reactivity to power stresses. *Journal of Personality and Social Psychology, 47,* 853–859.

Folkman, S., & Moskowitz, J. T. (2004). Coping: Pitfalls and promise. *Annual Review of Psychology, 55,* 745–774.

Fowles, D. C. (1980). The three arousal model: Implications of Gray's two-factor learning theory for heart rate, electrodermal activity, and psychopathy. *Psychophysiology, 17,* 87–104.

Fox, N. A., & Davidson, R. J. (1988). Patterns of brain electrical activity during facial signs of emotion in 10-month-old infants. *Developmental Psychology, 24,* 230–236.

Fraley, R. C. (2002). Attachment stability from infancy to adulthood: Meta-analysis and dynamic modeling of developmental mechanisms. *Personality and Social Psychology Review, 6,* 123–151.

Fraley, R. C., Garner, J. P., & Shaver, P. R. (2000). Adult attachment and the defensive regulation of attention and memory: Examining the role of preemptive and postemptive defensive processes. *Journal of Personality and Social Psychology, 79,* 816–826.

Fraley, R. C., & Shaver, P. R. (1998). Airport separations: A naturalistic study of adult attachment dynamics in separating couples. *Journal of Personality and Social Psychology, 75,* 1198–1212.

Frank, E., & Brandstätter, V. (2002). Approach versus avoidance: Different types of commitment in intimate relationships. *Journal of Personality and Social Psychology, 82,* 208–221.

Frank, L. K. (1939). Projective methods for the study of personality. *Journal of Psychology, 8,* 389–413.

Frank, M. J., & Claus, E. D. (2006). Anatomy of a decision: Striato-orbitofrontal interactions in reinforcement learning, decision making, and reversal. *Psychological Review, 113,* 300–326.

Frank, M. J., & O'Reilly, R. C. (2006). A mechanistic account of striatal dopamine function in human cognition: Psychopharmacological studies with cabergoline and haloperidol. *Behavioral Neuroscience, 120,* 497–517.

Frank, M. J., Seeberger, L. C., & O'Reilly, R. C. (2004). By carrot or by stick: Cognitive reinforcement learning in Parkinsonism. *Science, 306,* 1940–1943.

Frank, S., & Quinlan, D. M. (1976). Ego development and female delinquency: A cognitive-developmental approach. *Journal of Abnormal Psychology, 85,* 505–510.

Frankel, A., & Snyder, M. L. (1978). Poor performance following unsolvable problems: Learned helplessness or egotism? *Journal of Personality and Social Psychology, 36,* 1415–1423.

Frankl, V. E. (1969). *The doctor and the soul.* New York: Bantam.

Fransella, F. (1972). *Personal change and reconstruction.* New York: Academic.

Freedman, J. L. (1986). Television violence and aggression: A rejoinder. *Psychological Bulletin, 100,* 372–378.

French, E. G. (1955). Some characteristics of achievement motivation. *Journal of Experimental Psychology, 50,* 232–236.

Freud, A. (1966). *The ego and the mechanisms of defense* (Rev. ed.). New York: International Universities Press.

Freud, S. (1933). *New introductory lectures on psychoanalysis.* New York: Norton. (Translated by W. J. H. Sprott)

Freud, S. (1936). *The problem of anxiety.* New York: Norton. (Translated by H. A. Bunker; originally published, 1926)

Freud, S. (1949). *An outline of psychoanalysis.* New York: Norton. (Translated by J. Strachey; originally published, 1940)

Freud, S. (1953a). Three essays on sexuality. In J. Strachey (Ed.), *The standard edition of the complete psychological works of Sigmund Freud* (Vol. 7). London, England: Hogarth. (Originally published, 1905)

Freud, S. (1953b). The interpretation of dreams. In J. Strachey (Ed.), *The standard edition of the complete psychological works of Sigmund Freud* (Vols. 4 and 5). London: Hogarth Press. (Originally published, 1900)

Freud, S. (1955). Beyond the pleasure principle. In J. Strachey (Ed.), *The standard edition of the complete psychological works of Sigmund Freud* (Vol. 18). London, England: Hogarth. (Originally published, 1920)

Freud, S. (1959). Inhibitions, symptoms and anxiety. In J. Strachey (Ed.), *The standard edition of the complete psychological works of Sigmund Freud* (Vol. 20). London, England: Hogarth. (Originally published, 1926)

Freud, S. (1960a). *Jokes and their relation to the unconscious.* New York: Norton. (Translated by J. Strachey, originally published, 1905)

Freud, S. (1960b). Psychopathology of everyday life. In J. Strachey (Ed.), *The standard edition of the complete psychological works of Sigmund Freud* (Vol. 6). London, England: Hogarth. (Originally published, 1901)

Freud, S. (1961). The unconscious. In J. Strachey (Ed.), *The standard edition of the complete psychological works of Sigmund Freud* (Vol. 14). London, England: Hogarth. (Originally published, 1915)

Freud, S. (1962). *The ego and the id.* New York: Norton. (Originally published, 1923)

Freund, A. M., & Baltes, P. B. (2002). Life-management strategies of selection, optimization, and compensation. Measurement by self-report and construct validity. *Journal of Personality and Social Psychology, 82,* 642–662.

Freyd, J. J. (1987). Dynamic mental representations. *Psychological Review, 94,* 427–438.

Freyd, J. J. (1996). *Betrayal trauma: The logic of forgetting childhood abuse.* Cambridge, MA: Harvard.

Friedman, H. S., Tucker, J. S., Schwartz, J. E., Martin, L. R., Tomlinson-Keasey, C., Wingard, D. L., & Criqui, M. H. (1995). Childhood conscientiousness and longevity: Health behaviors and cause of death. *Journal of Personality and Social Psychology, 68,* 696–701.

Friedman, L. J. (1999). *Identity's architect: A biography of Erik H. Erikson.* New York: Scribner.

Fritz, H. L., & Helgeson, V. S. (1998). Distinctions of unmitigated communion from communion: Self-neglect and overinvolvement with others. *Journal of Personality and Social Psychology, 75,* 121–140.

Frodi, A. (1977). Sexual arousal, situational restrictiveness, and aggressive behavior. *Journal of Research in Personality, 11,* 48–58.

Fujita, K., Trope, Y., Liberman, N., & Leven-Sagi, M. (2006). Construal levels and self-control. *Journal of Personality and Social Psychology, 90,* 351–567.

Fukuyama, F. (2002). *Our posthuman future: Consequences of the biotechnology revolution.* New York: Farrar, Straus, & Giroux.

Fultz, J., Schaller, M., & Cialdini, R. B. (1988). Empathy, sadness, and distress: Three related but distinct vicarious affective responses to another's suffering. *Personality and Social Psychology Bulletin, 14,* 312–325.

Funder, D. C. (1991). Global traits: A neo-Allportian approach to personality. *Psychological Science, 2,* 31–39.

Funder, D. C. (2001). Personality. *Annual Review of Psychology, 52,* 197–221.

Funder, D. C., & Block, J. (1989). The role of ego-control, ego-resiliency, and IQ in delay of gratification in adolescence. *Journal of Personality and Social Psychology, 57,* 1041–1050.

Funder, D. C., Block, J. H., & Block, J. (1983). Delay of gratification: Some longitudinal personality correlates. *Journal of Personality and Social Psychology, 44,* 1198–1213.

Funder, D. C., & Colvin, C. R. (1991). Explorations in behavioral consistency: Properties of persons, situations, and behaviors. *Journal of Personality and Social Psychology, 60,* 773–794.

Funder, D. C., & Ozer, D. J. (1983). Behavior as a function of the situation. *Journal of Personality and Social Psychology, 44,* 107–112.

Furr, R. M., & Funder, D. C. (2004). Situational similarity and behavioral consistency: Subjective, objective, variable-centered, and person-centered approaches. *Journal of Research in Personality, 38,* 421–447.

Gable, S. L. (2006). Approach and avoidance social motives and goals. *Journal of Personality, 74,* 175–222.

Gable, S. L., Reis, H. T., & Elliot, A. J. (2000). Behavioral activation and inhibition in everyday life. *Journal of Personality and Social Psychology, 78,* 1135–1149.

Gacsaly, S. A., & Borges, C. A. (1979). The male physique and behavioral expectancies. *Journal of Psychology, 101,* 97–102.

Gallagher, W. (1994). How we become what we are. *Atlantic Monthly, 274,* 39–55.

Gallese, V. (2001). The "shared manifold" hypothesis: From mirror neurons to empathy. *Journal of Consciousness Studies, 8,* 33–50.

Gallistel, C. R. (1980). *The organization of action: A new synthesis.* Hillsdale, NJ: Erlbaum.

Ganellen, R. J. (1996a). Comparing the diagnostic efficiency of the MMPMI, MCMI-II, and Rorschach: A review. *Journal of Personality Assessment, 67,* 219–243.

Ganellen, R. J. (1996b). *Integrating the Rorschach and MMPI-2 in personality assessment.* Hillsdale, NJ: Erlbaum.

Gangestad, S. W., & Simpson, J. A. (2000). The evolution of human mating: Trade-offs and strategic pluralism. *Behavioral and Brain Sciences, 23,* 573–587.

Gangestad, S. W., & Snyder, M. (1985). "To carve nature at its joints": On the existence of discrete classes in personality. *Psychological Review, 92,* 317–349.

Garcia, J., & Koelling, R. A. (1966). Relation of cue to consequence in avoidance learning. *Psychonomic Science, 4,* 123–124.

Gardner, H. (1985). *The mind's new science: A history of the cognitive revolution.* New York: Basic Books.

Gauthier, J., & Ladouceur, R. (1981). The influence of self-efficacy reports on performance. *Behavior Therapy, 12,* 436–439.

Geen, R. G. (1981). Behavioral and physiological reactions to observed violence: Effects of prior exposure to aggressive stimuli. *Journal of Personality and Social Psychology, 40,* 868–875.

Geen, R. G. (1984). Preferred stimulation levels in introverts and extraverts: Effects on arousal and performance. *Journal of Personality and Social Psychology, 46,* 1303–1312.

Geen, R. G. (1998). Aggression and antisocial behavior. In D. T. Gilbert, S. T. Fiske, & G. Lindzey (Eds.), *The handbook of social psychology* (Vol. 2, 4th ed., pp. 317–356). Boston: McGraw-Hill.

Geen, R. G., Stonner, D., & Shope, G. L. (1975). The facilitation of aggression by aggression: Evidence against the catharsis hypothesis. *Journal of Personality and Social Psychology, 31,* 721–726.

George, D. T., Umhau, J. C., Phillips, M. J., Emmela, D., Ragan, P. W., Shoaf, S. E., & Rawlings, R. R. (2001). Serotonin, testosterone, and alcohol in the etiology of domestic violence. *Psychiatry Research, 104,* 27–37.

Gerst, M. S. (1971). Symbolic coding processes in observational learning. *Journal of Personality and Social Psychology, 19,* 7–27.

Giancola, P. R. (2004). Executive functioning and alcohol-related aggression. *Journal of Abnormal Psychology, 113,* 541–555.

Gibson, H. B. (1981). *Hans Eysenck: The man and his work.* London, England: Peter Owen.

Gigerenzer, G., & Goldstein, D. G. (1996). Reasoning the fast and frugal way: Models of bounded rationality. *Psychological Review, 103,* 650–669.

Gill, M. M. (1959). The present state of psychoanalytic theory. *Journal of Abnormal and Social Psychology, 58,* 1–8.

Gilovich, T. (1990). Differential construal and the false consensus effect. *Journal of Personality and Social Psychology, 59,* 623–634.

Giltay, E. J., Kamphuis, M. H., Kalmijn, S., Zitman, F. G., & Kromhout, D. (2006). Dispositional optimism and the risk of cardiovascular death: The Zutphen elderly study. *Archives of Internal Medicine, 166,* 431–436.

Glassman, N. S., & Andersen, S. M. (1999). Activating transference without consciousness: Using significant-other representations to go beyond what is subliminally given. *Journal of Personality and Social Psychology, 77,* 1146–1162.

Glue, P., Wilson, S., Coupland, N., Ball, D., & Nutt, D. (1995). The relationship between benzodiazepine receptor sensitivity and neuroticism. *Journal of Anxiety Disorders, 9,* 33–45.

Glueck, S., & Glueck, E. (1956). *Physique and delinquency.* New York: Harper.

Goddard, A. W., Mason, G. F., Almai, A., Rothman, D. L., Behar, K. L., Petroff, O. A. C., Charney, D. S., & Krystal, J. H. (2001). Reductions in occipital cortex GABA levels in panic disorder detected with H-Magnetic resonance spectroscopy. *Archives of General Psychiatry, 58,* 556–561.

Goldberg, A. (Ed.). (1985). *Progress in self psychology* (Vol. 1). New York: Guilford.

Goldberg, L. R. (1981). Language and individual differences: The search for universals in personality lexicons. In L. Wheeler (Ed.), *Review of personality and social psychology* (Vol. 2, pp. 141–165). Beverly Hills, CA: Sage.

Goldberg, L. R. (1982). From ace to zombie: Some explorations in the language of personality. In C. D. Spielberger & J. N. Butcher (Eds.), *Advances in personality assessment* (Vol. 1). Hillsdale, NJ: Erlbaum.

Goldberg, L. R. (1993a). The structure of personality traits: Vertical and horizontal aspects. In D. C. Funder, R. Parke, C. Tomlinson-Keasey, & K. Widaman (Eds.), *Studying lives through time: Approaches to personality and development* (pp. 169–188). Washington, DC: American Psychological Association.

Goldberg, L. R. (1993b). The structure of phenotypic personality traits. *American Psychologist, 48,* 26–34.

Goldenberg, J. L., Pyszczynski, T., Greenberg, J., & Solomon, S. (2000). Fleeing the body: A terror management perspective on the problem of human corporeality. *Personality and Social Psychology Review, 4,* 200–218.

Goldenberg, J. L., Pyszczynski, T., Greenberg, J., Solomon, S., Kluck, B., & Cornwell, R. (2001). I am *not* an animal: Mortality salience, disgust, and the denial of human creatureliness. *Journal of Experimental Psychology: General, 130,* 427–435.

Goldfield, G. S., & Epstein, L. H. (2002). Can fruits and vegetables and activities substitute for snack foods? *Health Psychology, 21,* 299–303.

Goldfried, M. R. (1971). Systematic desensitization as training in self-control. *Journal of Consulting and Clinical Psychology, 37,* 228–234.

Goldfried, M. R., & Davison, G. C. (1976). *Clinical behavior therapy.* New York: Holt, Rinehart, & Winston.

Goldfried, M. R., & Merbaum, M. (Eds.). (1973). *Behavior change through self-control.* New York: Holt, Rinehart, & Winston.

Goldiamond, I. (1976). Self-reinforcement. *Journal of Applied Behavior Analysis, 9,* 509–514.

Goldstein, J. H., & Arms, R. L. (1971). Effects of observing athletic contests on hostility. *Sociometry, 34,* 90–93.

Gollwitzer, P. M. (1999). Implementation intentions: Strong effects of simple plans. *American Psychologist, 54,* 493–503.

Gollwitzer, P. M, & Brandstätter, V. (1997). Implementation intentions and effective goal pursuit. *Journal of Personality and Social Psychology, 73,* 186–199.

Goranson, R. E. (1970). Media violence and aggressive behavior: A review of experimental research. In L. Berkowitz (Ed.), *Advances in experimental social psychology* (Vol. 5). New York: Academic.

Gosling, S. D. (2001). From mice to men: What can we learn about personality from animal research? *Psychological Bulletin, 127,* 45–86.

Gotlib, I. H. (1983). Perception and recall of interpersonal feedback: Negative bias in depression. *Cognitive Therapy and Research, 7,* 399–412.

Gottesman, I. I., & Shields, J. (1972). *Schizophrenia and genetics.* New York: Academic.

Gould, R. L. (1980). Transformations during early and middle adult years. In N. J. Smelser & E. H. Erikson (Eds.), *Themes of work and love in adulthood* (pp. 213–237). Cambridge, MA: Harvard University Press.

Govorun, O., Fuegen, K., & Payne, B. K. (2006). Stereotypes focus defensive projection. *Personality and Social Psychology Bulletin, 32,* 781–793.

Grammer, K., & Thornhill, R. (1994). Human facial attractiveness and sexual selection: The role of symmetry and averageness. *Journal of Comparative Psychology, 108,* 233–242.

Gray, J. (1992). *Men are from Mars, women are from Venus: A practical guide for improving communication and getting what you want in your relationships.* New York: HarperCollins.

Gray, J. A. (1982). *The neuropsychology of anxiety: An enquiry into the functions of the septo-hippocampal system.* New York: Oxford University Press.

Gray, J. A. (1987). Perspectives on anxiety and impulsivity: A commentary. *Journal of Research in Personality, 21,* 493–509.

Gray, J. A. (1990). Brain systems that mediate both emotion and cognition. *Cognition and Emotion, 4,* 269–288.

Gray, J. A. (1991). The neuropsychology of temperament. In J. Strelau & A. Angleitner (Eds.), *Explorations in temperament: International perspectives on theory and measurement* (pp. 105–128). New York: Plenum.

Gray, J. A. (1994a). Personality dimensions and emotion systems. In P. Ekman & R. J. Davidson (Eds.), *The nature of emotion: Fundamental questions* (pp. 329–331). New York: Oxford University Press.

Gray, J. A. (1994b). Three fundamental emotion systems. In P. Ekman & R. J. Davidson (Eds.), *The nature of emotion: Fundamental questions* (pp. 243–247). New York: Oxford University Press.

Gray, J. A., & McNaughton, N. (2000). *The neuropsychology of anxiety: An enquiry into the functions of the septo-hippocampal system* (2nd ed.). Oxford, England: Oxford University Press.

Gray, J. D., & Silver, R. C. (1990). Opposite sides of the same coin: Former spouses' divergent perspectives in coping with their divorce. *Journal of Personality and Social Psychology, 59,* 1180–1191.

Gray, J. R., & Braver, T. S. (2002). Personality predicts working-memory-related activation in the caudal anterior cingulate cortex. *Cognitive, Affective, & Behavioral Neuroscience, 2,* 64–75.

Graziano, W. G., & Eisenberg, N. H. (1999). Agreeableness as a dimension of personality. In R. Hogan, J. Johnson, & S. Briggs (Eds.), *Handbook of personality* (pp. 795–825). San Diego: Academic.

Graziano, W. G., Jensen-Campbell, L. A., & Hair, E. C. (1996). Perceiving interpersonal conflict and reacting to it: The case for agreeableness. *Journal of Personality and Social Psychology, 70,* 820–835.

Green, J. D., & Campbell, W. K. (2000). Attachment and exploration in adults: Chronic and contextual accessibility. *Personality and Social Psychology Bulletin, 26,* 452–461.

Greenberg, B. D., Li, Q., Lucas, F. R., Hu, S., Sirota, L. A., Benjamin, J., Lesch, K.-P., Hamer, D., & Murphy, D. L. (2000). Association between the serotonin transporter promoter polymorphism and personality traits in a primarily female population sample. *American Journal of Medical Genetics (Neuropsychiatric Genetics), 96,* 202–216.

Greenberg, G. (2005). The limitations of behavior-genetic analyses: Comment on McGue, Elkins, Walden, and Ianoco. *Developmental Psychology, 41,* 989–992.

Greenberg, J., Pyszczynski, T., & Solomon, S. (1982). The self-serving attributional bias: Beyond self-presentation. *Journal of Experimental Social Psychology, 18,* 56–67.

Greenberg, J., Pyszczynski, T., & Solomon, S. (1986). The causes and consequences of a need for self-esteem: A terror management theory. In R. F. Baumeister (Ed.), *Public self and private self* (pp. 189–212). New York: Springer-Verlag.

Greenberg, J., Solomon, S., & Pyszczynski, T. (1997). Terror management theory of self-esteem and social behavior: Empirical assessments and conceptual refinements. In M. P. Zanna (Ed.), *Advances in experimental social psychology* (Vol. 29, pp. 61–139). New York: Academic.

Greene, D. L., & Winter, D. G. (1971). Motives, involvements, and leadership among black college students. *Journal of Personality, 39,* 319–332.

Greenfield, N. S., & Sternbach, R. A. (1972). *Handbook of psychophysiology.* New York: Holt, Rinehart, & Winston.

Greenwald, A. G., & Banaji, M. R. (1989). The self as a memory system: Powerful, but ordinary. *Journal of Personality and Social Psychology, 57,* 41–54.

Greenwald, A. G., Banaji, M. R., Rudman, L. A., Farnham, S. D., Nosek, B. A., & Mellott, D. S. (2002). A unified theory of implicit attitudes, stereotypes, self-esteem, and self-concept. *Psychological Review, 109,* 3–25.

Greenwald, A. G., McGhee, D. E., & Schwartz, J. L. K. (1998). Measuring individual differences in implicit cognition: The implicit association test. *Journal of Personality and Social Psychology, 74,* 1464–1480.

Greenwald, A. G., & Pratkanis, R. A. (1984). The self. In R. S. Wyer, Jr., & T. K. Srull (Eds.), *Handbook of social cognition* (Vol. 3). Hillsdale, NJ: Erlbaum.

Greer, S., & Morris, T. (1975). Psychological attributes of women who develop breast cancer: A controlled study. *Journal of Psychosomatic Research, 19,* 147–153.

Grewen, K. M., Gridler, S. S., Amico, J., & Light, K. C. (2005). Effects of partner support on resting oxytocin, cortisol, norepinephrine, and blood pressure before and after warm partner contact. *Psychosomatic Medicine, 67,* 531–538.

Griffin, D., & Bartholomew, K. (1994). Models of the self and other: Fundamental dimensions underlying measures of adult attachment. *Journal of Personality and Social Psychology, 67,* 430–445.

Grigsby, J., & Stevens, D. (2000). *Neurodynamics of personality.* New York: Guilford.

Grimes, J. M., Ricci, L. A., & Melloni, R. H., Jr. (2006). Plasticity in anterior hypothalamic vasopressin correlates with aggression during anabolic-androgenic steroid withdrawal in hamsters. *Behavioral Neuroscience, 120,* 115–124.

Grings, W. W. (1973). The role of consciousness and cognition in autonomic behavior change. In F. J. McGuigan & R. Schoonover (Eds.), *The psychophysiology of thinking.* New York: Academic.

Grolnick, W. S., & Ryan, R. M. (1989). Parent styles associated with children's self-regulation and competence in school. *Journal of Educational Psychology, 81,* 143–154.

Grossmann, K. E., Grossmann, K., & Waters, E. (2005). *Attachment from infancy to adulthood: The major longitudinal studies.* New York: Guilford.

Grouzet, F. M. E., Kasser, T., Ahuvia, A., Fernández Dols, J. M., Kim, Y., Lau, S., Ryan, R. M., Saunders, S., Schmuck, P., & Sheldon, K. M. (2005). The structure of goal contents across 15 cultures. *Journal of Personality and Social Psychology, 89,* 800–816.

Gruber, A. J., & Pope, H. G., Jr. (2000). Psychiatric and medical effects of anabolic-androgenic steroid use in women. *Psychotherapy and Psychosomatics, 69,* 19–26.

Gruen, R. J., & Mendelsohn, G. (1986). Emotional responses to affective displays in others: The distinction between empathy and sympathy. *Journal of Personality and Social Psychology, 51,* 609–614.

Guisinger, S., & Blatt, S. J. (1994). Individuality and relatedness: Evolution of a fundamental dialectic. *American Psychologist, 49,* 104–111.

Gurin, P., Gurin, G., Lao, R. C., & Beattie, M. (1969). Internal-external control in the motivational dynamics of Negro youth. *Journal of Social Issues, 25,* 29–53.

Gutierres, S. E., Kenrick, D. T., & Partch, J. J. (1999). Beauty, dominance, and the mating game: Contrast effects in self-assessment reflect gender differences in mate selection. *Personality and Social Psychology Bulletin, 25,* 1126–1134.

Haaga, D. A. F., Dyck, M. J., & Ernst, D. (1991). Empirical status of cognitive theory of depression. *Psychological Bulletin, 110,* 215–236.

Haan, N. (1981). Common dimensions of personality development: Early adolescence to middle life. In D. H. Eichorn, J. A. Clausen, N. Haan, M. P. Honzik, & P. H. Mussen (Eds.), *Present and past in middle life* (pp. 117–151). New York: Academic.

Haas, H. A. (2002). Extending the search for folk personality constructs: The dimensionality of the personality-relevant proverb domain. *Journal of Personality and Social Psychology, 82,* 594–609.

Hackett, G., & Horan, J. J. (1979). Partial component analysis of a comprehensive smoking program. *Addictive Behaviors, 4,* 259–262.

Haemmerlie, F. M., & Montgomery, R. L. (1984). Purposefully biased interactions: Reducing heterosocial anxiety through self-perception theory. *Journal of Personality and Social Psychology, 47,* 900–908.

Hall, R. V., Lund, D., & Jackson, D. (1968). Effects of teacher attention on study behavior. *Journal of Applied Behavior Analysis, 1,* 1–12.

Halpern, J. (1977). Projection: A test of the psychoanalytic hypothesis. *Journal of Abnormal Psychology, 86,* 536–542.

Halverson, C. F., Jr., Kohnstamm, G. A., & Martin, R. P. (Eds.). (1994). *The developing structure of temperament and personality from infancy to adulthood.* Hillsdale, NJ: Erlbaum.

Hamilton, J. C., Greenberg, J., Pyszczynski, T., & Cather, C. (1993). A self-regulatory perspective on psychopathology and psychotherapy. *Journal of Psychotherapy Integration, 3,* 205–248.

Hamilton, W. D. (1964). The genetical evolution of social behavior. *Journal of Theoretical Biology, 7,* 1–52.

Hampson, S. E., Andrews, J. A., Barckley, M., Lichtenstein, E., & Lee, M. E. (2000). Conscientiousness, perceived risk, and risk-reduction behaviors: A preliminary study. *Health Psychology, 19,* 496–500.

Hampson, S. E., Goldberg, L. R., Vogt, T. M., & Dubanoski, J. P. (2006). Forty years on: Teachers' assessments of children's personality traits predict self-reported health behaviors and outcomes at midlife. *Health Psychology, 25,* 57–64.

Handley, S. L. (1995). 5-Hydroxytryptamine pathways in anxiety and its treatment. *Pharmacology & Therapeutics, 66,* 103–148.

Hankin, B. L., Kassel, J. D., & Abela, J. R. Z. (2005). Adult attachment dimensions and specificity of emotional distress symptoms: Prospective investigations of cognitive risk and interpersonal stress generation as mediating mechanisms. *Personality and Social Psychology Bulletin, 31,* 136–151.

Hansenne, M., Pinto, E., Pitchot, W., Reggers, J., Scantamburlo, G., Moor, M., & Ansseau, M. (2002). Further evidence on the relationship between dopamine and novelty seeking: A neuroendocrine study. *Personality and Individual Differences, 33,* 967–977.

Harackiewicz, J. M. (1979). The effects of reward contingency and performance feedback on intrinsic motivation. *Journal of Personality and Social Psychology, 37,* 1352–1363.

Hardy, K. R. (1957). Determinants of conformity and attitude change. *Journal of Abnormal and Social Psychology, 54,* 289–294.

Harmon-Jones, E., & Allen, J. J. (1997). Behavioral activation sensitivity and resting frontal EEG asymmetry: Covariation of putative indicators related to risk for mood disorders. *Journal of Abnormal Psychology, 106,* 159–163.

Harmon-Jones, E., Lueck, L., Fearn, M., & Harmon-Jones, C. (2006). The effect of personal relevance and approach-related action expectation on relative left frontal cortical activity. *Psychological Science, 17,* 434–440.

Harmon-Jones, E., & Sigelman, J. D. (2001). State anger and prefrontal brain activity: Evidence that insult-related relative left-prefrontal activation is associated with experienced anger and aggression. *Journal of Personality and Social Psychology, 80,* 797–803.

Harmon-Jones, E., Vaughn-Scott, K., Mohr, S., Sigelman, J., & Harmon-Jones, C. (2004). The effect of manipulated sympathy and anger on left and right frontal cortical activity. *Emotion, 4,* 95–101.

Harris, C. R. (2002). Sexual and romantic jealousy in heterosexual and homosexual adults. *Psychological Science, 13,* 7–12.

Harris, C. R. (2003). A review of sex differences in sexual jealousy, including self-report data, psychophysiological responses, interpersonal violence, and morbid jealousy. *Personality and Social Psychology Review, 7,* 102–128.

Harris, J. R. (1995). Where is the child's environment? A group socialization theory of development. *Psychological Review, 102,* 458–489.

Harrison, R. J., Connor, D. F., Nowak, C., Nash, K., & Melloni, R. H., Jr. (2000). Chronic anabolic-androgenic steroid treatment during adolescence increases anterior hypothalamic vasopressin and aggression in intact hamsters. *Psychoneuroendocrinology, 25,* 317–338.

Hart, D., Keller, M., Edelstein, W., & Hofmann, V. (1998). Childhood personality influences on social-cognitive development: A longitudinal study. *Journal of Personality and Social Psychology, 74,* 1278–1289.

Hart, H. M., McAdams, D. P., Hirsch, B. J., & Bauer, J. J. (2001). Generativity and social involvement among African Americans and white adults. *Journal of Research in Personality, 35,* 208–230.

Hartmann, H. (1958). *Ego psychology and the problem of adaptation.* New York: International Universities Press. (Originally published, 1939)

Hartmann, H. (1964). *Essays on ego psychology: Selected problems in psychoanalytic theory.* New York: International Universities Press.

Hassin, R. R., Bargh, J. A., & Uleman, J. S. (2002). Spontaneous causal inferences. *Journal of Experimental Social Psychology, 38,* 515–522.

Hassin, R. R., Uleman, J. S., & Bargh, J. A. (Eds.). (2005). *The new unconscious.* New York: Oxford University Press.

Hathaway, S. R., & McKinley, J. C. (1943). *MMPI manual.* New York: Psychological Corporation.

Hauser, S. T. (1976). Loevinger's model and measure of ego development: A critical review. *Psychological Bulletin, 83,* 928–955.

Haviland, J. M., McGuire, T. R., & Rothbaum, P. A. (1983). A critique of Plomin and Foch's "A twin study of objectively assessed personality in childhood." *Journal of Personality and Social Psychology, 45,* 633–640.

Hayes, S. C., Rincover, A., & Volosin, D. (1980). Variables influencing the acquisition and maintenance of aggressive behavior: Modeling versus sensory reinforcement. *Journal of Abnormal Psychology, 89,* 254–262.

Hayes-Roth, B., & Hayes-Roth, F. (1979). A cognitive model of planning. *Cognitive Science, 3,* 275–310.

Haynes, S. N., & O'Brien, W. H. (2000). *Principles and practice of behavioral assessment.* Amsterdam, The Netherlands: Kluwer.

Hazan, C., & Shaver, P. R. (1987). Romantic love conceptualized as an attachment process. *Journal of Personality and Social Psychology, 52,* 511–524.

Hazan, C., & Shaver, P. R. (1990). Love and work: An attachment-theoretical perspective. *Journal of Personality and Social Psychology, 59,* 270–280.

Hazan, C., & Shaver, P. R. (1994). Attachment as an organizational framework for research on close relationships. *Psychological Inquiry, 5,* 1–22.

Hazen, N. L., & Durrett, M. E. (1982). Relationship of security of attachment to exploration and cognitive mapping abilities in 2-year-olds. *Developmental Psychology, 18,* 751–759.

Heath, A. C., Neale, M. C., Kessler, R. C., Eaves, L. J., & Kendler, K. S. (1992). Evidence for genetic influences on personality from self-reports and informant ratings. *Journal of Personality and Social Psychology, 63,* 85–96.

Heckhausen, H. (1967). *The anatomy of achievement motivation.* New York: Academic.

Heckhausen, H., & Gollwitzer, P. M. (1987). Thought contents and cognitive functioning in motivational versus volitional states of mind. *Motivation and Emotion, 11,* 101–120.

Heckhausen, H., Schmalt, H. D., & Schneider, K. (1985). *Achievement motivation in perspective.* New York: Academic.

Heiby, E. M. (1982). A self-reinforcement questionnaire. *Behaviour Research and Therapy, 20,* 397–401.

Heider, F. (1944). Social perception and phenomenal causation. *Psychological Review, 51,* 358–374.

Heider, F. (1958). *The psychology of interpersonal relations.* New York: Wiley.

Heilbrun, K. S. (1980). Silverman's psychodynamic activation: A failure to replicate. *Journal of Abnormal Psychology, 89,* 560–566.

Helgeson, V. S. (1994). Relation of agency and communion to well-being: Evidence and potential explanations. *Psychological Bulletin, 116,* 412–428.

Helgeson, V. S. (2003). Gender-related traits and health. In J. Suls & K. A. Wallston (Eds.), *Social psychological foundations of health and illness* (pp. 367–394). Oxford, England: Blackwell.

Helgeson, V. S., & Fritz, H. L. (1998). A theory of unmitigated communion. *Personality and Social Psychology Review, 2,* 173–183.

Helgeson, V. S., & Fritz, H. L. (1999). Unmitigated agency and unmitigated communion: Distinctions from agency and communion. *Journal of Research in Personality, 33,* 131–158.

Helgeson, V. S., Reynolds, K. A., & Tomich, P. L. (2006). A meta-analytic approach to benefit finding and health. *Journal of Consulting and Clinical Psychology, 74,* 797–816.

Heller, M. S., & Polsky, S. (1975). *Studies in violence and television.* New York: American Broadcasting Companies.

Helmreich, R. L., LeFan, J. H., Bakeman, R., Wilhelm, J., & Radloff, R. (1972). The Tektite 2 human behavior program. *JSAS Catalog of Selected Documents in Psychology, 2,* 13 (MS no. 70).

Helson, R., & Moane, G. (1987). Personality change in women from college to midlife. *Journal of Personality and Social Psychology, 53,* 176–186.

Helson, R., & Roberts, B. W. (1994). Ego development and personality change in adulthood. *Journal of Personality and Social Psychology, 66,* 911–920.

Helson, R., Jones, C., & Kwan, V. S. Y. (2002). Personality change over 40 years of adulthood: Hierarchical linear modeling analyses of two longitudinal samples. *Journal of Personality and Social Psychology, 83,* 752–766.

Helson, R., Kwan, V. S. Y., John, O. P., & Jones, C. (2002). The growing evidence for personality change in adulthood: Findings from research with personality inventories. *Journal of Research in Personality, 36,* 287–306.

Helson, R., & Srivastava, S. (2002). Creative and wise people: Similarities, differences, and how they develop. *Personality and Social Psychology Bulletin, 28,* 1430–1440.

Henderlong, J., & Lepper, M. R. (2002). The effects of praise on children's intrinsic motivation: A review and synthesis. *Psychological Bulletin, 128,* 774–795.

Hennig, J., Reuter, M., Netter, P., Burk, C., & Landt, O. (2005). Two types of aggression are differentially related to serotonergic activity and the A779C TPH polymorphism. *Behavioral Neuroscience, 119,* 16–25.

Henriques, J. B., & Davidson, R. J. (1990). Asymmetrical brain electrical activity discriminates between previously depressed subjects and healthy controls. *Journal of Abnormal Psychology, 99,* 22–31.

Henriques, J. B., & Davidson, R. J. (1991). Left frontal hypoactivation in depression. *Journal of Abnormal Psychology, 100,* 535–545.

Hersch, P. D., & Scheibe, K. E. (1967). Reliability and validity of internal-external control as personality dimensions. *Journal of Consulting Psychology, 31,* 609–613.

Hersen, M., & Bellack, A. (Eds.). (1976). *Behavioral assessment.* New York: Pergamon.

Heschl, A. (2002). *The intelligent genome: On the origin of the human mind by mutation and selection.* New York: Springer-Verlag.

Hess, E. H. (1973). *Imprinting.* New York: Van Nostrand Reinhold.

Hewitt, P. L., & Genest, M. (1990). The ideal self: Schematic processing of perfectionistic content in dysphoric university students. *Journal of Personality and Social Psychology, 59,* 802–808.

Higgins, E. T. (1987). Self-discrepancy: A theory relating self and affect. *Psychological Review, 94,* 319–340.

Higgins, E. T. (1990). Personality, social psychology, and person–situation relations: Standards and knowledge activation as a common language. In L. A. Pervin (Ed.), *Handbook of personality: Theory and research* (pp. 301–338). New York: Guilford.

Higgins, E. T. (1997). Beyond pleasure and pain. *American Psychologist, 52,* 1280–1300.

Higgins, E. T., & Bargh, J. A. (1987). Social cognition and social perception. *Annual Review of Psychology, 38,* 369–425.

Higgins, E. T., Bond, R. N., Klein, R., & Strauman, T. (1986). Self-discrepancies and emotional vulnerability: How magnitude, accessibility and type of discrepancy influence affect. *Journal of Personality and Social Psychology, 51,* 1–15.

Higgins, E. T., & Brendl, C. M. (1995). Accessibility and applicability: Some "activation rules" influencing judgment. *Journal of Experimental Social Psychology, 31,* 218–243.

Higgins, E. T., King, G. A., & Mavin, G. H. (1982). Individual construct accessibility and subjective impressions and recall. *Journal of Personality and Social Psychology, 43,* 35–47.

Higgins, R. L., Snyder, C. R., & Berglas, S. (Eds.). (1990). *Self-handicapping: The paradox that isn't.* New York: Plenum.

Higgins, S. T., Wong, C. J., Badger, G. J., Haug Ogden, D. E., & Dantona, R. L. (2000). Contingent reinforcement increases cocaine abstinence during outpatient treatment and 1 year of follow-up. *Journal of Consulting and Clinical Psychology, 68,* 64–72.

Hill, C. A. (1987). Affiliation motivation: People who need people . . . but in different ways. *Journal of Personality and Social Psychology, 52,* 1008–1018.

Hill, C. A. (1991). Seeking emotional support: The influence of affiliative need and partner warmth. *Journal of Personality and Social Psychology, 60,* 112–121.

Hill, T., Lewicki, P., Czyzewska, M., & Boss, A. (1989). Self-perpetuating development of encoding biases in person perception. *Journal of Personality and Social Psychology, 57,* 373–387.

Hillix, W. A., & Marx, M. H. (1960). Response strengthening by information and effect on human learning. *Journal of Experimental Psychology, 60,* 97–102.

Hilton, N. Z., Harris, G. T., & Rice, M. E. (2000). The functions of aggression by male teenagers. *Journal of Personality and Social Psychology, 79,* 988–994.

Hinkley, K., & Andersen, S. M. (1996). The working self-concept in transference: Significant-other activation and self change. *Journal of Personality and Social Psychology, 71,* 1279–1295.

Hiroto, D. S., & Seligman, M. E. P. (1975). Generality of learned helplessness in man. *Journal of Personality and Social Psychology, 31,* 311–327.

Hirt, E. R., McCrea, S. M., & Boris, H. I. (2003). "I know you self-handicapped last exam": Gender differences in reactions to self-handicapping. *Journal of Personality and Social Psychology, 84,* 177–193.

Hobfoll, S. E., Rom, T., & Segal, B. (1989). Sensation seeking, anxiety, and risk taking in the Israeli context. In S. Einstein (Ed.), *Drugs and alcohol use: Issues and factors* (pp. 53–59). New York: Plenum.

Hobson, J. A. (1988). *The dreaming brain.* New York: Basic Books.

Hodgins, H. S., Koestner, R., & Duncan, N. (1996). On the compatibility of autonomy and relatedness. *Personality and Social Psychology Bulletin, 22,* 227–237.

Hodgkinson, S., Sherrington, R., Gurling, H., Marchbanks, R., & Reeders, S. (1987). Molecular genetic evidence for heterogeneity in manic depression. *Nature, 325,* 805–806.

Hoffman, E. (1988). *The right to be human: A biography of Abraham Maslow.* Los Angeles: Jeremy P. Tarcher.

Hoffman, E. (1994). *The drive for self: Alfred Adler and the founding of individual psychology.* Reading, MA: Addison-Wesley.

Hoffman, L. W. (1991). The influence of the family environment on personality: Accounting for sibling differences. *Psychological Bulletin, 110,* 187–203.

Hofstee, W. K. B., de Raad, B., & Goldberg, L. R. (1992). Integration of the big five and circumplex approaches to trait structure. *Journal of Personality and Social Psychology, 63,* 146–163.

Hogan, R., & Nicholson, R. A. (1988). The meaning of personality test scores. *American Psychologist, 43,* 621–626.

Hogan, R., DeSoto, C. B., & Solano, C. (1977). Traits, tests, and personality research. *American Psychologist, 32,* 255–264.

Hogansen, J., & Lanning, K. (2001). Five factors in sentence-completion test categories: Toward rapprochement between trait and maturational approaches to personality. *Journal of Research in Personality, 35,* 449–462.

Hokanson, J. E., & Burgess, M. (1962a). The effects of status, type of frustration, and aggression on vascular processes. *Journal of Abnormal and Social Psychology, 65,* 232–237.

Hokanson, J. E., & Burgess, M. (1962b). The effects of three types of aggression on vascular processes. *Journal of Abnormal and Social Psychology, 64,* 446–449.

Hokanson, J. E., Burgess, M., & Cohen, M. F. (1963). Effects of displaced aggression on systolic blood pressure. *Journal of Abnormal and Social Psychology, 67,* 214–218.

Hokanson, J. E., & Edelman, R. (1966). Effects of three social responses on vascular processes. *Journal of Personality and Social Psychology, 3,* 442–447.

Hokanson, J. E., & Shetler, S. (1961). The effect of overt aggression on physiological arousal. *Journal of Abnormal and Social Psychology, 63,* 446–448.

Hokanson, J. E., Willers, K. R., & Koropsak, E. (1968). The modification of autonomic responses during aggressive interchanges. *Journal of Personality, 36,* 386–404.

Holahan, C. J., Moos, R. H., Holahan, C. K., Cronkite, R. C., & Randall, P. K. (2003). Drinking to cope and alcohol use and abuse in unipolar depression: A 10-year model. *Journal of Abnormal Psychology, 112,* 159–165.

Holden, K. B., & Rotter, J. B. (1962). A nonverbal measure of extinction in skill and chance situations. *Journal of Experimental Psychology, 63,* 519–520.

Holmes, D. (1972). Aggression, displacement and guilt. *Journal of Personality and Social Psychology, 21,* 296–301.

Holmes, D. S. (1981). Existence of classical projection and the stress-reducing function of attribution projection: A reply to Sherwood. *Psychological Bulletin, 90,* 460–466.

Holroyd, C. B., & Coles, M. G. H. (2002). The neural basis of human error processing: Reinforcement learning, dopamine, and the error-related negativity. *Psychological Review, 109,* 679–709.

Holt, R. (1966). Measuring libidinal and aggressive motives and their controls by means of the Rorschach test. In D. Levine (Ed.), *Nebraska symposium on motivation.* Lincoln: University of Nebraska Press.

Holt, R. R. (1980). Loevinger's measure of ego development: Reliability and national norms for male and female short forms. *Journal of Personality and Social Psychology, 39,* 909–920.

Holtzworth-Munroe, A. (1992). Social skill deficits in maritally violent men: Interpreting the data using a social information processing model. *Clinical Psychology Review, 12,* 605–617.

Holyoak, K. J., Koh, K., & Nisbett, R. E. (1989). A theory of conditioning: Inductive learning within rule-based default hierarchies. *Psychological Review, 96,* 315–340.

Holyoak, K. J., & Spellman, B. A. (1993). Thinking. *Annual Review of Psychology, 44,* 265–315.

Hopkin, K. (1995). Programmed cell death: A switch to the cytoplasm? *Journal of NIH Research, 7,* 39–41.

Hoppe, C. (1972). *Ego development and conformity behavior.* Unpublished doctoral dissertation, Washington University, St. Louis, MO.

Hormuth, S. E. (1990). *The ecology of the self: Relocation and self-concept change.* Cambridge, England: Cambridge University Press.

Horney, K. (1937). *Neurotic personality of our times.* New York: Norton.

Horney, K. (1939). *New ways in psychoanalysis.* New York: Norton.

Horney, K. (1942). *Self-analysis.* New York: Norton.

Horney, K. (1945). *Our inner conflicts.* New York: Norton.

Horney, K. (1950). *Neurosis and human growth.* New York: Norton.

Horney, K. (1967). *Feminine psychology.* New York: Norton.

Horowitz, M. J. (1986). *Stress response syndromes* (2nd ed.). New York: Aronson.

Horvath, P., & Zuckerman, M. (1993). Sensation seeking, risk appraisal, and risky behavior. *Personality and Individual Differences, 14,* 41–52.

Hovland, C. I. (1937). The generalization of conditioning responses. I. The sensory generalization of conditioned responses with varying frequencies of tone. *Journal of General Psychology, 17,* 125–148.

Howard, G. S. (1990). On the construct validity of self-reports: What do the data say? *American Psychologist, 45,* 292–294.

Howard, G. S., Maxwell, S. E., Weiner, R. L., Boynton, K. S., & Rooney, W. M. (1980). Is a behavioral measure the best estimate of behavioral parameters? Perhaps not. *Applied Psychological Measurement, 4,* 293–311.

Hsee, C. K., & Abelson, R. P. (1991). The velocity relation: Satisfaction as a function of the first derivative of outcome over time. *Journal of Personality and Social Psychology, 60,* 341–347.

Hubbard, J. A., Dodge, K. A., Cillessen, A. H. N., Coie, J. D., & Schwartz, D. (2001). The dyadic nature of social information processing in boys' reactive and proactive aggression. *Journal of Personality and Social Psychology, 80,* 268–280.

Hull, C. L. (1943). *Principles of behavior.* New York: Appleton-Century-Crofts.

Hull, J. G. (1981). A self-awareness model of the causes and effects of alcohol consumption. *Journal of Abnormal Psychology, 90,* 586–600.

Hull, J. G., & Rielly, N. P. (1986). An information-processing approach to alcohol use and its consequences. In R. E. Ingram (Ed.), *Information processing approaches to clinical psychology.* New York: Academic.

Hull, J. G., Slone, L. B., Meteyer, K. B., & Matthews, A. R. (2002). The nonconsciousness of self-consciousness. *Journal of Personality and Social Psychology, 83,* 406–424.

Humphreys, L. G. (1939). The effect of random alteration of reinforcement on the acquisition and extinction of conditioned eyelid reactions. *Journal of Experimental Psychology, 15,* 141–158.

Hutchison, K. E., McGeary, J., Smolen, A., Bryan, A., & Swift, R. M. (2002). The DRD4 VNTR polymorphism moderates craving after alcohol consumption. *Health Psychology, 21,* 139–146.

Hy, L. X., & Loevinger, J. (1996). *Measuring ego development* (2nd ed.). Mahwah, NJ: Erlbaum.

Hyman, I. E., Husband, T. H., & Billings, F. J. (1995). False memories of childhood experiences. *Applied Cognitive Psychology, 9,* 181–197.

Hymbaugh, K., & Garrett, J. (1974). Sensation seeking among skydivers. *Perceptual and Motor Skills, 38,* 118.

Ilgen, M., McKellar, J., & Tiet, Q. (2005). Abstinence self-efficacy and abstinence 1 year after substance use disorder treatment. *Journal of Consulting and Clinical Psychology, 73,* 1175–1180.

Ingram, R. E. (Ed.). (1986). *Information-processing approaches to clinical psychology.* New York: Academic.

Isaacs, E. A., & Clark, H. H. (1987). References in conversation between experts and novices. *Journal of Experimental Psychology: General, 116,* 26–37.

Isabella, R. A., Belsky, J., & von Eye, A. (1989). Origins of infant–mother attachment: An examination of interactional synchrony during the infant's first year. *Developmental Psychology, 25,* 12–21.

Jacklin, C. N., Maccoby, E. E., & Doering, C. H. (1983). Neonatal sex-steroid hormones and timidity in 6–18-month-old boys and girls. *Developmental Psychobiology, 16,* 163–168.

Jackson, D. N. (1984). *Personality Research Form manual* (3rd ed.). Port Huron, MI: Research Psychologists.

Jackson, D. N., & Messick, S. (Eds.). (1967). *Problems in assessment.* New York: McGraw-Hill.

Jacob, S., McClintock, M. K., Zelano, B., & Ober, C. (2002). Paternally inherited HLA alleles are associated with women's choice of male odor. *Nature Genetics, 30,* 175–179.

James, W. (1890). *The principles of psychology* (Vol. 2). New York: Holt.

Jang, K. L., Hu, S., Livesley, W. J., Angleitner, A., Riemann, R., Ando, J., Ono, Y., Vernon, P. A., & Hamer, D. H. (2001). Covariance structure of neuroticism and agreeableness: A twin and molecular genetic analysis of the role of the serotonin transporter gene. *Journal of Personality and Social Psychology, 81,* 295–304.

Jang, K. L., Livesley, W. J., Angleitner, A., Riemann, R., & Vernon, P. A. (2002). Genetic and environmental influences on the covariance of facets defining the domains of the five-factor model of personality. *Personality and Individual Differences, 33,* 83–101.

Jang, K. L., Livesley, W. J., & Vernon, P. A. (1996). Heritability of the big five personality dimensions and their facets: A twin study. *Journal of Personality, 64,* 577–591.

Jang, K. L., McCrae, R. R., Angleitner, A., Riemann, R., & Livesley, W. J. (1998). Heritability of facet-level traits in a cross-cultural twin sample: Support for a hierarchical model of personality. *Journal of Personality and Social Psychology, 74,* 1556–1565.

Janoff-Bulman, R. (1992). *Shattered assumptions: Towards a new psychology of trauma.* New York: Free Press.

Janoff-Bulman, R., & Leggatt, H. K. (2002). Culture and social obligation: When "shoulds" are perceived as "wants." *Journal of Research in Personality, 36,* 260–270.

Jeffery, R. W. (1976). The influence of symbolic and motor rehearsal on observational learning. *Journal of Research in Personality, 10,* 116–127.

Jenkins, H. M. (1962). Resistance to extinction when partial reinforcement is followed by regular reinforcement. *Journal of Experimental Psychology, 64,* 441–450.

Jenkins, S. R. (1987). Need for achievement and women's careers over 14 years: Evidence for occupational structure effects. *Journal of Personality and Social Psychology, 53,* 922–932.

Jenkins, S. R. (1994). Need for power and women's careers over 14 years: Structural power, job satisfaction, and motive change. *Journal of Personality and Social Psychology, 66,* 155–165.

Jensen, M. B. (1987). Psychobiological factors predicting the course of breast cancer. *Journal of Personality, 55,* 317–342.

Jensen-Campbell, L. A., Adams, R., Perry, D. G., Workman, K. A., Furdella, J. Q., & Egan, S. K. (2002). Agreeableness, extraversion, and peer relations in early adolescence: Winning friends and deflecting aggression. *Journal of Research in Personality, 36,* 224–251.

Jensen-Campbell, L. A., Gleason, K. A., Adams, R., & Malcolm, K. T. (2003). Interpersonal conflict, agreeableness, and personality development. *Journal of Personality, 71,* 1059–1086.

Jensen-Campbell, L. A., & Graziano, W. G. (2001). Agreeableness as a moderator of interpersonal conflict. *Journal of Personality, 69,* 323–362.

Jensen-Campbell, L. A., Graziano, W. G., & West, S. G. (1995). Dominance, prosocial orientation, and female preferences: Do nice guys really finish last? *Journal of Personality and Social Psychology, 68,* 427–440.

Jessor, R., Costa, F., Jessor, L., & Donovan, J. E. (1983). Time of first intercourse: A prospective study. *Journal of Personality and Social Psychology, 44,* 608–626.

Jessor, S. L., & Jessor, R. (1975). Transition from virginity to nonvirginity among youth: A social–psychological study over time. *Developmental Psychology, 11,* 473–484.

Jockin, V., McGue, M., & Lykken, D. T. (1996). Personality and divorce: A genetic analysis. *Journal of Personality and Social Psychology, 71,* 288–299.

John, O. P. (1990). The big-five factor taxonomy: Dimensions of personality in the natural language and in questionnaires. In L. Pervin (Ed.), *Handbook of personality theory and research* (pp. 66–100). New York: Guilford.

John, O. P., & Robins, R. W. (1994). Accuracy and bias in self-perception: Individual differences in self-enhancement and the role of narcissism. *Journal of Personality and Social Psychology, 66,* 206–219.

Johnson, D. J., & Rusbult, C. E. (1989). Resisting temptation: Devaluation of alternative partners as a means of maintaining commitment in close relationships. *Journal of Personality and Social Psychology, 57,* 967–980.

Johnson, J. A., Germer, C. K., Efran, J. S., & Overton, W. F. (1988). Personality as the basis for theoretical predilections. *Journal of Personality and Social Psychology, 55,* 824–835.

Johnson, J. A., & Ostendorf, F. (1993). Clarification of the five-factor model with the abridged big five dimensional circumplex. *Journal of Personality and Social Psychology, 65,* 563–576.

Johnson, S. L. (2005). Mania and goal regulation: A review. *Clinical Psychology Review, 25,* 241–262.

Johnson, S. L., & Leahy, R. L. (Eds.). (2003). *Psychological treatment of bipolar disorder.* New York: Guilford.

Johnson, S. L., Sandrow, D., Meyer, B., Winters, R., Miller, I., Solomon, D., & Keitner, G. (2000). Increases in manic symptoms after life events involving goal attainment. *Journal of Abnormal Psychology, 109,* 721–727.

Johnson, W., & Kieras, D. (1983). Representation-saving effects of prior knowledge in memory for simple technical prose. *Memory & Cognition, 11,* 456–466.

Joireman, J., Anderson, J., & Strathman, A. (2003). The aggression paradox: Understanding links among aggression, sensation seeking, and the consideration of future consequences. *Journal of Personality and Social Psychology, 84,* 1287–1302.

Jonas, K. J., & Sassenberg, K. (2006). Knowing how to react: Automatic response priming from social categories. *Journal of Personality and Social Psychology, 90,* 709–721.

Jonas, E., Schimel, J., Greenberg, J., & Pyszczynski, T. (2002). The Scrooge effect: Evidence that mortality salience increases prosocial attitudes and behavior. *Personality and Social Psychology Bulletin, 28,* 1342–1353.

Jones, A., & Crandall, R. (1986). Validation of a short index of self-actualization. *Personality and Social Psychology Bulletin, 12,* 63–73.

Jones, E. E., & Berglas, S. (1978). Control of attributions about the self through self-handicapping strategies: The appeal of alcohol and the role of underachievement. *Personality and Social Psychology Bulletin, 4,* 200–206.

Jones, E. E., & Nisbett, R. E. (1971). The actor and the observer: Divergent perceptions of the causes of behavior. In E. E. Jones et al. (Eds.), *Attribution: Perceiving the causes of behavior.* Morristown, NJ: General Learning.

Jones, E. E., & Pittman, T. S. (1982). Toward a general theory of strategic self-presentation. In J. Suls (Ed.), *Psychological perspectives on the self* (Vol. 1). Hillsdale, NJ: Erlbaum.

Jones, J. T., Pelham, B. W., Carvallo, M., & Mirenberg, M. C. (2004). How do I love thee? Let me count the Js: Implicit egotism and interpersonal attraction. *Journal of Personality and Social Psychology, 87,* 665–683.

Jones, M. C. (1968). Personality correlates and antecedents of drinking patterns in adult males. *Journal of Consulting and Clinical Psychology, 32,* 2–12.

Jones, M. C. (1971). Personality antecedents and correlates of drinking patterns in women. *Journal of Consulting and Clinical Psychology, 36,* 61–69.

Jones, W. H., Hobbes, S. A., & Hockenberg, D. (1982). Loneliness and social skills deficits. *Journal of Personality and Social Psychology, 42,* 682–689.

Jöreskog, K. G., & Sörbom, D. (1979). *Advances in factor analysis and structural equations.* Cambridge, MA: Abt Associates.

Josephs, R. A., Sellers, J. G., Newman, M. L., & Mehta, P. H. (2006). The mismatch effect: When testosterone and status are at odds. *Journal of Personality and Social Psychology, 90,* 999–1013.

Jourard, S. M. (1974). *Healthy personality: An approach from the viewpoint of humanistic psychology.* New York: Macmillan.

Jung, C. G. (1933). *Psychological types.* New York: Harcourt, Brace, & World.

Jung, C. G. (1960). *The structure and dynamics of the psyche, Collected works* (Vol. 8). Princeton, NJ: Princeton University Press. (Originally published in German, 1926)

Jung, C. G. (1968). *Analytical psychology: Its theory and practice.* New York: Pantheon.

Juni, S. (1981). Maintaining anonymity vs. requesting feedback as a function of oral dependency. *Perceptual and Motor Skills, 52,* 239–242.

Juni, S., & Fischer, R. E. (1985). Religiosity and preoedipal fixation. *Journal of Genetic Psychology, 146,* 27–35.

Juni, S., & Lo Cascio, R. (1985). Preference for counseling and psychotherapy as related to preoedipal fixation. *Psychological Reports, 56,* 431–438.

Juni, S., Masling, J., & Brannon, R. (1979). Interpersonal touching and orality. *Journal of Personality Assessment, 43,* 235–237.

Jussim, L. (1991). Social perception and social reality: A reflection–construction model. *Psychology Review, 98,* 54–73.

Kagan, J. (1994). *Galen's prophecy: Temperament in human nature.* New York: Basic Books.

Kahn, M. (2002). *Basic Freud: Psychoanalytic thought for the 21st century.* New York: Basic Books.

Kahn, S., Zimmerman, G., Csikszentmihalyi, M., & Getzels, J. W. (1985). Relations between identity in young adulthood and intimacy at midlife. *Journal of Personality and Social Psychology, 49,* 1316–1322.

Kamin, L. J. (1968). Attention-like processes in classical conditioning. In M. R. Jones (Ed.), *Miami symposium on the prediction of behavior: Aversive stimuli* (pp. 9–32). Coral Gables, FL: University of Miami Press.

Kanayama, G., Gruber, A. J., Pope, H. G., Jr., Borowiecki, J. J., & Hudson, J. I. (2001). Over-the-counter drug use in gymnasiums: An underrecognized substance abuse problem? *Psychotherapy and Psychosomatics, 70,* 137–140.

Kanfer, F. H. (1977). The many faces of self-control, or behavior modification changes its focus. In R. B. Stuart (Ed.), *Behavioral self-management: Strategies, techniques, and outcomes.* New York: Brunner/Mazel.

Kanfer, F. H., & Busemeyer, J. R. (1982). The use of problem-solving and decision-making in behavior therapy. *Clinical Psychology Review, 2,* 239–266.

Kanfer, F. H., & Hagerman, S. M. (1981). The role of self-regulation. In L. P. Rehm (Ed.), *Behavior therapy for depression: Present status and future directions.* New York: Academic.

Kanfer, F. H., & Hagerman, S. M. (1985). Behavior therapy and the information-processing paradigm. In S. Reiss & R. R. Bootzin (Eds.), *Theoretical issues in behavior therapy.* New York: Academic.

Kanfer, F. H., Karoly, P., & Newman, A. (1975). Reduction of children's fear of the dark by competence-related and situational threat-related verbal cues. *Journal of Consulting and Clinical Psychology, 43,* 251–258.

Kanfer, F. H., & Marston, A. R. (1963). Human reinforcement: Vicarious and direct. *Journal of Experimental Psychology, 65,* 292–296.

Kanfer, F. H., & Saslow, G. (1965). Behavioral analysis: An alternative to diagnostic classification. *Archives of General Psychiatry, 12,* 519–538.

Kanfer, F. H., & Schefft, B. K. (1988). *Guiding the process of therapeutic change.* Champaign, IL: Research Press.

Kaplan, A. G., & Bean, J. P. (1976). *Beyond sex-role stereotypes: Readings toward a psychology of androgyny.* Boston: Little, Brown.

Kaplan, A. G., & Sedney, M. A. (1980). *Psychology and sex roles: An androgynous perspective.* Boston: Little, Brown.

Kaplan, J. R., Manuck, S. B., Fontenot, M. B., & Mann, J. J. (2002). Central nervous system monoamine correlates of social dominance in cynomolgus monkeys (*Macaca fascicularis*). *Neuropsychopharmacology, 26,* 431–443.

Karylowski, J. J. (1990). Social reference points and accessibility of trait-related information in self–other similarity judgments. *Journal of Personality and Social Psychology, 58,* 975–983.

Kasser, T. (2002). *The high price of materialism.* Cambridge, MA: Bradford Books.

Kasser, T., Koestner, R., & Lekes, N. (2002). Early family experiences and adult values: A 26-year, prospective longitudinal study. *Personality and Social Psychology Bulletin, 28,* 826–835.

Kasser, T., & Ryan, R. M. (1993). A dark side of the American dream: Correlates of financial success as a central life aspiration. *Journal of Personality and Social Psychology, 65,* 410–422.

Katigbak, M. S., Church, A. T., Guanzon-Lapeña, M. A., Carlota, A. J., & del Pilar, G. H. (2002). Are indigenous personality dimensions culture specific? Philippine inventories and the five-factor model. *Journal of Personality and Social Psychology, 82,* 89–101.

Kawada, C. L. K., Oettingen, G., Gollwiter, P. M., & Bargh, J. A. (2004). The projection of implicit and explicit goals. *Journal of Personality and Social Psychology, 86,* 545–559.

Kazdin, A. E. (1974). Effects of covert modeling and reinforcement on assertive behavior. *Journal of Abnormal Psychology, 83,* 240–252.

Kazdin, A. E. (1975). Covert modeling, imagery assessment, and assertive behavior. *Journal of Consulting and Clinical Psychology, 43,* 716–724.

Keane, T. M., Kolb, L. C., Kaloupek, D. G., Orr, S. P., Blanchard, E. B., Thomas, R. G., Hsieh, F. Y., & Lavori, P. W. (1998). Utility of psychophysiological measurement in the diagnosis of posttraumatic stress disorder: Results from a Department of Veteran Affairs cooperative study. *Journal of Consulting and Clinical Psychology, 66,* 914–923.

Keller, P. E., Wascher, E., Prinz, W., Waszak, F., Koch, I., & Rosenbaum, D. A. (2006). Differences between intention-based and stimulus-based actions. *Journal of Psychophysiology, 20,* 9–20.

Kelly, A. E., Klusas, J. A., von Weiss, R. T., & Kenny, C. (2001). What is it about revealing secrets that is beneficial? *Personality and Social Psychology Bulletin, 27,* 651–665.

Kelly, G. A. (1955). *The psychology of personal constructs* (Vols. 1 and 2). New York: Norton.

Kelly, G. A. (1962). Europe's matrix of decisions. In M. R. Jones (Ed.), *Nebraska symposium on motivation* (Vol. 10). Lincoln: University of Nebraska Press.

Kelly, G. A. (1969). In whom confide: On whom depend for what? In B. Maher (Ed.), *Clinical psychology and personality.* New York: Wiley.

Kendler, K. S. (1997). Social support: A genetic–epidemiological analysis. *American Journal of Psychiatry, 154,* 1398–1404.

Kendler, K. S. (2005). "A gene for . . .": The nature of gene action in psychiatric disorders. *American Journal of Psychiatry, 162,* 1243–1252.

Kenford, S. L., Fiore, M. C., Jorenby, D. E., & Smith, S. S. (1994). Predicting smoking cessation: Who will quit with and without the nicotine patch. *Journal of the American Medical Association, 217,* 589–594.

Kenrick, D. T., Groth, G. E., Trost, M. R., & Sadalla, E. K. (1993). Integrating evolutionary and social exchange perspectives on relationships: Effects of gender, self-appraisal, and involvement level on mate selection criteria. *Journal of Personality and Social Psychology, 64,* 951–969.

Kenrick, D. T., & Keefe, R. C. (1992). Age preferences in mates reflect sex differences in human reproductive strategies. *Behavioral and Brain Sciences, 15,* 75–91.

Kenrick, D. T., Neuberg, S. L., Zierk, K. L., & Krones, J. M. (1994). Evolution and social cognition: Contrast effects as a function of sex, dominance, and physical attractiveness. *Personality and Social Psychology Bulletin, 20,* 210–217.

Kenrick, D. T., Sadalla, E. K., Groth, G., & Trost, M. R. (1990). Evolution, traits, and the stages of human courtship: Qualifying the parental investment model. *Journal of Personality, 58,* 97–116.

Kenrick, D. T., & Stringfield, D. O. (1980). Personality traits and the eye of the beholder: Crossing some traditional philosophical boundaries in the search for consistency in all of the people. *Psychological Review, 87,* 88–104.

Kenrick, D. T., Sundie, J. M., Nicastle, L. D., & Stone, G. O. (2001). Can one ever be too wealthy or too chaste? Searching for nonlinearities in mate judgment. *Journal of Personality and Social Psychology, 80,* 462–471.

Kernberg, O. (1976). *Borderline conditions and pathological narcissism.* New York: Jason Aronson.

Kernberg, O. (1980). *Internal world and external reality.* New York: Jason Aronson.

Kessler, R. C., Kendler, K. S., Heath, A., Neale, M. C., & Eaves, L. J. (1992). Social support, depressed mood, and adjustment to stress: A genetic epidemiologic investigation. *Journal of Personality and Social Psychology, 62,* 257–272.

Keyes, C. L. M., Shmotkin, D., & Ryff, C. D. (2002). Optimizing well-being: The empirical encounter of two traditions. *Journal of Personality and Social Psychology, 82,* 1007–1022.

Kiecolt-Glaser, J. K., Bane, C., Glaser, R., & Malarkey, W. B. (2003). Love, marriage, and divorce: Newlyweds' stress hormones foreshadow relationship changes. *Journal of Consulting and Clinical Psychology, 71,* 176–188.

Kiecolt-Glaser, J. K., McGuire, L., Robles, T. F., & Glaser, R. (2002). Emotions, morbidity, and mortality: New perspectives from psychoneuroimmunology. *Annual Reviews of Psychology, 53,* 83–107.

Kieras, J. E., Tobin, R. M., Graziano, W. G., & Rothbart, M. K. (2005). You can't always get what you want: Effortful control and children's responses to undesirable gifts. *Psychological Science, 16,* 391–396.

Kihlstrom, J. F. (1987). The cognitive unconscious. *Science, 237,* 1445–1452.

Kimura, D. (1999). *Sex and cognition.* Cambridge, MA: MIT Press.

Kinder, L. S., Kamarck, T. W., Baum, A., & Orchard, T. J. (2002). Depressive symptomatology and coronary heart disease in type 1 diabetes mellitus: A study of possible mechanisms. *Health Psychology, 21,* 542–552.

Kirkpatrick, L. A. (1998). God as a substitute attachment figure: A longitudinal study of adult attachment style and religious change in college students. *Personality and Social Psychology Bulletin, 24,* 961–973.

Kirkpatrick, L. A., & Davis, K. E. (1994). Attachment style, gender, and relationship stability: A longitudinal analysis. *Journal of Personality and Social Psychology, 66,* 502–512.

Kirsch, I. (1985). Response expectancy as a determinant of experience and behavior. *American Psychologist, 40,* 1189–1202.

Kirsch, I. (1990). *Changing expectations: A key to effective psychotherapy.* Pacific Grove, CA: Brooks/Cole.

Kirsch, I., Mearns, J., & Catanzaro, S. J. (1990). Mood-regulation expectancies as determinants of dysphoria in college students. *Journal of Counseling Psychology, 37,* 306–312.

Kirschenbaum, D. S. (1987). Self-regulatory failure: A review with clinical implications. *Clinical Psychology Review, 7,* 77–104.

Kitcher, P. (1987). Précis of *Vaulting ambition: Sociobiology and the quest for human nature. Behavioral and Brain Sciences, 10,* 61–100.

Klein, G. S. (1970). *Perception, motives, and personality.* New York: Knopf.

Klein, J. (1987). *Our need for others and its roots in infancy.* London, England: Tavistock.

Klein, M. (1935). *The psychoanalysis of children.* New York: Norton.

Klein, M. (1955a). The psychoanalytic play technique. *American Journal of Orthopsychiatry, 112,* 418–422.

Klein, M. (1955b). The psychoanalytic play technique, its history and significance. In M. Klein, P. Heiman, & R. Money-Kyrle (Eds.), *New directions in psychoanalysis: The significance of infant conflict in the pattern of adult behavior.* New York: Basic Books.

Klinesmith, J., Kasser, T., & McAndrew, F. T. (2006). Guns, testosterone, and aggression: An experimental test of a mediational hypothesis. *Psychological Science, 17,* 568–571.

Klinger, E. (1975). Consequences of commitment to and disengagement from incentives. *Psychological Review, 82,* 1–25.

Klinger, E. (1987). Current concerns and disengagement from incentives. In F. Halisch & J. Kuhl (Eds.), *Motivation, intention, and volition* (pp. 337–347). Berlin, Germany: Springer-Verlag.

Klion, R. E., & Leitner, L. M. (1991). Impression formation and construct system organization. *Social Behavior and Personality, 19,* 87–98.

Klohnen, E. C. (1996). Conceptual analysis and measurement of the construct of ego-resiliency. *Journal of Personality and Social Psychology, 70,* 1067–1079.

Klohnen, E. C., Vandewater, E. A., & Young, A. (1996). Negotiating the middle years: Ego-resiliency and successful midlife adjustment in women. *Psychology and Aging, 11,* 431–442.

Knapp, R. R. (1976). *Handbook for the Personal Orientation Inventory.* San Diego: EdITS.

Knee, C. R., Lonsbary, C., Canevello, A., & Patrick, H. (2005). Self-determination and conflict in romantic relationships. *Journal of Personality and Social Psychology, 89,* 997–1009.

Knee, C. R., Patrick, H., Vietor, N. A., Nanayakkara, A., & Neighbors, C. (2002). Self-determination as growth motivation in romantic relationships. *Personality and Social Psychology Bulletin, 28,* 609–619.

Knickmeyer, R., Baron-Cohen, S., Raggatt, P., Taylor, K., & Hackett, G. (2006). Fetal testosterone and empathy. *Hormones and Behavior, 49,* 282–292.

Knutson, B., Wolkowitz, O. M., Cole, S. W., Chan, T., Moore, E. A., Johnson, R. C., Terpstra, J., Turner, R. A., & Reus, V. I. (1998). Selective alteration of personality and social behavior by serotonergic intervention. *American Journal of Psychiatry, 155,* 373–379.

Kobak, R. R., & Hazan, C. (1991). Attachment in marriage: Effects of security and accuracy of working models. *Journal of Personality and Social Psychology, 60,* 861–869.

Kochanska, G., Friesenborg, A. E., Lange, L. A., & Martel, M. M. (2004). Parents' personality and infants' temperament as contributors to their emerging relationship. *Journal of Personality and Social Psychology, 86,* 744–759.

Kochanska, G., & Knaack, A. (2003). Effortful control as a personality characteristic of young children: Antecedents, correlates, and consequences. *Journal of Personality, 71,* 1087–1112.

Koestner, R., Lekes, N., Powers, T. A., & Chicoine, E. (2002). Attaining personal goals: Self-concordance plus implementation intentions equals success. *Journal of Personality and Social Psychology, 83,* 231–244.

Koestner, R., Zuckerman, M., & Koestner, J. (1987). Praise, involvement, and intrinsic motivation. *Journal of Personality and Social Psychology, 53,* 383–390.

Koffka, K. (1935). *Principles of Gestalt psychology.* New York: Harcourt, Brace.

Kohler, E., Keysers, C., Umiltà, M. A., Fogassi, L., Gallese, V., & Rizzolatti, G. (2002). Hearing sounds, understanding actions: Action representation in mirror neurons. *Science, 297,* 846–848.

Köhler, W. (1947). *Gestalt psychology.* New York: Liveright.

Kohut, H. (1977). *The restoration of the self.* New York: International Universities Press.

Konecni, V. J. (1975). Annoyance, type and duration of postannoyance activity, and aggression: The "cathartic effect." *Journal of Experimental Psychology: General, 104,* 76–102.

Koole, S. L., Jager, W., van den Berg, A. E., Vlek, C. A. J., & Hofstee, W. K. B. (2001). On the social nature of personality: Effects of extraversion, agreeableness, and feedback about collective resource use on cooperation in a resource dilemma. *Personality and Social Psychology Bulletin, 27,* 289–301.

Korchmaros, J. D., & Kenny, D. A. (2001). Emotional closeness as a mediator of the effect of genetic relatedness on altruism. *Psychological Science, 12,* 262–265.

Kornhaber, R. C., & Schroeder, H. E. (1975). Importance of model similarity on extinction of avoidance behavior in children. *Journal of Consulting and Clinical Psychology, 43,* 601–607.

Kosfeld, M., Heinrichs, M., Zack, P. J., Fischbacher, U., & Fehr, E. (2005). Oxytocin increases trust in humans. *Nature, 435,* 673–676.

Kotler, M., Cohen, H., Segman, R., Gritsenko, L., Nemanov, L., Lerer, B., Kramer, I., Zer-Zion, M., Kletz, I., & Ebstein, R. P. (1997). Excess dopamine D_4 receptor (D4DR) exon III seven repeat allele in opioid-dependent subjects. *Molecular Psychiatry, 2,* 251–254.

Kotre, J. (1984). *Outliving the self: Generativity and the interpretation of lives.* Baltimore: Johns Hopkins University Press.

Kowaz, A. M., & Marcia, J. E. (1991). Development and validation of a measure of Eriksonian industry. *Journal of Personality and Social Psychology, 60,* 390–396.

Kramer, P. D. (1993). *Listening to Prozac: A psychiatrist explores anti-depressant drugs and the remaking of the self.* New York: Viking.

Krantz, D. S., & McCeney, M. K. (2002). Effects of psychological and social factors on organic disease: A critical assessment of research on coronary heart disease. *Annual Reviews of Psychology, 53,* 341–369.

Kretschmer, E. (1925). *Physique and character.* New York: Harcourt, Brace.

Krieger, S. R., Epting, F. R., & Leitner, L. (1974). Personal constructs and attitudes toward death. *Omega, 5,* 299.

Kriegman, D., & Knight, C. (1988). Social evolution, psychoanalysis, and human nature. *Social Policy, 19,* 49–55.

Krueger, R. F. (2002). Personality from a realist's perspective: Personality traits, criminal behaviors, and the externalizing spectrum. *Journal of Research in Personality, 36,* 564–572.

Krueger, R. F., Schmutte, P. S., Caspi, A., Moffitt, T. E., Campbell, K., & Silva, P. A. (1994). Personality traits are linked to crime among men and women: Evidence from a birth cohort. *Journal of Abnormal Psychology, 103,* 328–338.

Krueger, R. F., Watson, D., & Barlow, D. H. (Eds.). (2005). Toward a dimensionally based taxonomy of psychopathology [Special section]. *Journal of Abnormal Psychology, 114,* 491–569.

Kuhl, J. (2000). The volitional basis of Personality Systems Interaction Theory: Applications in learning and treatment contexts. *International Journal of Educational Research, 33,* 665–703.

Kuhl, J., & Helle, P. (1986). Motivational and volitional determinants of depression: The degenerated-intention hypothesis. *Journal of Abnormal Psychology, 95,* 247–251.

Kuiper, N. A., & Derry, P. A. (1981). The self as a cognitive prototype: An application to person perception and depression. In N. Cantor & J. Kihlstrom (Eds.), *Cognition, social interaction, and personality.* Hillsdale, NJ: Erlbaum.

Kukla, A. (1972). Foundations of an attributional theory of performance. *Psychological Review, 79,* 454–470.

Kulhavy, R. W., & Stock, W. A. (1989). Feedback in written instruction: The place of response certitude. *Educational Psychology Review, 1,* 279–308.

Kunda, Z. (1999). *Social cognition: Making sense of people.* Cambridge, MA: MIT Press.

Kunda, Z., & Thagard, P. (1996). Forming impressions from stereotypes, traits, and behaviors: A parallel-constraint-satisfaction theory. *Psychological Review, 103,* 284–308.

Kunzmann, U., & Baltes, P. B. (2003). Wisdom-related knowledge: Affective, motivational, and interpersonal correlates. *Personality and Social Psychology Bulletin, 29,* 1104–1119.

La Greca, A. M., & Santogrossi, D. A. (1980). Social skills training with elementary school students: A behavioral group approach. *Journal of Consulting and Clinical Psychology, 48,* 220–227.

La Greca, A. M., Stone, W. L., & Bell, C. R., III (1983). Facilitating the vocational–interpersonal skills of mentally retarded individuals. *American Journal of Mental Deficiency, 88,* 270–278.

La Guardia, J. G., Ryan, R. M., Couchman, C. E., & Deci, E. L. (2000). Within-person variation in security of attachment: A self-determination theory perspective on attachment, need fulfillment, and well-being. *Journal of Personality and Social Psychology, 79,* 367–384.

Lakoff, G. (1987). *Women, fire, and dangerous things: What categories reveal about the mind.* Chicago: University of Chicago Press.

Lamiell, J. T. (1981). Toward an idiothetic psychology of personality. *American Psychologist, 36,* 276–289.

Landreth, G. L. (1991). *Play therapy: The art of the relationship.* Muncie, IN: Accelerated Development.

Landy, F. J. (1986). Stamp collecting versus science: Validation as hypothesis testing. *American Psychologist, 41,* 1183–1192.

Lane, R. D., & Nadel, L. (Eds.). (2000). *Cognitive neuroscience of emotion.* New York: Oxford University Press.

Lang, P. J., & Lazovik, A. D. (1963). Experimental desensitization of a phobic. *Journal of Abnormal and Social Psychology, 66,* 519–525.

Langens, T. A., & Schmalt, H.-D. (2002). Emotional consequences of positive daydreaming: The moderating role of fear of failure. *Personality and Social Psychology Bulletin, 28,* 1725–1735.

Langner, C. A., & Winter, D. G. (2001). The motivational basis of concessions and compromise: Archival and laboratory studies. *Journal of Personality and Social Psychology, 81,* 711–727.

Langston, C., & Cantor, N. (1989). Social anxiety and social constraint: When "making friends" is hard. *Journal of Personality and Social Psychology, 56,* 649–661.

Lanning, K. (1994). Dimensionality of observer ratings on the California Adult Q-set. *Journal of Personality and Social Psychology, 67,* 151–160.

Lansing, J. B., & Heyns, R. W. (1959). Need affiliation and frequency of four types of communication. *Journal of Abnormal and Social Psychology, 58,* 365–372.

Larsen, R. J., & Ketelaar, T. (1991). Personality and susceptibility to positive and negative emotional states. *Journal of Personality and Social Psychology, 61,* 132–140.

Larstone, R. M., Jang, K. L., Livesley, W. J., Vernon, P. A., & Wolf, H. (2002). The relationship between Eysenck's P-E-N model of personality, the five-factor model of personality, and traits delineating personality dysfunction. *Personality and Individual Differences, 33,* 25–37.

Lassiter, G. D., Briggs, M. A., & Bowman, R. E. (1991). Need for cognition and the perception of ongoing behavior. *Personality and Social Psychology Bulletin, 17,* 156–160.

Lassiter, G. D., Briggs, M. A., & Slaw, R. D. (1991). Need for cognition, causal processing, and memory for behavior. *Personality and Social Psychology Bulletin, 17,* 694–700.

Lau, R. R. (1989). Construct accessibility and electoral choice. *Political Behavior, 11,* 5–32.

Laurenceau, J.-P., Barrett, L. F., & Pietromonaco, P. R. (1998). Intimacy as an interpersonal process: The importance of self-disclosure, and perceived partner responsiveness in interpersonal exchanges. *Journal of Personality and Social Psychology, 74,* 1238–1251.

Lazarus, R. S. (1966). *Psychological stress and the coping process.* New York: McGraw-Hill.

Lazarus, R. S., & Folkman, S. (1984). *Stress, appraisal, and coping.* New York: Springer.

Le Vay, S. (1991). A difference in hypothalamic structure between heterosexual and homosexual men. *Science, 253,* 1034–1037.

Le Vay, S. (1993). *The sexual brain.* Cambridge, MA: MIT Press.

Leak, G. K., & Christopher, S. B. (1982). Freudian psycho-analysis and sociobiology: A synthesis. *American Psychologist, 37,* 313–322.

Leary, M. R., & Baumeister, R. F. (2000). The nature and function of self-esteem: Sociometer theory. In M. P. Zanna (Ed.), *Advances in experimental social psychology* (Vol. 32, pp. 1–62). San Diego: Academic.

Lee, L., & Snarey, J. (1988). The relationship between ego and moral development: A theoretical review and empirical analysis. In D. K. Lapsley & F. C. Power (Eds.), *Self, ego, and identity: Integrative approaches* (pp. 151–178). New York: Springer-Verlag.

Lefcourt, H. M. (1976). *Locus of control: Current trends in theory and research.* Hillsdale, NJ: Erlbaum.

Lefcourt, H. M. (Ed.). (1981). *Research with the locus of control construct. Vol. 1, Assessment methods.* New York: Academic.

Lefcourt, H. M., Martin, R. A., Fick, C. M., & Saleh, W. E. (1985). Locus of control for affiliation and behavior in social interactions. *Journal of Personality and Social Psychology, 48,* 755–759.

Lefcourt, H. M., Von Baeyer, C. I., Ware, E. E., & Cox, D. J. (1979). The Multidimensional-Multiattributional Causality scale: The development of a goal specific locus of control scale. *Canadian Journal of Behavioral Science, 11,* 286–304.

Leit, R. A., Pope, H. G., Jr., & Gray, J. J. (2001). Cultural expectations of muscularity in men: The evolution of playgirl centerfolds. *International Journal of Eating Disorders, 29,* 90–93.

Leitner, L. M., & Cado, S. (1982). Personal constructs and homosexual stress. *Journal of Personality and Social Psychology, 43,* 869–872.

Lemann, N. (1994). Is there a science of success? *Atlantic Monthly, 273,* 83–98.

Lengfelder, A., & Gollwitzer, P. M. (2001). Reflective and reflexive action control in patients with frontal brain lesions. *Neuropsychology, 15,* 80–100.

Lepper, M. R., & Greene, D. (1975). Turning play into work: Effects of adult surveillance and extrinsic rewards on children's intrinsic motivation. *Journal of Personality and Social Psychology, 31,* 479–486.

Lepper, M. R., & Greene, D. (1978). *The hidden costs of reward.* Hillsdale, NJ: Erlbaum.

Lesch, K.-P., Bengel, D., Heils, A., Sabol, S. Z., Greenberg, B. D., Petri, S., et al. (1996). Association of anxiety-related traits with a polymorphism in the serotonin transporter gene regulatory region. *Science, 274,* 1527–1531.

Lesch, K.-P., & Mössner, R. (1998). Genetically driven variation in serotonin uptake: Is there a link to affective spectrum, neurodevelopmental, and neurodegenerative disorders? *Biological Psychiatry, 44,* 179–192.

Levenson, H. (1973). Multidimensional locus of control in psychiatric patients. *Journal of Consulting and Clinical Psychology, 41,* 397–404.

Levenson, H. (1981). Differentiating among internality, powerful others, and chance. In H. F. Lefcourt (Ed.), *Research with the locus of control construct. Vol. 1, Assessment methods.* New York: Academic.

Levenson, R. W., & Ruef, A. M. (1992). Empathy: A physiological substrate. *Journal of Personality and Social Psychology, 63,* 234–246.

Levine, D. S., & Leven, S. J. (Eds.). (1992). *Motivation, emotion, and goal direction in neural networks.* Hillsdale, NJ: Erlbaum.

Levinson, D. J. (1978). *The seasons of a man's life.* New York: Knopf.

Lewin, D. I. (1990). Gene therapy nears starting gate. *Journal of NIH Research, 2,* 36–38.

Lewin, K. (1951a). *Field theory in social science.* New York: Harper.

Lewin, K. (1951b). The nature of field theory. In M. H. Marx (Ed.), *Psychological theory.* New York: Macmillan.

Lewinsohn, P. M., Mischel, W., Chaplin, W., & Barton, R. (1980). Social competence and depression: The role of illusory self-perceptions. *Journal of Abnormal Psychology, 89,* 203–212.

Lewis, D. J., & Duncan, C. P. (1956). Effect of different percentages of money reward on extinction of a lever pulling response. *Journal of Experimental Psychology, 52,* 23–27.

Lewontin, R. C., Rose, S., & Kamin, L. J. (1984). *Not in our genes: Biology, ideology, and human nature.* New York: Penguin.

Li, N. P., Bailey, J. M., Kenrick, D. T., & Linsenmeier, J. A. W. (2002). The necessities and luxuries of mate preferences: Testing the tradeoffs. *Journal of Personality and Social Psychology, 82,* 947–955.

Li, T., Xu, K., Deng, H., Cai, G., Liu, J., Liu, X., Wang, R., Xiang, X., Zhao, J., Murray, R. M., Sham, P. C., & Collier, D. A. (1997). Association analysis of the dopamine D_4 gene exon III VNTR and heroin abuse in Chinese subjects. *Molecular Psychiatry, 2,* 413–416.

Libera, C. D., & Chelazzi, L. (2006). Visual selective attention and the effects of monetary rewards. *Psychological Science, 17,* 222–227.

Lichtenstein, E., & Danaher, B. G. (1976). Modification of smoking behavior: A critical analysis of theory, research, and practice. In M. Hersen, R. M. Eisler, & P. M. Miller (Eds.), *Progress in behavior modification* (Vol. 3). New York: Academic.

Lieberman, M. D., Gaunt, R., Gilbert, D. T., & Trope, Y. (2002). Reflection and reflexion: A social cognitive neuroscience approach to attributional inference. In M.

Zanna (Ed.), *Advances in Experimental Social Psychology* (pp. 199–249). San Diego: Academic.

Liebert, R. M., & Baron, R. A. (1972). Some immediate effects of televised violence on children's behavior. *Developmental Psychology, 6,* 469–475.

Liebert, R. M., & Fernandez, L. E. (1970). Effects of vicarious consequences on imitative performance. *Child Development, 41,* 841–852.

Light, K. C., Smith, T. E., Johns, J. M., Brownley, K. A., Hofheimer, J. A., & Amico, J. A. (2000). Oxytocin responsivity in mothers of infants: A preliminary study of relationships with blood pressure during laboratory stress and normal ambulatory activity. *Health Psychology, 19,* 560–567.

Lilienfeld, S. O., Wood, J. M., & Garb, H. N. (2000). The scientific status of projective techniques. *Psychological Science in the Public Interest, 1,* 27–66.

Linville, P. W. (1987). Self-complexity as a cognitive buffer against stress-related illness and depression. *Journal of Personality and Social Psychology, 52,* 663–676.

Litt, M. D. (1988). Self-efficacy and perceived control: Cognitive mediators of pain tolerance. *Journal of Personality and Social Psychology, 54,* 149–160.

Little, B. R. (1989). Personal projects analysis: Trivial pursuits, magnificent obsessions, and the search for coherence. In D. M. Buss & N. Cantor (Eds.), *Personality psychology: Recent trends and emerging directions* (pp. 15–31). New York: Springer-Verlag.

Locke, E. A., & Latham, G. P. (1990). *A theory of goal setting and task performance.* Englewood Cliffs, NJ: Prentice-Hall.

Locurto, C. M., Terrace, H. S., & Gibbon, J. (Eds.). (1980). *Autoshaping and conditioning theory.* New York: Academic.

Loehlin, J. C. (1992). *Genes and environment in personality development.* Newbury Park, CA: Sage.

Loehlin, J. C., & Nichols, R. C. (1976). *Heredity, environment, and personality.* Austin: University of Texas Press.

Loehlin, J. C., Willerman, L., & Horn, J. M. (1985). Personality resemblances in adoptive families when the children are late-adolescent or adult. *Journal of Personality and Social Psychology, 48,* 376–392.

Loehlin, J. C., Willerman, L., & Horn, J. M. (1988). Human behavior genetics. *Annual Review of Psychology, 38,* 101–133.

Loevinger, J. (1966). The meaning and measurement of ego development. *American Psychologist, 21,* 195–206.

Loevinger, J. (1969). Theories of ego development. In L. Breger (Ed.), *Clinical–cognitive psychology: Models and integrations.* Englewood Cliffs, NJ: Prentice-Hall.

Loevinger, J. (1976). *Ego development: Conceptions and theories.* San Francisco: Jossey-Bass.

Loevinger, J. (1987). *Paradigms of personality.* New York: W. H. Freeman.

Loevinger, J. (1993). Measurement of personality: True or false? *Psychological Inquiry, 4,* 1–16.

Loevinger, J., & Knoll, E. (1983). Personality: Stages, traits, and the self. *Annual Review of Psychology, 34,* 195–222.

Loevinger, J., & Wessler, R. (1970). *Measuring ego development 1. Construction and use of a sentence-completion test.* San Francisco: Jossey-Bass.

Loftus, E. F. (1997). Creating false memories. *Scientific American, 277,* 70–75.

Loftus, E. F., Coan, J. A., & Pickrell, J. E. (1996). Manufacturing false memories using bits of reality. In L. Reder (Ed.), *Implicit memory and metacognition* (pp. 195–220). Mahwah, NJ: Erlbaum.

Loftus, E. F., & Pickrell, J. E. (1995). The formation of false memories. *Psychiatric Annals, 25,* 720–725.

Lord, C. G. (1982). Predicting behavioral consistency from an individual's perception of situational similarities. *Journal of Personality and Social Psychology, 42,* 1076–1088.

Lovaas, O. I., Freitag, G., Gold, V. J., & Kassorla, I. C. (1965). Recording apparatus for observation of behaviors of children in free play settings. *Journal of Experimental Child Psychology, 2,* 108–120.

Lowell, E. L. (1952). The effect of need for achievement on learning and speed of performance. *Journal of Psychology, 33,* 31–40.

Lucas, R. E., & Diener, E. (2001). Understanding extraverts' enjoyment of social situations: The importance of pleasantness. *Journal of Personality and Social Psychology, 81,* 343–356.

Lucas, R. E., Diener, E., Grob, A., Suh, E. M., & Shao, L. (2000). Cross-cultural evidence for the fundamental features of extraversion. *Journal of Personality and Social Psychology, 79,* 452–468.

Lumsden, C., & Wilson, E. O. (1981). *Genes, mind, and culture.* Cambridge, MA: Harvard University Press.

Lundy, A. C. (1985). The reliability of the Thematic Apperception Test. *Journal of Personality Assessment, 49,* 141–145.

Lütkenhaus, P., Grossmann, K. E., & Grossmann, K. (1985). Infant-mother attachment at twelve months and style of interaction with a stranger at the age of three years. *Child Development, 56,* 1538–1542.

Lykken, D. T., & Tellegen, A. (1993). Is human mating adventitious or the result of lawful choice? A twin study of mate selection. *Journal of Personality and Social Psychology, 65,* 56–68.

Lynam, D. R., Leukefeld, C., & Clayton, R. R. (2003). The contribution of personality to the overlap between antisocial behavior and substance use/misuse. *Aggressive Behavior, 29,* 316–331.

Lynn, R. (2001). *Eugenics: A reassessment.* Westport, CT: Praeger.

Lynn, S. J., Myers, B., & Malinoski, P. (1997). Hypnosis, pseudomemories, and clinical guidelines: A sociocognitive perspective. In J. D. Read & D. S. Lindsay (Eds.),

Recollections of trauma: Scientific studies and clinical practice. New York: Plenum.

Maccoby, E. E., & Wilson, W. C. (1957). Identification and observational learning from films. *Journal of Abnormal and Social Psychology, 55,* 76–87.

MacKay, D. M. (1963). Mindlike behavior in artefacts. In K. M. Sayre & F. J. Crosson (Eds.), *The modeling of mind: Computers and intelligence.* Notre Dame, IN: University of Notre Dame Press.

MacKay, D. M. (1966). Cerebral organization and the conscious control of action. In J. C. Eccles (Ed.), *Brain and conscious experience.* Berlin, Germany: Springer-Verlag.

Macrae, C. N., & Boderhausen, G. V. (2000). Social cognition: Thinking categorically. *Annual Review of Psychology, 51,* 93–120.

Macrae, C. N., Milne, A. B., & Bodenhausen, G. V. (1994). Stereotypes as energy-saving devices: A peek inside the cognitive toolbox. *Journal of Personality and Social Psychology, 66,* 37–47.

Maddi, S. R. (1980). *Personality theories: A comparative analysis.* Homewood, IL: Dorsey.

Magnus, K., Diener, E., Fujita, F., & Pavot, W. (1993). Extraversion and neuroticism as predictors of objective life events: A longitudinal analysis. *Journal of Personality and Social Psychology, 65,* 1046–1053.

Magnusson, D., & Endler, N. S. (Eds.). (1977). *Personality at the crossroads: Current issues in interactional psychology.* Hillsdale, NJ: Erlbaum.

Mahler, M. S. (1968). *On human symbiosis and the vicissitudes of individuation: Infantile psychosis.* New York: International Universities Press.

Mahler, M. S., Pine, F., & Bergman, A. (1975). *The psychological birth of the human infant: Symbiosis and individuation.* New York: Basic Books.

Mahoney, M. J. (1977). Some applied issues in self-monitoring. In J. D. Cone & R. P. Hawkins (Eds.), *Behavioral assessment: New directions in clinical psychology.* New York: Brunner/Mazel.

Main, M., & Cassidy, J. (1988). Categories of response to reunion with the parent at age 6: Predictable from infant attachment classifications and stable over a 1-month period. *Developmental Psychology, 24,* 415–426.

Major, B., Cozzarelli, C., Sciacchitano, A. M., Cooper, M. L., Testa, M., & Mueller, P. M. (1990). Perceived social support, self-efficacy, and adjustment to abortion. *Journal of Personality and Social Psychology, 59,* 452–463.

Major, B., Richards, C., Cooper, M. L., Cozzarelli, C., & Zubek, J. (1998). Personal resilience, cognitive appraisals, and coping: An integrative model of adjustment to abortion. *Journal of Personality and Social Psychology, 74,* 735–752.

Malamuth, N. M., & Donnerstein, E. (Eds.). (1984). *Pornography and sexual aggression.* New York: Academic.

Malec, J., Park, T., & Watkins, J. T. (1976). Modeling with role playing as a treatment for test anxiety. *Journal of Consulting and Clinical Psychology, 44,* 679.

Mallick, S. K., & McCandless, B. R. (1966). A study of catharsis of aggression. *Journal of Personality and Social Psychology, 4,* 591–596.

Maltzman, I. (1968). Theoretical conceptions of semantic conditioning and generalization. In T. R. Dixon & D. L. Horton (Eds.), *Verbal behavior and general behavior theory.* Englewood Cliffs, NJ: Prentice-Hall.

Mancuso, J. C., & Adams-Webber, J. R. (Eds.). (1982). *The construing person.* New York: Praeger.

Maner, J. K., Luce, C. L., Neuberg, S. L., Cialdini, R. B., Brown, S., & Sagarin, B. J. (2002). The effects of perspective taking on motivations for helping: Still no evidence for altruism. *Personality and Social Psychology Bulletin, 28,* 1601–1610.

Manning, M. M., & Wright, T. L. (1983). Self-efficacy expectancies, outcome expectancies, and the persistence of pain control in childbirth. *Journal of Personality and Social Psychology, 45,* 421–431.

Mansfield, E. D., & McAdams, D. P. (1996). Generativity and themes of agency and communion in adult autobiography. *Personality and Social Psychology Bulletin, 22,* 721–731.

Manuck, S. B., Flory, J. D., Ferrell, R. E., Mann, J. J., & Muldoon, M. F. (2000). A regulatory polymorphism of the monoamine oxidase-A gene may be associated with variability in aggression, impulsivity, and central nervous system serotonergic responsivity. *Psychiatry Research, 95,* 9–23.

Manuck, S. B., Flory, J. D., McCaffery, J. M., Matthews, K. A., Mann, J. J., & Muldoon, M. F. (1998). Aggression, impulsivity, and central nervous system serotonergic responsivity in a nonpatient sample. *Neuropsychopharmacology, 19,* 287–299.

Manuck, S. B., Flory, J. D., Muldoon, M. F., & Ferrell, R. E. (2003). A neurobiology of intertemporal choice. In G. Loewenstein, D. Read, & R. F. Baumeister (Eds.), *Time and decision: Economic and psychological perspectives on intertemporal choice* (pp. 139–172). New York: Russell Sage Foundation.

Marangoni, C., Garcia, S., Ickes, W., & Teng, G. (1995). Empathic accuracy in a clinically relevant setting. *Journal of Personality and Social Psychology, 68,* 854–869.

Marcia, J. E. (1966). Development and validation of ego identity statuses. *Journal of Personality and Social Psychology, 3,* 551–558.

Marcia, J. E. (1976). Identity six years after: A follow-up study. *Journal of Youth and Adolescence, 5,* 145–160.

Marcia, J. E. (1980). Identity in adolescence. In J. Adelson (Ed.), *Handbook of adolescent psychology.* New York: Wiley.

Marcus, G. F. (1996). Why do children say "breaked"? *Current Directions in Psychological Science, 5,* 81–85.

Marcus-Newhall, A., Pedersen, W. C., Carlson, M., & Miller, N. (2000). Displaced aggression is alive and well: A meta-analytic review. *Journal of Personality and Social Psychology, 78,* 670–689.

Markey, C. N., Markey, P. M., & Tinsley, B. J. (2003). Personality, puberty, and preadolescent girls' risky behaviors: Examining the predictive value of the five-factor model of personality. *Journal of Research in Personality, 37,* 405–419.

Markon, K. E., Krueger, R. F., & Watson, D. (2005). Delineating the structure of normal and abnormal personality: An integrative hierarchical approach. *Journal of Personality and Social Psychology, 88,* 139–157.

Markus, H. (1977). Self-schemata and processing information about the self. *Journal of Personality and Social Psychology, 35,* 63–78.

Markus, H., & Nurius, P. (1986). Possible selves. *American Psychologist, 41,* 954–969.

Markus, H., & Sentis, K. (1982). The self and social information processing. In J. Suls (Ed.), *Psychological perspectives on the self* (Vol. 1, pp. 41–70). Hillsdale, NJ: Erlbaum.

Markus, H., & Wurf, E. (1987). The dynamic self-concept: A social psychological perspective. *Annual Review of Psychology, 38,* 299–337.

Martin, L. L., & Tesser, A. (1996). Some ruminative thoughts. In R. S. Wyer, Jr. (Ed.), *Advances in social cognition* (Vol. 9, pp. 1–47). Mahwah, NJ: Erlbaum.

Masling, J. M., & Bornstein, R. F. (Eds.). (1994). *Empirical perspectives on object relations theory.* Washington, DC: American Psychological Association.

Masling, J. M., Johnson, C., & Saturansky, C. (1974). Oral imagery, accuracy of perceiving others, and performance in Peace Corps training. *Journal of Personality and Social Psychology, 30,* 414–419.

Masling, J. M., O'Neill, R., & Jayne, C. (1981). Orality and latency of volunteering to serve as experimental subjects. *Journal of Personality Assessment, 45,* 20–22.

Masling, J. M., O'Neill, R., & Katkin, E. S. (1982). Autonomic arousal, interpersonal climate, and orality. *Journal of Personality and Social Psychology, 42,* 529–534.

Masling, J. M., Price, J., Goldband, S., & Katkin, E. S. (1981). Oral imagery and autonomic arousal in social isolation. *Journal of Personality and Social Psychology, 40,* 395–400.

Masling, J. M., Rabie, L., & Blondheim, S. H. (1967). Obesity, level of aspiration, and Rorschach and TAT measures of oral dependence. *Journal of Consulting Psychology, 31,* 233–239.

Masling, J. M., Weiss, L., & Rothschild, B. (1968). Relationships of oral imagery to yielding behavior and birth order. *Journal of Consulting and Clinical Psychology, 32,* 38–81.

Maslow, A. H. (1955). Deficiency motivation and growth motivation. In M. R. Jones (Ed.), *Nebraska symposium on motivation.* Lincoln: University of Nebraska Press.

Maslow, A. H. (1962). *Toward a psychology of being.* Princeton, NJ: Van Nostrand.

Maslow, A. H. (1968). *Toward a psychology of being* (2nd ed.). New York: Van Nostrand.

Maslow, A. H. (1970). *Motivation and personality* (Rev. ed.). New York: Harper & Row.

Maslow, A. H. (1971). *The farther reaches of human nature.* New York: Viking.

Maslow, A. H. (1979). *The journals of A. H. Maslow* (2 vols.). R. J. Lowry (Ed.). Monterey, CA: Brooks/Cole.

Mason, A., & Blankenship, V. (1987). Power and affiliation motivation, stress, and abuse in intimate relationships. *Journal of Personality and Social Psychology, 52,* 203–210.

Masson, J. M. (1984). *The assault on truth.* New York: Farrar, Straus, & Giroux.

Matas, L., Arend, R. A., & Sroufe, L. A. (1978). Continuity of adaptation in the second year: The relationship between quality of attachment and later competence. *Child Development, 49,* 547–556.

Matthews, K. A., Batson, C. D., Horn, J., & Rosenman, R. (1981). "Principles in his nature which interest him in the fortune of others . . .": The heritability of empathic concern for others. *Journal of Personality, 49,* 237–247.

Matthews, K. A., Owens, J. F., Kuller, L. H., Sutton-Tyrrell, K., & Jansen-McWilliams, L. (1998). Are hostility and anxiety associated with carotid atherosclerosis in healthy postmenopausal women? *Psychosomatic Medicine, 60,* 633–638.

Matthiesen, A.-S., Ransjö-Arvidson, A.-B., Nissen, E., & Uvnäs-Moberg, K. (2001). Postpartum maternal oxytocin release by newborns: Effects of infant hand massage and sucking. *Birth, 28,* 13–19.

May, R. (1953). *Man's search for himself.* New York: Norton.

May, R. (1958). The origins and significance of the existential movement in psychology. In R. May, E. Angel, & H. F. Ellenberger (Eds.), *Existence: A new dimension in psychiatry and psychology.* New York: Basic Books.

May, R. (Ed.). (1969). *Existential psychology* (2nd ed.). New York: Random House.

Mazur, A. (1985). A biosocial model of status in face-to-face primate groups. *Social Forces, 64,* 377–402.

Mazur, A., & Booth, A. (1998). Testosterone and dominance in men. *Behavior and Brain Sciences, 21,* 353–397.

Mazur, A., Booth, A., & Dabbs, J. M., Jr. (1992). Testosterone and chess competition. *Social Psychology Quarterly, 55,* 70–77.

McAdams, D. P. (1982). Experiences of intimacy and power: Relationships between social motives and autobiographical memory. *Journal of Personality and Social Psychology, 42,* 292–302.

McAdams, D. P. (1984). Human motives and personal relationships. In V. J. Derlaga (Ed.), *Communication, intimacy, and close relationships.* New York: Academic.

McAdams, D. P. (1985). *Power, intimacy, and the life story: Personological inquiries into identity.* New York: Guilford.

McAdams, D. P. (1989). *Intimacy: The need to be close.* New York: Doubleday.

McAdams, D. P. (1992). The five-factor model *in* personality: A critical appraisal. *Journal of Personality, 60,* 329–361.

McAdams, D. P. (1993). *The stories we live by: Personal myths and the making of the self.* New York: Morrow.

McAdams, D. P. (2001). The psychology of life stories. *Review of General Psychology, 5,* 100–122.

McAdams, D. P. (2006). *The redemptive self: Stories Americans live by.* New York: Oxford University Press.

McAdams, D. P., Anyidoho, N. A., Brown, C., Huang, Y. T., Kaplan, B., & Machado, M. A. (2004). Traits and stories: Links between dispositional and narrative features of personality. *Journal of Personality, 72,* 761–784.

McAdams, D. P., & Bryant, F. B. (1987). Intimacy motivation and subjective mental health in a nationwide sample. *Journal of Personality, 55,* 395–413.

McAdams, D. P., & Constantian, C. A. (1983). Intimacy and affiliation motives in daily living: An experience sampling analysis. *Journal of Personality and Social Psychology, 45,* 851–861.

McAdams, D. P., & de St. Aubin, E. (1992). A theory of generativity and its assessment through self-report, behavioral acts, and narrative themes in autobiography. *Journal of Personality and Social Psychology, 62,* 1003–1015.

McAdams, D. P., Diamond, A., de St. Aubin, E., & Mansfield, E. (1997). Stories of commitment: The psychosocial construction of generative lives. *Journal of Personality and Social Psychology, 72,* 678–694.

McAdams, D. P., Healy, S., & Krause, S. (1984). Social motives and patterns of friendship. *Journal of Personality and Social Psychology, 47,* 828–838.

McAdams, D. P., Jackson, R. J., & Kirshnit, C. (1984). Looking, laughing, and smiling in dyads as a function of intimacy motivation and reciprocity. *Journal of Personality, 52,* 261–273.

McAdams, D. P., & Pals, J. L. (2006). A new big five: Fundamental principles for an integrative science of personality. *American Psychologist, 61,* 204–217.

McAdams, D. P., & Powers, J. (1981). Themes of intimacy in behavior and thought. *Journal of Personality and Social Psychology, 40,* 573–587.

McAdams, D. P., Reynolds, J., Lewis, M., Patten, A. H., & Bowman, P. J. (2001). When bad things turn good and good things turn bad: Sequences of redemption and contamination in life narrative and their relation to psychosocial adaptation in midlife adults and in students. *Personality and Social Psychology Bulletin, 27,* 474–485.

McAdams, D. P., & Vaillant, G. E. (1982). Intimacy motivation and psychosocial adjustment: A longitudinal study. *Journal of Personality Assessment, 46,* 586–593.

McArthur, L. Z. (1981). The role of attention in impression formation and causal attribution. In E. T. Higgins, C. P.

Herman, & M. P. Zanna (Eds.), *Social cognition: The Ontario Symposium* (Vol. 1). Hillsdale, NJ: Erlbaum.

McClelland, D. C. (1961). *The achieving society.* Princeton, NJ: Van Nostrand.

McClelland, D. C. (1965). Toward a theory of motive acquisition. *American Psychologist, 20,* 321–333.

McClelland, D. C. (1979). Inhibited power motivation and high blood pressure in men. *Journal of Abnormal Psychology, 88,* 182–190.

McClelland, D. C. (1984). *Human motivation.* Glenview, IL: Scott, Foresman.

McClelland, D. C. (1985). How motives, skills, and values determine what people do. *American Psychologist, 40,* 812–825.

McClelland, D. C. (1989). Motivational factors in health and disease. *American Psychologist, 44,* 675–683.

McClelland, D. C., Atkinson, J. W., Clark, R. A., & Lowell, E. L. (1953). *The achievement motive.* New York: Appleton-Century-Crofts.

McClelland, D. C., & Boyatzis, R. E. (1982). Leadership motive pattern and long-term success in management. *Journal of Applied Psychology, 67,* 737–743.

McClelland, D. C., Davis, W. N., Kalin, R., & Wanner, E. (Eds.). (1972). *The drinking man.* New York: Free Press.

McClelland, D. C., Koestner, R., & Weinberger, J. (1989). How do self-attributed and implicit motives differ? *Psychological Review, 96,* 690–702.

McClelland, D. C., & Winter, D. G. (1969). *Motivating economic achievement.* New York: Free Press.

McClelland, J. L. (1999). Cognitive modeling, connectionist. In R. W. Wilson & F. C. Keil (Eds.), *The MIT encyclopedia of the cognitive sciences* (pp. 137–139). Cambridge, MA: MIT Press.

McClelland, J. L., Rumelhart, D. E., & PDP Research Group. (Eds.). (1986). *Parallel distributed processing: Explorations in the microstructure of cognition: Vol. 2. Psychological and biological models.* Cambridge, MA: MIT Press.

McCrae, R. R. (1993). Moderated analyses of longitudinal personality stability. *Journal of Personality and Social Psychology, 65,* 577–585.

McCrae, R. R. (1996). Social consequences of experiential openness. *Psychological Bulletin, 120,* 323–337.

McCrae, R. R., & Costa, P. T., Jr. (1987). Validation of the five-factor model of personality across instruments and observers. *Journal of Personality and Social Psychology, 52,* 81–90.

McCrae, R. R., & Costa, P. T., Jr. (1989a). Reinterpreting the Myers–Briggs type indicator from the perspective of the five-factor model of personality. *Journal of Personality, 57,* 17–40.

McCrae, R. R., & Costa, P. T., Jr. (1989b). The structure of interpersonal traits: Wiggins's circumplex and the five-factor model. *Journal of Personality and Social Psychology, 56,* 586–595.

McCrae, R. R., & Costa, P. T., Jr. (1997). Personality trait structure as a human universal. *American Psychologist, 52,* 509–516.

McCrae, R. R., & Costa, P. T., Jr. (2003). *Personality in adulthood: A five-factor theory perspective* (2nd ed.). New York: Guilford.

McCrae, R. R., Costa, P. T., Jr., & Busch, C. M. (1986). Evaluating comprehensiveness in personality systems: The California Q-Set and the five factor model. *Journal of Personality, 54,* 430–446.

McCrae, R. R., & John, O. P. (1992). An introduction to the five-factor model and its implications. *Journal of Personality, 60,* 175–215.

McCrae, R. R., Terracciano, A., et al. (2005). Universal features of personality traits from the observer's perspective: Data from 50 cultures. *Journal of Personality and Social Psychology, 88,* 547–561.

McCrae, R. R., Zonderman, A. B., Costa, P. J., Jr., Bond, M. H., & Paunonen, S. V. (1996). Evaluating replicability of factors in the Revised NEO Personality Inventory: Confirmatory factor analysis versus Procrustes rotation. *Journal of Personality and Social Psychology, 70,* 552–566.

McCullough, M. (2001). Freud's seduction theory and its rehabilitation: A saga of one mistake after another. *Review of General Psychology, 5,* 3–22.

McCullough, M. E., Emmons, R. A., Kilpatrick, S. D., & Mooney, C. N. (2003). Narcissists as "victims": The role of narcissism in the perception of transgressions. *Personality and Social Psychology Bulletin, 29,* 885–893.

McCullough, M. E., & Hoyt, W. T. (2002). Transgression-related motivational dispositions: Personality substrates of forgiveness and their links to the big five. *Personality and Social Psychology Bulletin, 28,* 1556–1573.

McCullough, M. E., Tsang, J., & Brion, S. (2003). Personality traits in adolescence as predictors of religiousness in early adulthood: Findings from the Terman longitudinal study. *Personality and Social Psychology Bulletin, 29,* 980–991.

McFall, R., & Twentyman, C. T. (1973). Four experiments on relative contributions of rehearsal, modeling and coaching to assertion training. *Journal of Abnormal Psychology, 81,* 199–218.

McGregor, H. A., & Elliot, A. J. (2005). The shame of failure: Examining the link between fear of failure and shame. *Personality and Social Psychology Bulletin, 31,* 218–231.

McGregor, I., & Marigold, D. C. (2003). Defensive zeal and the uncertain self: What makes you so sure? *Journal of Personality and Social Psychology, 85,* 838–852.

McGregor, I., Zanna, M. P., Holmes, J. G., & Spencer, S. J. (2001). Compensatory conviction in the face of personal uncertainty: Going to extremes and being oneself. *Journal of Personality and Social Psychology, 80,* 472–488.

McGue, M., & Lykken, D. T. (1992). Genetic influence on risk of divorce. *Psychological Science, 3,* 368–373.

McGuffin, P., Rijsdijk, F., Andrew, M., Sham, P., Katz, R., & Cardno, A. (2003). The heritability of bipolar affective disorder and the genetic relationship to unipolar depression. *Archives of General Psychiatry, 60,* 497–502.

McGuire, W. (Ed.). (1974). *The Freud/Jung letters: The correspondence between Sigmund Freud and C. G. Jung.* Princeton, NJ: Princeton University Press.

McGuire, W. J., & McGuire, C. V. (1986). Differences in conceptualizing self versus conceptualizing other people as manifested in contrasting verb types used in natural speech. *Journal of Personality and Social Psychology, 51,* 1135–1143.

McMahan, I. D. (1973). Relationships between causal attributions and expectancy of success. *Journal of Personality and Social Psychology, 28,* 108–114.

McNamara, P., McLaren, D., Smith, D., Brown, A., & Stickgold, R. (2005). A "Jekyll and Hyde" within: Aggressive versus friendly interactions in REM and non-REM dreams. *Psychological Science, 16,* 130.

Medin, D. L. (1989). Concepts and conceptual structure. *American Psychologist, 44,* 1469–1481.

Meehl, P. E. (1962). Schizotaxia, schizotypy, schizophrenia. *American Psychologist, 17,* 827–838.

Meehl, P. E. (1992). Factors and taxa, traits and types, differences of degree and differences in kind. *Journal of Personality, 60,* 117–174.

Megargee, E. I. (1966). Undercontrolled and overcontrolled personality types in extreme antisocial aggression. In E. I. Megargee & J. E. Moranson (Eds.), *Psychological Monographs.* New York: Harper & Row.

Megargee, E. I. (1971). The role of inhibition in the assessment and understanding of violence. In J. L. Singer (Ed.), *The control of aggression and violence.* New York: Academic.

Megargee, E. I., Cook, P. E., & Mendelsohn, G. A. (1967). Development and evaluation of an MMPI scale of assaultiveness in overcontrolled individuals. *Journal of Abnormal Psychology, 72,* 519–528.

Meichenbaum, D. (1971). Examination of model characteristics in reducing avoidance behavior. *Journal of Personality and Social Psychology, 17,* 298–307.

Meichenbaum, D. (1972). Cognitive modification of test anxious college students. *Journal of Consulting and Clinical Psychology, 39,* 370–379.

Meichenbaum, D. (1974). *Cognitive behavior modification.* Morristown, NJ: General Learning.

Meichenbaum, D. (1977). *Cognitive-behavior modification: An integrative approach.* New York: Plenum.

Meichenbaum, D. (1985). *Stress inoculation training.* New York: Pergamon.

Meichenbaum, D., & Goodman, J. (1971). Training impulsive children to talk to themselves: A means of developing self-control. *Journal of Abnormal Psychology, 77,* 115–126.

Meier, B. P., & Robinson, M. D. (2004). Does quick to blame mean quick to anger? The role of agreeableness in dissociating blame and anger. *Personality and Social Psychology Bulletin, 30,* 856–867.

Meier, B. P., Robinson, M. D., & Wilkowski, B. M. (2006). Turning the other cheek: Agreeableness and the regulation of aggression-related primes. *Psychological Science, 17,* 136–142.

Melamed, B. G., & Siegel, L. J. (1975). Reduction of anxiety in children facing hospitalization and surgery by use of filmed modeling. *Journal of Consulting and Clinical Psychology, 43,* 511–521.

Melamed, B. G., Weinstein, D., Hawes, R., & Katin-Borland, M. (1975). Reduction of fear-related dental management problems using filmed modeling. *Journal of the American Dental Association, 90,* 822–826.

Meltzoff, A. N. (1985). Immediate and deferred imitation in fourteen- and twenty-four-month-old infants. *Child Development, 56,* 62–72.

Mendoza-Denton, R., Ayduk, O., Mischel, W., Shoda, Y., & Testa, A. (2001). Person x situation interactionism in self-encoding (*I am . . . when . . .*): Implications for affect regulation and social information processing. *Journal of Personality and Social Psychology, 80,* 533–544.

Merluzzi, T. V., Glass, C. R., & Genest, M. (Eds.). (1981). *Cognitive assessment.* New York: Guilford.

Merluzzi, T. V., Rudy, T. E., & Glass, C. R. (1981). The information-processing paradigm: Implications for clinical science. In T. V. Merluzzi, C. R. Glass, & M. Genest (Eds.), *Cognitive assessment.* New York: Guilford.

Mershon, B., & Gorsuch, R. L. (1988). Number of factors in the personality sphere: Does increase in factors increase predictability of real-life criteria? *Journal of Personality and Social Psychology, 55,* 675–680.

Metcalfe, J., & Mischel, W. (1999). A hot/cool-system analysis of delay of gratification: Dynamics of willpower. *Psychological Review, 106,* 3–19.

Meyer, D., Leventhal, H., & Gutmann, M. (1985). Common-sense models of illness: The example of hypertension. *Health Psychology, 4,* 115–135.

Meyer, J. P. (1980). Causal attribution for success and failure: A multivariate investigation of dimensionality, formation, and consequences. *Journal of Personality and Social Psychology, 38,* 708–718.

Meyer, J. P., & Pepper, S. (1977). Need compatibility and marital adjustment in young married couples. *Journal of Personality and Social Psychology, 35,* 331–342.

Michalski, R. L., & Shackelford, T. K. (2002). An attempted replication of the relationships between birth order and personality. *Journal of Research in Personality, 36,* 182–188.

Mickelson, K. D., Kessler, R. C., & Shaver, P. R. (1997). Adult attachment in a nationally representative sample. *Journal of Personality and Social Psychology, 73,* 1092–1106.

Mikulincer, M. (1998). Adult attachment style and individual differences in functional versus dysfunctional experiences of anger. *Journal of Personality and Social Psychology, 74,* 513–524.

Mikulincer, M., Florian, V., & Hirschberger, G. (2003). The existential function of close relationships: Introducing death into the science of love. *Personality and Social Psychology Review, 7,* 20–40.

Mikulincer, M., Florian, V., & Weller, A. (1993). Attachment styles, coping strategies, and posttraumatic psychological distress: The impact of the Gulf War in Israel. *Journal of Personality and Social Psychology, 64,* 817–826.

Mikulincer, M., & Goodman, G. S. (2006). *Dynamics of romantic love: Attachment, caregiving, and sex.* New York: Guilford.

Mikulincer, M., Hirschberger, G., Nachmias, O., & Gillath, O. (2001). The affective component of the secure base schema: Affective priming with representations of attachment security. *Journal of Personality and Social Psychology, 81,* 305–321.

Mikulincer, M., & Horesh, N. (1999). Adult attachment style and the perception of others: The role of projective mechanisms. *Journal of Personality and Social Psychology, 76,* 1022–1034.

Mikulincer, M., & Nachshon, O. (1991). Attachment styles and patterns of self-disclosure. *Journal of Personality and Social Psychology, 61,* 321–331.

Mikulincer, M., & Shaver, P. R. (2001). Attachment theory and intergroup bias: Evidence that priming the secure base schema attenuates negative reactions to out-groups. *Journal of Personality and Social Psychology, 81,* 97–115.

Mikulincer, M., & Shaver, P. R. (2005). Attachment security, compassion, and altruism. *Current Directions in Psychological Science, 14,* 34–38.

Mikulincer, M., & Shaver, P. R. (2007). *Attachment in adulthood: Structure, dynamics, and change.* New York: Guilford.

Mikulincer, M., Shaver, P. R., Gillath, O., & Nitzberg, R. A. (2005). Attachment, caregiving, and altruism: Boosting attachment security increases compassion and helping. *Journal of Personality and Social Psychology, 89,* 817–839.

Mill, J. S. (1962). "On liberty." In M. Warnock (Ed.), *John Stuart Mill: Utilitarianism, On liberty, Essay on Bentham, together with selected writings of Jeremy Bentham and John Austin.* Cleveland, OH: World. (Originally published, 1859)

Miller, G. A., Galanter, E., & Pribram, K. H. (1960). *Plans and the structure of behavior.* New York: Holt, Rinehart, & Winston.

Miller, G. E., Cohen, S., & Ritchey, A. K. (2002). Chronic psychological stress and the regulation of pro-inflammatory cytokines: A glucocorticoid-resistance model. *Health Psychology, 21,* 531–541.

Miller, I. W., & Norman, W. H. (1979). Learned helplessness in humans: A review and attribution-theory model. *Psychological Bulletin, 86,* 93–119.

Miller, J. D., Lynam, D., & Leukefeld, C. (2003). Examining antisocial behavior through the lens of the five factor model of personality. *Aggressive Behavior, 29,* 497–514.

Miller, L. C., Putcha-Bhagavatula, A., & Pedersen, W. C. (2002). Men's and women's mating preferences: Distinct evolutionary mechanisms? *Current Directions in Psychological Science, 11,* 88–93.

Miller, N. E. (1944). Experimental studies of conflict. In J. McVicker Hunt (Ed.), *Personality and the behavior disorders* (Vol. 1, pp. 431–465). New York: Ronald.

Miller, N. E. (1948). Theory and experiment relating psychoanalytic displacement to stimulus–response generalization. *Journal of Abnormal and Social Psychology, 43,* 155–178.

Miller, N. E. (1951). Learnable drives and rewards. In S. S. Stevens (Ed.), *Handbook of experimental psychology.* New York: Wiley.

Miller, N. E., & Dollard, J. (1941). *Social learning and imitation.* New Haven, CT: Yale University Press.

Miller, N., Pedersen, W. C., Earleywine, M., & Pollock, V. E. (2003). A theoretical model of triggered displaced aggression. *Personality and Social Psychology Review, 7,* 75–97.

Miller, R. S. (1987). Empathic embarrassment: Situational and personal determinants of reactions to the embarrassment of another. *Journal of Personality and Social Psychology, 53,* 1061–1069.

Miller, S., Saccuzzo, D., & Braff, D. (1979). Information-processing deficits in remitted schizophrenics. *Journal of Abnormal Psychology, 88,* 446–449.

Mineka, S., & Zinbarg, R. (2006). A contemporary learning theory perspective on the etiology of anxiety disorders. *American Psychologist, 61,* 10–26.

Mirels, H. (1970). Dimensions of internal versus external control. *Journal of Consulting and Clinical Psychology, 34,* 226–228.

Mischel, W. (1961). Delay of gratification, need for achievement, and acquiescence in another culture. *Journal of Abnormal and Social Psychology, 62,* 543–552.

Mischel, W. (1966). Theory and research on the antecedents of self-imposed delay of reward. In B. A. Maher (Ed.), *Progress in experimental personality research* (Vol. 3). New York: Academic.

Mischel, W. (1968). *Personality and assessment.* New York: Wiley.

Mischel, W. (1970). Sex typing and socialization. In P. H. Mussen (Ed.), *Carmichael's manual of child psychology* (Rev. ed.). New York: Wiley.

Mischel, W. (1973). Toward a cognitive social learning reconceptualization of personality. *Psychological Review, 80,* 252–283.

Mischel, W. (1974). Processes in delay of gratification. In L. Berkowitz (Ed.), *Advances in experimental social psychology* (Vol. 7). New York: Academic.

Mischel, W. (1977). The interaction of person and situation. In D. Magnusson & N. S. Endler (Eds.), *Personality at the crossroads: Current issues in interactional psychology.* Hillsdale, NJ: Erlbaum.

Mischel, W. (1979). On the interface of cognition and personality: Beyond the person–situation debate. *American Psychologist, 34,* 740–754.

Mischel, W. (1990). Personality dispositions revisited and revised: A view after three decades. In L. A. Pervin (Ed.), *Handbook of personality: Theory and research* (pp. 111–134). New York: Guilford.

Mischel, W., & Baker, N. (1975). Cognitive transformations of reward objects through instructions. *Journal of Personality and Social Psychology, 31,* 254–261.

Mischel, W., & Ebbesen, E. (1970). Attention in delay of gratification. *Journal of Personality and Social Psychology, 16,* 329–337.

Mischel, W., Ebbesen, E., & Zeiss, A. (1973). Selective attention to the self: Situational and dispositional determinants. *Journal of Personality and Social Psychology, 27,* 129–142.

Mischel, W., & Liebert, R. M. (1966). Effects of discrepancies between observed and imposed reward criteria on their acquisition and transmission. *Journal of Personality and Social Psychology, 3,* 45–53.

Mischel, W., & Metzner, R. (1962). Preference for delayed reward as a function of age, intelligence, and length of delay interval. *Journal of Abnormal and Social Psychology, 64,* 425–431.

Mischel, W., & Moore, B. (1973). Effects of attention to symbolically presented rewards upon self-control. *Journal of Personality and Social Psychology, 28,* 172–179.

Mischel, W., & Shoda, Y. (1995). A cognitive–affective system theory of personality: Reconceptualizing situations, dispositions, and invariance in personality structure. *Psychological Review, 102,* 246–268.

Mischel, W., Shoda, Y., & Mendoza-Denton, R. (2002). Situation–behavior profiles as a locus of consistency in personality. *Current Directions in Psychological Science, 11,* 50–54.

Moffitt, T. E. (2005a). The new look of behavioral genetics in developmental psychopathology: Gene-environment interplay in antisocial behaviors. *Psychological Bulletin, 131,* 533–554.

Moffitt, T. E. (2005b). Genetic and environmental influences on antisocial behaviors: Evidence from behavioral-genetic research. *Advances in genetics, 55,* 41–104.

Moffitt, T. E., Caspi, A., & Rutter, M. (2006). Measured gene-environment interactions in psychopathology: Concepts, research strategies, and implications for research, intervention, and public understanding of genetics. *Perspectives on Psychological Science, 1,* 5–27.

Monson, T., Hesley, J., & Chernick, L. (1982). Specifying when personality traits can and cannot predict behavior: An alternative to abandoning the attempt to predict single-act criteria. *Journal of Personality and Social Psychology, 43,* 385–399.

Moore, B., Mischel, W., & Zeiss, A. (1976). Comparative effects of the reward stimulus and its cognitive representation in voluntary delay. *Journal of Personality and Social Psychology, 34,* 419–424.

Moore, J. W. (1972). Stimulus control: Studies of auditory generalization in rabbits. In A. H. Black & W. F. Prokasy (Eds.), *Classical conditioning II: Current research and theory.* New York: Appleton-Century-Crofts.

Moors, A., & De Hower, J. (2006). Automaticity: A theoretical and conceptual analysis. *Psychological Bulletin, 132,* 297–326.

Morf, C. C., & Rhodewalt, F. (1993). Narcissism and self-evaluation maintenance: Explorations in object relations. *Personality and Social Psychology Bulletin, 19,* 668–676.

Morgan, C. D., & Murray, H. A. (1935). A method for investigating fantasies. *Archives of Neurology and Psychiatry, 34,* 289–306.

Morilak, D. A., Barrera, G., Echevarria, D. J., Garcia, A. S., Hernandez, A., Ma, S., & Petre, C. O. (2005). Role of brain norepinephrine in the behavioral response to stress. *Biological Psychiatry, 29,* 1214–1224.

Morris, L. W., Davis, M. A., & Hutchings, C. H. (1981). Cognitive and emotional components of anxiety: Literature review and a revised worry–emotionality scale. *Journal of Educational Psychology, 73,* 541–555.

Morrone, J. V., Depue, R. A., Scherer, A. J., & White, T. L. (2000). Film-induced incentive motivation and positive activation in relation to agentic and affiliative components of extraversion. *Personality and Individual Differences, 29,* 199–216.

Moskowitz, D. S. (1994). Cross-situational generality and the interpersonal circumplex. *Journal of Personality and Social Psychology, 66,* 921–933.

Moskowitz, G. B. (1993). Individual differences in social categorization: The influence of personal need for structure on spontaneous trait inferences. *Journal of Personality and Social Psychology, 65,* 132–142.

Motley, M. T. (1985). Slips of the tongue. *Scientific American, 253,* 116–127.

Mowrer, R. R., & Klein, S. B. (Eds.). (2001). *Handbook of contemporary learning theories.* Mahwah, NJ: Erlbaum.

Mueller, C. M., & Dweck, C. S. (1998). Praise for intelligence can undermine children's motivation and performance. *Journal of Personality and Social Psychology, 75,* 33–52.

Mullen, B. (1986). Atrocity as a function of lynch mob composition: A self-attention perspective. *Personality and Social Psychology Bulletin, 12,* 187–197.

Muraven, M., & Baumeister, R. F. (2000). Self-regulation and depletion of limited resources: Does self-control resemble a muscle? *Psychological Bulletin, 126,* 247–259.

Muraven, M., Tice, D. M., & Baumeister, R. F. (1998). Self-control as a limited resource: Regulatory depletion patterns. *Journal of Personality and Social Psychology, 74,* 774–789.

Murray, E. J. (1985). Coping and anger. In T. M. Field, P. M. McCabe, & N. Schneiderman (Eds.), *Stress and coping.* Hillsdale, NJ: Erlbaum.

Murray, H. A. (1938). *Explorations in personality.* New York: Oxford University Press.

Murray, S. L., & Holmes, J. G. (1993). Seeing virtues in faults: Negativity and the transformation of interpersonal narratives in close relationships. *Journal of Personality and Social Psychology, 65,* 707–722.

Murray, S. L., Holmes, J. G., & Griffin, D. W. (2000). Self-esteem and the quest for felt security: How perceived regard regulates attachment processes. *Journal of Personality and Social Psychology, 78,* 478–498.

Murray, S. L., Holmes, J. G., Griffin, D. W., Bellavia, G., & Rose, P. (2001). The mismeasure of love: How self-doubt contaminates relationship beliefs. *Personality and Social Psychology Bulletin, 27,* 423–436.

Mussweiler, T. (2006). Doing is for thinking! Stereotype activation by stereotypic movements. *Psychological Science, 17,* 17–21.

Mustanski, B. S., Dupree, M. G., Nievergelt, C. M., Bocklandt, S., Schork, N. J., & Hamer, D. H. (2005). A genome-wide scan of male sexual orientation. *Human Genetics, 116,* 272–278.

Myers, M. B., & McCaulley, M. H. (1985). *Manual: A guide to the development and use of the Myers–Briggs Type Indicator.* Palo Alto, CA: Consulting Psychologists.

Nasby, W. (1985). Private self-consciousness, articulation of the self-schema, and the recognition memory of trait adjectives. *Journal of Personality and Social Psychology, 49,* 704–709.

Neale, M. C., & Stevenson, J. (1989). Rater bias in the EASI temperament scales: A twin study. *Journal of Personality and Social Psychology, 56,* 446–455.

Neimeyer, G. J., & Neimeyer, R. A. (1981). Personal construct perspectives on cognitive assessment. In T. V. Merluzzi, C. R. Glass, & M. Genest (Eds.), *Cognitive assessment.* New York: Guilford.

Neimeyer, R. A. (1985). Personal constructs in clinical practice. In P. C. Kendall (Ed.), *Advances in cognitive-behavioral research and therapy* (Vol. 4, pp. 275–339). New York: Academic.

Nell, V. (2002). Why young men drive dangerously: Implications for injury prevention. *Current Directions in Psychological Science, 11,* 75–79.

Nelson, R. O. (1977). Methodological issues in assessment via self-monitoring. In J. D. Cone & R. P. Hawkins (Eds.),

Behavioral assessment: New directions in clinical psychology. New York: Brunner/Mazel.

Netter, P., Hennig, J., & Rohrmann, S. (1999). Psychobiological differences between the aggression and psychoticism dimension. *Pharmacopsychiatry, 32,* 5–12.

Neuberg, S. L., & Newsom, J. T. (1993). Personal need for structure: Individual differences in the desire for simple structure. *Journal of Personality and Social Psychology, 65,* 113–131.

Neuringer, A. (2004). Reinforced variability in animals and people: Implications for adaptive action. *American Psychologist, 59,* 891–906.

Newcomb, M. D., & McGee, L. (1991). Influence of sensation seeking on general deviance and specific problem behaviors from adolescence to young adulthood. *Journal of Personality and Social Psychology, 61,* 614–628.

Newell, A., & Simon, H. A. (1972). *Human problem solving.* Englewood Cliffs, NJ: Prentice-Hall.

Newman, D. L., Tellegen, A., & Bouchard, T. J., Jr. (1998). Individual differences in adult ego development: Sources of influence in twins reared apart. *Journal of Personality and Social Psychology, 74,* 985–995.

Newman, J. P., Wallace, J. F., Strauman, T. J., Skolaski, R. L., Oreland, K. M., Mattek, P. W., Elder, K. A., & McNeeley, J. (1993). Effects of motivationally significant stimuli on the regulation of dominant responses. *Journal of Personality and Social Psychology, 65,* 165–175.

Newman, L. S., Duff, K. J., & Baumeister, R. F. (1997). A new look at defensive projection: Thought suppression, accessibility, and biased person perception. *Journal of Personality and Social Psychology, 72,* 980–1001.

Nezu, A. M. (1987). A problem-solving formulation of depression: A literature review and proposal of a pluralistic model. *Clinical Psychology Review, 7,* 121–144.

Niedenthal, P. M., Halberstadt, J. B., & Innes-Ker, A. H. (1999). Emotional response categorization. *Psychological Review, 106,* 337–361.

Niedenthal, P. M., Setterlund, M. B., & Wherry, M. B. (1992). Possible self-complexity and affective reactions to goal-relevant evaluation. *Journal of Personality and Social Psychology, 63,* 5–16.

Nielsen, T. A. (2000). A review of mentation in REM and NREM sleep: "Covert" REM sleep as a possible reconciliation of two opposing models. *Behavioral and Brain Sciences, 23,* 851–866.

Nigg, J. T. (2000). On inhibition/disinhibition in developmental pychopathology: Views from cognitive and personality psychology as a working inhibition taxonomy. *Psychological Bulletin, 126,* 220–246.

Nigg, J. T., John, O. P., Blaskey, L. G., Huang-Pollock, C. L., Willcutt, E. G., Hinshaw, S. P., & Pennington, B. (2002). Big five dimensions and ADHD symptoms: Links between personality traits and clinical symptoms. *Journal of Personality and Social Psychology, 83,* 451–469.

Nisbett, R. E., & Cohen, D. (1996). *Culture of honor.* Boulder, CO: Westview.

Nisbett, R. E., & Ross, L. (1980). *Human inference: Strategies and shortcomings of social judgment.* Englewood Cliffs, NJ: Prentice-Hall.

Nisbett, R. E., & Wilson, T. D. (1977). Telling more than we can know: Verbal reports on mental processes. *Psychological Review, 84,* 231–259.

Nolen-Hoeksema, S., Morrow, J., & Frederickson, B. L. (1993). Response styles and the duration of episodes of depressed mood. *Journal of Abnormal Psychology, 102,* 20–28.

Nolen-Hoeksema, S., Parker, L., & Larson, J. (1994). Ruminative coping with depressed mood following loss. *Journal of Personality and Social Psychology, 67,* 92–104.

Norman, D. A. (1981). Categorization of action slips. *Psychological Review, 88,* 1–15.

Norman, W. T. (1963). Toward an adequate taxonomy of personality attributes: Replicated factor structure in peer nomination personality ratings. *Journal of Abnormal and Social Psychology, 66,* 574–583.

Novaco, R. W. (1978). Anger and coping with stress: Cognitive behavioral interventions. In J. P. Foreyt & D. P. Rathjen (Eds.), *Cognitive behavior therapy: Research and application.* New York: Plenum.

Nowak, A., Vallacher, R. R., Tesser, A., & Borkowski, W. (2000). Society of self: The emergence of collective properties in self-structure. *Psychological Review, 107,* 39–61.

O'Connor, B. P. (2002). The search for dimensional structure differences between normality and abnormality: A statistical review of published data on personality and psychopathology. *Journal of Personality and Social Psychology, 83,* 962–982.

O'Connor, B. P., & Dyce, J. A. (2001). Rigid and extreme: A geometric representation of personality disorders in five-factor model space. *Journal of Personality and Social Psychology, 81,* 1119–1130.

O'Connor, S. C., & Rosenblood, L. K. (1996). Affiliation motivation in everyday experience: A theoretical comparison. *Journal of Personality and Social Psychology, 70,* 513–522.

O'Donnell, M. C., Fisher, R., Rickard, M., & McConaghy, N. (2000). Emotional suppression: Can it predict cancer outcome in women with suspicious screening mammograms? *Psychological Medicine, 30,* 1079–1088.

O'Donohue, W., & Kitchener, R. (Eds.). (1999). *Handbook of behaviorism.* San Diego: Academic.

O'Leary, K. D., & Becker, W. C. (1967). Behavior modification of an adjustment class: A token reinforcement program. *Exceptional Children, 33,* 637–642.

Ogilvie, D. M. (1987). The undesired self: A neglected variable in personality research. *Journal of Personality and Social Psychology, 52,* 379–385.

Öhman, A., & Mineka, S. (2001). Fears, phobias, and preparedness: Toward an evolved module of fear and fear learning. *Psychological Review, 108,* 483–522.

Oliver, M. B., & Hyde, J. S. (1993). Gender differences in sexuality: A meta-analysis. *Psychological Bulletin, 114,* 29–51.

Olson, J. M., Vernon, P. A., Harris, J. A., & Jang, K. L. (2001). The heritability of attitudes: A study of twins. *Journal of Personality and Social Psychology, 80,* 845–860.

Oreland, L. (2004). Platelet monoamine oxidase, personality and alcoholism: The rise, fall and resurrection. *Neurotoxicology, 25,* 79–89.

Oring, E. (1984). *The jokes of Sigmund Freud: A study in humor and Jewish identity.* Philadelphia: University of Pennsylvania Press.

Orlofsky, J. L., Marcia, J. E., & Lesser, I. M. (1973). Ego identity states and the intimacy versus isolation crisis of young adulthood. *Journal of Youth and Adolescence, 27,* 211–219.

Orr, S. P., Lasko, N. B., Metzger, L. J., Berry, N. J., Ahern, C. E., & Pitman, R. K. (1998). Psychophysiologic assessment of women with posttraumatic stress disorder resulting from childhood sexual abuse. *Journal of Consulting and Clinical Psychology, 66,* 906–913.

Öst, L. G., Ferebee, I., & Furmark, T. (1997). One-session group therapy of spider phobia: Direct versus indirect treatments. *Behavior Research and Therapy, 35,* 721–732.

Overall, N. C., Fletcher, G. J. O., & Friesen, M. D. (2003). Mapping the intimate relationship mind: Comparisons between three models of attachment representations. *Personality and Social Psychology Bulletin, 29,* 1479–1493.

Overmier, J. B., & Seligman, M. E. P. (1967). Effects of inescapable shock upon subsequent escape and avoidance learning. *Journal of Comparative and Physiological Psychology, 63,* 28–33.

Overwalle, F. V., & Siebler, F. (2005). A connectionist model of attitude formation and change. *Personality and Social Psychology Review, 9,* 231–274.

Owen, M. J., Williams, N. M., & O'Donovan, M. C. (2004). The molecular genetics of schizophrenia: New findings promise new insights. *Molecular Psychiatry, 9,* 14–27.

Oyserman, D., Bybee, D., & Terry, K. (2006). Possible selves and academic outcomes: How and when possible selves impel action. *Journal of Personality and Social Psychology.*

Oyserman, D., Bybee, D., Terry, K., & Hart-Johnson, T. (2004). Possible selves as roadmaps. *Journal of Research in Personality, 38,* 130–149.

Oyserman, D., Terry, K., & Bybee, D. (2002). A possible selves intervention to enhance school involvement. *Journal of Adolescence, 25,* 313–326.

Ozer, D. J. (1986). *Consistency in personality: A methodological framework.* New York: Springer-Verlag.

Ozer, D. J., & Benet-Martínez, V. (2006). Personality and the prediction of consequential outcomes. *Annual Review of Psychology, 57,* 401–421.

Ozer, D. J., & Reise, S. P. (1994). Personality assessment. *Annual Review of Psychology, 45,* 357–388.

Ozer, E. M., & Bandura, A. (1990). Mechanisms governing empowerment effects: A self-efficacy analysis. *Journal of Personality and Social Psychology, 58,* 472–486.

Paaver, M., Eensoo, D., Pulver, A., & Harro, J. (2006). Adaptive and maladaptive impulsivity, platelet monoamine oxidase (MAO) activity and risk-admitting in different types of risky drivers. *Psychopharmacology, 186,* 32–40.

Pang, J. S., & Schultheiss, O. C. (2005). Assessing implicit motives in U.S. college students: Effects of picture type and position, gender and ethnicity, and cross-cultural comparisons. *Journal of Personality Assessment, 85,* 280–294.

Panksepp, J. (1998). *Affective neuroscience: The foundations of human and animal emotions.* New York: Oxford University Press.

Panksepp, J., & Cox, J. (1986). An overdue burial for the serotonin theory of anxiety. *Behavioral and Brain Sciences, 9,* 340–341.

Park, C. L., Armeli, S., & Tennen, H. (2004). Appraisal-coping goodness of fit: A daily internet study. *Personality and Social Psychology Bulletin, 30,* 558–569.

Park, J.-W., Yoon, S.-O., Kim, K.-H., & Wyer, R. S., Jr. (2001). Effects of priming a bipolar attribute concept on dimension versus concept-specific accessibility of semantic memory. *Journal of Personality and Social Psychology, 81,* 405–420.

Parke, R. D. (1969). Effectiveness of punishment as an interaction of intensity, timing, agent nurturance, and cognitive structuring. *Child Development, 40,* 211–235.

Parnell, R. W. (1957). Physique and mental breakdown in young adults. *British Medical Journal, 1,* 1485–1490.

Partridge, T. (2005). Are genetically informed designs genetically informative? Comment on McGue, Elkins, Walden, and Iacono (2005) and quantitative behavioral genetics. *Developmental Psychology, 41,* 985–988.

Patterson, C. M., & Newman, J. P. (1993). Reflectivity and learning from aversive events: Toward a psychological mechanism for the syndromes of disinhibition. *Psychological Review, 100,* 716–736.

Paul, G. L. (1966). *Insight vs. desensitization in psychotherapy: An experiment in anxiety reduction.* Stanford, CA: Stanford University Press.

Paulhus, D. L. (1983). Sphere-specific measures of perceived control. *Journal of Personality and Social Psychology, 44,* 1253–1265.

Paulhus, D. L. (1998). Interpersonal and intrapsychic adaptiveness of trait self-enhancement: A mixed blessing? *Journal of Personality and Social Psychology, 74,* 1197–1208.

Paulhus, D. L., & Christie, R. (1981). Spheres of control: An interactionist approach to assessment and perceived control. In H. F. Lefcourt (Ed.), *Research with the locus of control construct. Vol. 1, Assessment methods.* New York: Academic.

Paulhus, D. L., & Suedfeld, P. (1988). A dynamic complexity model of self-deception. In J. S. Lockard & D. L. Paulhus (Eds.), *Self-deception: An adaptive mechanism?* Englewood Cliffs, NJ: Prentice-Hall.

Paulhus, D. L., Trapnell, P. D., & Chen, D. (1999). Birth order effects on personality and achievement within families. *Psychological Science, 10,* 482–488.

Paunonen, S. V. (1989). Consensus in personality judgments: Moderating effects of target–rater acquaintanceship and behavior observability. *Journal of Personality and Social Psychology, 56,* 823–833.

Paunonen, S. V. (1998). Hierarchical organization of personality and prediction of behavior. *Journal of Personality and Social Psychology, 74,* 538–556.

Paunonen, S. V., & Ashton, M. C. (2001a). Big five factors and facets and the prediction of behavior. *Journal of Personality and Social Psychology, 81,* 524–539.

Paunonen, S. V., & Ashton, M. C. (2001b). Big five predictors of academic achievement. *Journal of Research in Personality, 35,* 78–90.

Paunonen, S. V., & Jackson, D. N. (2000). What is beyond the big five? Plenty! *Journal of Personality, 68,* 821–835.

Paunonen, S. V., Jackson, D. N., Trzebinski, J., & Forsterling, F. (1992). Personality structure across cultures: A multi-method evaluation. *Journal of Personality and Social Psychology, 62,* 447–456.

Pavlov, I. P. (1927). *Conditioned reflexes.* Oxford, England: Oxford University Press.

Pavlov, I. P. (1955). *Selected works.* New York: Foreign Languages.

Payne, B. K. (2005). Conceptualizing control in social cognition: How executive functioning modulates the expression of automatic stereotyping. *Journal of Personality and Social Psychology, 89,* 488–503.

Peabody, D. (1984). Personality dimensions through trait inferences. *Journal of Personality and Social Psychology, 46,* 384–403.

Peabody, D., & De Raad, B. (2002). The substantive nature of psycholexical personality factors: A comparison across languages. *Journal of Personality and Social Psychology, 83,* 983–997.

Peabody, D., & Goldberg, L. R. (1989). Some determinants of factor structures from personality-trait descriptors. *Journal of Personality and Social Psychology, 57,* 552–567.

Peciña, S., Cagniard, B., Berridge, K. C., Aldridge, J. W., & Zhuang, X. (2003). Hyperdopaminergic mutant mice have higher "wanting" but not "liking" for sweet rewards. *Journal of Neuroscience, 23,* 9395–9402.

Pedersen, N. L., Plomin, R., McClearn, G. E., & Friberg, L. (1988). Neuroticism, extraversion, and related traits in adult twins reared apart and reared together. *Journal of Personality and Social Psychology, 55,* 950–957.

Pelham, B. W., Mirenberg, M. C., & Jones, J. T. (2002). Why Susie sells seashells by the seashore: Implicit egotism and major life decisions. *Journal of Personality and Social Psychology, 82,* 469–487.

Pennebaker, J. W. (1989). Confession, inhibition, and disease. In L. Berkowitz (Ed.), *Advances in Experimental Social Psychology* (Vol. 22, pp. 211–244). San Diego: Academic.

Pennebaker, J. W. (1993). Putting stress into words: Health, linguistic, and therapeutic implications. *Behaviour Research and Therapy, 31,* 539–548.

Pennebaker, J. W., & Beall, S. K. (1986). Confronting a traumatic event: Toward an understanding of inhibition and disease. *Journal of Abnormal Psychology, 95,* 274–281.

Pennebaker, J. W., & Chung, C. K. (2007). Expressive writing, emotional upheavals, and health. In H. Friedman & R. Silver (Eds.), *Foundations of health psychology* (pp. 263–284). New York: Oxford University Press.

Pennebaker, J. W., & Graybeal, A. (2001). Patterns of natural language use: Disclosure, personality, and social integration. *Current Directions in Psychological Science, 10,* 90–93.

Pennebaker, J. W., Kiecolt-Glaser, J. K., & Glaser, R. (1988). Disclosure of traumas and immune function: Health implications for psychotherapy. *Journal of Consulting and Clinical Psychology, 56,* 239–245.

Peplau, L. A., & Perlman, D. (Eds.). (1982). *Loneliness: A sourcebook of current theory, research, and therapy.* New York: Wiley.

Perkins, K. A. (1999). Nicotine self-administration. *Nicotine and Tobacco Research, 1* (suppl.), 133–137.

Pervin, L. A. (1983). The stasis and flow of behavior: Toward a theory of goals. In M. M. Page & R. Dienstbier (Eds.), *Nebraska symposium on motivation* (Vol. 31). Lincoln: University of Nebraska Press.

Pervin, L. A. (1985). Personality: Current controversies, issues, and directions. *Annual Review of Psychology, 36,* 83–114.

Pervin, L. A. (Ed.). (1989). *Goal concepts in personality and social psychology.* Hillsdale, NJ: Erlbaum.

Pervin, L. A. (1994). A critical analysis of current trait theory. *Psychological Inquiry, 5,* 103–113.

Peterson, C. (1995). Explanatory style and health. In G. M. Buchanan & M. E. P. Seligman (Eds.), *Explanatory style* (pp. 233–246). Hillsdale, NJ: Erlbaum.

Peterson, L. M. (1980). Why men have pockets in their pants: A feminist insight (or, If Freud had been a woman). *Society for the Advancement of Social Psychology Newsletter, 6,* 19.

Petri, H. L., & Mishkin, M. (1994). Behaviorism, cognitivism, and the neuropsychology of memory. *American Scientist, 82,* 30–37.

Petry, N. M., Martin, B., Cooney, J. L., & Kranzler, H. R. (2000). Give them prizes, and they will come: Contingency management for treatment of alcohol dependence. *Journal of Consulting and Clinical Psychology, 68,* 250–257.

Phares, E. J. (1957). Expectancy changes in skill and chance situations. *Journal of Abnormal and Social Psychology, 54,* 339–342.

Phares, E. J. (1976). *Locus of control in personality.* Morristown, NJ: General Learning.

Piedmont, R. L., McCrae, R. R., & Costa, P. T., Jr. (1992). An assessment of the Edwards Personal Preference Schedule from the perspective of the five-factor model. *Journal of Personality Assessment, 58,* 67–78.

Pierce, T., & Lydon, J. E. (2001). Global and specific relational models in the experience of social interactions. *Journal of Personality and Social Psychology, 80,* 613–631.

Pietromonaco, P. R., & Carnelley, K. B. (1994). Gender and working models of attachment: Consequences for perception of self and romantic relationships. *Personal Relationships, 1,* 3–26.

Pietromonaco, P. R., & Barrett, L. F. (1997). Working models of attachment and daily social interactions. *Journal of Personality and Social Psychology, 73,* 1409–1423.

Plaks, J. E., Stroessner, S. J., Dweck, C. S., & Sherman, J. W. (2001). Person theories and attention allocation: Preferences for stereotypic versus counterstereotypic information. *Journal of Personality and Social Psychology, 80,* 876–893.

Plomin, R. (1974). *A temperament theory of personality development: Parent–child interactions.* Unpublished doctoral dissertation, University of Texas at Austin.

Plomin, R. (1981). Ethnological behavioral genetics and development. In K. Immelmann, G. W. Barlow, L. Petrinovich, & M. Main (Eds.), *Behavioral development: The Bielefeld interdisciplinary project.* Cambridge, England: Cambridge University Press.

Plomin, R. (1989). Environment and genes: Determinants of behavior. *American Psychologist, 44,* 105–111.

Plomin, R. (1995). Molecular genetics and psychology. *Current Directions in Psychological Science, 4,* 114–117.

Plomin, R. (1997). *Behavioral Genetics.* New York: Freeman.

Plomin, R., & Crabbe, J. (2000). DNA. *Psychological Bulletin, 126,* 806–828.

Plomin, R., & Daniels, D. (1987). Why are children in the same family so different from one another? *Behavioral and Brain Sciences, 10,* 1–60.

Plomin, R., DeFries, J. C., Craig, I. W., & McGuffin, P. (Eds.). (2003). *Behavioral genetics in the postgenomic era.* Washington, DC: American Psychological Association.

Plomin, R., DeFries, J. C., & Loehlin, J. C. (1977). Genotype–environment interaction and correlation in the analysis of human behavior. *Psychological Bulletin, 84,* 309–322.

Plomin, R., DeFries, J. C., & McClearn, G. E. (1990). *Behavioral genetics: A primer* (2nd ed.). New York: W. H. Freeman.

Plomin, R., & Foch, T. T. (1980). A twin study of objectively assessed personality in childhood. *Journal of Personality and Social Psychology, 39,* 680–688.

Plomin, R., & Rende, R. (1991). Human behavioral genetics. *Annual Review of Psychology, 42,* 161–190.

Plomin, R., & Rowe, D. C. (1977). A twin study of temperament in young children. *Journal of Psychology, 97,* 107–113.

Plomin, R., Scheier, M. F., Bergeman, C. S., Pedersen, N. L., Nesselroade, J. R., & McClearn, G. E. (1992). Optimism, pessimism, and mental health: A twin/adoption analysis. *Personality and Individual Differences, 13,* 921–930.

Pollak, S., & Gilligan, C. (1982). Images of violence in Thematic Apperception Test stories. *Journal of Personality and Social Psychology, 42,* 159–167.

Pool, R. (1993). Evidence for homosexuality gene. *Science, 261,* 291–292

Posner, M. I., & DiGirolamo, G. J. (2000). Cognitive neuroscience: Origins and promise. *Psychological Bulletin, 126,* 873–889.

Postman, L. (1951). Toward a general theory of cognition. In J. H. Rohrer & M. Sherif (Eds.), *Social psychology at the crossroads.* New York: Harper.

Powell, J., & Azrin, N. (1968). The effects of shock as a punisher for cigarette smoking. *Journal of Applied Behavior Analysis, 1,* 63–71.

Powell, R. A., & Boer, D. P. (1994). Did Freud mislead patients to confabulate memories of abuse? *Psychological Reports, 74,* 1283–1298.

Powers, S. I., Pietromonaco, P. R., Gunlicks, M., & Sayer, A. (2006). Dating couples' attachment styles and patterns of cortisol reactivity and recovery in response to a relationship conflict. *Journal of Personality and Social Psychology, 90,* 613–628.

Powers, W. T. (1973). *Behavior: The control of perception.* Chicago: Aldine.

Prager, K. J. (1982). Identity development and self-esteem in young women. *Journal of Genetic Psychology, 141,* 177–182.

Pratt, M. W., Danso, H. A., Arnold, M. L., Norris, J. E., & Filyer, R. (2001). Adult generativity and the socialization of adolescents: Relations to mothers' and fathers' parenting beliefs, styles, and practices. *Journal of Personality, 69,* 89–120.

Pratto, F., & Hegarty, P. (2000). The political psychology of reproductive strategies. *Psychological Science, 11,* 57–62.

Prentice-Dunn, S., & Rogers, R. W. (1980). Effects of deindividuating situational cues and aggressive models on subjective deindividuation and aggression. *Journal of Personality and Social Psychology, 39,* 104–113.

Prentice-Dunn, S., & Rogers, R. W. (1982). Effects of public and private self-awareness on deindividuation and aggression. *Journal of Personality and Social Psychology, 43,* 503–513.

Prentice-Dunn, S., & Rogers, R. W. (1989). Deindividuation and the self-regulation of behavior. In P. B. Paulus (Ed.), *Psychology of group influence* (2nd ed., pp. 87–109). Hillsdale, NJ: Erlbaum.

Pressman, S. D., & Cohen, S. (2005). Does positive affect influence health? *Psychological Bulletin, 131,* 925–971.

Preston, K. L., Umbricht, A., Wong, C. J., & Epstein, D. H. (2001). Shaping cocaine abstinence by successive approximation. *Journal of Consulting and Clinical Psychology, 69,* 643–654.

Price, M. A., Tennant, C. C., Smith, R. C., Butow, P. N., Kennedy, S. J., Kossoff, M. B., & Dunn, S. M. (2001). The role of psychosocial factors in the development of breast carcinoma: Part I. The cancer-prone personality. *Cancer, 91,* 679–685.

Privette, G., & Landsman, T. (1983). Factor analysis of peak performance: The full use of potential. *Journal of Personality and Social Psychology, 44,* 195–200.

Pronin, E., Steele, C. M., & Ross, L. (2004). Identity bifurcation in response to stereotype threat: Women and mathematics. *Journal of Experimental Social Psychology, 40,* 152–168.

Pruessner, J. C., Champagne, F., Meaney, M. J., & Dagher, A. (2004). Dopamine release in response to a psychological stress in humans and its relationship to early life maternal care: A positron emission tomography study using [¹¹C] raclopride. *The Journal of Neuroscience, 24,* 2825–2831.

Pryor, J. B., Reeder, G. D., Yeadon, C., & Hesson-McInnis, M. (2004). A dual-process model of reactions to perceived stigma. *Journal of Personality and Social Psychology, 87,* 436–452.

Pyszczynski, T., & Greenberg, J. (1985). Depression and preference for self-focusing stimuli after success and failure. *Journal of Personality and Social Psychology, 49,* 1066–1075.

Pyszczynski, T., & Greenberg, J. (1987). Self-regulatory perseveration and the depressive self-focusing style: A self-awareness theory of reactive depression. *Psychological Bulletin, 102,* 122–138.

Pyszczynski, T., Greenberg, J., & Solomon, S. (2000). Proximal and distal defense: A new perspective on unconscious motivation. *Current Directions in Psychological Science, 9,* 156–160.

Pyszczynski, T., Greenberg, J., Solomon, S., Arndt, J., & Schimel, J. (2004). Why do people need self-esteem? A theoretical and empirical review. *Psychological Bulletin, 130,* 435–468.

Pyszczynski, T., Solomon, S., & Greenberg, J. (2002). *In the wake of 9/11: The psychology of terror.* Washington, DC: American Psychological Association.

Pytlik Zillig, L. M., Hemenover, S. H., & Dienstbier, R. A. (2002). What do we assess when we assess a big 5 trait? A content analysis of the affective, behavioral, and cognitive processes represented in big 5 personality inventories. *Personality and Social Psychology Bulletin, 28,* 847–858.

Quinn, S. (1987). *A mind of her own: The life of Karen Horney.* New York: Summit.

Rabin, A. I., Zucker, R. A., Emmons, R. A., & Frank, S. (Eds.). (1990). *Studying persons and lives.* New York: Springer.

Rachlin, H. (1977). Reinforcing and punishing thoughts. *Behavior Therapy, 8,* 659–665.

Rachman, J., & Teasdale, J. (1969). *Aversion therapy and behaviour disorders: An analysis.* Coral Gables, FL: University of Miami Press.

Rachman, S. (Ed.). (1978). *Advances in behaviour research and therapy* (Vol. 1). Oxford, England: Pergamon.

Rapaport, D. (1960). *The structure of psychoanalytic theory: A systematizing attempt* (Psychological Issues Monograph 6). New York: International Universities Press.

Raskin, P. A., & Israel, A. C. (1981). Sex-role imitation in children: Effects of sex of child, sex of model, and sex-role appropriateness of modeled behavior. *Sex Roles, 7,* 1067–1076.

Razran, G. H. S. (1940). Conditioned response changes in rating and appraising sociopolitical slogans. *Psychological Bulletin, 37,* 481.

Read, S. J. (1987). Constructing causal scenarios: A knowledge structure approach to causal reasoning. *Journal of Personality and Social Psychology, 52,* 288–302.

Read, S. J., Jones, D. K., & Miller, L. C. (1990). Traits as goal-based categories: The importance of goals in the coherence of dispositional categories. *Journal of Personality and Social Psychology, 58,* 1048–1061.

Read, S. J., & Miller, L. C. (Eds.). (1998). *Connectionist models of social reasoning and social behavior.* Mahwah, NJ: Erlbaum.

Read, S. J., & Miller, L. C. (2002). Virtual personalities: A neural network model of personality. *Personality and Social Psychology Review, 6,* 357–369.

Read, S. J., Vanman, E. J., & Miller, L. C. (1997). Connectionism, parallel constraint satisfaction processes, and Gestalt principles: (Re)introducing cognitive dynamics to social psychology. *Review of Personality and Social Psychology, 1,* 26–53.

Reason, J., & Mycielska, K. (1982). *Absent-minded? The psychology of mental lapses and everyday errors.* Englewood Cliffs, NJ: Prentice-Hall.

Redmore, C., & Waldman, K. (1975). Reliability of a sentence completion measure of ego development. *Journal of Personality Assessment, 39,* 236–243.

Reese, E. P. (1966). The analysis of human operant behavior. In J. A. Vernon (Ed.), *Introduction to psychology: A self-selection textbook.* Dubuque, IA: Brown.

Reinisch, J. M. (1981). Prenatal exposure to synthetic progestins increases potential for aggression in humans. *Science, 211,* 1171–1173.

Repetti, R. L. (1989). Effects of daily workload on subsequent behavior during marital interactions: The role of social withdrawal and spouse support. *Journal of Personality and Social Psychology, 57,* 651–659.

Rescorla, R. A. (1972). Informational variables in Pavlovian conditioning. In G. H. Bower (Ed.), *The psychology of learning and motivation* (Vol. 6, pp. 1–46). New York: Academic.

Rescorla, R. A. (1987). A Pavlovian analysis of goal-directed behavior. *American Psychologist, 42,* 119–129.

Rescorla, R. A. (1988). Pavlovian conditioning: It's not what you think it is. *American Psychologist, 43,* 151–160.

Rescorla, R. A. (1997). Response-inhibition in extinction. *Quarterly Journal of Experimental Psychology: Comparative and Physiological Psychology, 50B,* 238–252.

Rescorla, R. A. (1998). Instrumental learning: Nature and persistence. In M. Sabourin, F. Craik, et al. (Eds.), *Advances in psychological science, Vol. 2: Biological and cognitive aspects* (pp. 239–257). Hove, England: Psychology Press.

Reuter, M., Schmitz, A., Corr, P., & Hennig, J. (2005). Molecular genetics support Gray's personality theory: The interaction of COMT and DRD2 polymorphisms predicts the behavioural approach system. *International Journal of Neuropsychopharmacology, 9,* 155–166.

Revonsuo, A. (2000). The reinterpretation of dreams: An evolutionary hypothesis of the function of dreaming. *Behavioral and Brain Sciences, 23,* 877–901.

Reyna, C., Henry, P. J., Korfmacher, W., & Tucker, A. (2005). Examining the principles in principled conservatism: The role of responsibility stereotypes as cues for deservingness in racial policy decisions. *Journal of Personality and Social Psychology, 90,* 109–128.

Reynolds, S. K., & Clark, L. A. (2001). Predicting dimensions of personality disorder from domains and facets of the five-factor model. *Journal of Personality, 69,* 199–222.

Rhawn, J. (1980). Awareness, the origin of thought, and the role of conscious self-deception in resistance and repression. *Psychological Reports, 46,* 767–781.

Rhee, S. H., & Waldman, I. D. (2002). Genetic and environmental influences on antisocial behavior: A meta-analysis of twin and adoption studies. *Psychological Bulletin, 128,* 490–529.

Rhodewalt, F., & Morf, C. C. (1998). On self-aggrandizement and anger: A temporal analysis of narcissism and affective reactions to success and failure. *Journal of Personality and Social Psychology, 74,* 672–685.

Rholes, W. S., & Simpson, J. A. (2004). *Adult attachment: Theory, research, and clinical implications.* New York: Guilford.

Rholes, W. S., Simpson, J. A., & Friedman, M. (2006). Avoidant attachment and the experience of parenting. *Personality and Social Psychology Bulletin, 32,* 275–285.

Rholes, W. S., Simpson, J. A., & Oriña, M. M. (1999). Attachment and anger in an anxiety-provoking situation. *Journal of Personality and Social Psychology, 76,* 940–957.

Riedel, W. (1970). An investigation of personal constructs through nonverbal tasks. *Journal of Abnormal Psychology, 76,* 173–179.

Riordan, C. A., & Tedeschi, J. T. (1983). Attraction in aversive environments: Some evidence for classical conditioning and negative reinforcement. *Journal of Personality and Social Psychology, 44,* 683–692.

Risley, T. R. (1968). The effects and side effects of punishing the autistic behaviors of a deviant child. *Journal of Applied Behavior Analysis, 1,* 21–34.

Ritvo, L. B. (1990). *Darwin's influence on Freud: A tale of two sciences.* New Haven, CT: Yale University Press.

Rizzolatti, G., Fogassi, L., & Gallese, V. (2002). Motor and cognitive functions of the ventral premotor cortex. *Current Opinion in Neurobiology, 12,* 149–154.

Roberts, B. W., & Bogg, T. (2004). A longitudinal study of the relationships between conscientiousness and the social-environmental factors and substance-use behaviors that influence health. *Journal of Personality, 72,* 325–354.

Roberts, B. W., Caspi, A., & Moffitt, T. E. (2001). The kids are alright: Growth and stability in personality development from adolescence to adulthood. *Journal of Personality and Social Psychology, 81,* 670–683.

Roberts, B. W., & Del Vecchio, W. F. (2000). The rank-order consistency of personality traits from childhood to old age: A quantitative review of longitudinal studies. *Psychological Bulletin, 126,* 3–25.

Roberts, B. W., & Robins, R. W. (2000). Broad dispositions, broad aspirations: The intersection of personality traits and major life goals. *Personality and Social Psychology Bulletin, 26,* 1284–1296.

Roberts, B. W., Walton, K. E., & Bogg, T. (2005). Conscientiousness and health across the life course. *Review of General Psychology, 9,* 156–168.

Roberts, J. E., Gotlib, I. H., & Kassel, J. D. (1996). Adult attachment security and symptoms of depression: The mediating roles of dysfunctional attitudes and low self-esteem. *Journal of Personality and Social Psychology, 70,* 310–320.

Roberts, J. E., & Monroe, S. M. (1994). A multidimensional model of self-esteem in depression. *Clinical Psychology Review, 14,* 161–181.

Robins, R. W., Fraley, R. C., Roberts, B. W., & Trzesniewski, K. H. (2001). A longitudinal study of personality change in young adulthood. *Journal of Personality, 69,* 617–640.

Robins, R. W., John, O. P., Caspi, A., Moffitt, T. E., & Stouthamer-Loeber, M. (1996). Resilient, overcontrolled, and undercontrolled boys: Three replicable personality types. *Journal of Personality and Social Psychology, 70,* 157–171.

Robins, R. W., Noftle, E. E., Trzesniewski, K. H., & Roberts, B. W. (2005). Do people know how their personality has changed? Correlates of perceived and actual personality change in young adulthood. *Journal of Personality, 73,* 489–522.

Robins, R. W., & Pals, J. L. (2002). Implicit self-theories in the academic domain: Implications for goal orientation, attributions, affect, and self-esteem change. *Self and Identity, 1,* 313–336.

Robinson, F. G. (1992). *Love's story told: A life of Henry A. Murray.* Cambridge, MA: Harvard University Press.

Robinson, S., Sandstrom, S. M., Denenberg, V. H., & Palmiter, R. D. (2005). Distinguishing whether dopamine regulates liking, wanting, and/or learning about rewards. *Behavioral Neuroscience, 119,* 5–15.

Robles, T. F., Glaser, R., & Kiecolt-Glaser, J. K. (2005). Out of balance: A new look at chronic stress, depression, and immunity. *Current Directions in Psychological Science, 14,* 111–115.

Roccas, S., Sagiv, L., Schwartz, S. H., & Knafo, A. (2002). The big five personality factors and personal values. *Personality and Social Psychology Bulletin, 28,* 789–801.

Rogers, C. R. (1951). *Client-centered therapy: Its current practice, implications and theory.* Boston: Houghton Mifflin.

Rogers, C. R. (1959). A theory of therapy, personality and interpersonal relationships, as developed in the client-centered framework. In S. Koch (Ed.), *Psychology: A study of a science* (Vol. 3). New York: McGraw-Hill.

Rogers, C. R. (1961). *On becoming a person.* Boston: Houghton Mifflin.

Rogers, C. R. (1965). *Client-centered therapy: Its current practice, implication, and theory.* Boston: Houghton Mifflin.

Rogers, C. R., & Dymond, R. F. (Eds.). (1954). *Psychotherapy and personality change: Coordinated research studies in the client-centered approach.* Chicago: University of Chicago Press.

Rogers, C. R., & Stevens, B. (1967). *Person to person: The problem of being human.* New York: Simon & Schuster.

Rogers, T. B. (1981). A model of the self as an aspect of the human information-processing system. In N. Cantor & J. F. Kihlstrom (Eds.), *Personality, cognition and social interaction.* Hillsdale, NJ: Erlbaum.

Rogers, T. B., Kuiper, N. A., & Kirker, W. S. (1977). Self-reference and the encoding of personal information. *Journal of Personality and Social Psychology, 35,* 677–688.

Roney, J. R. (2003). Effects of visual exposure to the opposite sex: Cognitive aspects of mate attraction in human males. *Personality and Social Psychology Bulletin, 29,* 393–404.

Rorer, L. G. (1965). The great response-style myth. *Psychological Bulletin, 63,* 129–156.

Rorschach, H. (1942). *Psychodiagnostics.* Berne, Switzerland: Huber.

Rosch, E., & Mervis, C. (1975). Family resemblances: Studies in the internal structure of categories. *Cognitive Psychology, 7,* 573–605.

Rosekrans, M. A. (1967). Imitation in children as a function of perceived similarity and vicarious reinforcement. *Journal of Personality and Social Psychology, 7,* 307–315.

Roseman, I. J. (1991). Appraisal determinants of discrete emotions. *Cognition and Emotion, 5,* 161–200.

Rosen, C. M. (1987). The eerie world of reunited twins. *Discover, 8,* 36–46.

Rosenbaum, D. A. (1987). Hierarchical organization of motor programs. In S. Wise (Ed.), *Neural and behaviorial approaches to higher brain function* (pp. 45–66). New York: Wiley.

Rosenbaum, D. A. (1990). *Human motor control.* San Diego: Academic.

Rosenbaum, D. A. (2005). The Cinderella of psychology: The neglect of motor control in the science of mental life and behavior. *American Psychologist, 60,* 308–317.

Rosenthal, T. L., & Reese, S. L. (1976). The effects of covert and overt modeling on assertive behavior. *Behavior Research and Therapy, 14,* 463–469.

Rosenwald, G. C. (1972). Effectiveness of defenses against anal impulse arousal. *Journal of Consulting and Clinical Psychology, 39,* 292–298.

Ross, D. M., Ross, S. A., & Evans, T. A. (1971). The modification of extreme social withdrawal by modeling with guided participation. *Journal of Behavior Therapy and Experimental Psychiatry, 2,* 273–279.

Ross, M. (1989). Relation of implicit theories to the construction of personal histories. *Psychological Review, 96,* 341–357.

Ross, M., & Fletcher, G. J. O. (1985). Attribution and social perception. In G. Lindzey & E. Aronson (Eds.), *The handbook of social psychology* (3rd ed., pp. 73–122). Reading, MA: Addison-Wesley.

Roth, S. (1980). A revised model of learned helplessness in humans. *Journal of Personality, 48,* 103–133.

Rothbart, M. K., Ahadi, S. A., & Evans, D. E. (2000). Temperament and personality: Origins and outcomes. *Journal of Personality and Social Psychology, 78,* 122–135.

Rothbart, M. K., Ahadi, S. A., Hershey, K., & Fisher, P. (2001). Investigations of temperament at three to seven years: The Children's Behavior Questionnaire. *Child Development, 72,* 1394–1408.

Rothbart, M. K., & Bates, J. E. (1998). Temperament. In W. Damon (Series Ed.) and N. Eisenberg (Vol. Ed.), *Handbook of child psychology: Vol 3. Social, emotional and personality development* (5th ed., pp. 105–176). New York: Wiley.

Rothbart, M. K., Ellis, L. K., Rueda, M. R., & Posner, M. I. (2003). Developing mechanisms of temperamental effortful control. *Journal of Personality, 71,* 1113–1143.

Rothbart, M. K., & Posner, M. (1985). Temperament and the development of self-regulation. In L. C. Hartlage & C. F. Telzrow (Eds.), *The neuropsychology of individual differences: A developmental perspective* (pp. 93–123). New York: Plenum.

Rotter, J. B. (1954). *Social learning and clinical psychology.* New York: Prentice-Hall.

Rotter, J. B. (1966). Generalized expectancies for internal versus external control of reinforcement. *Psychological Monographs, 80* (1, Whole No. 609).

Rotter, J. B. (1982). *The development and applications of social learning theory: Selected papers.* New York: Praeger.

Rotter, J. B. (1990). Internal versus external control of reinforcement: A case history of a variable. *American Psychologist, 45,* 489–493.

Rotter, J. B., Seeman, M., & Liverant, S. (1962). Internal versus external control of reinforcement: A major variable in behavior theory. In N. F. Washburne (Ed.), *Decisions, values, and groups* (Vol. 2). New York: Pergamon.

Rowe, D. C. (1994). *The limits of family influence: Genes, experience, and behavior.* New York: Guilford.

Rowe, D. C. (2001). *Biology and crime.* Los Angeles: Roxbury.

Roy-Byrne, P. (2005). The GABA-benzodiazepine receptor complex: Structure, function, and role in anxiety. *Journal of Clinical Psychiatry, 66,* 14–20.

Roy-Byrne, P., Russo, J., Pollack, M., Stewart, R., Bystrisky, A., Bell, J., Rosenbaum, J., Corrigan, M. H., Stolk, J., Rush, A. J., & Ballenger, J. (2003). Personality and symptom sensitivity predictors of alprazolam withdrawal in panic disorder. *Psychological Medicine, 33,* 511–518.

Rozsnafszky, J. (1981). The relationship of level of ego development to Q-sort personality ratings. *Journal of Personality and Social Psychology, 41,* 99–120.

Rubin, R. T., Reinisch, J. M., & Haskett, R. F. (1981). Postnatal gonadal steroid effects on human behavior. *Science, 211,* 1318–1324.

Ruchkin, V., Koposov, R. A., af Klinteberg, B., Oreland, L., & Grigorenko, E. L. (2005). Platelet MAO-B, personality, and psychopathology. *Journal of Abnormal Psychology, 114,* 477–482.

Rushton, J. P. (1988). Genetic similarity, mate choice, and fecundity in humans. *Ethology and Sociobiology, 9,* 329–335.

Rushton, J. P. (1989a). Genetic similarity, human altruism, and group selection. *Behavioral and Brain Sciences, 12,* 503–559.

Rushton, J. P. (1989b). Genetic similarity in male friendships. *Ethology and Sociobiology, 10,* 361–373.

Rushton, J. P., & Bons, T. A. (2005). Mate choice and friendship in twins. *Psychological Science, 16,* 555–559.

Rushton, J. P., Brainerd, C. J., & Pressley, M. (1983). Behavioral development and construct validity: The principle of aggregation. *Psychological Bulletin, 94,* 18–38.

Rushton, J. P., Fulker, D. W., Neale, M. C., Nias, D. K. B., & Eysenck, H. J. (1986). Altruism and aggression: The heritability of individual differences. *Journal of Personality and Social Psychology, 50,* 1192–1198.

Rushton, J. P., Russell, R. J. H., & Wells, P. A. (1984). Genetic similarity theory: Beyond kin selection. *Behavior Genetics, 14,* 179–193.

Ryan, R. M. (1982). Control and information in the intrapersonal sphere: An extension of cognitive evaluation theory. *Journal of Personality and Social Psychology, 43,* 450–461.

Ryan, R. M. (1993). Agency and organization: Intrinsic motivation, autonomy, and the self in psychological development. In J. Jacobs (Ed.), *Nebraska symposium on motivation: Developmental perspectives on motivation* (Vol. 40, pp. 1–56). Lincoln: University of Nebraska Press.

Ryan, R. M., & Connell, J. P. (1989). Perceived locus of causality and internalization: Examining reasons for acting in two domains. *Journal of Personality and Social Psychology, 57,* 749–761.

Ryan, R. M., & Deci, E. L. (2001). On happiness and human potentials: A review of research on hedonic and eudaimonic well-being. *Annual Review of Psychology, 52,* 141–166.

Ryan, R. M., Rigby, S., & King, K. (1993). Two types of religious internalization and their relations to religious orientations and mental health. *Journal of Personality and Social Psychology, 65,* 586–596.

Ryan, R. M., Sheldon, K. M., Kasser, T., & Deci, E. L. (1996). All goals are not created equal: An organismic perspective on the nature of goals and their regulation. In P. M. Gollwitzer & J. A. Bargh (Eds.), *The psychology of action: Linking cognition and motivation to behavior* (pp. 7–26). New York: Guilford.

Sabini, J., & Green, M. C. (2004). Emotional responses to sexual and emotional infidelity: Constants and differences across genders, samples, and methods. *Personality and Social Psychology Bulletin, 30,* 1375–1388.

Sadalla, E. K., Kenrick, D. T., & Vershure, B. (1987). Dominance and heterosexual attraction. *Journal of Personality and Social Psychology, 52,* 730–738.

Samuel, D. B., & Widiger, T. A. (2006). Clinicians' judgments of clinical utility: A comparison of the DSM-IV and five-factor models. *Journal of Abnormal Psychology, 115,* 298–308.

Sarason, I. G. (1975). Test anxiety and the self-disclosing coping model. *Journal of Consulting and Clinical Psychology, 43,* 148–153.

Saucier, G. (1992). Benchmarks: Integrating affective and interpersonal circles with the big-five personality factors. *Journal of Personality and Social Psychology, 62,* 1025–1035.

Saucier, G., & Goldberg, L. R. (1998). What is beyond the big five? *Journal of Personality, 66,* 495–524.

Saucier, G., & Goldberg, L. R. (2001). Lexical studies of indigenous personality factors: Premises, products, and prospects. *Journal of Personality, 69,* 847–879.

Saucier, G., & Ostendorf, F. (1999). Hierarchical subcomponents of the big five personality factors: A cross-language replication. *Journal of Personality and Social Psychology, 76,* 613–627.

Saucier, G., & Simonds, J. (2006). The structure of personality and temperament. In D. K. Mroczek & T. D. Little (Eds.), *Handbook of Personality Development* (pp. 109–128). Mahwah, NJ: Erlbaum.

Saudino, K. J., McGuire, S., Reiss, D., Hetherington, E. M., & Plomin, R. (1995). Parent ratings of EAS temperaments in twins, full siblings, half siblings, and step siblings. *Journal of Personality and Social Psychology, 68,* 723–733.

Saudino, K. J., Pedersen, N. L., Lichtenstein, P., McClearn, G. E., & Plomin, R. (1997). Can personality explain genetic influences on life events? *Journal of Personality and Social Psychology, 72,* 196–206.

Scarr, S. (1985). Constructing psychology: Making facts and fables for our time. *American Psychologist, 40,* 499–512.

Scarr, S., & Carter-Saltzman, L. (1979). Twin method: Defense of a critical assumption. *Behavior Genetics, 9,* 527–542.

Scarr, S., & McCartney, K. (1983). How people make their own environments: A theory of genotype -> environment effects. *Child Development, 54,* 424–435.

Schank, R. C., & Abelson, R. P. (1977). *Scripts, plans, goals, and understanding.* Hillsdale, NJ: Erlbaum.

Schefft, B. K., & Lehr, B. K. (1985). A self-regulatory model of adjunctive behavior change. *Behavior Modification, 9,* 458–476.

Scheier, M. F., & Carver, C. S. (1983). Self-directed attention and the comparison of self with standards. *Journal of Experimental Social Psychology, 19,* 205–222.

Scheier, M. F., & Carver, C. S. (1988). A model of behavioral self-regulation: Translating intention into action. In L. Berkowitz (Ed.), *Advances in experimental social psychology* (Vol. 21, pp. 303–346). New York: Academic.

Scheier, M. F., & Carver, C. S. (1992). Effects of optimism on psychological and physical well-being: Theoretical overview and empirical update. *Cognitive Therapy and Research, 16,* 201–228.

Scheier, M. F., Carver, C. S., & Bridges, M. W. (2001). Optimism, pessimism, and psychological well-being. In E. C. Chang (Ed.), *Optimism and pessimism: Implications for theory, research, and practice* (pp. 189–216). Washington, DC: American Psychological Association.

Scheier, M. F., Matthews, K. A., Owens, J. F., Magovern, G. J., Lefebvre, R. C., Abbott, R. A., & Carver, C. S. (1989). Dispositional optimism and recovery from coronary artery bypass surgery: The beneficial effects on physical and psychological well-being. *Journal of Personality and Social Psychology, 57,* 1024–1040.

Scheier, M. F., Matthews, K. A., Owens, J. F., Schulz, R., Bridges, M. W., Magovern, G. J., Sr., & Carver, C. S. (1999). Optimism and rehospitalization following coronary artery bypass graft surgery. *Archives of Internal Medicine, 159,* 829–835.

Scheirer, M. A., & Kraut, R. E. (1979). Increasing educational achievement via self-concept change. *Review of Educational Research, 49,* 131–150.

Schell, T. L., Klein, S. B., & Babey, S. H. (1996). Testing a hierarchical model of self-knowledge. *Psychological Science, 7,* 170–173.

Schiedel, D. G., & Marcia, J. E. (1985). Ego identity, intimacy, sex-role orientation, and gender. *Journal of Personality and Social Psychology, 21,* 149–160.

Schimek, J. G. (1987). Fact and fantasy in the seduction theory: A historical review. *Journal of the American Psychoanalytic Association, 35,* 937–965.

Schimel, J., Arndt, J., Pyszczynski, T., & Greenberg, J. (2001). Being accepted for who we are: Evidence that social validation of the intrinsic self reduces general defensiveness. *Journal of Personality and Social Psychology, 80,* 35–52.

Schimel, J., Greenberg, J., & Martens, A. (2003). Evidence that projection of a feared trait can serve a defensive function. *Personality and Social Psychology Bulletin, 29,* 969–979.

Schimmack, U., Oishi, S., Furr, R. M., & Funder, D. C. (2004). Personality and life satisfaction: A facet-level analysis. *Personality and Social Psychology Bulletin, 30,* 1062–1075.

Schmidt, L. A. (1999). Frontal brain electrical activity in shyness and sociability. *Psychological Science, 10,* 316–320.

Schmidt, R. A. (1976). The schema as a solution to some persistent problems in motor learning theory. In G. E. Stelmach (Ed.), *Motor control: Issues and trends.* New York: Academic.

Schmidt, R. A. (1988). *Motor control and learning: A behavioral emphasis* (2nd ed.). Champaign, IL: Human Kinetics Publishers.

Schmitt, D. P. (2003). Universal sex differences in the desire for sexual variety: Tests from 52 nations, 6 continents, and 13 islands. *Journal of Personality and Social Psychology, 85,* 85–104.

Schmitt, D. P. (2004). Patterns and universals of mate poaching across 53 nations: The effects of sex, culture and personality on romantically attracting another person's partner. *Journal of Personality and Social Psychology, 86,* 560–584.

Schmitt, D. P., & Buss, D. M. (1996). Strategic self-promotion and competitor derogation: Sex and context effects on the perceived effectiveness of mate attraction tactics. *Journal of Personality and Social Psychology, 70,* 1185–1204.

Schmitt, D. P., & Buss, D. M. (2001). Human mate poaching: Tactics and temptations for infiltrating existing mateships. *Journal of Personality and Social Psychology, 80,* 894–917.

Schmitt, W. A., Brinkley, C. A., & Newman, J. P. (1999). Testing Damasio's somatic marker hypothesis with psychopathic individuals: Risk takers or risk averse? *Journal of Abnormal Psychology, 108,* 538–543.

Schneider, D. J. (1991). Social cognition. *Annual Review of Psychology, 42,* 527–561.

Schneider, K. J., Bugental, J. F. T., & Pierson, J. F. (Eds.). (2001). *The handbook of humanistic psychology: Leading edges in theory, research, and practice.* Thousand Oaks, CA: Sage.

Schneiderman, N., & Gormezano, I. (1964). Conditioning of the nictitating membrane of the rabbit as a function of the CS–US interval. *Journal of Comparative and Physiological Psychology, 57,* 188–195.

Schober, M. F., & Clark, H. H. (1989). Understanding by addressees and overhearers. *Cognitive Psychology, 21,* 211–232.

Schriesheim, C. A., & Hill, K. D. (1981). Controlling acquiescence response bias by item reversals: The effect on questionnaire validity. *Educational and Psychological Measurement, 41,* 1101–1114.

Schuckit, M. A., & Rayses, V. (1979). Ethanol ingestion: Differences in blood acetaldehyde concentrations in relatives of alcoholics and controls. *Science, 203,* 54–55.

Schultheiss, O. C. (2002). An information-processing account of implicit motive arousal. In P. R. Pintrich & M. L. Maehr (Eds.), *Advances in motivation and achievement: New directions in measures and methods* (Vol. 12, pp. 1–41). Amsterdam, The Netherlands: Elsevier.

Schultheiss, O. C., & Brunstein, J. C. (2001). Assessment of implicit motives with a research version of the TAT: Picture profiles, gender differences, and relations to other personality measures. *Journal of Personality Assessment, 77,* 71–86.

Schultheiss, O. C., & Brunstein, J. C. (2002). Inhibited power motivation and persuasive communication: A lens model analysis. *Journal of Personality, 70,* 553–582.

Schultheiss, O. C., Campbell, K. L., & McClelland, D. C. (1999). Implicit power motivation moderates men's testosterone responses to imagined and real dominance success. *Hormones and Behavior, 36,* 234–241.

Schultheiss, O. C., Dargel, A., & Rohde, W. (2003). Implicit motives and sexual motivation and behavior. *Journal of Research in Personality, 37,* 224–230.

Schultheiss, O. C., & Hale, J. A. (in press). Implicit motives modulate attentional orienting to facial expressions of emotion. *Motivation and Emotion.*

Schultheiss, O. C., & Pang, J. S. (in press). Measuring implicit motives. In R. W. Robins, R. C. Fraley, & R. Krueger (Eds.), *Handbook of Research Methods in Personality Psychology.* New York: Guilford.

Schultheiss, O. C., Pang, J. S., Torges, C. M., Wirth, M. M., & Treynor, W. (2005). Perceived facial expressions of emotion as motivational incentives: Evidence from a differential implicit learning paradigm. *Emotion, 5,* 41–54.

Schultheiss, O. C., & Rohde, W. (2002). Implicit power motivation predicts men's testosterone changes and implicit learning in a contest situation. *Hormones and Behavior, 41,* 195–202.

Schultheiss, O. C., Wirth, M. M., Torges, C. M., Pang, J. S., Villacorta, M. A., & Welsh, K. M. (2005). Effects of implicit power motivation on men's and women's implicit learning and testosterone changes after social victory or defeat. *Journal of Personality and Social Psychology, 88,* 174–188.

Schultz, C. B., & Pomerantz, M. (1976). Achievement motivation, locus of control, and academic achievement behavior. *Journal of Personality, 44,* 38–51.

Schultz, T. R., & Lepper, M. R. (1996). Cognitive dissonance reduction as constraint satisfaction. *Psychological Review, 103,* 219–240.

Schultz, W. (2000). Multiple reward signals in the brain. *Nature Reviews, 1,* 199–207.

Schultz, W. (2006). Behavioral theories and the neurophysiology of reward. *Annual Reviews of Psychology, 57,* 87–115.

Schutte, N. S., Kenrick, D. T., & Sadalla, E. K. (1985). The search for predictable settings: Situational prototypes, constraint, and behavioral variation. *Journal of Personality and Social Psychology, 49,* 121–128.

Schwartz, B. (1989). *Psychology of learning and behavior* (3rd ed.). New York: Norton.

Schwarz, N. (1990). Feelings as information: Informational and motivational functions of affective states. In E. T. Higgins & R. M. Sorrentino (Eds.), *Handbook of motivation and cognition: Foundations of social behavior* (Vol. 2, pp. 527–561). New York: Guilford.

Seamans, J. K. & Yang, C. R. (2004). The principal features and mechanisms of dopamine modulation in the prefrontal cortex. *Progress in Neurobiology, 74,* 1–57.

Sears, R. R. (1943). *Survey of objective studies of psychoanalytic concepts* (Bulletin 51). New York: Social Sciences Research Council.

Sears, R. R., Rau, L., & Alpert, R. (1965). *Identification and child rearing.* Stanford, CA: Stanford University Press.

Sechrest, L. (1977). Personal constructs theory. In R. J. Corsini (Ed.), *Current personality theories.* Itasca, IL: Peacock.

Sederer, L., & Seidenberg, R. (1976). Heiress to an empty throne: Ego-ideal problems of contemporary women. *Contemporary Psychoanalysis, 12,* 240–251.

Segal, N. L. (1993). Twin, sibling, and adoption methods: Tests of evolutionary hypotheses. *American Psychologist, 48,* 943–956.

Segal, N. L. (1999). *Entwined lives: Twins and what they tell us about human behavior.* New York: Dutton.

Segal, Z. V. (1988). Appraisal of the self-schema construct in cognitive models of depression. *Psychological Bulletin, 103,* 147–162.

Segerstorm, S. C., Miller, G. E. (2004). Psychological stress and the human immune system: A meta-analytic study of 30 years of inquiry. *Psychological Bulletin, 130,* 601–641.

Seidenberg, M. S. (2005). Connectionist models of word reading. *Current Directions in Psychological Science, 14,* 238–242.

Seifer, R., Sameroff, A. J., Barrett, L. C., & Krafchuk, E. (1994). Infant temperament measured by multiple observations and mother report. *Child Development, 65,* 1478–1490.

Seligman, M. E. P., & Hager, J. L. (Eds.). (1972). *Biological boundaries of learning.* New York: Appleton-Century-Crofts.

Seligman, M. E. P., & Maier, S. F. (1967). Failure to escape traumatic shock. *Journal of Experimental Psychology, 74,* 1–9.

Seltzer, R. A. (1973). Simulation of the dynamics of action. *Psychological Reports, 32,* 859–872.

Semmer, N., & Frese, M. (1985). Action theory in clinical psychology. In M. Frese & J. Sabini (Eds.), *Goal directed behavior: The concept of action in psychology.* Hillsdale, NJ: Erlbaum.

Sen, S., Villafuerte, S., Nesse, R., Stoltenberg, S. F., Hopcian, J., Gleiberman, L., Weder, A., & Burmeister, M. (2004). Serotonin transporter and GABA(A) alpha 6 receptor variants are associated with neuroticism. *Biological Psychiatry, 55,* 244–249.

Shane, M. S., & Peterson, J. B. (2004). Self-induced memory distortions and the allocation of processing resources at encoding and retrieval. *Cognition and Emotion, 18,* 533–558.

Shao, C., Li, Y., Jiang, K., Zhang, D., Xu, Y., Lin, L., Wang, Q., Zhao, M., & Jin, L. (2006). Dopamine D4 receptor polymorphism modulates cue-elicited heroin craving in Chinese. *Psychopharmacology, 186,* 185–190.

Shapiro, D., & Surwit, R. S. (1979). Biofeedback. In O. F. Pomerleau & J. P. Brady (Eds.), *Behavioral medicine: Theory and practice.* Baltimore: Williams & Wilkins.

Shaver, P. R., & Brennan, K. A. (1992). Attachment styles and the "big five" personality traits: Their connections with each other and with romantic relationship outcomes. *Personality and Social Psychology Bulletin, 18,* 536–545.

Shaver, P. R., & Rubenstein, C. (1980). *Childhood attachment experience and adult loneliness.* In L. Wheeler (Ed.), *Review of personality and social psychology* (Vol. 1, pp. 42–73). Beverly Hills, CA: Sage.

Shedler, J., & Block, J. (1990). Adolescent drug use and psychological health: A longitudinal inquiry. *American Psychologist, 45,* 612–630.

Shedler, J., Mayman, M., & Manis, M. (1993). The *illusion* of mental health. *American Psychologist, 48,* 1117–1131.

Sheeran, P., Webb, T. L., & Gollwitzer, P. M. (2005). The interplay between goal intentions and implementation intentions. *Personality and Social Psychology Bulletin, 31,* 87–98.

Sheldon, K. M. (2005). Positive value change during college: Normative trends and individual differences. *Journal of Research in Personality, 39,* 209–223.

Sheldon, K. M., & Elliot, A. J. (1998). Not all personal goals are personal: Comparing autonomous and controlled reasons for goals as predictors of effort and attainment. *Personality and Social Psychology Bulletin, 24,* 546–557.

Sheldon, K. M., & Elliot, A. J. (1999). Goal striving, need satisfaction, and longitudinal well-being: The self-concordance model. *Journal of Personality and Social Psychology, 76,* 482–497.

Sheldon, K. M., Elliot, A. J., Kim, Y., & Kasser, T. (2001). What is satisfying about satisfying events? Testing 10 candidate psychological needs. *Journal of Personality and Social Psychology, 80,* 325–339.

Sheldon, K. M., & Houser-Marko, L. (2001). Self-concordance, goal attainment, and the pursuit of happiness: Can there be an upward spiral? *Journal of Personality and Social Psychology, 80,* 152–165.

Sheldon, K. M., & Kasser, T. (1998). Pursuing personal goals: Skills enable progress but not all progress is beneficial. *Personality and Social Psychology Bulletin, 24,* 1319–1331.

Sheldon, K. M., Ryan, R. M., & Reis, H. (1996). What makes for a good day? Competence and autonomy in the day and in the person. *Personality and Social Psychology Bulletin, 22,* 1270–1279.

Sheldon, W. H. (with the collaboration of S. S. Stevens). (1942). *The varieties of temperament: A psychology of constitutional differences.* New York: Harper.

Sher, K. J., Bartholow, B. D., & Wood, M. D. (2000). Personality and substance use disorders: A prospective study. *Journal of Consulting and Clinical Psychology, 68,* 818–829.

Sherwood, G. G. (1981). Self-serving biases in person perception: An examination of projection as a mechanism of defense. *Psychological Bulletin, 90,* 445–459.

Shiner, R. L., Masten, A. S., & Tellegen, A. (2002). A developmental perspective on personality in emerging adulthood: Childhood antecedents and concurrent adaptation. *Journal of Personality and Social Psychology, 83,* 1165–1177.

Shoal, G. D., & Giancola, P. R. (2003). Negative affectivity and drug use in adolescent boys: Moderating and mediating mechanisms. *Journal of Personality and Social Psychology, 84,* 221–233.

Shoda, Y., Mischel, W., & Wright, J. C. (1989). Intuitive interactionism in person perception: Effects of situation–behavior relations on dispositional judgments. *Journal of Personality and Social Psychology, 56,* 41–53.

Shoda, Y., Mischel, W., & Wright, J. C. (1993). The role of situational demands and cognitive competencies in behavior organization and personality coherence. *Journal of Personality and Social Psychology, 65,* 1023–1035.

Shoda, Y., Mischel, W., & Wright, J. C. (1994). Intraindividual stability in the organization and patterning of behavior: Incorporating psychological situations into the idiographic analysis of personality. *Journal of Personality and Social Psychology, 67,* 674–687.

Shostrom, E. L. (1964). An inventory for the measurement of self-actualization. *Educational and Psychological Measurement, 24,* 207–218.

Shostrom, E. L. (1974). *Manual for the Personal Orientation Inventory.* San Diego: EdITS.

Showers, C. J., & Ryff, C. D. (1996). Self-differentiation and well-being in a life transition. *Personality and Social Psychology Bulletin, 22,* 448–460.

Shubsachs, A. P. W. (1975). To repeat or not to repeat? Are frequently used constructs more important to the subject? *British Journal of Medical Psychology, 48,* 31–37.

Sidanius, J., Pratto, F., & Bobo, L. (1994). Social dominance orientation and the political psychology of gender: A case of invariance? *Journal of Personality and Social Psychology, 67,* 998–1011.

Silverman, L. H. (1976). Psychoanalytic theory: "The reports of my death are greatly exaggerated." *American Psychologist, 31,* 621–637.

Silverman, L. H. (1983). The subliminal psychodynamic activation method: Overview and comprehensive listing of studies. In J. Masling (Ed.), *Empirical studies of psychoanalytic theories* (Vol. 1, pp. 69–100). Hillsdale, NJ: Erlbaum.

Silverman, L. H., Ross, D. L., Adler, J. M., & Lustig, D. A. (1978). Simple research paradigm for demonstrating subliminal psychodynamic activation: Effects of Oedipal stimuli on dart-throwing accuracy in college men. *Journal of Abnormal Psychology, 87,* 341–357.

Simon, D., Snow, C. J., & Read, S. J. (2004). The redux of cognitive consistency theories: Evidence judgments by constraint satisfaction. *Journal of Personality and Social Psychology, 86,* 814–837.

Simon, D. P., & Simon, H. A. (1978). Individual differences in solving physics problems. In R. S. Siegler (Ed.), *Children's thinking: What develops?* (pp. 325–348). Hillsdale, NJ: Erlbaum.

Simon, H. A. (1967). Motivational and emotional controls of cognition. *Psychological Review, 74,* 29–39.

Simpson, J. A. (1990). Influence of attachment styles on romantic relationships. *Journal of Personality and Social Psychology, 59,* 971–980.

Simpson, J. A., & Rholes, W. S. (Eds.). (1998). *Attachment theory and close relationships.* New York: Guilford.

Simpson, J. A., Rholes, W. S., & Nelligan, J. S. (1992). Support seeking and support giving within couples in an anxiety-provoking situation: The role of attachment styles. *Journal of Personality and Social Psychology, 62,* 434–446.

Simpson, J. A., Rholes, W. S., Oriña, M. M., & Grich, J. (2002). Working models of attachment, support giving, and support seeking in a stressful situation. *Personality and Social Psychology Bulletin, 28,* 598–608.

Simpson, J. A., Winterheld, H. A., & Chen, J. Y. (2006). Personality and relationships: A temperament perspective. In A. L Vangelisti & D. Perlman (Eds.), *The Cambridge handbook of personal relationships* (pp. 231–250). New York: Cambridge University Press.

Singer, J. A. (2004). Narrative identity and meaning making across the adult lifespan: An introduction. *Journal of Personality, 72,* 437–459.

Singer, J. A. (2005). *Personality and psychotherapy: Treating the whole person.* New York: Guilford.

Singh, D. (1995). Female judgment of male attractiveness and desirability for relationships: Role of waist-to-hip ratio and financial status. *Journal of Personality and Social Psychology, 69,* 1089–1101.

Skinner, B. F. (1938). *The behavior of organisms.* New York: Appleton-Century-Crofts.

Skinner, B. F. (1948). "Superstition" in the pigeon. *Journal of Experimental Psychology, 38,* 168–172.

Skinner, B. F. (1953). *Science and human behavior.* New York: Macmillan.

Skinner, B. F. (1974). *About behaviorism.* New York: Knopf.

Skinner, B. F. (1987). Whatever happened to psychology as the science of behavior? *American Psychologist, 42,* 780–786.

Skinner, B. F. (1989). The origins of cognitive thought. *American Psychologist, 44,* 13–18.

Skowronski, J. J., Carlston, D. E., Mae, L., & Crawford, M. T. (1998). Spontaneous trait transference: Communicators take on the qualities they describe in others. *Journal of Personality and Social Psychology, 74,* 837–848.

Sloman, S. A. (1996). The empirical case for two forms of reasoning. *Psychological Bulletin, 119,* 3–22.

Small, M. F. (1993). *Female choices: Sexual behavior of female primates.* Ithaca, NY: Cornell University Press.

Smith, A. (1969). *The theory of moral sentiments.* New Rochelle, NY: Arlington House. (Originally published in 1759)

Smith, C. P. (Ed.). (1992). *Motivation and personality: Handbook of thematic content analysis.* New York: Cambridge University Press.

Smith, E. E., Shoben, E. J., & Rips, L. J. (1974). Structure and process in semantic memory: A featural model for semantic decisions. *Psychological Review, 81,* 214–241.

Smith, E. R. (1996). What do connectionism and social psychology offer each other? *Journal of Personality and Social Psychology, 70,* 893–912.

Smith, E. R., Murphy, J., & Coats, S. (1999). Attachment to groups: Theory and measurement. *Journal of Personality and Social Psychology, 77,* 94–110.

Smith, G. M. (1967). Usefulness of peer ratings of personality in educational resarch. *Educational and Psychological Measurement, 27,* 967–984.

Smith, K. D., Keating, J. P., & Stotland, E. (1989). Altruism reconsidered: The effect of denying feedback on a victim's status to empathic witnesses. *Journal of Personality and Social Psychology, 57,* 641–650.

Smith, M. L., & Glass, G. V. (1977). Meta-analysis of psychotherapy outcome studies. *American Psychologist, 32,* 752–760.

Smith, M. L., Glass, G. V., & Miller, T. I. (1980). *The benefits of psychotherapy.* Baltimore: Johns Hopkins Press.

Smith, R. E. (1989). Effects of coping skills training on generalized self-efficacy and locus of control. *Journal of Personality and Social Psychology, 56,* 228–233.

Smolensky, P. (1988). On the proper treatment of connectionism. *Behavioral and Brain Sciences, 11,* 1–23.

Smolensky, P., Mozer, M. C., & Rumelhart, D. E. (Eds.). (1996). *Mathematical perspectives on neural networks.* Mahwah, NJ: Erlbaum.

Smyth, J. M. (1998). Written emotional expression: Effect sizes, outcome types, and moderating variables. *Journal of Consulting and Clinical Psychology, 66,* 174–184.

Snyder, C. R., & Higgins, R. L. (1988). Excuses: Their effective role in the negotiation of reality. *Psychological Bulletin, 104,* 23–35.

Snyder, M. (1974). The self-monitoring of expressive behavior. *Journal of Personality and Social Psychology, 30,* 526–537.

Snyder, M. (1987). *Public appearances/private realities: The psychology of self-monitoring.* New York: W. H. Freeman.

Snyder, M., & Gangestad, S. (1982). Choosing social situations: Two investigations of the self-monitoring process. *Journal of Personality and Social Psychology, 43,* 123–135.

Snyder, M. L., Stephan, W. G., & Rosenfield, D. (1976). Egotism and attribution. *Journal of Personality and Social Psychology, 33,* 435–441.

Snyder, M. L., Stephan, W. G., & Rosenfield, D. (1978). Attributional egotism. In J. H. Harvey, W. Ickes, & R. F. Kidd (Eds.), *New directions in attributional research* (Vol. 2). Hillsdale, NJ: Erlbaum.

Sobotka, S. S., Davidson, R. J., & Senulis, J. A. (1992). Anterior brain electrical asymmetries in response to reward and punishment. *Electroencephalography and Clinical Neurophysiology, 83,* 236–247.

Solms, M. (2000). Dreaming and REM sleep are controlled by different brain mechanisms. *Behavioral and Brain Sciences, 23,* 843–850.

Solomon, R. L. (1964). Punishment. *American Psychologist, 19,* 239–253.

Somer, O., & Goldberg, L. R. (1999). The structure of Turkish trait-descriptive adjectives. *Journal of Personality and Social Psychology, 76,* 431–450.

Sorg, B. A., & Whitney, P. (1992). The effect of trait anxiety and situational stress on working memory capacity. *Journal of Research in Personality, 26,* 235–241.

Sorrentino, R. M., & Field, N. (1986). Emergent leadership over time: The functional value of positive motivation. *Journal of Personality and Social Psychology, 50,* 1091–1099.

Soubrié, P. (1986). Reconciling the role of central serotonin neurons in human and animal behavior. *Behavioral and Brain Sciences, 9,* 319–364.

Spacapan, S., & Cohen, S. (1983). Effects and aftereffects of stressor expectations. *Journal of Personality and Social Psychology, 45,* 1243–1254.

Spangler, W. D., & House, R. J. (1991). Presidential effectiveness and the leadership motive profile. *Journal of Personality and Social Psychology, 60,* 439–455.

Spanos, N. P. (1996). *Multiple identities and false memories.* Washington, DC: American Psychological Association.

Spetch, M. L., Wilkie, D. M., & Pinel, J. P. J. (1981). Backward conditioning: A reevaluation of the empirical evidence. *Psychological Bulletin, 89,* 163–175.

Spielberger, C. D., & DeNike, L. D. (1966). Descriptive behaviorism versus cognitive theory in verbal operant conditioning. *Psychological Review, 73,* 309–326.

Spooner, A., & Kellogg, W. N. (1947). The backward conditioning curve. *American Journal of Psychology, 60,* 321–334.

Sprecher, S., Sullivan, Q., & Hatfield, E. (1994). Mate selection preferences: Gender differences examined in a national sample. *Journal of Personality and Social Psychology, 66,* 1074–1080.

Srivastava, S., McGonigal, K. M., Richards, J. M., Butler, E. A., & Gross, J. J. (2006). Optimism in close relationships: How seeing things in a positive light makes them so. *Journal of Personality and Social Psychology, 91,* 143–153.

Sroufe, L. A., & Fleeson, J. (1986). Attachment and the construction of relationships. In W. W. Hartup & Z. Rubin (Eds.), *Relationships and development* (pp. 51–71). Hillsdale, NJ: Erlbaum.

Srull, T. K., & Wyer, R. S., Jr. (1979). The role of category accessibility in the interpretation of information about persons: Some determinants and implications. *Journal of Personality and Social Psychology, 37,* 1660–1672.

St. Clair, M. (1986). *Object relations and self psychology: An introduction.* Monterey, CA: Brooks/Cole.

Staats, A. W. (1996). *Behavior and personality: Psychological behaviorism.* New York: Springer.

Staats, A. W., & Burns, G. L. (1982). Emotional personality repertoire as cause of behavior. *Journal of Personality and Social Psychology, 43,* 873–881.

Staats, A. W., & Staats, C. K. (1958). Attitudes established by classical conditioning. *Journal of Abnormal and Social Psychology, 57,* 37–40.

Staats, A. W., Staats, C. K., & Crawford, H. L. (1962). First-order conditioning of meaning and the parallel conditioning of a GSR. *Journal of General Psychology, 67,* 159–167.

Staats, C. K., & Staats, A. W. (1957). Meaning established by classical conditioning. *Journal of Experimental Psychology, 54,* 74–80.

Stanton, A. L., Danoff-Burg, S., Sworowski, L. A., Collins, C. A., Branstetter, A. D., Rodriguez-Hanley, A., Kirk, S. B., & Austenfeld, J. L. (2002). Randomized, controlled trial of written emotional expression and benefit finding in breast cancer patients. *Journal of Clinical Oncology, 20,* 4160–4168.

Stanton, A. L., & Snider, P. R. (1993). Coping with a breast cancer diagnosis: A prospective study. *Health Psychology, 12,* 16–23.

Steele, C. M. (1988). The psychology of self-affirmation: Sustaining the integrity of the self. In L. Berkowitz (Ed.), *Advances in experimental social psychology* (Vol. 21, pp. 261–302). New York: Academic.

Steele, C. M. (1997). A threat in the air: How stereotypes shape intellectual identity and performance. *American Psychologist, 52,* 613–629.

Steele, C. M., & Aronson, J. (1995). Stereotype threat and the intellectual test performance of African Americans. *Journal of Personality and Social Psychology, 69,* 797–811.

Sternberg, R. J. (Ed.). (1982). *Handbook of human intelligence.* New York: Cambridge University Press.

Steronko, R. J., & Woods, D. J. (1978). Impairment in early stages of visual information processing in nonpsychotic schizotypic individuals. *Journal of Abnormal Psychology, 87,* 481–490.

Stevens, R. (1983). *Erik Erikson: An introduction.* New York: St. Martin's.

Stevenson, H. W., Hale, G. A., Hill, K. T., & Moely, B. E. (1967). Determinants of children's preferences for adults. *Child Development, 38,* 1–14.

Stewart, A. J. (1980). Personality and situation in the prediction of women's life patterns. *Psychology of Women Quarterly, 5,* 195–206.

Stewart, A. J., & Vandewater, E. A. (1999). "If I had it to do over again. . ." Midlife review, midcourse corrections, and women's well-being in midlife. *Journal of Personality and Social Psychology, 76,* 270–283.

Stock, G. (2002). *Redesigning humans: Our inevitable genetic future.* Boston: Houghton Mifflin.

Stolberg, S. (1994, March 27). Genetic bias: Held hostage by heredity. *Los Angeles Times,* p. 1A.

Stone, L. J., & Hokanson, J. E. (1969). Arousal reduction via self-punitive behavior. *Journal of Personality and Social Psychology, 12,* 72–79.

Stotland, E. (1969). Exploratory investigation of empathy. In L. Berkowitz (Ed.), *Advances in experimental social psychology* (Vol. 4). New York: Academic.

Strack, F., & Deutsch, R. (2004). Reflective and impulsive determinants of social behavior. *Personality and Social Psychology Review, 8,* 220–247.

Straub, R. E., Jiang, Y., MacLean, C. J., Ma, Y., Webb, B. T., et al. (2002). Genetic variation in the 6p22.3 gene *DTNBP1*, the human ortholog of the mouse dysbindin gene, is associated with schizophrenia. *American Journal of Human Genetics, 71,* 337–348.

Strauman, T. J. (1989). Self-discrepancies in clinical depression and social phobia: Cognitive structures that underlie emotional disorders? *Journal of Abnormal Psychology, 53,* 14–22.

Strauman, T. J., & Higgins, E. T. (1987). Automatic activation of self-discrepancies and emotional syndromes: When cognitive structures influence affect. *Journal of Personality and Social Psychology, 53,* 1004–1014.

Strong, R. K., & Dabbs, J. M., Jr. (2000). Testosterone and behavior in normal young children. *Personality and Individual Differences, 28,* 909–915.

Strube, M. J. (1989). Evidence for the *type* in Type A behavior: A taxometric analysis. *Journal of Personality and Social Psychology, 56,* 972–987.

Stucke, T. S., & Sporer, S. L. (2002). When a grandiose self-image is threatened: Narcissism and self-concept clarity as predictors of negative emotions and aggression following ego-threat. *Journal of Personality, 70,* 509–532.

Stumpf, H. (1993). The factor structure of the Personality Research Form: A cross-national evaluation. *Journal of Personality, 61,* 27–48.

Stumphauzer, J. S. (1972). Increased delay of gratification in young prison inmates through imitation of high delay peer models. *Journal of Personality and Social Psychology, 21,* 10–17.

Sulloway, F. J. (1996). *Born to rebel: Birth order, family dynamics, and creative lives.* New York: Pantheon.

Sutton, S. K., & Davidson, R. J. (1997). Prefrontal brain asymmetry: A biological substrate of the behavioral approach and inhibition systems. *Psychological Science, 8,* 204–210.

Swann, W. B., Jr. (1987). Identity negotiation: Where two roads meet. *Journal of Personality and Social Psychology, 53,* 1038–1051.

Swann, W. B., Jr. (1990). To be adored or to be known: The interplay of self-enhancement and self-verification. In E. T. Higgins & R. M. Sorrentino (Eds.), *Handbook of motivation and cognition* (Vol. 2, pp. 408–448). New York: Guilford.

Swann, W. B., Jr., Bosson, J. K., & Pelham, B. W. (2002). Different partners, different selves: Strategic verification of circumscribed identities. *Personality and Social Psychology Bulletin, 28,* 1215–1228.

Swann, W. B., Jr., Pelham, B. W., & Krull, D. S. (1989). Agreeable fancy or disagreeable truth? Reconciling self-enhancement and self-verification. *Journal of Personality and Social Psychology, 57,* 782–791.

Swann, W. B., Jr., Wenzlaff, R. M., & Tafarodi, R. W. (1992). Depression and the search for negative evaluations: More evidence of the role of self-verification strivings. *Journal of Abnormal Psychology, 101,* 314–317.

Tajfel, H., & Turner, J. C. (1986). The social identity theory of intergroup behavior. In S. Worchel & W. G. Austin (Eds.), *Psychology of intergroup relations* (2nd ed., pp. 7–24). Chicago: Nelson-Hall.

Tangney, J. P., Baumeister, R. F., & Boone, A. L. (2004). High self-control predicts good adjustment, less pathology, better grades, and interpersonal success. *Journal of Personality, 72,* 271–324.

Tannen, D. (1990). *You just don't understand: Women and men in conversation.* New York: Ballantine.

Tavris, C., & Wade, C. (1984). *The longest war: Sex differences in perspective* (2nd ed.). New York: Harcourt Brace Jovanovich.

Taylor, M. C., & Hall, J. A. (1982). Psychological androgyny: Theories, methods and conclusions. *Psychological Bulletin, 92,* 347–366.

Taylor, S. E. (1983). Adjustment to threatening events: A theory of cognitive adaptation. *American Psychologist, 38,* 1161–1173.

Taylor, S. E. (2002). *The tending instinct: How nurturing is essential to who we are and how we live.* New York: Henry Holt.

Taylor, S. E., & Brown, J. D. (1988). Illusion and well-being: A social psychological perspective on mental health. *Psychological Bulletin, 103,* 193–210.

Taylor, S. E., & Fiske, S. T. (1978). Salience, attention, and attribution: Top of the head phenomena. In L. Berkowitz (Ed.), *Advances in experimental social psychology* (Vol. 11). New York: Academic.

Taylor, S. E., & Gollwitzer, P. M. (1995). Effects of mindset on positive illusions. *Journal of Personality and Social Psychology, 69,* 213–226.

Taylor, S. E., Klein, L. C., Lewis, B. P., Gruenewald, T. L., Gurung, R. A. R., & Updegraff, J. A. (2000). Biobehavioral responses to stress in females: Tend-and-befriend, not fight-or-flight. *Psychological Review, 107,* 411–429.

Taylor, S. E., Lichtman, R. R., & Wood, J. V. (1984). Attributions, beliefs in control, and adjustment to breast cancer. *Journal of Personality and Social Psychology, 46,* 489–502.

Tedeschi, R. G., & Calhoun, L. G. (1995). *Trauma and transformation: Growing in the aftermath of suffering.* Thousand Oaks, CA: Sage.

Tellegen, A. (1985). Structure of mood and personality and their relevance to assessing anxiety, with an emphasis on self-report. In A. H. Tuma & J. D. Maser (Eds.), *Anxiety and the anxiety disorders* (pp. 681–706). Hillsdale, NJ: Erlbaum.

Tellegen, A., Lykken, D. T., Bouchard, T. J., Jr., Wilcox, K. J., Segal, N. L., & Rich, S. (1988). Personality similarity in twins reared apart and together. *Journal of Personality and Social Psychology, 54,* 1031–1039.

Tesch, S. A., & Whitbourne, S. K. (1982). Intimacy status and identity status in young adults. *Journal of Personality and Social Psychology, 43,* 1041–1051.

Tesser, A. (1971). Evaluative and structural similarity of attitudes as determinants of interpersonal attraction. *Journal of Personality and Social Psychology, 18,* 92–96.

Tesser, A. (1986). Some effects of self-evaluation maintenance on cognition and action. In R. M. Sorrentino & E. T. Higgins (Eds.), *The handbook of motivation and cognition: Foundations of social behavior.* New York: Guilford.

Tesser, A. (1988). Toward a self-evaluation maintenance model of social behavior. In L. Berkowitz (Ed.), *Advances in experimental social psychology* (Vol. 21, pp. 181–227). New York: Academic.

Tesser, A. (1991). Social vs. clinical approaches to self psychology: The self-evaluation maintenance model and Kohutian object relations theory. In R. Curtis (Ed.), *The relational self: Theoretical convergences in psychoanalysis and social psychology* (pp. 257–281). New York: Guilford.

Tesser, A. (1993). The importance of heritability in psychological research: The case of attitudes. *Psychological Review, 100,* 129–142.

Tesser, A., & Campbell, J. (1983). Self-definition and self-evaluation maintenance. In J. Suls & A. G. Greenwald (Eds.), *Psychological perspectives on the self* (Vol. 2). Hillsdale, NJ: Erlbaum.

Thagard, P. (1989). Explanatory coherence. *Behavioral and Brain Sciences, 12,* 435–467.

Thagard, P., & Millgram, E. (1995). Inference to the best plan: A coherence theory of decision. In A. Ram & D. B. Leake (Eds.), *Goal-driven learning* (pp. 439–454). Cambridge, MA: MIT Press.

Theios, J. (1962). The partial reinforcement effect sustained through blocks of continuous reinforcement. *Journal of Experimental Psychology, 64,* 1–6.

Thelen, M. H., & Rennie, D. L. (1972). The effect of vicarious reinforcement on imitation: A review of the literature. In B. Maher (Ed.), *Progress in experimental personality research* (Vol. 6). New York: Academic.

Thiessen, D., & Gregg, B. (1980). Human assortative mating and genetic equilibrium: An evolutionary perspective. *Ethology and Sociobiology, 1,* 111–140.

Thomas, M. H., Horton, R. W., Lippincott, E. C., & Drabman, R. S. (1977). Desensitization to portrayals of real-life aggression as a function of exposure to television violence. *Journal of Personality and Social Psychology, 35,* 450–458.

Thompson, G. C. (1968). George Alexander Kelly (1905–1967). *Journal of General Psychology, 79,* 19–24.

Thompson, S. C. (1985). Finding positive meaning in a stressful event and coping. *Basic and Applied Social Psychology, 6,* 279–295.

Thompson, S. C. (1991). The search for meaning following a stroke. *Basic and Applied Social Psychology, 12,* 81–96.

Thompson, S. C., & Janigian, A. S. (1988). Life schemes: A framework for understanding the search for meaning. *Journal of Social and Clinical Psychology, 7,* 260–280.

Thorndike, E. L. (1898). Animal intelligence: An experimental study of the associative processes in animals. *Psychological Monographs, 2* (Whole No. 8).

Thorndike, E. L. (1905). *The elements of psychology.* New York: A. G. Seiler.

Thorndike, E. L. (1933). *An experimental study of rewards.* New York: Teachers College Press.

Thorne, A. (1987). The press of personality: A study of conversations between introverts and extraverts. *Journal of Personality and Social Psychology, 53,* 718–726.

Thrash, T. M., & Elliot, A. J. (2002). Implicit and self-attributed achievement motives: Concordance and predictive validity. *Journal of Personality, 70,* 729–755.

Thronquist, M. H., Zuckerman, M., & Exline, R. V. (1991). Loving, liking, looking, and sensation seeking in unmarried college couples. *Personality and Individual Differences, 12,* 1283–1292.

Timberlake, W. (1993). Behavior systems and reinforcement: An integrative approach. *Journal of the Experimental Analysis of Behavior, 60,* 105–128.

Toates, F. (2006). A model of the hierarchy of behaviour, cognition, and consciousness. *Consciousness and Cognition, 15,* 75–118.

Tobin, R. M., Graziano, W. G., Vanman, E. J., & Tassinary, L. G. (2000). Personality, emotional experience, and efforts to control emotions. *Journal of Personality and Social Psychology, 79,* 656–669.

Todd, M., Tennen, H., Carney, M. A., Armeli, S., & Affleck, G. (2004). Do we know how we cope? Relating daily coping reports to global and time-limited retrospective assessments. *Journal of Personality and Social Psychology, 86,* 310–319.

Tolman, E. C. (1932). *Purposive behavior in animals and men.* New York: Appleton-Century-Crofts.

Tolman, E. C. (1959). Principles of purposive behavior. In S. Koch (Ed.), *Psychology: A study of a science* (Vol. 2, pp. 92–157). New York: McGraw-Hill.

Tomich, P. T., & Helgeson, V. S. (2002). Five years later: A cross-sectional comparison of breast cancer survivors with healthy women. *Psycho-Oncology, 11,* 154–169.

Tomich, P. T., & Helgeson, V. S. (2004). Is finding something good in the bad always good? Benefit finding among women with breast cancer. *Health Psychology, 23,* 16–23.

Toner, I. J., & Smith, R. A. (1977). Age and overt verbalization in delay-maintenance behavior in children. *Journal of Experimental Child Psychology, 24,* 123–128.

Tooby, J., & Cosmides, L. (1989). Evolutionary psychology and the generation of culture, Part I. *Ethology and Sociobiology, 10,* 29–49.

Tooby, J., & Cosmides, L. (1990). On the universality of human nature and the uniqueness of the individual. *Journal of Personality, 58,* 17–67.

Trapnell, P. D., & Campbell, J. D. (1999). Private self-consciousness and the five-factor model of personality: Distinguishing rumination from reflection. *Journal of Personality and Social Psychology, 76,* 284–304.

Trapnell, P. D., & Wiggins, J. S. (1990). Extension of the interpersonal adjective scales to include the big five dimensions of personality. *Journal of Personality and Social Psychology, 59,* 781–790.

Triandis, H. C., Hui, H., Albert, R. D., Leung, S., Lisansky, J., Diaz-Loving, R., Plascencia, L., Marin, G., Betancourt, H., & Loyola-Cintron, L. (1984). Individual models of social behavior. *Journal of Personality and Social Psychology, 46,* 1389–1404.

Trivers, R. L. (1971). The evolution of reciprocal altruism. *Quarterly Review of Biology, 46,* 35–57.

Trivers, R. L. (1972). Parental investment and sexual selection. In B. Campbell (Ed.), *Sexual selection and the descent of man: 1871–1971* (pp. 136–179). Chicago: Aldine.

Trobst, K. K., Herbst, J. H., Masters, H. L., III, & Costa, P. T., Jr. (2002). Personality pathways to unsafe sex: Personality, condom use, and HIV risk behaviors. *Journal of Research in Personality, 36,* 117–133.

Trope, Y. (1975). Seeking information about one's own ability as a determinant of choice among tasks. *Journal of Personality and Social Psychology, 32,* 1004–1013.

Trope, Y. (1979). Uncertainty-reducing properties of achievement tasks. *Journal of Personality and Social Psychology, 37,* 1505–1518.

Trope, Y. (1980). Self-assessment, self-enhancement, and task preference. *Journal of Experimental Social Psychology, 16,* 116–129.

Trope, Y., & Fishbach, A. (2000). Counteractive self-control in overcoming temptation. *Journal of Personality and Social Psychology, 79,* 493–506.

Trope, Y., & Fishbach, A. (2005). Going beyond the motivation given: Self-control and situational control over behavior. In R. R. Hassin, J. S. Uleman, & J. A. Bargh (Eds.), *The new unconscious* (pp. 537–563). New York: Oxford University Press.

Truax, C. B., & Mitchell, K. M. (1971). Research on certain therapist interpersonal skills in relation to process and outcome. In A. E. Bergin & S. L. Garfield (Eds.), *Handbook of psychotherapy and behavior change.* New York: Wiley.

Tse, W. S., & Bond, A. J. (2001). Serotonergic involvement in the psychosocial dimension of personality. *Journal of Psychopharmacology, 15,* 195–198.

Tulving, E. (1972). Episodic and semantic memory. In E. Tulving & W. Donaldson (Eds.), *Organization of memory.* New York: Academic.

Tulving, E. (1993). What is episodic memory? *Current Directions in Psychological Science, 2,* 67–70.

Turk, D. (1978). Cognitive behavioral techniques in the management of pain. In J. P. Foreyt & D. P. Rathjen (Eds.), *Cognitive behavior therapy: Research and application.* New York: Plenum.

Turkheimer, E. (1998). Heritability and biological explanation. *Psychological Review, 105,* 782–791.

Turner, J. L., Foa, E. B., & Foa, U. G. (1971). Interpersonal reinforcers: Classification, interrelationship, and some differential properties. *Journal of Personality and Social Psychology, 19,* 168–170.

Turner, R. A., Altemus, M., Enos, T., Cooper, B., & McGuinness, T. (1999). Preliminary research on plasma oxytocin in normal cycling women: Investigating emotion and interpersonal distress. *Psychiatry, 62,* 97–113.

Twenge, J. M. (2000). The age of anxiety? Birth cohort change in anxiety and neuroticism, 1952–1993. *Journal of Personality and Social Psychology, 79,* 1007–1021.

Twenge, J. M. (2001). Birth cohort changes in extraversion: A cross-temporal meta-analysis, 1966–1993. *Personality and Individual Differences, 30,* 735–748.

Twenge, J. M. (2002). Birth cohort, social change, and personality: The interplay of dysphoria and individualism in the 20th century. In D. Cervone & W. Mischel (Eds.), *Advances in personality science* (pp. 196–218). New York: Guilford.

Twenge, J. M., Baumeister, R. F., Tice, D. M., & Stucke, T. S. (2001). If you can't join them, beat them: Effects of social exclusion on aggressive behavior. *Journal of Personality and Social Psychology, 81,* 1058–1069.

Twenge, J. M., & Campbell, W. K. (2001). Age and birth cohort differences in self-esteem: A cross-temporal meta-analysis. *Personality and Social Psychology Review, 5,* 321–344.

Twenge, J. M., & Campbell, W. K. (2003). "Isn't it fun to get the respect that we're going to deserve?" Narcissism, social rejection, and aggression. *Personality and Social Psychology Bulletin, 29,* 261–272.

Tyner, S. D., Venkatachalam, S., Choi, J., Jones, S., Ghebranious, N., Igelmann, H., Lu, X., Soron, G., Cooper, B., Brayton, C., Park, S. H., Thompson, T., Karsenty, G., Bradley, A., & Donehower, L. A. (2002). p53 mutant mice that display early ageing-associated phenotypes. *Nature, 415,* 45–53.

Udry, J. R., & Talbert, L. M. (1988). Sex hormone effects on personality at puberty. *Journal of Personality and Social Psychology, 54,* 291–295.

Underwood, B. J. (1975). Individual differences as a crucible in theory construction. *American Psychologist, 30,* 128–134.

Vaillant, G. E. (1977). *Adaptation to life.* Boston: Little, Brown.

Vallacher, R. R., & Nowak, A. (1997). The emergence of dynamical social psychology. *Psychological Inquiry, 8,* 73–99.

Vallacher, R. R., Read, S. J., & Nowak, A. (Eds.). (2002). The dynamical perspective in personality and social psychology [Special issue]. *Personality and Social Psychology Review, 6* (4).

Vallacher, R. R., & Wegner, D. M. (1985). *A theory of action identification.* Hillsdale, NJ: Erlbaum.

Vallacher, R. R., & Wegner, D. M. (1987). Action identification theory: The representation and control of behavior. *Psychological Review, 94,* 3–15.

Vallacher, R. R., & Wegner, D. M. (1989). Levels of personal agency: Individual variation in action identification. *Journal of Personality and Social Psychology, 57,* 660–671.

Vallerand, R. J. (1997). Toward a hierarchical model of intrinsic and extrinsic motivation. In M. P. Zanna (Ed.), *Advances in experimental social psychology* (Vol. 29, pp. 271–360). San Diego: Academic.

Van Honk, J., Schutter, D. J. L. G., Hermans, E. J., Putman, P., Tuiten, A., & Koppeschaar, H. (2004). Testosterone shifts the balance between sensitivity for punishment and reward in healthy young women. *Psychoneuroendocrinology, 29,* 937–943.

Van Maanen, J. (1973). Observations on the making of policemen. *Human Organization, 32,* 407–418.

Van Maanen, J. (1975). Police socialization: A longitudinal examination of job attitudes in an urban police department. *Administrative Science Quarterly, 20,* 207–228.

Vandenberg, S. G., Singer, S. M., & Pauls, D. L. (1986). *The heredity of behavior disorders in adults and children.* New York: Plenum.

Vandewater, E. A., Ostrove, J. M., & Stewart, A. J. (1997). Predicting women's well-being in midlife: The importance of personality development and social role involvements. *Journal of Personality and Social Psychology, 72,* 1147–1160.

Vaughan, K. B., & Lanzetta, J. T. (1980). Vicarious instigation and conditioning of facial expressive and autonomic responses to a model's expressive display of pain. *Journal of Personality and Social Psychology, 38,* 909–923.

Vernon, D. T. A. (1974). Modeling and birth order in responses to painful stimuli. *Journal of Personality and Social Psychology, 29,* 794–799.

Vernon, P. E. (1964). *Personality assessment: A critical survey.* New York: Wiley.

Veroff, J. (1957). Development and validation of a projective measure of power motivation. *Journal of Abnormal and Social Psychology, 54,* 1–8.

Verplanken, B., & Holland, R. W. (2002). Motivated decision making: Effects of activation and self-centrality of values on choices and behavior. *Journal of Personality and Social Psychology, 82,* 434–447.

Vertes, R. P. (2004). Memory consolidation in sleep: Dream or reality. *Neuron, 44,* 135–148.

Viken, R. J., & McFall, R. M. (1994). Paradox lost: Implications of contemporary reinforcement theory for behavior therapy. *Current Directions in Psychological Science, 3,* 121–125.

Viken, R. J., Rose, R. J., Kaprio, J., & Koskenvuo, M. (1994). A developmental genetic analysis of adult personality: Extraversion and neuroticism from 18 to 59 years of age. *Journal of Personality and Social Psychology, 66,* 722–730.

Vohs, K. D., & Baumeister, R. F. (2005). Self-regulation and self-presentation: Regulatory resource depletion impairs impression management and effortful self-presentation depletes regulatory resources. *Journal of Personality and Social Psychology, 88,* 632–657.

Vohs, K. D., Baumeister, R. F., & Ciarocco, N. J. (2005). Self-regulation and self-presentation: Regulatory resource depletion impairs impression management and effortful self-presentation depletes regulatory resources. *Journal of Personality and Social Psychology, 88,* 632–657.

Wacker, J., Chavanon, M., & Stemmler, G. (2006). Investigating the dopaminergic basis of extraversion in humans: A multilevel approach. *Journal of Personality and Social Psychology.*

Wade, S. L., Borawski, E. A., Taylor, H. G., Drotar, D., Yeates, L. O., & Stancin, T. (2001). The relationship of caregiver coping to family outcomes during the initial year following pediatric traumatic injury. *Journal of Consulting and Clinical Psychology, 69,* 406–415.

Wagner, A. R., Siegel, S., Thomas, E., & Ellison, G. D. (1964). Reinforcement history and the extinction of a conditioned salivary response. *Journal of Comparative and Physiological Psychology, 58,* 354–358.

Wahlsten, D. (1990). Insensitivity of the analysis of variance to heredity–environment interaction. *Behavioral and Brain Sciences, 13,* 100–161.

Wahlsten, D. (1999). Single-gene influences on brain and behavior. *Annual Review of Psychology, 50,* 599–624.

Walker, E. F., & Diforio, D. (1997). Schizophrenia: A neural diathesis-stress model. *Psychological Review, 104,* 667–685.

Walker, M. P. (2005). A refined model of sleep and the time course of memory formation. *Behavioral and Brain Sciences, 28,* 51–104.

Walker, R. N. (1962). Body build and behavior in young children. Body build and nursery school teacher ratings. *Monographs of the Society for Research on Child Development, 27* (Serial No. 84).

Wallace, H. M., & Baumeister, R. F. (2002). The performance of narcissists rises and falls with perceived opportunity for glory. *Journal of Personality and Social Psychology, 82,* 819–834.

Walls, R. T., & Cox, J. (1971). Expectancy of reinforcement in chance and skills tasks under motor handicaps. *Journal of Clinical Psychology, 27,* 436–438.

Wallston, B. S., & Wallston, K. A. (1978). Locus of control and health: A review of the literature. *Health Education Monographs, 6,* 107–117.

Wallston, K. A., & Wallston, B. S. (1981). Health locus of control scales. In H. F. Lefcourt (Ed.), *Research with the locus of control construct. Vol. 1, Assessment methods.* New York: Academic.

Walters, R. H., & Parke, R. D. (1964). Influence of response consequences to a social model on resistance to deviation. *Journal of Experimental Child Psychology, 1,* 269–280.

Walther, E. (2002). Guilty by mere association: Evaluative conditioning and the spreading attitude effect. *Journal of Personality and Social Psychology, 82,* 919–934.

Walton, K. E., & Roberts, B. W. (2004). On the relationship between substance use and personality traits: Abstainers are not maladjusted. *Journal of Research in Personality, 38,* 515–535.

Watson, D., & Clark, L. A. (1984). Negative affectivity: The disposition to experience aversive emotional states. *Psychological Bulletin, 96,* 465–490.

Watson, D., & Clark, L. A. (1994). Introduction to the special issue on personality and psychopathology. *Journal of Abnormal Psychology, 103,* 3–5.

Watson, D., Clark, L. A., McIntyre, C. W., & Hamaker, S. (1992). Affect, personality, and social activity. *Journal of Personality and Social Psychology, 63,* 1011–1025.

Watson, D., & Tellegen, A. (1985). Toward a consensual structure of mood. *Psychological Bulletin, 98,* 219–235.

Watson, D., Wiese, D., Vaidya, J., & Tellegen, A. (1999). The two general activation systems of affect: Structural findings, evolutionary considerations, and psychobiological evidence. *Journal of Personality and Social Psychology, 76,* 820–838.

Watson, J. B., & Raynor, R. (1920). Conditioned emotional reactions. *Journal of Experimental Psychology, 3,* 1–14.

Watt, J. D., & Blanchard, M. J. (1994). Boredom proneness and the need for cognition. *Journal of Research in Personality, 28,* 44–51.

Webb, T., & Sheeran, P. (2003). Can implementation intentions help to overcome ego-depletion? *Journal of Experimental Social Psychology, 39,* 279–286.

Wegner, D. M. (1989). *White bears and other unwanted thoughts: Suppression, obsession, and the psychology of mental control.* New York: Viking Penguin.

Wegner, D. M. (1994). Ironic processes of mental control. *Psychological Review, 101,* 34–52.

Wegner, D. M. (2002). *The illusion of conscious will.* Cambridge, MA: MIT Press.

Wegner, D. M., Schneider, D. J., Carter, S. R., III, & White, T. L. (1987). Paradoxical effects of thought suppression. *Journal of Personality and Social Psychology, 53,* 5–13.

Wegner, D. M., Shortt, J. W., Blake, A. W., & Page, M. S. (1990). The suppression of exciting thoughts. *Journal of Personality and Social Psychology, 58*, 409–418.

Wegner, D. M., Wenzlaff, R. M., & Kozak, M. (2004). Dream rebound: The return of suppressed thoughts in dreams. *Psychological Science, 15*, 232–236.

Wegner, D. M., & Wheatley, T. (1999). Apparent mental causation: Sources of the experience of will. *American Psychologist, 54*, 480–492.

Weinberger, D. A., Schwartz, G. E., & Davidson, R. J. (1979). Low-anxious, high-anxious, and repressive coping styles: Psychometric patterns and behavioral and physiological responses to stress. *Journal of Abnormal Psychology, 88*, 369–380.

Weinberger, J. L., & Hardaway, R. (1990). Separating science from myth in subliminal psychodynamic activation. *Clinical Psychology Review, 10*, 727–756.

Weinberger, J. L., & Silverman, L. H. (1987). Subliminal psychodynamic activation: A method for studying psychoanalytic dynamic propositions. In R. Hogan & W. H. Jones (Eds.), *Perspectives in personality* (Vol. 2, pp. 251–287). Greenwich, CT: JAI.

Weiner, B. (1979). A theory of motivation for some classroom experiences. *Journal of Educational Psychology, 71*, 3–25.

Weiner, B. (1986). *An attributional theory of motivation and emotion.* New York: Springer-Verlag.

Weiner, B. (1990). Attribution in personality psychology. In L. A. Pervin (Ed.), *Handbook of personality: Theory and research* (pp. 465–485). New York: Guilford.

Weiner, B., & Litman-Adizes, T. (1980). An attributional, expectancy–value analysis of learned helplessness and depression. In J. Garber & M. E. P. Seligman (Eds.), *Human helplessness: Theory and applications.* New York: Academic.

Weiner, B., Heckhausen, H., Meyer, W., & Cook, R. E. (1972). Causal ascriptions and achievement behaviors: A conceptual analysis of effort and reanalysis of locus of control. *Journal of Personality and Social Psychology, 21*, 239–248.

Weiner, B., Nierenberg, R., & Goldstein, M. (1976). Social learning (locus of control) versus attributional (causal stability) interpretations of expectancy of success. *Journal of Personality, 44*, 52–68.

Weinstein, N. D. (1989). Optimistic biases about personal risks. *Science, 246*, 1232–1233.

Weisberg, P., & Waldrop, P. B. (1972). Fixed-interval work habits of congress. *Journal of Applied Behavioral Analysis, 5*, 93–97.

Weiss, L., & Masling, J. (1970). Further validation of a Rorschach measure of oral imagery: A study of six clinical groups. *Journal of Abnormal Psychology, 76*, 83–87.

Weiss, R. S. (Ed.). (1973). *Loneliness: The experience of emotional and social isolation.* Cambridge, MA: MIT Press.

Wendelken, C., & Shastri, L. (2005). Connectionist mechanisms for cognitive control. *Neurocomputing: An International Journal, 65–66*, 663–672.

Wenzlaff, R. M., & Wegner, D. M. (2000). Thought suppression. *Annual Review of Psychology, 51*, 59–91.

Wenzlaff, R. M., Wegner, D. M., & Roper, D. W. (1988). Depression and mental control: The resurgence of unwanted negative thoughts. *Journal of Personality and Social Psychology, 55*, 1–11.

Westen, D. (1991). Social cognition and object relations. *Psychological Bulletin, 109*, 429–455.

Westen, D. (1998). The scientific legacy of Sigmund Freud: Toward a psychodynamically informed psychological science. *Psychological Bulletin, 124*, 333–371.

Westenberg, P. M., & Block, J. (1993). Ego development and individual differences in personality. *Journal of Personality and Social Psychology, 65*, 792–800.

Westmaas, J. L., & Silver, R. C. (2001). The role of attachment in responses to victims of life crises. *Journal of Personality and Social Psychology, 80*, 425–438.

Wheeler, R. E., Davidson, R. J., & Tomarken, A. J. (1993). Frontal brain asymmetry and emotional reactivity: A biological substrate of affective style. *Psychophysiology, 30*, 82–89.

Whitam, F. L., Diamond, M., & Martin, J. (1993). Homosexual orientation in twins: A report on 61 pairs and three triplet sets. *Archives of Sexual Behavior, 22*, 187–206.

Whitbeck, L. B., Hoyt, D. R., Simons, R. L., Conger, R. D., Elder, G. H., Jr., Lorenz, F. O., & Huck, S. (1992). Intergenerational continuity of parental rejection and depressed affect. *Journal of Personality and Social Psychology, 63*, 1036–1045.

Whitbourne, S. K., Zuschlag, M. K., Elliot, L. B., & Waterman, A. S. (1992). Psychosocial development in adulthood: A 22-year sequential study. *Journal of Personality and Social Psychology, 63*, 260–271.

White, K. M., Houlihan, J., Costos, D., & Speisman, J. C. (1990). Adult development in individuals and relationships. *Journal of Research in Personality, 24*, 371–386.

White, R. W. (1959). Motivation reconsidered: The concept of competence. *Psychological Review, 66*, 297–333.

White, R. W. (1963). *Ego and reality in psychoanalytic theory: A proposal regarding independent ego energies* (Psychological Issues Monograph 11). New York: International Universities Press.

Wickelgren, W. A. (1977). *Learning and memory.* Englewood Cliffs, NJ: Prentice-Hall.

Wicker, F. W., Brown, G., Wiehe, J. A., Hagen, A. S., & Reed, J. L. (1993). On reconsidering Maslow: An examination of the deprivation/domination proposition. *Journal of Research in Personality, 27*, 118–133.

Widiger, T. A., Trull, T. J., Clarkin, J. F., Sanderson, C., & Costa, P. T, Jr. (2002). A description of the DSM-IV personality disorders with the five-factor model. In P. T.

Costa, Jr. & T. A. Widiger (Eds.), *Personality disorders and the five-factor model of personality* (2nd ed., pp. 89–99). Washington, DC: American Psychological Association.

Wiedenfeld, S. A., O'Leary, A., Bandura, A., Brown, S., Levine, S., & Raska, K. (1990). Impact of perceived self-efficacy in coping with stressors on components of the immune system. *Journal of Personality and Social Psychology, 59,* 1082–1094.

Wiener, N. (1948). *Cybernetics: Control and communication in the animal and the machine.* Cambridge, MA: MIT Press.

Wiggins, J. S. (1973). *Personality and prediction: Principles of personality assessment.* Reading, MA: Addison-Wesley.

Wiggins, J. S. (1979). A psychological taxonomy of trait-descriptive terms: The interpersonal domain. *Journal of Personality and Social Psychology, 37,* 395–412.

Wiggins, J. S. (Ed.). (1996). *The five-factor model of personality: Theoretical perspectives.* New York: Guilford.

Wiggins, J. S., Phillips, N., & Trapnell, P. (1989). Circular reasoning about interpersonal behavior: Evidence concerning some untested assumptions underlying diagnostic classification. *Journal of Personality and Social Psychology, 56,* 296–305.

Willerman, L., Loehlin, J. C., & Horn, J. M. (1992). An adoption and a cross-fostering study of the Minnesota Multiphasic Personality Inventory (MMPI) Psychopathic Deviate scale. *Behavior Genetics, 22,* 515–529.

Williams, G. C., & Deci, E. L. (1996). Internalization of biopsychosocial values by medical students: A test of self-determination theory. *Journal of Personality and Social Psychology, 70,* 767–779.

Williams, G. C., Grow, V. M., Freedman, Z. R., Ryan, R. M., & Deci, E. L. (1996). Motivational predictors of weight loss and weight-loss maintenance. *Journal of Personality and Social Psychology, 70,* 115–126.

Williams, R. L., Moore, C. A., Pettibone, T. J., & Thomas, S. P. (1992). Construction and validation of a brief self-report scale of self-management practices. *Journal of Research in Personality, 26,* 216–234.

Wilson, E. O. (1975). *Sociobiology: The new synthesis.* Cambridge, MA: Harvard University Press.

Wilson, J. Q., & Herrnstein, R. J. (1985). *Crime and human nature.* New York: Simon & Schuster.

Wilson, M. I., & Daly, M. (1985). Competitiveness, risk-taking, and violence: The young male syndrome. *Ethology and Sociobiology, 6,* 59–73.

Wilson, M. I., & Daly, M. (1996). Male sexual proprietariness and violence against wives. *Current Directions in Psychological Science, 5,* 2–7.

Wink, P., & Helson, R. (1993). Personality change in women and their partners. *Journal of Personality and Social Psychology, 65,* 597–605.

Winson, J. (1985). *Brain and psyche: The biology of the unconscious.* Garden City, NY: Doubleday.

Winson, J. (1990). The meaning of dreams. *Scientific American, 263,* 86–96.

Winter, D. G. (1972). The need for power in college men: Action correlates and relationship to drinking. In D. C. McClelland, W. N. Davis, R. Kalin, & E. Wanner (Eds.), *The drinking man.* New York: Free Press.

Winter, D. G. (1973). *The power motive.* New York: Free Press.

Winter, D. G. (1988). The power motive in women—and men. *Journal of Personality and Social Psychology, 54,* 510–519.

Winter, D. G. (1993). Power, affiliation, and war: Three tests of a motivational model. *Journal of Personality and Social Psychology, 65,* 532–545.

Winter, D. G. (1994). *Manual for scoring motive imagery in running text.* University of Michigan, Ann Arbor: Unpublished manuscript.

Winter, D. G. (1996). *Personality: Analysis and interpretation of lives.* New York: McGraw-Hill.

Winter, D. G., & Barenbaum, N. B. (1985). Responsibility and the power motive in women and men. *Journal of Personality, 53,* 335–355.

Winter, D. G., John, O. P., Stewart, A. J., Klohnen, E. C., & Duncan, L. E. (1998). Traits and motives: Toward an integration of two traditions in personality research. *Psychological Bulletin, 105,* 230–250.

Winter, D. G., Stewart, A. J., & McClelland, D. C. (1977). Husband's motives and wife's career level. *Journal of Personality and Social Psychology, 35,* 159–166.

Wirth, M. M., Welsh, K., & Schultheiss, O. C. (2006). Salivary cortisol changes in humans after winning or losing a dominance contest depend on implicit power motivation. *Hormones and Behavior, 49,* 346–352.

Wise, R. A. (2004). Dopamine, learning and motivation. *Nature Reviews Neuroscience, 5,* 1–10.

Wisman, A., & Koole, S. L. (2003). Hiding in the crowd: Can mortality salience promote affiliation with others who oppose one's worldviews? *Journal of Personality and Social Psychology, 84,* 511–526.

Wispé, L. (1986). The distinction between sympathy and empathy: To call forth a concept, a word is needed. *Journal of Personality and Social Psychology, 50,* 314–321.

Woike, B. A. (1995). Most-memorable experiences: Evidence for a link between implicit and explicit motives and social cognitive processes in everyday life. *Journal of Personality and Social Psychology, 68,* 1081–1091.

Woike, B., Mcleod, S., & Goggin, M. (2003). Implicit and explicit motives influence accessibility to different autobiographical knowledge. *Personality and Social Psychology Bulletin, 29,* 1046–1055.

Wolberg, L. R. (1967). *The technique of psychotherapy.* New York: Grune & Stratton.

Wolfe, J. B. (1936). Effectiveness of token-rewards for chimpanzees. *Comparative Psychology Monographs, 12* (Whole No. 60).

Wolfe, R. N., & Kasmer, J. A. (1988). Type versus trait: Extraversion, impulsivity, sociability, and preferences for cooperative and competitive activities. *Journal of Personality and Social Psychology, 54,* 864–871.

Wolpe, J. (1981). Behavior therapy versus psychoanalysis: Therapeutic and social implications. *American Psychologist, 36,* 159–164.

Wong, M. M., & Csikszentmihalyi, M. (1991). Affiliation motivation and daily experience: Some issues on gender differences. *Journal of Personality and Social Psychology, 60,* 154–164.

Wood, J. M., Nezworski, M. T., & Stejskal, W. J. (1996a). The comprehensive system for the Rorschach: A critical examination. *Psychological Science, 7,* 3–10.

Wood, J. M., Nezworski, M. T., & Stejskal, W. J. (1996b). Thinking critically about the comprehensive system for the Rorschach: A reply to Exner. *Psychological Science, 7,* 14–17.

Wood, R., & Bandura, A. (1989). Impact of conceptions of ability on self-regulatory mechanisms and complex decision making. *Journal of Personality and Social Psychology, 56,* 407–415.

Wood, W., & Eagly, A. H. (2002). A cross-cultural analysis of the behavior of women and men: Implications for the origins of sex differences. *Psychological Bulletin, 128,* 699–727.

Wood, W., Quinn, F. M., & Kashy, D. A. (2002). Habits in everyday life: Thought, emotion, and action. *Journal of Personality and Social Psychology, 83,* 1281–1297.

Wood, W., Tam, L., & Guerrero Witt, M. (2005). Changing circumstances, disrupting habits. *Journal of Personality and Social Psychology, 88,* 918–933.

Woodruffe, C. (1985). Consensual validation of personality traits: Additional evidence and individual differences. *Journal of Personality and Social Psychology, 48,* 1240–1252.

Wortman, C. B., & Brehm, J. W. (1975). Responses to uncontrollable outcomes: An integration of reactance theory and the learned helplessness model. In L. Berkowitz (Ed.), *Advances in experimental social psychology* (Vol. 8). New York: Academic.

Wright, J. C., & Mischel, W. (1988). Conditional hedges and the intuitive psychology of traits. *Journal of Personality and Social Psychology, 55,* 454–469.

Wright, J. C., Lindgren, K. P., & Zakriski, A. L. (2001). Syndromal versus contextualized personality assessment: Differentiating environmental and dispositional determinants of boys' aggression. *Journal of Personality and Social Psychology, 81,* 1176–1189.

Wright, J. C., & Zakriski, A. L. (2003). When syndromal similarity obscures functional dissimilarity: Distinctive evoked environments of externalizing and mixed syndrome boys. *Journal of Consulting and Clinical Psychology, 71,* 516–527.

Wright, J. C., Zakriski, A. L., & Drinkwater, M. (1999). Developmental psychopathology and the reciprocal patterning of behavior and environment: Distinctive situational and behavioral signatures of internalizing, externalizing, and mixed-syndrome children. *Journal of Consulting and Clinical Psychology, 67,* 95–107.

Wright, R. A. (1996). Brehm's theory of motivation as a model of effort and cardiovascular response. In P. M. Gollwitzer & J. A. Bargh (Eds.), *The psychology of action: Linking cognition and motivation to behavior* (pp. 424–453). New York: Guilford.

Wrosch, C., Dunne, E., Scheier, M. F., & Schulz, R. (2006). *Journal of Behavioral Medicine, 29,* 299–306.

Wrosch, C., Scheier, M. F., Carver, C. S., & Schulz, R. (2003). The importance of goal disengagement in adaptive self-regulation: When giving up is beneficial. *Self and Identity, 2,* 1–20.

Wulfert, E., Block, J. A., Santa Ana, E., Rodriguez, M. L., & Colsman, M. (2002). Delay of gratification: Impulsive choices and problem behaviors in early and late adolescence. *Journal of Personality, 70,* 533–552.

Wyer, R. S., Jr., & Srull, T. K. (1986). Human cognition in its social context. *Psychology Review, 93,* 322–359.

Wylie, R. (1979). *The self concept* (Vol. 2). Lincoln: University of Nebraska Press.

Yates, B. T., & Mischel, W. (1979). Young children's preferred attentional strategies for delaying gratification. *Journal of Personality and Social Psychology, 37,* 286–300.

Yates, J., & Taylor, J. (1978). Stereotypes for somatotypes: Shared beliefs about Sheldon's physiques. *Psychological Reports, 43,* 777–778.

York, K. L., & John, O. P. (1992). The four faces of Eve: A typological analysis of women's personality at midlife. *Journal of Personality and Social Psychology, 63,* 494–508.

Young, J. E., & Klosko, J. S. (1993). *Reinventing your life.* New York: Plume.

Zald, D. H., & Depue, R. A. (2001). Serotonergic functioning correlates with positive and negative affect in psychiatrically healthy males. *Personality and Individual Differences, 30,* 71–86.

Zeidner, M., & Hammer, A. L. (1992). Coping with missile attack: Resources, strategies, and outcomes. *Journal of Personality, 60,* 709–746.

Zeldow, P. B., Daugherty, S. R., & McAdams, D. P. (1988). Intimacy, power, and psychological well-being in medical students. *Journal of Nervous and Mental Disease, 176,* 182–187.

Zelenski, J. M., & Larsen, R. J. (1999). Susceptibility to affect: A comparison of three personality taxonomies. *Journal of Personality, 67,* 761–791.

Zener, K. (1937). The significance of behavior accompanying conditioned salivary secretion for theories of the conditioned response. *American Journal of Psychology, 50,* 384–403.

Zentall, T. R., Sutton, J. E., & Sherburne, L. M. (1996). True imitative learning in pigeons. *Psychological Science, 7,* 343–346.

Zillmann, D. (1971). Excitation transfer in communication-mediated aggressive behavior. *Journal of Experimental Social Psychology, 7,* 419–434.

Zillmann, D. (1998). *Connections between sexuality and aggression* (2nd ed.). Mahwah, NJ: Erlbaum.

Zimmerman, D. W. (1957). Durable secondary reinforcement: Method and theory. *Psychological Review, 14,* 373–383.

Zinbarg, R. E., & Mohlman, J. (1998). Individual differences in the acquisition of affectively valenced associations. *Journal of Personality and Social Psychology, 74,* 1024–1040.

Zucker, A. N., Ostrove, J. M., & Stewart, A. J. (2002). College-educated women's personality development in adulthood: Perceptions and age differences. *Psychology & Aging, 17,* 236–244.

Zuckerman, M. (1971). Dimensions of sensation seeking. *Journal of Consulting and Clinical Psychology, 36,* 45–52.

Zuckerman, M. (1979). *Sensation seeking: Beyond the optimal level of arousal.* Hillsdale, NJ: Erlbaum.

Zuckerman, M. (1985). Biological foundations of the sensation-seeking temperament. In J. Strelau, F. H. Farley, & A. Gale (Eds.), *The biological bases of personality and behavior. Vol. 1. Theories, measurement techniques, and development.* Washington, DC: Hemisphere.

Zuckerman, M. (1991). *The psychobiology of personality.* New York: Cambridge University Press.

Zuckerman, M. (1992). What is a basic factor and which factors are basic? Turtles all the way down. *Personality and Individual Differences, 13,* 675–681.

Zuckerman, M. (1993). P-impulsive sensation seeking and its behavioral, psychophysiological and biochemical correlates. *Neuropsychobiology, 28,* 30–36.

Zuckerman, M. (1994). *Behavioral expression and biosocial bases of sensation seeking.* New York: Cambridge University Press.

Zuckerman, M. (1995). Good and bad humors: Biochemical bases of personality and its disorders. *Psychological Science, 6,* 325–332.

Zuckerman, M. (1996). The psychobiological model for impulsive unsocialized sensation seeking: A comparative approach. *Neuropsychobiology, 34,* 125–129.

Zuckerman, M. (2005). *Psychobiology of Personality.* New York: Cambridge University Press.

Zuckerman, M., Bernieri, F., Koestner, R., & Rosenthal, R. (1989). To predict some of the people some of the time: In search of moderators. *Journal of Personality and Social Psychology, 57,* 279–293.

Zuckerman, M., Kieffer, S. C., & Knee, C. R. (1998). Consequences of self-handicapping: Effects on coping, academic performance, and adjustment. *Journal of Personality and Social Psychology, 74,* 1619–1628.

Zuckerman, M., Koestner, R., DeBoy, T., Garcia, T., Maresca, B. C., & Sartoris, J. M. (1988). To predict some of the people some of the time: A reexamination of the moderator variable approach in personality theory. *Journal of Personality and Social Psychology, 54,* 1006–1019.

Zuckerman, M., Kuhlman, D. M., Joireman, J., Teta, P., & Kraft, M. (1993). A comparison of three structural models for personality: The big three, the big five, and the alternative five. *Journal of Personality and Social Psychology, 65,* 757–768.

Zuckerman, M., & Neeb, M. (1980). Demographic influences in sensation seeking and expressions of sensation seeking in religion, smoking, and driving habits. *Personality and Individual Differences, 1,* 197–206.

Zuckerman, M., & Tsai, F. Costs of self-handicapping. *Journal of Personality, 73,* 411–442.

Zuroff, D. C. (1986). Was Gordon Allport a trait theorist? *Journal of Personality and Social Psychology, 51,* 993–1000.

Zwanzger, P., & Rupprecht, R. (2005). Selective GABA-ergic treatment for panic? Investigations in experimental panic induction and panic disorder. *Journal of Psychiatry & Neuroscience, 30,* 167–175.